Thomas Jefferson

& The New Nation

Volume Two
Return to Monticello

Thomas Jefferson

& The New Nation

Volume Two
Return to Monticello

By

MERRILL D. PETERSON

Biography in two volumes:
To the Vice Presidency
Return to Monticello

Published by American Political Biography Press

Newtown, CT

Withdrawal and Return:

Vice President

CONTINUED

Adams and Jefferson

Jefferson became a candidate for the presidency in 1796 in spite of himself. He did not seek the office but the office sought him. He did not consent to run or, if elected, to serve; and lest he refuse, he was not even asked. His situation seemed to call for explanation. Having renounced public service, having repeatedly declared that nothing could drag him from the oblivion of Monticello, he found himself back on the field of combat in a contest for the nation's highest office. It had all been against his will, he protested, without concert or expectation or the lift of a finger on his part: "on my salvation I declare it." His friends would believe him; it was too much to expect of his enemies. Wasn't it marvelous, John Adams snorted, how political plants grew in the shade!

If Jefferson made no move in his own behalf, neither did he spurn the candidacy thrust upon him. He might have declared his unavailability in terms not to be misunderstood; but his candidacy was a *fait accompli* before he had knowledge of it, and he could not, consistent with his own character, set the public will at defiance. There was no escape. Nor is it at all certain that Jefferson wanted one. His attitude toward political life was always governed by some balance between reciprocal forces of attraction and repulsion, and their alternation set up the cyclical rhythm of withdrawal and return which, beyond the limits of consciousness, expressed the deep ambivalance of his nature. The cycle was again completing itself in 1796. The pastoral idyl he had imagined for himself three years earlier had not materialized. Retirement showed its darker side in crop failures, frustrations of building, dreary winters in isolation at Monticello, and cares of estate as unrelenting as his creditors. He had set out to recoup the fortune he believed he had lost by prolonged absence from home and inattention to private affairs, but after an experiment of several years devoted to these interests he could take little satisfaction in the results. "The unprofitable condition of Virginia estates in general," he said, "leaves it next to impossible for the holder of one to avoid ruin." Worst of all he began to detect feelings of self-pity and misanthropy in himself. Several years later, observing these symptoms in his younger daughter, he cited his own experience. "I remained closely at home," he recalled, "saw none but those who came there, and at length became very sensible to the ill effect it had upon my own mind . . . I felt enough of the effect of withdrawal from the world then, to see that it led to an anti-social and misanthropic state of mind which severely punishes him who gives in to it: and it will be a lesson I shall never forget as to myself." He was ready for "return to the world," though he could never actually consent to it or, once embarked, resign himself to the "splendid torments" of public life.

While thus disenchanted with his retreat to felicity, he also found that the nation's affairs still made an irresistible claim upon him. The tendency of the Federalist administration appeared even more disturbing from his private seat in Virginia than it had from his official one in Philadelphia. President Washington's retirement would create a vacuum in the national leadership. However it was filled, extreme partisanship, which the veneration for his name had checked, was sure to assert itself. The transition might well prove critical. The Republicans looked to Jefferson to convert crisis to opportunity. He gradually accustomed himself to the idea. But he neither expected nor wished to be elected President in 1796. Federalist power so impressively organized under Washington's aegis had not been spent, and Jefferson found compelling reasons both personal and political for preferring John Adams as Washington's successor. The vice presidency, on the other hand, would be tolerable. "The second office . . . is honorable and easy," he later said, "the first is but splendid misery." It carried no weighty responsibilities, yet would place him in an enviable position to steer his course as events might dictate. The calculation helped to reconcile him to return to the political arena.

Since his retirement, in Jefferson's opinion, the octopus of British policy had taken a stranglehold on the Washington administration. When British attacks on American neutral shipping brought the two countries to the verge of war in 1794, the administration, instead of adopting an experiment in commercial warfare such as he and Madison had long advocated, sent Chief Justice John Jay to London in a suit for peace. The mission was humiliating in itself, Jefferson thought, but the treaty Jay negotiated sounded the depths of national degradation. Britain was in no position to be stubborn with the United States when Jay and Lord Grenville sat down at the bargaining table in the later months of 1794. France was everywhere on the offensive: the armies of the republic had crossed the Pyrenees, invaded Italy, overrun the German Rhineland and Belgium, and all but conquered the Netherlands. An "armed neutrality" was shaping up among the Northern powers with France's blessing and the chance of American support. The monarchical coalition put together in 1793 was breaking up. Soon Britain, wracked within by sedition, grain shortages, rising unemployment, and fiscal crisis, would stand alone against France. Peace and commmerce with the United States had become vital to British survival. Yet the American envoy played his cards as if he held the losing hand.

The result was a treaty as disgusting to the Americans as it was pleasing to the British. Some satisfaction could be found in the British pledge to evacuate the Northwest posts, though this obligation descended from the Treaty of 1783. The Americans were admitted to direct trade with the British East Indies, but the far more important trade with the West Indies remained closed, except on terms too limiting and vexatious for the United States to accept. The treaty made special provision for settling the claims of British creditors on American citizens, most of them southern planters, but made no provision to indemnify the planters for slaves carried off by the enemy army. Nothing was said on the subject of impressment, nor of those principles of neutral commerce—free ships make free goods, the narrow definition of contraband, of blockade, and so on—the United States had championed from 1776 forward. The treaty assumed American acquiescence in British maritime rule and practice that had produced the crisis in the first place. No more drastic change in American foreign policy had occurred since the Revolution. Indeed for the first time since 1780 anywhere, an international treaty sacrificed the right of neutral flags to the barbarous rule of the medieval code, *consolato del mare*. France, bound by treaty to respect American commerce under liberal arrangements, could not be indifferent to this development. Article XV placed Anglo-American trade on the most favored nation basis and prohibited any new or higher tonnage duties on British vessels, yet reserved to Britain the right to impose countervailing duties on the American. So the United States not only extended valuable guarantees to a rival commercial power but ensured that favors henceforth granted to friendly nations should also go to Britain. As Madison observed, "It was hardly imagined that we were soon to grant everything to Great Britain for nothing in return; and to make it a part of this bad bargain with her, that we should not be able to make a good one with other nations." The commercial clauses of the treaty would draw the teeth of Republican doctrine and prevent legislation aimed at curbing British power. All considered, Jefferson said of Jay's work, it was "nothing more than a treaty of alliance between England and the Anglomen of this country against . . . the people of the United States."

The terms of the treaty became public only after it was ratified by the Senate in June 1795. A whirlwind of indignation rolled across the land. The treaty dismayed the Federalists, and men might read the Republican scribes' denunciations by the light of Jay's burning effigies. "So general a burst of dissatisfaction never before appeared against any transaction," Jefferson reported to Monroe, now the American Minister to France. The treaty would demolish the Federalists, he casually predicted. However, increasingly drawn into this political vortex, he grew alarmed at the resurgence of the Federalists under Hamilton's leadership. They had got themselves into "a defile, where they might be finished," he observed, but the Republicans, misled by a false security, failed to press the attack and were once again outmaneuvered by Hamilton. "Hamilton is really a colossus to the anti-Republican party. Without numbers, he is a host within himself." Only Madison could furnish an antidote strong enough for his poison. "For God's sake take up your pen," Jefferson begged his friend. The poison had infected the mass of merchants, at first open-mouthed against the treaty but now fearful of the political consequences of its defeat. "They have feared the shock would be too great, and have chosen to tack about and support both treaty and government, rather than risk the government. Thus it is," Jefferson said, "that Hamilton, Jay, etc., in the boldest act they ever ventured on to undermine the government, have the address to screen themselves, and direct the hue and cry against those who wish to drag them into light. A bolder party stroke was never struck." That the treaty was a blatant party measure Jefferson had not the slightest doubt. And, like Madison, he emphasized its commercial character: "an attempt of a party, which finds they have lost their majority in one branch [the House of Representatives] of the Legislature, to make a law by the aid of the other branch [the Senate] and of the executive, under color of a treaty, which shall bind up the hands of the adverse branch from ever restraining the commerce of their patron-nation."

The treaty was the capstone of the Hamiltonian system. How

else could its terms, so favorable to Britain, so insulting to France, be explained? Jefferson pondered the treaty at the same time he received the news of continuing French triumph in Europe. The latter conditioned his view of the former. With the establishment of the Executive Directory in France, the Revolution had been stabilized at last; and as liberation spread over Europe, Britain became isolated and vulnerable. It had really been in America's power, Monroe wrote from Paris, to dictate terms to Britain, provided she had been made to believe in our opposition. "Accomplishing this point, everything would have been accomplished; for of all possible calamities with which they are threatened now, a war with us is that which they most dread: not so much indeed from the fear of our maritime force, as the effect it would produce upon their commerce, by which they alone are enabled to support a war." Placing the Jay Treaty in this context, reading it after indulging lighthearted fancies of leaving his peas and clover for awhile, going to England in the fall, dining with General Pichegru in London, to "hail the dawn of liberty and republicanism in that island," Jefferson judged it to be a willful abdication of American interests.

For a time he held to the slender hope that Washington would refuse to sign the treaty. His faith in the President had been badly shaken several months earlier by the public denunciation of the democratic societies. No event prior to the Jay Treaty produced a stronger reaction at Monticello. These popular societies, thirty-five of them scattered from Maine to Georgia, championed the French Revolution and Republican men and measures. The Hamiltonians artfully accused them of fomenting the Whiskey Rebellion of 1794. A massive force of 15,000 militia, accompanied by Hamilton, overwhelmed a handful of fleeing insurgents against the whiskey excise in western Pennsylvania. Washington journeyed to the site, and after his return to the capital lashed out at the societies in language that betrayed intolerance of political opposition from outside the official channels of government. The denunciation was a bold act of repression, Jefferson said. "It is wonderful indeed, that the President should have permitted himself to be the organ of such an attack on the freedom of discussion, the freedom of writing, printing and publishing." He found it increasingly difficult to escape the conclusion that Washington had become the captive of the Anglican and "monocratic" party.

For Jefferson and for Republicans generally, Washington's decision to sign or not to sign the treaty became a final test of his politics. He withheld his signature in July on Secretary of State Randolph's plea to demand prior British repeal of a new order in council damaging to American trade. The next month Randolph was the victim of a bizarre plot fashioned by the British Minister Hammond, and Oliver Wolcott and Timothy Pickering, the successors to Hamilton and Knox in the cabinet. A British man-of-war had intercepted a dispatch from the French Minister in which Randolph appeared as the petitioner of a bribe. After tailoring the dispatch to their purposes, the Federalist marplots called the President to Philadelphia. Pickering pointed the accusing finger to Randolph: "That man is a traitor!" The plot worked. Believing that Randolph schemed to defeat the treaty as a favor to France, Washington signed it without further ado. The next day, in the presence of the accusers, he confronted the hapless Secretary, his friend and confidant of many years, with the incriminating document. Angered and humiliated, Randolph resigned at once, accused Washington of "treachery unexampled since Tiberius," and wrote a long public vindication in which he portrayed himself as the "meditated victim of party spirit" —a "not guilty" plea history is now inclined to accept. Jefferson read Randolph's *Vindication* with interest. It continued for him the secret cabinet history he had once known intimately, and it confirmed his judgment of the Jay Treaty. As for Washington, he erred with integrity, though the cost of his integrity was becoming unbearable. "I wish," Jefferson said, "that his honesty and his political errors may not furnish a second occasion to exclaim 'curse his virtues, they've undone his country.' " As for Randolph, he stood acquitted of charges of bribery and treason, but Jefferson shed no tears over this man's misfortunes. Had Randolph been firm in 1793, had he succeeded to Jefferson's policy as well as to his office, the President would have been kept from habitual concert with the Hamiltonians. The Republicans owed nothing to Randolph; to sustain him in a personal vendetta against the President was unthinkable. It was, in fact, the principal problem of the Republican leadership in the later months of 1795 to work out a strategy of opposition to the treaty free of the odium and disgrace of attacking the President, whose halo, while dimmed for many, still awed the mass of Americans.

Jefferson was a sometimes impatient bystander to the final Republican assault on the treaty. Though signed and ratified, its future waited on appropriations by the House of Representatives; and there the Republican majority tried to stifle the embryo monster. The strategy took form in the Virginia House of Delegates in November. Resolutions voted at Richmond asserted the right of the lower house of Congress to share in the making of treaties, to withhold appropriations, and to approve or disapprove stipulations on subjects, such as foreign commerce, within its legislative jurisdiction. Especially pleasing was the concession wrung from the ablest of the Virginia Federalists, John Marshall, that the treaty in all its commercial parts still fell under the power of the House of Representatives. At the opening of Congress in December, Washington confounded his foes by deferring communication of the treaty. "The situation is truly perplexing," Madison informed his friend. "It is clear that a majority, if brought to the merits of the Treaty are against it. But as the Treaty is not regularly before the House, and an application to the President brings him personally into the question . . . there is great danger that enough [congressmen] will fly off to leave the opponents of the Treaty in a minority."

Republican tempers simmered for three months. At Monticello, Jefferson commenced an inquiry into the powers of the House with respect to treaties. Finally, on March 1, after the exchange of ratifications in London, Washington sent the treaty to the House. The next day Edward Livingston, the young lion of the New York clan, seized the initiative with a resolution calling upon the President to lay before the House the instructions given to Jay in 1794 together with other pertinent papers. Such papers could be considered pertinent to the business of the House only on the assumption it possessed certain powers of decision as to treaties. Madison was dismayed by this turn of events. Apparently still uncertain of the correct constitutional ground, he worried too lest Livingston's motion force a showdown with the President. Untroubled by these doubts at Monticello, Jefferson applauded the radical move. Unfortunately, he did not complete the inquiry Madison had forced upon him. Defeated by his own party on an amendment softening the Livingston resolution, Madison had no choice but to fall in with it. The resolution passed by a decisive majority. The President, just as decisively, refused the call for papers. "The absolute refusal was as unexpected as the tone and temper of the message are improper and indelicate," Madison wrote. Jefferson searched his files for evidence that Washington had earlier taken a different view of the powers of the House. Had he searched a little farther he would have discovered that he too, in the case of the Creek Treaty of 1790, had earlier taken a different view, one in accord with the position he now combated. In response to the President, the Republican majority reaffirmed its rights in the matter. But this riposte did not decide the abstract question of constitutional law, nor was it ever finally decided. As the House proceeded to the substantive question, the majority "daily melted down" until at the end, April 30, it had become a minority by two votes.

The defeat deeply embarrassed the Republicans. Surveying the entire proceeding, Madison thought it "the most worrying and vexatious business" he had ever experienced, "and the more so," he told Jefferson, "as the causes lay in the unsteadiness, the follies, the perverseness, and the defections among our friends, more than in the strength, or dexterity, or malice of our opponents." The Republicans had yet to learn the discipline of party leadership. The effectiveness of the Federalists could not be discounted, however. They had frightened men with the danger of war. They had rallied merchants, bankers, and plain citizens in public meetings and deluged Congress with petitions. They had, at the last moment, pulled a rabbit out of the hat: a treaty negotiated by Thomas Pinckney with Spain, providing for the settlement of the southern boundary and the opening of the Mississippi to navigation. Fearing the effect of an Anglo-American rapprochement on her North American colonies, Spain chose a rapprochement of her own. The Pinckney Treaty fulfilled an old objective of Jefferson's diplomacy, ironically under Federalist auspices. It appealed strongly to western Americans, and to Republicans generally; but it stood little chance of ratification if the mainly Federalist and eastern interests associated with the Jay Treaty were sacrificed. Satisfying both interests, sacrificing none, was the simple solution.

Far from the scene, Jefferson wrote no postmortem analysis of the Republican debacle in Congress. He was disappointed but, sanguine as ever, lifted his gaze to the farther horizon. The treaty had been a "dear bought victory" for the Anglomen, he assured Monroe. "It has given the most radical shock to their party which it has ever received: and there is no doubt they would be glad to be replaced on the ground they possessed the instant before Jay's nomination extraordinary. They see that nothing can support them but the colossus of the President's merits with the people, and the moment he retires, that his successor, if a Monocrat, will be overbourne by the republican sense of his constituents, if a Republican he will of course give fair play to that sense, and lead them into channels of harmony between the governors and the governed. In the meantime, patience." Jefferson thus acknowledged what everyone tacitly assumed: the contest on the Jay Treaty was the opening gun in the presidential campaign.

The campaign was well advanced months before Washington issued his Farewell Address in September 1796. As early as January, John Adams was primping himself as "heir apparent." And Madison wrote to Monroe in February: "The Republicans, knowing that Jefferson alone can be started with hope of success, mean to push him." With friends and collaborators as close as Jefferson and Madison it is difficult to believe one would push the other into anything without his consent, yet this seems to have been the case. The subject of the presidency had entered into their correspondence more than a year before. Jefferson hoped that Madison would succeed to the highest office. Under no other helmsman would the nation's "political bark" be so safe, he wrote. As for himself, the insinuations of his enemies that he coveted the office had forced him to face the question in the privacy of his own heart and mind. And he did, finding them as quiet as the grave. To the old reasons—"reputation, tranquillity, labor"—were added others since his retirement—age and health and family—which still more insuperably barred the door. "The little spice of ambition which I had in my younger days has long since evaporated, and I set still less store by a posthumous than present name." The subject was closed. But Madison persisted. He would not for a moment entertain the idea of his own candidacy. "You ought to be preparing yourself, however," he warned, "to hear truths which no inflexibility will be able to withstand." These truths he reserved for "the latitude of a free conversation." Presumably the conversation occurred in the spring of 1795 when Madison and his bride of a few months, Dolley Payne Todd, visited Monticello. Presumably, too, Madison ran through the reasons why Jefferson should lead the Republicans. He possessed a national reputation; he had served with distinction in France and as Secretary of State; his name was identified with the Republican cause at home and abroad; and his retirement set an example of political abnegation meriting the esteem of his countrymen. Madison, on the other hand, was eight years Jefferson's junior; his career had been exclusively congressional; for years he had been in the thick of partisan controversy; and he lacked the arts of popularity. Besides, he intended soon to retire himself, overcome his bachelor ways, and devote his attentions for a time to a charming wife and fine estate. It was unthinkable that both Virginians could withdraw from the national scene. If Madison surrendered the reins of Republican leadership it had better be to Jefferson.

What part of this ground the two men traversed in "free conversation" at Monticello cannot be known. One thing seems certain: Jefferson did not consent to his name being brought forward in the forthcoming presidential contest. Doubtless other Republican leaders, like William B. Giles and the New Yorker Aaron Burr, who stopped at Monticello, tried their persuasions with no better results. Although events connected with the Jay Treaty revived Jefferson's interest in national affairs, he avoided any discussion of the presidency during this period, indeed until the election was over; nor did the political associates who placed his name at the head of the ticket discuss the subject with him. It was only half a day's ride from Montpelier to Monticello, but Madison did not make the trip in 1796. "I have not seen Jefferson," he explained to Monroe early in the fall, "and have thought it wise to present him no opportunity of protesting to his friends against being embarked in the contest." Silence was the only form of consent he could expect from Monticello.

Jefferson did not lead the Republicans in 1796—the role still belonged to Madison if to anyone—but he was the virtuous symbol around whom Republicans nation-wide could rally and unite. In newspapers, broadsides, and pamphlets, Jefferson was presented as the "steadfast friend to the rights of the people," while his opponent was portrayed as the "champion of rank, titles and hereditary distinctions." In Pennsylvania, where Jefferson's old friend John Beckley, Clerk of the House of Representatives, conducted a popular campaign without parallel, a Republican handbill invited the voters to compare the political views of the two candidates: "*Thomas Jefferson* first drew the declaration of American independence—he first framed the sacred political sentence that all men are *born* equal. *John Adams* says this is all a farce and a falsehood; that some men should be born kings, and some should be born nobles. Which of these, freemen of Pennsylvania, will you have for your President?" Republicans extolled Jefferson's character, his services, his philosophy. He was enlightened, dignified, modest, a man of unsullied integrity, without artifice, passion, rancor, or any ambition other than the freedom and well-being of his countrymen. "Of no party but the great party of human benefactions, he will allay the heats of our country, heal its divisions, and calm the boisterous elements of political controversy—Under the administration of a man, untinctured by party spirit, citizens may smoke the calumet of peace . . . , and every citizen sit down in quiet under his own vine and fig-tree." His retirement offered the surest proof of republican character. Like the renowned Cincinnatus, it was said, "he knows how to support the burden of high office with dignity, or to resign it without a sigh." Federalists heaped upon Jefferson fully as much abuse as their own candidate received. Under the pen name *Phocion*, South Carolina Congressman William L. Smith, probably assisted by Hamilton as usual, elaborated the partisan image he had drawn four years before. His stinging pamphlet, *The Pretensions of Thomas Jefferson the Presidency Examined*, denounced the candidate as an enemy of religion, of national credit, of Union, and of President Washington. Worst of all, Jefferson was a philosopher, and though not a very good one, his talents would be better employed as president of a university than as president of a great nation. The satire was heavy-handed, but the Federalists seemed determined to fashion a ludicrous, as well as a frightful, image of the Virginian.

Jefferson observed the campaign from his serene heights with mixed emotions. "In truth," he wrote when it was all over, "I did not know myself under the pens either of my friends or foes. It is unfortunate for our peace, that unmerited abuse wounds, while unmerited praise has not the power to heal." The wounds inflicted in Virginia probably hurt him most. It was said that he had been sued in federal court by British creditors for an amount exceeding the value of his entire estate—a story denied by John Marshall, with whom it allegedly began. Another libel charged a secret political alliance with Aaron Burr, his running-mate, entered into when the New Yorker visited Monticello in the fall of 1795—an allegation of bargain and corruption denied in a sworn deposition by two of Jefferson's neighbors present at Monticello when Burr called. His Virginia enemies raked up the old accusations of official negligence, personal cowardice, and resignation under fire when he was governor of Virginia. This was the kind of political ammunition the Federalists had been looking for, and they spent it freely in the propaganda barrage. It struck a sensitive nerve in Jefferson. His friends, old Dr. Currie in Richmond, John Taylor, John Beckley, and others, rushed to his defense. The charges probably had no bearing on the outcome of the election, but neither Jefferson nor his friends could ever put them to rest.

Of more direct consequence was the suspicion that Jefferson and his party were the puppets of France. Cultivating this idea, the Federalists received unexpected assistance from the alleged puppeteers on the eve of the election. Angered and dismayed by the Jay Treaty, the Directory resolved to treat American neutral shipping in the same manner as was permitted to Britain, to suspend normal diplomatic relations, and give the go-ahead to the plan of its minister in Philadelphia, Pierre Adet, to "revolutionize" the American government by securing the ascendancy of a man and a party known to be friendly to the French nation. French influence in American affairs was an old story, much exaggerated by men under British influence; but in this instance it was open and blatant. Timing his action with a view to maximum impact in the Pennsylvania election, Adet published four diplomatic notes between November 2 and 21. These notes, which had the color of campaign documents, announced the new policy of the Directory and appealed to the American people for a change in their government. The Republicans won a narrow victory in Pennsylvania in spite of Adet; and in the country generally his "diplomatic blunderbuss," like Genêt's in 1793, injured the friends rather than the enemies of France. Coming on the heels of Washington's Farewell Address, with its stern warning against "the insidious wiles of foreign influence," Adet's maneuver enabled the Federalists to point an accusing finger at their political foes. Nor were they wholly without blame. Republican leaders deplored Adet's intervention and bore no direct responsibility for it. Yet they had contributed to the impression in French governing circles that the American electorate was divided between a British party and a French party, and that once the latter attained power everything would be arranged to the satisfaction of France. Monroe had suggested as much in Paris. Incurable Francophiles, like Benjamin F. Bache, editor of the foremost Republican newspaper, the *Aurora*, which published Adet's pronouncements, daily nurtured the idea. In the political heats generated by the Jay Treaty, the opposition could not avoid impaling itself on the horn of French policy.

While all this was true, Adet acted on a calculation as fallacious as Genêt's before him. What it left out, as a former French official in the United States informed his government the next year, was the large "middle party" submissive to no foreign power and composed of the country's best men regardless of party affiliation. "This party, whose existence we have not even suspected, is the American party which loves its country above all and for whom preferences either for France or England are only accessory and often passing affections." And Adet too, after the tumult of the election, recognized this truth. Jefferson himself, so far as is known, never commented one way or another on Adet's misguided intervention in his behalf. Federalist zealots saw in the episode certain proof of Jefferson's subservience to France. Adet knew better. "Mr. Jefferson likes us because he detests Britain . . . ," the Minister reported to his government, "but tomorrow he might change his opinion of us if tomorrow Britain should cease to inspire his fears. Jefferson, though a friend of liberty and enlightenment, an admirer of the efforts we have made to break the bonds and dispel the ignorance which burden the human race, Jefferson, I say, is an American and, as such, he cannot be sincerely our friend. An American is the born enemy of all the peoples of Europe."

When the electoral vote was tallied, Adams emerged the victor 71 to 68. Jefferson had carried Pennsylvania, the southern states, except South Carolina, evenly divided, and a portion of the Maryland vote. As the recipient of the second highest vote he was elected Vice President, though of the opposite party from the President. The candidates entered by both parties for the second office were victims of political stratagems inseparable from the electoral system. Thomas Pinckney, the Federalist candidate, if supported fairly by all the electors of his party would have ended in a tie with Adams; but to avert this result, which would drop the contest into the House of Representatives, it was only necessary for some of the Federalist electors to deny their votes to one of the candidates. Hamilton preferred Pinckney to Adams, no warm admirer of the Treasury system, stubbornly independent, and, in Hamilton's opinion, a poor bet to defeat Jefferson. So he plotted to bring Pinckney in ahead of Adams by splitting the South Carolina vote between the native son and the Virginian. Suspecting this treachery, Adams's friends in New England threw more than enough votes away from Pinckney to offset the defection in South Carolina. The bitter seeds Hamilton sowed in the Federalist ranks would sprout dragons in the course of time. In the case of Aaron Burr, the other half of the Republican ticket, the Virginians had defected. Burr felt betrayed. Yet it does not appear that the Republicans nationally or in several of the states ever endorsed the New Yorker. The Virginia electors were pledged to Jefferson but not to Burr, and he received only one of the state's 21 electoral votes. Burr's reputation was already tainted. The Virginians distrusted him; and he now distrusted them. Jefferson would soon get to know Burr better. Whatever opinion he may have formed of him before or during his flying visit in 1795, he had no part in Burr's candidacy or in the slap administered by the Virginia Republicans.

Jefferson descended from his lofty perch in December when it appeared the electoral vote would be uncomfortably close. He wrote to Madison on the 17th that should he and Adams end in a tie, he wished the choice to go to the New Englander. He had always been his junior in office; he could accept second place a good deal more gracefully than Adams. And if this was not reason enough, he would consider himself fortunate to trade the presidency for a post safe from political buffettings and requiring his presence in Philadelphia only one-third of every year. A rumor was abroad that he would accept the first office but not the second. In fact, he said repeatedly, the reverse was true. "If I am to act . . . a more tranquil and unoffending station could not have been found for me, nor one so analogous to the dispositions of my own mind. It will give me philosophical evenings in the winter, and rural days in the summer." Political wisdom and personal preference were in perfect accord. Now was not the time to take the helm. Let Adams ride out the storm that had been brewing for four years and was about to burst.

Madison, in Philadelphia, could more readily assess the advantages of Jefferson's position. He urged acceptance of the vice presidency—a plea quite unnecessary—and drew Jefferson's attention to the prospects of political conciliation under Adams. "You know that his feelings will not enslave him to the example of his predecessor. It is certain that his censures of our paper system and the intrigues at New York for setting Pinckney above him have fixed an enmity with the British faction. Nor should it pass for nothing, that the true interest of New England particularly requires reconciliation with France as the road to her commerce, add to the whole that he is said to speak of you now in friendly terms and will no doubt be soothed by your acceptance of a place subordinate to him." Adams and moderate Federalists were, in fact, soothed by Jefferson's expressions in his letter of the 17th, which Madison quietly circulated in Philadelphia. The Hamiltonians were alarmed. This shameful piece of "hypocrisy" and "Jacobinical intrigue," they warned, masked "a deep design to cajole and deceive the public." Hamilton himself was soon writing, "Our Jacobins say they are well pleased, and that the *Lion* and the *Lamb* are to lie down together. Mr. Adams' *personal* friends talk a little in the same way. . . . If Mr. Adams has *Vanity*, 'tis plain a plot has been laid to take hold of." Republicans who but the other day were denouncing Adams as an apostate from the principles of American liberty now lavished him with compliment. The *Aurora* lauded his "republican character," such a welcome change from the ostentatious Washington; and even the Virginia firebrand, William B. Giles, was heard to say, "The old man will make a good President too." As the election year came to a close, men who had been bitter foes rubbed their tired eyes in amazement at the prospect of political concord founded in the renewal of the Revolutionary alliance of Adams and Jefferson, Massachusetts and Virginia.

Word of these developments had not reached Monticello when Jefferson took up his pen to write a warm, congratulatory letter to his old friend. No one could congratulate him with more disinterestedness, Jefferson said. "I have no ambition to govern men. It is a painful and thankless task. Since the day too on which you signed the treaty of Paris our horizon was never so overcast." Condolences, not congratulations, seemed to be in order; but Jefferson prayed that Adams might preserve the peace, warned him against the schemes and tricks of his "arch-friend" in New York, and pledged his loyal support. Having written the letter Jefferson laid it aside, discouraged by the difficulty of making himself believed, and worried, perhaps, lest his expressions of magnanimity and cordiality convey more than he intended. Only after reading Madison's heartening report from Philadelphia did he mail the letter. Still hesitant, he took the precaution of enclosing it under cover of his answer to Madison, who should intercept or forward the epistle as he thought best. "If Mr. Adams can be induced to administer the government on its true principles, and to relinquish his bias to an English constitution," Jefferson stated, "it is to be considered whether it would not be on the whole for the public good to come to a good understanding with him as to his future elections. He is perhaps the only sure barrier against Hamilton's getting in."

Madison was startled by the suggestion of an understanding, perhaps a coalition, between Adams Federalists and Republicans. If this was the kind of overture that lurked in the honeyed phrases of his friend's letter to Adams, it should go no farther. Seeing that it did not, Madison offered Jefferson half a dozen reasons for his action. Adams's conciliatory feelings toward Jefferson were already advertised, likewise Jefferson's toward him. Any forwardness on the Virginian's part might prove offensive to a man of Adams's prickly temperament. Moreover, overt expressions of friendship would cause embarrassment should subsequent events call for vigorous opposition to the administration. Nor could the interests of the Republican party, only now feeling its strength and demanding opposition as its life's blood, be neglected. Already, Madison noted, Republican zealots groaned at the idea of a rapprochement. Adams had everything to gain by it, the Republicans everything to lose. True policy lay in cultivating the New Englander's better nature, separating him from the High Federalists, and giving a fair start to his executive career without, however, compromising the freedom and independence of the Republican organization. Jefferson thanked his friend for suppressing the overture. While his feelings were as he stated them, there was a delicacy and probably too much mischief in the attempt to convey them. On this cautious note, January 30, the dialogue on conciliation closed, to be resumed when Jefferson arrived at the seat of government.

He had wanted to avoid the official ceremony of inauguration in Philadelphia, but out of respect for the public suffered himself to go through with it with as little formality as possible. On February 20 he was back on the road he had traveled so many times in the past. Exchanging his phaeton and pair for the anonymity of the stage at Alexandria, and announcing a later arrival than he planned, Jefferson meant to sneak into the capital unnoticed. In this he was unsuccessful. A troop of artillery met him at the gates of the city, signaled his approach, and marched before him bearing aloft a banner inscribed "Jefferson, The Friend of the People." He at once called on Adams. Cordiality was the keynote. For several weeks the friends of both men had laid the ground for reconciliation. Adams, though for some time troubled by Jefferson's traffic with Paine, Freneau, Bache, and other "pernicious" characters, never doubted his talents and love of country. Jefferson, though disappointed by Adams's retreat from the principles of 1776, "never felt a diminution of confidence in his integrity, and retained a solid affection for him." The friendliness of these professions easily survived the test of the first meeting.

The ice broken, Adams called on Jefferson the next morning, March 3, at Madison's lodgings, and broached the problem of France. The success or failure of the new administration hung on the resolution of this crisis. France marauded American commerce, and diplomatic relations between the two countries had collapsed.

Several months previous Washington had recalled Monroe, alleging failure to cushion the shock of the Jay Treaty in Paris and subservience of his embassy to partisan designs in the United States. In response to this "unpardonable" affront, the Directory snubbed Monroe's replacement, Charles Cotesworth Pinckney, leaving no avenue to negotiation. Jefferson believed that Hamilton and his lieutenants in Washington's cabinet, which Adams was about to inherit, aimed at war in alliance with Britain. The calamity might be averted if Adams assumed a posture perfectly neutral and independent at the outset. "I do not believe Mr. Adams wishes war with France; nor do I believe he will truckle to England as servilely as has been done," he wrote hopefully to Madison. The Virginian and the New Englander had different opinions of the French Revolution, but neither supposed the differences touched vital national interests. Adams, for his part, wished the benefit of Jefferson's experience and prestige in the present crisis. This was the object of his visit on March 3.

His first wish was to send Jefferson to Paris. The idea was a natural one—several of Adams's friends advocated it. "Indeed," he later wrote to one of them, "I made a great stretch in proposing it, to accommodate to the feelings, views and prejudices of the parties." Unfortunately, the dispatch abroad of the "crown prince" posed serious difficulties. Jefferson concurred, adding his personal repugnance to a European mission. So Adams unfolded the plan of a bipartisan commission. Pinckney, still cooling his heels in Paris, was mentioned, also Elbridge Gerry, Adams's close friend in Massachusetts, a moderate Federalist, who would be acceptable to the Republicans, and finally, Madison. Madison was the key to the plan. Would he go? Jefferson did not know but agreed to ask him. As expected, Madison declined. What passed between the two Virginians on this occasion is unknown. Madison had turned down foreign posts before and was about to take a well-earned rest from active service; but, more than likely, political considerations, such as those he had earlier stated to Jefferson, controlled the decision. On March 6 Jefferson and Adams dined at Washington's table. After leaving, as they walked down the street to their lodgings, Jefferson explained the result of his inquiry. Adams, somewhat embarrassed, said that objections had been raised to Madison's appointment and he had already dropped the idea. Jefferson suspected the reason. Years later Adams recalled that he had mentioned to Wolcott the plan of joining Madison in a French mission. Wolcott at once fell into "a profound gloom," then pouted, "Mr. President, we are willing to resign." Amazed, Adams discovered on further inquiry that Federalists in the cabinet and in the Senate would not tolerate the conciliatory gesture he had planned. As Jefferson remembered that evening stroll with his old friend, they came to Fifth Street "where our road separated, his being down Market Street, mine off along Fifth, and we took leave; and he never after that said one word to me on the subject or ever consulted me as to any measure of the government."

The spirit of an *entente cordiale* set the tone of the inauguration on March 4 and lingered wistfully for several weeks. Jefferson took the oath of office in the Senate chamber. Concluding his little address with an encomium on the "eminent character" who had preceded him in the office, Jefferson prayed he might be "long preserved for the Government, the happiness, and prosperity of our common country." The ceremony completed, the Vice President led the Senate to the lower chamber for the inauguration of the President. A brilliant assemblage filled the hall. Washington entered to shouts of applause, repeated when Adams, followed by his secretaries, marched down the aisle and mounted to the Speaker's chair. Attired in drab gray, a sword dangling at his side, Adams looked to Washington and Jefferson on his right, the former in black, the latter in a long blue frockcoat. Adams, Washington, and Jefferson: these three giants of the American republic had so much in common and felt so much confidence in each other that they could never quite acknowledge, much less understand, the forces that drove them apart. They sat together on the same platform for the last time, and for a fleeting moment the twenty-one-year-old nation seemed united with its history. When the hubub subsided, Adams rose to deliver his inaugural address. It was elegantly done, on his own view "the sublimest thing ever delivered in America." With an eye to the "heresies" that had been alleged against him, Adams spiritedly declared his loyalty to the Constitution and to republican government. "What other form of government, indeed, can so well deserve our esteem and love?" It had secured for America "immortal glory with posterity." Pledging to administer the government without favor to party or section, Adams extended the hand of friendship to all who would unite with him for the good of the nation. As to foreign nations, he expressed "an inflexible determination" to maintain peace, faith, and honor within the system of neutrality so long sanctioned by the American people. Concluding with a solemn invocation of divine providence, Adams then took the oath of office. Resuming his seat briefly, he rose, bowed all around, and left the hall, followed by Jefferson and Washington, after an amusing byplay on the matter of precedence. Most of huzzas were for the retiring President, who in a few days was on the road to Mount Vernon and peace at last.

Republicans were delighted with Adams's address. He had, said the *Aurora*, "declared himself the friend of France and of peace, the admirer of republicanism, the enemy of party." Some Federalists objected to his "temporizing." But the euphoria of harmony lingered. "God grant it may continue," a Federalist judge wrote, "and serve to allay that vile party spirit which does so much injury to our country." It was not destined to last, however. Cast as Washington's successor, Adams dared not hazard an abrupt change of administration or abdication of responsibility to the Federalist party. It was a pretty thought that parties might vanish, or even become friends, but a President who acted on this expectation in 1797 would soon find himself alone and helpless. With a more than average capacity for self-delusion, Adams bowed to the party yoke without knowing he was putting it on. He sealed his fate by the decision to retain Washington's cabinet: Pickering, Wolcott, and James McHenry, all High Federalists and Francophobes, who took their orders from Alexander Hamilton. The implications of this decision were at once apparent to Jefferson on March 6. Every effort would be made to keep foreign policy on a collision course with France, and nothing would be left untried to alienate Adams from him. So he went his own way, hoping for the best but fearing the worst.

Jefferson tarried in Philadelphia several days after the inauguration. Caught up in the city's society once again, he seemed to enjoy it. He attended a great farewell banquet in Washington's honor. (The Vice President's toast: "Eternal union of sentiments between the commerce and agriculture of our country.") He attended a meeting of the American Philosophical Society. He replenished his wardrobe, buying boots, coat, and waistcoat. He renewed his acquaintance with elk (75 cents) and elephant (50 cents). On the 13th, after settling his bill for ten days board, wood, and wine at Francis' Hotel, he returned to Virginia. It was "a delicious spring." Cherry and peach trees popped into bloom as he neared home. Monticello was empty. He expected to accomplish miracles of building before going to Philadelphia in the fall. But Adams disappointed him by calling Congress into special session to deal with the French crisis. Jefferson was back in Philadelphia on May 11.

Adams's "war message," as the Republicans dubbed it, dispelled the illusion of harmony. Recent dispatches from France showed the determination of the Directory to force its will upon the United States by a combination of insult, plunder, and blackmail, the President declared. He called upon Congress to strengthen the country's defenses on land and sea, not with an immediate view to war but with a view to commanding respect for the mission he intended to send to France in a last desperate effort to preserve the peace. The executive secretaries had withdrawn their opposition to the special mission though not to a bipartisan one. Adams did not know it but he had Hamilton to thank for that. The New Yorker, with sharper political calculation than he usually showed, made his underlings see that the mission was necessary to disarm the Republicans. If it failed, as he expected, high policy at home and abroad would be without effective opposition.

While the cabinet labored to put together an acceptable three-man commission, Congress fell into bitter wrangling over the President's preparedness program. In the Senate, where Jefferson presided, the Federalists had a clear majority. In the House the opposition blocked most of the "warlike" measures. Republicans turned on Adams in a rage: the hand held out to them two months before concealed a dagger! The stream of invective again poured from the *Aurora*. The response strengthened the Federalists' conviction that "the infernal French disease" was an incurable, and increasingly dangerous, affliction of Republicanism. In Geneva, Holland, and Spain "republicanization" by way of collaboration between native revolutionaries and the French armies had ended in conquest and subjection. Was this not the fate France decreed for the United States? French hostility, Adams declared in his message, showed "a disposition to separate the people from the government." Extreme Federalists might find fault with the mildness of this expression; to the Republicans it meant that their motives and aims had no title of patriotism.

Once again, as in 1793, Jefferson found himself at the center of a political inferno. The passions of debate extended to the streets and into the parlors; the pleasures of society, so refreshing in March, turned to ashes in May, and as the dreary session dragged on into June and then July, Jefferson saw few but political friends and talked little but politics. Political opinions, he reminded himself, ought to be as inoffensive in social intercourse as opinions in philosophy or mechanics. Unfortunately, his countrymen were a long way from that elysium. Recurring to an old thought, he wondered if the high style of partisanship in the United States was not "inseparable from the different constitutions of the human mind, and that degree of freedom which permits unrestrained expression." "Foreign influence" was the hue and cry. It was just, but, Jefferson observed, those most guilty of the evil were loudest in the cry. Whatever the President's intentions, the "British faction" in control of the administration aimed at war. The plan, supposedly, was to negotiate peace while preparing for war, but this was a transparent fraud, which could not succeed with Congress or the Directory. "The struggle to keep us [in session], while pretending to negotiate for peace, from provoking war by putting ourselves into all its attitudes, will be arduous and doubtful," Jefferson observed. In truth, Congress had nothing to do. The panic induced by Adams's address quickly subsided under the sobering news of events in Europe. Napoleon Bonaparte's victories over the Austrians, the failure of the Bank of England, mutiny in the British fleet, revolutionary agitation in Ireland, Lord Malmsbury's negotiations with the French—these events cooled the "war party," Jefferson said, and revived the spirit of peace in Congress. The next act would be played in Paris. The three envoys named to the special commission, C. C. Pinckney, John Marshall, and Elbridge Gerry, were moderate Federalists of varying hues. The commission, while partisan, was better than Jefferson had expected it to be.

The letters the Vice President wrote during the meeting of Congress suggest at least the outlines of the policy he would have pursued had he been President. Peace was the great object. "Interest and honor are also national considerations," he conceded. "But inter-

est, duly weighed is in favor of peace even at the expense of spoliations past and future; and honor cannot now be an object"—it had
been insulted by Britain for years. Exhortations of national honor
and dignity left him cold, not because he was any less patriotic than
the exhorters but because he suspected they were war-mongering.
He dreaded war: "I anticipate the burning of our seaports, havoc of
our frontiers, household insurgency, with a long train of et ceteras."
In war Louisiana and the Floridas might become French colonies,
for Spain could not hold them. War would multiply the debt with
all its evils. War conducted on the side of Britain would give a head
to foreign influence fatal to the republic. War would not unite but
divide the nation. "Our countrymen have divided themselves by
such strong affections, to the French and the English, that nothing
will secure us internally but a divorce from both nations; and this
must be the object of every real American, and its attainment is
practicable without much self-denial." Here he echoed the sentiments of "non-entanglement" expressed in Washington's Farewell
Address. Older commitments to the French republic seemed to have
no place in this new calculus of the national interest.

War being the great behemoth of danger, Jefferson would have
avoided bluster and recrimination, put off provocative military measures, and assumed a posture of friendship toward France. The European conflict moved rapidly to a climax. The present campaign
was probably the last, so it seemed better for the United States to
"rub through this fragment of a year" as it had four preceding ones.
He would have admitted the justice of the Directory's complaint
against the Jay Treaty, for, in fact, that abomination threw American "neutrality" into the scales of British power and provoked the
decrees of the Directory that led to the present crisis. His enemies
charged he would abrogate the treaty. While he never suggested
that, it was not at all clear how he proposed to maintain the treaty
and at the same time pacify the French in 1797. He certainly would
have seized every opportunity to force the British into a straight-
and-narrow respect for American neutrality. Failing in this, he
might have been expected to experiment with commercial coercion,
perhaps an embargo of American trade, such as he would adopt a
decade later. "War is not the best engine for us to resort to," he
wrote in a memorable restatement of an old position, "nature has

given us one *in our commerce,* which, if properly managed, will be a better instrument for obliging the interested nations of Europe to treat us with justice." Indeed, he declared, had his commercial policy been adopted at an earlier time, "we should at this moment have been standing on such an eminence of safety and respect as ages can never recover."

Clearly, Jefferson continued to believe that Britain held the nation in bondage, hence any policy risking war with France fastened the chains of oppression. The danger was greater now than before. The oppression was greater; moreover, Britain was going down in Europe and would sink the United States too if it did not get clear of the wreck. In a remarkable flourish, written for Gerry's benefit in May, Jefferson summed up the ledger of British monopoly and influence:

> When we take notice that theirs is the workshop to which we go for all we want; that with them center either immediately or ultimately all the labors of our hands and lands; that to them belongs either openly or secretly the great mass of our navigation; that even the factorage of their affairs here, is kept to themselves by factitious citizenships; that these foreign and false citizens now constitute the great body of what are called our merchants, fill our seaports, are planted in every little town and district to the interior country, sway everything in the former places by their own votes and those of their dependents, in the latter, by their insinuations and the influence of their ledgers; that they are advancing fast to a monopoly of our banks and public funds, and thereby placing our public finances under their control; that they have in their alliance the most influential characters in and out of office; when they have shown that by all these bearings on the different branches of the government, they can force it to proceed in whatever direction they dictate, and bend the interests of this country entirely to the will of another; when all this, I say, is attended to, it is impossible for us to say we stand on independent ground, impossible for a free mind not to see and to groan under the bondage in which it is bound.

The only surprise, he concluded, was that the British party had "been able so far to throw dust in the eyes of our citizens, as to fix on those who wish merely to recover self-government the charge of subserving one foreign influence, because they resist submission to another."

In this same letter Jefferson recurred to the unpleasant subject of his relationship with the President. Gerry had Adams's ear and offered himself as a friendly intermediary. Jefferson confessed that the maneuvers of the British faction to alienate the President from him made him uneasy on the point of Adams's trust. "It cannot but damp the pleasure of cordiality, when we suspect that it is suspected. I cannot help fearing, that it is impossible for Mr. Adams to believe that the state of my mind is what it really is; that he may think I view him as an obstacle in my way." He had no desire to influence the executive councils and from the nature of his office could not. If only Adams would understand . . . . But as the party warfare thickened in the spring, so did the President's suspicions of Jefferson. Assuming a posture of opposition to France Adams inevitably drew closer to the High Federalists for whom Jefferson was the enemy. In letters to Gerry, Adams repelled warnings of British influence and Hamiltonian intrigue, arguing rather that the danger came from a French party subversive of American independence since 1778. When Jefferson supplied fresh proofs of his association with this party, Adams reluctantly concluded the Vice President was his enemy too.

The *coup de grâce* was a letter addressed to Adams from Georgetown in June. The author, Uriah Forrest, an old personal friend and Federalist zealot, had been privy to certain "disgraceful insinuations" and "barefaced assertions" made by the Vice President in a confidential letter to Peregrine Fitzhugh, a Maryland Republican with whom Jefferson corresponded on agricultural and political topics. Covering a number of the latter, Jefferson pointedly criticized Adams for endangering the peace of the country. Although Fitzhugh was enjoined to hold these sentiments in confidence, he showed the letter to his friends, among them his kinsman Forrest. Struck by the discrepancy between the public reports of cordiality and the censorious tone of the letter, Forrest committed the major part to memory, then wrote it down and sent it to Adams. The revelation was "a serious thing," Adams replied; he was grateful to Forrest for putting him on guard against Jefferson's cunning. "You can witness for me how loath I have been to give him up," he said in re-

porting the affair to his son John Quincy. "It is with much reluctance that I am obliged to look upon him as a man whose mind is
warped by prejudice and so blinded by ignorance as to be unfit for
the office he holds. However wise and scientific as a philosopher, as
a politician he is a child and a dupe of party!" Adams thus subscribed, grudgingly, to the canonized Federalist opinion of Jefferson. The Virginian, at the same time, though he knew nothing of
the Forrest letter, believed Adams had become a "dupe of party."
The breach between them was complete.

The estrangement was part of a crowded political canvas. Jefferson entered his new office in the expectation it would be "honorable
and easy." He was rapidly disappointed. He became, as he complained, "the property of the newspapers, a fair target for every
man's dirt." And powerless as his office was, he discovered that he
had been thrust into another and unofficial role, that of party leader,
in which he was the second most powerful figure in the country.
The two roles, official and unofficial, were quite compatible. Had
the *entente* materialized he would have felt a measure of responsibility to the administration; as it was, he could oppose and criticize
without any of the disquieting ambiguity of his position in 1792–93.
He could no longer escape the leadership of the Republican party.
Madison had withdrawn to Montpelier. The only first-rate man the
Republicans could boast in Congress, Geneva-born Albert Gallatin,
who had already caught Jefferson's eye, lacked the credentials for
national leadership. As Vice President, Jefferson was nothing. As
party leader, he was everything. Upon him Federalists and Republicans alike, one in fear, the other in hope, fixed their gaze.

The alacrity with which he stepped into this new role has never
ceased to amaze students of his character. The change from the retired master of Monticello to the downright politician, all in a few
months' time, was a remarkable instance of Jefferson's adaptability
to the political environment. He urged greater discipline on the Republicans in the House. He took an active part in building up the
Republican press, assisting new party organs and political pamphleteers like James T. Callender. This most scurrilous of Republican
scribes had fled Edinburgh in 1793 under indictment for sedition
founded on his tract, *The Political Progress of Britain*, which Jefferson admired. If the author's "advertisement" of the American edi-

tion may be credited, it was reprinted in Philadelphia on Jefferson's recommendation. In June 1797 Jefferson befriended this poor, woebegone refugee, and under the mask of charity opened his purse to support his writings. Jefferson penned many ingratiating letters to political leaders in key states, to dissident Federalists like Edward Rutledge in South Carolina, to moderates like Gerry, and to valued allies like Aaron Burr. These letters were all studiously calculated for political effect. With Burr, in particular, Jefferson's connections were entirely political; and his elaborate overture to the New York chieftain in June was prompted by the desire to work out a strategy for "the penetration of truth into the Eastern States." Later in the month, obviously gratified by this mark of confidence, Burr traveled to Philadelphia to map plans with Jefferson. At Francis' Hotel, where Jefferson lodged, surrounded by congressmen, in quarters that had neither the elegance nor the privacy he had craved as Secretary of State, he found many opportunities for conversation easily blending philosophy with the politics of the day. His enemies wondered what treasonable schemes were hatching in this nest.

The vice presidency, Federalists came to believe, was an imposing front behind which the incumbent deviously, secretly, conducted a campaign against the government. Sly old Fisher Ames, fearing something of this kind in December, had warned that Jefferson's election to the second office would be disastrous. "In the Senate that will bring him into no scrapes . . . , responsible for no measures, acting in none that are public, he may go on affecting zeal for the people; combining the *antis*, and standing at the head, he will balance the power of the chief magistrate by his own. Two Presidents, like two suns in the meridian, could meet and jostle for four years, and the Vice would be first." To combat the danger Federalist politicoes spared no effort to expose the Vice President, to flush him out of his privileged sanctuary, and arraign him before the public in all the colors of political depravity. Nothing would do so well as Jefferson's own hidden words and deeds. Fortune smiled on the Federalists at the opening of Congress, and it was many years before Jefferson could trust his pen again.

The damaging document was a letter Jefferson had written to Philip Mazzei on April 19, 1796. Most of it concerned the Florentine's private affairs in Virginia, but Jefferson digressed to give his old friend a quick view of the changed political scene in the United States. He said that "an Anglican monarchical, and aristocratical party has sprung up, whose avowed object is to draw over us the substance, as they have already done the forms, of the British government." The mass of citizens remained republican, but against them were the executive, the judiciary, the Senate, traders on British capitals, speculators, stockjobbers, and so on. "It would give you a fever were I to name to you the apostates who have gone over to these heresies, men who were Samsons in the field and Solomons in the council, but who have had their heads shorn by the harlot England." Mazzei should not be alarmed, however. The Americans would "awake and snap the Lilliputian cords," and so preserve their hard-won liberty. Written in the angry aftermath of the Jay Treaty, the letter was an accurate summation of Jefferson's political views, though especially combustible because the rhetoric was highly compressed. Mazzei, quite combustible himself, turned the political portion of the letter into Italian and saw to its publication in a Florentine newspaper. The Paris *Moniteur* picked it up and lectured the "ungrateful children" of France, "their true mother country," for submitting to the harlot; and this French version, turned back into English, appeared in the American press in May 1797.

Jefferson met with the published letter while en route to Philadelphia. He at first thought he must buckle on his armor and take to the newspapers. Yet this posed difficulties. He could not disavow what he had in substance written. Nor could he altogether avow it, since in completing the circuit of three languages his own words had been altered in one or two particulars. For example, where he had referred to the *forms* of the British government, meaning "birth-days, levees, processions to parliament, inauguration pomposities, etc.," the letter as published referred to the *form*, meaning monarchy. Furthermore, since to avow was to defend, he would be compelled to go into proofs, explanations, and secret transactions which must, as he said, "embroil me personally with every member of the Executive, with the Judiciary, and others still," indeed with the nine-tenths of the people of the United States who worshipped Washington's character. So he decided to remain silent. Federalist pundits took his silence as admission of guilt: the treasonous guilt of maligning the government of the United States, of emboldening

571

French insult and aggression, above all of libeling General Washington. Who but Washington and his colleagues were the "Samsons in the field and Solomons in the council" of the infamous letter? Years later, not long before he died, Jefferson said his allusion had been to the Society of the Cincinnati; but the explanation seems not to have occurred to him in 1797, and had he made it few, least of all the Federalists, would have believed him.

With the publication of the Mazzei letter Jefferson stood accused of defaming Washington, and not only Washington but the American character of which he was the hero. The political value of this exposé was beyond calculation. It tumbled the lofty philosopher from his pedestal into the ranks of slanderers like Bache, Paine, and Beckley. Disclosing his deceit toward the first President, it showed, some said, the fundamental duplicity of Jefferson's character. The Federalists had labored to bathe their party in the radiance of Washington's fame. The Farewell Address, so largely Hamilton's work, was a testament to their success. Federalist policy was identified with the national interest, with patriotism, with Washington's name; and partisan opposition was denied any title of legitimacy. Hamilton spoke for himself when he later acknowledged that Washington had been "an *Aegis very essential to me*," yet it might have been said of the party generally. In Jefferson's opinion the personification of the Federalist party was the paramount fact of American political life until March 4, 1797, and he was not a little distressed that the candor of his own pen should now help to perpetuate this idolotrous influence.

His tone toward Washington was normally respectful. The Mazzei letter was, in this regard, an aberration. He thought Washington a great and good man who had been misled, gulled by flattery, and captured by the gang around him. Whether this view was any less flattering than the one which saw him as the conscious agent of Federalist power is an interesting question; for Jefferson, at any rate, it enabled him to reconcile his exalted idea of Washington's character with his profound distrust of Washington's administration. While Washington was President, Jefferson observed, the Republicans were virtually paralyzed by the spell he cast over the American public. For the people would always support him "without appealing to their own reason or to anything but their feelings toward him"; and his mind was "so long used to unlimited applause that it could not brook contradictions, or even advice offered unasked." Once Washington withdrew into retirement, Jefferson expected the magic of his name to fade too, ushering in the epoch of political self-possession. He was disappointed for a number of reasons, of which the Mazzei letter was more symptom than cause. Yet that letter, by serving to portray him as the assassin of Washington, helped the Federalists to bring back the charisma and to vilify him for wishing to obliterate it.

What Washington himself thought of the epistle can only be surmised. After his retirement to Mount Vernon, he did not see Jefferson again, nor did any letters pass between them—negative evidence in itself of their alienation. Seeds of suspicion and distrust had been planted in Washington's mind for years. Jefferson's anxiety to remove them had, in fact, occasioned the last of his letters to Washington, in the summer of 1796. He had learned that "a miserable tergiversator," Henry Lee, had been "dirtily employed in sifting the conversations of my table" and carrying the crumbs to Washington in order "to sow tares between you and me." To Jefferson's assurances of unfailing friendship, Washington responded with assurances of his own, saying he discredited all reports of Jefferson's enmity. Presumably the seeds sprouted with the disclosure of the Mazzei letter, and they came to harvest in Washington's mind four or five months later. Peter Carr, Jefferson's favorite nephew, who should have known better, wrote to Washington over the fictitious signature of John Langhorne, apparently with a view to eliciting political sentiments useful to the Republican cause in Virginia. Washington replied in a non-committal fashion. There the matter might have ended but for a Federalist snooper in the Charlottesville post office, "Clerk John" Nicholas, who informed the old hero that the Langhorne letter emanated from "the very headquarters of Jacobinism" and gave further proof of the "vile hypocrisy" of the author of the Mazzei letter. This time Washington was not incredulous. "Nothing short of the evidence you have adduced," he wrote Nicholas, "corroborative of intimations which I had received long before, through another channel, would have shaken my belief in the sincerity of a friendship, which I had conceived was possessed by me . . . ." In retirement, observing the conceit of France and the refractoriness of

the Republicans, Washington grew more and more fearful of subversion of the government. He could no longer separate this fear
from Jefferson—was he not chief of the subverters? So political
enmity slid into personal enmity, and Washington credited the testimony of a village gossip for the proof of suspicions he had earlier
repressed. Of course, Jefferson had no responsibility whatever for
the Langhorne letter. Any enmity he felt toward Washington was
political, not personal, and he was quite incapable of the silly little
scheme concocted by his nephew. Not for some time, in fact, did he
learn of this episode which closed the book, rather sadly, on a long
friendship.

The controversy over the Mazzei letter coincided with Jefferson's assumption of the Republican leadership. The former was not
necessary to the latter, but by raising Federalist censure to new
heights, by publicly exhibiting the Vice President in partisan garb,
by stinging his pride, it enabled him to accept his new role with
something like cheerfulness. Such an experience at an earlier time
would have excited all his old loathing for politics and sent him
scurrying back to Monticello. But not now. If he became more
guarded with his pen, he neither disguised his opposition to the
Adams administration nor evaded the responsibilities of leadership.
There were grave political risks in the advocacy of pacific policy
toward France in 1797, yet Jefferson ran the risk and severed the
lines of retreat to domestic conciliation and compromise. On July 1,
a few days before Congress adjourned, he attended a festive dinner
at Oeller's to welcome James Monroe, the recalled envoy from
France and defender of the old alliance. The party was a Republican
affair. Jefferson was toasted "The man of the people." Not only to
Federalists but to some Republican moderates as well, it was a celebration of Jacobinism. One of the latter, John Rutledge, Jr., the
young South Carolinian he had befriended in Paris years before, was
shocked by Jefferson's presence in such company. "It was a complete medley . . . . Here you saw an American disorganizer and
there a blundering Irishman—in another corner a banished Genevan
and in another a French Spy—on one side a greasy Butcher and on
the other a dirty Cobbler . . . ." Young Rutledge had recently
written his uncle that Jefferson was "a wonderfully great and good
man but I really believe that the severe persecution he has lately un-

dergone (and which continues) has occasioned a little fresh bias."
Now, after the Monroe fete, Rutledge was the more convinced, and
soon he would be counted among the most violent of the Federalists.

Several days later Jefferson exchanged "the roar and tumult of
bulls and bears" for the prattle of his grandchildren at Monticello.
He had left home in May as the Vice President; he returned in July
as the leader of the Republican party. There was no suspension of
politics when he entered his sanctuary. Madison, Monroe, and the
Albemarle friend and congressman Wilson Cary Nicholas, a comparative newcomer to the inner circle, came to the mountain to confer on political tactics. They reviewed Jefferson's silent treatment of
the Mazzei letter. Only Monroe thought he should take to print.
Monroe himself was preparing to do so in defense of his conduct as
minister to France. Jefferson, while rather cool to the project, lent
Monroe a helping hand. The notorious Reynolds affair, for five
years a well-kept secret among half-a-dozen Republicans including
Jefferson, blew up in the summer months. Beckley fed the scandal
to Callender, and he published it in a tract Jefferson neither approved nor disapproved. Although his scrupulous respect for privacy in affairs of personal honor would never permit him to indulge
his own pen on this tawdry episode in Hamilton's career, he could
not forbid it to hacks like Callender.* The political implications of
the publication must have been discussed at Monticello, especially as
it seemed likely for a time to produce a duel between Hamilton and
Monroe, whom the New Yorker held responsible. And there were
other political questions, such as the encroachment of the federal judiciary on freedom of speech, which began to agitate Jefferson. He
wrote few political letters during this season. The risk was too high
—he had learned his lesson. The affairs of state, while discouraging,
were not at the point of crisis, nor would they be as long as Americans and Frenchmen talked in Paris. So Jefferson found time and repose for children and grandchildren, building and farming, and
for intellectual activities that even in critical hours held high claim
on his mind.

* The affair had its beginnings in the controversy of 1790 over the ar-
rearages of soldiers' pay. (See pp. 414-15.) James Reynolds was one of a group
of speculators engaged in buying up the soldiers' certificates. The next year,

Science and Politics

When Jefferson journeyed to Philadelphia for the inauguration he carried with him a box of fossilized bones, the remains of some great unknown creature lately uncovered in Virginia. He had written a paper to announce this discovery to the scientific world from the rostrum of the American Philosophical Society. On the recent death of its second president, David Rittenhouse, the Society had elected Jefferson to the chair; and so he came to Philadelphia to be installed not only in the second office of the government of the United States but also in the first office of American science. He took the chair at the Society's evening meeting on March 10. On his left sat Joseph Priestley, the distinguished chemist, philosopher, revolutionary, and dissenting theologian, who had fled persecution in England, and on his right the peripatetic French rationalist Volney, also a refugee in the land of freedom. Jefferson, Priestly, Volney: a philosophical triumvirate of the Enlightenment. There was the usual business of the Society, and papers on "The Big Naked Bear" of the Delawares and

---

with blackmail his object, Reynolds employed the charms of his wife Maria to seduce Hamilton. Hamilton fell into the trap, and into the lady's boudoir, and was soon paying handsomely. When the amour ceased, and when fortune turned against Reynolds, this rake exposed Hamilton to three Republican congressmen, one of them Monroe, not only as an adulterer but as a speculator in the public funds as well. The Republicans, who were then, in 1792, looking into the Treasury, were especially interested in the charge of public misconduct. When they confronted Hamilton he confessed the adultery in order to save his public reputation. The three Republicans, apparently satisfied on the latter point, had no wish to make a scandal of Hamilton's private life. Nor did Jefferson, who knew of the affair. But in 1797 John Beckley, who also knew of it, and who had recently been dismissed by the Federalists from his position as Clerk of the House of Representatives, gave the entire story to Callender, without consulting Jefferson, Monroe, or others in the Republican leadership. As the affair was told by Callender in his *History of the United States for the Year 1796*, Hamilton was both an adulterer and a partner with Reynolds in corrupt financial transactions. Hamilton now defended his public morality by confessing his private vices in his *Observations* on Callender's tract. Jefferson, although not entirely satisfied that Hamilton had, in fact, cleared himself of public misconduct, showed no interest in pursuing the matter after Hamilton himself blasted his political future.

on the properties of land and sea air; but the feature of the meeting was Jefferson's "Memoir on the Discovery of Certain Bones of a Quadruped of the Clawed Kind in the Western Parts of Virginia."

These bones had been discovered by diggers of saltpeter in a limestone cave in Greenbrier County, beyond the Blue Ridge, in 1796. A local resident, John Stuart, had sent them to Monticello. For years, since his famous encounter with Buffon, Jefferson had been collecting the relics of mysterious vertebrate giants; no objects of natural history were more interesting to him, and the bigger they came the better he liked them. He was especially excited by this new discovery, for the bones belonged to an animal apparently unknown to science. Judging from the huge claws eight inches long, he thought it probably of "the family of lion, tiger, panther, etc., but as preeminent over the lion in size as the mammoth is over the elephant." Communicating this information to Rittenhouse, he named the animal the great-claw, or megalonyx. Although eager to write an account of the discovery for inclusion in the fourth volume of the Society's *Transactions*, soon to be published, Jefferson put it off in the hope that important missing parts of the skeleton would be found in the diggings. And more bones were found, but not the thigh bone necessary to fix the animal's stature, nor any teeth. He finally ventured to write the memoir anyway, and in February packed up the bones he had for presentation to the Society.

Arriving in Philadelphia he came upon an article recently published in London which shook his classification of the animal. The article described the skeleton of a huge creature unearthed in Paraguay, brought to Madrid, and mounted in the Royal Cabinet of Natural History. (Jefferson had actually received a sketch and description of the skeleton in 1789, but, unhappily, had forgotten all about it eight years later.) The animal had great claws and measured 12 feet long and 6 feet high; however, it was classed not with the lion but with the non-carnivorous sloth, hence named great-sloth, or megatherium. Jefferson at once recognized the similarities between this specimen and the one he was about to describe in Philadelphia, yet shunned the conclusion that they were, in fact, the same. The London article was "only an abstract" of a paper written by the French naturalist Cuvier; the engraving of the skeleton, reproduced in the magazine, struck him as unreliable; and so many bones were missing, particularly in his own specimen, there was no sure basis of analogy. Jefferson mentioned the abstract in a postscript to his paper; in fact, he went further, cautiously toning down his classification of the animal. Yet he stuck to the name, megalonyx, and compared it to the lion. With the largest of the bones on the table before him, he told the Society that the animal was at least three times the size of the lion and undoubtedly as worthy an antagonist of the mammoth as the lion was of the elephant. Buffon was long dead, but Jefferson was still combating his theories of New World pygmyism.

Having described the animal as best he could, Jefferson went on to argue that it continued to exist, like the mammoth, somewhere in the dark forest beyond the American frontier. He cited accounts of early adventurers in Virginia who mentioned lion-like creatures, of images carved on rock above the Ohio River, and tales of Indians and pioneers of "terrible roarings" and "eyes like two balls of fire" aglow in the forest. Of course, it was part of the economy of nature to check the rapid multiplication of so powerful a destroyer, and so megalonyx was probably the rarest of living creatures. "In fine," he concluded, "the bones exist: therefore the animal has existed. The movements of nature are in a never ending circle. The animal species which has once been put into a train of motion, is still probably moving in that train. For if one link in nature's chain might be lost, another and another might be lost, till this whole system of things would evanish by piece-meal." At bottom, Jefferson's faith in a divinely ordered universe made it impossible for him, as indeed for Buffon and most of the naturalists of his generation, to credit the extinction of species; and thus despite his enormous contribution to paleontology as a collector and a spokesman, he denied the proposition essential to the establishment of this young science.

In this particular instance, science would have been better served had Jefferson been able to overcome the prepossessions that caused him to link the mysterious creature to the leonine species. The excitement of the discovery conquered his usual skepticism of airy hypothesis. When he returned to Philadelphia for the meeting of Congress in May, he met with an impressive folio volume on the Paraguayan animal, which had been published in Madrid the preceding year. Here were the original descriptions and drawings of the skeleton mounted in Madrid—the authentic basis of Cuvier's paper and the London abstract. Very likely the Virginia megalonyx was the same animal. Yet Jefferson was not entirely convinced. "Since this discovery [of megalonyx] had led to questioning the Indians as to this animal," he informed Stuart, "we have received some of their traditions which confirm his classification with the lion." The nature of this questioning he did not explain, but he and his colleagues in the American Philosphical Society had not been inactive. At the May meeting they discussed a plan to amass information on the antiquities of North America, including the skeletons of giant creatures. Not for several years would Jefferson concede the identity of megalonyx and megatherium. Scientific judgment was still uncertain, so he had no cause for embarrassment; and in the end Cuvier himself, the first true scientist of fossil quadrupeds, paid high tribute to Jefferson for his work in paleontology as in the other sciences.

The episode is a notable instance of Jefferson's diligence in matters of scientific investigation and, at the same time, of the national pride that infused the enterprise. All his attachments, he once said, were to "science, and freedom, the first born daughter of science." Freedom was the first principle of inquiry, inquiry the beginning of freedom. The despots of the world, supported by slavish ignorance, feared science because they feared freedom. Priestley's riotous enemies in England, Jefferson told an admirer from that country, "think they have quenched his opinions by sending him to America, just as the pope imagined when he shut up Galileo in prison that he had compelled the world to stand still." Truth had no country. Men of science the world around spoke the same language and engaged in the same search even as their countries warred upon each other; and it always seemed to Jefferson that the relations among nations ought to be copied from the fraternal community of science. In republican America, certainly, there was no cause for political dissensions to impair the quest for knowledge. Science was apolitical. What did it matter whether a man called himself a Republican or a Federalist if his work contributed to the upbuilding of civilization in America and the improvement of mankind? When Jefferson accepted the presidency of the Philosophical Society he confessed to have one clear qualification for the post: "an ardent desire to see knowledge so disseminated through the mass of mankind that it may at last reach the extremes of society, beggars and kings." He held this post through all the years of his presidency and on into 1814. In the dual role of public leadership, in science and in government, he saw nothing incompatible; indeed he believed they were mutually supporting.

Unfortunately, his political foes did not agree. They ridiculed his scientific attainments, called him philosopher, visionary, speculator—opprobrious terms the rough coefficients of which were revolutionary, infidel, and incompetent—and set down science as a positive liability to statesmanship. Years later Jefferson reflected, "Of all the charges brought against me by my political adversaries, that of possessing some science has probably done them the least credit." And the least good, for, he added, "Our countrymen are too enlightened themselves, to believe that ignorance is the best qualification for service." The attack began in 1792, subsided, revived in 1796, and exploded from the moment of his election to the vice presidency.

His appearance on the platform of the American Philosophical Society offered a fitting picture for Federalist diatribe. William Cobbett, the English bookseller who had just commenced publication of *Porcupine's Gazette* in Philadelphia, was amused by the solemn discourse on an old bone and, taking note of Volney and Priestley, wondered what fate awaited the nation from this "triumvirate of *atheism, deism,* and *nothingism.*" Among the Federalist scribes Peter Porcupine was the master of invective. The Vice President was a regular recipient. Mocking his own would-be assassins sometime later, Peter printed his last will and testament. "To Thomas Jefferson, philosopher," one clause began, "I leave a curious Norway spider, with a hundred legs and nine pair of eyes; likewise the first black cutthroat general he can catch hold of, to be flayed alive, in order to determine with more certainty the real cause of the dark colour of his skin . . . ." As a philosopher Jefferson was a straw man, but had he believed him to possess solid merits, Cobbett would have thought no better of him in affairs of state. According to Cobbett, "if one characteristic more than another could disqualify Mr. Jefferson for the Presidency, it would be the charge of being a philosopher." Robert Goodloe Harper, the South Carolina Federalist, while more respectful, concurred in this opinion. "He possesses much knowledge, chiefly however of the scientific kind, the least useful for a statesman, whose business it is to judge and act, not to write books." A man who is "always pursuing certain visionary theories of the closet, which experience constantly contradicts . . . cannot be relied on for the performance of any duty, which might require . . . a manly decisive conduct in difficult situations." And so, Harper concluded in a public letter, "With this opinion of Mr. Jefferson, I might think him fit to be a professor of a college, President of a Philosophical Society, or even Secretary of State; but certainly not the first magistrate of a great nation." The republic of Jefferson's vision was one in which freedom and science advanced hand in hand—a republic of science. In the Federalist mind, Jeffersonian science—air balloons, philosphical plows, mammoth bones, salt mountains, the Negro's kidneys, vibrating pendulums, wirligig chairs—was absurd, and Heaven preserve the nation from the whimsies of its projector. "Science and government are two different paths," a Federalist tract summed up the argument in 1800. "He that walks in one, becomes, at every step, less qualified to walk with steadfastness or vigour in the other."

A direct challenge to Jefferson's reputation as a scientific man occurred within a month of his return to office. In the pages of *Porcupine's Gazette*, Luther Martin, Attorney General of Maryland, vehemently objected to the inclusion of "The Story of Logan, the Mingo Chief" in the program of readings and recitations of a Philadelphia actor. The story, of course, had been popularized by Jefferson's account in the *Notes on Virginia*. Already an American legend in 1797, it was the theme of drama and verse and Logan's tragic plaint the *ne plus ultra* of savage eloquence. In this impassioned utterance at the conclusion of Lord Dunmore's War in 1774, Logan blamed Michael Cresap for the murder of his family. From this circumstance the ensuing blood bath on the upper waters of the Ohio was sometimes called Cresap's War. Jefferson, who introduced the speech in the *Notes* to refute Buffon's aspersions on the Indians, went along with Logan and described Cresap as "a man infamous for many murders" on the frontier. In all the years since 1775, when the story was first published, no one had challenged its truth. Now Martin declared that the speech was a fraud and that Jefferson, by broadcasting it, had libeled an innocent man, the late Captain Cresap. Like the philosopher he was, said Martin, Jefferson had a ridiculous hypothesis to establish, the equality of the American savage with the civilized European, and he picked up Logan's story without stopping to verify it or to consider its injury to the good name of Cresap. The vindication of that name was a point of honor with Martin, for Cresap's daughter, now dead, was the mother of his children.

This profession of motive was transparently false. The more Jefferson pondered the matter the more convinced he became that Martin acted as "the cat's paw" of party. "After letting this matter remain uncontradicted for upwards of twenty years it has now been raked up from party hatred, as furnishing some with the design of writing me down." The timing of the letter, the place of its initial publication, its barbs and innuendo, the entire absence of evidence against the traditional account—Martin obviously had more interest in smearing the Vice President than in clearing the name of his father-in-law. Yet his motives are not easily assessed. A Marylander to whom Jefferson made inquiry supposed that Martin must have acted in "a state of drunkenness from which he is scarcely ever free." He was a sick man, often depressed, a Federalist but forever scarred by his Anti-Federal past, as well as by fondness for drink and an unruly temperament. In short, the Federalist leaders would not have trusted Luther Martin, for all his talents at the bar, as a "cat's paw" to tickle the Vice President. The attack was political because Martin made it so, and because in the climate then existing any blemish on Jefferson's character was bound to have political repercussions.

Had it been only for these repercussions, had it been merely an attack on Jefferson as a political man, he would have adhered to his rule of silence in such matters; but Martin struck at his reputation for science and truth, and this was a different matter. Intellectually, he was committed to the principles Logan's speech had been evinced to prove; moreover its truth or falsity, unlike political opinions, was open to investigation. So Jefferson quietly commenced an inquiry, pursued for nearly three years, to establish the authenticity of the story of Logan and Cresap. Witnesses to these events of a quarter-century past still lived. Jefferson knew some of them; as the investigation proceeded he learned of others who volunteered their testimony. In effect, he made himself the annalist and the historian of this small but illuminating episode in the American past. The methods he employed were in striking constrast to the invective and bombast of his enemies.

While Jefferson prepared to overwhelm his assassin with facts, that intemperate gentleman wrote more public letters. Furious that Jefferson would not enter into the contest at his own level, or even acknowledge his letters, Martin said that he condemned himself by his "obstinate, stubborn silence." In Maryland the Attorney General's accusations were having the desired political effect. The Governor, John Henry, tried to cool the controversy but was nearly consumed by it. Before his election to this post in November 1797, Henry had been in the United States Senate where, despite his party affiliation, he had formed a high opinion of the Vice President. He expressed this opinion at Annapolis, Martin's letters being the subject of conversation, and pointedly declared "that men of sense and moderation ought not to suffer their minds to be led awry by the wicked, malicious reports unprincipled men were daily circulating." He was astonished at the result. "Innocent and natural as this conversation appears, it nevertheless instantly kindled a flame which flew through all the boarding houses and so violently agitated the minds of the majority of the legislature, that I verily believe if they . . . had the power they would have displaced the man whom a few days before they had elected to the chief office in the state without a dissenting voice." Instead they elected to the Senate seat vacated by Henry a Federalist of the same violent stripe as Luther Martin. Compared with the animosities released by the Mazzei letter or the furies that raged around Jefferson in 1798, Luther Martin's vendetta was an annoying side-show. Still it was singularly instructive to Jefferson and his friends. The Federalist press participated in Martin's malice and misrepresentation, and in at least one instance that came to Jefferson's attention closed its columns to authentic testimony on Logan's speech. Truth, justice, probity—the rules of scientific inquiry itself—seemed to be at stake in the party struggle.

All the while Jefferson was quietly amassing documentary evidence, letters, depositions, versions of Logan's speech—two dozen separate items—some solicited, some unsolicited, some obtained by old friends like Mann Page, Harry Innes, and James Brown, some obtained from total strangers like the Reverend John Heckwelder, a

Moravian missionary to the Delawares who had known Logan, John Sappington, the killer of Logan's brother, and General John Gibson, the recipient of the famous address. By 1800 Jefferson was ready to publish these "fragments of evidence, the small remain of a mighty mass which time has consumed," and he did so in the form of an appendix to the *Notes on Virginia*.

The story as reconstructed from this evidence was more complex than he had imagined, yet in its essentials consistent with what he had believed since first hearing Logan's speech repeated by Dunmore's officers in Williamsburg. It was necessary to distinguish four separate massacres on the Ohio below Fort Pitt in the bloody spring of 1774. Frontiersmen, mostly Virginians, were occupying this land claimed by the Shawnee. Logan, a Cayuga sachem, whose Indian name was Tah-gah-jute, had married a Shawnee and established a settlement at the mouth of Yellow Creek on the north bank of the Ohio. As a boy he had frequented the Moravian mission and been baptized in the name of the Secretary of the Province of Pennsylvania. Among whites and Shawnee alike he was known as a friend of the Long Knives. Fears of Indian attack spread up and down the river in April. The frontiersmen looked to Cresap, later commissioned a captain by Dunmore, for leadership. At the head of a party on the south shore near Wheeling, he laid ambush and killed two Indians, then quickly moved down the river to Grove Creek and killed several more, including some of Logan's family settled there. The next day Cresap's party went up the river to Yellow Creek. However, Cresap dropped out, leaving Daniel Greathouse in charge. The party stopped at a place called Baker's Bottom, opposite Yellow Creek, where there was a tavern. When six or seven Indians from Logan's settlement came to the tavern the next morning, Greathouse and his men got them drunk and massacred everyone. Logan's brother and sister "big with child" were among the victims. Other Indians, on hearing the shots, paddled across the river to investigate. Some fled, some were killed. At this point Logan went on the warpath.

So the famous speech had erred in blaming Cresap for all the murders that extinguished Logan's blood from every living creature. Jefferson acknowledged the error but did not think it mitigated Cresap's crime. For in the massacre at Yellow Creek, Greathouse

584

was only pursuing the example set by Cresap. Further evidence brought to light at a later time suggested that Cresap was more directly implicated in the final murders than Jefferson claimed; even so, at the end of his researches the guilt remained where Logan had placed it. "Logan imputed the whole to Cresap . . . : the Indians generally imputed it to Cresap: Lord Dunmore and his officers imputed it to Cresap: the country, with one accord, imputed it to him: and whether he was innocent, let the universal verdict now declare." The documents spoke for themselves. As to the authenticity of the Indian's utterance, which Martin had denied, the evidence was equally convincing. Many of Jefferson's informants reported hearing the speech at the time, some at Dunmore's headquarters when peace was made—the same speech they had later seen in the newspapers or in the *Notes on Virginia*. Men who knew Logan, like the Moravians, believed him fully capable of such eloquence. In the final analysis, the point rested on the testimony of one man, General Gibson, who had been sent by Dunmore to obtain Logan's consent to the treaty. The Mingo spoke in his native tongue. Gibson, a man of some learning and also the father of a child by Logan's murdered sister, translated and took the words down in English. In his deposition Gibson gave an exact account of the incident and vouched for the accuracy of his translation. Another deponent testified that Gibson, on showing the speech in Pittsburgh, had said it was but "a poor picture of the original."

Jefferson's manner of treating the subject in his pamphlet-appendix, ignoring Martin altogether and relying, as he said, on "exact information of the historical past," caused rejoicing among his friends and proved definitive during his lifetime. When the controversy was revived after his death, the new accusers found one gaping hole in his scholar's armor. Regrettably, he had suppressed the one piece of testimony most damaging to his case. His old friend George Rogers Clark, the once idolized hero of the West, professed a "perfect recollection" of the entire transaction, which he related in a detailed narrative. Clark had known Cresap and been a member of his party in April 1774. The Marylander deserved a medal for good conduct, in Clark's opinion, and should not be blamed for any of the murders Logan charged to him. The speech was unquestionably Logan's, but he had been misinformed, Clark stated. On hearing it, Cresap had smiled and said he had a mind to tomahawk Greathouse. Why did Jefferson suppress Clark's letter? Not simply because it was favorable to Cresap, for he published other testimony of this character. And not simply because Clark alone of all the witnesses boasted a venerable name. Jefferson plainly did not think the Kentuckian's narrative trustworthy, and rather than expose it for what it was, "an attempt to rub out blood with whitewash," as Irving Brant has said, Jefferson mercifully buried it in his private papers. While his action may be regarded as a mark of charity for an old warrior who had lost all character for judgment, the indulgence was quite mistaken. Jefferson assumed the stance of a historian: let the documents speak, he said, and the testimony of all witnesses declare. But he withheld a singularly important document of a singularly important witness. The verdict would probably not have been different had he published Clark's narrative; and had he done so he would have removed the only basis for cavil with what was, in truth, a remarkable vindication of sober intelligence against vicious partisanship. Under Jefferson's barrage of facts Luther Martin was as silent as the grave. It would have been pleasant to dismiss him altogether, but in the passage of time Jefferson would have to fight off this "impudent Federal bull-dog" again and again, and with a good deal less success.

If Jefferson felt a somewhat romantic attraction for the American Indian, the methods and aims of his study were in the best tradition of science in his time. He had suggested the broad field open to investigation in the *Notes on Virginia.* Now as president of the American Philosophical Society he made a special point of advancing knowledge of the aborigines. Evidence of an archaeological nature tending to prove the red man capable of the civilizing arts was especially welcome. Languages remained Jefferson's principal interest. For years he had been placing his "blank vocabularies" into the hands of friends able to fill them up with the corresponding words of the different tribes. By comparing these languages with one another and also with Asiatic tongues, Jefferson hoped to construct the anthropology of the redmen. Supposing that the large number of radically different languages among the Indians could only have developed over an immense time, he had ventured the opinion in the *Notes* that these people were of greater antiquity than those of Asia, possibly as old as mankind itself. The opinion was a minority one. The Indians were generally traced to Asia, and thence back to the common cradle of the human race.

A prominent New York minister, the Reverend William Linn, challenged Jefferson's opinion in 1798. He replied that it had been "hazarded" on the state of knowledge a decade and a half ago; much had been learned since then, and there was still much more to learn. "My object being the true facts, I do not permit myself to form as yet a decisive opinion, and therefore leave the slight one I had hazarded to the result of further enquiry." When all the vocabularies were collected and then laid beside the Empress Catherine's great compendium of the Asiatic languages, perhaps men would be able to draw conclusions. Linn participated in Jefferson's enterprise but refused to credit his scientific purpose. In the presidential campaign two years later he blasted Jefferson as an infidel, including in his array of evidence the "profane" opinion advanced in the *Notes* that the Indians were indigenous to America. Politics and science did not mix, nor did religion and science. Benjamin Smith Barton, a colleague in the Philosophical Society, though he too disagreed with Jefferson on important points of Indian ethnology and linguistics, was considerably more generous than Linn. Recognizing Jefferson's leadership in this area of scientific investigation, Barton dedicated his book, *New Views of the Origin of the Tribes of Natives of America*, to him.

Describing his collection of vocabularies to Benjamin Hawkins, federal agent to the Creeks, Jefferson said he was "afraid to risk it any longer, lest by some accident it might be lost." So he was about to publish it. Unfortunately, he did not act on this premonition, which materialized in 1809, the whole collection being lost in the course of moving his household from Washington to Monticello. He wanted his collection to be as complete as possible before sending it forth. In 1800, when he wrote to Hawkins, he still did not have the languages of the great nations south of the Ohio. Hawkins would get for him the Choctaw, another the Chickasaw, and so on. But then entirely new tribes came into the white man's ken, even an entirely new kind of communication. From William Dunbar, in Natchez, Jefferson received the first information of "the language by signs" among the Plains Indians and hardly knew what to make of it.

The opening of the Mississippi Territory in the last years of the century commenced a new chapter in the natural history of America. Jefferson was exhilarated by every scrap of scientific intelligence from the unknown land. Andrew Ellicott, L'Enfant's successor in laying out the national capital, went down to run the boundary along the 31st parallel, as provided under the Pinckney Treaty, and he sent Jefferson his astronomical observations. In Dunbar, with whom he opened correspondence in 1799, Jefferson found a man whose learning and passion for inquiry equaled his own. "Sir William," the youngest son of a Scottish lord, who had lived near Natchez under the Spanish and only now became an American citizen, was unquestionably "the first character" for science and philosophy in that part of the world. He made the first meteorological observations in the Mississippi Valley. These records, together with the harvest of his curiosity on many subjects—Indians, astronomy, geography, agriculture—he sent to Jefferson, who referred most of it to the Philosophical Society.

Jefferson was captivated by the stories of wild horses of beautiful mien and strange colors roaming the lands west of the Mississippi. He wrote to Philip Nolan, the young man he had been told knew more about these mustangs than anyone else. Nothing was known in the Old World, Jefferson explained, of the horse in a state of nature, and with the rapid advance of civilization in America it would soon be too late to obtain this knowledge in the New. "The present then is probably the only moment in the age of the world, and the herds . . . mentioned the only subjects of which we can avail ourselves to obtain what has never yet been recorded, and never can be again in all probability." Nolan was a remarkable man, as Jefferson soon learned. For several years he had ranged far and wide in Texas rounding up wild horses, then breaking them, for the supply of the Spanish regiment in Louisiana. In Texas when Jefferson's letter reached New Orleans in 1799, he was expected at any time at the head of a cavalcade of a thousand mustangs. The next year, after the Spanish government became suspicious of Nolan's activities and revoked his license to trade in Texas, he planned to journey east with a string of horses, stopping at Monticello along the way to talk with Jefferson and present him with one of the beasts. Nolan was more than a horse-trader. He had mapped the north Texas country and explored all the way to the Rio Grande. Obviously he had more in mind than horses, as his association with the intriguing border commander, Brigadier General James Wilkinson, also suggests. From no American of that day could Jefferson have learned as much not only about wild horses but about the lands of the great Southwest. Instead of going east in 1800, however, Nolan set out on his fourth expedition to Texas, this time in defiance of the Louisiana government, and he met violent death near the Brazos River early in 1801. Decades later Edward Everett Hale used his name for *The Man Without a Country*, a character and a story with no resemblance to the historical Philip Nolan.

There was always a touch of the fabulous in Jefferson's intercourse with the West. Another, and more prosaic, side of his scientific personality expressed itself in agriculture. Nothing could be more prosaic than the plow, yet it was "the most useful of the instruments known to man," in Jefferson's opinion. While he was Vice President he presented his moldboard of least resistance to the agriculturists of two continents. He had worked out the mathematical principles of this improvement while in France. From New York, in 1790, he had sent the first model, cut in a block of wood, to his son-in-law. In retirement he had joined the mathematically perfect moldboard to the common bar share plow and tested it in his own fields. The results were amazing: the plow of his invention cut a furrow two inches deeper than the one it replaced, owing solely to the difference of resistance. Strickland saw the plow at Monticello and returned to England with a small model. In recognition of this and other contributions to the cultivator's science, Jefferson was elected an honorary member of the English Board of Agriculture in 1797. The Board mailed him books and reports and expressed further interest in the moldboard. In the early months of the next year he had a finished model executed in Philadelphia and wrote a detailed account of his invention in both its theoretical and practical aspects. After rigorous scrutiny by his mathematical friend Robert Patterson, model and paper were sent to London. The same paper was read before the Philosophical Society and printed in its *Transactions*, while another model went on exhibit in the Society's hall. Jefferson's moldboard was widely copied. He never thought of patenting it, for he opposed, in principle, the monopoly of any useful idea. How useful the invention actually proved to be is a matter of conjecture. But Benjamin Latrobe, the young architect and engineer, expressed wonderment at the performance of Jefferson's plow, and so did many others. In 1806 the Agricultural Society of Paris thought the invention worthy of a gold medal. Jefferson had made further improvements by then; still later he had the moldboard cast in iron. In time, of course, it was superseded, not by better moldboards, but by new and better plows.

Even an invention as practical as this one did not escape the jests of his political enemies. Jefferson paid no attention. By sharing his discovery with all nations, including "harlot" Britain, he testified to the cosmopolitanism of science. The societies of scientists, he once observed, "are always at peace, however their nations may be at war . . . they form a great fraternity spreading over the whole earth." What dreams might nations not realize if they would arrange their relations on the fraternal model of science! In the letter transmitting his account of the moldboard to Sir John Sinclair, Jefferson reflected sadly on the enormous gap between the two worlds of science and politics. "I am fixed in awe at the mighty conflict to which two great nations [Britain and France] are advancing and recoil with horror at the ferociousness of man. Will nations never devise a more rational umpire of differences than force? . . . Wonderful has been the progress of human improvement in other lines. Let us hope . . . that nations will at length be sensible that war is an instrument entirely inefficient toward redressing wrong; that it multiplies instead of indemnifying losses." His enlightened views addressed the future. Even as he wrote the drums of war were beating in his own country, and before long Jefferson, with many of his friends, witnessed the fanaticism of political man in America as in Europe.

The Terror of '98

In the annals of Jeffersonian Republicanism 1798 was the year of terror. It was, or rather seemed, an American Thermidor, a revolution of the right, a "reign of terror" not by the Jacobins but against them. It created a politics of hysteria, made opposition a crime, audacity a virtue, and turned breasting fears into insane political cults. The Jeffersonian Republicans survived this ordeal but were maimed by it. Some of them, assisted by Jefferson himself, raised their own cult around the "terror of '98."

Congress was in doldrums when the year began, waiting for the breeze from France that would propel the nation toward peace or war. Rumors filled the air, Jefferson reported, alternately favorable and unfavorable. "I begin to fear, not war from them [the French] but that they will refuse to have any settlement with us, only perhaps confining their depredations to provision vessels going to their enemies, and to enemy's goods in our ships, according to the English example: and that this may excite a war cry with us." Then he added, "The best anchor of our hope is an invasion of England." He was only half in earnest. Had he been primarily concerned with the balance of power in Europe, he could not have entertained this hope in any aspect; but, of course, he was primarily concerned with checking British maritime dominion, so much more pressing on the United States than French armies whether viewed as liberators or conquerors. Still, in a longer view of American interests, he could not embrace the hope, as he was careful to emphasize in other letters. "The subjugation of England would indeed be a general calamity," he said in sober truth. Jefferson continued to trace the American predicament to false commercial policy. Had the country earlier employed its commerce to force justice from Britain, instead of permitting its incorporation into Pitt's war machine, France could have been held at bay. When peace returned the error ought to be corrected. At present, while France belligerently contested British spoliation of the American trade, the nation had no weapon to command respect from either one. So the Federalists attempted to substitute a military engine for the discarded commercial one. The final provocation was all that was wanting to start a war.

The calm was unnerving. It was almost impossible to do business in the stormy political atmosphere at Philadelphia. From the moment of his arrival, Jefferson said, he had determined for the first time in his life to stand on the ceremony of the first visit, even with his friends, so as to sift out those who chose a separation. Pending the news from France, Congress had nothing to do, so it occupied its time with partisan brawls and recriminations. Day after day Jefferson walked to the historic hall on Chestnut Street to preside over the Senate. The chamber on the upper floor struck an English observer as both elegant and convenient, "just fitted in point of size for the accommodation of the Senators 26 [actually 32] in number, each of them having a large red morocco chair appropriated to him with a desk before it . . . , the whole furniture and arrangements being much superior to our House of Lords." The Vice President sat in a large, red, high-backed chair, slightly elevated, behind a mahogany table festooned with silk. His situation in this high-toned body was anything but pleasant. Being small, informal, and virtually leaderless, the Senate could not function without personal good humor, a commodity in dwindling supply even as to the Vice President himself. "More than once he has heard, in debates, and in terms which could not be mistaken, philippics pronounced against the author of the letter to Mazzei." The debates of the Senate were not reported, but such was the testimony of a Federalist member. The House of Representatives never had elegance and was fast losing all reputation for decorum. When the Connecticut Federalist Roger Griswold accused the Vermont Republican Matthew Lyon of wearing a wooden sword during the Revolution, the Vermonter spat in his face and narrowly escaped expulsion for the insult, which Griswold avenged personally on the floor by beating Lyon with his cane. Jefferson commented on the three-week-long imbroglio: "These proceedings must degrade the General Government, and lead the people to lean more on their state governments, which have been sunk under the early popularity of the former."

One of the vehicles of party rancor in the House was the Foreign Intercourse bill. Economy-minded Republicans sought to eliminate appropriations for the embassies in Prussia and Holland. Joshua Coit, of Connecticut, thought the move exhibited the abominable "political enthusiasm" of the Mazzei letter, which he read to the assembly. The Federalists seemed determined to make that letter a taboo against every expression of opposition, Albert Gallatin replied. "If we complain of the prodigality of . . . the Administration or wish to control it by refusing to appropriate all the money which is asked, we are stigmatized as disorganizers; if we oppose the growth of systems of treaties, we are charged with a design of subverting the Constitution and of making a revolution; if we attempt to check the extension of our political connections with European nations, we are branded with the epithet of Jacobins." The Federalists had turned everything around, the shrewd Genevan declared. The doctrine of the Mazzei letter was the doctrine of liberty. "Revolutions and Jacobinism do not flow from that line of policy we wish to see adopted. They belong, they exclusively belong to the system we resist; they are the last stage, the last page in the book of the history of government under its influence." Answering Gallatin, the ultraist Harper condemned the Mazzei letter, charged Jefferson with manipulating the "venal press," and ascribed to him the "war system"—war against Britain—that had guided the Republicans since 1793.

Little that passed in the political greenhouse at Philadelphia escaped Jefferson's senses. Monarchical fears, long present in his mind, now became a virtual obsession. It was the doctrine of the Mazzei letter, as Gallatin put it, "that a monarcho-aristocratic faction . . . wish to impose upon us the substance of the British government." Federalists insisted its author imputed this design to Washington; actually, Washington's presence at the helm had acted as a check on these fears. Adams was another matter. His prepossessions about government, his vanity, his political vulnerability made him highly susceptible to influence from the "monarcho-aristocratic faction." The evidence for this belief was inconclusive, but its political persuasiveness overcame all obstacles. From the standpoint of creating a popular ideology, it was in the Republican interest to portray Adams in monarchical colors, whereas the attempt would have been folly in the case of Washington.

In response to these fears and desires, Jefferson revised his conception of the party conflict in the early months of 1798. Earlier he had emphasized the economic basis of the division between the parties, accentuated by differences on the federal system and on foreign policy. Now he dusted off the old terms "Whig" and "Tory," reminiscent of the American Revolution, and fixed their meaning in the ideology of his party. "It is well understood that two political sects have arisen within the U. S.; the one believing the executive is the branch of our government which most needs support; the other that like the analogous branch in the English government, it is already too strong for the republican parts of the Constitution, and therefore in equivocal cases, they incline to the legislative powers; the former of these are called Federalist, sometimes aristocrats or monocrats and sometimes Tories, after the corresponding sect in the English government of exactly the same definition: the latter are still republicans, whigs, Jacobins, anarchists, disorganizers, etc." The names Federalist and Republican would not do, he said, because the mass on both sides were federalist *and* republican. All other terms were slanders, except Whig and Tory, which exactly described the issue between the parties. Toryism was associated with monarchy and aristocracy, of course—with opposition to the principles of the American Revolution. Jefferson kept his antennae extended for reports, anecdotes, and rumors of this heresy. The "anas" he recorded during these several months were mostly of this sort, for example:

> On his second election as vice president, when there were several votes cast for George Clinton, Adams said in the Senate chamber, gritting his teeth, "damn 'em, damn 'em, damn 'em, you see that an elective government will not do."
>
> On going out of office in 1794, Hamilton alluded to party differences and said, "I avow myself a monarchist; I have no objection to a trial being made of this thing of a republic, but . . . ."
>
> In an after-dinner conversation with Jefferson, the President expatiated on the vital importance of a strong senate, thinking ours not durable enough. As to trusting a popular assembly for the preservation of our liberties, Adams said it was the merest chimera imaginable.

These scraps of gossip and conversation from the President's table, from the congressional mess at Francis' Hotel, from the streets and the Senate corridors, Jefferson deemed worthy of record. The Constitution was threatened, he had no doubt, more mortally under Adams than under Washington; and monarcho-aristocratic Toryism described the threat in the political vocabulary of the time.

The suspense ended, the storm broke, in March. On the 5th, Adams prepared Congress for the failure of the mission to France; two weeks later he announced the end of negotiation and called for the prompt enactment of defense measures. This "insane message," Jefferson wrote to his Virginia friends, produced great effects: "Exultation on the one side, and a certainty of victory; while the other is petrified with astonishment." The President did not ask a declaration of war, but war was his aim in the guise of defense, Jefferson believed. (Unknown to him, Adams had, in fact, drafted a war message but discarded it in favor of the defense message of March 19.) However deplorable the Directory's rejection of American overtures, it offered no motive for war "plausible enough to impose even on the weakest mind." What, then, could account for the extraordinary impetuosity of the Federalists? War was a cover, he speculated, either for the monarcho-aristocratic conspiracy so long contemplated or for a disunionist scheme lately broached in the eastern states. However this might be, a war system would terrorize the opposition. Already the war fever was taking its toll among the Whigs in the House. The party would try its strength on three countermeasures, Jefferson said. First, a call for the executive papers bearing on the negotiation. "For if Congress are to act on the question of war, they have a right to information." Thus far Adams had withheld the envoys' dispatches. Second, a legislative countermand of Adams's order lifting the ban on the arming of merchantmen. This order, announced in the message, opened the way to armed conflict at sea. It was not overturned. Third, the adjournment of Congress at the earliest opportunity, permitting the legislators to return to their constituents. Jefferson was especially keen on the last point. In his conception it amounted to a popular referendum on the question of war. He had no doubt of the result: "it will be a means of exciting the whole body of the people from the state of inattention . . . , it will require every member to call for the sense of his district by petition or instruction; it will show the people with which side of the House their safety as well as their rights rest, by showing them which is for war and which for peace; and their representatives will return here invigorated by the avowed support of the people." The idea was impractical of course, treacherous from the Federalist standpoint, too exotic for the Republicans; yet in the light of subsequent events it had genuine merit.

Near the end of March, Jefferson felt "the most gloomy apprehensions." A treaty of alliance with Britain was rumored. The Senate was passing bills to purchase and arm vessels for convoy duty, to buy foundries, and to fortify the coast, this last measure the only one Jefferson could approve. How long could one-half the lower house stand up against the rest of the government? "In fact, the question of war and peace depends now on a toss of cross and pile. If we could but gain this season," he reiterated to Madison, "we should be saved." For the present, the first item on the agenda was the call for papers. Charges that Adams had misrepresented the negotiation in Paris and withheld the dispatches in order to incite a war were embarrassing the administration. "The Jacobins want them. And in the name of God let them be gratified . . . ," one Federalist pleaded, confident the dispatches would sink the Jacobins. On April 2 the High Federalists, by supporting the demand, invited the Republicans into the trap of their own making, and on the next day Adams, with a sigh of relief, forwarded the dispatches. Now the bizarre tale unfolded: how Talleyrand, the Minister of Foreign Relations, kept the envoys dangling for three months in Paris; how his agents, mysteriously named X, Y, and Z in the dispatches, demanded a large loan and a *douceur* as the price of treating; and how the Americans defended their nation's honor against swindle and intrigue. "The Jacobins in the Senate and House were struck dumb," Mrs. Adams gloated.

The Federalists saw to publication of the dispatches. Jefferson said it "produced such a shock on the republican mind, as has never been seen since our independence," and carried over to the war party many "wavering characters" anxious to wipe off the imputation of Jacobinism. The stupidity of Talleyrand's conduct, more than its depravity, which was not unexampled, astonished Jefferson. He did not attempt to defend it, yet the consequences of accepting the administration's version of the XYZ Affair were too frightful to contemplate. So he offered excuses and mitigations for France. The swindle, if actually attempted, was Talleyrand's private venture, unknown to the Directory, Jefferson said. On coming into office, in his May address, Adams had insulted France, and this on top of the outrage of the Jay Treaty had created the vindictive obstacle to negotiation. Despite these asperities, which led Talleyrand and his hucktering crew to toy with the commissioners, the French government wanted no war with the United States. Indeed, except in the mind of the war party, the negotiation was not at an end, for it was learned that Gerry, differing with his colleagues, remained in Paris to prevent a rupture. Jefferson's extenuations and half-truths had the useful function of enabling him to keep his eye on the domestic political enemy against the temptation offered by an illusory foreign one. He was right in his twin convictions that France desired peace and that the Federalist leadership wished to push matters to extremities. But by glossing over the XYZ Affair he put himself and his party in an exceedingly vulnerable position. Thrown on the defensive by the publication of the dispatches, which spoke for themselves, the Republicans had somehow to adhere to peace without risking the odium of cowardice and treason. In practical terms this meant consent to reasonable measures of defense but opposition to measures calculated on war. It was a narrow line. Jefferson was unsure the Republicans could walk it.

"Whatever chance was left us of escaping war after the publication of the dispatches," he wrote home in May, "the President's answers to the addresses pouring in on him from the great towns . . . are pushing the irritation to a point to which nobody can expect it will be borne." John Adams gloried in his new-found popularity. "We are wonderfully popular," Mrs. Adams remarked, "except with Bache & Co. who in his paper calls the President old querilous [*sic*], Bald, blind, cripled [*sic*], Toothless Adams." The President's bombastic speeches and answers to the numerous addresses of loyalty inflamed the war spirit. Even Hamilton, who was playing a more cautious game, thought them "intemperate and revolutionary." "Nor is it France alone," Jefferson observed, "but his own fellow citizens, against whom his threats are uttered." For Adams assailed "the delusions and misrepresentations" of party, "the calumnies and contempt against Constituted Authorities," and "the profligate spirit of falsehood and malignity" against the government. To the stout-hearted "soldier-citizens" of New Jersey, he declared that "the degraded and deluded characters may tremble, lest they should be condemned to the severest punishment an American suffers—that of being conveyed in safety within the lines of an invading enemy." No one could doubt for whom these grotesqueries were intended. Jefferson thought they must lead to a sedition bill silencing the Republican press.

The anti-Jacobin hysteria first settled on Philadelphia and then like a giant octopus lashed its arms to the farther reaches of the Union. The Federalist press screamed invasion, subversion, and revolution. "Our time, though delayed by the great projects of France in

Europe . . . will certainly come, when we are to be invaded by a body of their troops, who are expected to be joined by their friends among us, our Jacobins." *Ça Ira*, the *Marseillaise*, and the other French tunes, earlier so popular in Philadelphia, were hissed off the stage, and the spirited national hymn *Hail Columbia!* made its debut. In defiance of the tricolored French cockade, Federalists mounted the black cockade, said to have been the badge of the Continental Army, but jeered by Republicans for its resemblance to the British emblem. The President entered heart and soul into this spring madness. On May 7 nearly 1200 young men, suitably cockaded, paraded to martial music through Market Street to a swelling throng before the President's house. The young men came to offer their services in war against France. Adams, in full military regalia, received their delegation, heard their address, and answered with a rousing lecture on the ancestral piety that, he said, had inspired the American Revolution. The young men withdrew and proceeded to the State House yard. Adams's address was read to the cheers of the multitude and the ceremonies closed with *Hail Columbia!* The President had proclaimed May 9 "a day of solemn humiliation, fasting and prayer" throughout the United States. The churches and meetinghouses in Philadelphia were filled. There had been rumors of a Jacobin plot to terrorize the city on this sacred day. A few scuffles occurred—a sham battle of the cockades—and the lighthorse patroled the streets that night—but nothing disturbed the public peace. Years later, when old men traded clouded memories, Adams freely recalled the spectacle for Jefferson: "When even Governor Mifflin himself thought it his duty to order a patrol of horse and foot . . . ; when Market Street was as full as men could stand by one another, and even before my door; when some of my domestics, in frenzy, determined to sacrifice their lives in my defence; when all were ready to make a desperate sally among the multitude . . . ; when I myself judged it prudent and necessary to order chests of arms from the war office, to be brought through by lanes and back doors; determined to defend my house at the expense of my life . . . . What think you of terrorism, Mr. Jefferson?" The Sage of Monticello paid no attention to the parting jibe. He believed then, as in 1798, that the terror and the frenzy were whipped up by Federalist madmen, of whom Adams was indubitably one, and apparently, fifteen years later, the ancient delusion hung in his memory.

The old man at Quincy playfully supposed Jefferson was "fast asleep in philosophical tranquility" when these events took place. He was not so fortunate. "Party passions are indeed high," he wrote on May 9. "Nobody has more reason to know it than myself. I receive daily bitter proofs of it from people who never saw me, nor know anything of me but through Porcupine and Fenno. At this moment all the passions are boiling over, and one who keeps himself cool and clear of the contagion is so far below the point of ordinary conversation, that he finds himself insulated in every society." Once again the torment of politics settled over him. "Politics and party hatreds destroy the happiness of every being here. They seem, like salamanders, to consider fire as their element." Far pleasanter to contemplate the "Game of Goose" he had purchased for his grandchildren! Or to lose himself in intellectual diversions. According to tradition he found escape from the political tumult in Philosophical Hall. "I have changed my circle here according to my wish," he told Martha, "abandoning the rich, and declining all their dinners and parties, and associating entirely with the class of science." He later recalled "delightful conversations" with Benjamin Rush, which "served as an anodyne to the afflictions of the crisis through which our country was then laboring."

The war party overrode the thinning ranks of the opposition in Congress. Acts to renounce the French treaties, to suspend trade, to establish a navy department and build frigates, to authorize the capture of French ships, to raise new regiments of infantry and establish a large provisional army, to expel aliens and stamp out sedition, to borrow money and lay direct taxes—such legislation took the country to the Rubicon and the Federalists apparently had every intention of crossing it. Yet they held back, counting on France to force the decision. Some High Federalists criticized these Fabian tactics. "If we hesitate or pause now," one said, "the Jacobin faction will revive, and all the avenues for French poison and intrigue be again opened . . . . Nothing but an open war can save us and the more inveterate and deadly it shall be, the better will be our chance for security in the future." Open war would place the Republicans in an intolerable position. The longer it was averted, the more impatient the people must become with the evils of taxes, standing army, and oppressive laws. Such measures were sold to the public under the pretense of a threatening French invasion. What was to be done with this war machine when the invasion failed to materialize?

The inner circle of High Federalists around Hamilton had two grand objects in view. First, war against France, openly declared in due time, perhaps in outright alliance with Britain, for the joint conquest of the Spanish dominions from Louisiana to the Antilles and on down to South America. Under cover of the French war, the American army and the British fleet would descend on the tottering Spanish empire. The plot took form before the XYZ crisis broke. The chief plotters on the American side were Hamilton, who expected to command the army, Secretary of State Pickering, and Rufus King, the American Minister in London. King was in touch with the British foreign office, of course, and also with the first engineer of the enterprise, Franciso de Miranda, the aging Venezuelan adventurer and revolutionary. Britain was ready to commence the "revolution of South America," King wrote to Pickering in April, as soon as Spain fell under French arms. In the same month Miranda sent a personal emissary to Philadelphia to lay the plan before Adams. The President had known nothing of it. When it was broached, he would have nothing to do with it. The country was at peace with Spain, and Adams hoped, through the quasi-war with France, to create an American naval power independent of Britain. Hamilton and his allies, backed by the British Minister, Robert Liston, aimed at an alliance associated with the Miranda project. They were constrained but not squelched by the President's opposition. Conquest, both at home and abroad, was their mission. As King advised Hamilton in July, the enthusiasm and union excited in the United States could not last without "some sufficient object that will interest and employ the passions of the Nation. The mere defensive system of the [European] enemies of France," he went on, "has been a principal cause of her success, and if we adopt the error we shall be exposed to greater risks than by a bold and active system, which, exclusive of being the most certain means of safety, would promise the acquisition of great and lasting advantages."

Jefferson had no knowledge of this fantastic secret project. Of course, the war strategy was likely to encompass designs on Spain, since she offered tempting prizes of conquest, while France herself could be profitably attacked only in her commerce; and the Directory's known interest in the re-establishment of French empire in North America furnished an additional motive to the war party. This much Jefferson probably took for granted. But the audacity of the Hamiltonians exceeded even his imagination. In regard to the second object, domestic use of the war machine, Jefferson lacked neither information nor imagination. It was intended to terrorize the opposition and bring about a monolithic government on the English model. Exploitative taxes, standing army, British alliance, and so on were elements of this grand design, but it was best revealed by the Alien and Sedition Laws of 1798.

The laws were enacted during the second gyration of the war boom in mid-June. It began with the unauthorized publication in the *Aurora* of Talleyrand's long letter of March 18 to the envoys, in which he reviewed the French grievances and again spurned the commission, yet offered to negotiate with Gerry, who was believed friendly. Publication of the still secret document handed the Federalists a wonderul opportunity to denounce Republican subservience to France. Two days later, June 18, John Marshall returned to a hero's welcome in Philadelphia. Weary of the seemingly interminable session of Congress, Jefferson had planned to go home, but he decided to stay in the city to see what turn Marshall's reception gave to affairs. On the whole, Jefferson thought his Virginia kinsman a very able man whose huge land speculations and legal practice, unfortunately, had bound him hand and foot to Federalist moneyed interests. While this doubtless laid the foundation of political distrust, it had not yet placed Jefferson at swords' points with Marshall. The envoy was not at his lodgings when Jefferson called, so he left a note regretting—telling slip of the pen!—he had been "so lucky as to find that he was out." Whether Marshall warmed or cooled the war party, Jefferson could not be sure at the time, but before long he was writing scathingly of "the XYZ dish cooked up by Marshall." Rarely again would he speak a kind word for the Richmond Federalist. Apparently he held Marshall responsible for the escalation of the crisis in June mainly because upon his return Congress ordered the printing of 10,000 copies of the entire XYZ corpus for public distribution. This unprecedented act raised popular feeling to a still higher pitch.

Meanwhile, indeed on the very day Marshall returned, Jefferson found himself on the griddle of Congress and the press for aiding and abetting Dr. George Logan's personal mission to Paris. This newest "Jacobin plot" was uncovered several days after the self-appointed envoy's departure. Logan was one of Jefferson's dearest friends, a fellow agriculturist, a Republican, a Quaker, and an enthusiast for the French Revolution. Something of an eccentric too, he had the wild idea he could throw himself into the breach between France and the United States. Although Jefferson had some inkling of his plan, since he had furnished Logan a routine certification of citizenship and good character—the nearest equivalent of a passport—he later said with complete truth that the Doctor's venture was "dictated by his own enthusiasm, without consultation or communication with any one." The suddenness of his departure, added to his prominence and party connections, produced "a real panic" in the city. He was "Jefferson's envoy extraordinary"! He was the secret agent of the American Jacobins to concert invasion plans with the armies of France! *Porcupine's Gazette* screamed, "Watch, Philadelphians, or the fire is in your houses and the *couteau at your throats* . . . . Take care: when your blood runs down the gutters, don't say you weren't forewarned of the danger." In Congress, Harper gravely accused leading American Jacobins, presumably Bache, Logan, and Jefferson, of a "traitorous conspiracy" with their French masters. Treasury Secretary Wolcott rushed to New York to meet a returning traveler said to be bearing letters from France. He found and intercepted a packet addressed to Bache, which proved to be harmless, and a private letter to Jefferson from his friend Fulwar Skipwith, the Consul General in Paris, which he commandeered but left to his biographer to publish two generations later. Jefferson worried about Mrs. Logan. He rode out to Stenton, taking a circuitous route in order to elude snoopers, and begged this gentle lady to defy the accusers by making her rounds in the city as before. "He spoke of the temper of the time and the late acts of the legislature with a sort of despair," Deborah Logan remembered their conversation, "but said he thought even the shadow of our liberties must be gone if they attempted anything that would injure me." She acted on Jefferson's advice—it was a painful experience. Cobbett at once informed the public of Jefferson's trip to Stenton: "Quere: What did he do there? Was it to arrange the Doctor's *valuable manuscripts?*" Evidence of the "traitorous correspondence," no doubt. "Porcupine gave me a principal share in it, as I am told," Jefferson reported the affair to Madison, "for I never read his papers."

It was a maxim with Jefferson that "Falsehood will travel a thousand miles while truth is putting on her boots." Falsehood ran under whip and spur in June. Federalist versifiers hailed the "warlike spirit," derided the slinking Jacobins, and added new touches to their parody of Jefferson, half devil, half buffoon.

> Now each Jacobinic face
> Redden'd with guilt, with fear, disgrace,
> While thro' the land, with keenest ire,
> Kindles the patriotic fire!
> See Jefferson with deep dismay,
> Shrink from the piercing eye of day,
> Lest from the tottering chair of state,
> The storm should hurl him to his fate!
> Great Sire of stories past belief!
> Historian of the Mingo Chief!
> Philosopher of Indian's hair!
> Inventor of a rocking chair!
> The Correspondent of Mazze'!
> And Banneker less black than he!
> With joy we find these rise from coguing
> With Judge M'Kean, and "foolish Logan,"
> And reeling down the factious dance,
> Send Deborah's husband off to France,
> To tell the Frenchmen, to their cost,
> They reckon'd here without their host;
> Whilst thou, to smooth the ills of life,
> Held sweet communion with the wife.

Out of the sea of political violence emerged the Alien and Sedition Laws. The former was acutally but one of three laws enacted against aliens. The Naturalization Act raised from five to fourteen years the period required for citizenship; the Alien Enemies Act empowered the President to confine or banish aliens of an enemy country during a state of war; the Alien (or Alien Friends) Act authorized the President summarily to deport aliens deemed dangerous to the peace and safety of the United States. The sponsors of this legislation held that two large foreign-born groups, the French and the Irish, constituted a subversive fifth column. Political refugees of the Irish rebellion had fled to the United States, where, as Rufus King protested in London, they at once "arrayed themselves on the side of the malcontents." A lodge of the Society of United Irishmen was discovered in Philadelphia in the spring of 1798. Cobbett published an inflammatory pamphlet: *Detection of a Conspiracy Formed by the United Irishmen, with the Evident Intention of Aiding the Tyrants of France in Subverting the Government of the United States of America.* The Polish patriot and veteran of the American Revolution, General Thaddeus Kosciusko, with whom Jefferson had become friendly on his return visit to America, was prominently linked to the alien conspiracy against American liberty. Among the numerous French refugees were several "philosophers," always the indispensable "pioneers of revolution," according to Harper. Jefferson thought these philosophers, like his friend Volney, whose slashing attack on priestly religion, *The Ruins*, he had begun to translate, were the main targets of the Alien bill. He had learned at first-hand the risks of that vocation. "It suffices for a man to be a philosopher, and to believe that human affairs are susceptible to improvement, to look forward, rather than back to the Gothic age, for perfection, to mark him as an anarchist, disorganizer, atheist and enemy of the government."

As passed by the Senate, the Alien bill was "worthy of the eighth or ninth century" in Jefferson's opinion. One of its provisions would have required him, for example, to send a messenger 70 miles for the written permission of a federal judge before sitting down to dinner with a foreign guest at Monticello! Although this objectionable provision and some others were eliminated in the House, Jefferson did not think much better of the finished bill. The Republicans had opposed it. "The people will oppose, the States will not submit to its operation . . . ," Livingston had declared. "Thus, sir, one of the first effects . . . will be disaffection among the States; and opposition among the people to your Government; tumults, violations, and a recurrence to first revolutionary principles." To these sentiments Jefferson would only add the bill was "in the teeth of the Constitution." No authority could be found for it, and the Federalists had appealed to the dangerous concept of inherent national soverignty to sanction it. Adams signed the bill into law on July 6. By then most of the Frenchmen, including Volney, and other "dangerous aliens" like Kosciusko, had left American soil. Despite the administration's zeal, no alien was actually deported under the arbitrary provisions of this law.

The Sedition Act, on the other hand, was generously enforced. Twenty-five persons were arrested, fourteen indicted, and ten tried and convicted, all Republican printers and publicists. Jefferson had predicted the passage of a sedition bill as early as April 26, several weeks before one was introduced in Congress. "The object . . . is the suppression of the Whig presses," he said. For years, at least as early as Washington's denunciation of the Democratic Societies, he had observed Federalist intolerance of opposition. Only a crisis was wanting to arm it. An incident in Virginia a year before had alerted him to the danger. The grand jury of the federal Circuit Court at Richmond made a presentment against Samuel J. Cabell, the representative of Jefferson's own congressional district, upbraiding him for the dissemination of "unfounded calumnies against the happy government of the United States . . . [in order] to separate the people therefrom, and to increase or produce a foreign influence ruinous to the peace, happiness, and independence of the United States." Jefferson at once fastened on this perversion of the grand jury "from a legal to a political engine." The federal judiciary was implicated, specifically in the person of Judge James Iredell, whose high-handed charge to the jury invited the presentment. After his return to Virginia in July 1797, Jefferson drafted a petition to the General Assembly in which he pleaded not only the natural right of correspondence between a representative and his constituents but also the state's right to interpose its authority as necessary to safeguard freedom of opinion. He went on to request legislative action against the Richmond grand jurors, either by impeachment or by law of *premunire*, an old English proceeding invented to punish the introduction of papal authority against the authority of the crown. He wrote to Monroe in defense of the petition: "It is of immense consequence that the States retain as complete authority as possible over their own citizens. The withdrawing themselves under the shelter of a foreign jurisdiction, is so subversive of order and so pregnant of abuse, that it may not be amiss to consider how far a law of *premunire* should not be revived and modified, against all citizens who attempt to carry their causes before any other than State courts, in cases where those other courts have no right to their cognizance." In thus rushing to the defense of civil and political liberty Jefferson ran headlong into state rights remedies likely to prove as mortal as the disease. The petition, without any ascription of authorship, came before the House of Delegates in December. A resolution of that body denounced the Cabell presentment as a violation of "the fundamental principles of representation" and "the natural right of speaking and writing freely," but omitted any mode of redress at law. So the assembly stopped short of Jefferson's objective. The radical principles and tactics he pursued in this matter foreshadowed the course he would take in opposition to the Sedition Act.

The Sedition Act made it a federal crime, punishable by fine and imprisonment, for anyone to enter into conspiracy impeding the operations of the federal government or to publish "any false, scandalous and malicious writing" against the government, Congress, or the President. Aimed at "domestic traitors," it was conceived as a companion to the Alien Act. As first proposed in the Senate it was also a treason bill, vaulting constitutional safeguards by the prescription of death for adherence to France and lesser penalties for failure to divulge knowledge of treason. But these sections were omitted from the bill passed by the Senate on July 4. Federalists noted nothing ironic in the date. A Fourth of July rally toasted Adams: "May he like *Samson*, slay thousands of Frenchmen with the *jawbone* of Jefferson." Whether or not Jefferson was a direct target of the Sedition Act—some of his friends feared he was—he could not fail to notice the omission of the Vice President from the officers of the government placed under the mantle of protection.

In the House the bill came under heavy fire from the dwindling, yet stubborn, Republican ranks. It was unconstitutional, they said, since Congress had no delegated power in this sphere, and indeed the First Amendment guarantee of freedom of speech and press withdrew the entire subject from the national authority. The Federalists denied that the amendment gave immunity to libelous assaults on the government; they appealed to the sovereign authority of any government to protect itself, and said that, even without the benefit of statute, the federal courts could punish sedition under common law. The claim of federal jurisdiction over common law crimes was a bold one. Gallatin and his little band rejected it and wondered why, if the courts already had the authority to punish sedition, any statute was necessary. The answer was that it was desirable to introduce certain ameliorations in the common law of seditious libel. First, the jury should be authorized to return a general verdict, that is, guilty or not guilty, rather than simply a verdict on the fact of the publication of the alleged libel by the defendant. In this, as in their entire campaign of repression, the Federalists followed the British example, specifically Fox's Libel Act of 1792. But they went a step further by admitting truth as a defense of the libel. By thus relaxing the common law the Federalists prided themselves on their liberality. The Repubicans were unimpressed. The statute was retrograde since it assumed an authority where none existed and where none was wanted. The real purpose of the measure was political: to cripple and destroy the Republican opposition under the pretense of saving the country from anarchists, demagogues, and incendiaries. This was the cant employed against the patriots of every nation where rulers exalted their own despotic power. And in the climate of fear and suspicion the Federalists had created, what would be the benefit of the boasted safeguards? As it turned out they were of no use whatever to the defendants tried under the Sedition Act.

Jefferson was hard at work at Monticello when the act was finally signed into law on July 14. He had earlier planned to leave by June 1, then on the 18th, the day of Marshall's return, but he did not get away until the 27th. On the day before he had heard the first reading of the bill in the Senate and learned that Bache had been hauled into federal court for common law libels of the President and the government—evidence that the Federalists would not be bound by statutory authority. Staying at his post for seven cruel months, Jefferson had helped to stave off still more violent measures and to keep up the flagging hopes of Republicans throughout the Union. To the end of his days he believed this was one of his best services. While he now despaired of stemming the Federalist tide in Congress, he still expected it to recede as rapidly as it rose. The people were Republican. War scare, land tax, standing army, and Alien and Sedition Laws were sure to produce a reaction. Had the Federalists declared war, the prospects would have been dim. Jefferson had expected it, so had Adams, and almost every leading Federalist favored war outright to the ambiguous quasi-war—a war of frigates and privateers—that existed. Just why it was not declared is a difficult question. In July the congressional strategists watched helplessly as the opportunity slipped from their grasp. "Half measures are seldom generally intelligible, and almost never safe, in the crisis of great affairs . . . ," Fisher Ames wrote to Pickering with Machiavellian cunning. "Internal foes can do twice as much harm as they could do in an open war. The hope of peace is yet strong enough to furnish the means of popular influence and delusion; at any rate, it chills the spirit of the citizens, and distracts them in the exercise of duty." Jefferson, on the other hand, took comfort in the continuing "hope of peace." Of course, if France warred on the United States every American must rally to the defense of his country. But he had never thought this likely, unless from unsufferable provocation. France had too many reasons for wishing peace with the United States. Moreover, the prospects for peace in Europe were good. If the country could scrape through the ensuing winter without being overborne by the war party, everything should turn to rights. Finally, in his last message to Congress, Adams had declared he would not send another minister to France *unless* on assurances he would be properly received. For all his thunder he had not slammed and bolted the door to peace.

Jefferson reached Monticello on July 3. (Along the way he accepted the honor of a public reception on Sunday, a fact "trumpeted from one end of the continent to the other, as irrefutable proof of his contempt for the Christian religion, and his devotion to the new religion of France.") He had much to think about, more of it political than suited his taste, yet he found time and wit in this season of madness to write an essay on Anglo-Saxon grammar. He wrote few letters, not a single one for seven weeks after his return, and when he commenced again usually relied on messengers rather than trust the post. To a Maryland Republican who sent a press report alleging subversive activities against him, he replied that his principles were those of the people and well known, whereas "the delusion of the people is necessary to the dominant party." It was pointless to answer calumnies, he said, for while putting down one, twenty new ones would spring up. To an Irish refugee bewildered by the stumbling of the American republic, he sketched a long view of the phenomenon. "The system of alarm and jealousy which has been so powerfully played off in England, has been mimicked here, not entirely without success. The most long-sighted politician could not, seven years ago, have imagined that the people of this wide extended country could have been enveloped in such delusion, and made so much afraid of themselves and of their own powers, as to surrender it spontaneously to those who are maneuvering them into a form of government, the principal branches of which may be beyond their control. The commerce of England, however, has spread its roots over the whole face of our country. This," he said, "is a real source of all the obliquities of the public mind . . . ." Virginia was safe, however—an asylum for all the persecuted.

Although Jefferson repeatedly stated that the disease would produce its own remedy, he decided in the summer months to administer a shock treatment to aid the recovery. The political therapy took the form of the Virginia and Kentucky Resolutions. These famous resolutions had a double character. Called forth by oppressive legislation of the national government, notably the Alien and Sedition Laws, they represented a vigorous defense of the principles of freedom and self-government under the United States Constitution. But since the defense involved an appeal to principles of state rights, the resolutions struck a line of argument potentially as dangerous to the Union as were the odious laws to the freedom with which it was identified. One hysteria tended to produce another. A crisis of freedom threatened to become a crisis of Union. The latter was deferred in 1798–1800, but it would return, and when it did the principles Jefferson had invoked against the Alien and Sedition Laws would sustain delusions of state sovereignty fully as violent as the Federalist delusions he had combated.

His decision to take a stand in the states was carefully meditated. The action on the Cabell presentment set the course. When Madison came out of retirement in the spring and offered himself for election to the General Assembly, Jefferson remarked on the great good that might be done by "a proper direction of the local force." Still he did not then share the desperation of some of his friends and counseled against extreme measures. In May, John Taylor was saying it was time to consider, as men were considering, Virginia's secession from the Union. Jefferson agreed that Virginia and her neighbors were ridden hard by the eastern states. "But our present situation is not a natural one," he told Taylor. The cunning of Hamilton, played off behind the popularity of Washington, followed by the untoward events and the artifices of the Adams administration, disguised the weakness of the Federalist party. "Be this as it may," he continued philosophically, "in every free and deliberating society, there must, from the nature of man, be opposite parties, and violent dissensions and discords; and one of these, for the most part, must prevail over the other for a longer or shorter time. Perhaps this party division is necessary to induce each to watch and relate to the people the proceedings of the other. But if on a temporary superiority of one party, the other is to resort to a scission of the Union, no federal government can ever exist." And where would the evil stop? One confederacy would become two, then three, then four, until there was nothing left. "Seeing, therefore . . . that we must have somebody to quarrel with, I had rather keep our New England associates for that purpose, than to see our bickerings transferred to others." He concluded on an optimistic note: "A little patience, and we shall see the reign of witches pass over, their spells dissolved, and the people recovering their true sight, restoring their government to its true principles."

To this Taylor soberly replied that if the violence was "indeed owing to witchraft, the spell must be broken by incantations on the part of the Republicans." He suggested several. For example, "The right of the State governments to expound the constitution, might possibly be made the basis of a movement towards its amendment. If this is insufficient, the people in state conventions, are incontrovertibly the contracting parties and possessing the impinging rights, may proceed by orderly steps to the object." Jefferson carefully scored and underscored the planter's proposal for future reference. Taylor, with a hard knot of Virginia Republicans, had never overcome the Anti-Federalist dogma on the Constitution. Wrong in essential principles, the compact necessarily produced vicious effects, as in the centralized privilege and corruption of the Hamiltonian system, and no mere change of men or of party could set the government aright. Jefferson, on the other hand, with the mass of Republicans, believed the disease was in the governors rather than in the government, hence political change could be effective. The object was to restore the Constitution, not to reform it. His conviction weakened in 1798, however, and partly for this reason Virginia Republicans of the Taylor breed expected a good deal more of him in the way of reform than he was prepared to deliver when placed in the presidency.

In June, when he left Congress, Jefferson believed time was on the side of the Republicans; in August he was not at all sure. The delusion of the war party seemed limitless. "There is no event . . . , however atrocious, which may not be expected." Vigorous enforcement of the Sedition Act would crush the Republican press, terrorize public opinion, and block the regular avenues of change through the electoral process. Those laws were merely "an experiment on the American mind," he said, to see to what degradation it would submit. "If this goes down we shall immediately see attempted another act of Congress, declaring that the President shall continue in office during life, reserving to another occasion the transfer of the succession to his heirs, and the establishment of the Senate for life." No reliance could be placed in the federal judiciary, a party stronghold, to check the mad career. Some counterforce was necessary. And where could it be found but in the state legislatures? There was no novelty in the proceeding. As early as 1790 the Virginia assembly had declared its opinion that certain acts of the federal government were unconstitutional. Hamilton had denounced the action, yet it was well founded in the theory of the federal system, even as expounded by Hamilton. "It may safely be received as an axiom in our political system," he had written in *The Federalist*, "that the State governments will, in all possible contingencies, afford complete security against invasions of the public liberty by the national authority . . . . They can discover the danger at a distance; and possessing all the organs of civil power, and the confidence of the people, they can at once adopt a regular plan of opposition, in which they can combine all the resources of the community. They can readily communicate with each other in the different States, and unite their common forces for the protection of their common liberty." Jefferson would have found it difficult to improve on this statement. The right of a state legislature to expound the Constitution and, where necessary, to oppose usurpations by the national government not only safeguarded the liberties of the citizen but also maintained the balance of the federal system upon which the preservation of the Union depended.

On these general principles Jefferson and Madison drafted the Kentucky and Virginia Resolutions of 1798. An air of secrecy surrounded the business. Not for many years were the true authors of the documents known to the public. Perhaps Jefferson discussed ways and means of counteracting the Federalist program when he stopped at Madison's place on his return from Congress, but they did not agree upon a plan of action at this early date. Perhaps they conferred later in the summer, though the record bears no trace. At any rate, early in the fall Jefferson drafted a series of resolutions intended for the North Carolina legislature. He put the document in the hands of Wilson Cary Nicholas for disposition. Acting on his own, Nicholas entrusted it to John Breckinridge, a former resident of Albemarle and friend of Jefferson's, now prominent in Kentucky politics. Visiting his old home, Breckinridge probably convinced Nicholas that Kentucky offered more fertile ground for Jefferson's seed than North Carolina. In Kentucky, as in Virginia, a wave of local protests against war and the "unconstitutional" measures of the federal government rolled across the state. Jefferson approved the choice of Kentucky for the political test. Breckinridge steered clear of Monticello, lest a visit there expose the Vice President's part in the plan afoot. The Kentuckian packed the momentous document in his saddlebag and rode across the mountains the second week of October. A week or so later Madison saw a copy of Jefferson's resolutions at Monticello. Undoubtedly they discussed the question of parallel action in Virginia, as well as Jefferson's new plan, revising that of the previous year, for taking the selection of jurors away from executive and judicial authorities and placing it directly in the hands of the people. (The legislature was not ready for this radical democratic step.) The resolutions Madison then drafted for introduction in the Virginia assembly asserted the same fundamental theory of the Constitution without, however, entering into Jefferson's bolder conclusions. These were too extreme even for

Breckinridge, with the result that the Kentucky Resolutions, adopted at Frankfort on November 10, were milder than Jefferson had planned.

The Resolutions set forth the theory of the union as a compact among the several states. Certain powers only were delegated to the central government; acts beyond its powers were unconstitutional, void, and of no force; and since the contracting parties had created no ultimate arbiter of the Constitution, each state had "an equal right to judge for itself, as well of the infractions as of the mode and measure of redress." Jefferson thus extended the logic of the compact theory and of limited government—a logic almost no one openly disputed—to a conclusion few had faced and fewer still had reached before him. His doctrinaire friend Taylor had preceded him, but Jefferson required neither Taylor's prompting nor his political bias to take this step. It followed naturally from the principles of constitutional law Jefferson and his colleagues had been elaborating for eight or nine years, and its execution only awaited the impetus of legislation as potent as the Alien and Sedition Laws. Five of the nine resolutions were devoted to proving the unconstitutionality of these laws. Except for crimes specified in the Constitution, such as counterfeiting and treason, the federal government had no criminal jurisdiction. Freedom of speech and press had the same standing under the First Amendment, Jefferson maintained, as freedom of religion. Congress could legislate in no matter whatsoever. Yet he did not enter a broadly philosophical plea for freedom of speech, preferring rather to rest his case on state rights ground. It was for the states to determine, he said, "how far the licentiousness of speech and of the press may be abridged without lessening their useful freedom." The Alien Law fell for want of power, for violation of a specific constitutional provision relating to immigration (Article I, Section 9), and for the denial of jury trial and other fair procedures in the deportation of aliens. The sweeping claim made in the name of state rights transcended the immediate issue of civil liberties. The seventh resolution passed a blanket condemnation on federal actions taken under color of the "general welfare" and "necessary and proper" clauses. Matters of less urgency, they were allowed to stand for legislative correction at an early date.

It was in the action resolutions, numbers eight and nine, that the legislature departed from Jefferson's draft. Kentucky declared its opinion that the Alien and Sedition Laws were unconstitutional and communicated the Resolutions to the various state legislatures, and to its senators and representatives in Congress, in order to obtain their repeal. Jefferson's proposal went further. Making a valid distinction between *abuses* of delegated powers, in which the electoral process offered the constitutional remedy, and *assumptions* of powers not delegated, he declared that "a nullification . . . is the rightful remedy" for the latter. There was a certain ambiguity in his statement of the doctrine. Significantly, however, he did not say nullification was the constitutional remedy, holding rather "that every State has a natural right in cases not within the compact . . . to nullify of their own authority all assumptions of power within their limits." The right pertained to each state independently; nevertheless, Jefferson would have Kentucky communicate its actions to the other parties of the compact, inviting each of them to "concur in declaring these acts void and of no force" and to "take measures of its own providing that neither . . . shall be exercised within these respective territories." Had the legislature followed Jefferson's instructions to the letter, Kentucky would have placed itself in defiance of federal laws; and it would have made little practical difference whether the appeal was to natural or to constitutional right. Jefferson's Latinism, "nullification," which three decades later became a political shibboleth, did not appear in the Kentucky Resolutions. Although Breckinridge subscribed to the doctrine in the debate on the resolutions, he trusted with the majority that an early repeal of the obnoxious laws would make unnecessary the resort to nullification. In a second series of resolutions the following year, after the failure of repeal, the legislature declared its opinion in favor of nullification, using that specific term, yet pointedly disclaimed any idea of practicing the doctrine.

As a rule Madison was a man of cooler judgment than Jefferson, and the parts played by these two principals in the Virginia and Kentucky Resolutions illustrate the different traits of character. The younger man once remarked on "a habit in Mr. Jefferson as in others of great genius of expressing in strong and round terms, impressions of the moment." The habit was disclosed in the bolder expressions of Jefferson's draft, which did not come under Madison's judicious eye before its dispatch to Kentucky. The Virginia Resolutions were, by contrast, brief, cautiously worded, and softly spoken. The legislatures of the sister states were asked to join Virginia in adjudging the Alien and Sedition Laws unconstitutional and in taking necessary steps to maintain the rights and liberties reserved to the states or to the people. Nicholas, again the intermediary, took Madison's draft to Monticello. In Jefferson's view it did not take high enough ground. To overcome the impression of a mere declaration of opinion, he proposed adding the phrase, "that the said acts are, and were *ab initio*, null, void and of no force, or effect." Nicholas made the change, and the resolutions were introduced in this form by John Taylor on December 10. But in the course of debate, probably at Madison's instigation, Taylor moved to strike the voiding phrase and restore the declaratory wording of the original. The motion passed. The resolutions were adopted as a solemn expression of opinion, or at least so Madison always held. He plainly did not adhere to the extremity of Jefferson's logic by which the legislature of a single state could nullify federal laws within its borders. If there was an ultimate judge anywhere it was the people of the states, who were the true parties to the compact, not the legislatures. Madison thought the point important enough to bring to his friend's attention in December, for his resolutions seemed to subordinate the true sovereigns to their legislative agents. Confusion was compounded by his description of nullification as a "natural right," which could only mean the right of revolution, necessarily accompanied, in the instance of a compact, by secession.

In the final analysis it is impossible to say precisely what Jefferson's theory was in the Resolutions of '98. They were not conceived in the oracular realm of constitutional law but in a desperate struggle for political survival. Acts unconstitutional had passed, liberty was in jeopardy, war in prospect, and specters of monarchy loomed on the horizon. Jefferson, therefore, pursued "a political resistance for political effect," without much regard for nuances and ambiguities of doctrine. The important point was to declare the Alien and Sedition Acts unconstitutional, leaving the sequel to later decision as events might prudently dictate. "I would not do anything at this moment which would commit us further," he wrote to Taylor in November, "but reserve ourselves to shape our future measures or no measures, by the events which may happen." Politics was an art of maneuver, as Jefferson understood; and although some of the expressions in his draft resolutions were embarrassingly dogmatic, he clearly had no intention of committing himself, his party, or the legislatures to an inflexible position. By resistance on constitutional grounds he hoped to avoid extremes, yet he was prepared for them if pushed by events.

The same practical wisdom that shaped Jefferson's course in this regard was evident in his decision to address the defense of personal and political liberty to the immediate enemy, the federal government. No danger came from the states—it was not a live political question. So it was no part of his purpose to compose a philosophical manifesto of freedom of speech and press; nor could this purpose be encompassed within the strategy of state protest against federal usurpations. The limits of state authority in these vital areas of freedom was another matter altogether. He believed, unquestionably, that the states could regulate "the licentiousness of speech and of press" under statutory or common law. He was not an absolutist. But the republican experiment was insupportable without freedom of speech and press at all levels of government and in the widest latitude compatible with the experiment itself. The emphasis fell, realistically, on state rights in 1798. Jefferson's commitment to the revolutionary principles of freedom and self-government was not, for that reason, any less than it had ever been. The following year he wrote a ringing reaffirmation of the larger faith to a college student: "To preserve the freedom of the human mind . . . and freedom of the press, every spirit should be ready to devote itself to martyrdom; for as long as we may think as we will, and speak as we think the condition of man will proceed in improvement. The generation which is going off the stage has deserved well of mankind for the struggles it has made, and for having arrested the course of despotism which had overwhelmed the world for thousands and thousands of years. If there seems to be danger that the ground they have gained will be lost again, that danger comes from the generation your contemporary. But that the enthusiasm which characterizes youth should lift its parricide hands against freedom and science would be such a monstrous phenomenon as I cannot place among possible things in this age and country."

As the Resolutions went abroad to work on the public mind, Jefferson returned to Philadelphia for the short session of the Fifth Congress. Notwithstanding peace feelers from France, the Federalists voted substantial increases in the army and navy and authorized a loan of $5,000,000 to make good the deficit. Business was sluggish, money scarce; the Treasury floated the loan at 8 per cent interest, and Jefferson doubted the money could be raised even at that price. Spiraling taxes, expenses, and debt caused alarms. The fiscal picture was not as bleak as Jefferson painted it, but considering the poverty of the nation's productive resources, the drain into the federal Treasury was a legitimate concern. The revenue of $10,000,000 amounted to one-third the value of domestic exports, the principal source of national wealth. Interest charges on the debt took a huge bite in taxes, approximately 40 per cent of the total every year. The debt grew with the growth of the military establishment, for more new taxes would not be borne, even at the alternative of borrowing at usurious interest. An annual levy of from two to three dollars on every man, woman, and child was perhaps little enough for the people to bear in defense of the nation; still it was no small burden when the annual income per capita did not much exceed $200, when every resource was needed for productive growth, and when, alas, there was no enemy to fight.

Dr. Logan had returned from his mission in November with tidings of peace. Hundreds of American privateers roamed the seas; the infant navy patroled the harbors and went in hot pursuit of French men-of-war to the West Indies; and Washington came out of retirement to lead the provisional army that really belonged to Major General Hamilton, his second in command over the objection of the President. Yet Logan reported, straight from the horse's mouth, that France earnestly desired peace. The Federalists were enraged. The day Jefferson resumed the chair in the Senate, the leadership in the lower house initiated legislation to punish persons who usurped the executive authority by communicating with the government of a foreign state. In four hours of feverish eloquence Harper unraveled the skein of treason and subversion contrived, he made quite clear, by the Vice President. Whatever the merits of the Logan bill, as it was called, it had less to do with the conduct of diplomacy than with attainting the Republican party and its leader. Through Logan the Federalists sought to get at Jefferson, whose "poor addled cat's paw" the doctor allegedly was. The transparency of their motives was obvious to all, Jefferson noted, yet the bill would pass. When it came before the Senate, only two Republicans dared to vote against it.

The good Quaker's report fell in with mounting evidence of the Directory's desire for reconciliation. The warlike posture of the United States had something to do with the turnabout, though it was a factor Jefferson could never credit. Far more compelling, in his opinion, was Admiral Nelson's defeat of the French fleet at the Nile, surprising reverses on land, the regrouping of the monarchical coalition, and the ruin of Franco-American commerce, all of which must produce a recovery of sanity in the French government. Letters from American friends in France—Joel Barlow, John Brown Cutting, Fulwar Skipwith, and others—pointed out the path of accommodation. Jefferson had already helped to blaze the path, not by conspiratorial transactions but by assurances to Volney, Kosciusko, and Victor Dupont, men of substance who returned to France in 1798, that the American people would trade the sword for the olive branch if given the opportunity. Dupont was especially helpful. This young man, the son of Jefferson's physiocratic friend, had been sent to the United States as consul general in 1798 only to be turned back by Adams. Jefferson had talked to him in the spring. If the Directory would revise its decrees against the neutral trade, recall its corsairs from the West Indies, and declare its willingness to resume negotiations, he told Dupont, the tide would turn, sweeping before it all the feeble artifices of the war party. The recommendation was conveyed to Talleyrand, who followed it exactly. When Gerry departed later in the summer he brought with him an order revoking the most obnoxious of the decrees, and Talleyrand promptly commenced overtures through The Hague for a pacific settlement.

Jefferson found a letter from Gerry on his return to Philadelphia. His reply was a ten-page work of political art, combining a profession of republican faith, a partisan history of the XYZ furor, and a calculated appeal to this Massachusetts moderate to come over to the Republicans. Had not the Federalists abandoned him? He had risked himself by staying in Paris to preserve the peace, while his quondom colleague Marshall, followed by Pinckney, came back with tales branding him a traitor. "They openly wished you might be guillotined, or sent to Cayenne, or anything else." The Republicans, on the other hand, uniformly praised Gerry's conduct, a few only wishing he had done what the Federalists maliciously accused him of attempting and boldly made a treaty beyond his authority. Gerry had the choice, Jefferson frankly told him, either of sinking into "the humble oblivion" to which the Federalists had condemned him or of being borne aloft on the shoulders of a grateful citizenry. For glory would be his if he would communicate fully all the details of his mission. The people had a right to this information. "It is their sweat which is to earn all the expenses of the war, and their blood which is to flow in expiation of the causes of it." Jefferson counted on these disclosures to bring forth the radiant republicanism of the American mind. Needless to say, he also counted the political value of such a recruit as Gerry to the arduous Republican cause in New England.

Within six months Gerry, whose talent for political zigzag became legendary, was the Republican candidate for governor of Massachusetts. He had visited Adams at Quincy in October and found him a willing listener. Adams worried about the army. It was a dangerous engine, especially with Hamilton second in command; and he began to sense the public backlash to measures predicated on war. "If this nation sees a great army to maintain, without an enemy to fight," he warned the Secretary of War, "there may arise an enthusiasm that seems to be little foreseen. At present there is no more prospect of seeing a French army here, than there is in Heaven." About this time he received dispatches from William Vans Murray, American Minister at The Hague, reporting Talleyrand's devious overtures for peace. What he had learned at Quincy contributed to the moderation of his opening address to Congress. He gave a reluctant ear to Dr. Logan, a reluctant eye to what the scoundrel Barlow —"Tom Paine is not a more worthless fellow"—had written to Washington, only then to discover that his own son John Quincy, chargé d'affaires in Berlin, held the same opinion of French intentions. Finally, he received the required assurances from Talleyrand himself. On February 18, without forewarning or consultation, the President nominated Murray as minister plenipotentiary to the French republic.

Jefferson, reading the special message to the Senate, was no less amazed than the High Federalists by this "event of events." "Never did a party show a stronger mortification, and consequently, that war had been their object." Jefferson should have been delighted. Grasping the olive branch, Adams acted on the policy of his opponents. But this was incredible. Supposing the President as anxious for war as the Hamiltonians around him, Jefferson was unable to accept the nomination of Murray at face value. He conjectured that Adams, knowing he could not conceal the French assurances, took a step "which should parry the overture while it wears the face of acceding to it." He nominated Murray on the expectation the Federalists in the Senate would "take on their own shoulders the odium of rejecting it." But they would not; instead, they forced the President to adopt tactics of obstruction and delay which, if they did not negate the mission, "must at least keep off the day so hateful and so fatal to them, of reconciliation, and leave more time for new projects of provocation." This was the object, Jefferson thought, of the decision within a week of Murray's nomination to add two envoys to the mission under conditions that made it problematical whether they would ever leave home.

Jefferson was less than charitable in thus seeking to account for the President's conduct. Yet nothing had taken place to suggest that Adams was any less infatuated with the war policy than the ultras in Congress and the cabinet. He had gone on inflaming the public mind and treating the French republic in the most arrogant manner. He signed the Logan Act even as he profited from Logan's counsel; he enforced the Sedition Act and signed blank warrants for the arrest of aliens; and he gave no check to war preparations. On the very day of Murray's nomination, the new army bill for an eventual force of 30,000 regulars and 75,000 volunteers cleared the Senate for his signature. Several days earlier the Senate approved his appointment of envoys to negotiate treaties of commerce with Russia and Turkey, both new accessions to the second coalition against France. "All this helps," Jefferson said of this transaction, "to fill up the measure of provocation towards France, and to get from them a declaration of war, which we are afraid to be the first in making." And why, he wondered, if the President sincerely wished for reconciliation, did he wait until the end of the session, when all the war measures had passed, to spring his surprise? If Jefferson was mistaken in his view of Adams's intentions, it was not without reason.

What staggered belief among Republicans infuriated High Federalists. Secretary of State Pickering called the projected mission "the most unfortunate and the most humiliating event to the United States . . . since the commencement of the French Revolution." To appease his critics, Adams agreed to a three-man commission. Chief Justice Oliver Ellsworth and William R. Davie, of North Carolina, were joined with Murray. The result was delay, as Jefferson had predicted, and more than that, sabotage by Pickering and his colleagues. There was no appeasing them. They cried betrayal. Adams had been tricked by the combined sophistries of Jefferson and Talleyrand, they charged. The prospects of the Federalist party, soaring since the XYZ Affair, rested on opposition to France. The success of the war system hung on the public conviction of its necessity to force honor and justice from France. To act on the contrary proposition was like declaring "the emperor has no clothes." How was it possible to stamp out sedition, consolidate the national government, recruit an army, and go filibustering in the Spanish dominions when the rationale for these enterprises was taken away? Hamilton, still flirting with the Miranda project, had drawn up a far-reaching program for the Federalist warriors. A force should be collected to put Virginia, headquarters of the opposition, to "the test of resistance," Hamilton said. The great states should be subdivided to reduce their influence, the army should be established on its present footing, the planned naval force completed, a military academy instituted, the judicial arm of the federal government extended into every town and county, a more sweeping sedition law enacted, and all the "renegade aliens" still in the country sent away. Hamilton advocated these measures regardless of a settlement with France, though their prospects would be improved by war. The risk of civil war seems not to have disturbed him; indeed, to make the national authority "a question of force" was a necessary part of the plan. Similar sentiments were espoused by John Fenno, Jr., who took over the *Gazette of the United States* on his father's death in the fall epidemic that also claimed Bache of the *Aurora*. With Cobbett and several others of the press tribe, young Fenno bitterly assailed Adams's peace policy. But unlike Hamilton, who saw that the policy, once started, could not be undone, Fenno called for an immediate declaration of war on France, Spain, and Holland, and the conquest of their West Indies' possessions in collaboration with Britain. He would also do away with the state governments, "those egregrious baubles of sovereignty, those pestiferous incitements of demagogy," and revise the franchise so as to place the government securely in the hands of "the proprietors of the country." Declaring for peace, Adams unwittingly exposed naked reaction in the Federalist ranks.

It was a pity Jefferson could not appreciate the irony of the situation. Adams plunged a sword into the Federalist party, one which many of its leaders thought a betrayal to Jeffersonianism, but which to Jefferson was only a "parry" of French advances. Whether or not anything came of the new mission, its very existence rendered the war party desperate and must, Jefferson supposed, speed the progress of reform. "The spirit of 1776 is not dead. It has only been slumbering." As Congress neared adjournment a rebellion against the direct tax broke out in the eastern counties of Pennsylvania. (It was led, not by a Jacobin, but by a Federalist, John Fries.) The people were opening their eyes. "Pennsylvania, Jersey, and New York are coming majestically around to true principles." Petitions for repeal of the Alien and Sedition Laws poured into Congress. The first victim of the latter, Matthew Lyon, the Vermont congressman and editor, who had served his term in prison and whose fine had been paid by Jefferson and his friends, again sat in the House. Just before the session ended a special committee submitted a report in defense of the Alien and Sedition Laws. When the Republicans attacked it on the floor a strange scene ensued: the Federalists fell into laughing and coughing until, Jefferson reported, one would have needed "the lungs of a vendue-master to have been heard." As it was impossible to proceed, the report quickly passed. Several Federalist-dominated state legislatures, either at this time or soon after, also defended these laws in action on the Virginia and Kentucky Resolutions.

What, if anything, should be done about these Resolutions was one of the problems Jefferson took home with him in March. On the one hand, it was apparent that their doctrine, regardless of the public clamor against the federal laws, raised Unionist alarms in the states, even among Republican moderates in Virginia. To press the issue might very well arrest the "revolution of opinion" in midcourse. "Anything rash or threatening," he told Madison, "might check the favorable dispositions of the middle states, and rally them again around the measures which are ruining us." On the other hand, to let the doctrine lie idle in the face of rebuke, directly by several legislatures, indirectly by Congress, might be interpreted as a sign of weakness. Sometime during the long summer Jefferson decided that Virginia and Kentucky should renew their protests of the previous year. He was motivated, in part, by the clearer recognition of a danger only vaguely discerned in 1798. This was the threat of common law criminal jurisdiction in the federal courts. Edmund Randolph had taken up the subject and the two men exchanged opinions. Of all the claims ever made by the federal government it was, said Jefferson, the most dangerous. "All their other assumptions of un-given powers have been in detail. The bank law, the treaty doctrine, the sedition act, the alien act . . . , etc., etc., have been solitary, unconsequential, timid things, in comparison with the audacious, barefaced and sweeping pretension to a system of law for the U.S., without adoption of their legislature, and so infinitely beyond their power to adopt." The state courts might as well shut up. Perhaps the state legislatures too, for Congress might legislate on any matter within the boundless field of jurisdiction thus opened to the federal courts. It portended a complete consolidation. The claim, absurd as it was, should not go unchallenged. At least two Supreme Court justices openly championed it; many Federalists espoused the doctrine. "But, great heavens!" Jefferson exclaimed, "Who could have conceived in 1789 that within ten years we should have to combat such windmills."

On a Sunday in August, Madison came to Monticello to map plans for a second set of resolutions. Nicholas, though invited, was unable to attend. He was about to go over the mountains to look after the affairs of his late brother, long a leader in Kentucky politics, and so could arrange concerted action between that state and Virginia. Several days before the meeting Jefferson sketched his ideas in a letter to Madison. Not only should the principle of nullification be asserted but the protesting states should announce their intention, should the usurpations persist, to sever themselves from the Union. Such a statement would eliminate some of the ambiguity of the original doctrine by justifying secession as its sequel. If the

Hamiltonians were prepared to put the Union to the test of force, Jefferson seemed prepared to put it to the test of secession "rather than give up the rights of self-government which we have reserved, and in which alone we see liberty, safety and happiness." Six months earlier he had warned against extreme measures of this kind, believing they would check the progress of opinion. He now seemed to think the time had come to wield the threat of secession for political ends. In his opinion, as in the opinion of most men, the Union was an "experiment in liberty," and whether or not it would succeed was still an open question. The Union was neither imperishable nor indestructible. If it failed to serve liberty, becoming despotic instead, it repudiated the end of its being. Jefferson reached the nadir of his hopes for the Union in these notes, hastily sketched, as he admitted to Madison, in August 1799.

But Madison came to dinner—a cool breeze in a hot summer—and at once soothed his friend's feelings. Jefferson receded from the threat of secession, "not only in deference to his judgment, but because we should never think of separation but for repeated and enormous violations, so these, when they occur, will be cause enough of themselves." And so he modified his instructions to Nicholas. At the same time he proposed an addition to the resolutions: a protest against "the new pretensions to a *common law* of the U.S." The subject had doubtless been discussed at Monticello. When Madison came to write his Virginia Report on the Resolutions of 1798, he incorporated a lengthy rebuttal of these pretensions. The point was passed over by the Kentucky legislature. Its Resolutions of 1799 were hastily drawn, as Breckinridge informed Jefferson, and would not have been drawn at all but for Nicholas's appearance at the capital. Going back to Jefferson's draft of 1798, Breckinridge picked up the word and language of nullification, securing the first official usage of the doctrine in a series of resolutions that simply repeated the protest against the constitutionality of the Alien and Sedition Laws. The Virginia Report, adopted by the legislature in January, ran to the same effect. But this document was a masterful exposition of the theory of the federal union and a powerful defense of human rights. An appeal to reason, it affirmed republican liberty without incurring the heresy of disunion. Jefferson was delighted with the

Report, had it reprinted in Philadelphia, and believed it boosted Republican hopes at the opening of the fateful election year.

The Election of 1800

The country mourned the death of George Washington when Jefferson returned to Philadelphia for the meeting of the Sixth Congress in December 1799. He arrived late, too late to participate in the formal ceremonies honoring the first President and to hear Henry Lee proclaim him "first in war, first in peace, and first in the hearts of his countrymen." Black crepe hung from the walls and draped the Vice President's chair when he made his appearance in the Senate several days later. Inevitably, the solemnities of Congress carried partisan overtones. Washington died a Federalist, whether more Hamiltonian or Adamsite it would be difficult to say. He had been partly responsible, not long before his death, for the phenomenal upsurge of the party in Virginia, resulting in the election of Lee, Marshall, and six other Federalists to Congress. To whatever heights the ambitions of party might exalt Washington in death, he could not be more mercilessly exploited than in life. Jefferson must have shared the emotions common to his countrymen at this momentous passage in the nation's history; but he had learned to hide his feelings, especially where Washington was concerned, and so far as the record shows uttered not one word on his death.

Jefferson had small hope for the new Congress, elected months earlier at the peak of the war frenzy. For the first time in years the Federalists held commanding majorities in both houses. All the Republicans could do was to stand their ground, avoid anything rash, let the Federalist warriors consume each other, and prepare for the coming contest. Although worried by Republican backsliding in the southern states, Jefferson was cheered by the recent victory of Thomas McKean at the head of the state Republican ticket in Pennsylvania—evidence that public indignation was beginning to be translated into votes. If Pennsylvania, and perhaps New York, would unite with the Republicans of the southern and western states, there could be no doubt of the outcome in 1800. The balance of political forces was close. Every debate in Philadelphia was an electioneering skirmish. Congress, one observer wrote, was like "a conclave of cardinals, intriguing in the election of a Pope."

The Republican candidate weighed his moves with a view to the election. It was important for him to lead, yet he dared not lead openly. He was especially guarded in his correspondence, wrote few political letters, and declined to trust the post with those he ventured, "knowing that a campaign of slander is now open upon me, and believing that the postmasters will lend their inquisitorial aid to fish out any new matter of slander they can [to] gratify the powers that be." The press was the engine of reform. "Every man must lay his purse and his pen under contribution." He left the pen to others, to old friends like Edmund Pendleton and to unspeakable hirelings like James T. Callender; but he gave freely of his purse. He subscribed to dozens of newspapers (some of them fell victims of the Sedition Law), laid himself and his friends under assessment for new gazettes, and personally saw to the circulation of partisan tracts. In April he sent eight dozen of a single pamphlet, *Political Arithmetic*, by Thomas Cooper, the friend of Priestley, to the chairman of the Republican General Committee in Virginia for distribution to the county committees. Cooper was a seditious character. "I trust yourself only with the secret that these pamphlets go from me," Jefferson admonished the chairman. "You will readily see what a handle would be made by my advocating their contents." The contents, really not so radical, offered a dollars and cents argument on the economic superiority of agriculture and inland commerce to foreign trade supported by an expensive navy and financed by British capital. Jefferson supposed it would appeal to Virginia farmers. With party organization, as represented in the Virginia central committee and similar bodies in other states, he did not directly concern himself. He approved of it, of course, if not in principle, then because such organization seemed necessary to Republican success at the polls, which was the salvation of all principle. Although he was in touch with state leaders, like Burr in New York and McKean in Pennsylvania and John Langdon in New Hampshire, more often his influence at the state level was felt through Republican congressmen, with whom he conversed almost daily over the dinner table at Francis' Hotel. Federalists, seeing the improved Republican machine

—agents dispersed everywhere, committees within committees, every part working in unison—gave Jefferson more credit, or discredit, for the accomplishment than he deserved. He did not build the organization, yet it could not have been built without him. He did not direct it, yet he was the shaft on which the machine turned.

A heterogeneous coalition of the aggrieved, the discontented, and the ambitious, the party had no clearly defined principles and objectives. Jefferson's mind was well furnished with both, however; and although they were not broadcast to the electorate as in a "platform," they gave the Republican party whatever unity of creed it possessed. The creed was stated in private letters, especially those addressed to prospective converts, like Gerry, or to state leaders, like Gideon Granger of Connecticut, who were strangers to Jefferson. The fundamental doctrines were three. First, the preservation of the federal Constitution and the rights of the states. In this connection Jefferson expressed his long-standing opposition to a system of administration and finance that "monarchized" the Constitution, multiplied offices and taxes and debt, and sank the states under a consolidated government. "Our country is too large to have all its affairs directed by a single government. Public servants at such distance . . . , by rendering detection impossible to their constituents, will invite the public agents to corruption, plunder and waste. . . . The true theory of our Constitution is surely the wisest and best, that the states are independent as to everything within themselves, and united as to everyhing respecting foreign nations." Second, freedom of religion, freedom of the press, and the right of the people, inseparable from their sovereignty, to oppose and criticize the governing authorities. "And," he added with a characteristic flourish, "I am for encouraging the progress of science in all its branches; and not for raising a hue and cry against the sacred name of philosophy; for awing the human mind with stories of raw-head and bloody bones to a distrust of its own vision . . . , to go backwards instead of forward to improvement; to believe that government, religion, morality, and every other science were in perfection in the ages of darkest ignorance, and that nothing can ever be devised more perfect than what was established by our forefathers." And third, "free commerce with all nations, political connection with none." Jefferson reaffirmed his belief that the nation should "disentangle" itself from the affairs of Europe. Only in this way could the United States establish its national character and independence, untroubled by the sufferings and rivalries and passions of the Old World. These were his principles, Jefferson said repeatedly. They rested on the mother principle of democracy, since all were un-questionably, he believed, the principles of "the great body of our fellow citizens."

The shiftings and shadings of Jefferson's thought in response to changing circumstances illuminated rather than blurred its basic consistency. Thus the war hysteria, while it caused no change of principle, hardened his broad state rights commitment. The most significant adjustment occurred in the realm of foreign policy. His faith in France had been jolted over the years. He began to speak of disengagement in 1797, but as late as 1798 he justified his faith in the French republic and its cause in Europe. Finally, the 18th Brumaire of Napolean Bonaparte, which overthrew the republic and estab-lished the rule of a dictatorial consulate, crushed the last hopes Jef-ferson had for the Revolution. Once again, as at its birth, the Amer-ican republic stood alone in the world. He had looked upon France as a commercial ally, but French atrocities on American commerce well-nigh destroyed the country's liberties. He had looked upon France as a spearhead of republicanism in the Old World, but the poor, ignorant peoples' longings for freedom were harnessed to Na-poleon's imperial ambitions. He had looked upon the success of the French republic as indispensable to secure the American—nothing was left of this theory in 1800. Darkness had fallen in Europe, and Jefferson was resigned, at last, to an American destiny in a world of its own. "It is very material," he wrote to Breckinridge, "for the [people] to be made sensible that their own character and situation are materially different from the French; and that whatever may be the fate of republicanism there, we are able to preserve it inviolate here. . . . Our vessel is moored at such a distance that should theirs blow up, ours is still safe, if we will but think so." Partiality to France was no longer justified; neutrality, under whatever guise, was no longer enough. Isolation was the true policy. Commerce must go on, of course, but independently of treaties such as he had earlier advocated to upbuild American freedom and power. The French treaties were dead by congressional decree. The Adams administration, while continuing to seek treaties of commerce, had abandoned the liberal principles of the original plan, as had the Jay Treaty. Whatever justification the policy once had was gone. And Jefferson, with most Republicans, believed the system needlessly involved the United States in the quarrels of Europe.

The coming election was omnipresent in Congress. "Our campaign will be as hot as that of Europe," Jefferson philosophized. "But happily indeed in ink only; they in blood." In January, Senator James Ross, the defeated Federalist candidate for governor of Pennsylvania, moved the appointment of a committee to report a bill setting forth the procedures to be followed in the scrutiny of electoral votes cast for President and Vice President. The upshot was the Ross bill. The electoral certificates of the various states, after being opened in Congress, would be referred to a grand committee of six elected members from each house and the Chief Justice. The committee would meet in secret session and throw out any votes cast in an irregular manner or by unqualified electors or under bribery or intimidation of any kind. Its report would be final. Everyone recognized the true purpose of this party measure. The grand committee would be dominated by Federalists, who could be expected to scrutinize the votes for Republican candidates with particular care. William Duane, now editor of the *Aurora*, learned of these secret proceedings, accused the Federalists of a cabalistic plot, and published the bill in full before it passed the Senate. In the arts of exposure and vilification Duane had rapidly proved himself the equal of Bache; and when death cheated the Federalists of enemy number one, they turned to his successor. Duane was no easy mark, however. Pickering had wanted to deport him as a "wild Irishman," but the editor, though he had grown up in Ireland, boasted American birth. Twice arraigned under the Sedition Law, he squirmed free the first time, and by threat of embarrassing disclosures forced the authorities to drop the second case. Now the Federalist senators, enraged by Duane's exposure of the Ross bill, summoned him before the bar of the house to answer for the publication of a false, scandalous, and malicious libel of the Senate.

It made an awkward situation for the Vice President. How could he preside at the trial of the first Republican editor in the land for high breach of the privileges of the Senate? On the other hand, how could he refuse to do his sworn duty? The dilemma might be avoided by stalling the trial. Such was the strategy adopted by Duane's counsel, Alexander Dallas and Thomas Cooper, no doubt in consultation with Jefferson. Duane appeared, denied the jurisdiction of the Senate, and asked to be represented by counsel. The request was granted; counsel, however, would not be permitted to inquire into the question of jurisdiction. In accordance with the strategy, Duane then addressed letters to Dallas and Cooper asking their services, but these gentlemen declined to submit themselves to Star Chamber proceedings. Thus denied the benefit of counsel, Duane informed the Vice President he could not appear for trial. The Senate declared Duane in contempt and instructed the Vice President to issue a warrant for his arrest. Jefferson did his duty. Part of the Federalists' game, he realized, was to put him on the spot. The editor went into hiding at Stenton, out of reach of the process server. Friends and sympathizers, meanwhile, got up a petition and remonstrance in his behalf. On the question of receiving it, the yeas and nays were equal, and Jefferson made the majority with his casting vote. After hearing the petition, the Senate refused to amend its action. But it could not stay in session forever, and so, in a final face-saving gesture, requested the President to prosecute the wily editor for sedition. (He was again indicted in the fall, and again without success.) It was a humiliating defeat for the Federalists. The Ross bill, too, finally met defeat. This piece of Federalist arrogance revolted decency and common sense; fortunately, these virtues had not altogether disappeared in the lower house, which rejected the Senate measure.

Panic descended on the Federalist chieftains as the election approached. The danger of war had passed, but the Sedition Act was enforced even more vigorously, not only against such prominent propagandists as Duane and Cooper and Callender, the monstrous Jacobin trio some High Federalists imagined took their orders from Jefferson himself, but against poor, obscure Republican editors as well. "The onset on the presses is to cripple and suppress the Republican efforts during the campaign which is coming on," Jefferson observed. "In the meantime their own batteries are teeming with every falsehood they can invent for defamation." All signs pointed to returning peace with France. Ellsworth and Davie had finally sailed in November and, with Murray, were received by Napoleon in March. The war machine could no longer be kept up. Washington's death was a blow to the provisional army—Congress began to dismantle it in February. The Federalist engineers, frantic to restore the machine's operation for domestic purposes, only betrayed themselves. "The rapid progress of public sentiment warns them of their danger, and they are passing laws to keep themselves in power," Jefferson said. Having failed with the first line of defense, the Ross bill, they retreated to a second in March. The leadership brought forward a bill to reform the judiciary. The bill would create new courts, many new judges, and greatly extend federal jurisdiction. While not without merits, it was a blatantly partisan measure designed, in part, to make the judiciary a fortress against the rising Republicanism of the nation. By multiplying courts and jurisdiction, the means would be at hand, argued the Massachusetts Federalist Theodore Sedgwick, "to render the justice of the nation acceptable to the people, to aid the national economy, to overawe the licentious, and to punish the guilty." And Wolcott observed, "It is impossible, in this country, to render an army an engine of government, and there is no way to combat the state opposition but by an efficient and extended organization of judges, magistrates, and other civil officers." By the narrowest of margins, Republicans and moderates blocked passage of the bill. The morale of the opposition, at low ebb two years before, had fully revived when Congress broke up in May.

The election of the New York legislature in April provided the first crucial test of party strength. In that state, as in several others, the legislature appointed the presidential electors; as the legislature went, so too would go New York's electoral vote. And the result in the legislature would be controlled by the contest in New York City. There Burr concentrated his efforts. They were rewarded. The Republican ticket, which Burr had framed for the maximum popular appeal, including names of Revolutionary fame—George Clinton, Horatio Gates, Brockholst Livingston—was swept into the Assembly. The Federalists were deposed. Jefferson seemed virtually assured of New York's electoral vote. By his own calculations, victory in New York would mean victory in the nation. Others agreed. When he stopped to see Adams on some official business after the upset in New York, he was accosted with, "Well, I understand that you are to beat me in this contest. . . ." (Jefferson replied that it was not a contest between them but between two systems of political principles: "Were we both to die today, tomorrow two other names would be put in the place of ours, without any change in the motion of the machinery.") So alarmed was Hamilton by Burr's coup that he urged his old friend John Jay, the Governor, to convene the lame-duck legislature in order to nullify the Republican victory by a change of the electoral law. Otherwise, said Hamilton, "the OVERTHROW of the GOVERNMENT . . . a REVOLUTION, after the manner of BONAPARTE," was the prospect. Revolted by the proposition, Jay quietly buried it.

Thus the opening battle spread gloom in one party and irrepressible optimism in the other. The Republicans owed so much to Burr that his candidacy for the vice presidential nomination could not be denied. It should go to a New Yorker anyway. Clinton was approached but declined. Burr, though still bristling at the southerners for their treatment of him in 1796, agreed to stand if he would be fairly supported. When Republican congressmen caucused in Philadelphia in May, Burr was the unanimous choice for Jefferson's running-mate.

The Federalists also went into caucus to choose nominees and map strategy. Their decision to support Adams and Charles Cotesworth Pinckney equally was, in effect, a vote of "no confidence" in the President. As Hamilton saw it, Adams was a necessary sacrifice if the Federalists were to be saved from "the fangs of Jefferson." He assumed the two candidates would, in fact, be equally supported in every state except South Carolina, where the vote would be split between Jefferson and the native son Pinckney, who would, therefore outdistance Adams and, it was to be hoped, the Virginian. The party was still badly torn by Adams's second mission to France; and the principal cabinet officers, Pickering, Wolcott, and McHenry, still took their orders from Hamilton. This intramural conflict, while less public, was more fatal than the conflict with the Republicans. Adams at last woke up to the treachery of his ministers, or at least two of them, Pickering and McHenry, and while the party reeled from the shock of the New York election, dismissed them from office in May. This was the crowning insult to the Hamiltonians. "If Mr. Adams should be reelected," a Marylander wrote, "I fear our constitution would be more injured by his unruly passions, antipathies, and jealousies, than by the whimsies of Jefferson." The President's enemies accused him of striking a bargain with Jefferson: the two men would join forces in the election and swap offices. The cabinet dismissals were part of the bargain, as was Jefferson's casting vote confirming the President's nomination of his father-in-law as a commissioner of the stamp tax. "Mr. *Adams* and his dear friend Mr. *Jefferson* have been *twice closeted* together," wagged one Federalist tongue, "and it is generally understood to be agreed on between them that General Pinckney is not to be President—Adams declares for Mr. Jefferson—the only man in America qualified to fill the appointment, except himself." Malice alone inspired these rumors. Jefferson had no need for Adams's support, nor did he wish it. As for Adams, no doubt he considered the Virginian a small evil compared to the Federalist madmen of the "British faction," but the idea of a secret Adams-Jefferson coalition in 1800 was absurd. As Jefferson had said to Adams of the contest, "Its motion is from principle, not from you or myself."

When Jefferson climbed into the stage at Philadelphia on May 15, he took final leave of the city that had been the principal scene of his public life. Before his return to Congress, the government would be seated on the Potomac. Except for the loss of his associates in the scientific circle, he infinitely preferred the new capital to the old. He continued to view great cities "as pestilential to the morals, the health, and the liberties of man." Philadelphia, for all its charms, had given abundant evidence of that. Realizing he might never be so far east again, he abandoned his usual itinerary and took the long route down the eastern shore to Norfolk, thence along the southside of the James, some of it through country he had never seen. He intended to bypass Richmond but stopped briefly, without becoming "a manniquin of ceremony," to talk with Governor Monroe. From there he went to Mont Blanco, Maria's new home, where horses and servant waited. Maria had lost her first-born child. Anxious for her health, he took her to Monticello with him. He was soon busy with house and farm. He had taken a heavy loss on last year's tobacco because of the suspension of commerce with France. Fortunately, the wheat harvest was the finest ever in Albemarle, and the market was good.

While occupied with domestic cares, he found time to complete a manual of parliamentary procedure begun in February. *Jefferson's Manual* laid down rules for the conduct of the Senate. This was a matter of concern to him from the moment he became Vice President. Fair and orderly procedure in legislative bodies was, he recognized, an essential ingredient of representative government. Neither house of Congress was above criticism in this regard. Jefferson, faced with the task of presiding over the Senate, began to collect his thoughts on "parliamentary science" and later determined to make a permanent digest of precedent and practice before his term of office ended. Although he took account of the experience of American legislative bodies, he went back to the fountainhead, the English Parliament, for his standard. The *Manual*, first published in 1801, is still in use in the Senate of the United States.

He was a passive and, on the whole, silent observer of the presidential campaign. Around his own person the Republican party had achieved a unity of action and of feeling beyond anything previously known. His mind was at ease as the fall elections came on. He would have felt better about the outcome, however, had the Pennsylvania legislature broken the stalemate that threatened to deprive the state of its electoral vote. (The two houses, one Federalist, the other Republican, could not agree on an electoral law.) The persistence of Federalist strength in certain states, such as the Carolinas, also troubled him. Correspondents in the different states kept him abreast of developments. From New England, especially from Connecticut, came pitiful accounts of Republican helots pitted against an entrenched Federalist aristocracy. "There are at least four hundred Men of public education and possessed of public confidence for four or five of us to contend with," wrote Gideon Granger. It was a "System of Terror" managed by clerics and lawyers. "They are now bold enough to tell us that we must be destroyed *root* and branch." Jefferson had no hope of cracking this Federalist stronghold, or Massachusetts either; indeed New England's isolation from the prevailing Republicanism of the country made him anxious for his administration of the government. "It can never be harmonious and solid," he told Granger, "while so respectable a portion of its citizens support principles which go directly to a change of the federal constitution, to sink the state governments, consolidate them into one, and to monarchize that."

Even in Virginia sedition had its day. About the time Jefferson passed through Richmond, James T. Callender was indicted for the publication of *The Prospect Before Us*, his principal contribution to the Republican campaign. Two days later Jefferson advised Monroe, "I think it essentially just and necessary that Callender should be substantially defended." By this he meant the commonwealth should take a hand in the defense, thereby making the trial a test not only of freedom of the press but of state authority as well. Callender was a hard test. It was not simply that he thrived on scandal; he was himself a scandal. "The wretch has a most thief-like look, he is ragged, dirty, has a downcast with his eyes, leans his head towards one side, as if his neck had a stretch, and goes along working his shoulders up and down with evident signs of anger against the fleas and lice." Justice Samuel Chase, the most fanatical Federalist on the bench, had chosen his victim after Luther Martin, in Maryland, gave him a copy of the free-swinging tract in which Adams was called "a hoary headed incendiary." The ablest counsel in Virginia, including the state's attorney general, defended Callender, so far as Chase would permit. The trial, a travesty of justice, ended in conviction by an all-Federalist jury and sentence of a $200 fine and nine months in jail. Of comparatively little importance in the election of 1800, the trial was the central event in what would become the most damaging personal relationship of Jefferson's career.

The relationship began in 1797. Encouraged by the distinguished patronage he then received, Callender put his fangs into Jefferson and would not let go. With the passage of the Sedition Act, he was a marked man in Philadelphia, and so, leaving four motherless children behind him, fled to the asylum of Senator Mason's home in northern Virginia. He was sick of politics. He complained of being ill-used by the Republicans and hunted by the Federalists. Describing himself as "alone in the land of strangers," he implored Jefferson to give him a job at Monticello. The last place Jefferson wanted to see this miserable refugee from Grub Street was at Monticello; still he sympathized with Callender's plight and through a carefully disguised transaction sent him $50. The next year Callender went to Richmond where his talents were employed by the *Richmond Examiner*, the state's leading Republican newspaper. At the same time he began writing *The Prospect*, primarily, it seems, as a money-making venture. Jefferson saw some of this in page proof, predicted the "best effect" from it, and instructed his agent in Richmond to pay Callender $50 on account of the book. All these payments Jefferson later justified as "mere charities . . . , no more meant as encouragements to his scurrilities, than those I give to the beggar at my door are meant as rewards for the vices of his life." Interestingly, the confession acknowledged that Callender wrote "scurrilities" and omitted the premise on which the "charities" were given and, for that reason, concealed. It was a scurrilous time, of course. Political partisans sucked venom as if it were mother's milk. But Callender was no ordinary scandalmonger. His letters to Jefferson reveal a paranoic, embittered against the world, contemptuous of "the rascally society of mankind"—an unscrupulous hireling less interested in the Republican cause than in the money he could make by scandalizing the opposition. No one seemed to like Callender, and some of the most ardent Republicans feared him. John Taylor, for instance, sought to warn Jefferson that the Scotsman was quite capable, at the slightest provocation, of turning on his benefactor. And Jefferson became more guarded. Callender sent him ranting letters from the Richmond jail and advance sheets of the second volume of *The Prospect*. Jefferson made no acknowledgment, except to send another $50 to the wretch, again under the fiction of covering purchases of the book. Motives of charity and of politics had become thoroughly confused, yet it seems unlikely at this point that Jefferson regarded Callender as a worthy object of either one. Probably he considered more the harm than the good Callender could now do to him. At any rate, he had placed himself in the hands of a man not at all loath to blackmail a President or, failing in that, smear him with scandal.

The vilification Jefferson received in the campaign of 1800 was hardly calculated to excite his disgust of Republican hatchet-men like Callender. For nearly a decade the Federalists had been fashioning an ugly image of Jefferson. Little was added in 1800, but everything was raised to the *n*th dimension. The fear and distrust dedicated Federalists felt for Jefferson presumably had psychological validity in the Federalist political mind. And the more they voiced their apprehensions the more they were possessed by them. In 1800 they became the victims of a self-induced hysteria; yet it did not seize them blindly. Angry, humiliated, desperate, they set out quite deliberately to terrorize the American public with the monster of their imagination. So many things operated to divide and embarrass the Federalists, the thing to do, Fisher Ames advised, was to "sound the tocsin about Jefferson." And sound it they did. Infidelity, Jacobinism, Disunionism—these were the most dreadful evils the people had to fear from the lean and crafty Virginian.

The conception had a certain coherence. The source of Jefferson's malignity was French philosophy. He was a visionary theorist, "a *philosophe* in the modern French sense of the word," not only a dangerous profession but one that incapacitated him for the chief magistracy of a great nation. This was more, much more, than jest and satire; the threat was real, and the Federalists treated it with an earnestness that betrayed deep-seated suspicion of philosophical intelligence in affairs of state. Jefferson's democratic ideas, being imported from France, were bizarre. The propagandists could not decide whether democracy would prostrate the government by the dissipation of its energies or bring the people under the tyranny of a demagogue; but either result, impotence or despotism, would destroy constitutional government in the United States. Playing up the worst of these dangers, the Federalists stigmatized Jefferson as a Jacobin and predicted his reign would follow the same course as revolutionary democracy in France. "Murder, robbery, rape, adultery, and incest will be openly taught and practiced, the air will be rent with the cries of distress, the soil will be soaked with blood, and the nation black with crimes." And yet, while portraying Jefferson as this prodigious Robespierre-Danton-Bonaparte, the Federalists did not neglect the other side of his character, the side of weakness, vacilation, and cowardice, as first exhibited in the Virginia governorship. Here, too, the fatal French influence was at work: a head full of dreamy Rousseauist ideas could not govern a state. The Jeffersonian dogmas of state rights represented the extension of these ideas to the federal system. National breakdown must be the consequence. Jefferson's views favorable to emancipation of the slaves evinced ei-

637

ther cruel hypocrisy or speculative delusion. Southerners, at least, might be frightened by the specter of Santo Domingo, another violent offspring of the French Revolution. The Gabriel Conspiracy in Virginia, uncovered in September 1800, dramatized the danger. In the Federalist press it was reported that Gabriel was not, in fact, a Negro slave but the notorious Callender acting on Jefferson's orders. Whether a misguided child of light or a demonic child of darkness, Jefferson was more Frenchman than American, and between the treachery of the one and the treachery of the other there was not much to choose.

Both press and pulpit rang with anathemas on Jefferson the Infidel. The *Gazette of the United States* emblazoned the issue:

THE GRAND QUESTION STATED

At the present solemn moment the only question to be asked by every American, laying his hand on his heart, is "Shall I continue in allegiance to

GOD—AND A RELIGIOUS PRESIDENT;

or impiously declare for

JEFFERSON—AND NO GOD!!!"

Of course, Jefferson's infidelity stemmed from French philosophy. In 1798 New England religionists set up a hue and cry on the world-wide conspiracy against Christianity masterminded by a secret order, the Illuminati, which had overspread Europe under the aegis of the French Revolution and infiltrated seditious societies in the United States. This absurdity was exploded by 1800; but the notion of atheistical democracy seemed peculiarly congenial to many Federalists, and Jefferson offered an inviting target. Some of the shots were wild rumors, for example, that he had done away with the Sabbath and introduced the French calendar in his family. Some were twisted anecdotes. The two most prominent clerical pamphleteers, the Reverends John M. Mason and William Linn, published the story told by still another man of the cloth, John B. Smith, deceased, who had supposedly heard it from Philip Mazzei. While riding with Jefferson through the country, so the story went, Mazzei remarked on the rundown appearance of a church, and his companion declared "it is good enough for him who was born in a manger." Linn drew the moral: "Such a contemptuous fling at the blessed Jesus, could issue from the lips of no other than a deadly foe of his name and cause." (A Republican newspaper, the *Vermont Gazette*, printed what it attested to be the true story. Mazzei, commenting on the church, said that Italian priests would refuse to enter such a shabby place, to which Jefferson replied, "And yet meaner places were deemed grand enough to dispense truth in, by HIM who was born in a manger.") Principally, however, the accusers relied on the *Notes on Virginia*, elated that the culprit convicted himself out of his own mouth. His disbelief in the deluge, his opposition to Bible reading in the schools, his impious declarations—"What *is* he, what *can he be*, but a decided, a hardened infidel?"

Jefferson attributed the vehement attack to his role in overthrowing the establishment in Virginia. Emboldened by the success of political delusion, the Federalist clergy had revived the hope of "obtaining an establishment of a particular form of Christianity thro' the U.S." Whatever the clerical intent—and the record does not support Jefferson's worst fears—the premises of the argument ran directly counter to the principles underlying the disestablishment. These principles were so widely accepted by 1800 that Republicans did not hesitate to acclaim Jefferson for them. As they pointed out, the Federalist censure implied there should be a religious test for high office. Was orthodoxy to be prescribed in religion as well as in politics, all in the face of the First Amendment? Although they marshaled evidence to prove the purity of Jefferson's Christian belief, the Republicans preferred to take the ground—the only one Jefferson could have approved—that the entire question was irrelevant. Between this position and the Federalist religionists no compromise was possible. To the latter, the voice of the nation in calling a deist or infidel to the first magistracy would be "no less than rebellion against God." It would assuredly end in the destruction of the churches and the reign of infamy. Christian belief was the test of moral character. Jefferson, lacking belief, was a bad man. His relations with Washington illustrated his besetting vice, duplicity. Federalists kept the Mazzei letter in the public eye. Moreover, he had obtained his property by fraud, fraud upon his British creditors and—a pure invention—upon a poor widow in his capacity as executor of an estate. But it would take a renegade Republican, Callender, to fill up the catalogue of slander at a later date.

Although personally hurt by the smear campaign, Jefferson

nursed his wounds in quiet. What his friend Cooper said in reference to Adams, he probably considered good philosophy for himself: "Calumny is a tax which every man high in office must sometimes pay, but truth like gold will come out unsullied and undimmed from the fire of discussion." He patiently bore the tax, confident he would enjoy the ultimate reward. "I know that I might have filled the courts of the United States with actions for these slanders," he wrote to a sympathetic stranger, "and have ruined perhaps many persons who are innocent. But this would be no equivalent for the loss of character. I leave them, therefore, to the reproof of their own consciences. If these do not condemn them, there will yet come a day when the false witness will meet a judge who has not slept over his slanders." He could rely on his Republican friends to defend his character and principles. John Beckley was one. His *Address to the People of the United States* raked through most of the charges and appended a brief biography of the Republican candidate, the first to be written of him and the first of all campaign lives. Five thousand copies were printed and it was liberally excerpted in the Republican press. Out of the enthusiasm was born the first of America's election songs, "Jefferson and Liberty." Republican hearts exulted in this hymn of victory—

> Rejoice, Columbia's sons, rejoice
> To tyrants never bend the knee
> But join with heart with soul and voice
> For Jefferson and Liberty.

Federalists were astounded by the industry and organization of the Republicans, even in New England where they were "trouped, officered, regimented . . . in a manner that our militia have never yet equalled," according to Ames. "Every threshing floor, every husking, every party work on a house-frame or raising a building, the very funerals are infected with bawlers or whisperers against government." The report of Jefferson's "funeral" afforded momentary relief. A Massachusetts divine noted in his diary: "In the morning we had news of the death of Mr. Jefferson. It is to be hoped that it is true." First printed in the *Baltimore American*, a Republican gazette, on June 30, the rumor or hoax was credited even by some of Jefferson's closest associates; but on July 4, a day Republicans claimed as their own, the *American* rejoiced "Jefferson Lives."

In the enveloping gloom Federalist leaders wrung their hands, bickered and swore, conspired and commiserated with each other. "Have our party shown that they possess the necessary skill and courage to deserve . . . to govern?" wrote the deposed Secretary of War to Wolcott. "What have they done? . . . They write private letters. To whom? To each other, but they do nothing to give a proper direction to the public mind. . . . They meditate in private. Can any good come out of such a system?" Obviously not. A quarreling elite, distrustful of democracy, the Federalists were poorly equipped to conduct a campaign in the electorate. Adams inveighed against the British faction and the Essex Junto, its supposed north of Boston headquarters, "like one possessed," as Ames said. "His language is bitter even to outrage and swearing and calling names." He was reported to speak in friendly terms of his Republican rival; extremists like Ames believed he would see Jefferson President before he would yield to a true Federalist. For many Hamiltonians the choice between Adams and Jefferson was, at best, a choice between evils. The plot to abandon Adams for Pinckney was more easily conceived than executed, however. Hamilton's warmest admirers despaired of its success and feared it would expose the whole party to defeat. The New Yorker persevered. He wrote a vindictive brief against Adams intended for private circulation among the Federalist leaders. When part of the polemic fell into Republican hands, Hamilton threw caution to the winds and published it in full. Coming late in the campaign, in October, the sensational pamphlet had no effect on the outcome of the election, already determined in most states, but it exposed the sickness of the Federalist party more effectively than anything that appeared under Republican auspices.

At Monticello Jefferson kept tabs on the expected electoral vote. By December he counted 58 sure votes for the Republicans, 53 for the Federalists. The remaining 27 belonged to Rhode Island (4) and South Carolina (8), where he rated the chances as even, and to Pennsylvania (15), which stood little chance of voting at all. Adams had shown surprising strength in Maryland and North Carolina. Federalist hopes revived. The race was closer than men on either side had expected. Rhode Island soon joined her New England sisters in the Federalist column. The Republicans had proved their superiority at the polls in Pennsylvania, but a bare Federalist majority in the Senate still blocked the adoption of an electoral law. At the last moment the two houses reached a compromise which split the electoral vote 8 and 7, a disappointing net gain of one for the Republicans. So the two candidates were nearly even as the country awaited word from South Carolina. There the Republican cause was in the able hands of Charles Pinckney, United States senator and kinsman of General Pinckney, the Federalist candidate who was expected to draw votes away from Adams and given an outside chance of winning the presidency. The Republican manager sent Jefferson blow by blow reports on the contest. Since the choice of electors fell to the legislature, the state election was decisive. While disheartened by his party's poor showing in Charleston, always a Federalist stronghold, Pinckney confidently expected the inland counties to furnish a Republican majority. Taking nothing for granted, he went to Columbia, set up his command post, and caucused, coaxed, and bargained to ensure the success of the electoral slate pledged to Jefferson and Burr. On December 2 he dispatched a breathless note to Jefferson: "The election is just finished and we have (thanks to Heaven's goodness) carried it." Jefferson, then in Washington, received the news on December 12. At the same time he was reliably informed from Columbia that one vote would be withheld from Burr, thereby eliminating the possibility of a tie. In the electoral count, though the margin poorly reflected the popular standing of the two parties, Jefferson was the choice over Adams 73 to 65.

Republicanism had triumphed! The bright day dawned—no more "gags, inquisitions and spies," no more "herds of harpies" or "lordlings with gorging jaws" or "bigots with their holy laws." "The Jig's Up!" shouted the *Baltimore American*. "Be glad America!" rejoiced the *Readinger Adler*. Dismayed Federalists wore such long faces, it was said, that barbers doubled their prices. Direst consequences were predicted from seating a visionary, a demagogue, and a "howling atheist" at the head of the nation. But in the victory celebrations even church bells rang for Jefferson. The people had consummated a peaceful revolution in government. "Here ends the 18th Century," one enthusiast marked the year's end. "The 19th begins with a fine clear morning wind at S.W.; and the political horizon affords as fine a prospect under Jefferson's administration, with returning harmony with France—with the irresistible propagation of the Rights of Man, the eradication of hierarchy, oppression, superstition and tyranny over the world. . . ."

In fact, however, the horizon had clouded. Entry into the promised land of "Jefferson and Liberty" was blocked by the terrible abyss of the electoral system. For several days after December 12, Jefferson assumed with most men that his election to the presidency was secure. To be sure, certain states—Kentucky, Tennessee, Georgia, and Vermont—had not been heard from, but no one doubted how they would vote; and the possibility of a tie between the first and second Republican candidates, tossing the choice to the House of Representatives, was too great an absurdity to be credited. Jefferson began putting together his cabinet. On the 14th, in a long letter touching on steam engines and mammoth bones, he offered the Navy post to Robert R. Livingston. The next day he sent congratulations to Burr and expressed regret over the loss of his services to the new administration. "It leaves a chasm in my arrangements, which cannot be adequately filled up." He simply assumed that Burr had been elected Vice President. He mentioned the report from South Carolina and also the expectations as to Tennessee and Georgia: enough votes would be withdrawn from Burr to prevent a deadlock but he would surely top Adams in the final tally. "However," he went on, "it was badly managed not to have arranged with certainty what seems to have been left to hazard." Decency required that he take no part in these arrangements, but Jefferson supposed they had been made. Otherwise a Republican victory would be at least partially nullified, either by loss of one-half the ticket or, in the event of a tie, by political wheeling and dealing that risked everything. The desired result might have been secured in the Virginia "college of electors," allowing the Republicans elsewhere to display their unanimity. But the sting of Burr's accusation of bad faith in 1796 caused Madison, possibly with Jefferson's consent, to demand a unanimous vote for Burr in Virginia. He got it only because he was able to offer anxious Virginia Jeffersonians the assurances of Burr's personal agent that votes would be thrown away from the New York in other states. If there was honor among politicians, Burr was bound to take steps that would place Jefferson's majority beyond hazard. He did not, and so Republican electors, North and South, played Alphonse and Gaston to each other.

The trace of apprehension Jefferson expressed in his letter to Burr increased from day to day. The earlier report from South Carolina was finally discredited; the state's electors were unanimous for Jefferson and Burr. On the 19th "an absolute parity" between the Republican candidates seemed certain, he told Madison. "This has produced great dismay and gloom on the Republican gentlemen here, and equal exultation on the Federalists." The last faint hope of breaking the stalemate vanished on the 23rd when the votes from Georgia and Tennessee were reported in Washington. "Seventy-three for Mr. Jefferson and seventy-three for Mr. Burr," Adams brooded. "May the peace and welfare of the country be promoted by this result!" The fate of the election, perhaps of the nation, would be decided in the lame-duck House of Representatives elected in the year of terror.

What would the Federalists do? The virgin capital buzzed with speculation and rumor. Huddled together in a few boarding houses, with nothing else to amuse them, politics was the congressmen's sole element. "A few, indeed, drink, and some gamble," Gallatin informed his wife, "but the majority drink nought but politics, and by not mixing with men of different or more moderate activities, they inflame one another." Excitement first centered on a Federalist plan to prevent an election altogether and in the interregnum to commit the first magistracy to the president *pro tem* of the Senate or some other officer. "This opens upon us an abyss, at which every sincere patriot must shudder," Jefferson said. Usurpation was the only name for such an act. The Republicans would resist by force if necessary; and groups were soon said to be organizing in neighboring states to march on Washington and put to death any man bold enough to offer himself as the usurper. It was "a wild measure," as Gouverneur Morris, now the junior senator from New York, acknowledged. Only the most desperate Federalists would actually carry it through, though others supposed the threat of the project would frighten the Republicans into imbecility. Jefferson was sufficiently alarmed to call on the President. The plan to make a President by law was fraught with "incalculable consequences," he told Adams, which it was in his power to prevent by executive veto. But the defeated President, with more than a trace of irritation, thought such an act might be justified, and observed that Jefferson could end the crisis in an instant by making certain pledges to the Federalists—pledges he consistently refused to make. For the first time in their long acquaintance, Jefferson recalled the interview, he and Adams parted with displeasure—and it was probably their last parting. The Vice President was not powerless in this situation. As the Senate's presiding officer, he could rule out of order any motion to legislate a President, and he had, in fact, promised to do just that before he talked to Adams. But the danger of usurpation and interregnum gradually receded as the Federalist leadership in Congress decided to make a President of Aaron Burr.

For a time Jefferson seemed little disturbed by this alternate project to upset the will of the people. Under the Constitution a majority of the representatives of each of nine states was needed to elect in the House; and the Federalists simply could not produce the necessary votes for Burr. Republican defections were possible, of course, but the party was firmly united on Jefferson. More likely, if he could not win nine states, stalemate would revive the danger of usurpation. To cover this eventuality Madison proposed in January that Jefferson and Burr jointly convene the new Congress to choose the President. The Republicans in Washington passed over the plan because they did not think it necessary. Burr himself declined all competition with Jefferson. "Be assured," he wrote to Samuel Smith, the Maryland Republican leader, "that the Federal party can entertain no wish for such an exchange. As to my friends, they would dishonor my views and insult my feelings by a suspicion that I would be instrumental in counteracting the wishes and expectations of the people of the United States." Smith published the letter, immensely reassuring to the Republicans.

The fact that Burr's letter was dated December 16, from Albany, when northern Republicans were celebrating Jefferson's election on the basis of the erroneous report from South Carolina, should have prompted second thoughts. At that time Burr had little reason to think the election would go to the House. Nor could he be certain on the point a week later when he pledged his loyalty in a letter to Jefferson. Nonetheless, most Republicans, including the chief, took Burr's disclaimer in good faith. "His conduct has been honorable and decisive, and greatly embarrasses" the Federalists, Jefferson stated. If embarrassed, the Federalists were not dismayed. As if to prove the theory it takes a rascal to know one, they claimed to understand Burr better than the Jeffersonians did. "Burr is a cunning man," one of them wrote. "If he cannot outwit all the Jeffersonians I do not know the man." James A. Bayard, the Delaware congressman, told Hamilton that the Federalists interpreted the letter to Smith either as proceeding from "a false calculation" of the electoral vote or as "a cover to blind his own party." "By persons friendly to Mr. Burr," Bayard said, "it is distinctly stated, that he is willing to consider the Federalists as his friends, and to accept the office of President as their gift." This was all they needed to know, and having let it be known, all that Burr could do to promote his candidacy. Active intervention on his part would give the game away.

As the congressional Federalists closed ranks around Burr, Gouverneur Morris felt like the man who stays sober while the rest of the company drinks itself to death. Adams's feelings were not very different. Burr's good fortune exceeded that of Bonaparte, he reflected. "All the old patriots, all the splendid talents, the long experience, both of Federalists and Antifederalists, must be subjected to the humiliation of seeing this dexterous gentleman rise, like a balloon, filled with inflamable air, over their heads. . . . What a discouragement to all virtuous exertion, and what an encouragement to party intrigue and corruption! What course is it we steer, and to what harbor are we bound?" In this moment of truth men like Morris and Adams, who had worked with Jefferson and who knew him as a dedicated public official, could look with a degree of equanimity on his election to the presidency.

But his leading apologist in the ultimate contest was another former cohort, Alexander Hamilton. "I admit," said Hamilton, "that his politics are tinctured with fanaticism, that he is too much in earnest with his democracy . . . , that he is crafty and persevering in his objects; that he is not scrupulous about the means of success, nor very mindful of the truth, and that he is a contemptible hypocrite." But it was not true, Hamilton insisted, that he was an enemy of the executive authority or a slave to his principles. On the contrary, he was likely to temporize and to acquiesce in established systems; and added to these merits, he was incapable, unlike Burr, of being corrupted. "He is by far not so dangerous a man; and he has pretensions of character." Burr was an unprincipled adventurer, bold enough to institute "the Jacobin system," and if the Federalist party foolishly raised this Catiline to the presidency, it would die. It was rather late in the day for Hamilton, of all people, to be fretting over the suicide of the Federalist party. The congressional leaders, many of them angry at Hamilton for his clumsy attack on Adams, spurned his advice. Casting the balance between the candidates, they argued that Jefferson was weak, Burr strong; Jefferson theoretical, Burr practical; Jefferson imbued with Jacobinical principles, Burr imbued with passion for power. "In public affairs," Griswold observed, "it is much better to trust a knave than a fool." Burr's vices were those of more than ordinary ambition; and to gratify it he would bargain and conciliate with the Federalists. Jefferson's vices, being founded in democratic principles, were incurable and deadly. Secretary of State Marshall, soon named Chief Justice by the departing President, had "insuperable objections" to his Virginia cousin. He would weaken the presidency, sap the foundations of government, and at the head of the majority party "embody himself in the House of Representatives," thereby increasing his personal power at the expense of constitutional authority. The estimate stood in marked contrast to Hamilton's. Neither would be proven right, but neither would be proven entirely wrong. Right or wrong, Hamilton's plea fell on deaf ears in Washington.

Republicans were bewildered by the enemy's resolution to support Burr despite his disavowal of candidacy. Early in January, Smith, to whom the disavowal had been made, went to Philadelphia as the party's emissary to obtain positive assurances from Burr. From Benjamin Hichborn of Massachusetts, who joined Smith, Jefferson at once learned the disappointing results of the meeting. Several years later, in 1804, Hichborn filled in the details of his conversation with Burr.

"We must have a President, and a constitutional one, in some way," Burr said.

"How is it to be done?" Hichborn asked. "Mr. Jefferson's friends will not quit him, and his enemies are not strong enough to carry another."

"Why," said Burr, "our friends must join the Federalists, and give the President."

Jefferson was prepared to believe the worst of Burr in 1804. Whatever his measure of trust in him in 1801, it was shaken by Burr's refusal, at Philadelphia, flatly to withdraw from the contest. As the time of decision neared, the capital was alive with rumors of Burr's agents trading and bribing for votes. "What is it you want, Colonel Lyon?" the Vermonter later claimed to have been asked. "Is it office, is it money? Only say what you want, and you shall have it." These "agents" may have acted without Burr's knowledge; but if he did not actively enter the Federalist plot, he declined to aid his party in foiling it.

Congress, meanwhile, went on with its business. In the Senate a French treaty signed by the American envoys at Morfontaine in October 1800 was at first rejected and then ratified. Republicans applauded the treaty, known as the Convention of 1800. While it superseded the old treaties, it preserved their commercial principles and, of course, restored normal relations between France and the United States. The Federalist bill to strengthen and enlarge the judiciary, scaled down somewhat, moved toward certain passage. "I dread this above all the measures meditated," Jefferson said, "because appointments in the nature of freehold render it difficult to undo what is done." Such measures kept partisan feelings at a high pitch. One January evening a group of Connecticut Federalists called on the Vice President at Conrad's boarding house, where he lodged in congenial Republican company, to lay before him the firearms manufactured on the principle of interchangeable parts by the ingenious Connecticut Yankee Eli Whitney, already known for the invention of the cotton gin. While in France Jefferson had had an enthusiastic first glimpse of this revolutionary development in the industrial arts, and he pronounced Whitney's achievement even more remarkable. Regardless of partisan animosities and jibes of "philosophism," Jefferson qualified as an expert in the arts and sciences.

On Wednesday, February 11, the members of the House retired to the Senate chamber to hear the results of the electoral vote everyone knew. Jefferson, as presiding officer, broke the seals on the state certificates, handed them one by one to the tellers, and at the conclusion announced the totals. The representatives then returned to their hall, closed the doors, and in accordance with procedures already agreed upon began a marathon of balloting, without formal adjournment or interruption by other business. The first ballot showed eight states for Jefferson, six for Burr, and two divided. The shift of a single vote to Jefferson in one of the divided states, Maryland and Vermont, or in Delaware, whose lone representative, Bayard, voted for Burr, would settle the matter. Republicans were hopeful. A Maryland Federalist said he would switch to Jefferson if need be; some looked to Lyon's Vermont colleague, others to Bayard, to break the deadlock. Both sides were impenetrable, however, and the war of attrition commenced. Six additional ballots followed in rapid succession. An hour's respite for a bit to eat, then eight more, another breather, resumption at nine p.m., and continued balloting throughout the snowy night. "The scene was now ludicrous. Many had sent home for night-caps and pillows, and wrapped in shawls and great-coats, lay about the floor of the committee-rooms, or sat sleeping in their seats. At one, and two, and at half past two, the tellers roused the members from their slumbers and took the same ballot as before." And so it went through the 27th ballot at sunrise. The pace slackened now: one more ballot on Thursday, two on Friday, three on Saturday.

"Four days of balloting have produced not a single change of a vote," Jefferson reported to Monroe on Sunday. "Yet it is confidently believed by most that tomorrow there is to be a coalition." (Actually, several congressmen had switched from Burr to Jefferson, all in delegations already decided.) In his quarters at Conrad's, Jefferson knew of no foundation for this belief. Yet the arrangements were going on under his nose. The key man was Bayard. He could end this war of nerves in an instant. Tiny Delaware tipped the scales of the Union. The sudden taste of power went to Bayard's head. He had fallen in with the Federalist scheme to support Burr. But after 33 ballots he was ready to give up the New Yorker. The election was in Burr's power, Bayard said, yet he declined to bid for

Jefferson's votes. Military measures, precautionary to a usurpation in Washington, were reported from the capitals of Virginia and Pennsylvania. Feeling that continuation of the stalemate risked the Constitution and civil war for no purpose, Bayard resigned himself to Jefferson's election.

But the Delaware congressman, still beguiled by the king-maker role, supposed he could exact terms of capitulation from Jefferson. He had, in fact, opened communication with Jefferson's friends while still soliciting votes for Burr. He first approached John Nicholas of Virginia, asking him to obtain assurances from Jefferson on three points of cardinal interest to the Federalists: support of the public credit, maintenance of the navy, and guarantees against the removal of certain federal officers. Nicholas, while foreseeing no difficulty on these points, refused to take the proposition to Jefferson. Bayard then, on Friday, turned to Samuel Smith. The Marylander lodged at Conrad's and had already conversed with Jefferson on the first two of the three points mentioned by Bayard, for other Federalists had made similar inquiries. Smith now agreed to sound out the Virginian on the subject of political removals. He did so that evening, and the next day gave Bayard the assurances he had requested. On the basis of this transaction, it was later charged, most prominently by Bayard, that Jefferson bargained his way into the presidency. This was another libel. Smith talked with Jefferson, but as he later testified, "without his having the remotest idea of my object." Jefferson talked freely on many subjects with his friends, including Federalists like Gouverneur Morris. Even if he had known the object of Smith's conversation, he had not authorized the communication; nor could the honest expression of his opinions be fairly construed as terms of capitulation. He rebuffed all overtures of this kind. "Many attempts have been made to obtain terms and promises from me," he wrote to Monroe on the 15th. "I have declared to them unequivocally, that I would not receive the government on capitulation, that I would not go into it with my hands tied." He deserved no medals for political valor, for he did not need to bargain his way into the presidency. Perhaps Smith thought he did, and in his self-appointed role as intermediary took unwanted liberties with Jefferson's conversation. As for the Delaware Federalist, his delusion would have collapsed without the idea of extortion and bargain.

Bayard expected to break the deadlock when the balloting resumed on Monday. The Federalists in angry caucus persuaded him to wait another day in the hope that Burr, now in Baltimore, might be heard from. On Tuesday, February 17, the 36th ballot, Jefferson was elected. South Carolina and Delaware, previously for Burr, cast blank ballots, and the Federalist members from Vermont and Maryland abstained, presumably on the plan devised by Bayard, thereby giving Jefferson a majority of ten states to four. "Thus has ended the most wicked absurd attempt ever tried by the Federalists," Gallatin sighed. No leader of that party ever undertook to defend its conduct in this crisis. Henceforth, the American people might wonder at the party's professions of fidelity to the Constitution, the Union, and republican government, all recklessly jeopardized in this contest. Even in defeat they acted a miserable part, most Federalists withholding their votes from Jefferson to the bitter end—"a declaration of perpetual war," Jefferson supposed.

But the picture had its brighter side too, and Jefferson was sure to find it. The bitter-enders had little support outside of Congress. The mass of Federalists might be brought back to genuine republicanism. "I am persuaded," he wrote an old friend, "that weeks of ill-judged conduct here, has strengthened us more than years of prudent and conciliatory administration could have done. If we can once more get social intercourse restored to its pristine harmony, I shall believe we have not lived in vain; and that it may, by rallying them [the mass of Federalists] to true republican principles, which few of them had thrown off, I sanguinely hope." With this spirit he turned from the long night of Federalism to the dawn of a new day.

CHAPTER NINE

President:

First Administration

The people, under such a government [representative democracy], would seem to be naturally more engaged in preserving and enjoying what they already possess, than solicitous of acquiring what was not necessary to their security or happiness; or, at least, that they should resort to no other means of acquiring it than the exercise of their individual faculties; nor think of obtaining authority, or power, by the invasion of the rights of other individuals, or an improper appropriation of the public wealth; that from the principle of attachment to the rights which vest in them all, each citizen should feel and be affected by the injustice done to his neighbor by the public force, as a danger which menaced and concerned them all, and for which no personal favor could compensate.

*   *   *

This form of government does not call for nor need the constraint of the human mind, the modification of our natural sentiments, the forcing of our desires, nor the excitement of imaginary passions, rival interests, or seductive illusions; it should, on the contrary, allow a free course to all inclinations which are not depraved, and to every kind of industry which is not incompatible with good order and morals: being conformable to nature, it requires only to be left to act.

Destutt de Tracy, A Commentary and Review of Montesquieu's Spirit of Laws. *Philadelphia, 1811*

Washington was a city of promises in the first year of the nineteenth century. Nowhere else on the American landscape was the contrast between resplendent ideals and insistent realities so poignantly stated. Without wealth or industry or society, the embryo capital lived on the grandiose image of itself, in which Roman elegance and ambition mingled with American small-town boosterism. Strangers to the scene thought themselves "in the company of crazy people" suffering delusions of grandeur. In the sprawling vastness between Georgetown and Anacostia, three thousand people dwelled in scattered settlements redeemed from nature but little softened by the amenities of civilization. The village pretending to be a capital, "a place with a few bad houses, extensive swamps, hanging on the skirts of a too thinly peopled, weak and barren country," was a grotesque symbol of the aspiring nation itself.

The public sector of the city was fixed by two points, the President's House, elegant and gleaming under its coat of whitewash, and the Capitol, a great torso of a building, the north wing alone awkwardly dominating the summit. These "shining objects [stood] in dismal contrast to the scene around them." Along the mile and a half axis between them, a straight, broad clearing, Pennsylvania Avenue, had been cut through the forest and marsh. Carriages ventured at peril upon the roadway, still beset with stumps and mud holes, though pedestrians traveled more or less at ease on a newly laid stone footway. The avenue, unrelieved by a single house, passed through a deep morass fed by a creek the natives called Tiber long before they were dazzled by Roman dreams. Duck and snipe and partridge infested the marsh, and in the spring the Tiber was so thick with perch "that by shooting in among them one may get a good dish full, for as many will leap on shore with fright . . . as can be killed with the shot".

From Capitol Hill the panorama was breathtaking—wide Potomac, virgin forest, picturesque clearings, and distant heights. Men who came to Washington on the nation's business scoffed at the city's pretensions and groaned at its discomforts, but even the worst groaners and scoffers conceded that no city was ever more beautifully situated. The area just north of the President's House appeared

653

thickly settled. A new community clustered around the Capitol. Tailor, shoemaker, and printer plied their trades; there was a grocery, a stationer's shop, a dry goods store, and an oyster house, as well as seven or eight boarding houses erected for the accommodation of congressmen. The finest of these, the hostelry of Conrad & McMun, perched on the hillside just south of the Capitol, where the House Office Building now stands. Here the Vice President continued to lodge with his Republican friends while he waited to move into the house on Pennsylvania Avenue. Rooms were in short supply —most congressmen doubled up—but Jefferson had a bedroom and a parlor to himself. Everyone was equal at mess, however, "and he occupied during the whole winter the lowest and coldest seat at a long table at which a company of more than thirty sat down." Nor did he command a better seat on the 4th of March.

At twelve noon on that day the 57-year-old statesman, surrounded by friends and well-wishers, walked up New Jersey Avenue, through the square, and into the Capitol to be inaugurated President of the United States. Except for the parade of riflemen and the roar of artillery, the procession was without pomp or ceremony, as befitted the man, the place, and the occasion. The upstart capital was full of visitors and most of them had crowded into the Senate chamber, a cavernous, circular room with a spacious gallery, ranged with arches and massive Doric columns, richly entablatured in appropriate classical style, and withal trying very hard to be elegant. On the platform Aaron Burr, already sworn as Vice President, sat at Jefferson's right, and at his left John Marshall, the new Chief Justice, who would administer the oath of office. John Adams, at his inauguration, had been honored by the presence of his predecessor; but now Adams, embittered by defeat, was on the road to Quincy. The story of his early morning flight buzzed through the gallery. It seemed—more than the petulant act of a proud old warrior—a blunt gesture of Federalist defiance to the new President. What had occurred in 1797 was a succession; what was occurring on this blustery March day four years later was a transfer of power, indeed in Republican eyes and in Jefferson's a revolution in American government as momentous as the Revolution of 1776. The test of this idea lay in the future; it was enough for the present—a truly revolutionary achievement in itself—that power was changing hands by the peaceful and orderly processes of democratic government. The spectacle, for all its simplicity, was the most moving a free people could ever witness. "The changes of administration," a Washington lady noted in her diary, "which in every government and in every age have most generally been epochs of confusion, villainy and bloodshed, in this our happy country take place without any species of distraction, or disorder."

Without further ado, the tall, lanky Virginian, indistinguishable by garb or manner from the multitude, rose to deliver his Inaugural Address. He was no orator, as everyone knew, and few heard anything above the low mumble of his words. But this was an address to be studied and pondered in the cool reflection of the written word. One of the most elaborate of Jefferson's compositions, it had gone through three drafts before he was satisfied with it. Every word, phrase, and nuance had to be right. In style, as in content, it bore the personal insignia of its author. Never had he soared to higher or lovelier peaks of republican ideality. Never was his happy faculty of condensing whole chapters into aphorisms more brilliantly displayed.

The genius of the address lay in its seemingly artless elevation of the Republican creed to a creed of Americanism. Summing up "the essential principles of our government," Jefferson gave a national cast to the principles that had guided his party in the stormy years just past. The list was a long one. Of particular note were the following: "peace, commerce, and honest friendship with all nations—entangling alliances with none"; "the support of the State governments in all their rights, as the most competent administrations for our domestic concerns and the surest bulwarks against anti-republican tendencies; the preservation of the general government in its whole constitutional vigor, as the sheet anchor of our peace at home and safety abroad"; "economy in the public expense, that labor may be lightly burdened"; "the diffusion of information and arraignment of all abuses at the bar of public reason; freedom of religion; freedom of press; freedom of person. . . ." These principles, said Jefferson, were the gifts of American sages and heroes. "They should be the creed of our political faith—the text of civil instruction—the touchstone by which to try the services of those we trust; and should we wander from them in moments of error or alarm, let us hasten to retrace our steps and to regain the road which alone leads to peace, liberty, and safety." In the manner of stating these principles, the cutting edge of partisanship was softened or removed, doctrinaire rigidities were abandoned. Nine-tenths of the American people professed this creed, in Jefferson's opinion. As he once said, "the Republicans are the nation." No more than his predecessors was he reconciled to the permanence of party divisions and party warfare. He looked, rather, to the rapid disappearance of this pestilence and "a perfect consolidation" of political sentiments under Republican auspices.

Spelling out the principles on which the nation should unite, the address made a lofty appeal for the restoration of harmony and affection. Why should Americans emulate the fanaticism and the violence of European politics? "We have called by different names brethren of the same principle. We are all republicans: we are all federalists." The statement was as baffling as it was startling. Jefferson was always stingy with capital letters, otherwise he might have written, "We are all Republicans: we are all Federalists," which was the way many heard it and nearly everyone read it, usually with capitals, in the newspapers. In this sense it was a bold appeal for reconciliation of parties or, more accurately, a converting ordinance for erring Federalists. By erasing imaginary fears of Republicanism, the new President hoped to draw over the mass of Federalists to his cause. But the declaration had a deeper meaning at the foundation of Jefferson's conception of the American polity. Every true republican was a friend of federalism, that is, of the harmony and union of the states under the Constitution, not of the party that had corrupted this concept. The old polarities of liberty and power, rights and duties, individual enterprise and national purpose, the state and the central governments—these were swept away as the new President identified the principles of the federal union with the principles of republican freedom. "If there be any among us," he said, alluding to the delusions of '98, "who would wish to dissolve this Union or to change its republican form, let them stand undisturbed as monuments of the safety with which error of opinion may be tolerated where reason is left free to combat it."* And following this ringing

* In the first draft of the address Jefferson wrote, "I do not believe there is one native citizen of the United States who wishes to dissolve this Union.

affirmation of political freedom, he continued, "I know, indeed, that some honest men fear that a republican government cannot be strong; that this government is not strong enough. But would the honest patriot, in the full tide of successful experiment, abandon a government which has so far kept us free and firm, on the theoretic and visionary fear that this government, the world's best hope, may by possibility want energy to preserve itself? I trust not. I believe this, on the contrary, the strongest government on earth. I believe it is the only one where every man, at the call of the laws, would fly to the standard of the law, and would meet invasions of the public order as his own personal concern. Sometimes it is said that man cannot be trusted with the government of himself. Can he, then, be trusted with the government of others? Or have we found angels in the form of kings to govern him? Let history answer this question." Here was a radical conception of American power and purpose never gleaned by Alexander Hamilton and the Federalist leaders. Under the tyranny of Old World ideas, they supposed the strength of nations and governments consisted in armies and navies, aristocratic patronage, the support of "the rich, the well born, and the able," great treasury, central command, ministerial mastery, the panoply of office and the splendor of state. Jefferson, whom the Federalists had labeled "visionary" for supposing that the United States could dismiss the usual arms and armor of power, now turned around to rebuke them for *their* "theoretic and visionary fear," while declaring his own conviction that this government, in all its weakness by Old World standards, was "the strongest government on earth." The American republic found its unity in an idea. It drew its strength from the energies of a free, enlightened, and virtuous society; and, unlike great monarchies, it would remain strong only as it grew in the affections of the people.

This transmutation of freedom into power, if Jefferson won the stake placed in it, would solve the riddle of the ages. It was an audacious venture in the world of Pitt and Bonaparte. It would require "courage and confidence," Jefferson told his countrymen. Bright promises scarcely glimpsed before the American Revolution were

I am confident there are few native citizens who wish to change its republican features." Dissatisfied with this flat one-dimensional statement, he worked it over with the result quoted above, one of his most famous sentences.

657

within their grasp. "Kindly separated by nature and a wide ocean from the exterminating havoc of one quarter of the globe; too high-minded to endure the degradations of others; possessing a chosen country, with room enough for our citizens to the hundredth and thousandth generation; entertaining a due sense of our equal right to the use of our faculties . . . ; enlightened by a benign religion . . . ; with all these blessings, what more is necessary to make us a happy and prosperous people? Still one thing more, fellow citizens—" Jefferson answered, "a wise and frugal government, which shall restrain men from injuring one another, which shall leave them otherwise free to regulate their own pursuits of industry and improvement, and shall not take from the mouth of labor the bread it has earned. This is the sum of good government, and this is necessary to close the circle of our felicities." A just government, while necessary, was only a small arc of the circle formed by the blessings of American nature, the freedom of American society, and the virtues of American character. With the government restored to first principles, the republican experiment could now be put to the test. It was a solemn and elevated moment. "We can no longer say there is nothing new under the sun," Jefferson reflected to Joseph Priestley. "For this whole chapter in the history of man is new."

After taking the oath of office the new President left the hall and returned to his lodgings, where congressmen, officers, foreign dignitaries, and prominent citizens greeted him. It was a festive time not only in Washington but in towns across the land. "Drunken frolicks is the order of the day," a New York Federalist pouted, "and more bullocks and rams are sacrificed to this newfangled deity than were formerly by the Israelitish priests." In Richmond a public pageant dramatized the theme, "Union can only be maintained by preserving Liberty." In Philadelphia a great procession wound its way from the State House to the German Reformed Church, where the assemblage heard the Declaration of Independence, "Jefferson's March," an oration, and a hymn of praise, "The People's Friend," to the new President.

> Rejoice, ye States, rejoice,
>   And spread the patriot flame;
> Call'd by a Nation's voice,

To make his country's fame,
And dissipate increasing fears,
Our favorite JEFFERSON appears.

Henceforth for Republicans the 4th of March was a red-letter day,
like the 4th of July.

The inaugural address rapidly made its way in the public mind.
A citizens' committee in Lexington, Kentucky, reported to Jefferson: "Printers have vied with each other in printing it upon Satin,
and the whole of the large sized window glass to be found in the
state [has been] used to set it in frames for parlours—Teachers of
schools are causing the youths under their care to commit it to
memory—and your political creed is considered as a masterpiece."
Republicans called it "a Magna Charta in politics." "In fact," said
William B. Giles, "it contains the only American language I ever
heard from the Presidential chair." Federalists—many of them—were
not backward in praise. The Chief Justice, while he thought the address gave the lie to the violent party declamation that had elected
Jefferson, nevertheless considered it "well judged and conciliatory."
Henry Knox, Jefferson's old cabinet colleague, sent warm congratulations. If the rhetoric of concilation was followed by deeds, the
enemy would quietly fold their tends. This was Jefferson's wish,
and in the euphoria of the inaugural many Federalists embraced it
gladly. "His public assurances . . . ," one editor confessed, "Have
inspired us with a hope that *he is not the man we thought him.*—We
thought him a philosophist, and have found him a virtuous and enlightened philanthropist—We thought him a Virginian, and have
found him an American—We thought him a partisan and have found
him a president." Benjamin Rush was astonished by the effects in
Philadelphia. Old friends too long separated by party names were
reunited. Some of the Doctor's Federalist acquaintances read the address again and again. "It never occurred to them 'till last week, that
a Republic was a government of *more* energy than a monarchy."
The inaugural address opened a new era and every eye fixed on its
author.

He did not remain long in Washington after the inauguration. It
had been a long siege, since the end of November; he was tired,
mentally and physically, and needed a rest. Congress had adjourned.

No crisis threatened. The country was calm, calmer than it had been for years. The work of organizing his administration, though far from finished, went steadily forward. Nothing he did in this period jarred the "lullaby effect" of the inaugural address. Let it settle in the public mind, Jefferson reasoned, before the shock waves of reformation commenced. Meanwhile, his own domestic arrangements called for attention in Virginia as in Washington. Near the end of March he moved into the cavernous mansion on Pennsylvania Avenue and began to assemble his household. On April 1 he set out for Monticello. It was only a four-day trip now, but he had eight rivers to cross, without bridges or ferries, and the roads were so punishing he preferred the saddle or a one-horse chair to the gig or carriage. While at home he collected a parcel of books—there were few in Washington. Everything attended to, he was back at his post four weeks after he left it.

Reconciliation and Reform

"If I had a universe to choose from," Jefferson said not long after assembling his cabinet, "I could not change one of my associates to my better satisfaction." He never found occasion to revise this opinion and in retrospect considered the harmony of his official family during eight years a thing without parallel in political annals. It was, in truth, a remarkable feat, one which his own personality made possible as well as necessary.

Two of the four secretaries were indispensable to him. James Madison, the Secretary of State, was well qualified for his office, of course, but it was less in his public than in his private capacity that he made himself necessary to the President. In most important matters Jefferson would be his own Secretary of State, and no one could hold the portfolio who was not tuned in to his mind. The two Virginians acted in perfect friendship, intimacy, and trust. With Albert Gallatin, the Secretary of the Treasury, the case was somewhat different. The Pennsylvanian shared Jefferson's Republican principles and his scientific interests. He was thoroughly conversant with the perplexing politics of his own state and, through marital connection, was rapidly becoming an expert on New York.

He was completely loyal to his chief. These were not the qualifications that made him indispensable to the President, however. Gallatin was a financier, the only one the Republicans had; and in so far as the political reformation hung on fiscal management, as it did to no small extent, his importance to the new administration rivaled Hamilton's to the first. Were politics alone consulted, there were grave risks in the appointment of the 41-year-old congressman, whose Swiss birth, forensic prowess, and wizardry with Treasury figures had combined to make him a Federalist whipping boy. But Jefferson never considered a lesser man for the Treasury post. Rather than risk his loss to the administration by the lame-duck Senate's rejection of his nomination, he deferred formal action and in May gave Gallatin a recess appointment, afterwards confirmed by a Republican Senate.

The remaining cabinet posts, War and Navy, together with the attorney generalship, went to men of more ordinary talents. Henry Dearborn, the Secretary of War, was a physician by profession who had learned the arts of soldiering in the Revolution. Jefferson hardly knew him before the appointment, but Dearborn was reputed to be an excellent "man of business" and also the leading Republican in Maine, the appendage of Massachusetts that had the power to swing the commonwealth into the Republican column. This was a great object with Jefferson. It undoubtedly influenced the choice of Levi Lincoln for Attorney General. Lincoln, a Harvard graduate, a leader of the Massachusetts bar, a man long experienced in state politics, was new to the national scene. At 52 years of age he stood, next to the President himself, the oldest member of the official family. The attorney generalship remained a part-time office of something less than full cabinet status. Normally, Lincoln lived at home, in Worcester, where he acted as Jefferson's eyes and ears in the Bay State.

The designation of Robert Smith as Secretary of Navy, unlike the other appointments, was an act of desperation. Jefferson had first offered the post to his philosophical friend Robert R. Livingston, who occupied a pivotal position in New York politics. When he declined, becoming Minister to France instead, Jefferson turned successively to three prominent Republicans and was refused, not once but twice, by each of them. No man of stature wished to preside over the liquidation of the infant navy, which seemed decreed by the return of peace with France, the rage for economy, and Jefferson's supposed hostility. "I believe I shall have to advertise for a Secretary of the Navy," the President sighed in May. Two months later the fifth choice, Smith, accepted. A Baltimore lawyer with almost no experience in public office, Smith's principal claim to recognition was his brother, General Samuel Smith, the prominent Maryland congressman and merchant who had been Jefferson's second choice for the post and who, in fact, ran the affairs of the department until his brother came on in July. The Smiths were connected by marriage with important Virginians, Wilson Cary Nicholas, one of Jefferson's closest political friends, and Peter Carr, his beloved nephew. The circumstances of his appointment were not very flattering, but Robert Smith proved to be an able minister, popular with the navy, amiable in the cabinet, though he and Gallatin were often at loggerheads, and, like the others, loyal to his chief.

These men revolved around the President like satellites around a planet. The model of presidential unity had been set by Washington, but Jefferson dominated his administration more completely than Washington had done. There was rarely any doubt, in cabinet, in Congress, in the public mind, who was master. The importance of unity in the executive to unity in the party was generally understood, and for most Republicans the destiny, even the survival, of the American republic depended on the fortunes of the party. Jefferson, of course, had a deep aversion to dissension and controversy. By some magic of personality he inspired the same amiable temper and restraint in his colleagues. He led without having to command; he dominated without ruling. The cabinet was run like a Quaker meeting; on the rare occasions when a vote was taken, the President counted as one. Differences of opinion among his colleagues invariably yielded to unanimity in matters of policy. But this would not have happened, he once reflected, whatever the temper of his colleagues, had each acted independently. "Ill-defined limits of their respective departments, jealousies, trifling at first, but nourished and strengthened by repetition of occasions, intrigue without doors of designing persons to build an importance to themselves on the division of others, might from small beginnings, have produced persevering oppositions. But the power of decision in the President left no object for internal dissension, and external intrigue was stifled in embryo by the knowledge which incendiaries possessed, that no division they could foment would change the course of executive power." No doubt he remembered, in these observations, his quarrel with Hamilton as well as the breakdown of the Adams administration. It was the latter chapter that most impressed him. Thus he reversed the tendency toward ministerial independence that, he thought, had undermined his predecessor, and returned to Washington's practice of routing everything through the President and centering powers of decision in him. Business was dispatched, not primarily in the cabinet, which met infrequently, but in day-to-day consultation and communication with department heads. The procedures were quite informal, yet they secured the object of executive unity and responsibility because of the confidence that existed in his official family.

Although he was a very able administrator, Jefferson's leadership was not administrative in character. He did not believe, as Hamilton most assuredly did, in administration as a political engine. He was more concerned with the control than the organization of power, with responsibility than with energy, with administration as a simple tool rather than an awesome machine. Recalling the observation of Tocqueville, who epitomized his own view, "the grandeur is not in what the public administration does, but in what is done outside it or without it." He was perfectly capable of using the administrative arts, and did so with a fine hand when crisis forced him to it, but his theory of government gave little scope to them. After the initial reformation, returning the government to the original tack, "let alone" would be his watchword. "A noiseless course, not meddling in the affairs of others, unattractive to notice, is a mark that society is going on in happiness. If we can prevent the government from wasting the labors of the people, under the pretext of taking care of them, they must be happy." This was a faith in what free men could do for themselves, not in what government could do for them. It made more sense in his age than in ours.

Gallatin and Madison arrived on the scene in May, and the administration, makeshift until then, began to function as a unit. The cabinet took a fateful step on May 15. The conduct of the Barbary states had not improved since Jefferson last dealt with them. Several years past the United States had entered into treaties with all four of the pirate states. The peace purchased by tributes and presents to the tune of two million dollars only whet the appetites of the Mediterranean potentates. American commerce in the Mediterranean steadily increased—158 vessels cleared for those ports in 1801—but it was subjected to continued insult, humiliation, and blackmail. Tripoli was the main offender when Jefferson took office. The Pasha, weighing the paltry settlement Tripoli had made against the annual tribute and splendid presents given to Algiers, demanded a new and munificent treaty under the threat of war. For fifteen years Jefferson had opposed submission to the powers. It seemed obvious now, if not before, that there was no reliance on their agreements or any end to their demands. Perhaps the time had come for the United States to reply with cannon instead of gold. The navy was unemployed. Under the terms of the act fixing the peacetime establishment, signed by Adams on March 3, many of the vessels were to be sold, others laid up, and of course most of the officers discharged. Two squadrons consisting of six frigates and two schooners were to remain in service. Where could they be better employed than in the Mediterranean? It was hardly more costly to keep them there than in American waters, where they were unwanted. Jefferson had always advocated a navy to cruise against the Barbary states; and, in fact, Congress had founded the United States Navy in 1794 with this distinct purpose in mind. The Tripolitan ultimatum furnished the occasion to put an old theory to the test. Whether any European states would join in the enterprise, as he had hoped, remained to be seen; and there were limits beyond which he could not commit Congress. In the cabinet discussion, Gallatin alone seemed reluctant to proceed, holding that war would be more costly than tribute, but he supported the decision to send the first squadron under Commodore Richard Dale to protect American commerce in the Mediterranean from Tripolitan or other attacks. Dale was not authorized to start a war; on the contrary, he was instructed to soothe wounded feelings in Tripoli, as well as in Algiers and Tunis. Should war be declared, as seemed likely, he was to defend the American flag and punish the aggressor. The squadron sailed on June 1. When it arrived in the Mediterranean, Tripoli was already at war with the United States.

The rumbles from the Mediterranean barely ruffled the calm of America's foreign relations. The Atlantic storm that had engulfed the Adams administration had blown over, and the promise of peace in Europe held out the most flattering prospects. While the war continued the administration would adhere to the principles of neutral rights without, however, going to war or entering into any arrangements to secure them. "Peace is my passion," Jefferson repeatedly affirmed. Some Federalists feared, some Republicans hoped, the new administration would join the "armed neutrality" of the Northern powers. France backed the League of Armed Neutrals as a maritime weapon against Britain; indeed, Napoleon regarded the Convention of 1800, embodying the rule of free ships–free goods, in the same light. But Jefferson emphatically rejected this policy. "Determined as we are to avoid, if possible, wasting the energies of our people in war and destruction," he wrote to Thomas Paine, an advocate of the League, "we shall avoid implicating ourselves with the powers of Europe, even in support of principles which we mean to pursue." European interests were so different from the American, and so disruptive of American councils, it was better to have nothing to do with them.

One of the first acts of the administration was to suppress the embassies in Lisbon, Berlin, and The Hague—a preliminary declaration of withdrawal from Europe. Ministries were kept up with Spain, France, and Britain. Charles Pinckney went to Madrid, a reward for clinching the Republican victory of 1800. Unfortunately, his skills did not extend to diplomacy. Rufus King, the New York Federalist, was allowed to remain in London over vocal Republican opposition. Jefferson was the beneficiary of an Anglo-American rapprochement carefully nurtured by King for several years. A change of ministry at Westminster, coinciding with the Republican accession in Washington, brightened the picture even more. King was putting the finishing touches on a settlement of the old issue of Revolutionary debts. Other matters were in negotiation. The ministry opened the ports of Gibraltar, Minorca, and Malta to the American squadron in the Mediterranean. "The change of administration here," Jefferson boasted on receiving this news, "has impressed them with a necessity of treating this country with more justice and conciliation." And lest the ministry be misled by propaganda representing him as a creature of France and an enemy of Britain, he made it a point to assure Edward Thornton, the British chargé, of his friendliness and impartiality. Although Britain continued to violate America's neutral commerce, for the present this was not a fighting issue. More serious was the practice of impressment. If Britain would remove this "stumbling-block," nothing more would be wanting. As to France, the partiality Jefferson had once felt was gone. He viewed the Convention of 1800, writing terminus to the alliance of 1778, as another signpost on the road of withdrawal from European politics. The Convention had not yet been ratified in Paris, and certain matters remained to be disposed of under it. Livingston would handle these details; in fact, when he was appointed it did not appear he would have much else to do. But in May, about the time of the first cabinet meeting, rumors reached Washington of the secret Spanish cession of Louisiana to France. The prospect of Napoleonic rebirth of French empire in North America chilled the atmosphere in Washington. It was involved in so many contingencies, however, that Jefferson refused to take alarm, and instead slowly, quietly, set in motion a course of diplomacy that would end two years later in the greatest triumph of his presidency.

Nothing gave the President more trouble in these early months than the disposition of the federal offices. It took more time, caused more pain, personal and political, and made more enemies than all the other business of government. The agony was worse at the beginning but Jefferson never found any relief from it. "The transaction of the great interests of our country costs us little trouble or difficulty," he remarked in 1804. "But the task of appointment is a heavy one indeed. He on whom it falls may envy the lot of a Sisyphus or Ixion. . . . Yet, like the office of hangman it must be executed by someone." What made the office so irksome was Jefferson's effort to strike a balance between the twin principles of reconciliation and reformation enunciated in his inaugural address. Had he clung to one or the other, had he either acquiesced in the Federalist monopoly of the offices or thrown them out in favor of the Republican faithful, his problem would have been much simpler; but his politics made either solution quite impossible. So he rode the horns of the dilemma, now leaning to one side, now to the other, and though the dexterity of his performance was admirable, it failed to satisfy either his friends or his enemies.

Jefferson had been struggling with the problem since December, when the applications of office-seekers began to litter his desk. By the time of the inauguration he had set the guidelines. His object, clearly, was to make as few removals as possible in order to consolidate the mass of Federalists to his administration. "If we can hit on the true line of conduct which may conciliate the honest part of those who were called Federalists," he said, "I shall hope to be able to obliterate, or rather to unite the names Federalists and Republicans." He was repelled by the principle, already reduced to practice in Pennsylvania and New York, of making party affiliation the sole, or even the primary, test of service. The politics of spoils and proscription degraded republican government. Nothing more should be asked of civil servants than that they be honest, able, and loyal to the Constitution. As important as the principle might be considered abstractly, it was far more important practically from its obvious fitness to Jefferson's political strategy. Partisan removals would revolt converts from Federalism, ensure a following to the leaders of that exploded faction, invite foreign intrigue together with the dissensions of European politics, and thus defeat the great goal of "a perfect consolidation" on the "ancient Whig principles" of 1776.

Hearing this line, many Republicans were apprehensive. The Federalists were incorrigible, they said; any temporizing with them would only disgust the Republicans and subvert the administration. It was incumbent on the President "to clear the Augean stables." "A pretty general purgation of offices has been one of the benefits expected by the friends of the new order of things . . . ," William B. Giles candidly advised. "It can never be unpopular to turn out a vicious one and put a virtuous one in his room; and I am persuaded from the prevalence of the vicious principles of the late administration, and the universal loyalty of its adherents in office, it would be hardly possible to err in exclusions." A New York editor put the matter bluntly: "If this," a clean sweep of the offices, "should not be the case, for what, in the name of God, have we been contending." The idea of uniting the parties was a delusion, others warned. Principles of light and darkness, of democracy and royalty, could not be united or compromised; and the Republicans could not be satisfied unless the revolution of principle made itself manifest in a revolution of men throughout the federal establishment. Still others elevated partisan interest to a democratic theory of office. "*Rotation in office,*" a press columnist wrote, "is the essence of Republicanism by keeping the people on a level, disposing them to pursuits of industry, instead of making a trade of the public service, diffusing a knowledge of office more generally among the citizens . . . ; keeping awake and in action the power and energy of so many minds leads to improvement in system, fidelity in practice, general habits of vigilance among the people, with so many political advantages to society." Jefferson could not ignore these partisan pleadings. They had realism, perhaps even democracy, in their favor. But he held his ground.

The policy worked out in March limited removals to two classes of officeholders. First, Adams's "midnight appointments" and, on second thought, all executive appointments (except judges in good behavior) made after December 12, the day Adams knew he had been defeated. On March 3 the Senate was in session late into the night confirming a last batch of nominations, and Adams spent his final hours in the executive chair hurriedly signing nocturnal commissions. The indecency of the proceeding capped two crowded months of Federalist office-packing. What was this for unless to stack the cards against the new regime? Jefferson considered appointments in this category "nullities," therefore not chargeable as removals. The second class, officers guilty of negligence or misconduct, were the only proper subjects of removal. Here Jefferson especially had in mind federal marshals and district attorneys who had forfeited the public trust by their enforcement of the Sedition Act, the former packing juries, the latter prosecuting their fellow citizens with the bitterness of party. "The courts being so decidedly federal and irremovable," Jefferson said, "it is believed that Republican attorneys and marshals being the doors of entrance into the courts, are indispensably necessary as a shield to the Republican part of our fellow citizens." Other grounds for misconduct removal were electioneering, official favoritism, and delinquency or defalcation in accounts. A list drawn up by Jefferson in January 1802 counted twenty-one "midnight appointments," considered null and void, and fifteen removals for misconduct of any kind.

Jefferson bound himself by these rules only so long and so far as they furthered the political consensus he had in view. By making few removals, on the fairest grounds, he hoped to disarm the opposition, prove his political tolerance, and show that principle, not spoils, was the Republican cause. This required unusual patience from his followers while the stake was won. Death and resignation would open some places, careful spotting of delinquent officers would open others; inevitably, however, under a self-denying ordinance against partisan removals, the Republicans would be slow to realize their just claims to participation in the patronage of the federal government. If the policy failed to impress the administration's enemies and only succeeded in alienating its friends, Jefferson was quite prepared to make the necessary adjustments. When the subject came up for review in May, he decided that the case of New York, in particular, called for special treatment.

Every state was a case unto itself. It was the peculiarity of the Republican organization in New York to be split into three factions, each the bailiwick of a notable family or personage: the Clintons, the Livingstons, and Aaron Burr. At the outset Jefferson deferred to the Vice President in patronage matters. Burr submitted a slate of candidates endorsed by the New York congressional delegation. John Swartwout, a Burrite, was promptly named federal marshal and Edward Livingston, not on the slate but half a Burrite himself, became district attorney. The Livingstons held an enviable position, courted by both Clintonians and Burrites, and no one could be certain which way the clan's loyalties would gravitate. Jefferson did not understand the struggle for power then going on in New York, and he wanted as little to do with it as possible; but it soon became apparent to him that the Clintonians, who controlled the state's party machinery, would not tolerate Burr's rivalry. Fresh reports of Burr's intrigues in the electoral contest just passed reached Jefferson's ear. For reasons of policy he had deferred action on the three main recommendations made by Burr and the New York delegation, and now, in May, heeding the remonstrances of men in the Clinton interest, he wrote to the old patriarch, Governor George Clinton, asking his advice. A second channel, hostile to the Burr connection, was thus opened up between Washington and Albany, where De-Witt Clinton, the Governor's brilliant nephew, rapidly became the leading voice. Clinton controlled the Council of Appointment, and with that marvelous patronage machine was not only purging the Federalists from state offices but also securing his own domination. With the spoils of a great state in his hands, Clinton need not be greedy for federal patronage; Burr, on the other hand, had no other place to go. Jefferson shied away from the disgraceful "spirit of persecution" in New York, but he was reconciled to further appointments and removals in the state in order to mollify the warring factions, neither of which he thought very respectable. "We shall yield a little to their pressure," he said, "but no more than appears absolutely necessary to keep them together. And if that would be as much as to disgust other parts of the union, we must prefer the greater to the lesser part."

As it turned out, Jefferson's efforts to close the breach only helped to widen it. In July he appointed one of Burr's candidates, David Gelston, collector of the New York customhouse, but passed over the other two. Instead, a Clintonian was named supervisor and the incumbent naval officer, a reputed Tory named Rogers, was allowed to remain in his post. It had been slated by Burr for Matthew L. Davis, his young friend and political lieutenant who had helped engineer the Republican victory of 1800 in New York City. Burr repeatedly urged Davis's appointment. As the months passed and nothing materialized it came to be seen as the decisive test of Jefferson's political allegiance in New York. It was all very embarrassing to Davis, as well as to Burr, for they had counted on this lucrative office and every politician in New York knew it. In September, armed with letters, Davis pursued the President all the way to Monticello to plead his case. One of the letters was from Gallatin, whom Davis had stopped to see in Washington. If Rogers should be removed Gallatin knew no better man for the office than Davis, but he was revolted by the administration dirtying its hands in the spoils of New York. Dissatisfied with this, Gallatin hastily penned a second letter in which he carefully pointed out the implications of the Davis affair for Jefferson and his administration. After all that had been said on the subject, the rejection of Davis would be a deliberate affront to Burr and he, surely, would take it as "a declaration of war." Davis met with a cool reception at Monticello. Jefferson's doubts about his qualifications had centered on the question of "respectability," doubts not in the least overcome by the unheralded visit of this brash and importunate young man. He told him nothing had been decided, and Davis returned to New York empty-handed. In fact the decision was as plain as day. Jefferson made it quite aware of the political dynamite Matt Davis packed on his shoulders. He was not the cause of the explosion in New York Republicanism, as William Duane held, but he was, in a manner of speaking, the fuse. The explosion was still several months away. Jefferson had hoped by the discriminate use of patronage to avert it. Instead, he was forced to choose between Burrites and Clintonians. His increasing suspicions of the Vice President, carefully cultivated by the Clinton interest, together with a realistic appraisal of the political forces in New York, made that choice inevitable.

The problem of too many Republicans, rivals among themselves, such as Jefferson found in New York, had its counterpart in the problem of Republican poverty and weakness, which was the case in Connecticut. There the Republicans were few, outcasts of society, and systematically excluded from the state government. In this "land of steady habits," politics and religion worked hand in hand— "preachers were politicians, and politicians preachers." Republicans hovered in the shadows of Jacobinism and infidelity, while the Federalist elite stood secure behind massive barricades of law and opinion. Jefferson's election brought no change in the system of persecution and proscription; if anything, it only aroused the Federalist oligarchs to greater exertions. Not only was conciliation producing no converts in Connecticut, it was dimming the faint hopes of the beleaguered band of Republicans. "They are all mortified," the leadership protested, "to see their enemies triumphing in a day when they expected triumph and to be daily insulted and abused as not having merited the confidence of the administration, whose advocates they have been." In most of the states the Republican organization was secure, buttressed by opinion, lavishly furnished with offices. In Connecticut the cause would be lost without the aid of federal patronage. And yet it was a dangerous experiment to force Republicans into offices against the decided will of the community. The issue came to a head on the President's nomination of a Republican for the collectorship at New Haven, currently filled by a "nullity" of Adams's appointment.

Wishing not to ruffle the sensibilities of the state any more than necessary, Jefferson emphasized the importance of finding a Republican of some standing in society for this important post. The unanimous recommendation of the party leadership was Samuel Bishop, mayor of New Haven, chief judge of the county court, a deacon of the Congregational Church, and a firm Republican. In May, Bishop was appointed. At once a "hideous brawling" went up from the Federalists. On June 18 a large group of merchants, who claimed to own seven-eighths of the shipping in New Haven, drew up a remonstrance against the appointment. Elizur Goodrich, the Federalist congressman Adams had named to the post, suited the merchants exactly; Samuel Bishop, on the other hand, was a man of 77 years, so infirm he could hardly write his own name, ignorant of accounting and all things commercial, and entirely unsuitable. To be sure, he held certain offices from the legislature, but on commissions granted long ago and continued out of charity. Moreover, the merchants said, he had been recommended to the President in order to gratify the son, Abraham Bishop, to whom the work of the office would fall, unhappily with no better results. Young Bishop was a strutting democrat. He had earned the hatred of Connecticut Federalists by two orations, one on political delusion delivered at Yale College, of all places, and widely circulated in the election of 1800, the other, which contained an extended parallel between Thomas Jefferson and Jesus Christ, spouted at a Republican victory celebration. The burden of the remonstrance was clear: the President had been "taken in" by the Republican rabble of Connecticut.

Jefferson grew warm on this matter even before the remonstrance reached his desk. He read the reports from the state, the pitiful appeals of the Republicans, the unyielding hostility of the Federalists. On his return to Worcester, Levi Lincoln, the President's chief liaison with the New England Republicans, had endeavored to interpret the administration's conciliatory policy. Everywhere removals were the topic of conversation, he informed Jefferson; "vague reports and individual clamors had clothed the subject with many false circumstances," but on the whole the picture was bright. Connecticut offered the main exception. There the opinion was decidedly and unanimously for removals at full blast. It would be necessary for the administration to go along, though gradually, one blast at a time, so as not to revive the sinking Federalists. While still optimistic about his policy, Jefferson saw the need for flexibility to meet the circumstances of particular states. "In Connecticut alone a general sweep seems to be called for on the principles of justice and policy," he wrote in June. Ecclesiastical dominance made Connecticut a desperate case—she would "follow the bark of liberty only by the help of a tow-rope." When the New Haven remonstrance arrived, he seized the occasion for a public statement of the policy that, until now, had floated on the airy rhetoric of the inaugural address.

Jefferson's reply to the New Haven merchants began with a careful defense of the controversial appointment, then inquired whether his call for the restoration of harmony and affection could be fairly construed, as the Federalists had done, into assurances against removals from office. When all the facts were considered—the monopoly under the late administration and its defeat at the polls—was it to be imagined that the old establishment was to be left undisturbed? "Is it *political intolerance* to claim a proportionate share in the direction of the public affairs? Can they [the Federalists] not *harmonize* in society unless they have everything in their own hands? If the will of the nation . . . calls for an administration of government according with the opinions of those elected; if, for the fulfillment of that will, displacements are necessary, with whom can they so justly begin as with persons appointed in the last moments of an administration, not for its own time, but to begin a career at the same time with their successors. . . . If a due participation of office is a matter or right, how are vacancies to be obtained? Those by death are few; by resignation, none. Can any other mode than that of removal be proposed?" Heretofore the answer to the last question had been yes, the mode of patience and conversion, of making friends by extinguishing enmities. Heretofore the argument that tenure in subordinate offices should rotate with the popular will had been rejected. Heretofore political opinion and party allegiance in themselves had been inadmissible grounds of removal. By suggesting that the Republicans should receive a "proportionate share" of the offices, Jefferson, without quite realizing it, altered the terms of the original policy. "I lament sincerely that unessential differences of opinion should ever have been deemed sufficient to interdict half the society from the rights and blessings of self-government, to proscribe them as unworthy of every trust." Had the case been different he would have resigned himself to time and accident to right the injustice to the Republicans. "But their total exclusion calls for prompter corrections. I shall correct the procedure; but that done," he concluded, "return with joy to that state of things when the only questions concerning a candidate shall be, Is he honest? Is he capable? Is he faithful to the Constitution?"

The answer to New Haven, whatever its intention, dispelled the warm afterglow of the inaugural. Federalist irreconcilers dipped their pens in vinegar and gall to accuse the President of the vilest hypocrisy. "Is this the language of the mild, the philosophic, the wise, the patriotic and conciliatory Jefferson?" they asked. No, it was the language of Jacobinical bigotry and extermination. Republicans hailed the letter for its liberality, candor, and timely correction of sophistical reasonings drawn from the magnanimous clauses of the inaugural address. On the whole the reception pleased Jefferson. The answer to the New Haven merchants was really meant for the Republicans, he said, especially those who were beginning to think that conciliation had wiped out the hopes of reformation. "Appearances of schismatizing from us have been entirely done away." Unfortunately, however, escaping Scylla there was danger from Charybdis. The letter gave more expectation to the "Sweeping Republicans" than he thought the terms justified. This was especially true in Philadelphia where, in contrast to New York, the political nerve center of the federal establishment, the customhouse, remained a Federalist monopoly. His fears that the reply would check the current of "republican federalists" toward the administration were not borne out. Do not be alarmed by the newspaper barrage, Lincoln wrote. "Be assured it is contemptible, and kept alive by a few lying scribblers." The spirit of accommodation was still abroad in New England, he continued with more optimism than the case warranted, and nothing like a general retreat was in order. Jefferson seemed to agree. To heal the wounds of partisanship, restore harmony, rally all shades of Federalists except the monarchical, and thereby make the nation one: this was the real business of the administration. "I am satisfied it can be done," he told Governor McKean, "and I own that the day which should convince me of the contrary would be the bitterest in my life." Expressions of this kind suggest that Jefferson had not accurately calculated the impact of his own words, which plainly set patronage policy on a new course. If the inaugural address was in some sense a converting ordinance for the Federalists, the answer to New Haven was a covenant to secure the Jeffersonian church with the elect of Republicanism.

The conflict between the ideal of reconciliation and the realities of partisanship was never resolved, but as a political matter Jefferson increasingly faced up to the unpleasant responsibilities party government forced upon him. Just after the answer to New Haven, Gallatin forwarded for the President's approval a circular he proposed to issue to the collectors of customs. They would be instructed to award the subordinate offices in their gift wholly on the basis of merit and to abstain from electioneering or political activity of any kind. Jefferson approved the principle but thought the circular should be deferred until the Republicans achieved an equality in the federal offices. (Actually, at that time the restraints would have worked primarily on Federalists, not Republicans. Three years later, after the customhouses had been renovated, Jefferson told Gallatin the Republican officers were "meddling too much with the public elections" and asked that it be stopped. Recalling his proposal in 1801, Gallatin said the circumstances were now so different it would be "very delicate" to decree a political interdict, and he did not.) In the early months Jefferson had not been averse to appointing Federalists to office and did so in New England, much to the consternation of eager Republicans. In August, however, he urged his colleagues to be "inflexible against appointing Federalists." It was more important to satisfy the Republican faithful than to make Federalist converts.

Jefferson's public conscience led him to assign removals to almost any cause other than the political one of opening places for Republicans. He repeatedly drew up lists of removals catalogued under as many as nine headings according to the grounds of decision. While the lists testify to his uneasiness, and are accurate in the main, they are not an adequate record of his motivations in the disposition of

675

patronage. What number of officeholders were removed for political reasons alone, it is impossible to say, but they were probably not many at any time. In 1803, after two years, Jefferson listed only fourteen in this category. Double the figure and it is still a small percentage of the roughly 330 significant civil offices, of which about one-half changed hands during Jefferson's first term. The Federalists, of course, had their own system of bookkeeping which charged every transaction to political persecution. Instead of acknowledging the moderation of his policy, as Jefferson remarked a year after the New Haven remonstrance, these zealots made it the ground for more strenuous opposition; and so he went on, rewarding his friends, punishing his enemies, when he had every wish to stop.

While Jefferson often yielded to Republican patronage demands, he was also capable of monumental efforts to protect his design for political unity. Many cases might be cited. In New York, for example, he withstood for eight years the combined pressure of Republican politicians and merchants to keep in office the Federalist collector of the port of Hudson. But the case of Allan McLane, collector at Wilmington, Delaware, best illustrates the point. In Jefferson's report of the first cabinet discussion of removals, McLane enjoyed the distinction of being the only Federalist officeholder explicitly confirmed in his post. Perhaps this was because his name had figured in the February negotiations between Samuel Smith and James A. Bayard, for the latter has sought assurances of McLane's tenure in office and Smith had mentioned it to Jefferson. If so—and Bayard later testified it was so—the explanation fails to account for the removal of the other officeholder for whom Bayard had sought the same assurances, nor can it fairly account for Jefferson's extraordinary adherence to McLane. McLane had served his country long and ably during the Revolution, always a plus in Jefferson's book; he was well regarded by the Treasury Department and by the merchants along the Brandywine; even more important, Jefferson apparently decided to make him an example of principle, and he clung to it like the rock of salvation when the surrounding political terrain shook beneath him. The Delaware Republicans, still a minority party, panted for McLane's prestigious office. Young Caesar A. Rodney, their leader and a brilliant lawyer, whom the President liked at once, presented the case against McLane: he was unpopular; he had worked for Adams in 1800; he had used his office for personal advantage. The latter charge traced back to 1799, when Secretary of Treasury Wolcott investigated and acquitted the collector. The administration now conducted its own inquiry, with the same result.

The matter slept for a time, but the following spring Washington was again bombarded with demands for McLane's removal. Addresses came from Wilmington, in New Castle County, where the Republicans were strong, as well as from the heavily Federalist county of Kent. (The third and smallest county, Sussex, was also Federalist.) No man was more obnoxoius to the party than McLane, wrote Governor David Hall, the first Republican victor in the state. Rodney voiced the same opinion, though with obvious distaste. Conceding that the authors of the attack on the collector fixed their hungry gaze on the spoils of office rather than the good of the country, admitting the justice of McLane's acquittal, Rodney nevertheless felt that the current for removal could not be resisted without imperiling the Republican cause. "The county of Kent, and particularly the leading men will be paralyzed, unless their remonstrances succeed," he warned. Rodney was then preparing for the state-wide congressional contest in which he had agreed, at Jefferson's urgent solicitation, to take on the Federalist champion, Bayard. Without a respectable showing in Kent, Rodney could not hope to win. He painted a bleak picture of Federalist hegemony. The people needed a clear sign that power had changed hands nationally and Delaware was out of step. The sacrifice of McLane would be such a sign. "The consequences will be wonderful," Rodney said. To these pleadings Jefferson answered he could do nothing unless furnished with substantial evidence pointing to McLane's misconduct. He had at this time, July 1802, just learned of the life appointment of Napoleon as First Consul of France. This melancholy event, the latest of a series blasting republican hopes in Europe, may help to explain the elevated tone of his reply to Hall. "Nor are we," he said, "acting for ourselves alone, but for the whole human race. . . . The leaders of Federalism say that man cannot be trusted with his own government. We must do no act which shall replace them in the direction of the experiment. We must not by any departure from principle,

677

disgust the mass of our fellow citizens who have confided in us this interesting cause." After Hall and Rodney conferred with Jefferson in Washington, he seemed satisfied they would acquiesce so long as McLane abstained from politics.

McLane, meanwhile, was active in his own defense. He had a good friend in John Steele, the moderate Federalist Gallatin had retained as Auditor. Through Steele, principally, the Collector's version of the plot to remove him reached the President. McLane blamed his persecution on personal enmity, political jobbery, and commercial ambition. The last was represented by the city of New Castle, which had been outstripped by Wilmington in the trade of Delaware Bay and had sought, unsuccessfully, to be made a port of entry of the United States. McLane had opposed New Castle's pretensions, a service to Wilmington that earned him the gratitude of its merchants whether Federalist or Republican. But jobbery was the main consideration, McLane thought. If the struggling Republicans in the lower counties succeeded there would be "an Inspector for every Creek." "Here lays the whole matter," he told Gallatin, "the Collector . . . provides for a Deputy, a temporary Surveyor at New Castle, a temporary Surveyor at Lewis Town, an Inspector at Wilmington, a weigh master, a quaser measurer, etc."

Calls for McLane's scalp again went up after the October election. Rodney barely won his contest, but the loss of Kent ensured a continued Federalist majority in the legislature with the probability that Bayard, whom the President had ticketed for oblivion, would be named to the Senate. Rodney charged the defeat to the non-removal of McLane. Fortunately, the problem might soon solve itself, for McLane was quietly talking of retirement. He had concluded his enemies would not rest until the President was forced to remove him, and rather than suffer this disgrace, he asked Steele to seek the administration's indulgence until the coming spring when he would be able to close his books. Jefferson grabbed at the proposal, interpreted McLane's letter as a letter of resignation, and conferred with Rodney on a successor. This was more than McLane had bargained for; at least, so he contended in December when he went to Washington and had a long talk with the President. All he had meant to say, he now told Jefferson, was that *if* his removal was decreed he would like the privilege of resigning. So Jefferson, as unyielding as ever on the principle of the case, was still on the hook with the Delaware Republicans. Out of his loyalty to the President, Rodney tried to pacify them. It was a hopeless task. In 1804, by suffering McLane, Jefferson sacrificed the expectations of the Delaware Republicans together with his own hopes for a clean sweep of the electoral vote. Still he stood firm. And the Federalist collector, who never recanted his political opinions, was still in office when Jefferson left the presidency. Several factors accounted for the prolonged resistance: McLane's Revolutionary services, his powerful connections, especially among Brandywine merchants and manufacturers, the inability of the Delaware Republicans to unite on a candidate whose claims were too impressive to be ignored, and, most of all, the mantle of principle Jefferson had draped over Allan McLane.

As the case suggests, the problem of turning out Federalists was often complicated by the problem of finding suitable successors among the Republicans. Candidates were plentiful enough. Jefferson likened his predicament to that of a man with "one loaf and ten wanting bread." American society was still simple, not poor but far from rich, and the careers open to modest talent were few. The offices in the President's gift held the promise of status and influence, if not of great wealth, and hordes of men sought them. Finding the right candidate was never easy, however. The Republicans, east of the Hudson especially, lacked the high proportion of educated talent of their opponents. Jefferson's standards were high, and every appointment had political ramifications at some level, local, state, or national. Sometimes it seemed better to tolerate a Federalist holdover than by the choice of a successor to alienate a portion of Republicans. Jefferson spent countless hours sifting and weighing the qualifications of candidates. He sought the advice of state and congressional leaders, of course; and since the bulk of federal patronage lay in Gallatin's jurisdiction, he became the principal channel of influence to the President. Gallatin's counsel generally worked for moderation, but he had learned the political trade in Pennsylvania, a tough school, and was less squeamish than his chief in plying it.

For posts in the upper branches of the civil service, Jefferson actively sought men who measured up to his standards of education and respectability. He believed in a "natural aristocracy," which he considered perfectly compatible with republican government and indeed essential to its virtuous leadership. It was part of the conceit of Federalism that these materials did not exist in the Jeffersonian following. The Federalist base had been narrow, overweighed with eastern men of wealth and station who, in too many instances, were blood or affinal relations. Jefferson broadened the base, taking into the official elite more westerners, more men of talents without privileges of birth, and more of respectability without high social status. In marked contrast to his predecessor, he avoided appointments that smacked of nepotism and, leaving out the Livingstons, clannish preferments. As a result, Jefferson made the higher civil service significantly more representative of American society; and despite his elitist idea of the public service, which became an anachronism in the age of democracy, he nevertheless commenced the line of development usually supposed to have begun with Andrew Jackson a generation later.

It is equally true that Jefferson, not Jackson, introduced the partisan standard of removals in the federal government. This came about, however, only because the Federalist had adhered to a partisan standard of appointments, and they, as Jefferson saw it, violently rejected the hand of conciliation held out to them in 1801. When conciliation failed, Jefferson moved toward partisanship, yet never quite reached it. He was always too partisan for infatuated Federalists, never partisan enough for his more zealous followers. Taking the whole country and all the offices into view, his course was both gradual and moderate, slower and softer in the South, faster and harder in the northern states, though exceedingly flexible at all times. In New Jersey only five of 256 party "activists" received appointment to federal posts under Jefferson; the state posts, on the other hand, were manned by these people. In New York the impact of federal patronage was also slight. During his first term alone Jefferson gave appointment to forty New Yorkers, twelve of them to posts abroad; during both terms he removed only eight Federalists, for varying reasons, and in 1809 one-third of the appointees of Washington and Adams remained in office. In Massachusetts no collector was removed in the first year of the administration; five were ousted the next year, all in Essex County, where a strong cadre of Republicans successfully challenged the notorious Essex Junto. In

Boston, where conciliation made steady progress, the old collector, Benjamin Lincoln, enjoyed the rewards of his office almost to the end of Jefferson's presidency. In Massachusetts and New England generally, resistance to the embargo in 1808 probably produced more removals than in all the preceding years. Moderation, gradualism, flexibility: these points of Jefferson's policy cannot be too much emphasized. Because of them he found no rest from problems of removal and appointment, nor from any of the related problems of federal patronage, during eight long years.

President, Congress, and Court

Jefferson was still optimistic about the future of the political *détente* when he went to Monticello at the end of July 1801. While there the newspaper assault triggered by his answer to New Haven gave him something to think about. The attack on the removals policy rapidly slid into an attack on his personal character. Winthrop Sargent, for example, published a vindictive pamphlet in Boston, *Political Intolerance*, which accused the President of lying duplicity in the manner of forcing him out of the governorship of the Mississippi Territory. A Philadelphia gazette accused the President of "killing" John Wilkes Kittera, federal attorney for the eastern district of Pennsylvania, whose sudden death, it was said, had been brought on by insupportable grief over his removal. The Federalists raised a terrible commotion when they learned by way of Paris that Jefferson had invited Thomas Paine to return to the shores of liberty in an American warship. "What! Invite to the United States that lying, drunken, brutal infidel, who rejoiced in the opportunity of basking and wallowing in the confusion, devastation, bloodshed, rapine, and murder in which his soul delights?" Jefferson still honored Paine—the Paine of *Common Sense* and *The Rights of Man*—and wished the adopted country he had nurtured in liberty also to honor him; but many Americans detested the old revolutionary whose scoffing attack on Christianity, *The Age of Reason*, had made him in their eyes the arch apostle of infidelity. Jefferson must have realized that his patronage of Paine might inflame the embers of religious and political bigotry. Yet he risked the venture, relying on sentiments of national gratitude and the country's return to the sanity of former times to sustain him. But this virtuous act proved to be a political blunder. The darts Federalists flung at Paine were really meant for Jefferson who, they said, threw "the weight of presidential influence . . . into the scale of infidelity and vice." More than a year passed before Paine returned to the United States; the issue subsided in the interim, but Federalist editors manufactured others to feed the engines of alarm. They blamed a student riot at the College of William and Mary on "the Jeffersonian system of religion," and held him responsible for the vogue of William Godwin's rationalistic works, which he had allegedly imported to corrupt the nation's youth. They accused him of slavishly submitting to French demands for a million-dollar loan—a pure invention. They spread the rumor that he had ordered the removal of federal arms from the Springfield arsenal, in Massachusetts, to the southward. Thus the irrational fears Jefferson had hoped to allay were kept alive. And despite his efforts to create a national image, he still appeared in the Federalist prints "a caricature, a creature of imagination, a mere image of party, dressed up and exhibited for an electioneering fright."

There were cannon to the left of him as well. Among Republican ideologues who formed a cult around the "doctrines of '98," the patronage issue, which rank politicians viewed simply as a matter of spoils, involved the much greater question of whether the administration moved in the direction of consensus or reform. They were alarmed by the temporizing tone of the inaugural address. A magnanimous gesture was one thing, conciliation on the level of policy quite another. And they feared that Jefferson, in a mistaken quest for unity and calm, would let pass the glorious opportunity of returning the government to true Republican principles. The task called for aggressive assault on the Treasury establishment, reform of the judiciary, reduction of the powers of the "monarchical" executive and the "aristocratic" Senate, restriction of the treaty power, firmer lines of demarcation between the national and the state governments, and so on. Virginia was the center of this Republican unrest. Governor James Monroe was perhaps its principal spokesman to the President, though he heard these rumblings of discontent from other quarters as well. His old friend Edmund Pendleton wrote the platform of the Virginia militants in a tract, *The Danger Not Over,* published in October. Republicanism had triumphed but it would be folly to rely on the purity of its leaders for security. The true principles of the government ought to be fixed beyond reversal or contradiction, and Pendleton proposed a series of eight amendments to the Constitution to complete the work. Jefferson, while sympathetic to these pleas, hoped to contain reform within the limits of a growing national consensus. He was more attentive to the voices of prudence, especially to Madison and Gallatin, who had a different conception of the "revolution of 1800." This incipient division of opinion within the Republican ranks caused no immediate difficulty for the administration; but the seeds of a dangerous schism were already planted.

Jefferson found a useful diversion from politics at Monticello that summer. He had learned of the work of Dr. Benjamin Waterhouse, of Boston, in employing the cowpox virus as an inoculation against smallpox. Waterhouse had introduced the epic-making discovery of Edward Jenner into American medical practice. In December he had sent to Jefferson an account of his experiment. Impressed, deeply interested, the new President actively enlisted in this public health cause, and by his own patronage greatly contributed to its progress in the United States. Waterhouse badly needed such an ally to combat professional inertia and public fears. Early trials of the vaccine, in other hands than his, often failed, hence increasing the prejudice against it. Such was the result of the first two supplies sent to Jefferson in June and administered by an able physician in Washington. The vaccine had lost its potency in transit, probably because of exposure to heat, Jefferson thought; and so he made the ingenious suggestion of shipping the vial in a water filled container. In August Waterhouse sent two fresh supplies to Monticello, one that had come from Jenner in England, the other taken from his own patients. Jefferson now proceeded, with the assistance of a local physician, to vaccinate his plantation family. By the time he returned to Washington about 200 persons, including some of the neighbors, had been vaccinated with excellent results. Waterhouse was delighted.

Methodical in his conduct of the experiment, Jefferson paid particular attention to the rule laid down by Waterhouse to withdraw the live virus from the pustule exactly eight days after vaccination, thereby keeping up a constant supply of vaccine. So successful was Jefferson in this part of the undertaking that he was able to supply pioneer vaccinators in Washington, Richmond, Philadelphia, and elsewhere, and to introduce this gift of the Great Spirit among the Indians. The results were encouraging, but always a skeptic in medical matters, he preferred to await the evidence, and partly for this reason declined to permit his name to be used as an endorsement of vaccination. Waterhouse, however, sent one of Jefferson's letters to a medical friend in London, whence it appeared in an English treatise and immediately in another published in Philadelphia. He thus became publicly identified with the movement that promised to wipe out one of the ancient scourges of mankind. By 1806, when he penned a noble tribute to Jenner, he was convinced the vaccine would, in fact, fulfill its promise. "Medicine has never before produced any single improvement of such utility," he said with characteristic emphasis. "Harvey's discovery of the circulation of the blood was a beautiful addition to the knowledge of the animal economy. But on a review of the practice of medicine before and since that epoch, I do not see any great amelioration which has been derived from that discovery. You," he lauded Jenner, "have erased from the calendar of human afflictions one of its greatest. Yours is the comfortable reflection that mankind can never forget you have lived. Future nations will know by history only that the loathsome smallpox has existed and by you has been extinguished."

In 1806, or even in 1801, Jefferson would gladly have traded for such a fame any of the accolades reserved to statesmen. At Monticello, the "Summer White House," his principal business was to prepare an agenda for the Seventh Congress. Madison came over from Orange, and Jefferson regularly communicated with the other secretaries. Actually, the preparations had been going on since March. The secretaries had canvassed their departments, written reports, and made recommendations, all keyed to a reformation of government along moderate lines. Gradually the pieces fell into place and Jefferson drew up the critical statement of policy that became, on December 8, his first annual message to Congress.

Unlike the "state of the union" messages of his predecessors, Jefferson's was communicated in writing and read by a clerk. The customary practice smacked of the monarch's speech from the throne, in his opinion, and the tedious formalities of an answer embarrassed both Congress and President. Doing away with it was a simple republican gesture Jefferson all the more willingly made because of his aversion to public address; but the innovation endured through a score of presidents who did not feel this aversion and long after monarchical forms and ceremonies ceased to be an issue.

The message itself seemed as self-effacing as the method of its presentation. Those who expected bold utterance and bold reforms pitched to the strains of partisan warfare were disappointed. The message was tame. Jefferson began by felicitating the Congress on the long-awaited return of peace in Europe, alluded to the spirit of friendship among the Indians, then discussed the Tripolitan war as the one exception to this "state of general peace," and finally, announced the happy result of the census of 1800. A population in excess of five million, doubling itself every 22 years, suggested the almost unlimited possibilities of the species in the free American environment. Government could make but a small addition to the spontaneous energies of a free society. "Agriculture, manufactures, commerce, and navigation, the four pillars of our prosperity, are the most thriving when left most free to individual enterprise." Protection from "casual embarrassments" might sometimes justify departures from this rule, as in the instance of the carrying trade, the only one of the four pillars recommended to the care of Congress. The thrust of the message ran toward *laissez faire* and simple government, in accordance with the doctrines of the inaugural address. "When we consider," he said, "that this government is charged with the external and mutual relations only of these states; that the states themselves have principal care of our persons, our property, and our reputation, constituting the great field of human concerns, we may well doubt whether our organization is not too complicated, too expensive; whether offices and officers have not been multiplied unnecessarily, and sometime injuriously to the service they were meant to promote."

The President made no specific recommendations in this matter, nor indeed, with the exception of the judiciary, did he propose to dismantle any of the machinery of government the Federalists had built. "Some things," he remarked privately, "may perhaps be left undone from motives of compromise for a time, and not to alarm by too sudden a reformation, but with a view to be resumed at another time." The judiciary was another matter, especially the new circuit courts created by act of Congress in February. He had at once slated this act for repeal and now, in December, hinted the object to Congress. He also requested repeal of the law of 1798 fixing a residence of fourteen years for naturalization. "Shall oppressed humanity find no asylum on this globe?" he asked. As for the Sedition Law, the first draft of the message had included a paragraph developing the theory of the equal right of each of the three branches of government to decide questions of constitutionality for itself. The hated law expired upon Jefferson's entry into office, so he could not negate it by his own decision; but he promptly pardoned the unfortunate Republicans still suffering its penalties and dropped the prosecution of William Duane still pending under a resolution of the Senate. The latter action, particularly, was branded unconstitutional in the Federalist prints. In his own defense, and in defense of the principle enunciated in the Virginia and Kentucky Resolutions, Jefferson had thought to make a straightforward declaration of his opinion holding the Sedition Act "in palpable and unqualified contradiction to the Constitution, considering it then as a nullity." However, prodded by Gallatin, Smith, and probably Madison, Jefferson eliminated the entire paragraph "as capable of being chicaned, and furnishing something to the opposition to make a handle of." His silence implied a reluctance, in his official station, to broach doctrines sure to be controverted and to defend executive actions of doubtful constitutionality, as he knew the *nolle* entry in the Duane case to be. The message throughout was elaborately deferential to Congress. Jefferson and his party rose to power preaching the Whiggish doctrine of legislative supremacy against the allegedly monarchical tendencies of the Federalist administrations. To reduce executive influence and return the direction of the government to the legislative branch was a logical first step in the Republican reformation. Jefferson honored the theory, renouncing powers and begging legislative restraints; at the same time, however, he devised a subtle language of indirection with Congress, in which recommendations were suggestions and demands were veiled in obscurity. His actions with respect to the Sedition Law ill comported with the Whig theory, so silence seemed best.

So far as the message aimed at a reformation of the federal establishment, it was bottomed on fiscal policy. In the Jeffersonian scripture, debt and taxes were public evils of the first magnitude. They drained capital from the mass of citizens, diverted it from productive enterprise, and supported a system of coercion, corruption, and privilege that was the bane of every government and necessarily fatal to a free one. "Economy and liberty, profusion and servitude." A decade of opposition to Hamiltonian practice had polarized the issue, with the result that the Republicans could see no escape from these simple alternatives. If Jefferson was doctrinaire on the point, Gallatin was more so. The paramount concern of the administration must be the extinguishment of the debt and the reduction of taxes. If it was not done under Jefferson, it would never be done, Gallatin argued, and all the evils of oppressive taxes, moneyed influence, temptations to foreign wars, encroaching government, and so on would be entailed on future generations. In November, Gallatin worked out a plan to cut the revenue and yet extinguish the debt— an unprecedented piece of financial wizardry.

Reversing the usual order of things, the Secretary began with the needs of the debt rather than the operational needs of the government. The government could be rid of debt in four administrations (his first calculations had been for two) by the annual appropriation of $7,300,000 to service and retirement. When it is considered that the debt had increased ten million dollars during the Federalist years, the project for its extinguishment in 16 or 17 Republican years was amazing. Gallatin conservatively estimated the annual revenue at $10,500,000, more than 90 per cent of it from the impost, the remainder from internal taxes, public lands, and the post. This income, after the huge slice for the debt, would leave $3,200,000 for the operation of the government, an amount well below expenditures in any year since 1793. But Gallatin was also determined to reduce taxes, hence the income. The internal taxes produced $600,000 yearly, most of it from the whiskey excise so much detested in the interior parts of the country. Gallatin was reluctant to give up these taxes, not because he approved of them but because of his paramount interest in paying the debt. As they were the only federal taxes that touched the people directly, the political argument for doing away with them was unanswerable, and the great expense, patronage, and inconvenience involved in their collection made them difficult to defend on economic grounds. (As for the patronage, Jefferson rejoiced in the loss, though it would make his task of finding places for Republicans much harder.) Pressed by his chief, the Secretary relented; "let them all go," he said, "and not one remain on which internal taxes may hereafter be engrafted." With only $2,-600,000 to run the government, savings on the order of a million dollars would be necessary. Modest economies had already been effected, as in the diplomatic establishment, and others were anticipated by the suppression of revenue officers, the new judgeships, and the mint. But these were paltry items. The big budgetary items were the army and the navy. Defense expenditures could be expected to fall to a normal peacetime level of about $3,000,000. Gallatin proposed to cut the figure almost in half, taking the biggest bite from the army, which would be reduced to approximately 3000 men scattered between Michilimackinac and the Tombigbee. The cabinet ratified the plan, and Jefferson's message opened it to view, leaving the details to the Secretary's report to Congress.

The system was liable to the objection that it risked national development and national defense to prove a doubtful theory of political economy. If the theory was sound, government would be saved from manifold dangers and private capital would be "set afloat," as Jefferson expressed it, "to be employed in rescuing our commerce from the hands of foreigners, or in agriculture, canals, bridges, or other useful enterprises." The federal government might aid in this work of economic development. In due time it should, and Jefferson and Gallatin were anxious for that time to arrive. But it was first essential for the government to put the people in full possession of their own energies and resources. The idea that the nation could grow out of its debt by federal investment in economic development—by growing deeper into debt—assailed common sense and lay under the Hamiltonian incubus. But even assuming the success of the Jeffersonian experiment in the light of political economy, would the system of "wise and frugal government" secure the nation's respect abroad and its frontiers at home? Jefferson thought it would.

The Peace of Amiens in Europe buoyed his confidence. "It removes the only danger we have to fear. We can now proceed without risk, in demolishing useless structures of expense, lightening the burdens of our constituents, and fortifying the principles of free government." The prospect of war could never be dismissed, he conceded, "but sound principles will not justify our taxing the industry of our fellow citizens to accumulate treasure for wars to happen we know not when, and which might not perhaps happen but from temptations offered by that treasury." Furthermore, the vast circumference of the United States could be secured from invasion or attack only at astronomical cost. Later estimates placed the cost of fortifying the principal harbors at $50,000,000 and 2000 soldiers; even then the defenses would be vulnerable. Jefferson referred the matter to Congress, together with naval preparedness, but offered his own opinion that the most effectual defense would be found in a well-ordered militia.

The fiscal model was calculated on peace. Indeed, in a larger sense peace was its object. It expressed the Jeffersonian animus against systems of energy, force, and command, whether fiscal or military, which were simply different faces of a statecraft at war with the liberties and happiness of the people. Jefferson's plan to reverse the natural tendency of every government toward power and aggrandizement placed him on unassailable ground with Republicans, while in Europe, where the message did not pass unnoticed, men rubbed their eyes in disbelief at the spectacle of a chief magistrate renouncing patronage and power. It promised, said an English journal, "a sort of Millennium in government."

It required power to vanquish power, however, and the more the President exercised power with righteous purpose the less scrupulous he became toward the abjurations of Republican theory. This was to be the story of his administration, first disclosed in the solution he and his colleagues found for the control of Congress. In the Republican theory, of course, Congress should control the executive. The deferential clauses of official discourse honored the theory, as Jefferson was bound to do; but he was also bound to recognize that the political system demanded executive leadership if any majority, Federalist or Republican, was to carry out its program. Congress could not lead. During the Federalist ascendancy it had performed most effectively under Hamilton's ministerial guidance. The problem had been easier for the Federalists. They had had no dogmas to overcome and compared with the Republicans had formed a fairly cohesive body. The Republican majority was a coalition of widely assorted interests, experienced in opposition and obstruction, dogmatic on the point of legislative ascendancy, but thus far untried in the constructive work of government. Even when they had earlier controlled the House of Representatives, the Republicans had shown little talent for policy formation and legislation. Jefferson had frequently criticized their lack of discipline and would do so again and again. How then could he, consistent with the Republican theory, make Congress an effective instrument of the reformation in view?

The solution was found in the network of party leadership outside constitutional channels. As the unchallenged head of the Republican party, Jefferson acted with an authority he did not possess, indeed utterly disavowed, in his capacity as President. This was not the first time he had played a double role—the official and the unofficial, the public and the private, the open and the devious—but for the first time he filled both roles in amplitude. Toward the end of diminishing the powers of government, he did not hesitate to employ means that increased his personal power. The long arm of the President reached out, often through the cabinet, to Capitol Hill. Leaders of both houses of Congress were the President's lieutenants. Speaker of the House Nathanial Macon, a ten-year veteran liked by everyone, appointed the standing committees for the transaction of legislative business. He named his young friend John Randolph chairman of the important Ways and Means Committee. Between this erratic and haughty Virginian and the President there was always a barrier and an impasse would develop in time, but Randolph began as a faithful servant of the administration. He and Macon were especially friendly with Gallatin, who turned his home on Capitol Hill into a kind of Republican club and through this nest of associations exercised an influence on the course of legislation nothing short of Hamilton's in his time. William B. Giles, cooler and wiser now, was Jefferson's principal agent in the House and also the majority leader, the "premier or prime minister," as some called him. Through Giles, presidential leadership was locked into congressional leadership. Unfortunately, illness overtook Giles after the first session and Randolph tried to manage the majority. Effective for a brief time, Randolph was not cut out for the role. The success of Jefferson's system of command depended on trust and loyalty, a willingness to work behind doors, to hear hints as orders, to subordinate personal caprice to the business in hand, none of which suited a man of Randolph's vanity, morbid suspicions, and erratic temperament. Jefferson did not openly move against him but quietly cast about for a "man of business" who would work with the administration and "undertake to keep a file of the business before Congress and press it as he would his own docket in court." He hoped that Caesar Rodney would come into the Eighth Congress in 1803 and take charge; but Rodney was no match for Randolph on the floor of the House, and Jefferson watched his system turn into a "rope of sand." Things went a little more smoothly in the Senate. Until his death in 1803, Stevens Thompson Mason, a Virginian, was the recognized leader, ably assisted by Wilson Cary Nicholas and John Breckinridge. Their devotion to Jefferson was complete. Giles succeeded Mason, and his power was such, so it was said, that if he should move to expel a senator on account of his looks, it would probably be done.

Although his method with Congress never worked with unerring precision, and would not have worked at all without his personal magnetism, Jefferson effectively converted party leadership into executive leadership, thereby creating a strong presidency responsive to the majority will of the community. This was no small accomplishment in a party that contained many jarring elements, and with a volatile Congress. He utilized the press, especially the *National Intelligencer* established in Washington as a more or less official administration organ; he kept up a steady stream of communication to Congress and the public on the nation's business; he drafted bills and with his colleagues originated nearly all the important legislation during eight years; he spent countless weary hours and a large part of his salary entertaining congressmen; and at all times exerted great influence through his friends at the Capitol. Hamilton had been right in his prediction that Jefferson would be no enemy to the powers of the executive; yet Marshall too had been right, or partly so, for Jefferson embodied himself in Congress. Federalists bitterly complained of influences felt but unseen. "The President has only to act and the majority will approve"; "*behind the curtain,* [he] directs the measures . . . while in each house a majority of puppets move as he touches the wires"; "the whole system of administration seems founded upon this principle of carrying through the legislature measures by his personal or official influence." The face behind the mask, so gentle and reserved, was a face of power and intrigue. So thought the Federalists.

The system achieved remarkable results in the Seventh Congress. The internal taxes were repealed and 400 federal officers vanished with them. Congress approved Gallatin's plan for the redemption of the debt. The army was reduced to 3000 men. Naval expenditures were cut back despite the Tripolitan war, which Congress authorized the President to prosecute with such force as he saw fit. The Republicans restored the naturalization act of 1795, making new citizens in five years. The Indian Trade and Intercourse Act carried forward the humane policy begun by Washington, with certain additions recommended by Jefferson, among them a prohibition of the liquor traffic. An act authorizing statehood for Ohio and a compact with Georgia for the cession of the vast acreage—the last of the old western claims—between the Chatahoochee and the Mississippi manifested the President's interest in the West. All these measures passed easily, usually on straight party votes.

The Jeffersonian program for the judiciary brought on a long and arduous contest finally won by the Republicans, though at later times it would seem a sham victory. The Federalist-sponsored Judiciary Act of 1801 created a new system of circuit courts with sixteen new judgeships vested with trial jurisdiction in all cases of law and equity arising under the Constitution and laws of the United States. The arrangement would unquestionably facilitate the removal of litigation from the state to the federal bench, thereby strengthening the central government at the expense of the states. Moreover, it relieved the Supreme Court justices of the irksome duty of riding circuit in the far reaches of the Union—a persistent complaint with the justices. The entire matter came to a head in the Adams administration. The Federalists wished to expand the jurisdiction of the federal courts both as an aid to commercial and financial interests, handicapped by a multitude of state jurisdictions, and as a check on the Republican opposition mounted on a cavalry of political heresy. Their object was to make the judiciary an "engine of government" more acceptable than standing armies, more subtle than sedition laws, more enduring than fiscal systems. It had been anything but this during the first decade. The limping third wheel of government, without prestige or popular favor, the judiciary was an equal partner of the executive and the legislature in name only. While these two branches were elegantly—too elegantly in the opinion of some—provided for in the new capital, the Supreme Court was shunted into a parlor-sized office that had been designated for the Clerk of the Senate. The federal courts attained public notoriety in the suppressive atmosphere of 1798. Their ambitions were disclosed in the prostitution of justice to partisan purposes. It was then, and only then, that Jefferson and his followers felt the menace of a judicial establishment more formidable perhaps than the Hamiltonian system. Jefferson had always favored an independent judiciary as the guardian of individual rights against legislative and executive tyranny. His quarrel with the courts was, in fact, that they failed to check these overreaching powers and became the destroyers rather than the protectors of the Constitution and the liberties of the citizen. Under the circumstances, when the courts checked the people rather than the government, when they were the monopoly of a party from the marshals who packed the juries to the judges who harangued them, when they had not enough business to justify expansion unless by manufacturing litigation through sedition and bankruptcy laws, common law jurisdiction, and encroachment on state judicatures—under the circumstances Jefferson could not acquiesce in any enlargement of the offices and powers of the federal judiciary.

As finally passed in the last breathless weeks of Federalist supremacy, the Judiciary Act reached neither the hopes of one party nor the fears of the other. Yet it did create many new judgeships, with the marshals, attorneys, and clerks to go with them, and it expanded federal jurisdiction in several significant areas. The case of disputed land titles between claimants of different states was especially sensitive. Litigation of this type, already of massive proportions in Kentucky, Virginia, and Georgia, grew out of land speculation. So long as the states maintained control, resident claimants tended to be favored over absentees. The act of 1801 threatened to undermine the local authorities, throw land laws into confusion, and enrich the speculators, including a number of Federalist congressmen. Jefferson's sentiments were naturally on the side of the states and the mass of small holders. But this was a secondary consideration in his opposition to the law. He was outraged, as were his followers, by a discredited majority enacting legislation of such momentous consequences in plain defiance of public opinion. The crowning insult, which he could not help but feel personally, came with the appointment of the "midnight judges." Adams hurriedly put together a full list of nominations for the new judgeships (nineteen in all, counting a three-judge court for the District of Columbia) and the Senate just as hurriedly ratified them. All were prominent Federalists; one had captained a Loyalist regiment during the Revolution; some were political casualties of the recent election; one was John Adams's nephew and three were brothers or brothers-in-law of John Marshall. He was the reputed author of the new system he would also head as Chief Justice of the Supreme Court.

Determined upon the repeal of this last act of a dying administration, Jefferson occupied the firmest Republican ground. His enemies had retired to the judiciary as a stronghold, he said. "There the remains of Federalism are to be preserved and fed from the treasury and from that battery all the works or Republicanism are to be beaten down and erased." Repeal touched the sensitive point of tenure. It was easy enough to remove marshals and attorneys, but judges appointed to terms in good behavior could not be legislated out of their seats, even if they had yet to warm them, without seeming to jeopardize the independence of the judiciary. The objection gave Jefferson pause. The Constitution made judges irremovable except by impeachment. But could this protection be fairly used to support a fraud? Could it be used to sanction and maintain a Federalist phalanx in the judicial branch? Who but the Federalists had struck the first blow against the independence of the judiciary? In an era when party affiliation split society in two, not a single Republican sat on the federal bench! And after the election of 1800 not a single judge could claim to possess the full confidence of the people. So Jefferson finally saw the issue as the restoration, not the destruction, of judicial integrity. To bring the courts into line, to chastise them, what could be more appropriate than the elimination of this "parasitical plant" engrafted on the judicial body in 1801?

Jefferson's initial doubts on this question were erased by fresh instances of judicial arrogance in the months following his inauguration. One of these was a prosecution for libel against his young friend Samuel Harrison Smith, editor of the administration newspaper in Washington. In June, Smith published an article defending the President's removals of attorneys and marshals and assailing the irresponsibility of the judges to public opinion. The courts, it was charged, "have been prompt to seize every occasion of aggrandizing executive power, of destroying all freedom of opinion, of executing unconstitutional laws, and of inculcating by the wanton and unsolicited diffusion of heterodox politics, the doctrines of passive obedience and non-resistance." This was a comparatively mild piece of denunciation in a newspaper that was almost a model of political restraint. Nevertheless, the newly established circuit court for the District of Columbia promptly ordered prosecution. The grand jury returned a presentment, but then refused to indict. The matter was dropped. If the article in question had been found libelous, many editors and writers, including Jefferson's old mentor Edmund Pendleton, might have been indicted, for Republican resentment against the judiciary was widespread and, as in Pendleton's case, it often involved the demand to ensure responsibility by making judges removable on the concurrent vote of both houses of Congress.

In December, just after his message to Congress, the Supreme Court issued a direct challenge to the President. The action led to the case of the "midnight judges," known to history as *Marbury v. Madison*. William Marbury with three others alleged that, on March 3, 1801, they had been appointed justices of the peace for the District of Columbia but that their commissions, though complete in every respect, had been withheld by the incoming administration. By some oversight these four commissions in a batch of forty made out for justices of the peace had not been delivered before the midnight hour. On coming into office Jefferson intended to treat the whole lot as nullities (justices of the peace did not enjoy life tenure) and so at once suppressed the tardy commissions. He subsequently named thirty, not forty, District justices of the peace, of whom twenty-three were the original Adams appointees; but Marbury and associates, not being recipients of this generosity, challenged the legality of the administration's action. Accordingly, they petitioned the Supreme Court for a writ of mandamus ordering the Secretary of State to deliver their commissions. The issue was delicate. Not prepared to decide it at once, the Court granted a preliminary motion for a rule to the Secretary to show cause why the writ should not issue. This was enough to raise the hair on Republican heads. Whatever the legal propriety of the "show cause" order—and there was precedent for it—the circumstances made it a political act. Republicans saw it as a bold challenge to the administration, an invasion of the executive power, an incrimination of the President through his agent, Madison. The President's feelings can only be guessed. He and Madison ignored Marshall's order, and it seemed for a time nothing more would be heard of the case. For the present, the Chief Justice had overcome any hesitancy the President may still have felt toward repeal of the Judiciary Act.

Such was the background of the repeal. John Breckinridge, a man known to be close to the President, introduced and shepherded the bill through the Senate. He did not attack the judiciary but took the line that the new courts were unnecessary. The line had been laid down by Jefferson, who had appended to his annual message a statement of the cases instituted and pending in the circuit courts from their inception. There were embarrassing errors in this statement, which Jefferson subsequently corrected, yet the figures showed clearly that the dockets were not so crowded as to warrant an expensive addition to the system. The corrected statement counted 8358 cases during ten years, 1629 of them pending. The largest volume of business had been in the southern states, Virginia at the head, which helps to explain the special sensitivity of the southern Republicans to the federal judiciary. Breckinridge could fairly argue, however, that the amount of litigation was in decline. For instance, hundreds of suits of British creditors had been referred to an Anglo-American commission and would, in fact, soon be settled by a lump payment to Britain. Moreover, it could not be argued that the Supreme Court justices were too busy to travel the circuits. In twelve years the Court had heard but sixty cases and its annual business could be transacted in five or six weeks. Of course the past history of the federal judiciary offered no measure of Federalist aspiration for it. Much new business was contemplated; this, in turn, would call into existence national legislation of equal scope. If these pretensions reached the realm of common law jurisdiction, consolidation would be complete. Jefferson knew this, as did Breckinridge, but for tactical reasons he favored an oblique approach to the question of judicial power. Carefully avoiding the real, the substantial, issue of the scope of federal authority, he turned the spotlight on the side issue of money and efficiency.

The Federalists were no more forthright in their defense of the Judiciary Act. Gouverneur Morris, their leading spokesman in the Senate, lavished his eloquence on the inviolability of contract. Abolition of the offices, he said, struck down the independence of the judiciary. Morris painted a ghastly picture of democratic despotism. "Why are we here?" he asked. "To save the people from their greatest enemy; to save them from themselves." Unfortunately for his argument, the Constitution, of which he had been a framer and on which he professed to stand, left the establishment of the federal judiciary below the Supreme Court to the discretion of Congress, and it was absurd to hold that the shadow of an office remained after Congress abolished the substance. Having blazed their path on this ground, the Federalists then dragged across it the red herring of judicial review, specifically, that is, the power of the federal courts to declare acts of Congress unconstitutional. The question was irrelevant to the debate, said the Republicans, but since a fuss had been raised about it, a reply was in order. Breckinridge, Mason, and others denied the power if it was assumed to be ultimate, for that would make the courts rather than the people the true sovereigns of the country. Their theory conformed exactly to the one Jefferson had stated in the stricken passage of his annual message: each of the co-ordinate branches of the government is supreme in its sphere and may judge for itself the constitutionality of actions of the other branches. Judicial review was thus conceded, though not as a supreme power binding on the executive and the legislature or, indeed, on the people and the states. If Jefferson ever subscribed to another theory he never stated it. The "tripartite" balance belonged to the general theory of the functional separation of powers. It was part of Republican orthodoxy, while the theory of judicial supremacy as asserted by the Federalists had little to support it in 1802.

The prolonged debate did not much clarify the issue, so momentous for the American polity, since the conflict was political through and through.

The Repeal Act cleared the Senate early in February and the House, after a marathon of oratory, a month later. Federalists bewailed the death of the Constitution. "It is dead, it is dead," Morris was heard to moan. Republicans congratulated themselves, the President and the Congress, for thus annihilating Federalist jobbery, extravagance, and influence. "It demonstrates the inflexible determination of those who now hold the reins of authority, to adhere in power to the same principles, avowed by them out of power." Not one American in a thousand, said the *National Intelligencer*, would disapprove the Repeal Act. The act returned the judiciary to its original foundation, somewhat modified in April, however, by a law which, among other things, eliminated one of the semi-annual terms of the Supreme Court. The practical effect was to prevent the meeting of the Court for nearly a year, an expedient dictated, Federalists charged, by the administration's fear of judicial reprisal against the Repeal Act. On the contrary, answered the Republicans, the new arrangement would afford the justices more leisure to attend their circuits, where the bulk of the business lay, without any neglect of the high Court's work; and besides, if the justices meant to declare the Repeal Act unconstitutional they could do so as well in 1803 as in 1802. When the Supreme Court met in February 1803, it prudently upheld the constitutionality of the repeal. Not until after the Civil War was the federal judiciary placed upon the broader foundations projected by the Judiciary Act of 1801.

Only six days before the Court's decision in this matter, Chief Justice Marshall delivered the opinion in the case of *Marbury v. Madison*. In the absence of co-operation from Madison and the Senate, the Court could not prove that Marbury had, in fact, been confirmed and commissioned a justice of the peace. Nevertheless, Marshall, who had been Secretary of State on March 3, 1801, assumed he had been, went on to hold that non-delivery of the commission did not affect the plaintiff's legal right to the office, and that the proper remedy was a writ of mandamus to the Secretary of State. But, alas, the Supreme Court could not grant the remedy. With tortuous reasoning Marshall held that the power of the Court to issue writs of mandamus in the exercise of its original jurisdiction, although given by Congress in the Judiciary Act of 1789, violated the explicit provision of the Constitution and was, therefore, null and void. There is no need to enter into the fallacies of Marshall's reasoning. Jefferson thought it a piece of sophistry, and constitutional historians, while lost in admiration of Marshall's dexterity, have been inclined to agree. What is important is that the Chief Justice, after reading a lecture to the executive on the duty of performing valid contracts with federal appointees, backed away from an open confrontation in which the Court would certainly be the loser. The fact that the retreat was masked under an apparent show of strength by the assertion of judicial authority over acts of Congress made no impression on Republicans at the time, and, in truth, set up a highly ambiguous precedent for the later development of the doctrine of judicial review.

So far as the case excited notice, it was in its character as a duel between the executive and the judiciary. A Federalist gazette exulted, "it has been solemnly decided in the Supreme Court that Mr. Jefferson, the idol of democracy, the friend of the people, has trampled upon the charter of their liberties." The Republicans left to the Court its face-saving gesture. The *National Intelligencer* and Duane's *Aurora* were silent. So was the President. Yet he could not be dispassionate toward anything John Marshall did, and his reflections on the case years later disclose deep resentment, not because the Court claimed the ultimate power to interpret the Constitution, for in fact it did not go that far in the mandamus case, but because Marshall traveled out of the case, pretending a jurisdiction he then disclaimed, in order to make a gratuitous stab at the President. Politics alone, not law, could account for the Chief Justice's behavior. Jefferson passed over the Court's declaration against the constitutionality of an act of Congress, presumably because he regarded this as a proper exercise of power in a matter directly affecting a co-ordinate branch of the government. It should have stopped there—nothing more was needed to dispose of the case—but Marshall ran on into the political field and accused the executive of a trespass on constitutional rights.

Jefferson was not finished with the judiciary. The Repeal Act and the mandamus case were but two skirmishes in a long campaign.

In retrospect, he must have wondered if in his anxiety to achieve reform within the limits of conciliation he had not been too gentle with the judiciary. The Virginia dogmatists later came to this conclusion. In things that counted the courts were remarkably acquiescent to the Jeffersonian regime, and partly for that reason the foundations of judicial power, even if somewhat narrowed, remained intact, ready for Marshall to build upon when the political climate was right. A more radical assault might have secured important Jeffersonian objectives; but the President was not prepared for it in 1802–03. Firmness in the executive and in the Congress, vigilance in the states, would hold the judiciary within constitutional limits. If this trust proved unjustified, he was quite ready to revive the subject in one shape or another. And so the problem of the Federalism of the bench was not solved but surrendered to political contingencies which, as it turned out, made impossible any constructive Republican solution.

Pitched on the horns of his dilemma, reformation and reconciliation, Jefferson agonized a good deal more about the fiscal system than about the judiciary. "When the government was first established," he said, "it was possible to have kept it going on true principles, but the contracted, English, half-lettered ideas of Hamilton destroyed that hope in the bud. We can pay off his debt in 15 years; but we can never get rid of his financial system. It mortifies me to be strengthening principles which I deem radically vicious, but the vice is entailed on us by the first error. In other parts of the government we shall be able by degrees to introduce sound principles and make them habitual. What is practicable must often control pure theory." His intellectual bent was toward the organization of government around principles that embodied political truth, but he was too much the statesman to deny the claims of practice. The conflict ran throughout his life, one accent succeeding the other as the mood or the occasion or the circumstances dictated. Hamilton's legacy was especially annoying. The machine he had erected could be made to work with more efficiency, the nuts and bolts could be tightened, its accountability to the public secured; but it could not be dismantled without ruining the economy together with the hopes of conciliation.

Banking was a case in point. Jefferson believed the government should separate itself from the banks of the country. At the head

of the system stood the Bank of the United States, which he thought
an institution of "the most deadly hostility . . . against the principles and form of our Constitution." A creature of privilege, it was
also too large, too independent, and too centralized. "I deem no
government safe which is under the vassalge of self-constituted authorities, or any other authority than that of the nation, or its regular functionaries," he lectured Gallatin in 1803. Looking to the day
eight years hence when Bank's charter would expire, he urged the
secretary to "make a beginning towards an independent use of our
own money," wherein the government would be its own banker.
But Gallatin thought the BUS a highly servicable institution both to
the government and to the economy. He actually expanded its operations by the addition of new branches and kept the bulk of federal funds in its vaults, where they supported the loans and note
issues of capitalistic enterprise. Jefferson was equally distrustful of
state banks. Between 1801 and 1811 their number grew threefold,
from thirty to ninety, and most of the new ones were Republican.
The demand for bank credit in an expanding economy was insatiable.
Republican administrations in the state capitals would have courted
disaster had they made no provision for it, and, of course, they were
eager for a share of the fiscal spoils that, like the patronage spoils,
had been a Federalist monopoly. A banking interest rose up in the
Republican party. Jefferson felt its pressures and on occasion gave
in to them. He instructed the Treasury to distribute the banking
business as widely as possible in order to keep it competitive and to
attach the banks to "the reformed order of things." Speaking of a
politically well-disposed bank in Providence, he told Gallatin, "I
am decidedly in favor of making all the banks Republican, by sharing deposits among them in proportion to the dispositions they
show." Yet he did not press the point—it ran against the grain. On
the whole, the administration conducted its business through the
BUS and made no positive effort to create a competing system centered in the Republican state banks. Either system played havoc with
Jefferson's faintly archaic ideal of a plain and dignified republican
order. But unable to discover a workable alternative, he acquiesced
in Gallatin's essentially Hamiltonian practice as well as in the relentless expansion of bank credit. "What is practicable must often control pure theory."

These problems of judicial and fiscal power went beyond the

first Jeffersonian Congress when the reforms were, if incomplete, nevertheless exceedingly gratifying to the Republicans. The Federalists muttered prophesies of doom. Everything was crumbling in ruins, they said. "Many of the members of Congress think there will not be another session under the present government." (Presumably the President would drop the hocus pocus of Congress and come forth openly as a dictator.) Jefferson rejoiced in the record of Congress. "They will pretty completely fulfil all the desires of the people," he wrote as the session drew to a close in April. "They have reduced the army and navy to what is barely necessary. They are disarming executive preponderance, by putting down one-half the offices of the United States, which are no longer necessary. These economies have enabled them to suppress all the internal taxes, and still to make provision for the payment of the public debt as to discharge that in eighteen years. They have lopped off a parasitic limb, planted by their predecessors on their judiciary body for party purposes; they are opening the doors of hospitality to fugitives from the oppressions of other countries; and we have suppressed all those public forms and ceremonies which tended to familiarize the public eye to the harbingers of another form of government." Indeed, so satisfactory was the reformation worked by Congress that later in the year, when he turned his thoughts to the coming session, the President scarcely knew what remained to be done. "We have almost nothing to propose to them but 'to let things alone'. . . . My chief object is to let the good sense of the nation have fair play, believing it will best take care of itself." Gallatin congratulated the President on the difficulty of collecting stuff for a message, since it suggested that the administration would afford "but few materials to historians." Fortunately or unfortunately, the historian of Jefferson's administration has not suffered from the want of materials.

Man in the White House

The phenomenon of Jefferson's popularity, mounting rapidly in the second year of his administration, made a puzzling problem for his political enemies. The country was going to ruin, but the man who, Nero-like, presided over the disaster was the hero of the populace.

Were the people corrupt or corrupted? Probably both. In 1800 the nation had sold its soul to a demagogue; the republic of 1787 had been overturned, the vile temple of democracy reared in its place; and all history testified that worship at this altar led straight to the graves of despotism. "The hopes and fears of the people are two windlasses, which the political machine obeys, as implicitly as any machine can. Those who turn the windlass, are as blind as the French revolutionists to the ruin that is sure to reach them." Old Fisher Ames, who wrote thus, was among the gloomiest of the Cassandras, but the Burkian theme of democratic despotism ran through the Federalist discourse. The true hero of democracy is the demagogue. The demagogue feeds on popularity; all his measures are calculated to obtain it. The younger Adams ascribed to Jefferson an irrepressible "itch for popularity," while the father spoke of "a mean thirst for popularity." Whether itch or thirst, it obliterated all truth, all morality, all nobler ambition, all interests of state beyond the apprehension of the multitude. The multitude is flattered by these attentions but cannot rule; it surrenders itself to the demagogue, and so by a new route the nation is conducted back into tyranny. The Federalists had sought to save the people from themselves; the Republicans, by exalting the popular will, consolidated their own power. Jefferson's "trust the people" was either a cunning façade or an insane delusion.

It hardly needs saying that these classical notions of democracy run through the mill of the French Revolution had little or no relevance to the new style of popular leadership Jefferson embodied. A free government grew strong not by opposing the popular will but by sympathizing with it. "He who would do his country the most good he can," Jefferson observed, "must go quietly with the prejudices of the majority until he can lead them into reason." What was "reason" for him, in the final analysis, was perhaps not very different from that of most Federalists, but he preferred to find it in the majority opinion of the community rather than in the conceits of self-styled guardians of the public interest. Hence popularity was a positive value; had he not possessed it, Jefferson would have deemed his presidency a failure. It held no terrors for him. "If I know myself I have no passion adverse to the interests of man. I have no pleasure in the exercise of power . . . ," he wrote, touching an old theme at the height of his power. "The love of popularity may induce some of those who come after me to practice what their natural dispositions might not otherwise lead them to." But this need not happen if, as in his own case, popularity was a means to virtuous ends. And he added, "If a sense of correct principles can be established among our citizens . . . they will be enabled to keep their governors in the right way."

The more popular Jefferson became, the deeper became the gloom of the shrinking Federalist remnant. "Our country is too big for union, too sordid for patriotism, too democratic for liberty," Ames lamented. The best that could be hoped for was that the cycle would quickly run its course—democracy to despotism to anarchy— after which the saving remnant of the wise and the good would restore the ravished republic. Hamilton, now a practicing lawyer in New York, often slipped into this mood; at other times, his morbidity reached the outer limits of despair. "Mine is an odd destiny," he wrote in 1802. "Perhaps no man in the United States has sacrificed or done more for the present Constitution than myself; and contrary to all my anticipations of its fate . . . I am still laboring to prop the frail and worthless fabric. . . . Every day proves to me more and more, that this American world was not made for me." If it was, indeed, a Jeffersonian world, Hamilton by his own pertinacity had helped to make it so. Young Adams, no admirer of the New Yorker, agreed with his pessimistic diagnosis of the national condition but, puncturing false hopes, pronounced the Federalist system dead and best forgotten. "The experiment . . . has failed, and to attempt its restoration would be as absurd, as to undertake the resurrection of a carcass seven years in the grave." After the election of 1802 the Republicans controlled all but two or three state governments and their majority in the next Congress would be unbeatable. Adams could not understand why "the pilots at the helm" remained so sensitive to opposition. "What they take for breakers are mere clouds of unsubstantial vapour."

Jefferson was disposed to agree and act accordingly. Yet the vapors were peculiarly obnoxious, and despite impressive electoral gains, the results fell below Republican expectations. This was true in Massachusetts, for instance, where Elbridge Gerry, the hope of Republican conciliation, lost the party stronghold, Boston, and met defeat in his third successive contest for the governorship. Young recruits to the Federalist ranks were renewing the vigor of the party as older leaders seemed to give up in dismay. The *Palladium*, a newly renovated Federalist newspaper, spewed venom upon the President and Republicans generally. Jefferson's Massachusetts friends concluded that a daring opposition would be pursued with all possible rancor. "There can be no reconciliation," Lincoln reported sadly in October. The demand for removals rose. Jefferson had made but a handful in Massachusetts. In Boston the weight of the collector's office could tip the scale against the Republicans in any election. Yet Jefferson ran the risk. Without hiding his disappointment over the election, he refused to admit failure in the Bay State and struck the line he would maintain, with but momentary lapses, against the violent Federalists. "This bitterness increases with their desperation," he told Lincoln. "They are trying slanders now which nothing could prompt but a gall which blinds their judgment as well as their consciences. I shall take no other revenge, than, by a steady pursuit of economy and peace, and by the establishment of republican principles in substance and in form, to sink Federalism into an abyss from which there shall be no resurrection for it."

Although Jefferson did not say what particular slanders he had in mind, he probably meant those fathered by James T. Callender, the most notorious of which had been published in Virginia several weeks before and had since made the rounds of the enemy press. The Sedition Act victim got out of jail just as Jefferson became President. Expecting to be rewarded for his past services—crowned for his martyrdom—he at once cast covetous eyes on the Richmond post office. It was beyond his grasp. Jefferson made a point to Monroe of finding "a gentleman of respectable standing in society" for this post. Callender proceeded to make himself obnoxious to the administration by raising a storm over the remission of the $200 fine imposed upon him by Judge Chase. Jefferson, holding the Sedition Act a nullity, at once issued a pardon and ordered remission of the fine. The money was still in the hands of the marshal at Richmond, a Federalist, and he was slow to co-operate. Callender blamed the President who, he said, was sacrificing him as "a scapegoat to political decorum." After five years' labor in the Republican cause he had no money, no job, no reputation, no prospects. "In a word," he raved, "I have been equally calumniated, pillaged, and destroyed by all parties." In hopes of placating this angry man, Jefferson asked Monroe to see if the refund could not be paid by private charities. He would give fifty dollars. Two or three days later Callender appeared in Washington. He pressed his claims, job and fine, upon Madison, who was amazed to discover that to his less endearing passions Callender had added the passion of love—a Richmond damsel in a station above him but hopefully his if he could be named postmaster. To relieve his distress, Jefferson sent fifty dollars. His private secretary returned from this mission with an alarming account of Callender's behavior. "He intimated that he was in possession of things which he could make use of in a certain case; that he received the $50 not as a charity but as a due, in fact as hush money; that I [the President] knew what he expected, viz. a certain office, and more to this effect." The threat of blackmail, intimated before, was now real. This put an end to his charities, Jefferson told Monroe, adding assurances on the idleness of Callender's boasts. "He knows nothing of me which I am not willing to declare to the world myself."

Callender returned to Virginia empty-handed (though he soon collected the $200) and apparently determined to make the President squirm. The Richmond Federalists now sheltered the man they had earlier chased out of town. Augustine Davis, the Federalist editor and postmaster, whose job Callender had sought, and David M. Randolph, the marshal, who had jailed him and repaid his fine, became his partners in libel. A new Federalist weekly, the *Richmond Recorder; or Lady's and Gentleman's Miscellany*, which catered to the taste for scandal, employed Callender. For several months he stored his depraved mind with scraps of gossip about Jefferson that circulated in Virginia, then in the spring of 1802 opened his infamous campaign by charging the President with aid and encouragement in the publication of the pamphlets that had led to the writer's conviction for seditious libel. Mortified by this "base ingratitude," which perverted "charities" into patronage of a lying renegade, Jefferson authorized Monroe to make a full disclosure of his connections with Callender should the Governor think it wise. Callender kept the initiative by printing Jefferson's letters which mingled money with politics in such a way that it required an act of naïveté to separate them. Now that he had dragged his victim down to his own level, Callender smeared him with the dirty gossip of his private life. On September 1 there appeared in the *Recorder* a slanderous little piece, "The President Again," signed by Callender in the conviction that Jefferson would realize at last the heavy cost of his betrayal. "It is well known," the article began, "that the man *whom it delighteth the people to honor*, keeps, and for many years past has kept, as his concubine, one of his own slaves. . . . By this wench, Sally, our President has had several children. . . . The African Venus is said to officiate as housekeeper at Monticello."

Thus was launched the prolific public career of a tale that had titilated Jefferson's enemies in the neighborhood of Monticello for years. The African Venus, Sally Hemings, was apparently the mulatto offspring of John Wayles and Elizabeth Hemings, his concubine, and hence the half-sister of Jefferson's departed wife. Sally it was who had accompanied Polly to Paris in 1787. After her return she had a number of children, all light skinned, whose paternity some wanton men ascribed to Jefferson. Like most legends, this one was not created out of the whole cloth. The evidence, highly circumstantial, is far from conclusive, however, and unless Jefferson was capable of slipping badly out of character in hidden moments at Monticello, it is difficult to imagine him caught up in a miscegenous relationship. Such a mixture of the races, such a ruthless exploitation of the master-slave relationship, revolted his whole being. It is of no historical importance, but the best guess is that Sally's children were fathered by Peter Carr, the same wayward nephew who was responsible for the Langhorne letter and who was now married to Hetty Smith of Baltimore, sister of the Maryland congressman and of the Secretary of the Navy. This circumstance, if true, taken together with a desire to shield his own family from the truth of the Hemings genealogy—a point of delicacy with him—may account for the tight-lipped silence Jefferson maintained on this matter not only when Callender brought it into the open but to the end of his days. His friends issued indignant denials, but succeeded only in feeding the scandal. It was too enticing, too good a snare for the lofty Jefferson, too neat an offset to the tale of Hamilton's amours told by Callender, and coming from him too smashing an example of retributive justice. Political poetasters had a gay time with Jefferson and his African harem. * And so a popular legend was born. Callender had his revenge. It was not sweet, however. He had proved himself a more dangerous friend than enemy. Federalists spread his libels but did not trust him. Damned in infamy for his dirty work, in July 1803, still at it, he drowned, drunk, in the James River.

To one of the malicious charges aired by Callender, Jefferson pleaded guilty. He had, he confessed, "when young and single . . . offered love to a handsome lady," Mrs. John Walker, the

---

* The most widely repeated verses were the following, published originally in the *Boston Gazette:*

A Song
supposed to have been written by the
Sage of Monticello
(to the tune of Yankee Doodle)

Of all the damsels on the green
  On mountain, or in valley,
A lass so luscious ne'er was seen
  As Monticellian Sally.

Yankee doodle, who's the noodle?
  What wife were half so handy?
To breed a flock, of slaves for stock,
  A blackamoor's the dandy.

Search every town and city through,
  Search market street and alley;
No dance at dusk shall meet your view,
  So yielding as my Sally.

Verse

When pressed by loads of state affairs,
  I seek to sport and dally,
The sweetest solace of my cares
  Is in the lap of Sally.

Verse

Let Yankee parsons preach the worst—
  Let Tory Wittling's rally!
You men of morals! and be curst,
  You would snap like sharks for Sally.

Verse

wife of his good friend. The story had been bandied about for some time before Callender got hold of it. Walker had demanded satisfaction fifteen years or so after the event. After the election of 1800, Henry Lee, a political turncoat still seeking to recover solvency and reputation as a Federalist, took up Walker's cause out of malice toward Jefferson. Knowledge of the affair passed from Lee and other Virginia Federalists to the press. During the fall elections of 1802 it was hinted at in Washington, rumored in New York, and freely circulated in Connecticut, allegedly by the agency of the Federalist attorney David Daggett, who, in turn, was said to have got it from Hamilton. (Jefferson later said that Hamilton had threatened disclosure at the time he was put on the carpet for the Reynolds affair.) Walker was still seeking satisfaction when the old scandal cropped up in debate in the Massachusetts legislature in January 1805. This was quickly followed by the "celebrated letter" of Thomas Turner, a Virginian connected with the Walker family, first published in a Boston journal. The letter traversed the whole field of Jefferson libels and became a kind of text for the Federalists. Here and elsewhere the seduction yarn was bawdily elaborated until it read like a chapter in a Richardsonian novel. The rake lewdly assailed the lady's virtue but, alas, was repulsed by a pair of scissors! Not finally, however, for he pursued her for ten years. "We have heard of a ten year siege of Troy," Paine remarked incredulously, "but who ever heard of a ten year siege to seduce?" Meanwhile, negotiations were going on through Lee for honorable amends. Walker demanded that the President make an apology before the whole world. He would not go that far, but in 1806 he formally acknowledged his youthful transgression in a document presented to Walker, who seemed satisfied with this private apology. But nothing could quiet the public slander.

The intricate relationship between these assaults on Jefferson's private character and ordinary political skirmishes is well illustrated by the case of the Geffroy letters. Early in the administration an informant who signed himself Nicholas Geffroy reported official favoritism and waste in the construction of fortifications at Newport, Rhode Island. It seemed just the kind of malfeasance Jefferson expected to uncover when he came into office—and to his distress never did—so he ordered Dearborn to launch an investigation and politely thanked his informant. Only then did he learn from Christopher Ellery, Republican senator from Rhode Island, that the Geffroy letters (there was a second one) were forgeries. Ellery pointed an accusing finger at John Rutledge, Jr., the South Carolina Federalist, who summered at Newport. Just why Rutledge, or any Federalist, should have written these letters was never made clear. It certainly was not clear to Jefferson who, accepting the idea of forgery, promptly dropped the matter. The next year the Republican legislature in South Carolina juggled the congressional districts so as to deprive Rutledge of his seat. He recklessly blamed the President for this maneuver and at the same time joined the little band of Federalists who secretly brooded over the eggs Callender dropped in their midst months before they were ready to hatch. When they hatched, Ellery attacked Rutledge as the trouble-making author of the Geffroy letters, a charge later detailed at length by William Duane. Vehemently denying the charge, Rutledge claimed he had been framed by Jefferson, Ellery, and Duane in order to divert attention from the Callender scandals. In October he asked Jefferson's permission to see the incriminating letters. Apparently he never received a reply. Jefferson knew of his connection with Callender—with what right did he ask any favor of the President? He had once held high hopes for this scion of a distinguished Revolutionary family, but like many of the Carolina aristocrats, Rutledge had gone over to Federalism in the 'nineties and rendered himself useless to his country.

The Callender libels, as Jefferson believed, opened the floodgates of personal vilification. One thing led to another. Thus "Clerk John" Nicholas, the Charlottesville gossip, came to Rutledge's aid by offering to publish a Jefferson forgery, the "Langhorne letter" of 1797, and in fact did publish it in 1803. Thus the Walker scandal triggered the revival of accusations of misconduct and cowardice—"a dastardly traitor to the trust reposed in him"—in his governorship of Virginia. This was part of Turner's catalogue. Charles Symmes, still in 1805 collector of the port at Alexandria, by Adams's appointment and Jefferson's grace, had first aired the subject in 1796. Jefferson's young friend and Virginia congressman, William A. Burwell, now gathered a vast array of evidence for a public vindication in the *Richmond Enquirer*. A Virginian who had loaned fifty pounds to Jefferson in 1773 charged that his offer six years later to discharge the debt in depreciated Revolutionary currency had been a dishonest, nay a criminal act. Similar accusations, all groundless, had been made before. In this instance Jefferson made an exception to his rule against noticing Federalist calumnies and wrote out a statement subsequently printed, quite anonymously, in the *Enquirer*. By these attacks on his private character the Federalist enemies hoped to deflate his immense popularity with the public. "There is not a feature of that character allowed to be fair," the *National Intelligencer* pointedly observed. "Candor is stigmatized as hypocrisy, decision rashness, and learning pedantry." It is doubtful if they accomplished anything aside from stiffening their own last-ditch resistance to the Jeffersonian regime and Republican ardor to maintain it at all cost.

If Jefferson was, in some sense, responsible for Callender, he also had some responsibility for Thomas Paine, another problem visited upon him in 1802. The prophet of reason and revolution arrived in Baltimore on October 30 and hastened to Washington. He had returned to America aboard a private vessel, not the public one earlier offered, but this did not in any way deter the bigoted Federalist sect. "My arrival has struck it as with an hydrophobia," Paine wrote; "it is like the sight of water to canine madness." The President gave him a warm embrace: the prophet was not without honor in his own country. Jefferson's fireside was brightened that winter by a visit from his daughters; they had known Paine in Paris, and though never a favorite with the ladies, he was a frequent guest at the President's House. Paine was a great talker (especially with the assistance of brandy), a supreme egotist, earthy, anecdotal, and full of ideas on all manner of things. He was sixty-five now, bloodied but unbowed by his revolutionary experience. Like the Abbé Sieyes he could say, "I survived," and add mockingly for his detractors, "by the protecting favor of heaven." He was sad about France. "You see they have conquered all Europe, only to make it more miserable than it was before." America, having recovered its sanity, was again the light of the world. He talked to Jefferson of these things, showed him the latest model of the ingenious iron bridge he was still promoting, and exchanged ideas about dry docks, gunboats, Louisiana, the Barbary pirates, and other subjects of current interest to both men. Various stories were afloat: that Paine would receive a post in the administration, that Jefferson had brought him back as a hack writer, that he was preparing a sequel to the *Age of Reason*. In the Federalist press he was "that creeping thing," lower than vermin; at the hotel where he dined curious people came and stared, it was said, as at an orang-outang; in Boston a young poet of the same name petitioned the General Court to permit him to take "a Christian name." A series of public letters, "To the Citizens of the United States," which Paine commenced soon after his arrival, fanned the flames of controversy. Even warm Republicans, like Duane, grew uneasy when Paine, in his third letter, started up the subject of religion. No one could talk him out of it, though if he continued to ride this hobby he would lose the last friends he had. Old Samuel Adams pleaded with him in the name of the people of New England: "Will you excite among them the spirit of angry controversy at a time when they are hastening to unity and peace?" But Paine called "all this war-whoop of the pulpit" a Federalist "stalking horse" and went his own way.

Jefferson, too, felt concern over the unruliness of Paine's opinions, particularly on religion. The two men, whose tempers were as different as fire and water, agreed in the essentials of their theistic faith, but Paine was a zealot, a propagator of the gospel, a prophet of a new religion as well as a new society, while Jefferson was tolerant of religious differences, only wishing that they might not foul the republican nest. In answer to a Connecticut Baptist address some months earlier, he had declared his conviction that the First Amendment erected "a wall of separation between church and state"; however, wishing not to offend the church order in New England, he struck from his reply an explicit refusal to follow his predecessors in proclaiming fast days and thanksgivings, and instead let it ride as an inference from the stated principle. Not long after Paine's visit he composed a "Syllabus . . . of the Doctrines of Jesus," which he described as a statement of his religious creed. It was done for his personal satisfaction, for his children and a handful of intimate friends. The public had no right to know his religious profession, nor did he have any desire to proselytize in its behalf. In these matters of separation of church and state and freedom of religious conscience, he differed from Paine not in principle but in the manner of pursuing it. After Congress convened in December it was said that Jefferson grew very sensitive to criticism of his friendliness with Paine, saw less of him, and made it a point regularly to attend Sunday worship in the Capitol. Paine himself detected a coolness in the President's attitude and, nothing abashed, reprimanded him for it before leaving the city in January. Jefferson had, "by a sort of shyness, as if . . . in fear of federal observation," precluded conversation, Paine said, adding that he was "not the only one who makes observations of this kind." Jefferson denied anything of the sort; on the contrary, he had been perfectly open with Paine, not only out of respect but in defiance to Federalist censure. "As to fearing it, if I ever could have been weak enough for that, they have taken to cure me of it thoroughly!" Yet he may, in fact, have shown the reserve he denied. Paine had imposed on their friendship for years and proven himself imprudent and overbearing. Jefferson could not risk, and did not want, a personal intimacy with him. Whatever the cause, the reunion of the old comrades failed of consummation, and Paine went north, lonely, unloved, literally a man without a country, to live out the remainder of his days in the obscurity of a New York village.

Jefferson had been reading an old favorite, Seneca, when he remarked to a European correspondent: "Nero wished all the necks of Rome united in one, that he might sever them at one blow. So our Federalists, wishing to have a single representative of all the objects of their hatred, honor me with that post, and exhibit against me such atrocities as no nation has ever before heard or endured." He had no intention of playing Nero. From a political standpoint the newspaper opposition was beneath contempt. It made a great noise, being concentrated in the commercial cities, but produced few reverberations in the vast agricultural spaces of America. Jefferson had the good sense not to confuse newspaper opinion with public opinion. He read dozens of newspapers, Republican and Federalist (his account books show that he personally subscribed to about a hundred dollars' worth annually), and thought the bulk of it trash. "When I read the newspapers and see what a mass of falsehood and what an atom of truth they contain, I am mortified with the consideration that 99/100ths of mankind pass through life imagining they have known what was going forward when they would have been nearer the truth had they heard nothing." Still, bad as the journalism of the time was, the press had a right to exist and even at its worst performed a useful service to society.

He was capable of being quite philosophical on the point. "They [the Federalists] fill their newspapers with falsehoods, calumnies and audacities far beyond anything you witnessed while here," he informed his friend Volney, "and happily these vehicles, like the flues of our chimneys, give an innocent conveyance and discharge to smoke and vapours which might be dangerous if pent up in their bowels." He then went on in the language of a true liberal to describe the "experiment" he was making "whether freedom of discussion, unaided by coercion, is not sufficient for the propagation and protection of truth, and for the maintenance of an administration pure and upright in its actions and views." Conducted under the auspices of one who was the object of so much malignity, what a noble experiment this would be! Jefferson stated his commitment in unequivocal terms. "I shall protect them," his libeling critics, he said, "in the right of lying and calumniating, and still go to merit the continuance of it, by pursuing steadily my object of proving that a people, easy in their circumstances as ours are, are capable of conducting themselves under a government founded not on the fears and follies of man, but on his reason. . . . This is the object now nearest my heart." It was still close to heart two years later, in 1804, when the German scientist Alexander von Humboldt visited him in Washington. Glancing at a violent newspaper in the President's office, the Baron asked, "Why are these libels allowed?" And he was answered, "Put that paper in your pocket, Baron, and should you hear the reality of our liberty, the freedom of our press questioned, show this paper, and tell where you found it."

But Jefferson was not always so philosophical. The Callender libels, especially, jarred his faith in the experiment; a press that was capable of inhaling these noxious vapors could not be considered either innocent or useful. Republican leaders in several states took alarm. In Pennsylvania, for instance, Governor McKean told the legislature it was time "that the good sense of the people, aiding the authority of the magistrate, should interpose to rescue us from a tyranny, by which the weak, the wicked and the obscure, are enabled to prey upon the fame, the feelings and the fortunes of every conspicuous member of the community." The following February,

McKean protested to the President that the "infamous and seditious libels" published almost daily had become intolerable. "If they cannot be altogether prevented, yet they may be greatly checked by a few prosecutions." He was quite ready to make the attempt under Pennsylvania law, but as the problem was a national one he wished to clear it with the President. Jefferson took over a week to answer, and when he did yielded to the Governor's pleas. "Not a general prosecution," he said, "for that would look like a persecution: but a selected one." And he enclosed a newspaper that might serve as a starter. In thus departing from his own far nobler experiment, Jefferson succumbed to partisan political pressures. His own preference, as he told another Republican leader, was to acquiesce in the atrocities of the press, but he could not demand this from numberless Republicans who frothed with indignation. He did not doubt, no more than when he wrote the Kentucky Resolutions, the lawfulness of state prosecutions for defamatory publications. Truth should be admitted as a defense, which amended the common law, but he continued to hold that government could be criminally assaulted by the publication of malicious falsehoods, by bad words, as well as by deeds of violence.

In his letter to McKean he offered still another justification for proceedings against journalistic scandalmongers. "The Federalists having failed in destroying the freedom of the press by their gag-law," he said, "seem to have attempted it in an opposite form, that is by pushing its licentiousness and its lying to such a degree of prostitution as to deprive it of credit. And the fact is that so abandoned are the tory presses in this particular that even the least informed of the people have learned that nothing in a newspaper is to be believed. This is a dangerous state of things and the press ought to be restored to its credibility if possible." In short, the aim was not to suppress freedom but to save it, not to muzzle political debate but to make it meaningful, not to destroy the press—it was destroying itself—but to lead it into a career of "useful freedom." Jefferson's statement may be interpreted as a mask for tyranny or, conversely, as a responsible answer to a sickness that demanded some rather strenuous purgatives. The Federalist press seemed to exist for no higher purpose than calumny, and Jefferson's opinion of its Republican counterpart was not much better. Until the condition was corrected the press must fail to fulfill its essential role in a free government. He once told Paine that the licentiousness of the press produced the same effect as the restraint of the press was intended to do. "The restraint was to prevent things being told, and the licentiousness prevents things being believed when they are told." He was not, then, by his own reckoning, engaging in masquerade when he spoke of restoring the integrity of newspapers. It is equally clear, however, that the means he approved in this instance were badly suited to the end in view. Either he did not recognize the danger a few "wholesome" prosecutions posed to all freedom of opinion or he had allowed the vomit of defamation to poison his vision of the truth.

There were very few principles he held as absolutes, and freedom of the press was not one of them. A press unrestrained to truth had not earned the right to unrestrained freedom. To be useful in the larger strategy of freedom the press must be truthful. It was not that; nevertheless, with rare exceptions, Jefferson stuck to high principle. His waverings were momentary, followed by more and more emphatic declarations of faith. Trust the people! And so he could say to John Taylor in 1804 just the opposite of what he had said to Governor McKean in 1803. "The firmness with which the people have withstood the late abuses of the press, the discernment they have manifested between truth and falsehood," he wrote, "show that they may safely be trusted to hear everything true and false, and to form a correct judgment between them." Republicans in New York tried a Federalist editor for seditious libel in 1804, and Pennsylvania did the same in 1805. Jefferson did not intervene in either of these suits under state jurisdiction. When he came to his second inaugural address, he dwelled at length on the experiment, not uninteresting to the world, "whether freedom of discussion, unaided by power, is not sufficient for the propagation and protection of truth—whether a government, conducting itself in the true spirit of its constitution, with zeal and purity, and doing no act which it would be unwilling the whole world should witness, can be written down by falsehood and defamation." The experiment, he went on with justifiable pride, had been fairly made and the suffrages of the people had pronounced the verdict. A free press could not be dangerous to republican government; it remained to be seen whether it could be useful.

The major test of Jefferson's commitment occurred in his second term. In 1806 the federal circuit court in Connecticut indicted several editors and ministers on charges of libeling the President. The Federalist terror persisted in that state. In the two-year period 1804–06, several Republican editors or printers were tried and convicted of seditious libel; a county judge who had turned Republican was dismissed for marching in a procession celebrating the Louisiana Purchase; Josiah Meigs, professor of mathematics at Yale College, was cashiered for his party affiliation; and a group of local justices, all Republicans, were hauled before the General Asssembly and summarily removed from office because they had dared to question the legitimacy of the state government still without a *bona fide* constitution. These circumstances help to explain Jefferson's initial acquiescence in the Connecticut prosecutions. "That a spirit of indignation and retaliation should arise, when an opportunity should present itself," he wrote to one of the Republican martyrs, "was too much within the human constitution to excite either surprise or censure, and confined to an appeal to truth only, it cannot lessen the useful freedom of the press." Yet this endeavor to recall the press within the pale of truth not only ran in the face of the great experiment but also contradicted the Republican principle against common law jurisdiction in the federal courts. Moreover, as Gideon Granger, the Postmaster General from Connecticut, warned the President, the prosecutions would supply the Federalists with martyrs to the injury of the arduous Republican cause. "Let the Federalists tyranize but let us maintain the correct principles of civil liberty," Granger pleaded. As a matter of principle, also of policy, Jefferson agreed; but, as always, he was reluctant to interfere in state contests. Only when he learned that one of the libels touched the Walker affair did he decide to act on the principle. The affair had, at last, been settled to everyone's satisfaction. None of the principals, neither Walker nor Jefferson nor Lee nor others who might be called to testify, wished to see it revived in a court of law. The prospect, Jefferson said, was "harrowing all our feelings." At his request Granger arranged for the dismissal of the prosecution for want of jurisdiction. (Five years later, in 1813, the moot case was taken up by the Supreme Court as the *United States v. Hudson and Goodwin* in order to determine the question of common law jurisdiction, with a result entirely favorable to the Republican opinion.)

The career of Federalist defamation continued throughout Jefferson's presidency, and well beyond, though nothing further occurred in the way of prosecution. It was a great thing to have made the experiment in freedom of the press; it would have been greater still had Jefferson never relaxed his faith in the ultimate result.

People who formed their mental images of the President from what they read in the gazettes usually discovered upon acquaintance that the supposed Satan had no horns. "He appears to be a gentleman of polite manners," a new Massachusetts congressman wrote, "and had I been entirely free from prepossession I should have viewed him in a favorable point of light." Some Federalists overcame their prepossessions. William Plumer, the New Hampshire senator, after four years in Washington was prepared to concede, at least to himself, that he had done the President injustice. A more striking case was Margaret Bayard Smith, the charming bride of the young man Jefferson brought to Washington in 1800 to publish the Republican newspaper. From an elegant Federalist family in Philadelphia, she possessed the prejudices of her class; but they were at once dissolved in Jefferson's presence. "And is this," she asked herself after their first meeting, "the violent democrat, the vulgar demagogue, the bold atheist and profligate man I have so often heard denounced by the Federalists? Can this man so meek and mild, yet dignified in his manners, with a voice so soft and low, with a countenance so benignant and intelligent, can this be that daring leader of a faction, that disturber of the peace, that enemy of all rank and order?" The Smiths became part of the small circle Jefferson drew from the new Washington society and in which he found more pleasure than in the hordes of congressmen.

The qualities of openness, modesty, gentleness, benevolence, and intelligence so much admired by Mrs. Smith struck other friendly observers as well, and they are the qualities young Rembrandt Peale captured in his portrait of 1800, which quickly became the best known likeness of the President. If not a handsome man, he was equally far from being the "tall, large-boned farmer" of Federalist caricature. The lean and lanky frame, spare of flesh—his most striking physical characteristic—easily lent itself to caricature, whence the unflattering appellative "Long Tom." The frame's attire came in for special remark. Men generally agreed it was casual and plain, whatever the color of the breeches, but some thought it coarse and slovenly as well. After calling at the President's House in 1804, Plumer described him as better dressed than usual. "Though his coat was old and threadbare, his scarlet vest, his corduroy small clothes, and his white linen hose, were new and clean—but his linen was much soiled, and his slippers old.—His hair was cropt and powdered." Even his worst enemies thought him among the most agreeable of men in society, "naturally communicative" on small and large subjects alike, "goodnatured, frank and rather friendly." One who was his friend thought him a bit grave, "but without any tincture of pomp, ostentation, or pride, and occasionally [he] can smile, and both hear and relate humourous stories as well as any other man." He relished anecdote and only humorless men supposed he lacked a sense of humor. He tended to be reticent with strangers, yet this was not always the case. Joseph Story, on first encounter, found himself immediately at ease. "Open to all, he seems willing to stand the test of inquiry. . . . You may measure if you please, and cannot easily misjudge." An English Quaker traveling in America dropped by the President's office and was received as if he were an old friend. "From his disregard of all useless forms and ceremonies, not excepting those in religion," the Englishman said, "his enemies accuse him of being deficient both in religion and politeness. But there are men, that have seen a good deal of the world, who believe, on good grounds, that where true religion and true politeness most abound, there we see least of forms and ceremonies, and that true religion and true politeness positively go hand in hand." In truth, Jefferson was no Quaker; but in his august station he endeavored to substitute natural good humor and common civility for the artificial forms of foreign courts. If manners were judged on the standard not of refinement but of consideration, the President had few peers. "He has more ease than grace—" Mrs. Smith keenly observed, "all the winning softness of politeness, without the artificial polish of courts."

The presidency was not all business. Outside the strict line of official function, Jefferson hit upon a course of conduct that dramatized the democratic character of the office. One of the first accomplishments of the new administration, he felt, was the suppression of "all those public forms and ceremonies which tended to familiarize the public eye to the harbingers of another form of government." The annual speech to Congress fell into this category, as did the appointment of fast days, the elegant birthday balls of his predecessors (he even refused to make his birth date public), the splendors of livery and equipage, and, above all, the weekly levees. "What a contrast!" exclaimed a visitor who knew the old regime. "Coteries and drawing rooms are no more; the promenade of superciliousness and dissipation, no longer excites disgust. . . . No vanities obstruct duties. No pomp or show is now seen to puzzle the unthinking, no etiquette is established to impede business or forbid the access of simply clad honesty." Instead, the simple grace of a young republic, whose rugged hills and rude winds and plain manners rebuked all regal ostentation! Conceiving of himself as one of the people, their chosen servant for the time being, Jefferson wished to relieve the presidency of any suggestion of age-old notions of kingship, arrogance, and lofty superiority. He gave an openness, an accessibility, even a familiarity to the office. As John Adams said, though he did not mean it as a compliment, "Jefferson's whole eight years was a levee." While this democratic approach was a deliberate expression of his own mind, it was so much aided and abetted by the conditions of life in the village capital that it might well have been impossible in Philadelphia.

Sociability was built into the President's daily routine. He rose at sunrise, breakfasted at a fixed hour, worked at his desk until one p.m., rode on horseback for an hour or two, in mid-afternoon entertained at dinner, in the evening withdrew to the privacy of his domestic circle, and generally retired at ten. In the morning hours he kept his door ajar for callers both official and unofficial. While he did not seek out common citizens, many accounts testify to the cordiality with which they were met when, perhaps responding to the image of "the man of the people," they sought him out. For instance, a Pennsylvania farmer and his daughter traveling on horseback to Virginia stopped in Washington and begged their congressman to be taken to the President. It was the dinner hour, but the congressman consented, and the three of them soon found themselves seated at the President's table, conversing of clover, stock, and fertilizer. The moral was readily drawn: Jefferson was one "who in his inter-

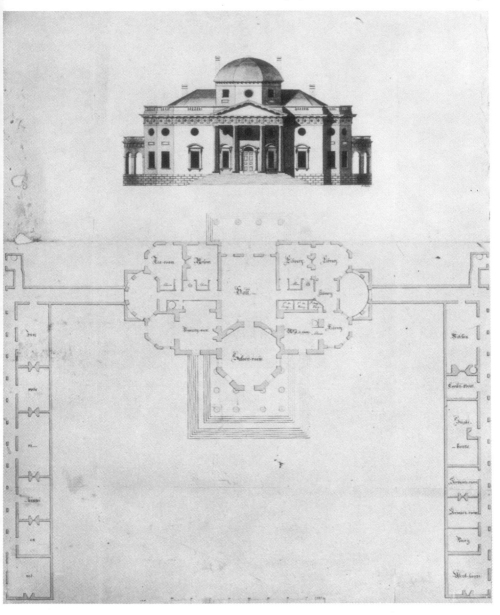

Monticello renewed. Elevation, west front, and plan of first floor and
dependencies. Drawn by Robert Mills, about 1803.

The President. Portrait
by Gilbert Stuart, 1805.

The President.
Medallion portrait
by Gilbert Stuart, 1805.

The President. Portrait by Rembrandt Peale, 1805.

Sage of Monticello. Portrait by Thomas Sully, 1822.

course with his fellow man was as plain, as simple and as free from artificiality or sham as the humblest man in the nation."

The daily ritual of riding horseback acquainted the President with every foot of ground in and around the capital and brought him into contact with all manner of men—the workmen at the navy yard, the mechanics in their shops, gardeners, builders, and so on. He rode alone, usually on his handsome bay Wildair, as obscure as any rider one was apt to meet. Once, it was said, he fell into conversation with a stranger who upbraided the President mercilessly, and Jefferson, without giving the game away, won the gentleman's consent to be introduced to this horrible personage on the morrow. When he called and at last realized his plight, the stranger was full of apology, but Jefferson quickly put him at ease by disclaiming any relationship with the imaginary being to whom apology was owing, and after a long talk the stranger went away as good a friend as he had been an enemy. The enemies labeled his equestrian saunterings a species of democratic ostentation. He sank the dignity of his station, which he well knew how to maintain, in an artful appeal to popular feelings. Thus Joseph Dennie, the same Federalist editor who would be tried for libel in Pennsylvania, made this entry in his "Imaginary Diary of the President:" "Ordered my horse—never ride with a servant—looks proud—mob doesn't like it—must gull the boobies—Adams wouldn't bend so—would rather lose his place—knew nothing of the world."

Actually, although Jefferson wished to be a people's President, there is no need to search the political recesses of his mind for an explanation of his solitary rides. Immediately upon becoming President he had ordered a suitable carriage, "as neat as it can possibly be without any tawdriness," made for him in Philadelphia. Counting the plated harness and the two postillion saddles, the outfit cost him over $1200, to which must be added the cost of four full-blooded bays, $1600, acquired in Virginia. But Washington, its roads rutted and muddy, was no place for a coach and four. If anyone on his domestic staff had a sinecure, it was the coachman, who saw service only at the rare intervals when Jefferson played host to his children. Furthermore, riding horseback was a kind of therapy both mental and physical. For several years Jefferson's health had been so good that he sometimes dreaded the prospect of living too long. But a flaw appeared, a persistent diarrhea, occasionally violent, just at the time he became President. He mentioned the complaint to Benjamin Rush, who prescribed the usual regimen of diet, exercise, bathing, and medication, together with cessation of Jefferson's practice—his prescript against colds—of bathing his feet every morning during the winter. Said Rush, "The bowels sympathize with the feet above any other external part of the body, and suffer in a peculiar manner from the effects of cold water upon them." Well, Jefferson never had much confidence in physicians, even the learned Dr. Rush. Yet he was put on the right track, or so he came to believe, by another physician, Dr. William Eustis of Boston, who evidently believed the bowels sympathized with that part of the body most exercised by a horse. For more information on the "trotting cure," Eustis referred him to the great Dr. Sydenham, "the English Hippocrates." Jefferson got Sydenham's book and at once began to ride a couple of hours daily; by 1804, the bowels strengthened, he was completely cured of his "visceral complaint." One thing is sure: in this instance the bowels sympathized with democracy.

Emblematic of the popular image Jefferson projected, of "Jeffersonian simplicity," was the presentation of the "mammoth cheese" on New Year's Day, 1802. This free-will offering by the farmers of the town of Cheshire in the Berkshire hills of Massachusetts measured four feet four and one half inches in diameter, 15 inches thick, and weighed 1235 pounds. If Federalists could deride, Republicans could exalt Jefferson's fame as the champion of American mammoths. The cheese had been made in the summer, strictly from "Republican cows"—900 of them—then transported by land and by sea in the charge of Parson John Leland, an indefatigable Jeffersonian, Baptist, and crusader for religious liberty. It arrived in Washington on the first morning of the new year in a wagon drawn by four horses richly caparisoned. "It is an ebullition of the passion of Republicanism in a state where it had been under heavy persecution," Jefferson wrote with obvious delight. The present was accompanied by an address inscribed "The Greatest Cheese in America, for the Greatest Man in America." It was a trifle, "a peppercorn," not the enforced offering of a lord to his monarch nor a bribe for lofty titles or offices, but, said the address, "a mite [cast] into the scale of democracy" and a token of the esteem free men felt for their President. (Actually, Jefferson paid a sum of $200 for the cheese in keeping with a strict personal rule against the acceptance of gifts.) Federalist wits made easy jest of the cheese, "this monument of human weakness and folly," to which Republicans returned, "Do what they can —and say what they please, Rats love to nibble at good Cheshire Cheese." Federalist congressmen were insulted by the introduction of Parson Leland in the Capitol pulpit the following Sunday, especially as he chose as his text, the President in attendence, "And behold a greater than Solomon is here." For a year and a half the great cheese reposed in the "mammoth room," as Jefferson dubbed the unfinished east room of the mansion, where it was an object of curiosity. Finally, on July 4, 1803, in celebration of the Louisiana Purchase, Jefferson broke into this "far fam'd and far fetch'd" cheese and served it to his guests. Republicans raved, while Federalists pronounced it wretched.

Twice a year, on New Year's Day and the 4th of July, the President threw open his doors to the public. The latter, he said, was the only birthday he ever celebrated. The festivities in Washington followed the same pattern from year to year. A dawn salute, a military parade, the President in mufti standing in review on his steps, then an oration. At noon the citizens, a hundred or two hundred, flowed into the Executive mansion, greeted by the President himself. Four large sideboards in the dining room offered cake, wine, punch, and other refreshments. From an adjacent room the Marine Band played partiotic airs. (Less than satisfied with the band, which also played at the Sunday services in the Capitol and summer concerts on the grounds of the Executive mansion, the President, in 1805, imported a band of Italian musicians such as he had dreamed of at Monticello.) There were always picturesque additions to the company: the turbaned Tunisian minister and his entourage, all richly garbed, or a delegation of Osage Indians in full regalia from the great Missouri. At two p.m. the citizens departed to wind up the festivities at a public dinner.

The President took only a modest part in the social life of the city. Public dinners, the dancing assembly, theatrical performances (by a touring company from Philadelphia) could boast his patronage but rarely his presence. He was a widower, of course, and that made a difference. Dolley Madison graciously filled the role of first lady as occasion required, and so did his daughter Martha during her visits. Martha possessed none of Dolley's buxom beauty and bubbling charm. She was described as "rather homely, a delicate likeness of her father." But she won the admiration of everyone. Jefferson had put the amusements of the *bon ton* behind him with one exception, horse racing. The turf season in the fall, on the heights beyond Georgetown, was the social event of the year. The races featured the finest blooded-stock of Virginia and Maryland, the human with the equinine. Congress, if it happened to be in session, found excuses to adjourn; hundreds of fashionable carriages surrounded the turf; four or five hundred people of both sexes, all ages and conditions, from the President to the meanest beggar, attended the races. In his love of the turf, Jefferson showed his Virginia colors. Some New Englanders were offended, regarding it as the sport of nabobs, extravagant, immoral, and vulgar; yet they too could be seen at the races. Senator Plumer talked with the President after a day at the turf: "His conversation was vapid—mere commonplace observations on the weather—crops and sickness of particular districts. From these he went into an elaborate defense of horse racing—he said it was an effectual means to improve the breed of horses . . . that all people will have their amusements—that horse racing is less injurious to the people than playing at cards or dice as the Bostonians do."

For eight long years the President played host to congressmen and, in fact, to all official Washington. One of his successors, John F. Kennedy, on the occasion of a dinner for Nobel laureates of the Americas, called his guests "the most extraordinary collection of talents . . . that has ever been gathered together at the White House, with the possible exception of when Thomas Jefferson dined alone." But the President seldom dined alone. Nothing in the presidency, he once remarked, equaled the trials of the table. The burden of entertaining 176 congressmen, as well as foreign diplomats, cabinet officers, and local or visiting dignitaries, was thrust upon him by the meager conveniences of social life in the capital. The President's House, unfinished, scantily furnished though it was, offered to congressmen trapped in this wasteland the only certain refuge from social misery.

By nature and training a hospitable man, Jefferson would have opened his doors to these poor creatures without any ulterior motive. Given the situation, however, he could not help but recognize the political value of what he was doing. In the opinion of unfriendly observers, it was all part of the game of subverting Congress to the executive will. Jefferson ignored the criticism when it came from Federalists who, after all, were pleased to accept his hospitality; but when it came from a Republican who wished to place his independence beyond the shadow of suspicion, he explained the practice in terms which, though political, disclaimed any motive of improper influence. "I cultivate personal intercourse with the members of the legislature," he said, "that we may know one another and have opportunity of little explanations of circumstances, which, not understood might produce jealousies and suspicions injurious to the public interest, which is best promoted by harmony and mutual confidence among its functionaries. I depend much on the members for the local information necessary on local matters, as well as for the means of getting at public sentiment." The President did not turn his house into a kind of congressional club for nothing. He expected, and apparently got, a more sympathetic Congress because of it.

His procedure was well described by a Federalist representative three weeks after the opening of the Seventh Congress: "Under the new order of things, there are no Levees, but the members are invited to dine with the President in rotation, and what is strange . . . only Federalists or only Democrats are invited at the same time. The number in a day is generally eight, and there is one of the heads of Departments, which makes nine." The entertainment of Federalists and Republicans, occasionally called Democrats in derision, was thus separate but equal. Also, Jefferson tried to break down the political cohesiveness of certain boardinghouse groups by mixing the congressmen together. Eight or ten was the usual number; but with other guests, as many as eighteen dined at Jefferson's table. Every other day or so he sent a batch of billets to the Capitol. Guests were invited for 3:30 p.m., the hour Congress usually rose. Down Pennsylvania Avenue they came, to the great white house barren of landscape and (until late in Jefferson's presidency) surrounded by a crude post and rail fence. Servant or private secretary met them at the door and ushered them into a reception room, where the President joined the party and conversed for perhaps half an hour before dinner. Pell-mell was the rule of the house; the guests, accordingly, found what place they could at the table. The dining room, needless to say, was not the resplendent state dining room of the present-day White House. Jefferson had furnished the smaller dining room with an oval table, which he considered more democratic than the rectangular table used by his predecessors. There was neither head nor foot. Green canvas, instead of a bothersome Brussels carpet, covered the floor. Clergymen remarked that no blessing was ever offered. To facilitate the service Jefferson introduced some of his own contrivances, for example, a set of circular shelves on a revolving door that quickly dispatched dishes between kitchen and dining room with the minimum traffic, and dumb waiters sometimes set beside the guests at the table. The food was abundant and good, a combination of French and Virginia cookery, and if hardly of gourmet quality a great treat in this "land of hog, hominey and hoecake." Manesseh Cutler of Massachusetts described the menu of a dinner he rated below par for the President's table: "Rice soup, round of beef, turkey, mutton, ham, loin of veal, cutlets of mutton or veal, fried eggs, fried beef, a pie called macaroni. . . . Ice cream very good, crust wholly dried, crumbled into thin flakes; a dish somewhat like pudding—inside white as milk or curd, very porous and light, covered with cream sauce—very fine. Many other jimcracks, a great variety of fruit, plenty of wines, and good." Cutler had never tasted macaroni before, thought it some kind of onion, and did not like it. Ice cream was a delicacy, though Jefferson served it in all seasons by virtue of his ice house, filled every winter with two-inch thick cakes of ice cut from a pond below the house. As for the wines, they gave a truly Epicurean finish to the dinners. There were many kinds, all sent to Jefferson by consuls and friends in a dozen ports. No healths or toasts were ever drunk. "You drink as you please, and converse at your ease." The ladies, when ladies were present, retired to another room; tea and coffee were served; games of cards, the usual evening diversion in other houses, were never played, general conversation taking its place. The guests were gone by eight o'clock. "We enjoyed ourselves very well," Cutler wrote, "were social, and handsomely received and entertained."

Part of the enjoyment was the President's talk. Everyone expected him to take the lead, and he usually did, tactfully drawing out even the most retiring guests in conversation that encompassed the table. He made it a rule to avoid political talk lest it cause any uneasiness to his guests. Politeness, he once lectured his grandson and namesake, is "artificial good humor," the sacrifice of one's own little preferences and conveniences to the gratification of others. "Good humor and politeness never introduce into mixed society a question on which they foresee there will be a difference of opinion." At any other table than Jefferson's conversation on such a rule was almost sure to be insipid. But he could discourse on so many subjects, from travels in France to the natural history of parrots, there was never a void. Benjamin Latrobe rated a dinner at the President's House "an elegant mental treat." "Literature, wit, a little business, with a great deal of miscellaneous remarks on agriculture and building, filled every minute." John Quincy Adams, who came into Congress from Massachusetts in 1803, had long ago severed his youthful attachment to the Virginian, yet could still be enchanted by his talk. "You never can be an hour in this man's company without something of the marvellous." Once when the conversation turned to the French Revolution, Jefferson reflected how contrary to all expectations "this great bouleversement" had ended, as if the last dozen years had been a dream, and then said with casual aplomb that the French should return where they had started in 1789 and call back the old family. With an eye to good table talk, Jefferson played certain favorites among the congressmen. Dr. Samuel L. Mitchill, of New York, was his special delight. A physician educated at Edinburgh, learned in many scientific fields, actively associated with Robert Livingston and DeWitt Clinton in both scientific and political enterprise, Mitchill exemplified enlightened republicanism. Jefferson called him his "Congressional Dictionary."

Concern over the President's backstairs influence dampened the pleasure of the Federalist guests. The concern seemed justified. "No one can know Mr. Jefferson and be his personal enemy," one Federalist observed. And political enmity was no certain proof against the charms of his personality. Federalist anxiety on this point went back several years to the time when, as Secretary of State and Vice President, Jefferson had supposedly made many good men dupes by his "philosophizing dinners." Moreover, it soon became apparent that he was not averse to using his hospitality, or rather withholding it, as a political whip. In 1803 he declined to send invitations to the most forward Federalists, Bayard, Rutledge, and Griswold, who had offended him personally in one fashion or another. Word of this "marked neglect" passed through congressional corridors. In February four Connecticut members indignantly refused presidential invitations, and at the last minute Jefferson had to scurry to Georgetown for gentlemen to fill their places at the table. When Congress assembled in November 1804, Senator Plumer noted that the President had altered the form of his invitations. No longer "The President of the United States" but "Thomas Jefferson" requested the congressmen's pleasure at dinner. Asking Giles about this change, Plumer was told it was introduced to give Jefferson greater freedom, since as a private gentleman he was under no obligation to invite any member who abused him. "It discovers a littleness of mind unworthy of the President of the United States," Plumer noted. "As President—he ought never to act toward an individual as if he knew what was said for or against him or his measures." An excellent rule, one which Jefferson took into the presidency and always approved in the abstract. But, as he saw it, certain Federalists had traveled outside the bounds of political opposition and muddied the waters of social intercourse by participating in slanderous attacks on his personal character. Why should he honor men who thus trafficked in dishonor? And how could the easy sociability of his dinners be maintained in the presence of such men? Unfortunately, what began as a selective exclusion traced the typical route of a vicious circle—insult from one side produced insult from the other, until in his second term many Federalists were refusing to call on him even at New Year's, and he, at the same time, was refusing to invite them to dinner.

By then, too, dissension in the Republican ranks caused Jefferson to strike the names of schismatics from his guest lists. The chief of these was John Randolph. There is in Jefferson's papers a detailed record in his most minikin hand of the persons entertained at every dinner from December 1, 1804, to the end of his presidency. The record for the previous years has not survived, though the general picture that emerges for the later period probably holds good for the former. During the second session of the Eighth Congress, a total of 110 days, the President entertained upwards to 600 guests on fifty occasions. The great number were congressmen, and three of them, Randolph, Giles, and Mitchill, were his guests as many as five times. Randolph was eliminated in 1806. Clearly, Republicans as well as Federalists could fall from executive grace. It does not follow that those who remained in his grace, supping at his table, voted any differently in Congress because of it, though this was sometimes said. Asked to explain the Senate's consent to an unpopular executive appointment, Vermont Republican Stephen Bradley snapped, "The President's dinners have silenced them." In these matters the lines of cause and effect cannot be traced.

Entertainment on so large a scale required a well-managed household and considerable expense. The President's annual salary of $25,000 adequately covered his expenses, or so it would seem, but made no contribution toward the solvency of his still precarious estate. The principal items in his Washington accounts were food, wine, and servants. The first ran in the neighborhood of $6500 a year. Wine was an extravagance he could not do without. During his first term he spent about $2400 annually on wines; in his second, the cellar being stocked, considerably less. He personally attended to the wines, no small job in itself, and after a time computed his orders on the basis of actual consumption. Over a given period champagne, for instance, was consumed at the rate of one bottle to three and one-seventh persons, so he fixed the annual requisition at 500 bottles. There were usually eight to ten servants, whose combined wages came to something over $200 annually.

The day-to-day management of the household belonged to the *maître d'hotel* Etienne Le Maire, who Jefferson retained in August 1801, instructing him "that while I wish to have everything good in its kind, and handsome in style, I am a great enemy of waste and useless extravagance, and see them with real pain." One observer described Le Maire as "a very smart man, well educated, and as much a gentleman in his appearance as any man." He evidently met the President's exacting standards, for he remained in his service to the end. Almost any morning of the week he could be seen in the market at Georgetown purchasing supplies of meat and eggs, fruit and vegetables, often to the tune of $50 a day. The French chef, M. Julien, ran the kitchen under Le Maire's supervision, but no detail of domestic management, least of all this one, escaped Jefferson's personal attention. He still imported from abroad certain more or less standard items in his menu, macaroni, for example, and acquired others from Richmond or elsewhere. His unfailing interest in all things botanical and culinary is exhibited in an elaborate table arranged under the heading "A Statement of the Vegetable market at Washington, during a period of 8 years, wherein the earliest and latest appearance of each article within the whole 8 years is noted." Here it becomes apparent that he and his guests generally enjoyed broccoli for only two weeks in April, artichokes from early June to mid-July, tomatoes from mid-July until November, raspberries for but one week in the spring, lima beans for but three short weeks in late summer, and so on. On his daily excursions Jefferson often talked to gardeners with a view to improving the market of the federal city. In the winter months, salads were a special problem. "Would it be within the scope of Mr. Bailey's plan of gardening for the common market," he inquired in 1802, "to make a provision of endive for the ensuing winter, so as to be able to furnish Th. J. with a salad of endive every day through the winter till the spring salading shall commence . . . ?" Evidently it was not, for in December two and one-half years later Jefferson was sending to Baltimore for lettuce and endive.

The President's hospitality, easy and informal in the Virginia manner, presented no problem to his American guests—it was the custom of the country—but to foreign diplomats trained in another school, taught to insist on points of honor, it could be a jolt. The introduction into official society of "the principle of equality, or *pêle-mêle*," was the sequel to his revolt against the "courtly" forms of his predecessors; and although he might have excepted foreign envoys from the rule, he determined not to do so. For a time things went swimmingly. The only foreign minister of rank, Don Carlos Martinez de Yrujo, spent most of his time in Philadelphia, some of it in search of a French chef for the President. He had recently married the daughter of Governor McKean, and being indebted to Jefferson for interceding with the Spanish court to prolong his tour of duty in the United States, he made no protest against the new democratic canons. Nor did the new Dutch minister. This was reserved for Anthony Merry, the first British minister credited to the Jeffersonian court, who arrived in November 1803. He had been portrayed by Rufus King as "a plain, unassuming, and amiable man," as perhaps he was; but his imperious lady, certainly, had pretensions of another order.

The Merrys arrived in a dreary season. They could not find a decent house, and when they acquired an indecent one (actually two small houses side by side) could not find the servants to staff it. They despised Washington from the first moment. "Why it is a thousand times worse than the worse parts of Spain!" Merry exploded. The manner of his reception by the President contributed to these jaundiced feelings. He went with Madison and, finding the reception room empty, they proceeded down the hall to the President's study when he suddenly appeared, as casual as may be, and there in the awkwardness of the hallway Madison made the introductions. "Mr. Jefferson's appearance soon explained to me that the general circumstances of my reception had not been accidental, but studied," Merry reported. "I, in my official costume, found myself at the hour of reception he had himself appointed, introduced to a man as president of the United States, not merely in undress, but *actually standing in slippers down at the heels*, and both pantaloons, coat, and under-clothes indicative of utter slovenliness and indifference to appearances, and in a state of negligence actually studied." It was a deliberate insult to his government, Merry concluded. Perhaps it was. Perhaps Jefferson recalled that morning the insults Americans had received from British ministers and chose this occasion to return the injury. More likely, however, his appearance and conduct were quite unaffected. He was in his usual working attire, the same casual morning dress he wore to receive all and sundry, and presumably saw no reason to affect another appearance for the British Minister. He may have hoped to dispel false expectations and bring the Englishman promptly to American ground. If Merry failed to take the hint and, instead, chose to interpret the reception as a humiliating affront to his sovereign, it could not be helped.

A day or two later Jefferson entertained the Merrys at dinner. The Madisons were there, as were the Yrujos and the Pichons (Louis Pichon, the French chargé d'affaires) and several others. Supposing that the dinner was in his honor, Merry silently fumed at

Pichon's presence, a mere chargé and an enemy Frenchman to boot. He did not realize that the President gave no official dinners, eschewed rank, and, as Madison later explained, at his table threw a mantle of oblivion over hostile relations. When dinner was announced Jefferson offered his arm to Dolley Madison and over her demurring whispers, "Take Mrs. Merry," escorted her to the place at his right. Mrs. Merry was two seats further down the table, while her poor husband scurried to find any seat at all. "This will be cause of war," the Marchiones Yrujo was heard to remark. Four days later the Merrys received the same treatment at a dinner given by the Secretary of State. So it went. Merry poured his heart out to his government, thereby threatening to turn a social spat into an international incident. He refused further social intercourse with the President. Yrujo, who had had a falling-out with the administration, took sides with Merry. The two diplomats' wives turned heel on the cabinet wives. It was, said Madison, a "display of diplomatic superstition, truly extraordinary in this age and in this country."

The arrival on the embattled social scene of Jerome Bonaparte and his American bride introduced a new element which tended to confirm Merry in his belief that he was the victim of a rapprochement between the United States and France following upon the Louisiana Purchase and the resumption of hostilities in Europe. Several months earlier, while on a visit to the United States, Napoleon's youngest brother had dazzled, courted, and wed Elizabeth Patterson of Baltimore. She was not only a raving beauty but also a niece of the Maryland Smiths, who prated on this remarkable family alliance. Jefferson felt uncomfortable about the marriage. It was sure to invite Napoleon's wrath, and he might think the President of the United States should have prevented it. Yet Jefferson did not wish to displease the Smiths or allow reasons of state to come between the course of true love. He entertained the glittering young couple, with the Smiths and others, at a gala dinner. Merry exploded when he learned that the President, who had snubbed his wife, had escorted Mme Bonaparte to dinner. Etiquette did not justify this discrimination, but the ladies themselves did. Mrs. Merry was a large puffed-up woman, as gaudy as a peacock. Everybody in Washington tittered over her grotesque attire—a mélange of satin and crepe and spangles with shawl fantastically draped from head to heels—and her garish display of diamonds at the Robert Smiths' ball for the Bonapartes. Mme Bonaparte, on the other hand, was a bewitching young lady clothed in the highest, and scantiest, of Parisian fashions. Her appearance at the ball "threw all the company into confusion . . . , no one dared to look at her but by stealth," and men who did said "they could put all the clothes she had on in their vest pocket."

If the President was amused by this comic opera, he was not unaware of possibly serious repercussions. It was his turn to be snubbed. When he invited Merry and Yrujo alone to dine with him, they excused themselves, saying they would have to write to their governments for instructions. "It is unheard of," Jefferson fumed, "that a foreign minister has need of the permission of his court to sit down at the table of the head of state: I shall be highly honored when the King of England is good enough to let Mr. Merry come and eat my soup." He wrote an explanation of the whole affair to Monroe, at that time the American envoy in London. Merry himself should not be blamed; he appeared to be an amiable enough man, but his wife, a perfect virago, "has established a degree of dislike among all classes which one would have thought impossible in so short a time." As to the sticking point of precedence, "We have told him [Merry] that the principle of society as well as of government with us is the equality of the individuals composing it; that no man here would come to a dinner where he was to be marked with inferiority to any other; that we might as well attempt to force our principle of equality at St. James's as he his principle of precedence here." Of course, nothing in the application of the principle to social and public occasions was meant to degrade a foreign government or its minister, only, rather, that where the latter happened to sit at dinner, who escorted his wife to the table, and so on had no bearing whatever on the respect accorded him and his government. Jefferson had been in the habit, he explained, of asking one of the cabinet wives "to come and take care of the company, and as she was to do the honors of the table I handed her to dinner myself." Merry had objected, seconded by Yrujo, and so he had discontinued the practice in favor of strict adherence to pell mell, that is, giving his hand to the lady who happened to be nearest him. Alas, the practice was no more acceptable to the dissident ministers. The pretension, he said, "that agents of foreign nations should assume to dictate to us what shall be the laws of our society" had excited emotions of indignation and contempt in the United States, and he feared that the Merrys would "put themselves in coventry" because of it. This proved to be the case. Officially, Merry went about his business in the usual fashion. But unable to enlist the support of the foreign office for his claims, unwilling to yield to the rule of pell mell, he and his wife remained virtual exiles from Washington society to the detriment of Anglo-American relations.

As ludicrous as this little drama was, it was acted on a stage and with players that gave it sober meaning and purpose. Jefferson, in his role, endeavored to fashion a national style in the forms, the ceremonies, the manners of the state. It was an old but as yet unfulfilled passion. He had winced at Washington's levees, at Adams's pomposity, at an American diplomacy alternately futile and servile —the spirit of the nation rebelled at these expressions of the government. To adapt the outward demeanor of the government to the inner spirit of the people was a work of enduring importance beyond the trifles that occasioned it. The work took tangible form in a series of "Rules of Etiquette" approved by the cabinet and published in the press. The rules codified the experience of the administration in the Merry affair: foreign ministers were to pay the first visit to executive heads (Merry had expected the first visit), differences of rank or grade among diplomats and their wives gave no precedence, and when brought together in society they were perfectly equal to everyone else. The experience that led to these rules helped to put the nation in possession of itself. Viewed in this light the President's duel with Anthony Merry was a gesture, modest but dramatic, on behalf of American nationality.

The constant round of entertainment together with weighty affairs of state left Jefferson little time for intellectual pursuits. "It is rare I ever indulge myself in the luxury of philosophy," he apologized to a kindred spirit in 1802, and he would have to repeat himself many times during the next seven years. Year after year he was reelected president of the American Philosophical Society, although he never actually presided and his main service was as a transmission belt of other men's ideas. His presence at the head of the nation lent prestige to scientific endeavor. The National Institute of France elected him, alone among Americans, one of eight foreign associates. He continued to act as a kind of Johnny Appleseed for European flora. Being a farmer on leave, as it were, he tried to keep abreast of things agricultural. On the hint of a Pennsylvania agriculturist, he adapted the pointed toe to his moldboard of the plow, had new models made, and a circular printed to describe the method. According to Mrs. Smith, his favorite room in the elephantine house on Pennsylvania Avenue was the one he called his "cabinet." Books, maps, and charts lined the walls; scientific instruments, garden and carpenter tools lay on the table; in the window recesses were the flowers and plants he tended; and suspended over the roses and geraniums was a mocking bird in a cage. When alone he often opened the cage and the bird perched on his shoulder and sang as he worked at his desk.

Believing that he and his party embodied the sentiments of the great majority of farmers of the country, Jefferson wished his administration to make a positive contribution to agricultural science. He at once took steps to implement an idea drawn from the example of the English Board of Agriculture and first recommended to Congress by Washington in 1796. The project was to unite all the state agricultural societies through a central organization in the capital. Madison, Dr. Mitchill, and the versatile Isaac Briggs, of Maryland, helped to bring this incipient national board of agriculture into being in 1803. Each local society designated delegates, usually congressmen, to the national society. Madison was elected president at the first meeting. The society laid plans to establish an experimental agricultural garden in Washington and resolved to publish nationally the best contributions sifted from the proceedings of the local associations, thereby ensuring, in Jefferson's words, "that not a useful thought of any individual of the nation at large may be lost." Unfortunately, however, an entirely voluntary society, without an active executive secretary, without government subvention, lacked the most important attributes of the English Board, as Arthur Sinclair, its secretary, pointed out to Jefferson. For all his expressed opposition to government intervention in the economy, Jefferson was usually quite prepared to suspend the principle where a scientific purpose could be shown. In this instance, apparently, he did not think the national interest would be served by the creation of a quasi-public agency for the encouragement of agriculture.

Of the more esoteric sciences paleontology remained his principal interest. In 1801 Charles Willson Peale, that wonderful impresario of American science, was excavating the bones of a mammoth discovered on a New York farm. The place was deep in water, and Peale asked Jefferson for the loan of a pump from a naval vessel. The loan was promptly authorized, but Peale, with money borrowed from the American Philosophical Society, devised his own scheme for draining the pit. Jefferson must have marveled at Peale's ingenuity: a great wheel 20 feet in diameter, wide enough for men to walk within "as squirrels in a cage," which turned a revolving chain of buckets that conveyed the water out of the pit, and thus enabled the workmen to dig the bones from the mud. (The scene is wonderfully portrayed in Peale's painting, "Exhuming the Mastadon.") It was a precious cache. Within a few months Peale mounted the first skeleton of the mammoth (or mastadon), indeed the first fossil skeleton ever mounted in America and probably the second in the world—the megatherium in Madrid, about which Jefferson had learned in 1797, being the first. It would have made an interesting addition to the *Notes on Virginia* had the author ever found time to revise that prophetic work. Peale exhibited the skeleton in his famous museum in Philadelphia, where it attracted unusual attention. His artist sons Raphael and Rembrandt took a second skeleton, also mounted from the New York remains, for exhibition in Europe, whose savants had never seen this curiosity of the New World. (To celebrate their departure Peale staged a "feast within the breast of the mammoth" for a dozen men!) Jefferson was a distant spectator to these proceedings, but he kept in close touch with Peale, Caspar Wistar, and others, and served as an unofficial clearing house for all discoveries in paleontology. Later, in his second term, he sponsored a private venture of his own at the Big Bone Lick on the Ohio, the legendary source of ancient remains which George Rogers Clark had first tapped for him in 1781. Now, a quarter-century later, he sent William Clark (of Lewis and Clark fame) to the Lick to unearth everything he could. From the great collection of fossil bones Clark shipped to Washington, Jefferson presented some to the Society in Philadelphia, kept a few for his cabinet at Monticello, and gave the rest to the National Institute in Paris. The last were promptly displayed in the Museum of National History, where they enabled George Cuvier to reconstruct not one but two extinct species of the mammoth.

Jefferson's connections with Peale went beyond paleontology. Philosophical Hall could no longer contain his museum. In 1802 he revived his old dream of a national institution and wrote to Jefferson proposing such an establishment in Washington. The vision was grand—Jefferson would have loved to forward it. But he pointed to the constitutional obstacle, and without stating his own opinion of congressional power to encourage science and learning, declined to take up this hazardous cause, at least for the present. Two years later he was meditating a plan for the support of the museum in Washington by contributions from the several states. On his own scale of values, the advancement of science had more importance than political concepts like state rights; but, with the natural history museum as with the agricultural institution, he was unwilling to run the gamut of opposition sure to be formidable, especially among his own followers who possessed his constitutional scruples without his commitment to enlightenment. In the field of invention Peale introduced Jefferson to two new marvels sprung from the mechanical genius of John Isaac Hawkins, who had built him a piano some years before. The physiognatrace was a device for making silhouettes. Raphael Peale visited Washington to take Jefferson's profile, which was reproduced in quantity and distributed as a souvenir to viewers of the mammoth at Peale's Museum. This was a bagatelle. More useful was the polygraph, a new type of copying machine, which Jefferson pronounced "a most precious invention." It was a desk mounting two pens in such a way that what was written by one was perfectly duplicated by the mechanical arm of the other. At Peale's instigation Jefferson introduced the polygraph in his office in February 1804, and as any researcher in the President's letters (duplicates for the most part) can testify it was a vast improvement on the copying press. Jefferson suggested many refinements, and Peale, who took over the machine from Hawkins, incorporated them in later models that often got their first test in the President's office. He was the machine's best salesman, actually wrote a testimonial for Peale's use, and sent polygraphs to friends and heads of state on three continents.

During the first two weeks of June 1804, Jefferson was honored with a visit from the brilliant young scientist-explorer Baron Alexander von Humboldt. He had just completed a five-year expedition in Spanish America, from the Caribbean to the remote provinces of the southern continent, a thousand miles on the Orinoco by canoe, to Quito and Lima in the Andes, thence to Acapulco by sail, and a year's exploration of Mexico. Announcing himself from Philadelphia, Humboldt said he had been inspired by Jefferson's liberalism from his earliest youth. Peale, who afterwards painted his portrait, escorted Humboldt and his companions to Washington. The Baron came to see not the President of the United States but Thomas Jefferson, author of the *Notes on Virginia*, votary of New World enlightenment, and luminary of science and freedom. Although the visitor stayed at Stelle's Hotel on Capitol Hill, he was given the freedom of Jefferson's house and spent many hours in easy conversation with him. On one occasion the Baron came upon his host romping on all fours with his grandchildren in the drawing room. "You have found me playing the fool, Baron," Jefferson remarked, "but I am sure to you I need make no apology." In truth, the Baron was as modest and friendly as he was enlightened. He admired the village capital, did not condescend, unlike so many foreigners, and from the vastness of his knowledge of Mexico and the southern hemisphere was able to capture the immensity of the American future in the year after the Louisiana Purchase. Just at the time New Spain came within the orbit of Jefferson's plans and transactions, Humboldt generously provided maps, statistical reports, information on mines, roads, crops, Indian tribes, settlements, and so on, information that until then had been locked up in Spanish archives. "We all consider him a very extraordinary man . . . ," Gallatin said. "I am not apt to be easily pleased, and he was not prepossessing to my taste, for he speaks . . . twice as fast as anybody I know, German, French, Spanish, and English all together." He poured forth his knowledge—geographical, geological, meterological, ethnological—in volcanic eruptions at Jefferson's table. There were at least three dinners at the President's House. According to Peale, "Not a single toast was given or called for, or politics touched on, but the subjects of Natural History, and improvements of the conveniences of life, manners of different nations described, or other agreeable conversation animated the whole company." The eighteenth century had passed but its spirit still glowed in the conversation of scientists and philosophers of the Old World and the New gathered around the President's table. When Humboldt departed, Jefferson did not hesitate to name him "the most scientific man of his age he had ever seen." The Baron, for his part, went away more convinced than before that the future of civilization lay with America, and that Jefferson, "the most virtuous of men," was its prophet.

The boundaries between science and government overlapped vaguely in a number of areas, some already noted, others still to be observed, while in quite another area, architecture, as related to the planning of the federal city, the President's responsibility was not only definite but cheerfully accepted. Since his association with the early planning of the city, it had fallen on hard times. Very few government lots had been sold at auction, and great private speculators in real estate had failed and landed in debtors' prison. Public morale had been shattered. The original scheme of financing public buildings and improvements by the sale of lots had of necessity been abandoned to a considerable degree, and loans from Maryland and Virginia became the last resort, amounting to $250,000 when Jefferson took office. Revenue from sales proved insufficient to service the loans, to say nothing of repaying them. It was difficult to see how the city, so deficient in active capital, could ever become a going concern. "The situation of Washington is certainly very fine," a visiting Philadelphian observed, "but it has long been ascertained that people cannot live much less grow rich upon prospects. . . . No houses are building; those already built are not finished and many are falling rapidly to decay." In the ghoulish vision of some men Washington was already beginning to resemble the ruins of Palmyra or some other ancient city. Because of the chronic complaints of the city, the capital suffered. Shortages of money, workmen, and materials delayed progress on the public buildings, and congressmen grew impatient at the inconveniences they endured. Bills were introduced to move the capital to Baltimore or Philadelphia. They found little support, but a dissident minority, appealing to the local sentiment for self-government in the District of Columbia, launched a movement to retrocede large portions of the "ten mile square" to Maryland and Virginia, and this could only be seen as a first step in the liquidation of the Potomac capital. Jefferson had to contend with this opposition and at the same time contribute what he could to fulfilling the grand design of the federal city.

In 1801 the President's authority continued to be exercised through the Board of Commissioners; the following year, however, Congress abolished the board, devolving its functions on a superintendent. The same legislation incorporated Washington as an independent municipality, thereby placing it on an equal footing with the sister cities of Georgetown and Alexandria, except that the mayor, like the superintendent, was a presidential appointee. The mayor, Robert Brent, who presided over an elected council, was a personal friend, as were most of the men at the center of the city's affairs. Jefferson's influence was constant. He found some difficulty determining where his authority started and stopped in the perfect maze of jurisdiction—state, congressional, presidential, municipal— that had grown up around the city and the district. Clearly he had responsibility for the execution of the original plan of the city, which included streets, squares, parks, buildings, and so on for the use of the United States. These concerns could not be separated into air-tight boxes, however, so Jefferson's hand reached into almost every phase of the city's development, from the granting of liquor licenses to the building of the navy yard, from markets and canals to schools and militia.

In the condition of the city as he found it, the L'Enfant plan was still largely a blueprint dependent upon the appropriation of money by Congress. Jefferson at once directed the commissioners to give top priority to two projects. First, the completion of a good roadway from Georgetown down Pennsylvania and New Jersey Avenues, a distance of four miles, to the Eastern Branch. By 1804 Pennsylvania Avenue assumed the form Jefferson had designed for it: a broad thoroughfare bordered by rows of trees, behind these on either side narrow roadways, a second row of trees, gutters, and footpaths. The trees were Lombardy poplars, a special favorite, though he loved all trees, planted them at every opportunity, and could not bear to see precious specimens destroyed. (Once in conversation with Mrs. Smith, he exclaimed, "How I wish that I possessed the power of a despot!" Met with disbelief, he went on, "Yes, I wish I was a despot that I might save the noble and beautiful trees that are daily falling sacrifice to the cupidity of their owners, or the necessity of the poor," who cut them for firewood.) The grandeur of a mall, such as he had conceived and L'Enfant had embellished, was a luxury far out of reach in his time; but Pennsylvania Avenue brought to the city a touch of splendor and it endured in the form Jefferson gave to it for over thirty years. The second priority item was the construction of the south wing of the Capitol for the accommodation of the House of Representatives. The Capitol had been a colossal headache form the beginning. A succession of superintendents had struggled with William Thornton's grand design; no sooner had the Senate taken possession of the north wing than it was in need of major repairs and alterations; and another ten years passed before the House moved into its own quarters. The expense, inconveniences, and delays nettled Congress and spurred on opponents of the Washington venture.

Acutely aware of these problems, Jefferson made up his mind to place the Capitol, together with the other buildings, under the superintendence of the best man he could find. In March 1803, three days after he signed into law a far-reaching act of Congress appropriating $50,000 to the public buildings, Jefferson appointed Benjamin H. Latrobe to the post. Nothing in the letter of the statute authorized this appointment, but seeing in the law an opportunity to banish forever all doubts as to the future of the capital, he determined to make the most of it. Latrobe, born and trained in England, had come to Virginia in 1796. There he had planned the penitentiary in Richmond and completed the façade of Jefferson's capitol. Jefferson had known him personally for five years, first in Philadelphia when at work on his Greek Revival building for the Bank of Pennsylvania. Only the year before Jefferson had called him to Washington to plan a dry dock for the navy yard. Latrobe's combination of architectural and engineering genius (he was currently the engineer for the Delaware and Chesapeake Canal) could not be matched by anyone in the United States. He admired Jefferson both as a statesman and as the father of the arts in his adopted country. The respect each man had for the other became the foundation of a fruitful partnership, one that actually benefitted from their contrasting tastes in architecture. Both were classicists, but Latrobe confessed to being "a bigoted Greek," while Jefferson, if not so ready to confess it, was an equally bigoted Roman. The enthusiasm of one checked the enthusiasm of the other.

Latrobe formed his plan for the Capitol after consultation with the President. He was to adhere to the Thornton design so far as practicable, not because it was beyond improvement in Jefferson's eyes but because it had been emphatically endorsed by Washington and accepted without question for a decade. Latrobe obeyed reluctantly, for he was "shocked" by Thornton's conception. Of course, the exterior style was already set: the south wing must repeat the façade of the north wing. The interior was another matter. Jefferson himself put forth the idea of raising the Senate chamber from the basement level to the main floor. And this was done, releasing the lower floor to the Supreme Court after extensive repair and remodeling of the entire wing. As to the House wing, its inner walls in the elliptical shape Thornton had prescribed were already partially built, covered over with a temporary roof under which the House had met since December 1801 when work on the Capitol stopped. But the walls were faulty and had to come down. Starting from the foundations, Latrobe was free to propose his own ideas for the House chamber. Jefferson met him halfway, insisting that the principal feature of the hall, a semicircular colonnade supporting a gallery, be retained, but allowing Latrobe to straighten the sides of Thornton's oval chamber. Thornton objected, the architects quarreled, and Jefferson tried to sooth feelings on both sides. To carve the frieze, the capitals for the columns (Corinthian on his orders) and other decorative stone work, he sent to Italy for craftsmen more richly endowed than native sculptors of ships' heads and mantelpieces. In 1806 his faithful friend Mazzei sent Giuseppe Franzoni and Giovanni Andrei, the vanguard of an Italian invasion in the decorative arts. The former executed an American eagle (specifications provided by Peale) to adorn the frieze and a statue of liberty placed above the Speaker's chair. These did not withstand the British torch in 1814, but the "corn cob capitals"—ears of corn rising upon columns fluted as cornstalks—carved in the basement of the north wing from Latrobe's highly original design, survived the wreckage. While Jefferson applauded this touch of Americanism, he was revolted by Latrobe's plan to raise a lantern (a cupola-like ornament to admit light) above the roof of the House wing. No classical model showed lantern, belfry, or cupola, and Jefferson considered them among the "degeneracies of modern architecture." Conceding the historical point, Latrobe nevertheless thought they might be beautiful in the proper place, as atop the Capitol. He lost this little skirmish yet finally prevailed. In his reconstruction of the Capitol after the War of 1812, Latrobe placed a lantern above each wing.

Jefferson's only serious problem with Latrobe was holding him to the appropriation sparingly doled out by Congress year by year. In his eagerness to finish the House chamber in 1807, Latrobe ran a deficit of $52,000, about 70 per cent over his total budget. Jefferson apologized to Congress and read the architect a stiff lecture on public economy and the principles of American government. Piled on top of the criticism he was receiving for acoustical and other defects in the new chamber, together with partisan rumors of executive displeasure, this was the last straw. The harassed architect threatened to resign. Jefferson hastened to reassure him; no one else, he was convinced, could do the job. Latrobe stayed on, finishing the two wings not long after Jefferson left the presidency. "I think," he then wrote to the architect, "that the work when finished will be a durable and honorable monument to our infant republic, and will bear favorable comparison with the remains of the same kind of the ancient republics of Greece and Rome." It is a pity that Jefferson never saw Latrobe's post-war reconstruction of the Capitol, complete with the modestly domed middle building, for it was, as he always believed it would be, "the first temple dedicated to the sovereignty of the people, embellishing with Athenian taste the course of a nation looking far beyond the range of Athenian destinies."

His own residence, the White House as it would later be called, remained in a half-finished state throughout his presidency. For the first several years the roof leaked, no elegant staircase was in place, the bedrooms were without paint, the east room (where Jefferson kept mammoth cheese and mammoth bones, hence called the mammoth room) had yet to receive plaster, furnishings were sparse, and the grounds barren of landscape. Gradually, under Latrobe's supervision, most of these deficiencies were removed: a new roof went on (sheet iron, by direction of the President, who had used it at Monticello and would direct Latrobe to use it on the Capitol as well), the staircase went up, the apartments were painted, new fur-

743

niture, though never enough, went in; finally, stone wall and stone steps rose outside, and the grounds—the President's sheep pasture—were gracefully sloped and seeded with grass. Jefferson developed a plan for landscaping the mansion but never found the money to carry it out. He did succeed in building colonnaded terraces on either side, like those he had designed for Monticello, and committed to the same services—meat house, wine cellar, storage, privies, stable, and so on.

Jefferson was a planner by instinct, of governments, buildings, farms, gardens, and towns. The last, town planning, is usually overlooked except in connection with Washington. Actually, his vision ranged much farther, and had the times been different and he free to practice his ideas, the face of America might have been changed for the better. The year before he became President, in the course of conversation with William Henry Harrison of the Northwest Territory, Jefferson spoke of the epidemics that so often besieged American cities and suggested that a remedy might be found in a modification of the common gridiron, or checkerboard, pattern of urban design. Leave every alternate square open, he said, and the infection would not spread. He had noted in Philadelphia that the yellow fever raged at its worst in the most crowded parts of the city, that it did not reach into the country and, in fact, that the contagion could not even be carried into this pure atmosphere. His theory as to the disease was wrong, of course, though he was not the only one to hold it at the time. Noah Webster set forth a similar theory, ascribing epidemics to the morbid state of the atmosphere in congested places, in his *Treatise on Pestilential Diseases* in 1801. It convinced Benjamin Rush and confirmed Jefferson's opinion, which, it might be observed, went along with his general prejudice against cities. Harrison, at any rate, liked Jefferson's idea. In 1802, after becoming Governor of Indiana Territory, he directed that a new town planned near the falls of the Ohio and called Jeffersonville be laid out on the Jeffersonian principle. The President was delighted by this innovation. "In Europe," he wrote, "where the sun does not shine more than half the number of days . . . it does in America, they can build their towns in a solid block with impunity. But here a constant sun produces too great an accumulation of heat to admit that. Ventilation is indispensably necessary." Unfortunately, when

Jeffersonville, Indiana, was finally laid out, diagonal streets in imitation of the L'Enfant plan were superimposed on the grid, cutting every open square into four small triangles; and within two decades the irrepressible commercial spirit had invaded what was left of Jefferson's "ventilating system." He recommended the plan to Governor Claiborne in New Orleans with no visible results; and apparently the only town in the United States built on the Jeffersonian grid was Jackson, Mississippi. The country being a Jeffersonian paradise of opportunity, above all in real estate, had little patience with the beauties and the pleasantries of the Jeffersonian style of life.

Louisiana!

The two administrations of Thomas Jefferson turned on two gigantic facts of geography, the Mississippi River and the Atlantic Ocean. In the first administration, the Mississippi occupied the foreground, and the President's efforts to secure the freedom of its navigation culminated in the Louisiana Purchase. The great effort of the second administration, directed to the freedom of America's seafaring frontier with Europe, met with crushing defeat. The two frontiers, of land and of ocean, westward and eastward, had divided American energies from the beginning; but now, with the acquisition of the vast spaces beyond the Mississippi, the nation's destiny seemed fixed in its direction, and so fabulous was the triumph of Jefferson's western vision that it greatly mitigated the costs of defeat in the Atlantic.

The vision took form in Jefferson's mind about the time of the American Revolution. In confronting the problems of Virginia's far-flung frontiers, he caught the idea of an "empire of liberty," an empire not of the ocean's deep where Albion roamed but a contiguous landward empire formed by the accretion of free and equal states as the Americans took possession of a nearly vacant continent. There were, in fact, almost no limits to his dreams of expansion. "Our confederacy must be viewed as the nest from which all America, North and South is to be peopled," he wrote in 1786. "We should take care not to think it for the interest of that great continent [South America and its appendages] to press too soon on the Spaniards.

Those countries cannot be in better hands. My fear is that they are too feeble to hold them till our population can be sufficiently advanced to gain it from them piece by piece. The navigation of the Mississippi we must have. This is all we are as yet ready to receive." In his inaugural address he spoke of the United States as "a chosen country, with room enough for our descendants to the hundredth and thousandth generation." What country? Surely not the one bounded by the 31st parallel, the Great Lakes, and the Mississippi, when nearly a million Americans already lived beyond the Appalachians; the country, rather, of Jefferson's imagination, certain to materialize in easy stages as Americans multiplied and pressed westward. Several months after the inaugural, he was meditating a resolution of the Virginia legislature, forwarded by Monroe, for the colonization of insurgent slaves and free Negroes in the empty spaces of North America or elsewhere. While in sympathy with the object, he opposed the settlement of the blacks any where on the continent. "However our present interests may restrain us within our limits," he explained, "it is impossible not to look forward to distant times, when our rapid multiplication will expand itself beyond those limits, and cover the whole northern, if not the southern, continent, with a people speaking the same language, governed in similar forms, and by similar laws; nor can we contemplate with satisfaction either blot or mixture on that surface." He did not think it necessary that this "empire" be united under one government, but it must be of one people united in the enterprise of freedom, his own country serving as common parent, midwife, and nurse of the entire "American system."

In 1801, as before, the Spanish colonies of Louisiana and the Floridas presented obstacles to American expansion. The danger lay, as Jefferson said, not in Spain's possession of these lands, but in Spanish dispossession by a strong and vigorous power, either Britain or France. So long as Spain remained lord of this domain it was America's for the asking. The Americans might, paraphrasing Montesquieu, thank God for putting Spain in the world, since of all nations she knew best how to possess a great empire with insignificance. There were but 50,000 people in Louisiana and the Floridas, the whole garrisoned with 1500 troops; the American trade at New Orleans outstripped the Spanish two to one; and the colonies showed a deficit of several hundred thousand dollars a year in the imperial accounts. The Spanish governors tried various schemes to check the onrushing Americans, but nothing seemed to work. "Their method of spreading themselves, and their policy [of forming new states] are so much to be feared by Spain as are their arms," one of the governors had said. For these reasons His Catholic Májesty had not been averse to using the North American colonies as pawns in the power plays of European diplomacy. In 1796 he had offered to give Louisiana to France if France could deliver Gibraltar to Spain. French interest in the recovery of the great colony she had lost in 1763 went back a number of years. Moustier, the second French Minister to the United States, had written an enthusiastic memoir on the subject in 1789. After the collapse of the Family Compact during the Revolution, the Girondists espoused liberation of the Spanish colonies, and Edmond Genêt sought to enlist American aid to foment rebellion in Louisiana. Then, in the aftermath of the Jay Treaty, the threat of an Anglo-American alliance, presaging an attack on Louisiana and the Floridas, isolating the French Antilles, closing all North America to French vessels, and wiping out, perhaps forever, the only basis for the re-establishment of French empire in the New World—these considerations impressed the Directory and its successors, including Napoleon Bonaparte.

In 1800 France was supreme in Europe, peace was in the offing, and Napoleon turned his fantastic energies to rebuilding the overseas empire. Louisiana and the Floridas were essential elements of a grand design centered on Santo Domingo, the richest of the colonies, then in the hands of the rebel blacks led by Toussaint L'Ouverture. The mainland colonies would provide the necessary economic and strategic support for a reconquered Santo Domingo and ensure French hegemony not only in the wide littoral from Florida to the Rio Grande but, ultimately, in the West Indies as well. By the Treaty of San Ildefonso, in October 1800, Spain secretly ceded Louisiana to France conditioned on an Italian throne for the Duke of Parma, Charles IV's brother-in-law. The King was content. France could far better defend Louisiana, and its principal value to Spain was as a buffer between the Americans and Mexico. He refused to part with the Floridas, however, despite the importunities of Napoleon's emissaries in Madrid. These negotiations continued. Meanwhile, Napoleon mounted an expedition to take possession of Louisiana at the great port of New Orleans.

Jefferson got wind of the retrocession in May 1801. At once an ominous shadow fell over his administration, so promising in every other aspect. Ominous, but nothing more at this time or for some months to come. Napoleon's plans of New World empire were involved in so many contingencies that they might never materialize. A bargain had presumably been made, but Napoleon had yet to fulfill his part of it. (He would, though not to Spain's satisfaction.) Whether or not the Floridas were included was unknown to the Americans, but without the Floridas Louisiana would be of doubtful value to France. And how could France take possession of Louisiana, much less garrison and colonize it, without first subduing the blacks in Santo Domingo? Moreover, Britain would surely not be indifferent to the revival of French power in the New World. The Peace of Amiens lay only a few months ahead (the preliminary articles were announced in November) but any Napoleonic peace was likely to prove unstable, and without peace in Europe the First Consul could not raise an empire in America. In view of these contingencies, Jefferson wisely resisted the temptation to sound alarms. While prudently moving to strengthen the American force at Fort Adams, just above the Spanish line on the Mississippi, he seemed anxious to make as little noise as possible. It was important to keep the country calm if diplomacy was to work. And given the ambiguity of the situation itself, a strategy of delay and maneuver improvised to meet events as they unfolded seemed to be called for.

Santo Domingo, as Jefferson appreciated, was the nub of Napoleon's problem. American policy toward that tormented island underwent a change with the coming of the new administration. During the Franco-American conflict of 1798–1800, Toussaint, the military commander of the colony, assumed the character of an independent ruler, and in order to maintain the island's commercial lifeline, he entered into a secret agreement with Britain and the United States which secured to those countries a trading monopoly. The arrangement lapsed, of necessity, with the Convention of 1800. The United States quit the rebels as part of the price of peace. But while acknowledging French sovereignty in Santo Domingo, Jefferson was also anxious to preserve America's flourishing trade with the island,

and this was impossible without dealing with the *de facto* sovereign, Toussaint. Inevitably, then, American policy was pitched to ambiguity, an ambiguity France must dispel as she fought to regain control of Santo Domingo. Assigned this task, Pichon, the newly arrived chargé d'affaires in 1801, sought positive assurances from Madison that the United States would uphold French sovereignty in Santo Domingo even in the face of a declaration of independence, which Toussaint had threatened to issue from time to time. Dissatisfied with the Secretary's yes-and-no response, Pichon took the problem to the President in July. France did not wish the cessation of American commerce with the island, since that would only drive Toussaint into British arms, Pichon said, but he was anxious for American cooperation in the restoration of French rule. To this Jefferson replied, first make peace with Britain, "then nothing will be easier than to furnish your army and fleet with everything and to reduce Toussaint to starvation." He reminded the chargé that the country had no love for the Negro leader: his example menaced every slaveholding state. Britain too, he believed, with good reason, would join in the concert, both to secure her own colonies and to put down "another Algiers in the seas of America." Pichon reported the conversation to Talleyrand, the Foreign Minister, and it apparently played some part in Napoleon's decision to go ahead with his plans for Santo Domingo. In the light of events still to come, Jefferson had aroused false expectations of American collaboration in the destruction of this incipient black republic in the Caribbean. Perhaps he had, in fact, promised too much to Pichon. But whatever he promised as to Santo Domingo carried an implicit warning as to Louisiana, which in his mind called for the same consideration of American interests on the Mississippi as France requested for her interests in the Caribbean.

In 1802 Jefferson not only failed to deliver the support allegedly promised for the subjugation of the rebel government but showed every disposition to let the French army rot in Santo Domingo. General Victor Leclerc, Napoleon's esteemed brother-in-law who was given command of the reconquest, landed his first army of 10,-000 men in January. He had been instructed to obtain money and supplies and other assistance from the United States. Pichon, pressing these claims, found the President "reserved and cold," hearing

749

from him as from Madison the familiar story that while the government wished France success it dared not make an enemy of Toussaint. When Leclerc proclaimed a blockade of the ports in rebel control, Jefferson refused to co-operate. Most of the supplies of both armies, rebel and French, were American, and Leclerc's high-handed treatment of merchants and expulsion of the consul were added irritants. For a time the war went well for the French. Toussaint, betrayed by his own generals and acting on Napoleon's assurances of his liberty and the liberty of the blacks, gave himself up to Leclerc. On first hearing of this event, Jefferson was incredulous. "What has been called a surrender of Toussaint to Leclerc, I suspect was in reality a surrender of Leclerc to Toussaint." Wish was father to the thought, and he erred in this detail. Yet his intuition proved sound. Toussaint's surrender was followed by arrest and deportation and imprisonment high in the Jura Mountains, ending in cold and solitary death a few months later. When the authentic report reached Jefferson he predicted that Leclerc's perfidy would be his undoing: "some other black leader will arise, and a war of extermination will ensue: for no second capitulation will ever be trusted by the blacks." And so it happened. "Rid us of these gilded Africans," Bonaparte lectured his general, "and we shall have nothing more to wish." Slavery would be restored, the island's sugar, coffee, indigo, and other tropical produce would again enrich French commerce, and the troops in Santo Domingo would be sent to possess Louisiana. But black arms and yellow fever annihilated one French army after another. In October, Leclerc estimated the nine months' loss at 24,000 men, and still he was not master of the island. A month later he too was dead. The implications of this catastrophe for Louisiana were, throughout, as clear to Jefferson as they were to Bonaparte. A great expedition destined for the Mississippi was mounting at Dunkirk in the summer of 1802, but no sooner were troops and supplies assembled than they were diverted to Santo Domingo. The Louisiana expedition never sailed.

Meanwhile, Robert R. Livingston, the American Minister in Paris, tried to conduct negotiations on Louisiana. Livingston was deaf, spoke no French, and quarreled with every public agent—the consul, the secretary of legation—with whom he had anything to do. As if these handicaps were not enough, neither his own government

nor the French ministry paid much attention to him. Talleyrand, recalled to service by Napoleon to direct the imperial policy he had
himself largely conceived, despised the Americans. Jefferson traced
his enmity to the XYZ incident, but it probably went back to his
unhappy experience in the United States as a refugee from revolution. He had, at any rate, been badly burned by the Americans in
1798 and did not intend to make the same mistake again when so
much depended on American good will. On matters of claims and
other business left over from the Convention of 1800, Talleyrand
was eminently approachable, but he turned into a Sphinx at the
mention of Louisiana. Only in June 1802 did Livingston learn that
the Floridas were not included in the bargain with Spain, though
the matter was still in negotiation.

Livingston's original instructions on Louisiana were as mild as
the situation would permit. He was to press reasons against the cession, but should he meet with resistance, he was to do nothing that
would "unnecessarily irritate our future neighbors, or check the liberality which they may be disposed to exercise in relation to the
trade and navigation through the mouth of the Mississippi." This
was the first and only imperative of American policy. It seemed little enough—the continuation of existing Spanish policy on the river.
But France had other plans for control of the trade and refused to
budge. "There never was a government in which less could be done
by negotiation than here—," Livingston reported. "There is no people, no legislature, no councillors—One man is everything. He seldom asks advice and never hears it unasked—his ministers are mere
clerks and his legislators and councillors parade officials." Communication between Washington and Paris was painfully slow. Partly for
these reasons, Jefferson and Madison conducted their own negotiation quite apart from Livingston's. Their official channel was Pichon. In dispatches to Talleyrand he presented the American case
against the French policy more effectively than an interested native
could possibly do. He cited the pertinent figures on trade and population in Louisiana, pointed to the dangers of again making enemies
of the Americans, argued that a strong and independent United
States was France's best hope, and begged his country to accede to
"that which the force of events will give them in spite of us." The
same words in Livingston's mouth seemed not to be heard. Frus-

trated, Livingston turned to Rufus King, hoping to arouse a sympathetic response in Whitehall. But Britain would not risk the Peace of Amiens on the chance of strengthening ties with the United States. Britain acquiesced in the reconquest of Santo Domingo. As to Louisiana, King reported, Lord Hawkesbury only grunted "highly interesting." If the United States could no longer play off one European power against another, it was difficult to see what leverage the country had left in the tasks of diplomacy.

Undismayed, Jefferson nevertheless struck a new course in April predicated on an old theory, in this case that he could summon the winds of Albion to carry him safely into port. His good friend Dupont de Nemours, who had come to the United States with his family in 1799 and plunged into various enterprises destined to make his name a household word, was returning to France, and out of his deep friendship for the President ("the American Turgot," Dupont called him, after his own master) offered his services in the matter of Louisiana. Unlike Pichon, unlike an influential group of Americanists in Paris, sometimes called the Ideologues, Dupont was not inalterably opposed to the Napoleonic policy. He was going home partly to raise capital for his American enterprises, partly with a view of making peace with the First Consul and securing a high post in the government. Napoleon might listen to him. As a sincere friend of both countries, anxious for a mutually advantageous settlement between them, he seemed peculiarly fitted for the role of an honest broker in the Louisiana negotiation. Jefferson seized the opportunity to use him. He had written an important letter to Livingston which he now entrusted to Dupont and left open for his inspection.

The letter began gravely. The retrocession of Louisiana formed a new epoch in America's foreign relations. Heretofore the country had looked upon France, of all the great powers, as its natural friend, but France astride the lower Mississippi assumed the attitude of defiance. "There is on the globe one single spot, the possessor of which is our natural and habitual enemy. It is New Orleans, through which the produce of three-eights of our territory must pass to market, and from its fertility it will ere long yield more than half of our whole produce and contain more than half our inhabitants. . . . The day that France takes possession of New Orleans fixes the sentence which is to restrain her forever within her low water mark. It seals the union of two nations who in conjunction can maintain exclusive possession of the ocean. From that moment we must marry ourselves to the British fleet and nation." After flourishing this thunderbolt, after warning that the first cannon fired in the next European war would be the signal for tearing up any settlement France may have made on the Mississippi, Jefferson returned to his usual posture of peace and friendship. If in the face of an enlightened view of her own interests France persisted in the present policy, she ought, at least, to cede the island of New Orleans and the Floridas, since this would put off the threatened alliance with Britain and compensate the United States for the risk of a quarrel with France on the Mississippi. "Every eye in the United States is now fixed on the affair of Louisiana. Perhaps nothing since the revolutionary war has produced more uneasy sensations through the body of the nation." Yet Jefferson refused to be an alarmist, and lest the American Minister be inclined in that direction, he pointed out that time was on the American side and Livingston would be able "to return again and again to the charge, for the conquest of St. Domingo will not be short work." In covering this letter, Jefferson underscored several of its points for Dupont's benefit. The cession of New Orleans and the Floridas would be a "palliative" only. Repossession of Louisiana must eventually annihilate France on the ocean and appropriate all America to Britain and the United States as a consequence. The New World, he warned, could no longer be considered a plaything of Europe, "a mere make-weight in the general settlement of accounts,—this speck," Louisiana, "which now appears as an almost invisible point in the horizon, is the embryo of a tornado which will burst on the countries on both sides of the Atlantic, and involve in its effects their highest destinies."

The President's letters stunned Dupont. Gestures of bravado were not apt to impress the conqueror of Europe, the man who, in the words of the Abbé Sieyes, "knows everything, wants everything, and can do everything." And if Jefferson seriously contemplated an alliance with Britain he was sadly deceived. Nothing had changed as to that power: Britain still saw in the United States a formidable rival to her commercial dominion. Dupont did not mention, though both he and Jefferson understood the point, that the proposed marriage to the British fleet would be difficult to manage under the European peace just now, in April, being signed at Amiens. He probably suspected the President was bluffing. Perhaps he was. But the gravity of his analysis of the American position, taken together with the fragility of the Peace of Amiens, raised great risks for the nation that would call his bluff. Dupont thought France would listen if the American demands were limited to the left bank of the Mississippi, and he advised Jefferson to offer gold for New Orleans and the Floridas, assuming the latter were France's to sell.

The proposition of a purchase did not originate with Dupont. It had been earlier mentioned in Washington. On May 1, just before the Frenchman's letter arrived, Madison asked Livingston to ascertain the price, though without any commitment to buy. A startling idea, it could only have arisen in a nation and with an administration determined to settle international disputes without resort to force. In Paris, Livingston redoubled his diplomatic efforts and wrote a powerful memoir against the French course in North America. But the timing was off. Leclerc was taming the "gilded Africans," or so it seemed, and the Louisiana expedition was going forward. Talleyrand refused to bargain. Nor did Dupont succeed in mediating the dispute. Still he was highly useful. He had an audience with Napoleon and talked with Talleyrand and other high officials. Louisiana figured in these discussions. In contrast to Livingston, whose patience was nearly exhausted, Dupont kept up the hopes of the administration in a negotiated settlement.

As the months passed, and Jefferson summered at Monticello and returned to Washington at the first touch of fall, the Louisiana imbroglio seemed no closer to resolution. Simply to bide his time, waiting for something to turn up, may have been a poor excuse for a policy, yet his only alternative was a rupture with France, and this was premature. The situation remained fluid—he did not wish to freeze it beyond the possibilities of chance. Napoleon had yet to make good his policy; a British accord must await a *démarche* in Europe; and war with all its calamities was the last resort. In October he cautioned Livingston against any impetuous move that might commit the United States to one side or the other of the European power balance. We stand, he said, "completely corrected of the error, that . . . France has any remains of friendship for us," moreover "that no consequence, however ruinous to them, can secure us with certainty against the extravagance of her present rulers." Nevertheless, the country would wage unremitting peace with France. "No matter at present existing between them and us is important enough to risk a breach of peace—peace being indeed the most important of all things for us, except the preserving an erect and independent attitude." France was about to possess herself of the Mississippi, yet, without denying anything said from the other side of his mouth, Jefferson insisted that nothing in the present situation warranted a breach with France.

He was still playing for time. In October, within a week of his letter to Livingston, an event at New Orleans turned the clock ahead dramatically. The Spanish intendant revoked the right of deposit in violation of the Pinckney Treaty. Some Americans believed this virtual stoppage of the river traffic had been secretly ordered by Napoleon as a step preparatory to French occupation. Suspicions were also directed at the government in Madrid, which might have ordered the closure with a view to embarrassing their successors in New Orleans. In Washington, fortunately, neither government was blamed. Yrujo assured Jefferson and Madison that the intendant, acting on some mistaken idea of his authority, was alone responsible for the provocative measure. Informed Americans at New Orleans made the same report. Prudence lay on the side of accepting this explanation, especially as Yrujo moved rapidly to heal the breach. A letter from Dupont arrived at this anxious moment to check suspicions of French intrigue. Dupont named a price: six million dollars for New Orleans and the Floridas on condition that France receive the same commercial rights as the Americans. "If you are willing to go that far, I do not despair of success." Dupont wrote with some semblance of authority. As long as diplomatic channels remained open, there was no cause for panic.

In fact, the closure of the Mississippi had been authorized from Madrid, primarily in retaliation for American abuses of the privileges of the entrepôt; but even had the truth been known in Washington, it would not have served Jefferson's purposes nearly so well as the fiction that blamed the crisis on an erratic colonial official. The President sought to calm the soaring war fever among his friends in the West as well as his enemies in the East, who together, whatever the contrary nature of their motives, might topple his administration and throw away the opportunity to gain the Mississippi via the surer pacific route. The crisis came at a busy time. Jefferson was secretly preparing an expedition to explore the Trans-Mississippi country. Congress convened in an agitated frame of mind. He made no mention of the closure of the Mississippi in his message at the opening of the session. When information was demanded, he adroitly persuaded the House to let the administration handle the problem. The West assumed a higher tone, called for troops, and talked of marching on New Orleans. The West did not disturb him. He could control the West, though up to a point its ardor now served his diplomatic objectives. The Federalists were less tractable. Almost to a man they demanded war, not from any sudden conversion to Western interests (they had, many of them, looked upon the retrocession of Louisiana as a political blessing) but from a desire to embarrass the administration. Jefferson viewed the agitation under its varied aspects in January: "In the western country it is natural and grounded on honest motives. In the seaports it proceeds from a desire for war which increases the mercantile lottery; in the Federalists generally and especially those of Congress the object is to force us into war if possible, in order to derange our finances, or if this cannot be done, to attach the western country to them as their best friends, and thus get again into power." The measures thus far taken, being invisible, had not quieted these clamors. Something "sensible," yet in the diplomatic line, had become necessary.

Thus it was that on January 11 Jefferson nominated James Monroe minister extraordinary to join Livingston in negotiations for the purchase of New Orleans and the Floridas. Monroe was an ideal choice. He possessed the confidence of the West; he knew France and, after Jefferson himself, had been the only American minister to win the confidence of that nation. He was ending his term as Governor of Virginia, and although he toyed with the idea of retiring to the practice of law, he was, as Jefferson once remarked, one of those men "born for the public" and bound to serve. As Jefferson's neighbor in Albemarle, Monroe had seen the President often during the summer; doubtless they had conversed at length on the Mississippi question. The appointment was a *fait accompli* before Monroe even knew about it. "The measure has already silenced the Federalists here," Jefferson told him on the 13th. "Congress will no longer be agitated by them: and the country will become calm as fast as information extends over it. All eyes, all hopes, are now fixed on you; and were you to decline, the chagrin would be universal, and would shake under your feet the high ground on which you stand with the public. Indeed I know nothing which would produce such a shock, for on the event of this mission depends the future destiny of this republic." Closure only offered the excuse for Monroe's appointment—a gesture to calm the war hawks—for that problem was silently on its way to solution. The trade of New Orleans, in fact never effectively closed, regained its old footing in April. The larger problem remained. Upon the mission depended, as Jefferson saw it, whether by purchase of New Orleans and the Floridas the United States would "insure to ourselves a course of perpetual peace and friendship with all nations" or go to war with France at no distant time, "get entangled in European politics, and . . . be much less happy and prosperous" than now.

The purchase project, as strongly recommended by Dupont, was taking form. Jefferson felt vaguely distrustful of Livingston in a negotiation of this kind. It was apt to assume so many shapes that he preferred to send a minister who could speak "straight from the horse's mouth," as it were, and upon whom he could rely implicitly. Livingston had lost caste in Washington by including in his memorial to the French government a blatant appeal to Franco-American solidarity against British "tyranny," just when the administration waved a British alliance as its trump card. London protested and Washington hastened to cover its embarrassment. The errant Minister's response to the news of closure and of near disaster in Santo Domingo was to open a new channel of negotiation, Joseph Bonaparte, the elder brother, through whom he hoped to reach the First Consul. Livingston offered a whole series of propositions, some of them wild (the cession of the Florida littoral as a future refuge for the Bonapartes), all of them hinting at bribery, and one of them involving for the first time the acquisition of territory beyond the Mississippi. This proposal called for the sale of New Orleans and the small province to the east, West Florida, as well as that part of Louisiana above the Arkansas River. It raised no enthusiasm in

Washington since it appeared to install France on the Gulf and to make the United States a buffer between British Canada and the French in lower Louisiana. Not surprisingly, Livingston was nettled by Monroe's appointment. When he learned of it in March he was still angling with Joseph Bonaparte—New Orleans in exchange for certain "personal advantages"—but promptly gave it up. "With respect to Louisiana," he wrote despondently, "I fear nothing will be done here."

Yet at this very time the affair rapidly approached a climax. In Washington the Federalists resumed the drumbeats of war, and the administration, while muffling these alarms at home, amplified them for foreign ears. Things threatened to get out of hand in February when James Ross, the Pennsylvania Federalist, introduced in the Senate an inflamatory resolution authorizing the President to take New Orleans by force. "Plant yourselves on the river, fortify the banks, invite those who have an interest to defend it . . . ," said Ross, "and leave the event to him who controls the fate of nations." The resolution failed. Keeping the crisis in the track of diplomacy, Jefferson and Madison played upon Pichon's nerves, and he, in turn, transmitted every perturbation to Paris. "I noticed at his table," Pichon reported after one of the President's dinners, "that he redoubled his civilities and attentions to the British chargé." To the British chargé, Jefferson declared that should the United States be forced to it, "they would throw away the scabbard." No overture was actually made to Britain, though it was well understood, at least by Pichon, that one would be made if Monroe failed in his mission.

Jefferson gave Monroe a letter to Dupont in which he reiterated his view in an urgent manner. "For our circumstances are so imperious as to admit of no delay to our course; and the use of the Mississippi so indispensable, that we cannot hesitate one moment to hazard our existence for its maintenance. If we fail in this effort to put it beyond the reach of accident, we see the destinies we have to run, and prepare at once for them." The preparations went forward in silence: army recruitment was stepped up, arms, troops, and supplies concentrated at Fort Adams, Indian tribes on the left bank pressed to cede their lands, and the passage of western mail expedited. Of course, Jefferson told Dupont, the country would go on in peace if the rights of navigation and deposit were respected by France. Realistically, however, French control of the Mississippi must produce such a state of irritation that the two countries could not long remain at peace. "And how long would it be hers, with such an enemy, situated at its door, added to Great Britain?" Jefferson asked. "I confess, it appears to me as essential to France to keep at peace with us, as it is to us to keep at peace with her." Monroe's instructions authorized the purchase of New Orleans and the Floridas for upwards to ten million dollars—a tremendous stretch on the part of the economy-minded President and Congress. Should the offer be rejected, the ministers were to make the best bargain they could to ensure the rights of navigation and deposit. An addendum after Monroe's departure covered the last resort: alliance with Britain.

But the Louisiana Purchase was made in France, not in America, and it owed more to the vagaries of Bonaparte's ambition than to Jefferson's cautious diplomacy. The dream of New World empire faded fast in the early months of 1803. After Leclerc's death, Napoleon despaired of Santo Domingo. Because of it precious time, to say nothing of blood and treasure, had been lost in the planting of the French flag on the Mississippi; and without Santo Domingo, without the Gulf ports of the Floridas, which Spain would not yield, Louisiana was useless to France. Napoleon still had empire in his eyes. Turning from failure in the Western seas, he revived the dream of empire in the East—Egypt, the Levant, India. Malta stood in his way. He had surrendered the island fortress to Britain in 1800 and now demanded it back. War was again imminent in Europe. Jefferson, hearing this news early in May, convened the cabinet, which decided that on the outbreak of hostilities American neutrality would be withheld and used as a weapon of bargain for New Orleans and the Floridas. "In this conflict," he wrote, "our neutrality will be cheaply purchased by a cession . . . , because taking part in the war, we could certainly seize and securely hold them and more." A British alliance, so much deprecated, would probably not even be necessary. The United States would win its objectives with the armory Jefferson had always advocated. He had calculated at long-range on war coming to his rescue, and now, *mirabile dictu*, the gamble was paying off.

In Paris, meanwhile, everything was settled. Napoleon could not defend Louisiana while marching to the East. He could not march without gold, gold Louisiana would buy. He could not destroy the remains of British power without American friendship, and he could not have that without removing the causes of dissension on the Mississippi. "Irresolution and deliberation are no longer in season," he declared at St.-Cloud on April 11. "I renounce Lousiana." Monroe arrived in Paris the next day. Livingston, to whom Talleyrand had already made the extraordinary proposition of selling the whole of Louisiana, had been so taken aback that he could only repeat the litany of New Orleans and the Floridas. When it dawned on him and Monroe, who joined in the final negotiations, what a noble acquisition this would be, they did not hesitate to conclude a treaty beyond their instructions. After some haggle, the price was set at $15,000,000, one-fourth of which represented the assumption of French debts owed to American citizens. For this the United States received the immense uncharted country between the Mississippi and the Rocky Mountains or beyond. No one knew its size, its limits were obscure, but it virtually doubled the land area of the United States at a cost, omitting the interest, of approximately 13-1/2 cents an acre. "We have lived long," Livingston said at the signing of the treaty, "but this is the noblest work of our whole lives. . . . From this day the United States take their place among the powers of first rank."

News of the treaty reached Washington on the eve of the 4th of July, befitting an event many hailed as the greatest since the Declaration of Independence. All but the most choleric Federalists were overjoyed. Fifteen million dollars for a howling wilderness! Why, said the Federalists, stack the dollars one upon another and the pile would be three miles high. Twenty dollars from every taxpayer in the United States. And for whose benefit? Southern planters and western frontiersmen. The country was already too big—if the distant domain ever grew to statehood, its congressmen would have to go to Washington by way of Cape Horn! The transaction made no sense unless as tribute Thomas Jefferson paid to Napoleon Bonaparte for the conquest of Britain. Well, if the triumph was not enough to turn every fair-minded Federalist into a Republican, then the petulant utterances of the lunatic fringe were certain, in Jefferson's opinion, to bury the Federalist party under a heap of scorn.

Jefferson never boasted that *he* bought Louisiana. Yet he resented the grumblers and doubters who would deny to him and his administration any credit for the accomplishment. To those who had demanded war as the only solution, the President had looked too much "like Sterne's ass, which when . . . kicked, cuffed, and spat upon, turns up his piteous, imploring eyes and says 'pray don't beat us.' " From such a posture, obviously, no good could come. But Jefferson's posture, while pacific, was far more subtle than any political caricature and much better attuned to realities than the war-mongering of his critics. In the two-year-long campaign, he never overextended himself, never cut off his lines of retreat, never risked the consequences of an armed encounter, yet kept the objective steadily in view. Inaction was as much a part of his strategy as action, and he knew when to wave the sword and when to sheath it. While not neglecting defensive preparations, he made them without bluster or fanfare. While holding control of the warlike propensities of the West, he was able to use them for diplomatic effect. From easy beginnings he steadily tightened the springs of diplomacy. The entire proceeding was an impressive vindication of the ways of peace in the conduct of American affairs. In the final analysis, of course, he was saved by European war. But this was not simply a piece of dumb luck. The prospect of war, like the prospect of French defeat in Santo Domingo, entered into his calculations. He correctly weighed the imponderables of the European power balance, shrewdly threatened to throw his weight into the British scale, gauged the effect of renewed war on Napoleon's imperial design, and prepared to take advantage of the *démarche* when it came. He wrote in retrospect: "I did not expect he [Napoleon] would yield till a war took place between France and England, and my hope was to palliate and endure, if Messrs. Ross, Morris, etc. did not force a premature rupture, until that event," when the country could be obtained as the price of neutrality or in reprisal for wrongs sure to be received. "The war happened somewhat sooner than was expected," he said, "but our measures were previously taken, and the thing took the best turn for both parties."

Great affairs of state are always surrounded in chance, and victory hangs as much upon making the right wagers in the matters depending on the will of others as it does upon the efficient marshaling of one's own forces. In the Louisiana crisis Jefferson played the game to perfection. Indeed he won much more than he played for, the whole of Louisiana instead of New Orleans and the Floridas. The negotiations centered on the latter because, realistically, the United States was not threatened in Louisiana, and making it an object would only have weakened the force of a claim involving the nation's vital interests. This does not mean that Jefferson had no eyes for Louisiana, itself of small importance to France, only that it was not an immediate object. From the first and primary acquisition, the rest would certainly follow. Instead it came all at once, which altered the timetable of American expansion but not its destination.

For several months Jefferson had been planning to chart the path of destiny to the farthest shore. By happy coincidence the man he had chosen for this task, Meriwether Lewis, set out from Washington on July 4th with the acclaim of the Louisiana Purchase ringing in his ears. From the sixteenth-century conquistador Cabeza de Vaca to Alexander Mackenzie, who traversed the continent on the Canadian side in the 1790's, the work of exploration had gone forward, impelled by the centuries old dream of a Northwest Passage; yet the country of the Missouri River and beyond was still virtually unknown, either a blank on the map, often the only honest cartography, or filled up with imaginary seas, mountains, rivers, and deserts. Jefferson had long been fascinated by the challenge of this great country, first in his relationship with George Rogers Clark during the American Revolution, then with the eccentric Yankee traveler John Ledyard while in France, and in 1793 with the politically aborted expedition of André Michaux. The first requisite was to possess the country for the mind. Geographical knowledge would prepare the way for economic penetration, to be followed eventually by political mastery. The fact that a country held neither title nor jurisdiction in unknown lands and seas was not considered by enlightened rulers and philosophers a bar to "voyages of discovery." "The field of knowledge," Jefferson later said in defense of an expedition into the Spanish borderlands, "is the common property of all mankind, and any discoveries we can make in it will be for the benefit . . . of every other nation, as well as our own."

Both ruler and philosopher, he felt a keen desire to distinguish his administration in works of science as well as of government. His political creed was not well adapted to this purpose, however, and he had been in the presidency nearly two years without taking a single significant step toward the union of the hopes of science with the hopes of republicanism. Some of his philosophical friends candidly confessed their disappointment. "No naturalist travels at the public expense to explore our immense Country and make us acquainted with the infinite resources it contains upon its surface, in its waters and within its bowels, from whence great national advantages would result . . . ," William Dunbar complained, "but it would seem that the speculations of the generality of our politicians are confined within the narrow circle of the customs and the excise, while literature is left to weep in the background." The Mississippi savant still had hopes that under the illustrious Jefferson "Arts, Sciences, and Literature may take a flight, which will at length carry them as far beyond those of our European brethren, as we soar above them in the enjoyment of national liberty." In the end Dunbar would not be disappointed; in fact, he would have a part in the on-going enterprise of exploration launched by the Lewis and Clark Expedition.

The expedition had been in preparation since November 1802. Lieutenant Meriwether Lewis, the President's private secretary, had served in the 1st Infantry; he knew the posts above the Ohio, and had ranged far into the interior. This knowledge of the western country, combined with Jefferson's long acquaintance with his family and upbringing in Albemarle, had prompted the President to call him to Washington in 1801. He came to know the young man intimately. So impressed was he with Lewis's qualities of leadership, talent for observation, knowledge of the Indians, honesty, understanding, and so on—all the qualifications providentially united in one person for the mission Jefferson had in mind—that he did not hesitate to place him in command. Of Lewis's ardor for exploration there could be no doubt: a decade earlier, when only eighteen years of age, he had applied to Jefferson to head the expedition confided to Michaux. "To fill up the measure desired," Jefferson later wrote, "he wanted nothing but a greater familiarity with the technical language of the natural sciences, and readiness in the astronomical observations necessary for the geography of his route." To acquire these he was sent to Philadelphia and placed under the tutelage of its eminent scientists: Benjamin Smith Barton and Caspar Wistar in natural history, Robert Patterson and Andrew Ellicott (in Lancaster) in astronomy, Benjamin Rush in medicine. And, of course, he pored over the maps and travels of Mackenzie and others. After this brief exposure, Lewis hardly qualified as a learned man in any branch of science; nor was his second in command, William Clark of Kentucky, or any member of his party, a scientific specialist. But Jefferson's judgment of Lewis proved correct. He was a remarkably astute observer, and possessing this untrained intelligence under the gloss of science, together with the ability to lead men and the "know how" to survive in the wilderness, he possessed all that was necessary, unencumbered by the superfluous, for blazing the trail to the Pacific in which others might follow.

Jefferson announced the plan of the expedition to Congress in a secret message on January 18. The explorers would trace the Missouri to its source, cross the highlands—how high and how far no one knew—and follow the best water course to the Pacific. This was straightforward, but the purpose of the mission was quite ambiguous, deliberately so. To the ministers of foreign countries, like Yrujo, whose king remained the sovereign of the territory pending its actual transfer to France, Jefferson indicated that the mission was of a "literary" nature. To Congress, which would never approve anything so speculative, he emphasized its commercial aspect. The peltry trade of the Indians along the whole course of the Missouri and beyond might be diverted from Canada to a continuous line of navigation in the lower latitudes all the way to the Atlantic coast. The opening of water communication across the continent was a proper object of congressional legislation under the power to regulate commerce.

Commerce and Indian relations were certainly among the purposes Jefferson had in mind; of first importance, however, was geographical and, more generally, scientific knowledge. In his message he alluded to these objects as merely "incidental." "While other civilized nations have encountered great expense to enlarge the boundaries of knowledge, by undertaking voyages of discovery, and for other literary purposes, in various parts and directions," he said, "our nation seems to owe to the same object, as well as to its own interests, to explore this, the only line of easy communication across the continent, and so directly traversing our own part of it." Here spoke the philosopher-statesman, and it is impossible to read the detailed instructions he penned for Lewis in April without realizing the importance the acquisition of knowledge had in his conception of the expedition. Observations of latitude and longitude were to be taken with "great precision and accuracy" at all points along the route, carefully recorded, and kept in multiple copies. An acquaintance with the various Indian tribes—their languages, customs, occupations, moral and physical circumstances—had obvious bearing on commerce. Among other things meriting attention: "the soil and face of the country . . . the animals . . . the remains . . . the mineral productions of every kind . . . volcanic appearances . . . climate . . . the dates at which particular plants put forth or lose their flowers, or leaf, times of appearance of particular birds, reptiles or insects." Of course, Lewis could not unveil the whole arcanum of western nature. His mission was exploratory. What Jefferson later said to Dunbar in connection with the Red River expedition, he might have said to Lewis: "The work we are now doing is, I trust, done for posterity, in such a way that they need not repeat it. . . . We shall delineate with correctness the great arteries of this great country: those who come after us will extend the ramifications as they become acquainted with them, and fill up the canvas we begin."

Public interest in the expedition rose after the news of the Louisiana Purchase. "The Federalists alone treat it as philosophism, and would rejoice in its failure," Jefferson wrote to Lewis at his winter quarters near the mouth of the Missouri. The vein of raillery, "philosophism," began to flow in the fall when Jefferson sent to Congress a most remarkable document, An Account of Louisiana, in which Indian lore, western apocrypha, and similar scraps of knowledge were mixed with much hard data on the strange new world. The President told of Indian tribes of gigantic stature, of soil too rich for the growth of trees, and of astounding geological phenomena. A paper received from an army officer in the West, sent to Congress and published, reported a great salt mountain—180 miles of glittering white rock salt.* Fabled land indeed! Why, the New York *Evening*

---

* Jefferson later said he had not read the paper when it was posted through him to Congress and first learned of the salt mountain from lampooning Federalist writers who ascribed the prodigious tale to him. Yet he soberly

Post wondered, had not the President gone on to tell of "the immense lake of molasses" and the "extensive vale of hasty pudding, stretching as far as the eye could see." Perhaps Louisiana overexcited Jefferson's "itch for telling prodigies," which was John Quincy Adams's way of describing his capacity for enchantment; still, even if Lewis and Clark did not meet with fantastic mammoth or Indians descended from Welchmen or mountain "sous'd in pickle"—items mentioned in a satire from Adams's pen—the land proved to be as fabulous as Jefferson's imagination. From Fort Mandan 1600 miles up the Missouri, Lewis described the country he and his party had traversed on the first leg of the journey as "one of the fairest portions of the globe"; and from this point he sent back a barge full of specimens, of soil, plants, animals, Indian artifacts, and so on, which excited great curiosity when they finally arrived in Washington in August 1805. Some of these specimens, like the prairie dog (American badger) were unknown to science, others, like the magpie, heretofore unknown in America. Jefferson experimented with the maize sent by the explorers, filed the Indian vocabularies for future reference, and mounted the great horns of a wapiti in the entrance hall at Monticello. Nearly everything else was sent on to the scientists in Philadelphia. Meanwhile, the explorers descended the Columbia River, wintered near its mouth, then commenced the 3500-mile return trek, reaching St. Louis in September 1806.

Many years would be required to sort out and organize the wealth of information gained by the explorers. As a scientific enterprise, the expedition was a spectacular success. In terms of its practical purpose, the discovery of a feasible commercial route to the Pacific, it was not. The gap between the Missouri and the Columbia proved much greater than anyone had imagined in 1803: 340 miles, much of it, as Lewis said, "over tremendous mountains . . . covered with eternal snows." But such formidable obstacles did not discourage Jefferson nor the many Americans touched by his vision of a continental destiny. As Henry Nash Smith has said, "The importance of the Lewis and Clark expedition lay on the level of imagina-

entertained the possibility of its truth. Nothing in nature was against it. Salt mountains had been mentioned by Pliny and described by modern explorers in various places. In 1804 Osage Indians told him of a great salt plain on the Arkansas. Many laughed at this too.

tion: it was drama, it was the enactment of a myth that embodied the future."

The Louisiana Purchase did not solve the problem of the American West but changed its terms radically. In the summer of 1803, while Lewis descended the Ohio on his way to the continent's end, Jefferson and his colleagues turned their attention to urgent questions of law, government, and diplomacy arising under the treaty of cession. What were the boundaries of Louisiana? The treaty did not declare. The acquisition amounted to a revolution in the American Union. Was it warranted? Could the Union withstand the shock? Could the new lands be governed under the Constitution? How? As colonies subject to the will of Congress or as free and independent states? The people of Louisiana were predominantly French. Could they, or should they, be assimilated to American institutions? What were the bearings of Louisiana on Indian relations, on slavery, on land policy, on foreign policy? A great new frontier—a whole series of frontiers—had been created. How should it be secured and settled?

To these questions Jefferson had no certain answers, and they would be decided finally, like the event that produced them, more by forces of circumstance than by his own agency. On July 16, ten days after the treaty came into his hands, he convened the cabinet to take the first measured steps toward implementation. Congress was called into session October 17. Ratification was a foregone conclusion, but Jefferson made a point of urging prompt attendance on the Kentucky congressmen in particular. The American Consul in New Orleans, Daniel Clark, and the Governor of the Mississippi Territory, William C. C. Claiborne, were put on the alert should any problems arise in the transfer of Louisiana. Since Spain was still in possession, the territory must be handed to the French before it could be handed to the Americans; and in this process everything might be lost unless Washington was prepared to back its claim with force. Congress must provide a government for the province. For this work reliable information was essential. With the help of the secretaries, Jefferson drew up a long list of "Queries as to Louisiana," which he dispatched to the men most likely to supply the answers, such as Claiborne, Clark, and Dunbar. Gallatin, meanwhile, attended to the financial arrangements according to a separate convention coupled with the treaty of cession. The terms were not entirely to his liking, but blessed with an abundant treasury and hopeful of further economies, especially in the Navy Department, Gallatin managed to pay for Louisiana by ready money and the sale of new government stock, without resort to taxes or borrowing.

The treaty gave no precise limits to Louisiana, thereby opening one of the most tortuous and least edifying chapters in the history of American empire. France sold to the United States what she had acquired from Spain. And what was that? "Louisiana with the same extent as it now has in the hands of Spain, and that it had when France possessed it." But these were different things. When France possessed Louisiana it included the whole of the Mississippi Valley between the Great Lakes and the Gulf of Mexico. The portion east of the Mississippi, including the Floridas, passed to Great Britain at the conclusion of the Seven Years War, while the western part, with the Isle of New Orleans, went to Spain. When Spain obtained the Floridas by the treaty of peace in 1783, she did not reincorporate them into Louisiana but governed them as separate colonies. The retrocession of 1800 must have referred to the province France had ceded to Spain in 1762, and its eastern boundary was fixed at the Mississippi and the Iberville encompassing New Orleans. Such was the simple logic of the matter, the logic Livingston had consistently advocated in Paris when Spain's title to the Floridas, unmutilated, comported with American interest. But now that the United States had acquired Louisiana, Livingston found it convenient to read the vague clauses of the treaty as covering West Florida at least to the Perdido River east of the Bay of Mobile. (When he broached the claim to Talleyrand, the old fox snapped, "You have made a noble bargain for yourselves, and I suppose you will make the most of it"; and Napoleon, who could play the fox as well as the lion, commented on the boundary enigma, "If an obscurity did not exist, perhaps it would be good policy to put it there.") Jefferson read Livingston's preliminary argument of the point several days before the cabinet met on July 16. If it was discussed, it was not adopted. Instead, the cabinet decided Monroe should endeavor to purchase the Floridas, the West if not the East, and failing that fall back on the "natural right" Jefferson had always claimed against Spain, to wit, the navigation of rivers rising within American limits through Spanish territory to the Gulf. "We are more indifferent about pressing the purchase of the Floridas, because of the money we have to provide for Louisiana," Jefferson noted this decision, "and because we think they cannot fail to fall into our hands." The conviction that the Floridas would remain Spanish only so long as it suited American convenience was the point on which Jefferson's policy turned.

Still he could not be complacent about the Floridas. The American settlements on the Tombigbee and Alabama demanded access to Mobile, and Mobile was in some ways a superior harbor to New Orleans. The revenue of the Gulf trade, which Gallatin eyed with Midas delight, would waste away if American collectors were confined to New Orleans. Security was also a consideration, for Spanish presence on the east bank of the Mississippi would prove troublesome and the transfer of the Floridas to Britain could never be dropped out of the reckoning. When he retreated to Monticello near the end of July, Jefferson plunged into the books, maps, and documents in his collection of western Americana in order to see to what limits the United States might legitimately press its claims, not only on the east but on the west as well. The western limits were, in fact, more confused than the eastern. Whether they lay on the far or the near side of the Rocky Mountains in the north, whether the Sabine or the Rio Bravo or some river between formed the southwestern boundary, were questions veiled in obscurity. In time Jefferson would consider the distant Oregon country part of the acquisition, but he was not prepared for this leap in 1803. He summed up the results of his investigation in a somewhat hesitant fashion in August: "The unquestioned bounds of Louisiana are the Iberville and Mississippi, on the east, the Mexicana (Sabine) or the highlands east of it, on the west. . . . We have some pretensions to extend the western territory of Louisiana to the Rio Norte, or Bravo; and still stronger the eastern boundary to the Rio Perdido between the rivers Mobile and Pensacola." He marshaled the evidence for these pretensions in a brief memoir, An Examination of the Boundaries of Louisiana. Apparently he was not yet convinced of their legitimacy. While escalating the treaty as far as possible in order to strengthen his bargaining position with Spain, he was unwilling to commit the government to points he regarded as negotiable. But by the following February, the pretended limits had become the true limits in Jefferson's mind, though he would sacrifice Texas for all the Floridas and throw a million dollars into the bargain.

The brilliance of the Louisiana Purchase was somewhat dimmed for Jefferson from the first moment by the gagging conviction it exceeded the limits of the Constitution. For a President, an administration, a party that made a boast of constitutional morality, the problem seemed inescapable. Jefferson had seen it in January when shaping up the purchase offer. The Attorney General had then advised that since the Constitution predicated the Union as it was in 1787, an amendment would be necessary to sanction the acquisition of territory and the addition of new states carved from it. Lincoln's logic had been promptly demolished by Gallatin, who argued that despite the absence of explicit provision, the United States, as a sovereign nation, might acquire territory by treaty, govern it or, Congress approving, incorporate it into the Union. Jefferson appeared to be satisfied, at least to the point of authorizing a bargain in the national interest. "You are right . . . ," he told Gallatin, "there is no constitutional difficulty as to the acquisition of territory, and whether, when acquired, it may be taken into the Union by the Constitution as it now stands, will become a question of expediency." Yet he wished to hold expediency within the limits of principle, adding, "I think it will be safer not to permit the enlargement of the Union but by amendment of the Constitution."

When news of the cession reached him in July, he promptly drafted an amendment intended, in part, to sanction the treaty retroactively. "The Constitution has made no provision for our holding foreign territory, still less of incorporating foreign nations into our Union," he explained to Senator Breckinridge. "The executive in seizing the fugitive occurrence which so much advances the good of this country, have done an act beyond the Constitution. The legislature in casting behind them metaphysical subtleties, and risking themselves like faithful servants, must . . . throw themselves on their country for doing for them unauthorized, what we know they would have done for themselves had they been in a situation to do it." In his opinion this "act of indemnity" would "confirm and not weaken the Constitution, by more strongly marking out its lines." And indeed, on the premises of the Virginia and Kentucky Resolutions and the first inaugural address, no other opinion was respectable. To suppose that the whole shape and substance of the nation could be revolutionized on "fugitive occurrences" by the exercise of the treaty power was so outlandish that Federalist apostles of "implied powers" and "inherent sovereignty" might weep at their timidity.

But Jefferson's contemplated amendment had a prospective as well as a retrospective purpose. In the latter character it authorized the incorporation of Louisiana into the Union; this, however, was the lesser part, actually about one-fifth of the 375 words of Jefferson's draft. The greater part established a policy for all but the most southerly portion of the ceded territory. It would be "locked up," the lands reserved to the Indians, American settlement prohibited for an indefinite period, and no territorial government or state could be erected above the 33rd parallel except by further amendment of the Constitution. This was a startling bid to control the future of the Trans-Mississippi West. Unheralded in Jefferson's thinking, its sources may be discovered in considerations of national unity, defense, political economy, disposition of lands, and, above all, Indian policy.

In the President's eyes the acquisition opened a grand new chapter in the "empire of liberty." "The world will here see such an extent of country under a free and moderate government as it has never yet seen." But, while raising these hallelujahs, he was not blind to certain sobering realities. The country must for some time be virtually as defenseless under the Americans as it was under the Spanish. Would it not be wise, then, to create an Indian buffer between the Mississippi and the nation's borders with the British and Spanish dominions, and allow it to recede as the Americans themselves actually occupied the land? The title deeds still belonged to the savage tribes. To extinguish them peacefully and fairly would require years of patient negotiation; to open the wild lands to indiscriminate settlement would cost incalculable blood and treasure in Indian wars and let loose a whirlwind of speculation not unlike the Yazoo land frauds in the Georgia claim from which the country, and the administration, was only beginning to grope its way toward an honorable solution.

Louisiana promised to fulfil the prophesies of economic abundance, natural increase, and freehold farming, all contained within Jefferson's design of republican empire. While wrestling with the problems of policy, he again read Thomas Malthus's *Essay on Population,* now in revised edition. He thought it "masterly," no doubt true for the mass of mankind in its dismal forecast of population remorselessly outrunning food supply, yet fortunately "inapplicable" to the United States. Indeed the United States, after the Louisiana accession if not before, when the country already had 120 acres of land per capita, reversed the Malthusian rule. "Our food then," Jefferson wrote, "may increase geometrically with our laborers, and our births, however multiplied, become effective." But land wrested from cultivators by the avarice of speculators, land—an unprecedented immensity of virgin land—spread too thin with settlers and too hastily draining labor and capital from the still impoverished East could become more a curse than a blessing. The economic argument against the dispersal of American resources would be made repeatedly, especially by New England Federalists attached to oceanic commerce and fearful of waning political power in the Union. Their motives were suspect. Jefferson paid little attention to them, though he recognized the force of the argument in other hands, including his own.

He discounted too, as politically inspired, the curious revival under Federalist auspices of old Anti-Federalist fears of a union too big to survive in liberty. "We rush like a comet into infinite space," Ames declared. The western country would separate from the eastern and form a confederation of its own, some said. This was all speculation on remote contingencies. Yet, Jefferson asked, what if it should finally come to that? "The future inhabitants of [both] the Atlantic and Mississippi states will be our sons. . . . We think we see their happiness in their union, and we wish it. Events may prove it otherwise; and if they see their interest in separating why should we take side with our Atlantic rather than our Mississippi descendants? It is the elder and the younger son differing. God bless them both, and keep them in union if it be for their good, but separate them if it be better." Liberty was the ultimate value, Union the means, to be cherished only so long as it furthered the end of its being. Such was Jefferson's philosophical view of the matter, drawn out, it should be noted, in answer to captious Federalists.

Nothing could be more mistaken than to suppose that he resigned himself to separation and disunion. On the contrary, he believed the acquisition would strengthen the Union even as it strengthened liberty. The American experiment that upset Malthus also upset Montesquieu. "By enlarging the empire of liberty," Jefferson observed, "we multiply its auxiliaries, and provide new sources of renovation, should its principles at any time degenerate, in those portions of our country which gave them birth." The federal system bottomed on the equality of individuals and of states overcame the objection to republican government in a large empire. The acquisition shut the avenues of foreign intrigue, so dangerous to freedom and union. It extended the agricultural base of a virtuous republic and enabled the nation to cultivate its own garden at peace with the world. It opened the way to orderly possession of the continent, first of the vacant lands east of the Mississippi, then in progressive stages westward. "When we shall be full on this side, we may lay off a range of states on the Western bank from the head to the mouth, and so, range after range, advancing compactly as we multiply."

Advancing compactly as we multiply: the key to the program lay in Indian policy. The tribes east of the Mississippi would be resettled in Louisiana, thereby eliminating the Indian problem where it existed, filling up the eastern country, and garrisoning the western until the Americans were ready to possess it. "If our legislature dispose of it with the wisdom we have a right to expect," Jefferson explained, "they may make it the means of tempting all our Indians on the east side of the Mississippi to remove to the west, and of condensing instead of scattering our population." Searching for a policy to govern the new problem, Louisiana, Jefferson was led to the point of abandoning the policy he had consistently pursued toward the old problem, the Indians. That policy aimed at the rapid acquisition of Indian lands by treaty, the control of the tribes by commercial intercourse under federal supervision, accompanied by a variety of expedients to draw the savages into agriculture, thus by degrees civilizing them until ultimately they were incorporated with the whites. "In truth," Jefferson had recently written to his old friend Benjamin Hawkins, agent to the Creeks, "the ultimate point of rest and happiness for them is to let our settlements and theirs meet and blend together and to intermix, and become one people." Hawkins was the chief exemplar of this assimilationist policy, and Jefferson stood by him against the wrath of Georgians who believed his first loyalty was to the Indians. The Jeffersonian policy had the appearance of deviousness, even hypocrisy: the great white father runs his red children into debt, kills off the game, acquires one tract of land after another, crowding the savages into smaller and smaller reserves, until they are compelled to take the white father's view of their own interests and turn to agriculture and the domestic arts. Whatever the appearances, Jefferson insisted the policy breathed "pure morality" toward the Indians; for, realistically, the only alternative to assimilation was destruction, and if they had to be drawn into the paths of civilization by devious routes, the end justified the means.

The policy seemed to be working in 1803. Millions upon millions of acres were being acquired from the Indians, mostly above the Ohio. Hawkins, at least, was experiencing some success in his civilizing agency to the Creeks. Protestant missionaries, like Samuel Kirkland among the Iroquois, were helping tribes to discover avenues of accommodation. Still, where the problem was critical, where frontiersmen swarmed and the government pressed for land, roads, trading houses, and other concessions, among the confederacies of Creek, Cherokee, Choctaw, and Chickasaw in the booming cotton lands south of the Tennessee, frustrations bore hard upon the President. The tribes in the Mississippi Territory resisted every advance, yet the compact with Georgia in 1802 obligated the government to extinguish Indian titles in return for the state's cession of western claims extending to the Mississippi. The process was proving slow, tedious, and costly. The removal of the southern tribes west of the Mississippi would not only solve this problem but several others as well. So attractive a prospect warranted, in Jefferson's mind, suspension of the enlightened goals of civilization and amalgamation in favor of the entirely different set of directives contained in the policy of Indian removal. "Instead of inviting Indians to come within our limits," Jefferson now said, "our object is to tempt them to evacuate them."

Such was the prospective intent of Jefferson's planned amendment of the Constitution. His more pressing concern was with the constitutional difficulty, however. Dispatches from Livingston reached him in August urging prompt ratification without fuss or bother. "Be persuaded that France is sick of the bargain; that Spain is much dissatisfied; and that the slightest pretense will lose you the treaty." The Minister's fears might be groundless, but Jefferson could not afford to ignore them. In September, Yrujo submitted the caviling protest of his government, which was quite futile, and Senator Nicholas pointedly warned the President not to raise the issue of the competency of the treaty power lest he furnish the Federalists the lever to upset the treaty. Nicholas himself, like most Republicans, denied the want of constitutional power. Jefferson stuck to his opinion. He still wanted the amendment. But given the hazards, he concluded that the less said about it the better and asked his friends in the Senate to do what was necessary *sub silento*. "I had rather ask an enlargement of power from the nation, where it is found necessary, than to assume it by construction which would make our powers boundless," he told Nicholas. "Our peculiar security is in the possession of a written Constitution. Let us not make it a blank paper by construction." Yet what is practical, as he was want to say, must sometimes control what is true in theory, and if ever an instance proved the rule it was the Louisiana Purchase. So without yielding the principle he yielded the position. "If . . . our friends shall think differently," he advised Nicholas, "certainly I shall acquiesce with satisfaction; confiding, that the good sense of the country will correct the evil of construction when it shall produce ill effects."

The matter was dropped. Jefferson made no mention of the constitutional difficulty in his message to Congress on October 17. Federalists raised the issue but to no avail. A revolution in the American Union became, perforce, a revolution in the Constitution. A momentous act of Jeffersonian statesmanship unhinged the Jeffersonian dogmas and opened, so far as precedent might control, the boundless field of power so much feared. Critics then and since found the President inconsistent. In the narrow view he was, but a statesman riding the current of events cannot indulge narrow points of consistency. In the larger view of the national interest, Jefferson's dominant purpose remained what it had always been, indeed leaped far ahead of him, and he would deal with any untoward side-effects when they occurred.

Yielding the constitutional point, he also yielded his far-sighted plan for the disposition of the country between the Red River and the far reaches of the Missouri. The plan was an altogether separate matter; it might have been the subject of a constitutional amendment or put on the more hazardous footing of statutory law. Neither was done. Jefferson talked about it with certain congressmen, with Breckinridge, for instance, who approved the "lock up" in principle but doubted that a constitutional barricade floated on the waters of the Mississippi would check the westerners. Congress did, in 1804, empower the President to offer Trans-Mississippi lands to eastern tribes in exchange for their homelands. In his numerous addresses to visiting tribal delegations in Washington, Jefferson often recommended this course. (These addresses have a rhetoric all their own—child-like, metaphorical, bucolic, and affectedly naïve—which he did not originate but developed into a literary art.) The chiefs showed little interest, however, and Americans on the Mississippi filed indignant protests. By 1805 Jefferson had returned to the old theme of amalgamation. In truth, he had never actually given it up. The policy ran against the grain of both red men and white, and its chances of success dimmed with each passing year, yet Jefferson clung to it as the only humane solution. A quarter-century later the federal government adopted the alternate policy of Indian removal. Jefferson's early gestures in the same direction, and in quite another context, had been forgotten.

The machinery of government worked smoothly to effect the transition of authority in Louisiana. Jefferson reconvened the cabinet in Washington the first week of October. Gallatin had completed the financial arrangements. Information on the conditions and prospects of Louisiana was flowing in and being digested in Madison's department, which held administrative responsibility for territorial government. Dearborn dispatched orders to General James Wilkinson at Fort Adams, near Natchez, to prepare a force competent to take New Orleans should the Spanish refuse to deliver the province to the French. The Senate, meanwhile, quickly approved the treaty and with the House proceeded to frame legislation to implement it.

Jefferson signed the Enabling Act on October 21. The act empowered the President to take possession of Louisiana and, until Congress made provision for its government, vested him or his agents with full powers civil and military. Federalists said this provisional government made the President "as despotic as the Grand Turk" and marveled that the Republican cry of "monarchy" had so soon lost its sting. Directed by the statute to protect the inhabitants of Louisiana in their "liberty, property and religion" during the transition, Jefferson simply continued the local Spanish law in force, in accordance with historical precedent drawn from the example of conquered provinces. He appointed W. C. C. Claiborne temporary governor. He and Wilkinson were charged with seeing that the territory was delivered, first into French, then into American custody. Wilkinson's small force of regulars and militia paraded the colors. On November 30 France came into possession; twenty days later, at the Cabildo in New Orleans, in a ceremony so meager it seemed an impertinence, the Tricolor came down and the Star Spangled Banner waved over Louisiana. When the news reached Washington a thousand miles away near the end of January, cannon dragged up from the navy yard boomed on Capitol Hill and a great festival, in which the President joined, hailed the conclusion of a transaction that still staggered the imagination.

For many weeks Congress labored to bring forth a regular government for the territory. "There appear to be about as many opinions as to the mode of governing Louisiana as there are members of the National Legislature," Gideon Granger informed Claiborne. Like everything else about the Louisiana Purchase, the problem of the form of government answered to no precedent and challenged every theory. Never before had a republic set out to incorporate an alien province almost as big as itself. The rules of conquest did not apply, not only because the relation of conqueror and conquered violated the American scheme of things but also because the purchase treaty bound the United States to admit, "as soon as possible," the ceded territory and its inhabitants into the Union. The legal obligation only reinforced the nation's moral commitment, one that Jefferson himself had laid deep in the polity twenty years before, and he had no thought of backing away from it. But how it should be managed, through what preliminiary stages the territory should pass, and on what timetable—on these questions he was flexible, governed by facts not theories, and responsible to the test of practice.

His plans for upper Louisiana have been noted. As to the lower settled portion, soon to become the Orleans Territory, with the same limits as the present state of Louisiana, Jefferson's first thought was to annex it to Mississippi. Of the approximately 50,000 inhabitants nearly half were slaves, and a majority of the whites were natives of French descent, Creoles, who knew nothing of American government. "We shall certainly endeavor to introduce American laws there," Jefferson had written in July, "and that cannot be done but by amalgamating the people with such a body of Americans as may take the lead in legislation and government." Actually, Mississippi was the last place to look for leadership. The eastern territory had similar problems to the western. Claiborne encountered the same difficulties as his Federalist predecessor, Sargent, in governing this refractory populace. "In no part of the Union are the citizens less informed of the principles of our government, and (generally speaking) involved in as much mental ignorance," he had written. On reflection, Jefferson decided against annexation. Mississippi was governed by the provisions of the Northwest Ordinance of 1787, except for the no-slavery proviso, and had just passed from the first to the second grade of territorial government. Jefferson had supposed the government of lower Louisiana might be founded on the same basis. Early in November, he changed his mind. The old ordinance would not do for Louisiana—"it would turn all their laws topsy turvy." As indeed it would. An instrument framed for state-making in vacant domain would not do for a settled province formerly the colony of France and Spain. So Jefferson turned his thoughts to a plan of government adapted to the specific case.

What led him on, down paths of government never ventured in his political philosophy, was the detailed information funneled into Washington. The picture was discouraging. By American standards the old Spanish government was a complete despotism. Supreme authority, civil and military, rested in a governor who reported to the captain-general in Havanna. There was a kind of executive council, the Cabildo, which also acted as a court, and which represented the interests of the great Creole planters. The offices of the Cabildo were purchased; in fact, venality, bribery, and corruption ruled in all things. Except for 6 per cent duties on imports and exports, commonly evaded by smuggling and bribery, there were no taxes, and the Crown met the whole cost of the civil and military establishment. The law, like the church, was Roman, being based on Spanish codes and compilations as ancient as the thirteenth century, though in actuality the law was largely executive or dispensative. The common law was unknown, so too the palladium of Anglo-American liberty, trial by jury. French was the language of the courts, and lawyers had no place in the judicial system. Land titles were in a state of confusion. Not one-fourth of the lands granted by the colonial government were held on complete titles; most of the remainder depended on the written provision of some commandant. Moreover, according to one estimate, 30,000,000 acres of Louisiana had been bargained away by Spanish officials in fraudulent grants, some to Americans who descended on the territory like a flock of buzzards, subsequent to the Treaty of San Ildefonso or even the French cession. So troublesome was the inherited land system that the matter of titles would not finally be disposed of until 1879. Slavery existed, of course, the brutal slavery of the sugar plantations that consumed Negroes as fast as they could be imported. The large, concentrated slave population, together with several thousand free Negroes in and around New Orleans, aroused fears that Louisiana might become another Santo Domingo. Nor was this the only worry for the territory's security. Many of the Creoles, Washington was warned, wished for the return of the province to France, possibly Spain, and they could count the deposed colonial officials as allies.

Ignorance, the unfailing legacy of despotism, was perhaps the worst curse of all. Religious bigotry abounded. Schools were all but non-existent; over half the people were illiterate; at Point Coupee, the second largest place, renowned for wealth and polish, not one-third of the free inhabitants could write their own names. The Quaker Isaac Briggs, Surveyor General south of the Tennessee, spoke of the "vicious, luxurious, and oppressive habits" of the Louisianans, which in his opinion barred their entrance into the "blessings of Republican liberty." Claiborne thought the natives mild and submissive, a good people, but peculiarly vulnerable to the intrigues of ambitious men, Creole or American. "Sudden and total reformation is best calculated for enlightened minds; the experiment may prove

779

hazardous with Creole ignorance." Claiborne agreed with other informants on the need for a firm and strong hand, though he did not go as far as some, Wilkinson and Clark, for example, who advocated virtually a military government. Daniel Clark, the Irish-born consul, rich and ambitious, was by all odds the most knowledgeable American on the civil state of lower Louisiana. His memoranda reached Washington about the first of November and made a deep impression on the President and his colleagues. The imprint could be seen in the Account of Louisiana sent to Congress on November 14. More than any other report, Clark's seems to have crystalized the President's thoughts on the plan of government for lower Louisiana.

Clearly, in his opinion, the Louisianans must serve an apprenticeship before entering the estate of American liberty. They were ignorant of its principles, laws, and forms. The introduction of representative government on the American model would almost certainly put the territory at the hazard of the dominant Creole class, retard improvement, foment discord, and check the influx of Americans who alone could lay the foundations of a free state. Jefferson envisioned a gradual transition to republicanism paced to the advance of American settlement. "In proportion as we find the people there ripe for receiving these first principles of freedom," he told Gallatin, "Congress may from session to session confirm their employment of them." Sometime after the middle of November he discussed his ideas with Breckinridge, who apparently agreed to draw up a plan of government, but sensing the Senator's reluctance, Jefferson began the task himself.

The plan he sketched gave the people of Louisiana no voice in their government. The President would appoint the governor and the secretary for a term of years. Judges, too, would be appointed by the President, not to terms in good behavior but for four years. This was a necessary safeguard, Jefferson said, for "shall the judges take a kink in their heads in favor of leaving the present laws of Louisiana unaltered, that evil will continue for their lives unamended by us, and become so inveterate that we may never be able to introduce the uniformity of law so desirable." Otherwise, except for the elimination of the requirement of large freehold estates for territorial officers, the provisions for the executive and judiciary conformed to the first grade of government under the Northwest Ordinance.

With respect to the legislative power, Jefferson's plan went beyond the first grade, wherein governor and judges made the laws, and yet did not attain the second, wherein the power was shared with a representative assembly. Lower Louisiana easily satisfied the population requirement for the latter, but Jefferson declined to trust the largely alien populace with legislative power. Instead, he proposed an "assembly of notables": twenty-four distinguished characters annually appointed by the governor and sharing with him the lawmaking power. The concept was French, of course. Jefferson supposed it would be more acceptable to the Louisianans than "a legislature of judges." Still, as he confessed to Breckinridge, it was "a sudden conceit" to which he was not attached.

Jefferson also proposed in the government bill a ban on the importation of slaves from abroad—the same as had been imposed on the Mississippi Territory five years before. Moreover, to cover the peculiar case of South Carolina, which had reopened its doors to the African trade, slaves could be brought in only from those American states that prohibited foreign importation. Since the treaty obligated the United States to protect the property of the inhabitants, including slave property, the only place the institution could be legally attacked was at the gates to the territory. Jefferson proposed to close the foreign entrance but leave open the domestic. Realistically, he could do no more. To lock up this rich country to slaves, to prohibit southern planters from migrating there, to force the territory into an economic pattern alien to itself and to its neighbors—Jefferson never even considered these propositions. He did, at one point, consider tacking on a clause pledging emancipation to the grandchildren of slaves henceforth carried to Louisiana. But he quickly dropped the idea. Lower Louisiana was not very promising ground on which to test the federal power to restrict slavery in the territories.

Jefferson sent his plan to Breckinridge in the strictest confidence. No one should know he had even "put pen to paper" on the subject. "I am this particular," he said, "because you know with what bloody teeth and fangs the Federalists will attack any sentiment or principles known to come from me, and what blackguardisms and personalities they make it the occasion of vomiting forth." Eleven days later the Kentuckian moved the appointment of a committee to prepare a plan of government for Louisiana. The bill reported to the Senate on December 30 was in all essentials Jefferson's, though known then and to history by the name of the reporting chairman, Breckinridge. It was vigorously attacked in both houses, and not only by Federalists. "It really establishes a complete despotism," said a Tennessee congressmen. Other Republicans spoke of "the wear and tear of conscience" they suffered from the measure, as well as from the revenue bill (taxation without representation!) that accompanied it. The issue of principle traced back to the fountainhead, the Declaration of Independence. If the United States could tax and govern the people of Louisiana without their consent, the American Revolution had been a sham. Adams, more a purist than most, returned to the charge again and again. The United States had no right to make laws for Louisiana. He conceded that theory could not always control practice. The bandying of the people from one sovereign to another by scratches of a pen violated natural right, yet the treaty of cession was justified. But between "a momentary departure from the inflexible rigor of theory" and "the total sacrifice of all principle" there was a wide difference. Nothing in the situation prevented the United States from obtaining the consent of the Louisianans to a government formed for them.

Adams, who also stoutly advocated a constitutional amendment to take the new country into the Union, would insist for the rest of his life that the management of the Louisiana Purchase subverted every sound principle of the Jeffersonian party. "It made the Union totally different from that for which the Constitution had been formed," he wrote in 1821. "It gives despotic power over territories purchased. It naturalizes foreign territories in a mass. It makes French and Spanish laws a large part of the laws of the Union. It introduced whole systems of legislation abhorrent to the spirit and character of our institutions, and all this done by an administration which came in blowing a trumpet against implied power. After this," he concluded, "to nibble at a bank, a road, a canal, the mere mint and cummin of the law was but glorious inconsistency." And so it was, if Republicanism demanded consistency of this kind. Jefferson, for his part, justified the departure from principle in the permanent interest of liberty and Union. He had little patience with purists who let theory tyrannize over facts. He had seen the consequences of this passion in France. Louisiana was unique, yet perhaps not unlike France under the Old Regime. The only responsible statesmanship was to deal with it on its own terms. "Although it is acknowledged that our fellow citizens are as yet as incapable of self-government as children," Jefferson observed, "yet some cannot bring themselves to suspend its principles for a single moment." It was a suspension, not a subversion, of principle that he called for.

As finally passed in March (51 to 45 in the House) the Breckinridge Act was limited to one year, all power being vested in the President and his appointees during that time. The act prohibited the foreign slave trade. It annulled Spanish land grants after October 1800. Many federal laws were extended to lower Louisiana, or the Orleans Territory as it was named. The country above the 33rd parallel, called the District of Louisiana, was temporarily annexed to the Indiana Territory, interdicted to slavery.

New Orleans already seethed with discontent. Planters and merchants complained of the loss of ancient privileges. The trade with Spain and her colonies had previously been free; now, of course, it paid the same duties as all other trade. The sugar growers had been privileged under the laws of the Indies to pay their debts with the product of their harvest; but the court of justice introduced by Claiborne knew nothing of these laws, it was said, and executions for debt, in lands, slaves, and equipment, were ruining the planters. This court, like the city council, conducted its business in the English language, a grievance voiced repeatedly, usually coupled with complaint against the Governor, whose ignorance of the language and the customs of the country affronted the native populace. Trivial events rising out of the conflict of cultures threatened to explode into international incidents. For example, at a public ball in January, French officers and civilians boisterously interrupted an American country dance, *contre danse, anglais* in their lingo, hence partial to the English, and demanded a waltz instead. Swords were drawn, a riot ensued, a French officer was arrested. No blood flowed but tempers flared for weeks to come. The French commissioner took an interest in the matter. His continued presence, along with the former Spanish officials, proved a constant irritant and an invitation to intrigue by the disaffected of every nationality.

Thrown into this cauldron of troubles, the government act

brought things to a boil. Etiénne Boré, mayor of New Orleans by Claiborne's appointment, resigned his office charging that the new government scheduled to begin October 1 annihilated the rights of the people. Boré joined the growing party of malcontents. While mainly French, it counted among its leaders several ambitious Americans. Clark was one of these. Hating Claiborne, wishing the governorship himself, he was especially dangerous because of his close association with the old Spanish officialdom and the Creole merchants and planters. Another troublemaker, Edward Livingston, had just arrived in the territory, seeking a fresh start for a blighted career. As Jefferson's attorney general for New York, he had defaulted to the government in a huge amount. Forced to resign, he had then joined a battery of lawyers to argue Madrid's contention that France, not Spain, as Washington insisted, was responsible for the spoliations of American commerce in Spanish waters before the Peace of Amiens. A Jeffersonian outcast, Livingston had nothing to lose in taking up the cause of the opposition in Louisiana.

At a public meeting called by this party on June 1, it was decided to prepare a memorial to Congress. Livingston wrote the memorial—a petition of rights and grievances mimicking the style of American petitions to George III a generation before. Adopted at a second public meeting a month later, it then circulated far and wide for signatures. The memorial complained of many things: the tyranny of the English language, the unsettlement of land titles, the substitution of licensing for monopoly in the Indian trade, the high import duties, and so on. But the principal thrusts were against a system of government in which the people had no voice and the prohibition of the slave trade. Taxation without representation, the domination of the executive, the dependence of the judiciary—these forms of tyranny had been repudiated in 1776 and American government had been raised on opposite principles "fundamental, indefeasible, self-evident, and eternal." "Are truths, then, so well founded, so universally acknowledged, inapplicable only to us?" the petitioners asked. "Do political axioms on the Atlantic become problems when transferred to the shores of the Mississippi?" The memorialists, having thus shoved Jefferson's own words down his throat, went on to construe the third article of the treaty of cession as a guarantee of immediate statehood, since only by statehood could the inhabitants be "incorporated in the Union." Jefferson would find little merit in the argument. Whatever that ambiguous phrase meant, it clearly did not impose an obligation of immediate statehood. The strident demand became more understandable when linked with the demand for reopening the slave trade. As a state Louisiana would be free to import slaves, at least until 1808 when the federal constitutional prohibition would take effect. The demand for slaves was urgent and emphatic. The Louisianans, observed the former French commissioner, "could not have been attacked in a more vulnerable spot." On this point alone, Claiborne told Washington, the memorial accurately reflected the opinion of the inhabitants both French and American. Jefferson became convinced that the bar to the slave traffic lay at the bottom of the dissension in Louisiana. And he must have reflected sadly on the irony of a people petitioning for their rights that they might import and enslave Africans.

During the summer Jefferson tended the tedious business of filling offices in the territory. The principal difficulty was with the legislative council which Breckinridge had substituted for his "assembly of notables" and then made appointive of the President instead of the Governor. He tried to appoint bilinguists only and to strike a balance between the French and the American, giving the edge to the latter on the 13 member council. Unfortunately, he had to proceed with the commissions before receiving Claiborne's recommendations reflecting the shift of political loyalties since June. As a result, most of those nominated for the council, Clark and Boré at the head of the list, declined to serve. Not until December was Claiborne able to fill out enough blank commissions to make a quorum in the council and thus put the government in motion.

The decision to retain Claiborne as Governor was no more popular in Congress than in the territory. Claiborne had come into Congress from Tennessee in 1797, having barely attained his majority, and grown men continued to think of him as a mere boy. Jefferson recognized his limitations for the office he now considered the second most important in the United States. Inability to speak French was only his most obvious handicap. Observers described him as "awkward," "slovenly," and "below his place." He had neither the wealth nor the fame nor the dignity Louisianans seemed to expect in a governor. Jefferson had hoped to allay discontents with a master

785

stroke: the appointment of the Marquis de Lafayette. The Revolutionary hero had been stripped of fame and fortune in France. In 1802, at Jefferson's bidding, Congress had voted Lafayette a huge grant of land north of the Ohio in the hope that he would return to live and die in the country of his dreams. With the acquisition of Louisiana, reason and interest came to the aid of sentiment. Jefferson asked Congress to amend the terms of the grant so as to permit Lafayette to take up his lands in Louisiana. This was done, but Lafayette became an absentee lord and declined the governorship. Monroe had been the President's next choice, but he could not be spared from diplomatic assignment in Europe and, when that was finished, spurned the offer. After canvassing other prospects Jefferson reluctantly concluded to stick with Claiborne. He had a year's experience (and two years in Mississippi); he was loyal, trustworthy, and well intentioned; and his rejection while under fire would only embolden the opposition. Claiborne proved a sound choice after all. Nonetheless, it was perhaps the most unpopular appointment Jefferson ever made.

As the plot thickened in New Orleans, Jefferson decided that even if the Louisianans were not ready for representative government, Congress should go ahead and introduce it in order to avoid a calamity infinitely worse. The grievances alleged by the malcontents did not impress him, yet it would be foolhardy to ignore them. Mounting dissension, disunionism, appeals to the First Consul, foreign intervention—vague reports of these dangers came to Jefferson from New Orleans, from Paris, even from London. Whatever the evils to be anticipated from the extension of representative government to the Louisianans, he told Madison in August, they "will not be so serious as leaving them the pretext of calling in a foreign empire between them and us." He returned to the point a week later: "I am so much impressed with the expediency of putting a termination to the right of France to patronize the rights of Louisiana, which will cease with their complete adoption as citizens of the United States, that I hope to see that take place on the meeting of Congress." No hasty retreat to the safety of republican dogma, no sudden conversion to the immutable rights of untutored Creoles, produced this decision. It was a political response to a political situation, one that still wore a dangerous foreign complexion in the President's eyes. The same "expediency" that caused him to oppose representative government for Louisiana in 1803 caused him to advocate it in 1804. Without changing his direction, he changed his timetable, advancing the stage of representative government ahead of the gradual process of Americanization that he still believed the only permanent solution.

Jefferson came to this decision before he read the Louisiana Memorial. Three deputies of the opposition group, Derbigny, Destréhan, and Sauvé, presented the memorial to Congress in the fall. Their principal object, Claiborne advised Madison, was the opening of the African trade, the demand for statehood being only a convenient façade. Republican rhymsters got the point, as evidenced by the concluding lines of "The Louisiana Memorial Abridged":

> O spread lov'd Freedom far and wide.
> Receive us to your arms as Brothers
> And grant us *to make slaves of others.*

Federalists welcomed and Republicans shunned the Creole deputies. The President's reception was especially frigid; by their own account "he studiously avoided conversing . . . upon every subject that had relation to their mission." They found a better listener in the Vice President, to whom they were introduced by General Wilkinson. These two gentlemen had already concocted plans for a conspiracy in the Southwest that depended on the agitation at New Orleans for its success.

Although Congress rejected the petition for immediate statehood, the act of March 2, 1805, introduced the second stage of territorial government, including a representative assembly, on the plan of the Northwest Ordinance, omitting its freehold qualification for the franchise. A companion bill called local land titles into question and demanded that they be proved to the satisfaction of the United States. The three deputies found little consolation in these measures. They returned to New Orleans mortified and discouraged. Creole opposition grew bold. To no one's surprise the first legislature, convened in November, was dominated by the old inhabitants. A virtual stalemate ensued in the government. Backed by the President, Claiborne endeavored to speed the progress of Americanization. The assembly worked just as hard to turn it back. Plans for an educational system in which Claiborne, like Jefferson, placed great stock came to nothing. He vetoed bills to introduce a black code and to restrict membership in the assembly to native Louisianans. The showdown came when he vetoed legislation to retain the old Spanish civil law. The assembly quit in protest. Claiborne and Clark thought to settle their differences with dueling pistols, alas, without success. (It was not the Governor's only duel. He had been wounded once, his secretary had been killed in defense of the Governor's honor, and disease had robbed him of a wife and daughter.) The presence of the Spanish in West Florida contributed to this persistent hostility to Americanization. Jefferson would make almost any sacrifice to get West Florida, not just for itself but for its bearing on the future of Louisiana. This chronicle of misadventure began with the government's claim under the treaty and continued its troubled course in Jefferson's second administration. Claiborne, meanwhile, discovered the path of political conciliation. Smuggling, tolerated if not approved by the government, together with relaxation of controls over domestic imports, overcame the shortage of slave labor. In 1808 the Governor acquiesced in the adoption of Livingston's civil code derived from the Roman law, thus terminating happily what had seemed an irresoluble conflict. The road to statehood in the Orleans Territory would never be smooth, yet after nearly a decade of strife and confusion born of the clash of cultures, laws, and nationalities, the end would be reached in 1812.

It was, all considered, an unprecedented achievement. The nation incorporated a foreign dominion and committed it to the status of equality in a union of free men. Freedom followed the flag in Louisiana. First one, then many new states fastened on the land; and the nation grew by accretion rather than by conquest and domination. None of this was fated to happen. Under a different leadership it might not have happened. To be sure, the principles of the American polity set the direction and the Northwest Ordinance provided a working formula, but neither the principles nor the formula had been made with a view to foreign territory, foreign laws and institutions, or a foreign populace. The acquisition of Louisiana presented the government with a situation quite new. To have imposed, arbitrarily, rules addressed to another condition would have been the height of folly in Jefferson's opinion, not because they were wrong —on the contrary they were eternally right—but because they would be permanently jeopardized by dogmatism and precipitancy in their application. Jefferson's approach was eminently pragmatic. Never losing sight of the end, he improvised the means, constantly making adjustments to the changing balance of risks in Louisiana, so far as he was able to assess them in Washington. He could not always be right in such a situation. He overreacted to fears of subversive foreign influence, for instance. But he did not make any big mistakes, and whatever the faults of his improvisation, it was vindicated in its workings over the longer run of history.

An event of the magnitude of the Louisiana Purchase profoundly affected everything to come after. Because of it the prospects of the Union were at once far grander and far more terrifying than before, and government must assume new responsibilities addressed to this condition. Because of it the United States acquired greater independence and self-assurance in the affairs of nations, which would be reflected in the diplomacy Jefferson practiced toward Spain and in the developing crisis over neutral rights. Because of it the Republicans tightened their political grip on the nation, growing bold in power and making freaks and fanatics of their opposition. These tendencies would show themselves in Jefferson's second administration, but they were already in evidence at the close of the first.

Triumph on the Mississippi made the President ten feet tall in the public eye, his re-election a foregone conclusion many months before the long, drawn-out contest began. The election did not pass without the usual Job-like utterance from Jefferson. Oh what he would give to exchange "the deadly feuds of party" for "the affections of domestic society"! The protest had become almost a ritual, transparently false, some thought, for no man could go on living in what he hated and despised. But so it had been for many years, and the death of his younger daughter Maria in April gave a peculiar poignancy to the old sadness. Maria, always the delicate one, never recovered from the birth of a second child earlier in the year. Jefferson reached her near the end of a lingering illness, immediately transported her four miles on a litter from Martha's home at Edgehill to Monticello, nursed her, and watched her die in the bright flush of spring. He poured out his grief to the oldest of his friends,

John Page. "Others may lose of their abundance, but I, of my want, have lost even the half of all I had. My evening prospects now hang on the thread of a single life. . . . The hope with which I had looked forward to the moment when, resigning public cares to younger hands, I was to retire to that domestic comfort from which the last great step is to be taken, is fearfully blighted." There had been so much affliction and slaughter since he and Page had come on the scene in the first moments of the Revolutionary torrent that he felt like a lonely straggler marking the footsteps of the fallen. He put on no mourning this sad spring and quickly resumed his usual rounds. People said, "What a Stoic Mr. Jefferson is." But it was not that. "I have had experience enough in the school of affliction," he said, "to know that time and silence are its best medicines and occupation as soon as the state of mind can bear it." One of the letters of condolence came from Abigail Adams, who had taken Polly to her heart many years ago in London. Jefferson was pleased by the letter, not just for the sentiments it contained but for the opportunity to renew a friendship that ought to have been safe from the slings and arrows of party warfare. Whatever their differences of opinion, he had never closed his heart to John Adams nor to his wife, Jefferson wrote. He went on to say in a spirit of candor that only one act of Adams's political life, the midnight appointments, ever gave him a moment's personal displeasure. Instead of grasping this overture, Abigail replied in a tone of political recrimination. Another exchange of letters closed the correspondence on a discordant note. The time had not yet come for the revival of the old friendship.

While Jefferson had no desire to prolong his confinement in office, he was far less willing to gratify his enemies by going into retirement. Apparently he did not commit himself to a second term until early in the election year. The "unfounded calumnies of the Federal party," he said at that time, had obliged him to throw himself on the verdict of the country despite his "decided purpose" to retire. He realized too that his continued leadership was necessary to secure the permanent ascendancy of the party that carried all his hopes for the American experiment. Whatever his misgivings about a second term, he was quite ready to undertake it.

Virtually unanimous in support of the President, Republicans centered their attention on the vice presidential nomination. A constitutional amendment, the 12th, then in the process of ratification by the states, would prevent any recurrence of the near abortion of the popular will in 1801 by requiring separate ballots for President and Vice President. The amendment would close the only loophole through which the Federalists might evict the President, and they fought it vigorously for two years. Some of them were still flirting with Aaron Burr. Burr had lost caste in his own party. Suspicions aroused by his conduct in the contest of 1801 were never quieted and, in fact, tended to be confirmed by his less than ardent support of the administration and his cautious pandering to Federalists in Washington. Jefferson's coolness toward the wily New Yorker first showed itself in patronage decisions. His political death warrant was signed, however, not in Washington, not by the President, but by DeWitt Clinton in New York. The ensuing factional struggle went on for three years, in the press, in the courts, at the polls, and on the dueling grounds. For sheer political violence the spectacle was unsurpassed. Jefferson watched from afar with mingled horror and fascination. Through James Cheetham, a Clintonian editor, whom the administration employed to publish the laws in New York and who regularly supplied the President with pamphlets and newspapers, he received a blow by blow account of the proceedings. It was a biased account, of course, constantly insinuating that the would-be usurper of 1801 still plotted to snatch the presidency from Jefferson by an unprincipled coalition with the Federalists. Burrites, on the other hand, accused the Clintons, uncle and nephew, of using the President as a front for their schemes while waiting in ambush for the administration. Caught between this crossfire, Jefferson must have been puzzled to distinguish his friends from his enemies. The choice was difficult morally, politically much easier, for the Clintonians controlled the state organization.

In January 1804 Burr came to Jefferson and offered to give up the battle, thus ending a dangerous schism in the party, if he could avail himself of an honorable retreat, some mark of favor, perhaps appointment as Livingston's successor in Paris, which would declare to the world that he retired in the President's confidence. Jefferson coolly parried this overture. In 1800 he had needed Burr; now Burr, this "modern Machiavel," as Republicans called him, was a political liability. Reflecting on the interview, he said he had never trusted Burr, who seemed a man "always at market," and their association being entirely political, had never been intimate with him. Burr returned to New York and at once plunged into a race for the governorship against the Clintonians, or regular Republicans. Both factions laid claim to Jefferson's support. He honestly deplored the schism, saying, in effect, "a plague on both your houses." Officially he was neutral, but his "secret wishes" were all on the side of the Clintonians and their candidate, Morgan Lewis.

Near the end of February, as the New York campaign gathered momentum, the congressional Republicans caucused in Washington to nominate candidates for President and Vice President. Jefferson maintained his hands-off policy. The caucus was just as unanimous in its rejection of the Vice President as it was in its endorsement of the President. Burr received not a single vote, and as if to underscore the humiliation, the caucus nominated George Clinton. Burr was virtually read out of the party. The frightful din set up in New York embarrassed the party nationally, and the reverberations of the state conflict convinced Republicans nation-wide that Burr had indeed intrigued against Jefferson in the election of 1800. Jefferson and his friends had been reluctant to draw this conclusion, even less to admit it publicly. It disgraced the party. But what would have been disgrace if admitted in 1801 had the appearance of political valor in 1804. Repudiated in Washington, Burr nevertheless clung to Jefferson's coattails in the gubernatorial contest. The New York Federalists supported him almost to a man. It was 1801 all over again. Voting for Burr, Federalists hoped to sow seeds of discord in the Republican ranks, rally northern Republicans against Virginia domination, perhaps even create in New York the nucleus of the Northern Confederacy some of the Federalist witch-doctors had been prescribing since the affliction of the Louisiana Purchase. Again, as in 1801, Alexander Hamilton opposed their scheme. Through the New York *Evening Post,* established largely under his auspices, Hamilton had kept up a constant barrage against the administration. He had no love for Jefferson or his works; but he hated Aaron Burr and again tried to turn the Federalists from him. His pleas were no more heeded than before, but Burr, crushed in the election, chose to take his revenge on Hamilton, killing him on a bright July morning on the dueling grounds at Weehawken. Checked at every turn, hunted as a murderer, Burr became a political desperado. Jefferson himself, thus far a silent partner in his destruction, would have to bring the culprit to justice at last.

Although Burr was defeated, the New York contest underscored the importance of vigilance and unity in the Republican ranks. The problem was not confined to New York; intramural quarrels split the party in Pennsylvania, for instance, and each faction accused the other of flirting with the Federalists. Jefferson dissected the motives of the opposition in a letter to the Postmaster General. "The Federalists know, that, *eo nomine*, they are gone forever. Their object, therefore, is how to return into power under some other form. Undoubtedly, they have but one means, which is to divide the Republicans, join the minority, and barter with them for the cloak of their name. . . . Thus a bastard system of federo-republicanism will rise on the ruins of the true principles of our revolution." He did not think this "crooked scheme" would work—the mass of Republicans were sound—but the danger was ever-present and, henceforth, never far from his mind. Partly for this reason he became more and more insistent that recipients of the federal patronage have Republican credentials. Any adulteration of the official corps, any schism in the party, any insurgency in Congress, any agitation of a crisis atmosphere played into Federalist hands and must, accordingly, be suppressed.

Disunionism and foreign intrigue, Jefferson generally assumed, entered into the schemes of ultra Federalists. In the early months of 1804 the political air wafted rumors of a disunionist conspiracy in New England. They undoubtedly reached Jefferson's ear, and he could hardly fail to suspect some connection between Burr's candidacy in New York and the alleged plot of Senators Pickering, Tracy, Griswold, Plumer, and their followers in New England. For these men, New England, omitting Rhode Island, was the last refuge of sanity in an America gone mad with democracy. Time was running out. The Virginians ruled the nation with "a rod of iron," New England's power waned as the Union expanded westward, while at home Republicans beat at the doors of the state houses. The only solution lay in secession and the formation of a Northern Confederacy. Leading New York Federalists were let in on the plot, as was Burr, who smiled agreeably without committing himself, and Anthony Merry, who gleefully reported it to his government. The conspiracy collapsed after Burr's defeat and Hamilton's death. Very likely it would have met the same fate in any event, for most ultraists, while they sympathized with the disunion scheme, thought it foolhardy in 1804 and preferred to wait for the redeeming crisis democracy was sure to produce at no very distant time. The inner secrets of this misadventure were quite beyond Jefferson's ken in 1804. But he knew enough to realize that New England, at least, was still vulnerable to Federalist intrigue, for which the only certain remedy was the Republicanization of these states.

The secession plot, engineered by men who had helped raise the structure of federal union and power, was the most extreme partisan reaction to a Jeffersonian nationalism that increasingly used this structure for its own ends. The Louisiana Purchase threatened the power of the eastern states. The interests of dominant groups in these states had been well served by Federalist nationalism. Jeffersonian nationalism, on the other hand, seemed designed for the aggrandizement of the South and the West with interests of another kind. The sectional politics of the dispirited Federalists was thus a logical sequel to nationalism on the constricted Hamiltonian model. And the author of the Kentucky Resolutions of 1798 occupied six years later broader national ground than any president before him. The ultra Federalist fear of Jeffersonian nationalism combined also the fear of democracy. Democracy was the country's real disease, Hamilton lectured the disunionists the day before his death; separation might briefly retard but could not cure it. By relaxing restraints on the popular will and investing its agents with paramount authority, by perfecting the party machinery in every state, the Jeffersonian system worked relentlessly toward a democratic consolidation of power much more awesome than the Federalist version based on elitist politics, fiscal manipulation, and ministerial leadership.

The issue was most clearly drawn in the partisan encounter over the impeachment of two federal judges, John Pickering of the New Hampshire District and Samuel Chase of the Supreme Court. The Repeal Act of 1802 had not touched the foundations of judicial power. As the branch of the government still in Federalist control, the judiciary possessed the means to humble and humiliate the Republican administration and make a farce of democratic principle. Were the people or the judges sovereign? "We shall see who is master of the ship," Caesar Rodney boldly stated the issue. "Whether men appointed for life or the immediate representatives of the people agreeably to the Constitution are to give laws to the community." Since the federal judiciary was largely the creation of Congress, the issue might have been settled in more or less permanent fashion by legislation curtailing the jurisdiction of the courts, by packing them with Republicans, or by devices to secure their responsibility. None of these avenues was taken, as Jefferson and his friends stumbled upon the least effective and most offensive of all expedients, impeachment.

In February 1803, three weeks before Marshall's opinion in the case of *Marbury v. Madison*, Jefferson referred the complaint against Judge Pickering to the House of Representatives, the body charged with the power of impeachment for "high crimes and misdemeanors." The judge was a Federalist, but his bizarre conduct proceeded from intoxication and insanity, and it was this condition, not political malice or criminal behavior, that called for his removal from the bench. Unfortunately, while the Constitution provided for the appointment of judges in "good behavior," it made no provision for removal in cases of "bad behavior" unless by way of impeachment, limited, however, to offences indictable at law. In England and in a number of the states, judges were subject to removal by the executive on the address of the legislature. Jefferson and most Republicans favored a federal procedure of this kind. Had it existed, it would have reached the peculiar case of the New Hampshire judge as well as the general problem of partisanship on the federal bench. But amending the Constitution seemed a risky and tedious business. Although advocated by doctrinaire Virginians, it was not seriously considered in Washington. Nor were other reforms, such as an appellate jurisdiction in the legislature over controverted judicial opinions, which the Chief Justice himself seemed willing to concede. Jefferson resorted to the constitutional process, impeachment, without realizing its pitfalls. To impeach and then convict Pickering, the Republicans were forced to argue that the constitutional provision extended to cases of misbehavior, hence could be used to remove a judge who had committed no crime. The process was transformed from a criminal proceeding into a method of removal. Federalists accused the administration of launching a reign of terror in the judiciary. "The Judges . . . are, if possible, to be removed. Their judicial opinions, if at all questionable through mere errors of judgment, are interpreted into crimes and to be ground of impeachment." And so what began as an honest attempt to remove an unfit judge developed into a heated political controversy in which the two parties became more and more committed to opposed doctrines of judicial responsibility and judicial supremacy.

The Chase impeachment seemed to justify the worst Federalist fears. On May 2, 1803, Justice Chase, one of the most irascible Federalists, delivered a slashing attack on democratic tendencies to the federal grand jury in Baltimore. In the course of his harangue he assailed equal rights, universal suffrage, the Repeal Act, and outrages against property. "Our republican Constitution," he predicted, "will sink into a mobocracy—the worst of all possible governments." Tory language from a signer of the Declaration of Independence! A few days later Jefferson wrote to Joseph Nicholson, a Republican stalwart who was managing the Pickering impeachment in the House. "Ought this seditious and official attack on the principles of our Constitution . . . go unpunished," he asked, "and to whom so pointedly as yourself will the public look for the necessary measures?" In this roundabout fashion Jefferson invited the impeachment of Chase, declining at the same time any further interference in the matter. Republicans remembered Chase as the violently partisan judge in several sedition trials, especially Callender's, and in the treason trial and conviction of John Fries for opposing the direct tax of 1798. His charge to the grand jury again brought politics into the administration of justice and, in addition, announced principles that to Republican ears were incompatible with the Constitution he was sworn to uphold. Inevitably, the impeachment of Chase was a political act. Jefferson had no illusions on the point. Of course, the Federalists held him responsible. In their opinion the Chase impeachment was only one of a series intended to drive every Federalist from the bench. The fact that the House voted the indictment on the same day, March 12, 1804, that the Senate passed the verdict of guilty on Pickering seemed to substantiate their fears. But if Jefferson pursued a grand strategy against the judiciary, he left no record of it. The

Chase impeachment was a piece of improvisation, like every other encounter in the so-called "war on the judiciary," and when the smoke of battle finally cleared no one should have been surprised by how little had been accomplished.

Despite party schism, judicial arrogance, Federalist malice, and the treacherous shoals navigated in Louisiana, the President rode the crest of the wave as the election of 1804 came on. In foreign affairs, where he had been especially fortunate, three problems claimed his attention, and toward each of them he acted with the greater freedom and assurance born of the Louisiana Purchase. The defense of neutral rights, primarily against British infractions, increasingly troubled the administration. The Anglo-American rapprochement commenced by the Federalists had been carried forward by the Republicans under the incentive of French danger on the Mississippi. Considerable progress had been made. The long vexatious issue of Revolutionary debts had been settled. And prospects held out for settlement of the boundary with Canada, liberalization of commerce, and perhaps even curtailment of the British practice of impressment. The Louisiana Purchase relieved the pressure for conciliation on the American side. Edward Thornton, the former British chargé, now back in the foreign office, comparing Merry's reports with his before the Louisiana Purchase, could scarcely credit the evidence of deterioration in "the manifest ill-will discovered toward us." On the British side, the exigencies of war with France led to renewed naval activity in American waters, impressments, and captures on a rising scale. France, too, offended against neutral rights. But her rivalry on the paths of commerce had never threatened the Americans. Moreover, in 1804, Jefferson pandered to France in order to secure her support for American demands against Spain. In this turn of affairs, he took a higher tone with Britain.

West Florida was an especially sticky problem. Having set up a claim to the colony under the Louisiana treaty, Jefferson hastened to use the European war to force the concession of the claim. The theory was that Spain could not defend West Florida, and that France, preferring to see it in American than in British hands, would press the cession on the Spanish court. In order to cover this eventuality and, at the same time, to impress Spain with the earnestness of American intentions, the President asked Congress for authority to establish a customs district in the area of Mobile. Congress obliged with the so-called Mobile Act in February 1804. Since Mobile Bay belonged to Spain and the act gave no clue of a hypothetical character, as something contingent on Spanish cession, it had the appearance of an arrogant invasion of foreign sovereignty. Yrujo, already short-tempered with the administration, went into a rage, unappeased by Madison's reassuring words or the President's careful exclusion of lands outside American jurisdiction from the revenue district on the Mobile. Jefferson later stated publicly that the act had been misunderstood by Spain, that it was wholly prospective; but even Gallatin thought the explanation less than candid. Yrujo finally carried his campaign to the newspapers, writing in the disguise of an American. When he was found out, as he soon was, Jefferson and Madison wanted nothing more to do with him. A similar fate overtook Pinckney in Madrid. This man, a political appointee Jefferson had come to regard as "a standing reproach" to himself, boiled over because Spain made the Mobile Act an excuse for refusing to ratify the claims convention he had negotiated two years earlier. Spanish-American relations were in a torrid state in the fall. Spanish officials rallied the Indians in the Floridas; Jefferson ordered more troops to the borderlands; and both ministers were discredited.

The Mediterranean was the third theater where Jefferson stiffened his posture. The Tripolitan campaign dragged on from year to year with feeble results. "We are . . . now exactly where we were 18 months ago," he wrote dejectedly in September 1803. The "two years' sleep," as he was soon calling it, had been induced by Commodore Morris, Dale's successor in command, who cruised the Mediterranean instead of blockading Tripoli. Jefferson also blamed meddling American consuls more interested in trade with the Barbary states than in their chastisement. Back home Gallatin took an appeasing tone, while Secretary of the Navy Smith consistently advocated a hard line in the modest debate between "hawks" and "doves" in the administration. The President repeatedly demanded a peace forced on Tripoli without a cent of tribute, yet seemed unwilling to supply the fighting ships necessary to the task. He angrily recalled Morris and then, after a court-martial finding of negligence, cashiered him from the service.

When Louisiana was secure, the President gave more attention to this "little speck of Tripoli" that alone marred the horizon. He entrusted the command to a resourceful young officer, Commodore Edward Preble. Indignities continued to pile up. The frigate *Philadelphia* ran aground and gave up its crew to the pirate-enemy. Soon, however, the tide turned. Preble blockaded and bombarded Tripoli, winning a hero's fame. Stephen Decatur's gallant exploit, destroying the captive frigate under the Pasha's nose, earned him the same renown and struck a decisive blow for American honor and courage. Jefferson now determined to push matters to a victorious conclusion. The Mediterranean squadron was powerfully reinforced—scarcely a sea-worthy vessel remained in American waters. Confident that peace could be won by diplomacy backed with naval force, he refused to endorse more extreme measures, such as the audacious plan put forth by William Eaton, formerly consul at Tunis, to lead a motley insurrectionary army overland against Tripoli. The intrepid adventurer was nevertheless permitted to return to the Mediterranean and await the progress of events. Instead he proceeded at once with his fantastic scheme. And he might have won his stake but for the fact that the stepped-up naval bombardment and blockade, assisted by the real threat of his desert army, brought the Pasha to his senses before Eaton could reach Tripoli. In 1805, after four years of war, the Pasha signed a peace that freed commerce of tribute, though the United States paid $60,000 to ransom prisoners. It was not all the President had hoped for, and Smith was downright disappointed by the treaty. But Jefferson had waited twenty years for this victory—when it came he rejoiced in it.

This leaps ahead of the story, beyond Jefferson's electoral victory at home, into the thickening morass of foreign affairs. He stood on the highest public ground in 1804. Federalists seemed resigned to their fate, a shrinking minority, though they fielded a national ticket. The candidates, C. C. Pinckney and Rufus King, were virtually invisible, as the Republicans ran against John Adams, conveniently revived as the monster symbol of the evils from which the Republican Moses had delivered the people. The contrast between four years of Adams and four of Jefferson was striking: new taxes —no taxes; profusion—economy; mounting public debt—rapid extinguishment of the debt; multiplication of offices—elimination of judges, tax-gatherers, and other useless functionaries; Indian wars—

peaceful acquisition of Indian lands; alien and sedition laws—freedom and equality; judicial arrogance—judicial chastisement; oppressive armies and wasteful navies—defensive arms only; trade burdened with restrictions—flourishing commerce; war and subservience to foreign powers—peace, independence, and national expansion.

Republicans stood on the President's record and the people responded. The seventeen states (Ohio had been added) cast 162 electoral votes for Jefferson and Clinton against 14 for Pinckney and King. Only Delaware and Connecticut, with two Maryland electors, landed in the Federalist column. Even Massachusetts went Republican. Nothing gave the President greater satisfaction. "This is truly the case wherein we may say, 'this our brother was dead, and is alive again: and was lost, and is found.' " As long as Massachusetts strayed "out of the fold," the Union could not be sound. Everything would now turn to rights; Connecticut and the remaining grumblers and disorganizers would succumb, and the "perfect consolidation" Jefferson had prophesized four years before would come to pass. "The new century opened itself by committing us on a boisterous ocean," the President mused. "But all this is now subsiding, peace is smoothing our paths at home and abroad, and if we are not wanting in the practice of justice and moderation, our tranquility and property may be preserved, until increasing numbers shall leave us nothing to fear from without." And at the close of another four years he might embrace "the nunc dimittis Domine with a satisfaction leaving nothing to desire but the last great audit."

CHAPTER TEN

President:

Second Administration

And many have imagined republics and principalities which have never been known to exist in reality; for how we live is so far removed from how we ought to live, that he who abandons what is done for what ought to be done, will rather learn to bring about his own ruin than his preservation. A man who wishes to make a profession of goodness in everything must come to grief among so many who are not good. Therefore it is necessary for a prince, who wishes to maintain himself, to learn how not to be good, and to use this knowledge and not use it, according to the necessity of the case.

Machiavelli, The Prince, *1532*

In March 4, 1805, three months after Napoleon Bonaparte crowned himself Emperor of France midst the splendor of Notre Dame in Paris, Thomas Jefferson rode up Pennsylvania Avenue to the half-finished Capitol, strolled into the half-empty Senate chamber, and in a ceremony more austere than the last again swore the Presidential oath, delivered, inaudibly, an inaugural address, and quietly departed. He conceived of this address as a *compte rendu*, showing the conformity of his administration to the principles of the first inaugural. "The former was *promise:* this is *performance.*" Jefferson's empire was one of principles, and if principles could have worn a crown, he would have crowned them. A self-congratulatory tone pervaded the address, though he was careful to remove any impression of self-applause, ascribing the merits of his administration, rather, "to the reflecting character of our citizens at large." Of foreign affairs he said little other than to reiterate his belief "that with nations, as with individuals, our interests, soundly calculated, will ever be found inseparable from our moral duties." But he was effusive about domestic affairs. Because of the elimination of internal taxes, he observed, "it may be the pleasure and pride of an American to ask, what farmer, what mechanic, what laborer, ever sees a tax-gatherer of the United States." The rapid retirement of the debt and the continuing promise of peace and prosperity pointed to the day, not far distant, when the federal revenue would be liberated, after constitutional amendment, for internal improvements—"rivers, canals, roads, arts, manufacturing, education, and other great objects." The expansion of the Union had given an urgency to this task unfelt before. He took the occasion to rebuke those who feared for the survival of the Union from the great enlargement of territory. "But who can limit the extent to which the federative principle may operate effectively?" he asked. The larger the association, the more remote its extremities, the more varied its interests, the less would the center be shaken in any crisis of affairs; and expansion within continental limits secured the nation from foreign enemies.

The longest passage of the address was a kind of allegory in which Indian savages stood in the place of bigoted Federalists, the "anti-social doctrines" of the latter being condemned by inference from the pitiful state of the former. Jefferson explained his civilizing policy toward the Indians overwhelmed by progress, his efforts to enlighten and bring them to reason against the obstacles of ignorance, prejudice, pride, and the influence of crafty chieftains who inculcated "a sanctimonious reverence for the customs of their ancestors." In short, he said, "they, too, have their anti-philosophers, who find an interest in keeping things in their present state, who dread reformation, and exert all their faculties to maintain the ascendancy of habit over the duty of improving our reason, and obeying its mandates." The force or even the recognition of the allegory was lost by cautious pruning of the address at the behest of his colleagues, Gallatin especially, who thought the terms too broad and unnecessarily offensive to "old school" New Englanders. Thus, for instance, Jefferson eliminated an allusion to the charge of "philosophism" against him: "that science disqualifies men for the direction of the public affairs of the nation is one of the artful dogmas of ignorance and bigotry." In his discussion of press and pulpit, too, he cut out the thornier passages. The draft throughout was more direct, more pungent, and more personal than the final product.

Jefferson had planned to declare in this second inaugural address that he would not again seek re-election to the presidency. He had stated his intentions privately to personal friends. As he wrote to one of them, he had come to believe that a single constitutional term of seven years, his earlier preference, was not as good as the term of four years with re-eligibility, and although the danger persisted "that reelection through life shall become habitual, and election for life follow that"—the way of France to Napoleonic despotism—the example of Washington offered a safeguard which Jefferson hoped to force into an unwritten tradition of the Constitution. In the draft he approached this question indirectly through the discussion of freedom of the press. The experiment he had made proved that truth could not be put down by the calumnies of a licentious press; the people had pronounced their verdict at the polls. But instead of going on to say, as he had intended, that it would not now be necessary for him to appeal to the public again, he held his tongue and substituted a new paragraph in defense of state laws against false and defamatory publications. It was best, Jefferson had been persuaded, "not to put a continuance [in office] out of my power in defiance of all circumstances."

This was sound judgment; unfortunately, by privately confessing his true sentiments, Jefferson signaled the race for the next presidential election three years in advance, dangerously widening factional rifts among Republicans and undercutting his own position politically. Looking confidently now, in the second inaugural, to the completion of that "harmony of sentiment" envisioned in the first— to that "entire union of opinion, which gives to a nation the blessings of harmony, and the benefit of all its strength"—he was also uncomfortably aware that the problem of recalcitrant Federalists was being succeeded by the problem of dissident Republicans. Writing to Nicholas he said he had thought his situation four years ago, facing a humiliated opposition, the most unenviable to be imagined. "But I consider that as less painful than to be placed between conflicting friends. There my way was clear and my mind made up. I never for a moment had to balance between two opinions." Division and discord among friends, all Republicans, contributed to the ordeal of his second administration.

Within a week of the inauguration Jefferson went to Monticello for his usual spring holiday. The Eighth Congress, climaxed by the trial and acquittal of Justice Chase, had adjourned on March 3—many congressmen fled the capital before the inauguration. The President returned to his desk in April, then in mid-July, at the onset of the "sickly season" in the tidewater, again made the bruising four-day trek to Monticello, this time for a long stay, until early October. Such was the regular pattern. During this season the department heads scattered to their homes as well, and government was carried on by underlings in Washington through a network of postal communication. Jefferson said he passed more hours in public business at Monticello than he did in Washington, and it was more laborious because everything had to be written. In August or September Madison usually came over from Montpelier, some twenty miles distant, to take stock with his friend; on occasion one of the other secretaries visited the mountain with his family. Except for an annual excursion to his plantation in Bedford County, Jefferson did not stir from home.

The Republicans in Massachusetts, after scoring impressive gains in the spring canvass, begged him to make a tour through the Northeast; but he declined popular exposure of this kind, offering the press of business as an excuse for what he found personally distasteful. Had politics or popularity been paramount considerations with him he would have undertaken the northern tour, perhaps a southern as well, as President Washington had done before him; but "the man of the people" would not stoop to the little arts of leadership that his own political convictions, and his own legend, far more than Washington's, recommended. He was still anxious to complete the rout of the Federalists in Massachusetts. Lincoln's resignation opened the way for a cabinet reshuffle that would strengthen the Bay State's influence in the administration. Jacob Crowninshield, the

Salem merchant and congressman, was slated to become Secretary of the Navy, replacing Smith who would take the more congenial office of Attorney General. But Crowninshield backed out in March, and Jefferson, after prevailing on Smith to stay in his post, spent the next several months shopping for an Attorney General. He finally had to rob the Senate of one of his most reliable lieutenants, John Breckinridge; but no sooner was the Kentuckian appointed in December than he died. Jefferson now robbed the House of a primary leader, Caesar A. Rodney. With his appointment the cabinet was again complete and would not be disturbed until Jefferson's last days in office.

Trials of Foreign Policy

During these months between the old Congress and the new the administration engaged in a major reassessment of foreign policy. With the formation of the Third Coalition against Napoleon all Europe was engulfed in war. Jefferson could again, as he had written to an English friend, "bless the almighty being who in gathering together the waters under the heavens . . . divided the dry lands of your hemisphere from the dry lands of ours, and said 'here, at least, be there peace.' " But war ravaged the blessed ocean too, hence there could be no easy peace for America; and such were the stakes in the European conflict that Jefferson's system of manipulating American neutrality to force concessions from the great adversaries faced its severest trial. The nature of the problem would become clearer in the fall, after Trafalgar ensured British supremacy on the seas, and clearer yet in December, after Austerlitz heralded the collapse of the Third Coalition. "What an awful spectacle does the world exhibit at this instance," Jefferson would then observe. "One nation bestriding the continent of Europe like a Colossus, and another roaming unbridled on the ocean." If there was comfort in the division of the continent and the ocean between the belligerents, it was also this division that made America's position increasingly difficult. For Britain could play fast and loose with the United States in the Atlantic with little danger to herself, and France, master of a continent, had small need of any assistance the United States might supply. Jefferson continued to perceive the European power balance in the conventional image of scales—a balancing machine—which if depressed on one side caused reciprocal action on the other. But with the polarization of European power this conception grew obsolete. The damage the United States could inflict on British sea power was scarcely enough to engage Napoleon's interest; and the United States could do virtually nothing for Britain on the Continent. Between these extremities of power, neutral America could discover little leverage for action, though Jefferson would grasp at every elusive opportunity. The lesson he had been painfully learning was now driven home: The enemy was not Britain or France or Spain but Europe itself.

All the signs in the early months of 1805 pointed to the end of the decade-long Anglo-American rapprochement. The commercial articles of the Jay Treaty had expired. William Pitt had returned to power and in a few month's time moved the country from complacent to aggressive belligerency. The Third Coalition had been formed, embracing the Northern powers, Russia and Sweden, heretofore the fitful champions of neutral rights in Europe, now leaving the United States alone in their defense. The Royal Navy stepped up its harassment of American commerce; the impressment of American seamen soared to new heights; privateers infested American waters and plundered American trade. Before he left Washington in July, Jefferson sent out a small naval force to cruise against the privateers and, without a stitch of authority, ordered the arrest of any found within the limits of the Gulf Stream.

On July 23 the British vice-admiralty judge Sir William Scott abruptly reversed the country's policy on the neutral carrying trade from enemy colonies. This decision in the case of the ship *Essex* marked a return to strict interpretation of the Rule of 1756, which Britain had tried to interpolate into international law during the Seven Years War. According to the rule, a trade closed in time of peace could not be legitimately opened in time of war; hence a neutral, like the United States, could not carry the produce of the French and Spanish West Indian colonies to the Continent. Strictly British, the rule had no standing in international law, and Great Albion herself observed it only at convenience. She had revived it with devastating effect on American carriers late in 1793. The United

States then evaded the restriction by doing indirectly what it allegedly could not do directly. Enemy cargoes were landed in American ports, passed through customs, and re-exported to belligerent ports on the Continent. For a time the British admiralty courts contended this was fraudulent: the insertion of a neutral port did not neutralize cargoes in "continuous voyage" from one enemy port to another. But by 1801 the judges, without retracting the Rule of 1756, had accepted the principle of the "broken voyage": the landing of the cargo and the payment of duties, even if withdrawn on re-export, broke the continuity of the voyage and neutralized the trade. Now, in 1805, the esteemed Scott ruled that unless the neutral shipper could prove original intent to terminate the voyage in an American port, ship and cargo were subject to seizure and condemnation. Intent being subjective, the ruling could not be fairly applied, and it transferred the burden of proof from the captor to the shipper. The re-export trade floated American prosperity. By 1805 over one-half the country's exports were re-exports, from the colonies of all belligerents including the British. The United States had become the great entrepôt for Europe. Quite aside from the rights of the case, the trade was too valuable to be put to hazard.

What had motivated this shift of policy in Britain? A quasi-official explanation soon appeared in the form of a pamphlet, *War in Disguise; or the Frauds of the Neutral Flags*, whose anonymous author was James Stephen. After a long sleep Britain had awakened to the true character of the American re-export trade, the argument began. It was not a *bona fide* trade, pursued on its own account, but a fraudulent trade, a war in disguise, in tacit alliance with the enemy. Its effect was to negate British maritime and naval superiority in a struggle for survival against the land monster, Napoleon. The military costs of surrendering this superiority were quite evident; what was particularly notable in Stephen's defense of the new policy was the emphasis placed on the commercial costs of the old. The United States, as the last neutral of consequence, took possession of a great trade from which Britain had previously reaped huge profits, from freights, insurance, duties, and mercantile charges. By repossessing this trade Britain would put down a dangerous commercial rival and force it back into channels profitable to herself, even at the risk of supplying her own enemies on the Continent. At the same time, British West Indian commodities, currently under-sold on the Continent because of the American competition, would regain the market; British seamen fled to American vessels would re-turn; and a license to plunder neutral traders would be extended to the whole British marine. Such was the spirit of the new policy. Meanwhile, in the United States, Madison assembled the legal am-munition to demolish it. His learned report, published in January, tore away the fictitious defenses of the *Essex* policy and revealed the real motive as British jealousy of American commerce. He and Jef-ferson had been fighting on this front for a quarter century. Reason revolted, as Jefferson observed, at the idea that "a belligerent takes to himself a commerce with its own enemy which it denies to a neu-tral, on the ground of its aiding that enemy in the war." The preten-sion, inconsistent in itself, was yet entirely consistent with British strategy since the Revolution to subvert American wealth and power.

On the very day of the *Essex* decision Monroe returned to Eng-land, where he had succeeded Rufus King. He at once sensed the stiffening of British posture toward the United States. The new pol-icy, with the wave of seizures in the West Indies, was an experi-ment, he said, to see how much the Americans would bear. It must be resisted. But could the country take on both Britain and Spain at the same time? Having just come from a special mission to Spain, Monroe was impressed by the interconnections between these two American quarrels and inclined to think success with one, as proof of strength, would promote success with the other. France, more-over, was the crucial link to both. A satellite of France, weak and de-pressed, Spain was at Napoleon's command. He had no interest now in the Floridas or in an altercation between Spain and the United States; and he must see that the sooner this dispute was settled the sooner the United States could give its full attention to Britain. The fact that money would change hands or, better yet, that American stock would be thrown to European speculators in any transaction for the Floridas, seemed to offer further inducement to Napoleon, Talleyrand, and company. Monroe had passed through Paris to ob-tain the good offices of the French government on his way to Spain to negotiate a settlement. Amazingly, France shunned these over-tures and, instead, by taking sides with her ally ensured the defeat of Monroe's mission.

For five months Monroe and the discredited minister, Pinckney, had pressed the American demands at Aranjuez. These demands were harsh. First of all, Spain must ratify unconditionally the spoliations convention of 1802. The convention provided for the settlement of claims, estimated at between five and eight million dollars, arising from depredations in Spanish waters since 1796. Much of the damage had been inflicted by French cruisers, for which Spain said she could not be held responsible, and Yrujo assembled a battery of Philadelphia lawyers to support this position. Washington insisted that since the spoliations had occurred in Spanish jurisdiction, Madrid was responsible; and contrary to a later argument invented in Madrid, neither the Convention of 1800 nor the Louisiana Treaty with France covered the indemnification claim. In January 1804 the Senate had reluctantly ratified Pinckney's compromise reserving the disputed claims for subsequent negotiation. Don Pedro de Cevallos, the Spanish Foreign Minister, now required the suppression of this article and revocation of the offensive Mobile Act as well. The claims issue was less important in itself than as an irritant, both in Madrid and in Washington, where Jefferson saw it as further evidence, along with vexatious border incidents, of Spanish hostility. The issue might be circumvented, Monroe was instructed, by a general settlement that camouflaged the indemnification claim. Such a settlement would reach the greater issues of the Floridas and the western boundary of Louisiana. First, West Florida, to the Perdido, must be acknowledged as American under the Louisiana Treaty. Not only was this right, in the administration's view, but a title dated 1803 would annul the lavish Spanish land grants in the interim, while the United States would be stuck with them under a title dated 1805. Second, Spain must cede East Florida, for which the envoys were authorized to offer two million dollars. The negotiation of this demand might easily take account of the indemnification claim. Third, the western limit: the United States claimed, as had France, to the Rio Bravo; however, this was negotiable in the light of the arrangement on the Floridas. Humboldt, during his visit in June, had impressed the President with the value of the lands lying beyond the Sabine and the Colorado. Madison at once informed Monroe of the President's new felt aversion to the perpetual relinquishment of any of this domain, though he was agreeable to a neutral barrier state between the Rio Bravo and the Colorado or the Sabine for a term of twenty to thirty years. By still later instructions the envoys were authorized to fix the Colorado as the boundary if Spain demanded it in return for the Floridas. This was part of the final offer tendered to Cevallos in May. It was firmly rejected. And Monroe returned to more bad news in England. "It is evident that we have no sincere friends anywhere," he wrote from London, "that all the powers, with whom we have the most immediate relations are jealous of us, by some motives which are common to all." The Americans would have to stop playing games with European rivalries, take the country's interest into their own hands, and repel insult and injury with force.

The news from Cadiz reached Monticello near the end of July. Jefferson's immediate reaction was to conjure again, as in the Louisiana crisis, with a British alliance. "I infer a confident reliance on the part of Spain on the omnipotence of Bonaparte," he wrote to Madison, "but a desire of procrastination till peace in Europe shall leave us without an ally." A pacific settlement with Spain turned on the continuation of the European war; moreover, after a victorious peace the Emperor of France might turn his guns on the United States. "I am strongly impressed with a belief in the hostile and treacherous intentions against us on the part of France, and that we should lose no time in securing something more than a mutual friendship from England." To this startling proposition, Madison demurred. Any bargain struck with Britain, involving as it must a commitment to British arms, would prove more costly than the gains sought from Spain. Jefferson appreciated the point; nevertheless, fresh dispatches in the early weeks of August strengthened his attachment to the idea of a British alliance. He explained himself further to Madison. "The treaty should be provisional only, to come into force on the event of our being engaged in war with either France or Spain during the present war in Europe. In that event we should make common cause, and England should stipulate not to make peace without our obtaining the objects for which we go to war, to wit, the acknowledgment by Spain of the rightful boundaries of Louisiana . . . and 2, indemnification for spoliations, for which purpose we should be allowed to make reprisal on the Floridas and *retain them* as an indemnification." Britain would find sufficient inducement in the American pledge of co-operation, Jefferson thought, and the event of American belligerency would probably never materialize, since the mere fact of the treaty would force France and Spain to seek a settlement. He had not abandoned his old strategy of conquest through peace and diplomacy but simply proposed a change of tactics that, if Britain was willing, still kept the game in American hands.

The Spanish dispatches circulated among the secretaries in four cities and Jefferson collected their opinions at Monticello. Dearborn's cannot be documented; presumably he gave it directly to the chief during a September visit. Smith, as usual, took an aggressive stance: build the naval force for an offensive war, but if there was no time for this, ally with Britain and take Cuba and both the Floridas. Gallatin, surprisingly, agreed with Smith on the need for naval expansion to combat the European idea of the "passive endurance" of the United States; however, he opposed anything war-like including, it seems, a provisional alliance with Britain. American claims on Spain were excessive, in his opinion; surely they offered no just cause for war, a war that would destroy prosperity, plunge the country into debt, and, all together, cost far more than the adventure was worth. Gallatin called for a resumption of negotiation on more modest American demands backed up by defensive preparations. Madison's advice was similar, though he came halfway around —just far enough to appear sympathetic—to the chief's idea of a British alliance. By the middle of September, Jefferson also had the latest counsel of the American minister, John Armstrong, who had succeeded Livingston in Paris. The former Revolutionary general, with a mind that ran more to military than to diplomatic arts, advised the administration to seize Texas as hostage, suspend intercourse with the Spanish colonies, and then negotiate. France, having herself claimed to the Rio Bravo, while declining to claim the Floridas, would take the American side to settle this quarrel. Monroe seemed to concur in Armstrong's opinion, certainly in spirit if not in detail. Jefferson blended these various opinions with his own notion of an alliance and communicated the whole package to Madison. "Supposing a previous alliance with England to guard us in the worst event," he wrote, "I should propose that Congress should pass acts (1) authorizing the Executive to suspend intercourse with Spain at discretion; (2) to dislodge the new establishments of Spain between the Mississippi and Bravo; (3) to appoint commissioners to examine and ascertain all claims for spoliation." With this formulation he was ready to meet the cabinet on October 4 in Washington.

The cabinet met but reached no definite conclusion. Madison had been detained in Philadelphia by his wife's illness, and Jefferson was reluctant to proceed in his absence, especially on the question of a British alliance. Madison inclined to think it best at present to do nothing, and before he returned to Washington at the end of the month, Jefferson had come to the same conclusion. Not knowing which way to move, surrounded by dangers, it was perhaps best to stand still. The latest intelligence from Europe pointed to a long war, while a month or so earlier Jefferson had feared a short one. "This gives us our great desideratum, time," he said. "In truth it places us quite at our ease." The sense of crisis disappeared. All thought of a British alliance vanished, never to materialize again. "This new state of things [in Europe]," he observed, "is the more fortunate in proportion as it would have been disagreeable to have proposed closer connections with England at a moment when so much clamor exists against her for her new encroachments on neutral rights." Relieved of this embarrassment, which ought to have been equally obvious in August when driven to it by a kind of desperation, he fell back on the more congenial tactics skewed to French interest in Spanish affairs. "Our question now is what way to give Spain another opportunity," he wrote Gallatin, and by his rhetorical questions supplied the answer: "Is not Paris the place? France the agent? The purchase of the Floridas the means?"

On November 12, only three weeks before the President's message would go to Congress, the cabinet met and adopted the new plan of proceeding with Spain. First, purchase of both the Floridas: "the exciting motive with France, to whom Spain is in arrears for subsidies, and who will be glad also to secure us from going into the scale with England." Second, American cession of the land between the Rio Bravo and the Guadalupe, the Texas stream south of the Colorado: "the soothing motive with Spain which France would press bona fide because she claimed to the Rio Bravo." Third, Spanish payment of spoliations under her own flag only, before and since the abortive convention of 1802, in an amount not to exceed $5,-

000,000, for which she would hypothecate to the United States the strip between the Guadalupe and the Bravo. After two years of failure Jefferson was still speculating on France's good offices. Marvelously, on the next day a dispatch from Armstrong gave renewed substance to the speculation. Talleyrand had sent a confidential agent to Armstrong inviting the United States to resume negotiations with Spain and outlining the plan France would support. The old fox struck a hard bargain but, in general, his proposition fell within the range of accommodation, and Jefferson at once reconvened the cabinet. The United States, it was now decided, would pay $5,000,000 (Talleyrand had said ten and the agent had come down to seven) for the Floridas, fix the western boundary on the Colorado, and agree to settlement of spoliations under the Spanish flag by a joint commission, reserving the land south of the Colorado as security for payment of these indemnities.

So agonizing weeks and months of vacillation and indecision terminated in a Spanish policy. Jefferson proceeded with cautious optimism. Congress would have to co-operate, instantly, before a change in the winds at the Tuileries, and secretly, as diplomacy required in a transaction of this kind. He had thought to send immediate orders to Armstrong to arrange for the purchase of the Floridas or, at the very least, to pledge the government for the down-payment. But Gallatin had objected: the assent of Congress, while probable, was not certain and might take time. The cabinet agreed to suspend instructions until Congress could act. To throw the matter into Congress in any shape called for the utmost finesse. Money was wanted —$2,000,000 at the start—for a specific object in secret diplomacy at Paris. If Congress inquired too closely into the object, if it scrupled with the proposition of paying France for Spanish possessions or, indeed, for one possession, West Florida, the United States already claimed to own, the game might be lost. Jefferson had buried his scruples on these points. The claim that the nation had already paid for West Florida was a detail, one Monroe had willingly sacrificed in his efforts at Aranjuez. As to the money, "We need not care who gets that," Jefferson said; even if it were paid in Madrid it would find its way into Napoleon's coffers. Congress, in addition, must be willing to adopt secretly one policy looking to peace and bargain, and another policy, in public, pitched to war in defense of American demands on Spain. This seemed a necessary precaution against diplomatic failure and a useful means of exerting influence on France and Spain. Every part of the President's plan made excellent sense viewed as a whole, while each part was vulnerable to attack if left to itself. The difficulty came in blending the parts together to the satisfaction of Congress.

The hazards on the other side, in France, were largely beyond Jefferson's control. Again, as with Louisiana, the whim of Napoleon was likely to prove decisive. Whether or not he would dictate terms to Spain depended on any number of variables: the circumstances of the war, the adroitness of the American negotiator, the profitability of the transaction, his estimate of American determination and, above all perhaps, of the administration's willingness to subordinate neutrality to French objectives. On the last point Jefferson was ready to offer assurances within the generous limits of neutrality. The matter of profit went beyond the Emperor; it concerned Talleyrand, whose talent for turning public business into private lucre was well known, and a nest of bankers and speculators in Paris, including some Americans, who eyed the Floridas purchase as a handsome job for themselves. Their avarice had been excited by the administration's success in floating the Louisiana Purchase, which pushed American stocks to new heights; but this job had brought no money into their shop. Beginning with Livingston a year and a half before, every informed American in Paris warned the administration that a deal for the Floridas could not be arranged unless the moneylenders and stockjobbers got into the act and, in fact, could not fail if they did. This meant payment in securities, which afforded opportunity for speculation and had all the effect of a *douceur*. The final November cabinet decision provided that the $5,000,000 to be offered for the Floridas would be in the form of stock redeemable in three years. If that turned the proposition into a "French job," it could not be helped.

While wrapping up the Spanish policy, Jefferson drafted his fifth annual message, delivered on December 3. The Republicans dominated the Ninth Congress without hindrance except from themselves. In the Senate were only seven Federalists, though they moved as a phalanx against weak Republican leadership. The huge majority in the House—even the Massachusetts delegation was now predominantly Republican—continued to be led by the triumvirate of Speaker Macon, John Randolph, and Joseph Nicholson. As everyone expected, the message focused on foreign affairs. Jefferson denounced the British system of "hovering" on American coasts and harbors to the annoyance of commerce, and he pledged "effectual and determined opposition" to new principles "interloped into the law of nations." His tone towards Spain was perhaps a little higher. Alluding to the various grievances—spoliations, boundaries, obstructions at Mobile, and aggressions across the Sabine—he seemed to despair of a peaceful settlement. But he quickly broke off, deferred Spanish affairs to a subsequent message, and went on to recommend defensive preparations against belligerent powers generally. "We ought still to hope that time and a more correct estimate of interest, as well as of character, will produce the justice we are bound to expect. But should any nation," he warned, "deceive itself by false calculations, and disappoint that expectation, we must join in the unprofitable contest of trying which party can do the other the most harm. Some of these injuries may perhaps admit a peaceful remedy. Where that is competent it is always the most desirable. But some of them are of a nature to be met by force only, and all of them may lead to it." So the seaport towns should be fortified and furnished with gunboats, the militia system reformed, the export of arms and ammunition prohibited; and consideration should be given to building ships-of-the-line and strengthening the army. Jefferson had planned to call for a reduction of taxes. The Mediterranean Fund, serviced by a small added duty on imports, was scheduled to expire with the termination of the Tripolitan war; instead, Jefferson preferred to keep this revenue derived mainly from the rich and to eliminate the salt tax, which fell on the poor and brought about equal value to the Treasury. Some might think it improvident, he had written in the draft, to abolish taxes in the present circumstances, but he answered, "if we never discontinue taxes while there is a cloud of war visible on our horizon, all taxes will become perpetual." This was carrying economy too far for Gallatin. If the great war should end, the revenue would fall, as it would also if the United States undertook commercial retaliation against Britain. Aside from fiscal considerations, Gallatin pointed out that the tenor of the passage on taxes contradicted the tenor of the passages on foreign affairs. The belligerents, he said, "never can think us serious in any intention to resist if we recommend at the same time a diminution of our resources." Besides, the Treasury would need all the money it could get to pay for the Floridas without impairing the planned retirement of the debt. Jefferson struck all mention of reduced taxes. Nor did he return to the idea thrown out in the inaugural address of applying the surplus revenue, running at a million dollars a year, to internal improvements. Arms and defense would swallow up the surplus. Such was the sad reality again forced on the young nation that pursued wealth and power in an Atlantic world constantly torn by war.

Some quarters heard the message as "war-like." So far as it addressed foreign ears, this was Jefferson's intention. He meant to produce an effect in the Tuileries; and lest that effect, with respect to Spain, be lessened by too mild a notice of "the greater enormity" arising from the British system, Jefferson tried to balance his strictures. He did not mean to arouse belligerent dispositions at home, but in a message addressed to the American public as well as to foreign chancelleries he could not avoid giving the same impression to both; moreover, he fully realized now, if not before, that success abroad demanded challenge to the Quakerish reputation of the administration in Europe and manifest readiness to back up appeals to justice and interest with force. But the military preparations were still calculated on peace. They were meant to overcome the "false calculations" of belligerents who imagined they could kick and cuff the United States with impunity and hence had lost the incentive to pursue peace with the last great neutral.

On December 6, Jefferson communicated his confidential message on Spain, together with a bundle of diplomatic documents. After briefly reviewing the history of the controversy, he alluded to France's interest in preventing a rupture and indications of support for a comprehensive settlement on a plan acceptable to the United States. "The present crisis in Europe is favorable for pressing such a settlement: and not a moment should be lost in availing ourselves of it. Should it pass unimproved, our situation would become much more difficult. Formal war is not necessary. It is not probable it will follow. But the protection of our citizens, the spirit and honor of our country, require that force should be interposed to a certain degree. It will probably contribute to advance the cause of peace. But the course to be pursued will require the command of means which it belongs to Congress exclusively to yield or to deny." The language was obscure: Jefferson neither named the object nor the means wanted. Such were the counsels of prudence. The diplomacy on the French side was secretive and unofficial; he wished to keep it in the same course on the American, so far as the forms of government would permit. He recognized the political risks of the proceeding. Every Federalist editor would raise the cry of French influence and blackmail, and eastern jealousy of southerly expansion of the Union would again rear its head. It was part of his style of personal leadership to employ hints instead of commands, to move circuitously, to rule by a show of submissiveness to Congress. The system had worked in the past. In fact, the congressional procedure with respect to the Spanish business followed precisely the course pursued with respect to Louisiana. It was, Gallatin argued, "the smoothest mode of doing business in Congress." Read by itself the confidential message seemed to call for an act of clairvoyance; but it was meant to be read as part of a system, in relationship to the public message and the real views of the administration. Only the details were wanting, and they could be privately obtained from the executive by those charged with the business in Congress.

Randolph was the man in charge. He had effectively handled the Louisiana appropriation under similar circumstances. The House at once referred the Spanish message to a special committee under his chairmanship. He promptly called on the President and learned, what he already knew vaguely, that $2,000,000 was wanted to purchase the Floridas. He said he could never agree to the measure. The President had not publicly asked for the money but thrown the whole responsibility upon the House; even if he were to make an explicit request, however, Randolph would oppose the grant because, after the failure of the Spanish negotiation, the payment of money would be a kind of extortion and would disgrace the country forever. Nicholson joined Randolph in opposition, leaving only one of the seven members of the House committee to whom the President could confidently turn. This was Barnabas Bidwell, a prestigious lawyer from Massachusetts who had just come into the House and already caught the President's eye as the leader he was

817

seeking. Without any prompting from the President, Bidwell unhesitatingly interpreted the message as a request for money and moved the grant. Randolph adopted the fiction that no such grant was meant, rather the message looked to war-like measures on the southern frontier. The committee rejected Bidwell's motion, he alone voting for it, and did not meet again for two weeeks. Meanwhile, Randolph's hauteur rose. He talked to Madison, who frankly told him that a peaceful settlement with Spain depended on the payment of money to France. "I considered it a base prostration of the national character," Randolph later wrote of the interview, "to excite one nation by money to bully another nation out of its property." The administration pleaded the costs of delay. Snubbing the plea, Randolph galloped off to Baltimore for a week. On his return Gallatin pressed him for action. The Virginian said he would not vote a shilling for the purchase of the Floridas and blurted, "I do not understand this double set of opinions and principles—the one ostensible, the other real; I hold true wisdom and cunning to be utterly incompatible." The administration now confided its cause to Bidwell. The committee continued to support Randolph; finally, on January 3, it reported a resolution calling upon the President to raise troops for the southern frontier and chastise the aggressor. After a week's stormy debate behind closed doors, the House rejected Randolph's motion and adopted Bidwell's substitute, 76 to 54, appropriating $2,000,000 for extraordinary expenses of foreign intercourse. The Senate concurred in the Two Million Act on February 7. Formal instructions finally went to Armstrong in March, six months after the secret overture from Talleyrand.

Randolph's revolt spread confusion and dismay in Washington. For four years, in the service of the administration, he had terrorized the House with his bludgeoning talents, his javelin-like wit, and his loss to the administration could not be easily repaired. As the session wore on his revolt became permanent and systematic, causing the only notable party schism of Jefferson's presidency. At first, during the odious Spanish business, it appeared that Randolph would draw off a large troop of Republicans. But he soon astounded everyone by his mad ravings and conceits, and at the end was left with but a handful of ardent followers, mostly Virginians, who took the name Quids. The Federalists, of course, rallied to him simply to embarrass the administration. With a huge majority, Jefferson could still control Congress, though he would never find a satisfactory replacement for Randolph in the House leadership. The real damage of the schism was this: it rattled the confidence of Republicans in an administration that had seemed invincible, sent waves of suspicion and distrust through the ranks, and shook the pedestal under the President himself. Jefferson's loss was less of followers than of prestige—the aura of invincibility that surrounded him—and as prestige declined so did the zeal and trust and unity of his followers. The crisis of morale appeared not only in Congress but in crucial Republican states such as Virginia, Pennsylvania, and New York. In March, before the troubles in Congress became public knowledge, William Duane informed Jefferson of pernicious reports circulating in Pennsylvania. It was said the President had abandoned the firm Republicans of the South and thrown himself into the arms of a New England party, that he was building a third party composed of moderates, both Federalist and Republican, that he had lost control of his cabinet, and so on. Contributing to this infectious discontent was the question of the Presidential succession, not yet in the open but gnawing at the Republican vitals.

Whether or not any of this might have been avoided had the President taken a different course in Spanish affairs is questionable. As to Randolph, at least, he was spoiling for a fight and would doubtless have found excuse for one on some issue. His principal accusation against the administration, that it followed a double set of opinions, one ostensible and honorable, to go before the public, the other real, devious, and dishonorable, was true in a naïvely moralistic view of politics and diplomacy. Jefferson, preparing materials for an answer to Randolph's exposé of the affair under the mask of "Decius" in the Richmond *Enquirer* in August, denied any duplicity or contradiction of opinions. Both were parts of a single system, both equally official, both the responsibility of the Executive. The two messages perfectly harmonized; the latter, he said, without directly requesting an appropriation, "asked the means of negotiation in such terms as covered the purchase of Florida as evidently as it was proper to speak it out." Perhaps he had carried caution too far in this instance. But if he had chosen to "speak it out," trusting Congress to protect the policy, Randolph would still have found fault on grounds of "double dealing," "bribery," and "backstairs influence." As to the first of these, Jefferson thought it necessary if he was to cover both possibilities, negotiation and force, with Spain. The second was pious nonsense. Even Randolph had declared "there is no Spain," no Pyrenees, no sovereignty except at the sufferance of Napoleon. So the Floridas could be obtained only through France; and for such an accession to the peace and well-being of the nation, Jefferson could neither close his eyes to European realities nor wash his hands of European methods. The charge of "backstairs influence" came with ill grace from a man who had been its principal beneficiary for four years. "But," said Jefferson indignantly, "when he differed from the executive in a leading measure, and the executive, not submitting to him, expressed its sentiments to others, the very sentiments (to wit, the purchase of Florida) which he acknowledges they expressed to him, then he roars out on backstairs' influence." This cant got under the President's skin. Defending his methods to Bidwell, he observed, "if the members [of Congress] are to know nothing but what is important enough to be put into a public message, and indifferent enough to be made known to all the world, and if the executive is to keep all other information to himself, and the House to plunge on in the dark, it becomes a government of chance and not design."

The Florida business was the occasion of Randolph's revolt, not the cause. It was foreclosed in the previous session. His strident opposition to the administration-backed compromise in the case of the Yazoo lands revealed traits of political purism, exhibitionism, and hauteur that were scarcely tolerable in a deliberative body, let alone in a majority leader. In 1795 some 35,000,000 acres in the wild Yazoo country of Mississippi and Alabama had been fraudulently deeded away to speculative companies by the Georgia legislature, which then rescinded the sale after the companies had begun to unload on innocent buyers. The federal government fell heir to the problem of conflicting claims when Georgia ceded its western lands in 1802, and a commission, which included Madison and Gallatin, recommended a settlement that would award 5,000,000 acres to Yazoo purchasers. It was a fair and just compromise; moreover, because of the large New England interest in the Yazoo claims, it was important for the developing national consensus in the Republican party. But Randolph, who despised this consensus, thundered against the settlement as a national disgrace—a legislative reward of fraud and corruption —and his opposition kept "Yazooism" alive for ten years. Successful in this bitter encounter, his self-esteem suffered a crushing blow in the next, the impeachment trial of Justice Samuel Chase. Randolph was the manager, or chief prosecutor, of the case. Indeed he boasted "that this was *his* impeachment—that every article was drawn by *his* hand, and that *he* was to have the whole merit of it." This was true in the main. Jefferson, although he had suggested the move against Chase twenty months before, no longer believed in the efficacy of impeachment and took little interest in the Chase trial. In the end, while the judge was acquitted, Randolph practically hanged himself. His long closing summation, Adams noted, "was without order, conviction, or argument; consisting altogether of the most hackneyed commonplaces of popular declamation, mingled up with panegyrics and invectives upon persons, with a few well-expressed ideas, a few striking figures, much distortion of face and contortion of body, tears, groans, and sobs, with occasional passes of recollection, and continual complaints of having lost his notes." Randolph's management, some observers thought, had determined the verdict. Jefferson never expressed himself on the point, but Madison, it was said, rejoiced in his fellow Virginian's disgrace.

In view of his temperament and politics it is remarkable that Randolph submitted to the role of a backstairs councillor for four years. His corrosive talents demanded opposition. He was notoriously sensitive to any personal affront. As a young friend observed, "He was a man without a skin," though in appearance, gaunt face on a slight frame, he seemed to be all skin. Sullen and angry after the humiliation of the Chase trial, he returned to Washington in December half convinced by rumors that the administration had lost confidence in him. These rumors were not without foundation, especially as they touched Bidwell, actively courted by the administration and the personal representative, for Randolph, of the New England interest. He was despondent, as were many of his friends in Virginia, over the course of the administration. A doctrinaire Virginia Republican, his creed had been firmly fixed in 1798, when he came on the national scene, and with others of this school he felt the administration had strayed from the true path, put conciliation ahead of reform, sacrificed principles to prudence, and continued under different forms the dangerously "monarchical" practices of its predecessors. The evil genius of this betrayal, as Randolph saw it, was the Secretary of State. The symbol of political appeasement, Madison was tainted with Federalism, with Yazooism, and in foreign affairs, Bonapartism. His succession to the presidency would be a disaster. Randolph, therefore, sought to discredit him and at the same time to induce Monroe to contest the succession. The Quids courted Monroe for two years, finally to no avail because the mass of Republicans, including many who preferred Monroe or some other candidate, closed ranks behind the President to avert disaster. All of these factors—personal temperament, ideological disagreement, and animosity to Madison, as well as the collision on foreign policy—entered into Randolph's insurgency. (Randolph himself, ruminating many years later, blamed everything on a game of chess in which he had dared to beat the President!) It was later said of this classic Virginian, who flaunted Virginia manners and prejudices in Congress for years of madness to come, "He has so long spoken parables, that he now thinks in them." And so he was thinking even in 1806. In the final analysis the clash of these two Virginians, Jefferson and Randolph, so antithetical as types it affronts reason to embrace them in the same category, was a paradigm of the conflict between the pragmatic statesman and the political ideologue, the one yielding to circumstances, the other ceremoniously clinging to dogma, the one actively seeking realizable goals within the limits of principle, the other careless of prudence, wary of power, and exalting principle to a fetish.*

* Several stanzas of John Greenleaf Whittier's "Randolph of Roanoke," although written after the Virginian had become a symbol of the "slave power," accurately capture the perverse brilliance of the earlier Randolph.

> Mirth, sparkling like a diamond shower,
>   From lips of life-long sadness;
> Clear picturings of majestic thought
>   Upon a ground of madness
>
> While others hailed in distant skies
>   Our eagle's dusky pinion,
> He only saw the mountain bird
>   Stoop o'er his Old Dominion!

Several items of congressional business related to the negotiation for the Floridas. Jefferson nominated Armstrong and James Bowdoin as the special commissioners, an unfortunate pairing as it turned out. Bowdoin, also from Massachusetts, had been earlier appointed to Madrid as Pinckney's successor. The Senate made no objection to him, but so odious had Armstrong become that he was only finally confirmed, with the casting vote of the Vice President, in March. The result was further delay. A bill prohibiting intercourse with rebel-held Santo Domingo genuflected toward Napoleon. The blacks on the western part of the island (Haiti) had declared their independence in 1804. France did not recognize the claim, nor did any other nation; in international law, if not in fact, the island remained a French possession. The Americans carried on a lucrative trade with the rebels, which Jefferson wished to continue and Napoleon could not prevent. Strictly speaking, the trade was illicit; but when Pichon complained Madison told him it was up to France to stop it. The government's responsibility could not be so lightly dismissed, however. Because the trade was unprotected, American ships armed (the law prohibiting the arming of private vessels had expired in 1802) and also carried on a large traffic in arms with the rebels. French and Spanish privateers set upon the American traders. And Merry complained that the trade violated the law of neutrality because both armed vessels and arms, by capture or purchase, became the property of the King's enemies. (He did not mention Britain's interest in eliminating the Americans and monopolizing the trade for herself.) Responding to those pressures the President had laid the problem before the second session of the Eighth Congress. A bill passed to regulate the clearance of armed vessels and to require them to post bond against the use of their armament except in self-defense. The act, limited to one year, had no effect on the illicit trade. Through General Turreau, the scrappy new minister, France filed bitter complaint. But Jefferson made no mention of the matter in his annual message.

It was left to his old friend George Logan, senator from Penn-

> All parties feared him; each in turn
> Beheld its schemes disjointed,
> At right or left his fatal glance
> And spectral finger pointed.

823

sylvania, to take up the subject on his own initiative. When the Clearance bill was before the Senate, Logan had tried unsuccessfully to set it aside in favor of his own bill calling for total non-intercourse; and now, a year later, he sought enactment of this stiffer measure. Merchant Republicans, like Senator Smith of Maryland, vehemently objected, pointing to the loss of profits and revenue from a trade interdict that could be of no benefit to France and only enrich Britain. Undecided, the Senate called on the President for information. He sent notes from Talleyrand and Turreau demanding the trade be stopped. With little ado the Senate gave leave to Logan to bring in his bill, and it rapidly passed through both houses, the Federalists alone objecting. Randolph, it might be noted, steered clear of this matter altogether. Southern Republicans generally thought the black republic a menace to themselves and would gladly see it abandoned. These fears had no bearing on Jefferson's shifting policy toward Santo Domingo. Black rule of the island was a *fait accompli* in his opinion; nothing the United States or France could do would reverse the course. Commerce and diplomacy were his springs of action. That he was willing to sacrifice the former to the latter, to stop the American trade in order to advance his territorial ambitions in the Floridas, seemed the obvious explanation for the Logan bill, and the Federalists at once pounced on it. When the bill was before the House, Timothy Pickering dispatched an eleventh hour warning to the President. All the world knew—Logan had declared it in the Senate and the President's own son-in-law, John W. Eppes, had echoed it in the House—that the bill was before Congress on French demand. "Sir, the moment you sign this act (and you will sign it, if it passes the House of Representatives) you seal the disgradation of your country. . . . One act begets further unwarrantable demands. . . . While we thus yield obedience to France, we shall become the object of her contempt, and the pawn of Europe. Save then your country, while you may, from such ignominy and thralldom."

Pickering would make good his warning. The Santo Domingo bill was a sop to Napoleon, the Federalists said, and from the moment of its passage to the end of Jefferson's administration they accused him of subservience to the French Emperor. The old canard, now fully revived, would merit no attention were it not for the grain of truth it contained with respect to the Santo Domingo legislation. Although the bill originated with the Quaker senator from Philadelphia who, at this very time, strongly opposed the whole Florida venture, it became, in effect, an administration measure. A fortnight before he signed the act, Jefferson pointedly brought it to Armstrong's attention as a means of scoring a hit at the Tuileries. Yet he knew very well that the statute was unenforceable. It simply required bond and clearance for American vessels sailing *under orders* for rebel-held ports; but vessels seldom sailed for the West Indies under orders to specific ports—they surely would not now—and the act contained no effective penalties for violation or fraud. Every congressman considered it "a dead letter," according to Adams. Jefferson found the legislation chiefly valuable as another piece of "double dealing": a gesture of good will toward Napoleon, earning, it was hoped, his gratitude, and a signal to the merchants to continue the lucrative trade with the rebel island at their own peril. The little truth in the Federalist accusation was thus more subtle than they perceived or were willing to admit.

But in Spanish affairs nothing seemed to go right for the President. Randolph "assassinated" the negotiation. From New York, in February, Francisco de Miranda, the inveterate Latin American adventurer, embarked his vessel, the *Leander,* on an expedition against Caracas that the Spanish minister angrily charged, and many Americans believed, had the clandestine backing of the administration. Meanwhile, in Europe, the Third Coalition collapsed and Napoleon marched to hegemony. No sooner did the two envoys, Bowdoin and Armstrong, take up their business in Paris than they quarreled. Armstrong seemed to resent the newcomer; and Bowdoin unfairly suspected the New Yorker of jobbery. Because of the cloud Armstrong was under, tending to jeopardize any treaty he might make, Jefferson wished to add a third member to the commission and asked Nicholas to take the assignment. He declined, and no suitable alternate appeared; sometime later, when the situation became desperate, he wanted to send William Short but believed the Senate would reject the nomination. Hope remained despite difficulties. Napoleon did not want the annoyance of a Spanish-American war and he valued American neutrality, especially if it put the United States on a collision course with Britain. He consented to aid the purchase settlement with Spain, and the Prince of Peace, Manuel Godoy, agreed to name a negotiator in Paris. But as Godoy played for time, Napoleon talked as if the business belonged wholly to Spain and declined to mandate terms. Nothing had been accomplished when the Emperor went off to Prussia in September. The Battle of Jena, eliminating Prussia, occurred in October. With that the game was probably lost. Napoleon's domination over Europe, and the Berlin Decree inaugurating the Continental System, forced the United States into a line of neutrality that virtually removed the risk of war; and both he and Jefferson became preoccupied with British affairs. Tensions on the Mobile and the Sabine mounted. But Jefferson patiently avoided every occasion for war, even as he continued to threaten it. "We ask but one month to be in possession of the City of Mexico"; yet, as he reminded Bowdoin after waving this thunderbolt, he had just suppressed Burr's conspiracy in that direction as evidence of pacific dispositions. Bowdoin felt that Jefferson had over-impressed Spain and France on this point. Fearing nothing, they would grant nothing. But the stockjobbers were the principal obstacle, in his opinion. Not satisfied that they could make money on the American plan, they refused to throw their weight into the scale. France kept up the pretense of seeking a settlement for many months. Finally, in 1808, the Spanish revolt against Napoleon upset all the old calculations. Jefferson returned to consideration of a military solution; but when he left office the Spanish problem was still unsettled—the greatest single defeat of his statesmanship.

If the President dictated Spanish policy to the Congress, he seemed remarkably quiescent about British policy. In January he forwarded several memorials from the seaport cities protesting British invasions of neutral rights and acknowledged that the government's representations in this matter, as also in the matter of impressment, had not been met; but he declined to point out a course of action. Monroe, to whom the case had been committed two years before, had no hopes for an agreement and only awaited word from Washington to return home. The Pitt ministry adhered to the *Essex* decision, which put at hazard every American ship and cargo in the re-export trade to the Continent. Embarked on a war of survival, Britain showed little patience with American claims, though she wished to maintain her ascendancy in the American market and the flow of supplies to her ports.

Until the wave of captures following the *Essex* decision caused an uproar among the coastal merchants, the administration viewed impressment as the more vital issue. To merchants and shipmasters seamen were an expendable commodity, but to a sovereign state the forcible seizure and impressment of its citizens into foreign service was an attack on the nation itself. Every forcible seizure of American citizens was a stinging reminder of the revolutionary nation's continued subservience to the imperious mother country. The problem was peculiar to Anglo-American relations. No other civilized nation practiced impressment on the British plan; no other nation suffered its penalties like the United States. And, of course, it had no sanction in international law. The problem went back to 1790, first became serious in 1796, and then alarming during the last two or three years. Since the beginning of the present European war in 1803, Madison reported to Congress in March, 2273 American seamen had been impressed, on the record, that is—additional hundreds and thousands had been lost without a trace. Every ship in His Majesty's navy was manned in part by American seamen. The navy and marine consumed seamen and justified impressment not only to obtain them but also to check desertion from the barbarous British to the safer, better paid, and generally more humane American service. The American marine, growing by leaps and bounds, actively encouraged desertion; many of the impressed seamen, though a fraction of the total, were undoubtedly His Majesty's subjects. Washington did not claim that the American flag protected absconding British subjects, nor did London claim the right to impress citizens of the United States. But who was British and who was American? Both spoke the same language. Physical identification was difficult, if not impossible, and efforts to get seamen to carry citizenship papers failed. The root of the problem was the conflict of law. In English law a natural-born subject could never throw off his allegiance; so Britain denied the efficacy of American naturalization of British emigrants. Only natives and resident Englishmen in the United States in 1783 were considered *bona fide* American citizens. Under this rule thousands of naturalized American seamen were claimed as British subjects.

Thus impressment assaulted the very existence of American nationality. It forced Jefferson back to one of his fundamental principles, the right of expatriation, embracing the equivalent right of free citizenship. "Every man has a right to live somewhere on the earth, and if somewhere, no one society has a greater right than another to exclude him." The only proper line, he said, was between transient persons and *bona fide* residents of a country. But he did not expect to impose this sweeping principle on Great Britain or even to secure the protection of the American flag for everyone sailing under it. Monroe was authorized to offer two concessions. First, Britain might impress her own subjects aboard American ships in her own ports. Rufus King had gained this point—the abandonment of the practice on the high seas—with the Foreign Office in 1802, only to lose it at the last minute when the Admiralty insisted on the reservation of the "narrow seas" around the British Isles. Second, as a *quid pro quo*, the United States would agree to a plan for the return of deserters. Britain considered any alien seaman in the national service for two years a British subject; Madison proposed to apply the same rule to American seamen, in effect naturalizing every seaman in American sanctuary for two years. London refused to negotiate a convention on these terms. American nationality could concede no more.

Congress was moved more by the losses of trade than by the scourge of seamen. General Smith, himself a great merchant, seized the initiative in the Senate. He had already pressed the administration to adopt a selective non-importation act in retaliation against British discriminatory tonnage duties and extraordinary duties levied on exports to the United States. (Smith estimated the cost of the latter to American consumers at over half a million dollars annually.) The Baltimore senator now united this project with a comprehensive protest against British captures, impressments, and other aggressions on neutral rights. The plan that finally materialized in the Senate embraced two related courses of action. Resolutions strongly advised the President to seek redress and indemnification through the agency of an extraordinary mission. As an aid to the mission, a selective non-importation act was passed to take effect November 15, 1806, barring satisfactory adjustment. The House proceeded along similar lines. After several weeks, during which Randolph bottled up the British business in the Committee on Ways and Means, the House took the matter into its own hands. Andrew Gregg, the veteran Pennsylvania congressman, now startled everyone by proposing a total non-importation on British goods. This was at once attacked by Republicans of varying hues as a war-like measure. Randolph now upbraided the President for failing to show the way to Congress. A whirling tornado, he exhausted himself against the Gregg resolution as if the administration were for it. "After shrinking from the Spanish jackal,'" he fumed, "do you presume to bully the British lion!" Nicholson offered a substitute calling for selective non-importation, similar to, though milder than, the ban proposed by Smith. Madison summarized the confused situation for Monroe's benefit in early March. "The merchants are zealous for an extraordinary commission for the negotiating experiment. In this they are seconded by those who are averse to any legislative remedies [e.g. Randolph], and by some, perhaps generally, by those who wish a negotiation to be armed with legislative provision. The President has decided nothing on this point as yet." And he did not. He was nevertheless grateful to Nicholson for burying the Gregg resolution. The Marylander's weaker motion passed, followed by a bill to implement it, in which the Senate concurred. "What is it?" Randolph asked scornfully. "A milk and water bill, a dose of chicken broth to be taken nine months hence. Good God!" For once his scorn was merited.

Offering no plan of his own, Jefferson acquiesced in this congressional determination of policy toward Britain. Smith said it was forced on him by the Senate, and Jefferson admitted as much at least as to the extraordinary mission. The Senate demanded it under the cover of resolutions, he later told Monroe. "The members of the other House took up the subject, and set upon me individually . . . , and represented the responsibility which failure to obtain redress would throw on us both, pursuing a conduct in opposition to the opinion of nearly every member of the Legislature. I found it necessary, at length, to yield my own opinion to the general sense of the national council, and it really produced a jubilee among them." Non-importation, like a sword suspended over the British, seemed to arouse no more conviction in him than it would at Downing Street. Commercial coercion, on a meaningful scale, was his trump card with Britain and he was not ready to play it in the spring of 1806. Monroe had written eloquently of the stubbornness, almost the futility, of negotiation. A comprehensive settlement such as Congress proposed must take the form of a treaty, with concessions on both sides; and Jefferson wanted no successor to the Jay Treaty, preferring, rather, to deal with British problems *ad hoc* as they arose. An extraordinary mission must also involve an associate with Monroe. The joint commission was the usual practice, to which Jay had been the main exception, as if to prove the rule. Jefferson may have guessed Monroe's sensitiveness on this point; and he could hardly fail to see that some of the sponsors of the treaty project were interested in furthering their own political ambitions at Monroe's expense. At any rate, Jefferson was stuck with an unwanted policy. In its legislative aspect it marked the revival of old Republican doctrine of commercial retaliation. While Congress debated, Republican editors dug into the archives and reprinted Madison's commercial resolutions of 1794 and other more distant landmarks of the doctrine. It still had an important place in Jefferson's strategy. Significantly, however, it was not Jefferson, or even Madison, though he was more sympathetic, but the Republicans in Congress who resurrected this doctrine in 1806 before, in his judgment, the country was ready to prove its usefulness.

The President nominated William Pinkney to join Monroe in the special mission and then succeed him as minister. A Maryland lawyer with diplomatic credentials and a Federalist background, Pinkney was not a popular choice, certainly not among Republicans vexed by Jefferson's temporizing politics. (Had they known of his first choice for the post, Rufus King, they would have been outraged.) The fact that Smith, and perhaps Randolph, wanted the commission for himself contributed to the discontent. Monroe was deeply offended. The appointment of an associate envoy, his successor as well, reduced him to a cypher, he later said. "From that day I considered myself as nothing." Monroe suffered the anxieties of a politician too long absent from home. He felt neglected, unappreciated, and now stabbed in the back by his fellow triumvers; and friends to encourage him in this delusion were not wanting. Jefferson and Madison believed they were acting in accordance with his stated desire to return home, and they were the more inclined to indulge him in order to protect themselves from the political charge of keeping a rival for the presidency disarmed in Europe. Monroe may have felt, too, as Randolph insinuated, that he was being made to hold the candle for high-toned demands in Britain while the administration pussyfooted with France and Spain. Jefferson sensed his friend's displeasure and went out of his way to reassure him, but three years passed before their friendship regained its old footing.

Suddenly, before diplomacy could be put on the new track, the entire situation changed to the advantage of the United States. News of Napoleon's victories at Austerlitz and Pressburg reached Washington the latter part of March, accompanied by the announcement of Pitt's death and the formation of a new government which brought Charles James Fox, a long-time friend of the United States, into the foreign ministry. A bright prospect opened. From his first interview with Fox, Monroe confidently predicted a fair settlement of differences. Jefferson felt the same optimism. He now hoped the swords rattled by Congress would not perplex negotiations. Explaining the awkward predicament to Monroe, he wrote, "We had committed ourselves in a line of proceedings adapted to meet Mr. Pitt's policy and hostility, before we heard of his death, which self-respect did not permit us to abandon afterwards. . . . It ought not to be viewed by the ministry as looking towards them at all, but merely as a consequence of the measures of their predecessors, which this nation has called on them to correct." In the formal instructions of May 17 Madison also explained away the threatening legislation. The non-intercourse act looked to the encouragement of domestic manufactures, he said. The abandonment of impressment remained the ultimatum of any settlement. Pursuant of the example of the Anglo-Russian treaty of 1801, the United States would relinquish, during the present war, the principle of "free ships make free goods," conditional on full protection of neutral rights in the colonial re-export trade. The guiding principle was that neutrals may trade with all ports of the enemy not in effective blackade and in all articles except military contraband. There must be provision to curb the hovering of British cruisers in coastal waters; American commerce and navigation, generally, must be fairly treated; and indemnities for captures and injuries demanded, though this might be sacrificed in the interest of future safeguards. The problem of "hovering" had been recently aggravated by the *Leander* affair. The captain of this British cruiser, while searching for seamen and contraband at the entrance to New York harbor, fired a "warning" cannon shot that struck a vessel and killed an American sailor. Amidst great public outrage, Jefferson received a solemn apology from Merry and assurances that the *Leander,* her captain, and the two sister vessels would be recalled. The forbearance of the American government and Britain's prompt response boded well for the upcoming negotiations in London.

Unfortunately, the negotiations were in suspension for over two vital months while Monroe awaited Pinkney's arrival and the formal instructions. Jefferson grew anxious in July. Reports continued to be favorable. But, he observed, "the best founded hopes of an advantageous accommodation with England may possibly be blasted by our own indiscretions." Publications had appeared in the Federalist press, and copied in London papers, charging the administration with pursuing opposite lines of conduct toward Britain and Spain and offering a bribe of two million dollars to Napoleon. Randolph's exposé followed in August. These irresponsible political attacks would arm Fox's opponents, perhaps fatally. "Our affairs there, therefore, are in danger of being all in the wind." Jefferson's fears on this score may have been exaggerated. More fatal, certainly, to the American project was Fox's death in September. Illness had overtaken the Foreign Secretary about the time of Pinkney's arrival; further delay resulted, and in August, as Fox slowly slipped away, the negotiation he had begun on the British side was transferred to Lords Holland and Auckland, neither of whom inspired Jefferson with confidence. The bargaining went forward in the fall, but from the moment he learned of Fox's death Jefferson sealed his hopes for a favorable treaty with Britain.

In his annual message Jefferson had called for the rapid acceleration of the nation's defenses. Not all injuries admitted peaceable remedies, and European warlords must understand the defensive capabilities of the United States. Military force was accessory to a foreign policy premised on the efficacy in nearly all cases of American commerce and neutrality to secure the respect of European powers, but the credibility of this policy required disposable military force in the United States. So Jefferson had recommended improved fortifications of seaport cities, gunboats in considerable number, reorganization of the militia, and consideration of building six ships-of-the-line (74 guns) for which materials were already at hand. Congress responded by appropriating $150,000 for fortifications, insufficient for the defense of a single harbor, and $250,000 for 50 gunboats, well below the number wanted. The legislators voted no money for 74's and returned the navy—a victim of Randolph's blunderbuss—to a peacetime establishment of 900 men and three frigates plus a few smaller vessels. Congress rejected the administration's bill to put the militia on a firm basis, though it gave the President authority he did not ask, and did not use at this juncture, to require the governors of the several states to maintain 100,000 militia in readiness. The army remained at the old level of 3000 men, primarily on western stations. Having earlier put Congress on the track of peace and economy, the President seemed unable to switch it to another.

His proposals, which he would repeat in subsequent years, formed part of a comprehensive system of national defense. He never articulated the system in entirety and only isolated parts of it were enacted into law. On land the system placed primary reliance on the militia. Republican ideology from the Revolution forward had enforced the axiom against standing armies. In a country where peace was a moral commitment and the normal state of things, a regular army was as wasteful and unnecessary as it was dangerous. "Were armies to be raised whenever a speck of war is visible on our horizon, we never should have been without them," Jefferson told Congress in 1806. "Our resources would have been exhausted on dangers which have never happened, instead of being reserved for what is really to take place." And should war actually take place, a well-trained militia, promptly called into the field, could hold the ground until sufficient regulars were raised. But the present "promiscuous militia" would never do. That system, loosely governed by the act of Congress of 1792, slightly improved in 1803, lumped all able-bodied men together, abdicated responsibility to the states, and was generally inefficient. Jefferson's report to Congress on the state of the militia in 1804—the first of its kind—showed over half the state militias unarmed and other shocking deficiencies.

In the fall of 1805, before Congress met, Jefferson developed with Dearborn and Smith a new "classification" system, which provided, essentially, for a national military reserve, incorporating a naval militia as well. It seems to have been suggested to him by Napoleon's success with a similar, if more rigorous, system. His secret, Jefferson said, lay in conscripting the service of the young, the healthy, and the enthusiastic; and he would conquer the New World after he finished with the Old unless Congress formed the militia on the same principle. The bill provided for the enrollment of all able-bodied white males betwen the ages of 18 and 45, except those enrolled in the naval militia, and their division into four classes: minor (18–20), junior (21–25), middle (26–34), and senior (35–45). The burden of training and service would rest on the junior class, enrolling approximately 40,000 new recruits annually. They would be furnished with arms at the expense of the United States, trained one day each month, and be liable for active service for one year within the United States or adjacent countries. The minor class would receive the same training but, with the seniors, be liable to service only within their own states. The middle class, mustered twice a year, could be called to duty in adjacent states for three months. Under this plan the entire nation would be in arms within a few years. The country would be able to meet sudden emergencies wherever they arose.

Jefferson "earnestly" recommended the classification system to Congress. In the House a select committee under Joseph B. Varnum of Massachusetts reported against the bill. The plan was too systematic, too rigorous, too expensive, too centralizing for the committee's taste. Whatever the faults of the present loose and heterogeneous system, the committee thought it the only realistic one for a people spread over a vast terrain, governed under different local laws, and little inclined to compulsory service of any kind. Another favorite scheme, viewed by Jefferson as a companion measure, also met defeat. Addressed to the twofold problem of the defense and the Americanization of the Orleans Territory, the bill offered land bounties in return for two years' liability for military service to able-bodied men who settled in the territory. "If by giving 100 miles square of that country we can secure the rest," he observed, "and at the same time create an American majority before Orleans becomes a state, it will be the best bargain we ever made." If it worked in Orleans, the plan would be extended to other frontier areas. Devised to meet an urgent need of his own time, Jefferson's plan looked back to colonial practice and forward to the Homestead Act of 1862. He again pressed it on Congress in 1807, again without success. The classification system, especially, he considered "the most essential thing the United States have to do," and he would rather have it than new regiments of regulars. "No efforts should be spared to bring the public mind to this great point," he said in referring some material for publication in the *National Intelligencer*. But the verdict in Congress again went against him.

Jefferson's naval system took shape gradually in the debate on two issues. Should American naval power be for the protection of commerce or for territorial defense only? This was the first and larger question, and it proved too difficult for Jefferson. He never decided it definitely. His Mediterranean policy, the policy that gave birth to the United States Navy, returned one answer, and his invitation to Congress to built a fleet of 74's seemed consistent with it. But a naval skirmish against pirate nations did not decide the question, nor would the building of a few ships-of-the-line where mighty Albion was the adversary. The question was as old as the republic. Northern commercial interests had generally favored a navy as an arm of trade, while the staple producers of the South, relying mainly on British bottoms, had objected both on grounds of costly discrimination and the inability, practically, of a national fleet to defend the long exposed coastline from the Chesapeake southward. Considerations of cost and practicality influenced Jefferson's thinking. While a friend of foreign commerce in the still undeveloped state of the national economy, he did not believe its defense warranted the expense of a large navy and the attendant risk of war. European experience proved that large navies bred wars, sank a nation's finances, cruelly oppressed thousands upon thousands of seamen, all for the enrichment of a few merchants. Gallatin constantly preached the wastefulness of navies, including Smith's tiny fleet, and the President heard the same line from Thomas Cooper and Tench Coxe, who spoke as political economists, as well as from southern Republicans steeped in prejudice. Jefferson's fundamental objection was economical: not the original costs of a navy but the costs of upkeep, the costs of decay, during long intervals of peace. Reflecting on the problem years later, he wrote, "It has been estimated in England that, if they could be sure of peace a dozen years it would be cheaper for them to burn their fleet, and build a new one when wanting, than to keep the old one in repair during that term."

Jefferson hit on a novel solution to this problem during his second year in the presidency. He proposed to build a "lock-dock" at the navy yard in Washington for laying up ships of war on stocks, out of the water, and protected from the weather. The plan incorporated the principle of the drydock with a canal and lock and a storage facility or "naval arsenal." Benjamin Latrobe was called in to work out the engineering, draw the plans, and produce a model. Vessels would be floated up from the tidal basin, via lock, canal, and the Tiber, to Stoddert's Spring, there dried out, masts lowered, and settled on stays under a great domed roof constructed in the manner of the Halle aux Bleds, free of supports interfering with the movement of vessels in and out. As many as twelve frigates could be kept this way, ready to launch at a moment's notice, for a capital investment estimated by Latrobe at $417,000. The scheme was unprecedented, though Jefferson had heard of something similar in Venice and Benjamin Vaughan brought to his attention Peter the Great's experiment along the same line. The principal defect, as another old Philadelphia friend pointed out, was the impossibility of launching one ship without floating all the rest, and this ingenious man, Robert Leslie, suggested the remedy. Jefferson exhibited Latrobe's model to members of Congress. Aside from its other merits he thought it offered the basis of compromise between commercial and agricultural interests: the former would have their ships and the latter would be spared the ruinous costs of maintaining them. "But," as he recalled the episode, "the advocates for a navy did not fancy it, and those opposed to building of ships altogether were equally indisposed to provide protection for them. Ridicule was also resorted to, the ordinary substitute for reason, when that fails, and the proposition was passed over." He did not again press the plan with Congress; but it remained a part of his naval system, and he would have been much readier to build ships had there been some means of preserving them in times of peace.

Once the choice was made for a mainly defensive navy, the issue became "gunboats versus fortifications." The Federalists had gone into the latter system, that is conventional harbor forts and batteries. Jefferson estimated it could not be completed for less than $50,000,000 and an army to man it of 2000 in peacetime and 5000 in war. Even then fortifications promised no secure defense of certain seaports, such as New York. In 1805 DeWitt Clinton proposed that the administration erect four forts in New York harbor. The cost was astronomical; and ships could easily slip by the batteries through the mile-wide channel. A fort rested on geometrical principles; where a place, like New York, did not lend itself to enclosure or protection by a polygon, the defense was ineffectual. Other expedients were considered. Dearborn later investigated the idea of running a chain with heavy blocks across the harbor entrance, but this figured out to a million dollars and looked impractical besides. In 1805 Jefferson turned from fortifications to the gunboat system of defense for the fifteen principal seaports from Portsmouth to New Orleans. Fortifications were not abandoned altogether, but mobile land batteries, such as he recommended in his message to Congress, were viewed as adjuncts to the gunboat system.

The use of a guerrilla-like "mosquito fleet" in harbor defense had been first suggested in the crisis of the closure of New Orleans in 1802. The crisis passed before the law of Congress authorizing the construction of fifteen gunboats could be implemented, and the administration deferred the project until various models of these small vessels could be studied. Meanwhile, American naval officers in the Mediterranean were discovering the utility of gunboats. In 1804 Commodore Preble obtained six 25-ton craft on loan from Sicily; and on his return to a hero's acclaim the following year he prevailed upon the President to send gunboats to the Mediterranean. Nine of ten already built or building were at once equipped and manned; they sailed from different ports and, amazingly, all reached their destination in July, then played a prominent role in the final stage of operations. Jefferson was delighted. The test helped to convince him of the expediency of gunboats for American coastal defense. Even before he talked to Preble, prompted perhaps by Clinton's outrageous proposal, he had sketched the outlines of the gunboat system: 240 vessels, costing perhaps a million dollars, built as circumstances required over a period of years, hauled up under sheds or partly or fully manned, again as circumstances dictated. The cost of the system was a pittance compared with land fortifications, and Jefferson believed it superior. History had proven the effectiveness of gunboats many times. Mediterranean and North European nations concerned, like the United States, with territorial defense against great naval powers, had used them extensively. Russia offered the most famous example: in 1788, in the Liman Sea at the mouth of the Dniester, a Russian flotilla of 22 gunboats and 27 galleys destroyed the greater part of a Turkish fleet consisting of 16 ships-of-the-line and several frigates. Gunboats had many advocates in the United States, but their most indefatigable champion was Thomas Paine. In 1798 Paine had submitted to Napoleon the plan of a gunboat armada for the invasion of England. He furnished Jefferson a copy of this plan, and on his return to the United States adapted his ideas to American coastal defense, repeatedly advocating the gunboat solution in letters to Jefferson and in the press. Specifications varied, but the gunboats built in the United States were generally 50 feet long, rigged with oars and sails, mounted with medium cannon in bow and stern, and fully manned with a crew of twenty or more. A hundred gunboats could be bought, at about $5000 each, for the cost of a single ship-of-the-line. One of their principal advantages was the shallow draft that gave the boats superior maneuverability in American bays, inlets, and rivers. They presented a difficult target and the low trajectory of their cannon improved the gunners' accuracy against an enemy. Gunboats were flexible: they could be moved from one place to another with ease or be laid up when not wanted. They multiplied the opportunities for young officers to command, which helps to explain the navy's early tolerance of the system.

With all these advantages, attested by experience, seemingly so well adapted to the extended coastline and pacific dispositions of the United States, Jefferson fully subscribed to the gunboat system in 1805. Unfortunately, even more than his "lock-dock," it lent itself to ridicule. Things got off to a bad start in the fall of 1804 when the first of the diminutive fleet, Gunboat Number 1, was blown by a hurricane off the Georgia coast into a cornfield on Whitemarsh Island. "Every federal *type sticker*, from 'Marshall Coleman' down, down, down, took up the subject, and *hammered* their noodles for weeks together to *make* a paragraph about it." * Gunboats were

* Coleman was the editor of the New York *Evening Post*. A specimen of his lampooning voyage in command of Gunboat Number 1 follows: "Marshall

humbug, visionary, Jeffersonian "philosophism" run amuck. The President absorbed this punishment and went right on pressing his system with Congress. Congress followed, but without enthusiasm, and after 1806 lagged behind. When he left office approximately 180 gunboats were stationed in American ports; if he had had his way there would have been at least three hundred.

Much of the criticism of the system, so far as it was serious, turned on the invidious comparison of gunboats with frigates or other seagoing fighting ships. The boats were not intended to go to sea; their mission was inner-coastal defense; they were mainly a substitute for land fortifications, indeed sometimes described as "movable fortifications." But the system was subject to criticism on other grounds. As James Fenimore Cooper, himself a midshipman in 1808, later observed, one of the arguments Jefferson advanced for the system, the extended coastline, was equally an argument against it, for that defense required outer as well as inner-coastal maneuverability. Gunboats offered no effective defense against blockade, for instance. In the long run these unheroic objects of jest and ridicule probably lowered rather than raised naval morale. In the long run too, the costs gun for gun were perhaps not less than for frigates or 74's, which proved their superiority in every situation other than shoal waters. The gunboat system did not exclude other means of defense, but because of his faith in this particular weapon Jefferson tended to downgrade the importance of supporting weapons at sea and on shore. The gunboats tended to become a substitute for frigates and land fortifications rather than a valuable adjunct to them; as a result the system lacked the balance necessary for its success. The navy turned against the system, and when war came in 1812 it was abandoned.

Congress adjourned on April 21, 1806. Jefferson must have breathed a sigh of relief—it had been an ordeal. His leadership had

C. left 'Carter's Mountain' on the 6th ult. and met with a variety of 'highly interesting' incidents on his passage—among them are the following. In the lat. of Carolina, discovered a 'field of corn,' bore down upon her and fired a gun—she hove to, and after examining how many bushels she produced to an acre, left her. Capes of Virginia in sight, spoke 'Black Sal' and her two tenders, steering for 'Monticello.'—Saw 'Gabriel Jones' . . . and heard a ship, supposed to be the 'Prairie *Dog*,' firing signal guns. Same day, hailed 'Mrs. Walker' bound, bound to Boston. . . ."

been seriously challenged for the first time. Randolph had sent shivers through the party and embarrassed the administration at home and abroad. In the closing hours of the session the Virginian's unbridled fury threatened the President's personal peace as well, as an exchange of insults produced an affair of honor between the Randolph cousins in Congress, the other member of the pair being Thomas Mann Randolph, the President's son-in-law; but a duel was happily averted. Congress gave the President most of the legislation he wanted, some he did not really want, and defeated or passed over other items he considered important. He pretended to be satisfied. The Randolph schism, except for its side-effects on diplomacy, did not disturb him. Randolph had made a scene, indeed a whole drama in which he cast himself as the tragic hero; but his performance was pathetic, and he destroyed himself politically by his own recklessness and violence. To contain it all but a handful of Republicans rallied to the administration. It was a case of rebellion strengthening the government, Jefferson thought. Summing up for Monroe's benefit at the end of the session, he wrote, "Timid men consider it as a proof of the weakness of our government, and that it is to be rent into pieces by demagogues, and to end in anarchy. I survey the scene with a different eye and draw a different augury from it. In the House of Representatives of a great mass of good sense, Mr. Randolph's popular eloquence gave him such advantages as to place him unrivaled as the leader of the House. . . . The sudden defection of such a man could not but produce a momentary astonishment, and even dismay; but for a moment only. The good sense of the House rallied around its principles; and without any leader pursued steadily the business of the session, did it well, and by a strength of vote which has never before been seen." This calmly philosophical view, while not unwarranted as to the danger of Randolph himself, passed too easily over the real damage he had done by discomfiting the Republican majority. Henceforth it would support the administration on great points but prove uncontrollable on lesser ones; and the loyalty of many would be given less in trust than in fear of injuring the party that revolved on the prestige of the President. He might have rid Congress of Randolph by kicking him into a foreign mission, which he craved, but that would be exchanging one risk for another. He did get rid of the principal confederate, Nicholson, by appointing him to a district judgeship; and he tried to smooth over relations with Speaker Macon and to retain or recruit men of trust and talent for leadership roles in Congress.

The summer was quiet. Jefferson made his usual excursion, surveying the worst drought in Virginia since 1755. Nothing of consequence came from American ministers abroad. But mysterious rumblings of disunion and conspiracy in the West, vaguely audible before, grew in volume and became a matter of national concern when he returned to Washington in October. "Having been so long in the midst of a family," he wrote sadly to Martha, "the loneliness of this place is more intolerable than I ever found it. My daily rides too are sickening for want of some interest in the scenes I pass over, and indeed I look over the two ensuing years as the most tedious of my life." And so they proved to be.

The Burr Conspiracy

Rumors of a great conspiracy in the West with Aaron Burr at its head had been afloat for over a year when the President convened the cabinet on October 22, 1806, to ponder an official course of action. Burr's designs were still involved in mystery, but fragmentary evidence pointed to criminal and possibly treasonable acts, and implicated General James Wilkinson, the commanding officer of the United States Army and Governor of Louisiana. To move fast might be tilting at windmills or perhaps arresting the evidence of the crime before it was ripe, the ringleaders going free; to move cautiously, on the other hand, might prove disastrous. In this dilemma the cabinet finally decided, at its third meeting on October 25, on a policy of watchful waiting. A confidential agent, John Graham, was sent down the Ohio to investigate, uncover the designs of the conspirators, and put civil and military authorities on guard. More vigorous steps approved only the day before, such as ordering a naval force under Preble's command to New Orleans, were rescinded. Legal technicalities entered into this decision, much to Smith's irritation. The navy was starved for funds and the statutes gave no authority for the use of the public forces of the United States to suppress conspiracies or insurrections. As to Wilkinson, it was decided to leave him alone pending further information.

Burr's conspiracy had been germinating for over two years. His political career ruined, indictments for the murder of Alexander Hamilton hanging over him in two states, New York and New Jersey, neither fame nor fortune in prospect, this indomitable adventurer turned his gaze to the convulsive Southwest frontier. In the summer of 1804, while still Vice President, he communicated to the British minister a scheme for separating the western states and creating an independent confederacy south of the Ohio. Money and a small fleet, to secure the Mississippi and possibly take the Floridas, were wanted from Britain. Merry at once forwarded this interesting proposition to his government. The ensuing winter in Washington, Burr courted the Creole delegates from New Orleans and in conversations with Merry centered his designs on Louisiana. The Minister again pressed the project with the Foreign Office in London. Just when Burr linked his vague scheme for revolutionizing the West to General Wilkinson's old ambition for the conquest of Mexico is uncertain; but from 1805 the two projects were so deceptively blended that it would be impossible to separate them.

The General was also active in Washington in the early months of the year. His talent for intrigue, his intimacy with Burr, his popularity with the old inhabitants of Louisiana were well known. For years he had been suspected of being in Spanish pay, as indeed he had been intermittently, but Jefferson's predecessors in the chief magistracy had passed over these suspicions, and so did he. A scoundrel to the core, Wilkinson had nevertheless rendered useful service to the government, especially in Jefferson's administration, as in the negotiation of treaties with the southern tribes and the transfer of Louisiana to the United States. The latter event, unknown to the administration, provided him the occasion for renewing his old connections with the Spanish authorities. After Congress created the Louisiana Territory, Jefferson named Wilkinson governor. The appointment provoked a good deal of criticism, less from suspicions of the middle-aged general than from the principle of separation of civil and military authority. Jefferson subscribed to the principle; in fact, on this ground he had earlier withstood the pressure of Wilkinson's ardent friends in Congress to appoint him governor of the Mississippi Territory. "But in the appointment to Louisiana," Jefferson said in answer to congressional strictures, "I did not think myself departing from my own principle, because I consider it not as a civil government, but merely as a military station." He was still working on the theory that closed Louisiana to American settlement. Wilkinson agreed with this policy and went to St. Louis in 1805 with orders to plan the removal of all settlers to the east bank of the Mississippi. Viewing Louisiana as a great Indian reserve, Jefferson associated it with military government and Indian affairs, both within the jurisdiction of the War Department. Moreover, the danger of war with Spain, involving action on the frontier, suggested the wisdom of blending civil and military authority in the office of a commandant. Wilkinson seemed admirably qualified for the post. What Jefferson overlooked was the danger the vainglorious general himself presented to the peace and harmony of the Union. At St. Louis he was in an enviable position to carry on conspiratorial enterprises either with Burr or the dons as he chose.

Burr set out to reconnoiter the West in April 1805. He had already recruited several prominent associates, and as he moved down the Ohio, across Kentucky to Nashville, thence down the Cumberland and the Mississippi to New Orleans, he picked up others. Without disguising his bitterness toward the administration, he artfully conveyed the idea of an expedition against New Spain with the covert support of the government. At New Orleans he fell in with Clark, Livingston, and the Creole opposition to the Claiborne regime. The city was ripe for revolt, Burr concluded. Here the revolution of the western states might begin, or alternately, or perhaps in conjunction with that revolution, an expedition launched against Mexico. Burr conferred with Wilkinson both on the downward leg of his journey, at Fort Massac on the Ohio, and on his return at St. Louis, the base of Wilkinson's overland maneuvers. Western newspapers followed Burr's movements with suspicion. That he was engaged in conspiratorial intrigue seemed likely, but he had so effectively decoyed his object that no one could be sure of it.

Back in Washington in November, Burr reported enthusiastically to Merry. With British assistance the western revolt might commence in the spring. If Britain abstained, he warned, France would regain control of the dissevered country. Nothing official came from London. The ministry, while interested in Burr's project, was preoccupied with France on the Continent. Disappointed, Burr now sought to sell the scheme to Spain. In Philadelphia he sent his trusted aide Jonathan Dayton, the former New Jersey senator, to the disgraced Spanish minister, Yrujo, who was still feuding with the administration. Yrujo at first backed off, but after Dayton fabricated for his benefit the story of Madison's clandestine support of Miranda's expedition against Caracas, Yrujo took him seriously. The plot changed. It still aimed at revolution in the West but not at Mexico or the Floridas, as Yrujo had earlier believed when Britain was to be the protector. A *coup d'état* in Washington would commence the revolution. The President and other officers of the government would be seized, the banks plundered, the navy yard taken, and a naval expedition sent to New Orleans, where it would operate jointly with Wilkinson's army. Such a project only appeared insane, the Marquis wrote to the government in Madrid. Actually, given a host of adventurous men, who were not wanting, and the soft-headedness of the professors of goodness in Washington, it was perfectly easy of execution; and it would be well worth a million Spanish dollars to destroy the American colossus. But Spain declined to speculate in this venture. In fact, it may not have been the venture Burr had in mind. Perhaps he was simply engaging in a swindle of Spain on his own account, as Wilkinson and other Americans had done in the past. Or perhaps he was only trying to quiet apprehensions of a filibustering expedition against Mexico.

But neither of these contingencies was present in Burr's invitation to General William Eaton to join the conspiracy. Yet the plot he unfolded to Eaton was much the same as the one Dayton had described to Yrujo, with the added touch of assassination of the President. " 'Hang him!'—'throw him into the Potomac!'—'send him to Carter's mountain!' " Such was Eaton's recollection under oath of Burr's language. It is easy enough to understand Burr's approach to him. The hero of Derne was also something of a desperado. He had been, he felt, shabbily treated by the administration for his services in the Tripolitan campaign; and he had impressive military and political connections in Washington. But Eaton possessed the saving virtue of patriotism. In March, after hearing Burr's proposition, he went to the President and in a roundabout way warned him of the impending insurrection. Could not Burr be sent on a mission abroad? "The President . . . seemed to think the trust too important, and expressed something like a doubt about the integrity of

Mr. Burr," Eaton later testified. But if Burr was not put out of the way, Eaton warned, there would be a revolution on the western waters within eighteen months. "The President said he had too much confidence in the information, the integrity and attachment of the people of that country to the Union, to admit any apprehensions of that kind." Jefferson's response might have been different had Eaton disclosed all the facts and their source, but he feared Burr would "turn the tables" on him. As a result, his guarded warning carried no more weight with Jefferson than the general run of rumor and gossip. Eaton was scarcely to be trusted anyway. Known to be friendly with Burr, his errand to the President may have been at Burr's instigation. Only a few weeks before Burr himself had begged Jefferson for high employment of some kind and warned him of the great harm he could do from outside the government. Jefferson politely informed him that he no longer possessed the public confidence; as to the threat of injury, he had never conducted business on motives of this kind and had no fear of injury from Burr.

What injury could the serpentine New Yorker have in mind? Jefferson believed with most men that he was capable of almost any treachery. "I never . . . thought him an honest, frank-dealing man," he later said, "but considered him a crooked gun, or rather perverted machine, whose aim or shot you could never be sure of." But Burr was no fool: he could not undertake anything so chimerical as a western revolution. Averse on principle to considering any man his personal enemy, Jefferson continued to treat Burr politely for several weeks and entertained him at dinner—for the last time—on April 8. A week later he learned from Senator Smith that Burr had been actively soliciting depositions in Washington in proof of the Federalist canard that Jefferson had bargained his way into the presidency in 1801. Smith and Bayard were the principal deponents. Their testimony being contradictory proved of little value to Burr, who had hoped to transfer the onus of his own downfall to the President's head. Jefferson was indignant. He may have seen Burr's threat embodied in this fabrication. At any rate, it probably did more to discredit the New Yorker in Jefferson's eyes than anything he had seen or heard of the rumored western conspiracy in the spring of 1806.

An early warning had come from a responsible source, Joseph

H. Daveiss, the federal district attorney for Kentucky. His first confidential letter in January pointed the finger of suspicion at Wilkinson; subsequent letters implicated him with Burr in a conspiracy with Spain, and Daveiss named Dayton and John Brown, the Ohio senator, together with several prominent Kentucky Republicans. Daveiss later accused the President of heedless indifference to this intelligence. In fact, when the first report reached him in February, Jefferson at once showed it to the secretaries and within a week instructed Daveiss to communicate any new information he could turn up. The attorney diligently pursued his investigation, but the evidence he forwarded was of little use. Much of it belonged to ancient history: the old Spanish conspiracy of the 1780's and '90's, including the old suspicions of Wilkinson. Daveiss piled up hearsay and conjecture, gossip and rumor; nothing in his reports firmly linked Burr to Wilkinson or offered evidence respectable in a court of law. There was also the question of the attorney's credibility. He was a Federalist carried over from the Adams administration. The possibility that he was engaged in a political game, actuated as well perhaps by personal or family resentments, could not be discounted. His list of suspects read like a roster of Kentucky Republicanism. Even John Breckinridge, the President's deceased attorney general, appeared on the list. That some of these men, old friends like Brown and Judge Harry Innes, had once dallied with Spain, Jefferson did not doubt, but that was all in the dim past before the opening of the Mississippi and the acquisition of Louisiana. Suspicions of Daveiss on this head increased in July when John Wood, an unprincipled Federalist editor, formerly associated with Burr and more recently with Augustine Davis and his libeling crew in Richmond, established a newspaper, *The Western World*, in Frankfort, devoted to sinking the Republicans under the weight of the old Spanish conspiracy. Brown alerted Jefferson to this development and mentioned Daveiss, an inveterate personal enemy, together with John Marshall's brothers-in-law, as partners in Wood's press. Daveiss, angered by the President's neglect, filed his last report in August. He shuffled the list of suspects and said that the nature of the conspiracy had changed. It was no longer with Spain but directed against the Spanish colonies, though still premised on the severance of the western states and territories. After all this Daveiss concluded, "I must further observe, that I have often doubted whether the whole of this matter might not be a mere swindling trick played off on the Spaniards by our countrymen." This possibility had occured to the men in Washington. In Wilkinson's history, particularly, a vague line separated swindle from treason; and the former was no crime in public law.

Beginning in September, however, the administration received weighty items of information on the unfolding conspiracy that fit into the picture Daveiss had sketched. By then Burr, having done all he could in the East, had already gone to the Ohio to make final preparations for the expedition down the river. In this connection he visited the home of Colonel George Morgan just below Pittsburgh. Without revealing his plans he talked freely to Morgan and his sons of the imbecility of the federal government ("with two hundred men he could drive the president and congress into the Potomac") and western separatism ("the separation of the Union must take place"). To this the Colonel exclaimed, "God forbid!" and wrote to the President. About the same time a former New York congressman reported that one Comfort Tyler had recently returned from the West much richer than he had ever been and begun recruiting men for an expedition on the Ohio. Other reports identified Harman Blennerhassett, a well-to-do Irish émigré who lived on an island opposite Marietta, Ohio, as the author of newspaper articles advocating western separation; moreover, Burr had visited Blennerhassett's Island, the staging area of the expedition, in the fall. In October, Gideon Granger brought to Jefferson the unabridged version of Burr's overture to General Eaton. The pieces of the puzzle fell into place; the picture, while still mysterious, the object still obscure, clearly revealed Burr at the head of a western conspiracy. Such was the state of Jefferson's knowledge near the end of October when he took the first hesitant steps to cope with the conspiracy, a conspiracy so strangely public by then that men wondered at the timidity of the government. Jefferson's hesitancy stemmed from two main considerations. First, the dilemma already mentioned: to spring the trap before crimes had been committed would be to let the traitors, if traitors they were, go free. Second, he had too much confidence in the loyalty of the West, and just enough in General Wilkinson, to believe that Burr could cause any real damage to the Union. So, for the present, he sent Graham on Burr's trail and put governors and commanders in the West on guard.

Wilkinson, meanwhile, had gone to the Sabine to deal with Spanish encroachments on the Texas frontier. Ordered on this mission in May, the General had only finally descended the river in September. Jefferson was shocked by the commander's disobedience to orders and supposed it related in some way to Burr's plans. Cautiously suspending judgment on Wilkinson's complicity with Burr, he grasped the opportunity to ease him out of the governorship of Louisiana. The House had censured the appointment on principle; the territorial government had been in turmoil since Wilkinson's arrival in St. Louis; and judges, junior officers, and prominent civilians clamored for his removal. He had powerful pleaders for his cause in Washington, none more powerful than Senator Smith of Maryland. Smith staunchly defended his comrade of Revolutionary days against the "cabal" in St. Louis and the vicious rumors of disloyalty. Only two days before ordering the General to the Sabine, Jefferson assured Smith that he had no intention of dumping Wilkinson the Governor. But Smith interpreted the orders as just that, a convenient way of dumping the Governor; and so did Wilkinson, and so, in fact, did Jefferson. He at once pressed the office on Monroe, and when Monroe was detained in England held it open for Meriwether Lewis, who came to his long journey's end in the fall. Mortified by the military order, his enemies jubilant, Wilkinson was sorely tried, and he tarried in St. Louis as long as he dared to take stock of his future. If he chose he could ignite war with Spain on the Sabine. This fit the prescription of the twofold plan of conquest and revolution he had concocted with Burr. If, on the other hand, he wished to recover power and prestige with the government, he could make peace on the Sabine, turn on Burr, and present himself as the savior of both his own country and New Spain.

He had probably not committed himself to either of these interesting options before he reached the post at Natchitoches, east of the Sabine. But his actions led to the prevention, not to the instigation, of war. The Spanish commander at once responded to his threat by withdrawing across the river into Texas. Several weeks later Wilkinson marched to the Sabine and signed the neutral ground treaty which secured peace on the frontier pending the final determination of boundaries. At the same time he grandly dispatched an aide to the Viceroy in Mexico City with his bill of $120,000 for services rendered His Catholic Majesty! Between these two events, the Spanish retreat and the treaty, an emissary bearing a ciphered dispatch from Burr reached Wilkinson's camp. All was in readiness. British protection was secured. Commodore Thomas Truxton, the hero of the quasi-war with France who had resigned from the navy under unpleasant circumstances after Jefferson came to power, was going to Jamaica to pick up a British squadron, sail to New Orleans, and join parts of the American fleet at the mouth of the Mississippi. Detachments from various quarters would rendezvous on the Ohio in November; Burr would lead the first of 500 or a thousand men and coalesce with Wilkinson at Natchez in early December. They would then decide the exact course of the campaign. "The gods invite to glory and fortune; it remains to be seen whether we deserve the boon." Wilkinson questioned the emissary on military objectives. Presumably Louisiana would be revolutionized, New Orleans seized, an expedition sent to Vera Cruz, thence to Mexico. If Wilkinson had not by this date, October 8, decided to abandon Burr, the contents of the dispatch turned him toward that treachery rather than the harder one. To conquer Mexico without a war was absurd; to revolutionize the West, if that was still an object, almost as difficult when the plot had become a scandal from Pittsburgh to New Orleans. And Wilkinson must have known that Burr lied in boasting British support. Still the General hesitated for nearly a fortnight; then, on October 21, he sent a fast riding courier with a dispatch to the President. He described the "daring enterprise" and professed to be uninformed of its "prime mover and ultimate objects," but expecting a revolt in the territory, he had decided to make peace with the Spaniards and throw his army into the defense of New Orleans. Two days later Wilkinson marched to the Sabine; a month later he reached New Orleans.

On the receipt of Wilkinson's dispatch, November 25, the President convened the cabinet. There was no longer room to doubt a conspiracy, its general design, or its prime mover. Jefferson at once issued a proclamation denouncing the "criminal enterprise," enjoining all participants to withdraw, and calling all authorities to take appropriate action. Orders went out to officers from Pittsburgh to New Orleans. Graham had already spurred Ohio's governor to action; and Wilkinson had nicely anticipated the President's orders to him to arrange an accommodation on the Sabine and hurry to New Orleans. The proclamation, while vigorous, was also guarded: it neither named Burr nor so much as implied treason, positing rather an unlawful enterprise against the Spanish dominions. But Jefferson was probably now convinced of Burr's complicity in treason. Clearly, he had two main objects in view and, depending on the circumstances, would pursue either or both. One was an attack on Mexico, the other Western disunion and independence. Given the military requirements of the first, it could not be accomplished without the aid of the second, at the very least the possession of New Orleans. A possible third object entered the picture in November. On leaving Blennerhassett's Island, Burr passed through Kentucky and along the way purchased part of an old disputed Spanish land claim, the Bastrop grant, on the Washita River. The grant, which was quite worthless, figured in Burr's plans as a cover or refuge. As Jefferson later said, "This was to serve as the pretext for all his preparations, an allurement for such followers as really wished to acquire settlements in that country, and a cover under which to retreat in the event of final discomfiture of both branches of his real design." The desperate and disaffected had joined Burr for obvious reasons; some of his confederates were obsessed with dreams of western empire; many well-meaning citizens had been seduced by assurances of the government's secret patronage; and still others had been lured by the promise of land.

Congress convened in a state of alarm. The spectacle of conspirators stalking the land in broad daylight struck astonishment. Few, if any, congressmen doubted the reality of the conspiracy. Some questioned the energy of the administration in quelling it. Others secretly hoped for its success and Jefferson's disgrace. Yet as to Burr, the reports strained credulity. Senator Plumer, who remembered Burr's sympathy with the New England disunionists two years earlier, observed, "Burr is capable of much wickedness—but not so much folly." Jefferson, too, was puzzled whether to treat Burr as a Catiline or a Don Quixote. In his December message to Congress he stuck to the premise of the proclamation: the expedition was against the Spanish provinces—the criminal attempt of private individuals "to decide for their country the question of peace or war." If this was not the whole truth it was still a necessary fiction, for the government did not have the authority, which he now requested, to employ the nation's public forces to suppress enterprises "preparing against the United States."

Jefferson waited anxiously through the month of December to learn the fate of the conspiracy. It became in his mind a test of the loyalty of the West, and even more, a test of the power of a free government to maintain itself. He expected his faith to be vindicated. The proclamation, which he later described as "an instantaneous levee en masse," would mobilize the citizens to crush the conspiracy. Burr's true strength was unknown in Washington. Yet only Smith, in the cabinet, pushed for more vigorous measures. Jefferson agreed they would be needed if the expedition now on the Ohio was not broken up before the end of the year. In the West, meanwhile, where the President's proclamation had yet to be heard, the conspirators celebrated the only kind of triumph they would ever know, in the courts in law. In the district court at Frankfort, Daveiss secured a grand jury to inquire into Burr's enterprise. When the attorney's principal witness failed to appear he moved dismissal. Two weeks later he applied for a new grand jury, only this time to be foiled by the rulings of the judge as well as the absence of a key witness under subpoena. The jury returned no indictment. Daveiss thus proved the honorableness of his intentions throughout, even if his precipitancy embarrassed the government. (When he sometime later issued a diatribe against the President for the opposite of precipitancy he was at once removed from office.) For the hardy Federalist attorney to win an indictment in Kentucky against the former Vice President who professed to be acting in concert with the government in a popular cause against Spain—this was impossible in early December. The conspirators were upset on the river, however. The first blow fell on Blennerhassett's flotilla on the Ohio. Many of the recruits drew off when the President's proclamation became known. Few boats ever reached the Mississippi.

By the beginning of the new year Jefferson believed the conspiracy had been crushed. Burr remained at large with a few stragglers on the Mississippi, where he learned of the proclamation, the Ohio seizures, and Wilkinson's betrayal. The General turned New Orleans into an armed camp, subverted the civil authority, arrested several of Burr's associates, and when they were released on writs of habeas corpus bound two of them under military escort to Washington for trial. His zeal could not have been greater, but he wantonly induced panic and trampled on the law. Jefferson excused these actions without approving them. "We are obliged to estimate them," he wrote the General reassuringly, "not according to our own view of the danger, but to place ourselves in your situation and only with your information." Wilkinson expected a British fleet from below, Jefferson thought, and an expedition of several thousand men descending on the city from above. In that situation the law of self-preservation became the higher law, and Wilkinson had earned the nation's gratitude for risking himself to save the country. This, of course, is precisely what the turncoat commander wanted his chief to believe. Jefferson had remained anxious about the General even after the fall dispatches. He had gone this far with him on the hunch he was a safer friend than enemy, less dangerous inside the government than outside of it, and in the final reckoning a more prudent patriot than frontier adventurer. That he had been embarked in some way with Burr seemed likely, especially if the design was Mexico in a national war on Spain; but that he would abandon rank, reputation, and power to become a dubious second in Burr's fantastic scheme seemed incredible. All doubts were dispelled by Isaac Briggs, the Quaker surveyor, who broke into the New Year's festivities at the President's House with dispatches from New Orleans. "Is Wilkinson sound in this business?" he asked the trusted Briggs. "There is not the slightest doubt about it." From this moment Jefferson never wavered in his support of Wilkinson's conduct.

The principal malefactor remained at large but Jefferson felt justified in announcing the suppression of the conspiracy in a special message to Congress on January 22. Sent in response to resolutions of the House, the message gave a clear and straightforward account of what had taken place so far as it was known to the executive. Unfortunately, Jefferson allowed himself to declare that Burr's guilt had been "placed beyond question." This was very likely the case. The President voiced the prevailing opinion. Even Senator Plumer, for a long time "an infidel" on the subject, asserted, "There cannot now remain any doubt of Burr's seditious and treasonable designs—unless multitudes . . . have conspired to establish falsehood." Old John Adams, in Quincy, doubtless agreed. "But if his guilt is as clear as the noonday sun," he remarked, "the first magistrate of the nation ought not to have pronounced it so before a jury had tried him." The message disclosed that three of Burr's associates had been liberated by habeas corpus in New Orleans and, further, that two of them had been sent hither in the belief they could not receive an impartial trial in that turbulent city. The next day William B. Giles, who had returned to the post of leadership in the Senate, moved the suspension of habeas corpus for a limited time. A bill was at once reported, restricted to arrests for treason or other high crimes under the authority of the President, and passed over one dissenting voice on the same day. This was not the President's bill. It originated with Giles and Smith, in fact with both Smiths, for the secretary had been advocating suspension of the writ for a month; and as friends of Wilkinson, these gentlemen were enraged by judicial trifling with his stern measures in New Orleans. William Burwell, the Virginia congressman, formerly the President's private secretary, asked Jefferson about the suspension bill on the day it passed the Senate. He said it could not be justified and if approved in the House would give him great pain. Burwell and Eppes, Jefferson's son-in-law, fought the bill in the House, where it met defeat in some measure because of the covert hostility of the administration.

Burr's western odyssey came to a close on February 19. Three weeks earlier he had prudently surrendered to civil authority in Mississippi. Again a grand jury refused to indict. Burr had not committed any offence in the jurisdiction of the territorial court of Mississippi, and for this reason the attorney general had moved to send the prisoner to Washington, but the court overruled him. Still under recognizance in the sum of $10,000 to the court, Burr fled to the sanctuary of West Florida. In the Tombigbee country, just above the boundary, the fugitive was captured, placed under military arrest, then conducted under armed guard more than a thousand miles to Richmond.

Just where Burr should be tried was a problem. The trail of conspiracy ran its devious course from the Atlantic coast to the mouth of the Mississippi, but if he was to be convicted of treason in a court of law it was necessary to hold him to overt acts, with witnesses to these acts, at some particular place. On the whole, Blennerhassett's Island seemed the most eligible spot, and that being in Virginia jurisdiction the case would go to the federal circuit court in Richmond, where John Marshall, the President's old enemy, would preside. The judge tipped his hand at the end of February when he released the two prisoners, Eric Bollman and Samuel Swartwout, Wilkinson had sent from New Orleans, on grounds of insufficient evidence. This decision, Nicholson's release of two other accomplices in Baltimore on the same grounds, the rising outrage against Wilkinson, the instinctive public sympathy for the hunted, the persecuted, the heroes of misfortune, artfully sounded for political effect—already in March the trial of Burr and company threatened to become a trial of the President and his commanding general.

Jefferson had never underestimated the difficulty of securing legal evidence of Burr's guilt. This had been the problem from the beginning, and it continued to plague him as he turned to the task of gathering the evidence. The culprit was guilty beyond a shadow of doubt in Jefferson's mind. Burr had earned his hatred, but this was not a vindictive personal judgment, though that played a part inevitably. It was, rather, the judgment of the President who viewed the conspiracy in its totality and in the light of his responsibility for the peace and safety of the nation. Whether Burr could be convicted in a court of law conducted on other views was a different matter, but he was guardedly optimistic. It was more important that the conspiracy had been crushed. "On the whole," he wrote, "this squall, by showing with what ease our government suppresses movements which in other countries require armies, has greatly increased its strength by increasing the public confidence in it." The event had vindicated republican government against the old canard of weakness and imbecility, vindicated the experiment of republican liberty over a vast territory, vindicated the federal system and the virtue of the people, and above all, the power of the law where every citizen has a stake in its preservation.

In the tumult and confusion of the Burr Conspiracy, Congress mercifully finished its business in three months and went home. When the session opened no change had occurred in the nation's foreign relations. In January, after the revelations of Eaton and

Truxton started public speculation of foreign assistance in Burr's schemes, Jefferson spiked these rumors which, he said, were "to be imputed to the vauntings of the author of the enterprise, to multiply his partisans by magnifying the belief of his prospects and support." Except for quickening the pace of defense preparations nothing was wanted but patience in foreign affairs. Much of the President's annual message dealt with western affairs, not only the conspiracy and the neutralization of the Sabine, but with such subjects as Indian relations, defense, settlement, and exploration. The return of Lewis and Clark gave great satisfaction. Jefferson also reported the exploration of the Red River by Thomas Freeman and Zebulon Pike to the sources of the Mississippi. Not all the contours of the immense country had been traced but enough was now known to commence an accurate map of the Mississippi and its waters. Jefferson especially recommended to Congress enactment of the bounty bill for settling Americans on the river above New Orleans. Burr's enterprise pointed up the vulnerability of the territory, and Jefferson saw no real security apart from planting young and hardy men on the spot to defend it. Congress again passed over the recommendation. A more fundamental one, associated with western development but national in scope and aim, met the same fate.

Jefferson called for amendment of the Constitution to authorize the federal government to apply its resources to "the great objects of public education, roads, rivers, canals, and such other objects of public improvement as may be thought proper." He had tossed out the idea in the second inaugural address, when the plan was to distribute the funds among the states. Since then Gallatin had persuaded him to retain federal control. "By these operations," Jefferson said to Congress, "new channels of communication will be opened between the states; the lines of separation will disappear, their interests will be identified, and their union cemented by new and indissoluble ties." Roads and canals would knit the Union together, facilitate defense, furnish avenues of trade, break down local prejudices, and consolidate that "union of sentiment," so essential to the national polity, that had been his polestar since entering the presidency. This was a new departure, but it did not mark any shift of principles. He had never flatly opposed public improvements under federal auspices. In the past, however, his hostility to privilege in any shape and his concern for the sanction of the Constitution had led him to oppose various plans and projects in this line, including some his judgment otherwise approved. He had not moved earlier to secure the constitutional authority mainly for fiscal reasons. The debt had first claim on the revenue. Now, thanks to the profits of the neutral trade, the debt was well on the way to extinction and still the surplus piled up, exceeding the new outlays for defense and such hypothetical demands as the Florida purchase. The source of these profits produced a strong motive for investment in the country's internal development. A national prosperity founded on an extraordinary war in Europe was highly precarious. Whether in a state of war or of peace, the carrying trade was no more than a temporary mainstay of the economy, essential until the country got on its feet but to be gradually replaced by the home market. The object of political economy, Adam Smith had taught, was to increase the productive resources of a nation, and to that end a capital employed at home was generally many times more productive than a capital employed in the roundabout and uncertain traffic of foreign commerce. At least for the United States, Smith's example of China, with its extensive interior and virtual isolation, was a better model than the example of Britain with which the nation had set up a perilous rivalry on the oceans. Jefferson had always recognized this. The primacy he had given to agricultural industry reflected his view, in perfect accord with Smith's, of the natural order of economic development. But powerful circumstances had impinged on theory. The inducements offered by foreign commerce and the primitive state of the home economy had given ascendancy to the carrying trade. This would change in time, and it would change sooner if the federal government lent a hand to the development of arteries of internal commerce, the primary infrastructure of the home market. Investment of the national capital in works of peace instead of war strongly appealed to the President. Nor did he confine his views to such mundane things as roads and canals. His proposal gave equal rank to "a national establishment for education," despite Gallatin's plea to subordinate this unpopular innovation to the business-minded interest in routes of trade. But whether Congress would be sufficiently enlightened to adopt any part of the plan, or whether the warring powers would permit the country to invest its resources in works of peace, remained to be seen.

Certain Republican precedents were available. In 1806 Congress authorized the President to lay out a road, by commissioners of his appointment, from Cumberland, Maryland, on the Potomac, to Ohio. Gallatin had conceived this measure. When Ohio became a state in 1802 he had arranged for 5 per cent of the proceeds from the sale of public lands in Ohio to be paid into a fund for the making of roads to link the state to the East. By subsequent legislation the take had been lowered to 2 per cent, but enough money had been accumulated by 1806 to warrant the beginning of what would become the National Road, running all the way to Illinois. When the commissioners reported two years later Jefferson learned at firsthand the political hazards of federal responsibility for fixing routes of trade. Every town considered the road for its benefit. The commission's route bypassed the aspiring metropolis of Washington, in southwestern Pennsylvania, which at once roared its disapproval. The county, Gallatin reminded the President, had always given a 2000-vote majority to the Republican party, and if its allegiance shifted the Federalists might win Pennsylvania in the next election. From these political pressures Jefferson recoiled in disgust; still he submitted, directing the commissioners to survey a route through Washington. Because of the uniqueness of the Ohio fund, the National Road offered a doubtful precedent. So, too, did western roads through the Indian country principally for postal communication. In 1804 Jefferson had directed Briggs, going out to New Orleans as surveyor-general, to map a better and shorter route to that distant quarter than the existing 1200-mile passage over Indian traces and treacherous mountains and rivers. Briggs accomplished his mission, and Congress voted money for the new post road. (Since Congress had not authorized Briggs's expenses, Jefferson reimbursed him out of his own pocket.) Money had previously been voted for lighthouses and harbor improvements. In 1806, by an appropriation for the survey of the coast between Cape Hatteras and Cape Fear, the government began under Jeffersonian auspices the United States Coastal Survey. But neither this nor the Lewis and Clark Expedition nor anything thus far undertaken could be considered on the same plane with the systematic planning and construction of roads and canals through the states. A constitutional amendment seemed expedient for the innovation, and had it been obtained the political morass that trapped and muddled federal enterprise in this area over the next thirty to forty years might have been avoided.

Congress did not respond to Jefferson's proposal. Except for a Senate resolution calling on Gallatin to submit a comprehensive report on roads and canals, which eventuated in an admirable plan of development, no further action was recorded before the gusts of war shriveled this enlightened venture of Jeffersonian nationalism. The chances for the educational part of the plan had never been good. The idea of a national university had originated with George Washington. Its champions were not politicians but statesmen of science, art, and literature who regarded Jefferson as their leader. They were men like Dr. William Thornton, designer of the Capitol and superintendent of patents; Benjamin Latrobe, the architect and engineer; Dupont de Nemours, who had prepared a national plan of education at Jefferson's request; George Logan, senator and agriculturist; and, above all, Joel Barlow, that wayfaring poet and propagandist of revolution, who returned to his native land in 1805 seventeen years after Jefferson met him in Paris at the beginning of his European odyssey. All these men felt a deep interest in national pursuits of peace, in commercial freedom, and in the hardware of internal improvements, as well as in higher education under the patronage of the federal government. For years Barlow had been associated with Robert Fulton, the inventor-promoter of the submarine and torpedo, which would supposedly render naval power ineffectual against seagoing commerce, and the steamboat, already tested on the Seine and by others in American waters, which seemed providentially designed for the inland waterways of the United States. Jefferson failed to grasp the full significance of the steamboat. Few men did; Robert Livingston, Fulton's partner and patron of the *Clermont* voyage in 1807, was the exception. Barlow introduced his ingenious friend to the President, and he showed much more interest in the torpedo, as a weapon against British naval power, than in the steamboat. But Barlow and Fulton, together with Latrobe and perhaps others, all enthusiasts for canal navigation, undoubtedly influenced Jefferson's thinking on this phase of internal improvements; and Barlow, in particular, sparked the idea of a national university.

Barlow settled in Washington in the fall of 1805. For several years Jefferson had been urging him to come home and write a history of the United States. Marshall's *Life of Washington*, now beginning to appear, horrified the President. During the ensuing winter he set Barlow to work, with boxes upon boxes of material supplied from Monticello and easy access to all the offices of government, to write a Republican history of the new nation. The past did not seriously interest Barlow, however, and he turned his restless mind to the university project. He discussed it at length with the President, wrote a prospectus for him, and at his direction drafted a bill which Logan introduced in the Senate. Influenced in part by Napoleon's National Institute, the bill contemplated both a scientific academy and an educational institution, combining teaching and research in a fashion unknown to American universities of that time. Jefferson hoped that Peale's Museum might find shelter in this national institution. The result, had it materialized, would have had the characteristics of the American Philosophical Society, the University of Virginia, and the Smithsonian Institution all rolled into one. But Congress showed little interest. The mass of Republicans were indifferent or hostile from niggardly views of public economy or state rights, while the Federalists feared political influence, despite the safeguards contained in the bill. Jefferson's recommendation in his sixth annual message gave the project higher standing than before, but the sequel confirmed Gallatin's judgment that it was too unpopular to be considered. Jefferson did not press the measure again. A year later, at the commencement of the Tenth Congress, he wrote disappointingly to Barlow, "I had fondly hoped to set those enterprises [internal improvements generally] into motion with the last legislature I shall meet. But the chance of war is an unfortunate check." Roads and canals were more popular than science and education, of course, but "the narrow and niggardly views of ignorance working the suffrage of ignorance" doomed both halves of the system. "There is a snail-paced gait for the advance of new ideas on the general mind, under which we must acquiesce," he philosophized. "A forty years' experience of popular assemblies has taught me that you must give them time for every step you take. If too hard pressed, they balk, and the machine retrogrades." An ultimate faith in the machine—this was the final solace.

Toward the close of the session Jefferson was able to communicate two items of good news from abroad. The American ministers in London had concluded a treaty, and Armstrong had been reliably informed in Paris that Napoleon's Berlin Decree, making lawful prize of all traffic with Britain, would not extend to American carriers. Without this exemption or the protection of Britain, American neutrality was obliterated. If Monroe and Pinkney had, in fact, secured a treaty "satisfactory on all points," then Britain had presumably yielded to the American ultimatum on impressment under the alarm of the Berlin Decree. For in November the envoys had informed the administration that the British commissioners would not recede from impressment in the treaty, though they would deliver informal assurances of caution and forbearance in the practice. The American team considered the Auckland-Holland note on the subject satisfactory and were proceeding on their own responsibility to conclude the treaty. This startled Jefferson. "I believe the *sine qua non* we made is that of the nation," he told Madison, who entirely agreed, "and that they would rather go on without a treaty than one which does not settle this article." He convened the cabinet on February 2. The question was put: Should the United States yield the principle of the non-importation act in return for a treaty, even if satisfactory on other points, that did not secure its citizens against impressment? "Unanimously not. Because it would be yielding the only peaceable instrument for coercing all our rights." In other words, it was not simply the failure of the *sine qua non* that caused dissent but this failure in conjunction with treaty stipulations that would undoubtedly annihilate commercial legislation against Britain. As to neutral rights generally, Jefferson again expressed his belief that the two emperors, Napoleon and Alexander, would enforce them in the eventual peace treaty, surely with more latitude than Britain would now allow. The cabinet agreed to maintain a friendly attitude, to renew the executive suspension of the non-importation act, and to adhere to the original ultimatum. Writing to the envoys the next day, Madison said flatly that no treaty omitting firm guarantees against impressment would be acceptable. He recognized, of course, a treaty might already have been signed. Such was the case, on December 31, but by then Britain would have had time for sober second thoughts under the duress of the Berlin Decree and might have yielded to the American demand. This was Jefferson's hope when he announced the accord to Congress on February 19. In fact, the British ministry's reaction to the decree had been just the opposite; in the end it was Monroe and Pinkney, not Auckland and Holland, who had been frightened by Napoleon.

A copy of the treaty reached David Erskine, the new, young, and likeable British Minister, on March 3, the day before the expiration of the Ninth Congress. Erskine rushed the document to Madison who, in turn, took it to the President. Not only was the treaty silent on impressment but a British note had been annexed reserving to His Majesty's government the right to reciprocate the Berlin Decree and, in this connection, to violate engagements with the United States unless France revoked the decree or the American government openly combated it. That evening a joint committee of Congress rode in a carriage to the President's House to inquire of any last-minute business. When the treaty was mentioned, Dr. Mitchill asked if the Senate might expect an early call to consider it. "Certainly not!" Jefferson snapped. His irritability was compounded by a migraine attack. He could not imagine why his envoys had signed such a humiliating treaty, unless they had panicked at the first news of the Berlin Decree, supposing war with France inevitable. Talking to Erskine the next day, he said the informal note on impressment was worthless and waxed indignant at the pre-condition binding the United States to resist the injuries of another nation while Britain, an equal party to the contract, left herself free to wreak whatever injuries she pleased. Congress wound up its affairs agog at the President's peremptory rejection of the treaty. He took a heavy responsibility on himself, Senator Smith observed. Coerced into making the treaty by the Senate, he nevertheless refused its advice on acceptance. And why? Because he did not get everything asked. If British depredations increased would not he be responsible? Would not Monroe and Pinkney be insulted? Would not he and Madison be accused of seeking to discredit Monroe and curry favor with Napoleon? All these embarrassing questions had no effect whatever on the President's determination to refuse "a hard treaty" with Britain.

Indeed the more he pondered the treaty the worse it became in his eyes. When the official text arrived he subjected it to close scrutiny, arranging his "observations" in three columns: the specific article and the *pros* and *cons*. Most of the ink was in the third column. He had at first, somewhat impulsively perhaps, brushed the accord aside for two or three reasons; now he eagerly searched out and found many additional objections. The prior objections focused on the notes rather than the treaty itself. In the absence of an article on impressment the question became whether the United States could accept the note of the British commissioners as an "implied abandonment" of the practice. Monroe insisted this was the case: the note conceded the substance without the shadow of the right. It ought to be viewed, Monroe said, as if it were a stipulation of the treaty itself. He should have known better. On the British side the assurances were cautionary only, made no part of the treaty, and had no application to "British seamen," however they might be defined. Jefferson, for his part, viewed the omission of security against impressment as constructive recognition of the right, hence prejudicial to the American claim in the future. Without again entering into the argument over impressment, he thought Britain better able than the United States to make the necessary concession. More American than British seamen were seized on the high seas and the practice assailed the sovereignty of the United States, itself a greater consideration than any on the other side. Two additional things should be said of Jefferson's reaction to the note on the Berlin Decree. First, the British ministry waited only seven days after its commissioners signed the treaty before retaliating against the decree. The American government was given no time to comply with the demand, and the order in council of January 7, throwing a "paper blockade" along most of the European coast, attacked an American-dominated trade between Continental ports. After this blow, what reliance could be placed in British engagements? Second, the note in particular, but certain articles of the treaty as well, would force the United States into an unneutral attitude toward France. Jefferson said it "clearly squinted at the expectation that we would join in resistance to France, or they [Britain] would not regard the treaty." The country could not permit itself to be bullied into war. While Napoleon straddled the Continent, while the Florida purchase still depended on his good offices with Spain, Jefferson wished to avoid a fiasco with France, such as the Jay Treaty had invited a decade before.

But what of the treaty articles themselves? On a superficial view Article XI was the most valuable. It secured the re-export trade on the landing of the cargo and the payment of token duties in the American port. But as Jefferson read the article it restricted the re-export of colonial produce to European markets and the supply of the colonial markets to European articles. Moreover, this British retreat from the *Essex* decision was confined to the period of "the present hostilities." So if peace were made tomorrow the concession would be worthless. Article III covered the East India trade, highly prized by American merchants. Monroe thought it was returned to the footing of the Jay Treaty. Actually, the new provision put an end to indirect voyages to East India ports. The cargoes and the capital for this labyrinthian trade were obtained by coastal voyages in Europe and at other intermediate points; limited to direct voyages, it would be severely handicapped to the advantage of the British East India Company, even more so now than at the time of Jay's Treaty because fewer native princes were independent of British control. The treaty provided for equal tonnage duties, but this remained a fiction because of the added town port charges levied in Britain though not in the United States. The treaty acquiesced in the discriminatory duties on exports to the United States. Since the Constitution denied to Congress the power to lay export duties, reciprocity in this area was impossible, at great cost to American consumers and also to traders placed at a competitive disadvantage in the trans-shipment of British wares. The articles on contraband and blockade marked some advance for the American position, but recognition of the British doctrine on neutral flags, the status of the cargo determining the status of the ship, was a retrograde step. Other articles secured to British cruisers favorable treatment in American ports and to British privateers privileges that the United States was bound to deny the enemies of France. This was inadmissible. Finally, the "most favored nation" article barred the United States from retaliatory legislation against Great Britain. While so many wrongs remained to be righted by that power, "we will never," Jefferson emphatically declared, "tie our hands by treaty, from the right of passing a non-importation or non-intercourse act, to make it in her interest to become just."

Expert testimony confirmed Jefferson's judgment on the commercial articles of the treaty. In April, Madison laid these articles before Tench Coxe, Jacob Crowninshield, William Jones, and Senator Smith, perhaps others, all men who qualified as experts on the intricacies of foreign trade. The result was wholesale condemnation. Coxe, for instance, said that Britain surrendered nothing of importance and secured every present advantage in the Anglo-American trade. Better the United States should withdraw from the ocean and concentrate on internal trade and manufactures, he thought. Smith, who had earlier upbraided the President for cavalierly dismissing the treaty, now said it would "completely prostrate our commerce at the foot of Great Britain." The Senate would never ratify it. There was no informed public opinion of the accord since only its general outlines were known. The fact that it was silent on impressment justified its rejection to most Republicans. The President's popularity was unbounded, Nicholson wrote sourly to Monroe, and his will that of the nation. The only criterion of judgment on events was his approval or disapproval. If he were in favor of Jay's Treaty, the people would enthusiastically applaud it. "Such is our present infatuation," said Nicholson.

The treaty, meanwhile, was in the course of re-negotiation in London. That, at least, was the fiction adopted by the administration. Monroe and Pinkney had been instructed to renew the negotiation before the treaty reached Washington, so nothing had been concluded for the advice and consent of the Senate. In April, before Jefferson went to Monticello, the cabinet approved a long list of revisions to be sought. It considered Madison's proposal to surrender the employment of British seamen in exchange for the abolition of impressment. Pending Gallatin's report on the impact of this measure on the American marine, the new bill of particulars for the envoys was held up. When Gallatin estimated that nearly one-half the able seamen in the foreign trade were British—an estimate Jefferson thought high—the cabinet shelved Madison's plan and returned to the earlier proposition to reciprocate the British practice of nationalizing alien seamen after two years' service. The formal instructions were dispatched on May 20, just after Jefferson's return to Washington. An understanding on impressment thus remained the primary object; it was not in itself the decisive one, however. The United States might have shuffled along without an impressment article had it not been for the annex on the French decree, the unsatisfactory commercial articles, and the utterly intolerable sacrifice of commercial coercion.

By this time a new Tory, or "Pittite," ministry had come to power in Britain. The cabinet change doomed what slender hope Jefferson still had for an accommodation. Indeed, from the receipt of the treaty he viewed the continued negotiations in London as a kind of shadow play to save Monroe's face, to keep up expectations at home, and to gain precious time. He wrote to Gallatin in April, "Time strengthens my belief that no equal treaty will be obtained. . . . Perhaps we may engage them to act on certain articles, including their note on impressment, by a mutual understanding, under the pretext of further time to arrange a general treaty. Perhaps too the general peace will in the meantime establish for us better principles than we can obtain ourselves." Procrastination was his policy. While the negotiation took "a friendly nap," time, always "the most precious thing to us," would again be granted the opportunity to rescue the country from difficulties. He had not really wanted a treaty in the first place, preferring, rather, separate accords on critical issues. And when the envoys returned a treaty that dealt badly with the minor issues, made no provision on the major one in direct violation of their instructions, put the United States in hostile relation to France, and disarmed the country of its most potent weapon of defense, Jefferson felt justified in trotting this abomination out the back door. Having rejected accommodation with Britain, he now had to see if he had other means to vindicate American claims.

The opportunity would arise sooner than he expected. Meanwhile, the Burr trial got under way at Richmond. The executive officer responsible for the government's case was the Attorney General, Caesar A. Rodney, who was handicapped by illness in his family at Wilmington. Partly for this reason, but also because he knew that he as well as Burr was on trial, Jefferson took a more active role in the collection of evidence and the conduct of the prosecution than constitutional duty alone seemed to require. When Burr arrived in Richmond and appeared before Judge Marshall, the court decided to hold him on no higher charge than misdemeanor and admit him to bail in the amount of $10,000. Jefferson exploded. Demanding proof of overt acts of treason in order to commit the prisoner on that charge, Marshall placed an impossible burden on the government and twisted the law itself in the interest of the criminal. "We had always before understood that when there was reasonable ground to believe guilt, the offender must be put on his trial," Jefferson observed. "That guilty intentions [of treason] were probable, the judge believed. And as to overt acts, were not the bundles of letters of information in Mr. Rodney's hands, the letters and facts published in local newspapers, Burr's flight, and the universal belief or rumor of his guilt, probable ground for presuming the facts of enlistment, military guard, rendezvous, threats of civil war, or capitulation, so as to put him on trial? Is there a candid man in the U.S. who does not believe some one, if not all, of these overt acts to have taken place?" But the evidence could not be collected and the witnesses brought to Richmond under several months. Burr's crimes were sown from the Atlantic through all the western waters to New Orleans. Why are the crimes not proved? the judge asked. "As if an express could go to Natchez, or the mouth of the Cumberland, and return in five weeks, to do what has never taken place in twelve," Jefferson acidly retorted. Why, if troops were assembled on the Ohio in November or December, had not affidavits been obtained by the end of March? "But I ask the judge where they should have been lodged? At Frankfort? at Cincinnati? at Nashville? St. Louis? Natchez? New Orleans? These were the probable places of apprehension and examination. It was not known at *Washington* till the 26th of March that Burr would escape from the Western tribunals, be retaken and brought to an Eastern one: and in 5 days after (neither 5 months nor 5 weeks as the judge calculates) he says, it is 'impossible to suppose the affidavits could not have been obtained.'"

The decision was bad enough in its immediate effect; far worse were its implications for the trial still to come. For under a rigid interpretation of the Constitution's treason clause—two witnesses to the same overt act—Burr and his accomplices might go free. "The first ground of complaint was the supine inattention of the administration to a treason stalking through the land in open day. The present one, that they have crushed it before it was ripe for execution, so that no overt acts can be produced." Still impaled on the horns of this dilemma, Jefferson nevertheless felt that the government, if given a little time, could produce the evidence to convict the malefactors of treason even in a partisan court.

In April, and throughout the ordeal at Richmond, the President channeled his feelings not against Burr or his poor deluded followers but against the court and the circle of Federalists who made Burr's cause their own. Of course, he wished the culprit hanged for his crime. It was no ordinary crime. The integrity of the nation had been assaulted. This was the root of his passion, not the person of Aaron Burr, who had already destroyed himself regardless of the verdict at the bar of justice. In any fair and impartial trial that verdict must be guilty. The President himself had pronounced it and the public had thundered its approval. So when the course of justice opened in seeming defiance of the nation, Jefferson fell back on his old conviction in the Federalism of the bench. The mass of Republicans shared his opinion on the politicization of the trial. When Burr came out on bail in April, Marshall attended a dinner party hosted by John Wickham, a leading Richmond Federalist and chief counsel of the accused, who was also a guest. Thomas Ritchie, editor of the Richmond *Enquirer,* denounced the Chief Justice for this "wilful prostration of the dignity of his own character" and "wanton insult" to his country. To the Governor of Virginia, a mild and usually soft-spoken Republican, William H. Cabell, this notorious incident gave the plot away. "The Federalists have completely made this [trial] a party question," he wrote to a brother. "They unblushingly say that the prosecution originated with Mr. Jefferson in revenge and is kept up by the Republicans from the same motives. God damn their souls, they do not see that it is their enmity to Mr. Jefferson that makes them in love with misdemeanors and treasons, provided they can bring his administration into contempt." A year before the Federalists had used the Miranda case in the same way. The defendants then, charged with aiding and abetting an unlawful enterprise against Spain, were hailed as the martyred victims of a deceitful and persecuting administration. The government's chief prosecutor at Richmond, federal attorney George Hay, commented philosophically, "There is amongst mankind a sympathy for villainy, which sometimes shows itself in defiance of every principle of patriotism and truth." But with the Federalists it was more than that. They patronized and lionized Burr—the murderer of Hamilton—in order to assassinate the President politically. As the trial developed, Jefferson and Burr changed places and it rapidly became, on their side, a prosecution of the President, also of his general-in-chief, for driving an innocent lamb to slaughter.

"There never was such a trial from the beginning of the world," Hay remarked. Never, certainly, in the United States had a trial aroused so much interest or been accompanied by so much fanfare nation-wide. Late in May Burr and several accomplices were arraigned before a grand jury. Hay sought indictment for treason as well as misdemeanor, but things began inauspiciously. Several prospective jurors, including the distinguished Republicans Giles and Nicholas, though not John Randolph, were successfully challenged by the defense. The final complement of two Federalists, four Quids, and ten Republicans struck the President as unrepresentative. He traced it to the error of a wholly independent judiciary, "which from the citadel of the law can turn its guns on those they [the judges] were most meant to defend." Setting up a dispatch rider between Richmond and Washington, he was in constant touch with counsel. Hay complained of the court's rejection of affidavits on technical grounds of form, though it seemed to admit others similarly at fault from the defense side. The government had counted on the damaging testimony of Eric Bollman, one of the confederates earlier brought in custody to Washington, where he had given his story to the President orally and in writing on the pledge it would never be used against him or go out of executive hands. Jefferson had honored this man, the famed rescuer of Lafayette from prison, when he came to the United States; but he had fallen in with Burr. He was expected to give the same testimony in court, under the protection of executive pardon, he had given in Washington. Now Bollman refused the pardon and stood on the right against self-incrimination. At the same time he accused the President of betrayal of trust by delivering the Washington statement to Hay—a delicate point of ethics perhaps but one Jefferson resolved easily enough in his own mind on the ground that the offer of pardon fulfilled the promise and that Hay was a hand of the executive. At any rate,

Bollman's testimony was lost to the government. The man on whom the prosecution's case principally turned was General Wilkinson. Days and weeks passed and Wilkinson did not appear. Burr's partisans gloated: the Janus dared not show himself. He finally arrived, however, with ten witnesses wrested from the arms of the courts in New Orleans, and promptly opened a noose large enough for his own neck together with Burr's.

The defense counsel realized that the acquittal of their client depended on the conviction of Wilkinson. Partly for this reason, partly to harass the President, Burr himself moved that Jefferson be subpoened to appear in court with certain letters bearing on Wilkinson's actions. Marshall issued the subpoena on an opinion that could only be interpreted, like *Marbury v. Madison,* as a slap at the President. Jefferson's temperature had been mounting steadily. The judge tolerated the grossest invective against him from the defense counsel's most vocal member, Luther Martin, the "unprincipled and impudent Federal bull-dog," as Jefferson called him. And on one occasion Marshall openly avowed his opinion that the prosecution seemed more interested in a conviction than a fair trial—a statement he blushingly retracted when called to account by one of Hay's associates, William Wirt. The subpoena further strained Jefferson's feelings, yet he never lost control. The same maneuver had been attempted in the Miranda case; within two months it would be attempted, on Madison, in the Connecticut libel case. Were the President and his executive officers to be hailed into courts all across the country? "The Constitution enjoins his constant agency in the concerns of six millions of people. Is the law paramount to this, which calls on him on behalf of a single one?" Jefferson asked. He went on to reiterate his tripartite theory of the federal balance. "But would the executive be independent of the judiciary, if he were subject to the *commands* of the latter, and to imprisonment for disobedience; if the several courts could bandy him from pillar to post, keep him constantly trudging from north and south and east and west, and withdraw him entirely from his constitutional duties?" With this parade of horribles the question answered itself, so convincingly, in fact, that Marshall might have squirmed had he seen the opinion. But it was written for Hay's benefit; Jefferson would not dignify the subpoena with a formal answer and he would resist any effort to enforce it. Actually, as Hay pointed out, the President's appearance on the scene was the last thing wanted by the defense. No demand to enforce the subpoena embarrassed the judge. Nor did justice require it. Jefferson co-operated promptly and fully with the request for papers and offered to give testimony by way of deposition should the court desire. It was never requested.

On June 24–25 the grand jury returned indictments for treason and misdemeanor against Burr, Blennerhassett, Dayton, Smith, Tyler, and two others. The chief accuser, Wilkinson, barely escaped indictment himself. For Jefferson the General's part in suppressing the conspiracy covered the multitude of his sins, and he could readily sympathize with the man whose plight—the scapegoat of criminals—was similar to his own. Burr was thrown into the Richmond jail; two days afterwards, on the plea of counsel, the court permitted him to lodge under guard in the comfort of the house occupied by Luther Martin. The other defendants received no such generosity. On August 3, Burr's treason trial began. Impaneling a jury was tedious work. After several days, forty-eight had been called and only four chosen. Nearly everyone, Hay reported, was convinced of Burr's guilt and said so. "Have you not said that Col. Burr ought to be hung?" went one interrogatory. "No, I said hanging was too good for him." A jury was finally secured and Hay opened the case for the government. The indictment charged Burr with assembling troops and "levying war" against the United States at Blennerhassett's Island on December 10, 1806, and further with descending the western rivers in order to take possession of New Orleans. Hay dwelt at length on the fine line between conspiracy and treason, between the design and the act of treason, between the procurement of a treasonable force and the actual levying of war. It was incumbent on the prosecution to show, he concluded, that Burr had a treasonable design and assembled a force to effect that design. In this Hay believed he was supported by Marshall's opinion in the habeas corpus case of Bollman and Swartwout only a few weeks before. If there is "an actual assemblage of men for the purpose of executing a treasonable design," Marshall declared, "all those who perform any part, however minute, or however remote from the scene of action, and who are actually leagued in the general conspiracy are traitors." This seemed to adhere to the common law rule, "in treason all are principals." It followed, then, that the testimony of two witnesses to Burr's *procuring* a treasonable assemblage on the island, regardless of his whereabouts or war-like acts, would constitute proof of treason.

The testimony of Eaton, the Morgans, and others went to establish Burr's treasonable designs. Several witnesses to the goings-on at the island proved that armed men, boats, military stores, and provisions had been assembled, and that Blennerhassett, Tyler, and company had named the division of the Union as one of their objects. But it soon became apparent, before most of the witnesses had been called, that the prosecution could not fix Burr's presence on the island at the time of the overt act laid in the indictment or prove by the positive testimony of two witnesses that he procured such an assemblage in force as constituted "levying war." At this point the defense moved to arrest the evidence. After ten days of argument Marshall, on August 31, delivered his opinion accepting the motion and sent the case to the jury. The opinion, if it did not contradict that in the former case, unraveled its obscurities in favor of the defendant. In *Bollman* the judge had emphasized "the assemblage of men"; he now required "the employment and exhibition of force" in proof of "levying war." The question of Burr's procurement of treasonable acts became irrelevant unless the acts procured were, in fact, treasonable. "The legal guilt of the person who planned that assemblage on Blennerhassett's island depends . . . on the criminality of that assemblage. If those who perpetrated the fact be not traitors, he who advised the fact cannot be a traitor. His guilt, then . . . depends on theirs; and their guilt can only be established in a prosecution against themselves." The opinion amounted to a directive of acquittal to the jury. The jury returned an unusual verdict. The defendant, it said, "is not proved to be guilty by any evidence submitted to us."

Jefferson, quiet throughout this trial, had prepared himself for the decision. "The event has been what was evidently intended from the beginning . . . ," he wrote to Hay, "that is to say, not only to clear Burr but to prevent the evidence from ever going before the world." The whole conduct of the trial—the assault on him personally, the flattering attentions to Burr, the Jesuitical reading of the law—had been political, in his opinion. At first he seemed disinclined to go to trial on the lesser charge of misdemeanor for mounting an expedition against the Spanish dominions. Hay advised against it, at least in Richmond and before Marshall, where everything must again turn on the events at Blennerhassett's Island. But Jefferson ordered Hay to proceed, perhaps less with a view to the conviction of Burr than the embarrassment of Marshall. "If defeated," he said, "it will heap coals of fire on the head of the Judge; if successful, it will give time to see whether a prosecution of treason against him [Burr] can be instituted in any, and what other court." The trial commenced immediately. Another subpoena issued to the President, which he ignored as before; and the final result was much the same as before. The court arrested the evidence at the threshold by excluding any testimony not directly connected with the spot laid in the indictment. Hearings were then begun on the commitment of Burr and Blennerhassett for treason and misdemeanor in Ohio and Kentucky. The court, on October 20, remanded the prisoners for trial in the former state on the lesser charge only. Burr posted a small bail, at once forfeited, and fled to England.

Jefferson supposed the rulings at Richmond "equivalent to a proclamation of impunity to every traitorous combination which may be formed to destroy the Union." Fortunately, however, the public revulsion against the court would produce a more than adequate compensation in the form of a constitutional amendment making the federal judiciary, "this colossal power, which bestrides the legislative and executive authorities," responsible to the will of the nation. In November he laid the trial proceedings before Congress so that it might judge whether the defect lay in the testimony, or in the law, or in the administration of justice, and furnish whatever remedy needful to secure the nation from treason. The legislatures of Massachusetts and Pennsylvania instructed their respective delegations to work for a constitutional amendment rendering judges removable by the President on the address of both houses of Congress. Giles and Randolph introduced legislation to widen the scope of the treason clause beyond the construction Marshall had given to it. Jefferson was a silent observer of these proceedings; and Congress, preoccupied with foreign affairs, as he was, came to no final resolution of the problem. The Senate, at least, left no doubt of its opinion of the Burr Conspiracy. A committee under Adams's chairmanship moved the expulsion of John Smith, the Ohio senator, for his participation in the criminal combination "against the *peace, Union,* and *liberty* of the people of the United States." Adams's report warmly commended the administration for suppressing the conspiracy that would, "in a very short lapse of time, have terminated not only in war, but in a war of the most horrible description, in a war at once foreign and domestic." It went on to declare, without entering into technical legal questions of criminality, "that if the daylight of evidence, combining one vast and complicated intention, with overt acts innumerable, be not excluded from the mind by the curtain of artificial rules, the simplest understanding cannot but see what the subtlest understanding cannot disguise, crimes before which ordinary treason whitens into virtue—crimes of which war is the mildest feature." Several Republicans stood by Smith in the belief he had been duped by Burr. The vote on the expulsion resolution, 19 to 10, fell one short of the two-thirds needed. But the Senator resigned under the force of censure.

"Some circumstantial evidence is very strong, as when you find a trout in the milk." Thoreau's aphorism fits the case nicely. The verdict of common sense, of morality, and of history on Burr was, and must remain, guilty; the verdict of law was, and must remain, innocent. He might have been convicted on a less stringent interpretation of the treason clause, and but for Marshall's political bias this would surely have been the result. In the long run, however, the nation was better served by his bias than by Jefferson's. For conviction would have introduced into American law the ancient English principle of "constructive treason," founded in this case on Burr's "constructive presence" at Blennerhassett's Island, where the evidence failed to pin overt acts of treason on him. It was better that the scoundrel go free than be convicted on evidence outside the indictment or on a constructive definition of the act of "levying war." Jefferson could hardly be expected to take this view of the matter. Although he knew all along the defect of the evidence, the unfortunate constraints of the indictment, and so on, he also believed these difficulties could be surmounted by a court that placed the protection of the government above the protection of criminal assailants. In cases where the nation itself was attacked, as he believed it was in this case, the judiciary ought not to conjure with the law to cover traitors. At another time, in another place, he might have condemned reasoning of this kind as dangerous to liberty; but with the responsibilities of the chief magistrate at a time when the experiment in liberty and union was still perilous, he could not afford the luxury of abstract opinion. Democracy, too, placed him at odds with the Chief Justice. Jefferson had exchanged the independence of the judiciary, once thought an essential safeguard of civil liberties, for a vaguely plebicitarian conception—a judiciary responsible to the will of the nation. There could be no doubt of that will in the case of Aaron Burr. Over and over Jefferson emphasized the judgment of the people, so alarmingly at issue with the judgment of the court.

In the last analysis it was the popular judgment that counted, and partly for this reason Jefferson could tame his anger at the court. The Catiline went into exile. First in London, then in Paris, he tried to market a disunionist conspiracy with much the same western plot as before. He failed, of course. The foreign offices distrusted him. At times he lived on the edge of starvation. Finally, in 1812, he returned home in disguise and disgrace. How the mighty had fallen! If Jefferson took any comfort from the perdition that pursued Burr to his grave, he never mentioned it. Wilkinson fell too, but with the agility of a cat landed on his feet. Jefferson astutely anticipated the uproar in Congress against Wilkinson, and referred the charges of collaboration with Spain to a military court of inquiry. The artful dodger passed through this ordeal, another and longer and inconclusive one in Congress, and finally, in 1811, won acquittal from a court-martial. Through all this Jefferson stood by him, not from any fondness for the blustering commander but because his actions, crooked or straight, defeated the Burr Conspiracy. "As to the rest of his life," Jefferson wrote in 1812, "I have left it to his friends and his enemies, to whom it furnished matter enough for disputation. I classed myself with neither." In the end it seemed to him that the evils of Burr or Wilkinson or Marshall were small and transient compared with the permanent good wrought by the Burr Conspiracy in fixing the Union in the affections of the American people.

The Embargo

On June 25, when Jefferson was supposedly under subpoena to appear in Richmond, Captain Charles Gordon of the USS *Chesapeake* burst into the President's House to report the outrage committed on his ship off Norfolk three days before. The *Chesapeake*, under way for the Mediterranean, had been hailed by the HMS *Leopard*, one of a squadron patrolling off Hampton Roads, and ordered to submit to search for British deserters. Refused by Commodore James Barron, in command, the *Leopard* poured repeated broadsides into the defenseless frigate, killing three and wounding eighteen before its flag could be struck. Four alleged deserters were then removed and the *Chesapeake* limped back to port. The British government, in all the extremity of its pretensions, had never claimed the right to search national vessels. The assertion of the claim was an insult; accompanied by force, in the attack on the *Chesapeake*, it was an act of war.

Jefferson learned from Gordon that the captain of the *Leopard* acted under orders from Vice Admiral George C. Berkeley, commander of the fleet in American water. Berkeley, a typical specimen of admiralty arrogance and influence that intimidated government itself, was responsible for intercepting enemy vessels and contraband from the St. Lawrence to the Caribbean. His ships—roughly a score of different sizes and descriptions, with others building in Bermuda —depended on the services of American ports, and the same ports constantly depleted their crews. In May he learned that several British deserters had enlisted aboard the *Chesapeake* at Norfolk and, in addition, that three vessels of his fleet, earlier proscribed on the President's order for the *Leander* affair in New York, had been forced to leave Charleston. Boiling angry, he issued the order to search the *Chesapeake*. Of the four seamen taken, one was a genuine deserter, and he would later hang at Halifax; the other three were American citizens who had "deserted" from impressment aboard the HMS *Melampus*. They, too, would be condemned at Halifax, and then pardoned on condition of returning to the British service.

As the news of the *Chesapeake* affair spread across the country, the populace rose with thunderous voice against Britain. "I have never seen so large an assemblage—" Senator Smith wrote of the public meeting in Baltimore, "every man almost of respectability of whatever party was present—There appeared but one opinion— War." The same sentiment echoed and re-echoed in mass meetings up and down the land during the next several weeks. In Virginia, Governor Cabell ordered the militia into the Norfolk area. In Philadelphia the public assaulted a British armed brig, believed to be loading provisions for the Norfolk squadron, and left her crippled and dismantled. "This country has never been in such a state of excitement since the battle of Lexington," Jefferson remarked. And even Lexington had not produced the same unanimity. With such ardor did the Federalists rally to the administration that the President was tempted to exclaim with the Psalmist, "Lord, what have I done that the wicked should praise me!"

What he did, essentially, was to tap the war fever for vigorous measures in pursuit of peace, if possible, in preparation for war, if necessary. The cabinet officers reassembled in Washington and met on July 2. By proclamation the President proscribed all British warships from American waters. The Mediterranean squadron was recalled. The frigate *Revenge* was dispatched to Britain with instructions for the American ministers. They were to demand disavowal of the attack and the principles on which it rested, reparations for injuries, return of the four seamen, Berkeley's recall, and security against future outrages. Since the last could not be obtained while impressment existed, the demand was linked to the old ultimatum. The policy was redress, not war. But placing this price tag on his suit for redress, the President realized he ran the risk of war. We operate on three principles, he said in explaining the policy to his son-in-law Randolph: first, that the usage of nations calls for seeking satisfaction before going to war and, besides, peace is still a great object; second, that 40,000 seamen and property worth many millions scattered through all the seas and oceans ought to be brought home before a declaration of war; third, that Congress is the arbiter of war and should not be committed by any act of the President. Interestingly, he did not convene Congress at once, though some war-minded advisers urged him to do so. The call went out for more than three months hence, on October 26, by which time tempers would have cooled and the *Revenge* should have returned with the verdict of the British ministry on the suit for redress. Even if the verdict proved negative, it was by no means certain in his mind that war should follow. Non-intercourse, or commercial coercion in some form, had not yet been tried, only threatened; and this, not war, was the next logical step. In July, such was "the torrent of passion," Jefferson had only to snap his fingers to plunge the country into war with the old enemy. Instead he used the power in his hands for peace. As so often before in foreign crises, he played for time: Napoleon's time, time for military preparations at home, time for Britain to show her hand.

In the immediate crisis it could not be known whether Berkeley, the admiralty, or the ministry had been the author of the attack on the *Chesapeake*. If the orders were ministerial, as Jefferson first suspected, Britain had already thrown down the gauntlet and no American vessel was safe on the seas. But perhaps the Admiral's orders were equivocal, leaving him free to employ force in given circumstances; perhaps they had been timed to exploit the expected turmoil of the Burr Conspiracy or to coincide with renewed Indian incitements on the Great Lakes frontier. The main fear in July was an attack on Norfolk. "Blows may be hourly possible," Jefferson warned on the 7th. Governor Cabell, while keeping up his guard, was under strict orders not to strike the first blow. An anomalous situation existed at Hampton Roads. The men and ships of the British squadron, by virtue of defying the President's proclamation, were considered "enemies *de facto*." Communication with them was by flag only. When a small party foraging on shore for supplies was captured, Jefferson agreed with Cabell on the right to treat them as prisoners-of-war but prudently directed their release lest an enemy *de jure* be recognized. He was satisfied by the end of July that the squadron's intentions were pacific, though it did not withdraw beyond the capes until October. All the while the administration made extensive military preparations. These were defensive in part, addressed immediately to the enforcement of the proclamation in American harbors; but they also contemplated offensive war. The governors of the several states were ordered to ready their respective quotas of 100,000 militia for a winter campaign against Canada. Artillery, ammunition, and camp equipage were ordered to rendezvous points near the frontier. The discretionary act of the last Congress for the acceptance of volunteer companies, organized and placed on standby, was put into effect. The Army and Marine Corps were brought up to authorized limits, and the naval complement raised above the maximum fixed by law. Materials for additional gunboats were procured in anticipation of congressional appropriation. Fortifications were pushed, especially at New York, Charleston, and New Orleans.

And Gallatin quietly sounded out the banks on annual loans to support a war. The public knew nothing of these preparations. Rather than manufacturing a war hysteria around national defense, as his predecessor had done in another crisis, Jefferson worked silently, made no answer to the numerous addresses he received, and said "our greatest praise shall be, that we *appear* to be doing nothing."

Cooling the crisis in the hope of peace, Jefferson nevertheless remained skeptical of its chances. Where British pride and jealousy were concerned, the nation had learned not to expect justice, least of all from a Tory ministry. "I suppose our fate will depend on the successes or reverses of Bonaparte," he mused. This was a hard fate indeed. "It is really mortifying that we should be forced to wish success to Bonaparte and to look to his victims as our salvation." But, as he said repeatedly, "the English being equally tyrannical at sea as he is on land, and that tyranny bearing on us in every point of either honor or interest, I say 'down with England,' and as for what Bonaparte is then to do to us, let us trust to the chapter of accidents. I cannot, with the Anglomen, prefer a certain present evil to a future hypothetical one." Near the end of August news of the Battle of Friedland and the Treaty of Tilsit, conscripting Russia in Napoleon's Continental System, reached him at Monticello. Once again the fortunes of European war seemed to come to America's rescue. British reflexes to this blow ought to prove conciliatory, yet he reminded himself that Tory behavior upset all the laws of reason and nature. If war should come he intended to make the most of it, not only in Canada but in the Floridas as well. "I had rather have war against Spain than not, if we should go to war against England," he told Madison. "Our southern defensive force can take the Floridas, volunteers for a Mexican army will flock to our standard, and rich pabulum will be offered to our privateers in the plunder of their commerce and coasts. Probably Cuba would add itself to our confederation." This was boldly stated, as if in relief from the pent-up tensions of peace. War was an easy temptress; still he remained faithful to the demanding mistress of peace.

In London the brilliant young foreign secretary, George Canning, who gloated in the Tory name, learned of the *Chesapeake-Leopard* encounter only a week after the Emperor Alexander's betrayal at Tilsit. Canning's response when cornered was to attack, specifically in this instance the Danish and Russian fleets; and as for the United States, he would rather invite hostilities with contempt than surrender to an "insidious neutrality." He had powerful support. Monroe dispatched his estimate of the situation in early August. "There has been at all times . . . a strong party here for extending [the war's] ravages to the [United States]," he wrote. "This party is combined of the ship-holders, the navy, the East and West India merchants, and certain political characters of great consideration in the State. So powerful is this combination that it is most certain that nothing can be obtained by this government on any point, but what may be extended of necessity. The disasters of the North ought to inspire moderation, but it seems to have produced directly the opposite effect." A month later Monroe presented his formal note on the *Chesapeake* affair. The government had already disavowed the act and recalled Berkeley; the only question remaining, in Canning's view, was the amount of the reparations to families of the victims. With colossal arrogance Canning turned everything around: the real act of aggression was the President's proclamation. (In Washington his minister, Erskine, had demanded indemnification for some British water casks destroyed by the people of Hampton after the *Chesapeake* murders, a demand which reminded Jefferson of the man who broke his cane over the head of another and then sued for the cost of the cane.) By the proclamation the President took reprisal into his own hands and could not, accordingly, demand anything of Britain, said Canning, though she generously volunteered reparations. And since the attack was unauthorized there was no basis for joining the general issue of impressment in the settlement. Jefferson, on the other hand, considered an abuse of impressment in one branch of practice as involving every other and flowing from what was authorized. "Certain it is," he added, "there can never be friendship, nor even the continuance of peace with England so long as no American citizen can leave his own shore without danger of being seized by the first British officer he meets." Canning, on his side, discovered "extraordinary circumstances" for Berkeley's attack in the employment of deserters on American ships of war. These cavils, combined with the imperatives of British naval supremacy in the fall of 1807, doomed the prospect of settlement. The Monroe-Pinkney treaty met the same fate. It was buried by mutual consent in October. Near the end of that month Canning transferred this annoying little *Chesapeake* business to a special envoy, George Rose, to the United States. Rose's instructions barred any proposition on impressment, and placing the United States in the wrong, demanded the recall of the President's proclamation prior to negotiations. The mission had no chance of success.

Meanwhile, the Tenth Congress convened. The *Revenge* had not yet returned, but the President was pleased to discover—what he had hardly dared to hope—that the war spirit had cooled and the members of Congress, almost to a man, seemed disposed to peace or, at most, to coercive measures short of war. He found encouragement in the withdrawal of the British squadron from Hampton Roads and mercantile reports of fewer captures at sea since the *Chesapeake* encounter. Peace was still his passion, peace was still pending, and if it failed let the onus be on Britain. So he had no idea of provoking Congress to war. He worked through three drafts of his annual message in order to strike just the right balance between patriotic indignation and pacific intentions. In the opinion of Gallatin and Smith, who, strangely, found themselves doves together, the first draft had the appearance of a war-like manifesto. Jefferson softened a few expressions without altering the substance or the tone of the message, which was firm but calm and not at all war-like. While warning the nation that it might not long be permitted to remain in the quiet pursuits of peace, he called for patience pending the outcome of negotiations and accelerated military preparations while the outcome was uncertain. In due time Congress would appropriate several million dollars for national defense.

It was an open secret in Washington that Jefferson would not meet another Congress. He had made his decision to retire long ago. The pleas of Republican leaders had alone restrained him from public announcement. "The pivot we have been spinning upon is yourself," one of them had written. Without his leadership, it was feared, the party would fly apart, each faction or sect spinning into a little orbit of its own. And the fate of the republic itself was bound up with the fate of the Republican party. Some thought the Randolph schism and the party turmoils in Pennsylvania and elsewhere had been produced by the reports two years past of the President's decision to retire in 1809. Officially, Jefferson had given no credence to these rumors; privately, however, all his words and actions pointed to retirement. Congressmen noted as early as February 1807 that he was beginning to send his things to Monticello; and when he went there the ensuing spring he carried a great quantity of trees and shrubs for the gardens of repose that increasingly occupied his idle moments. Newspaper subscriptions were allowed to expire, beginning—no better place, he said—with the *Evening Post* in November. Since the first reports of his intentions, Republican committees, legislative assemblies, religious associations, and citizens in number had showered him with addresses and resolutions urging him to stay on the job. Occasionally he answered private citizens. The infirmities of age and the principle of rotation in office were his pleas. The former were not only physical—rheumatism, an infected jaw, and so on—but psychological. "The principal effect of age . . . ," he observed, "is an indisposition to be goaded by business from morning to night, from laboring in an Augean stable, which cleared out at night presents an equal task the next morning." Duty to principle supported desire. "If some period be not fixed, either by the Constitution or by practice, to the services of the First Magistrate," he wrote to one petitioner, "his office, though nominally elective, will in fact, be for life; and that will soon degenerate into an inheritance." Yet Randolph accused him of creating a "masked monarchy."

Finally, in December, because he could wait no longer, despite the critical juncture of national affairs, the President announced his impending retirement by way of answer to the addresses of the state legislatures. "The die is cast," a Pennsylvanian wrote. And while the President's decision was a matter of profound regret, the principle at the bottom of it entitled him to immortal renown. "If anything were wanting to stamp Jefferson great and good; to place him highest on the list of the benefactors of mankind, the voluntary surrender of the first office in the gift of a free people, entitles him to precedence." The succeeding January the Republican caucus met in Washington, and with surprising ease, though not without opposition from Clintonians in New York and Quids, mainly Virginians, whose reluctant candidate was James Monroe, the party nominated Madison for President and renominated George Clinton for the second office. Thus, in the face of increaisng factionalism, Jefferson managed to control the choice of a successor and to hold the party together.

Administration and Congress marked time for several weeks awaiting dispatches from abroad. From Erskine, late in November, Madison learned of Canning's uncompromising position in the *Chesapeake* affair. London newspapers teemed with speculation on more drastic measures of impressment and new orders in council that would place the entire European continent under blockade. Some American merchants voluntarily kept their ships in port. Napoleon, partly in anticipation of the British move, announced that the Berlin Decree would be extended to the United States. The regulations had yet to be promulgated and, of course, Napoleon could no more blockade the British Isles than he could the United States; but between the tightening Continental System and the expected British orders, American commerce was caught in the jaws of a vise, a maniacal war of blockades, from which there seemed to be no appeal to reason or justice or right. The ruthless had combined to slaughter the innocent.

In this rapidly deteriorating situation, Jefferson's cabinet met on three successive days at the end of November. Nothing final was decided, but between war, a total embargo on American commerce, and acquiescence in the European decrees, Jefferson reported to his son-in-law, "the middle proposition is most likely." Madison clearly favored this course. Gallatin favored something less drastic, perhaps a sweeping non-importation act against Britain to take effect two months hence. The long-suspended selective non-importation law was allowed to go into operation in December. On the 18th, after further consultation, Jefferson sent a brief confidential message to Congress calling attention to "the great and increasing dangers with which our vessels, our seamen, and merchandise, are threatened on the high seas and elsewhere," and to the efficacy of a general embargo for the protection of "these essential resources." The message communicated the papers on the new construction of the Berlin Decree and the proclamation of George III recalling all his natural-born subjects from foreign service and ordering the vigorous enforcement of impressment to this end. Both houses closed their doors. The Senate, suspending its rules, passed the Embargo Act on the same day (22 yea, 6 nay), the House three days later (82 yea, 44 nay), and it became law on December 22. A self-blockade of the nation's commerce, the embargo prohibited American vessels from sailing to foreign ports and foreign vessels from taking on cargo in the United States.

With barely a ripple of protest the government launched an experiment of incredible magnitude, one that dwarfed all previous undertakings and held momentous consequences for the peace of the United States and the world. There was nothing novel in the idea of an embargo; it was part of the Jeffersonian canon, and as an expedient of defense or diplomacy had been in the course of speculation for two years. But no one, not even Jefferson himself, fully grasped the significance or in December 1807 foresaw the consequences of the Embargo Act. A certain obscurity surrounded the measure, which would be the source of abuse and recrimination in the months to come. In part this resulted from the President's failure to present to Congress one of the principal grounds of action, the British orders in council of November 11. Briefly, these orders made fair prize of neutral carriers trading with Continental ports controlled by the enemy, unless under license from Britain. The Continent was placed under quarantine to neutrals with the object of forcing their trade into British channels. At the commencement of the Rose mission, Canning designedly held back the communication of these decrees. They had not been officially received in Washington when Jefferson sent his embargo message to Congress, so he omitted any notice of this new outrage. But the orders had been anticipated for several weeks. They were widely rumored in the English press and confirmed by foreign correspondents. Years later Jefferson said he distinctly recalled having seen the King's proclamation of the state of siege against the Continent in the London newspapers; and Madison went further, saying a copy of the unsigned orders lay on the President's desk when he wrote his message. The first draft of the message referred to the fact as something known, yet not officially communicated, and pointedly declared "the whole world is thus laid under interdict by these two nations." But Jefferson struck both reference and declaration, apparently at Madison's cautious suggestion, with the result that the administration opened itself to the charge of embarking on unprovoked commercial warfare against Britain, presumably at the dictate of Napoleon. Among Federalists and Randolphians the dogma was implanted that the embargo originated in hostility to Britain and friendship for France. The dogma would have taken root, indeed it already had, regardless of anything Jefferson might have said. His critics were undaunted by the receipt and publication of the British orders in January. Yet the embargo would have been better understood and protected from malice had it been grounded unequivocally in the renewed British aggression against neutral rights.

A greater error in this regard was the President's failure to inform the public of the objectives of the embargo. He called the nation to surrender its foreign commerce, the basis of prosperity, furl the sails of hundreds of ships, discharge tens of thousands of seamen from employment, renounce markets for grain, cotton, tobacco, lumber, fish, and other products, hitting the producers as well as the merchants, and shrivel the profits and revenue of foreign imports. Why were these sacrifices required? Jefferson did not explain. He issued no proclamation. To Congress he stated, at most, half his thought, and that without elucidation. The embargo was wanted, he said, to protect the "essential resources" of the country employed in foreign commerce. According to one reliable estimate, 1500 vessels, 20,000 seamen, and $60,000,000 worth of cargo were on the high seas when the embargo became law. (This was about one-third less than in the summer just past, for in the interim many shipholders had voluntarily embargoed their vessels.) The intention of the embargo, then, seemed to be protective and precautionary: to secure from marauding belligerents as much of the nation's seaborne wealth as possible, meanwhile closing the ports to departures and meditating measures to be taken when the ships were safely home. The usual period allowed for this maneuver was ninety days, though the Indiamen required up to twice as long. In that interval, too, the outcome of the Rose mission would become known and the nation's defenses strengthened. Depending on events, war with either, conceivably both, of the belligerents seemed likely. From the President on down, everyone agreed that war was preferable to *permanent* embargo. Of his advisers, however, only Gallatin argued for a statutory time limit scaled to the immediate objective, and Congress hurriedly passed the legislation without fixing a terminal date. To have done so, in Jefferson's opinion, while consistent with the theory of the embargo as

884

a protective measure, would have been to weaken its effect as a coercive measure, and he also had this undisclosed theory in view.

In Jefferson's conception the embargo was not simply a short-run measure preliminary to war but an experiment at longer run—how long he did not know—to discover a peaceable substitute for war. The antecedents of the policy went back over four decades, and its varied career included the non-importation associations before the American Revolution, Madison's retaliatory measures in the First Congress, Jefferson's Report on Foreign Commerce, followed by the resolutions of January 1794, and the non-importation act of 1806. That the United States could enforce justice on European nations by withholding or restraining its commerce in some fashion was a first principle of Jeffersonian diplomacy and of Jeffersonian Republicanism. The dependence of the European colonies in the West Indies on American provisions, especially in wartime, the importance of American neutral carriers and their cargoes of grain, naval stores, tropical produce, and raw materials for European belligerents, the enormous value of the American market, above all to British merchants and manufacturers—these factors in the transatlantic economy placed an ultimate weapon of peace in American hands which, if put to a fair test, Jefferson believed, might not only secure his own country from the ravages of European war but also demonstrate the efficacy of commercial coercion to peace-loving peoples everywhere. "I place immense value in the experiment being fully made," he said, "how far an embargo may be an effectual weapon in [the] future as well as on this occasion." But this aim, which must appear visionary to many at home and unfriendly as well to governments abroad, was held in reserve until the rescue of American property from the seas forced the acknowledgment of a rationale for the continuation of the embargo other than the one first advanced.

Yet the history of Republican ideology and statecraft, especially as exhibited in the public careers of the President and the Secretary of State, pointed to this rationale from the beginning. While they maintained official silence, the *National Intelligencer* at once expounded the general theory of the embargo in several articles which discerning readers ascribed to the Secretary. "It is singularly fortunate that an embargo, whilst it guards our essential resources," the first article stated, "will have the collateral effect of making it the interest of all nations to change the system which has driven our commerce from the ocean." Universal and impartial in its terms, the embargo offered no cause for war to any nation, though on the author's own reckoning it would prove more injurious to Britain than to her enemies. What counted, at any rate, were the injuries and the privations certain to be inflicted by this great weapon on nations abroad, not the injuries and privations at home. The latter were of small moment, the second article endeavored to show, while the third pointed to positive economic benefits, as in the liberation of the country from debilitating foreign fashions and luxuries, the growth of domestic manufactures, and the expansion of the home market. Finally, the experiment promised to secure the American people, through the virtuous practice of peace rather than the dubious glories of war, the "national character" that had so long eluded them. "Let the example teach the world that our firmness equals our moderation; that having resorted to a measure just in itself, and adequate to its object, we will flinch from no sacrifices which the honor and good of the nation demand from virtuous and faithful citizens." These articles in the administration gazette explained the embargo better than anything else published at the time. Yet they were not a substitute for a declaration by the President himself. If political and diplomatic considerations made such a declaration unwise in December, this was not the case in April or May. But even then he failed to take the nation into his confidence and to establish in public opinion the credibility of a policy no longer defensible on protective grounds. He betrayed his own principles of leadership, which underscored official openness and public trust, and contributed to the bewilderment and confusion surrounding the embargo. The field of exegesis was left to his enemies while his friends were reduced to pleading implicit faith in him.

Confidence ran high during the early months of the experiment. Jefferson put himself personally in charge of enforcing the embargo. He did not expect the task would be easy, but it proved far more difficult than he imagined at the outset. Administratively the law fell within Gallatin's jurisdiction. Although he had approved the policy with reservations, Gallatin labored like a Hercules to ensure it the fair trial he, no less than his chief, wanted. He at once discovered several deficiencies in the basic law. If the embargo was to be effective it must control the coastal trade and hold navigation within its confines; but the law levied no extraordinary penalties on ships sailing without clearance and omitted coasting vessels from the bonds—double the value of craft and cargo—exacted of ocean-going vessels. To close these loopholes Congress promptly passed the first supplementary act. A second suppplementary act, in March, laid additional penalties and, further, extended the embargo to exports by land as well as by sea. The latter provision slammed the gates on the flourishing traffic across the Canadian frontier. Six weeks later, in the waning hours of the session, Congress passed still another act, the fourth in the series of embargo laws. Again the coastal trade was the object. Collectors were empowered to search and detain vessels ostensibly bound coastwise but suspected of fraudulent trading, and the President was fully authorized to employ the navy in enforcement. This piling up of legislation, each law more severe than the last, also injured the experiment. Had the basic law been more carefully drawn, habits of evasion—hard to stop once started—might never have started, and the sense of mounting federal tyranny might have been avoided. As the mere recital of these laws suggests, the administration had the bear by the tail and could neither tame him nor let go.

Considering the dimensions of the task and the paucity of administrative means, the embargo was diligently and, on the whole, effectively enforced. It was manifestly impossible to plug all the leaks by sea and by land. Congress opened a huge leak by inserting in the second supplementary act "an insidious clause," as Jefferson labeled it, permitting anyone, with the President's approval, to send a ship for valuable property held abroad. Administering this provision Jefferson tried to maintain the integrity of the embargo while also meeting the intention of Congress. If, as was said, Jamaica owed two million dollars to New York merchants, 30 or 40 vessels would be required to settle the account in sugar and rum, whereas three or four could settle it in specie. Obviously, then, the latter course was preferred. The complexity of cases was such that Jefferson declined to formulate general rules and, instead, judged each application on its merits. Some New York merchants owned $100,000 worth of sandalwood in the Friendly Islands. The Orient was its only market.

Should they be permitted to send a ship, sell the sandalwood in the Orient, and bring home the proceeds in a return cargo, despite the legal provision barring traffic and trade in retrieved property? Yes, said Jefferson. "The bringing home of property being the main object, if it be in an impracticable form, it affects the intention of the law to let it be commuted into a practicable form." Before he called a halt to applications under the provision in August, 594 vessels had sailed to foreign ports, and many of them did not return, gladly forfeiting bond for the freedom and profits of the neutral trade.

On the coast infractions were serious from New York eastward. The most zealous of Gallatin's collectors could not always detect vessels loading secretly and sailing without clearance for foreign parts. The penalties of the supplementary acts, followed by increasing naval surveillance, reduced this leak to a trickle, however. The consul in Havana reported that in the period January 17–February 25, forty-five American flags arrived there compared with only four in a second period March 1–April 11. To be sure, American traders continued to ply the seas. Yankees reportedly landed thirty cargoes of cotton at Liverpool in the spring; and General Armstrong warned the President of Americans who came in under French colors, saying they were from the French islands when they were really from Baltimore. But this was expected and within tolerable limits. Many of the strays never returned. Some carriers jumped the embargo, of course. But the ships trading abroad at their own risk were a tiny fraction of the American marine, probably less than 5 per cent. Ingenious merchants and shipmasters quickly discovered new and, for a time, safer ways of evading the embargo. For example, ships went off without clearances or supposedly bound coastwise, and put their cargoes aboard British vessels hovering offshore, then sneaked back to the mainland or sailed to Nova Scotia or the West Indies. From these ports captains were likely to plead distress. The excuse, "blown off course," became the mariners' tiresome refrain. Jefferson's patience finally gave way under petitions of this kind. "We know that the fabrication of proofs of leaking ships, stress of weather, cargoes sold under duress, are a regular part of the system of infractions of the embargo, with the manufacture of which every foreign port is provided, and that their oaths and forgeries are a regular merchandise in every port. We must therefore consider them as nothing," he said, "and that the act of entering a foreign port and selling the cargo is decisive evidence of an intentional breach of the embargo." Most coastal merchants were loyal and law-abiding; some of them zealously supported the embargo. But Jefferson's encounters with mercantile avarice and knavery lowered still further his estimate of the class generally, especially the New Englanders.

Transactions of the market place that had been of no consequence to government suddenly assumed major importance under the embargo. As the commissar of the nation's economy, Jefferson made decisions on such trifling matter as the flour bakers used, the bread people ate. This particular question arose because of the amazing increase of flour shipments from the Middle Atlantic ports, ostensibly in the coastal trade. The President thought every seaboard city, Charleston excepted, ought to be able normally to supply itself with flour from the hinterland, even if of inferior quality to flour from the Delaware. Hence all flour cargoes were suspect. A Treasury circular to the collectors on May 6 called attention to the powers of detention they now possessed and urged their exercise on shipments of grain, flour, provisions, and so on to places where they could not be required for actual consumption. At the same time Jefferson instructed the governors of Georgia, South Carolina, Massachusetts, New Hampshire, and the Orleans territory, where local flour stocks might prove insufficient, to issue import licenses to reliable merchants directed, in turn, to the collector at the place of export. Gallatin was unhappy with this system. He did not trust all the governors; licensing risked mercantile favoritism or monopoly; and the unexpected flood of applications caused a massive administrative problem. The country, it appeared, was more specialized in its productions, more interdependent economically, than had been realized. With the extension of cotton cultivation in South Carolina and Georgia those states were substantial importers of provisions; and northern seaport towns, like Boston, imported more flour coastwise than they brought from the interior. The licensing system was relaxed within a month. Coastal shipments of flour and provisions not exceeding one-eighth of the cargo were permitted to move freely. The limitation, it was thought, would remove temptations to evasion and speculation and at the same time meet the needs of the people. "I do not wish a single citizen to be deprived of a meal of bread,"

Jefferson said, "but I set down the exercise of commerce, merely for profit, as nothing when it carries with it the danger of defeating the objects of the embargo." The licensing system remained, however, to cover emergency situations.

Massachusetts, alone of the states, seemed to be in a perpetual emergency. When Governor James Sullivan continued to issue licenses in large number, Jefferson ordered him to stop. Sullivan, the Bay State's first Republican executive, said he would, if demanded, but within three weeks the scarcity of bread would produce "mob riots and convulsions" and the enemies of the embargo would triumph. The people would then believe, as they did not now, the Federalist accusations "that the President has no confidence in the northern part of the nation, but relies on Virginia, etc., etc., etc." Jefferson reconsidered. Still suspecting the honesty of this traffic, he asked Levi Lincoln to investigate. Sullivan was a political alarmist, always in a bustle; Lincoln, cool and composed, could correctly estimate the situation in Massachusetts. The former Attorney General acknowledged that some of the imported flour had been carried out of the country but, on the whole, vindicated the Governor. The superfluity of flour for Massachusetts continued to vex the President on into the fall. It was small comfort perhaps, but of all the crimes charged against him in that quarter, he could not be accused of taking bread from the mouths of its citizens.

Another critical area for the enforcement of the embargo was the northern frontier of New York and New England. On and about Lake Champlain, in particular, a brisk smuggling trade was carried on with Canada by boat, wagon, and sled. Rising prices of potash, lumber, pork, and other articles returned exorbitant profits. By the summer, it was said in Plattsburg, "there was not a poor man in debt in the country." The Canadians encouraged the traffic and paid the Americans, in part, in proscribed English wares. The collectors, harassed and intimidated, were unable to suppress the traffic; and the second line of defense, manned by federal marshals, district attorneys, and judges, was ineffectual in the hostile environment. Here, as on the Passamaquoddy, actual shooting broke out, revenue boats were fired on, and smuggling gangs forcibly recaptured property legally seized by collectors. (There was a frontier traffic in the South as well, on the St. Mary's, but it was small by comparison.) In April, on Gallatin's advice and with cabinet approval, Jefferson issued a proclamation placing the Champlain region in a state of insurrection. The insurgents were ordered to disperse and the Governor authorized, if necessary, to call out the militia. Jefferson did not contemplate the use of the army, though he possessed the authority under the act of Congress provoked by the Burr Conspiracy. Very soon, as the situation deteriorated, Gallatin asked for and got a small force of regulars to aid in quelling the disturbance. The citizenry of the area treated the President's proclamation with contempt. Resolutions from one town called it an act of "military despotism." There was no insurrection, it was said, only violations of the law by a few desperate characters, but the law being arbitrary and wrong, the people refused to aid in its enforcement.

In the summer, the area of Oswego, on Lake Ontario, became a trouble spot. By this time, Gallatin confessed, commercial avarice and Federalist politics had combined to "baffle all our endeavors" along the northern frontier. Collectors and district attorneys wanted energy and even Republican juries declined to convict malefactors. The President himself, after the first humiliation, hesitated to risk a second proclamation of insurrection. Gallatin went to the Governor of New York, Daniel D. Tompkins, and prevailed upon him to call out the militia on his own authority, which did not require a public declaration. Tompkins doubted an insurrection actually existed at Oswego. Perhaps not in the popular sense, Jefferson conceded, but men arrayed in war-like manner against the laws, firing on public guards, and seizing confiscated property fell within the legal definition of insurrection. "I think it is so important in example to crush these audacious proceedings, and to make the offenders feel the consequences of individuals daring to oppose a law by force, that no effort should be spared to compass this object." Tompkins yielded to the President's appeal. To the two companies of New York militia, the administration added, in September, a small contingent of regulars. The situation improved, but half the army of the United States could not have put a stop to illicit trade on the wide northern frontier.

Dwelling on infractions, one is apt to lose perspective on the embargo. The mass of people everywhere obeyed the law. Indeed, Jefferson's zeal against violators stemmed as much from his concern for equitable enforcement throughout the Union as from concern for the embargo's impact abroad. A harsh law could not be maintained with justice anywhere if hundreds or thousands exploited it for personal gain in one section of the Union. Most collectors were reliable. Those who were not, commonly Federalist holdovers, resigned or were removed. With rare exceptions the federal machinery of law enforcement stood up under the ordeal. In general, public suppport of the embargo was excellent in the South, reasonably good in the Middle Atlantic states, and fair to poor east and west of the Hudson. Beginning in the spring, public morale declined in all sections and fell precipitously in the eastern states in the fall. Many factors, varying from place to place, caused this deterioration over the months but most of them may be grouped under three general headings: economic hardship and denial, partisan political opposition, and the growing sense of the failure of the experiment in its effects abroad. Running through all this was the belief that the embargo, however noble or ignoble its purposes, exacted too high a price from a free people.

The embargo struck a hard blow to the economy, but a comfortable cushion of prosperity saved the country from disaster. Most merchants and farmers had large reserves from the profits of previous years. So, too, did the federal Treasury, a whopping $17,000,000 surplus, part of which Jefferson still hoped to divert to internal improvements. Except for a few imported materials (antimony, wire, dyestuffs) the country suffered no acute shortages. Inventories were high when the embargo took effect, and omitting the banned "luxury" items from Britain, foreign goods continued to come into the country, at about half the normal rate. The prices of most articles were surprisingly stable. Many merchants covered their losses by raising prices on import goods in stock. Their maritime capital, if partially immobilized, was not seriously impaired, and may have been improved by diversion to manufactures. Domestic prices declined, of course. The southern staples, cotton and tobacco, were hardest hit, falling 40 to 50 per cent. Wholesale commodity prices, on the average, fell about 15 per cent in 1808.

The seaport cities showed the most immediate and dramatic effects of the embargo. An estimated 30,000 seamen were idled, together with longshoremen, ships' craftsmen, and other workers in maritime industry. Many seamen, British and American, signed on foreign vessels as if in mockery of Jefferson's effort to secure this national resource; but the seamen probably suffered more than any other economic group. And Massachusetts, with one-third of the nation's tonnage in foreign commerce, as well as a great fishing fleet, perhaps had more reason to complain of the embargo than any other state. Yet the loudest complainants, merchants generally, suffered little shrinkage of capital, and the stories of ships' rotting at the wharves and grass growing in the streets were embellished for political effect. Chancellor Livingston, after touring coastal New England in the winter of 1808–09, reported to Madison, "Never have I at any time witnessed more ease and comfort, more building and improvement." Livingston hardly qualified as an unbiased observer. He was pro-embargo, pro-French, and, like the host of Republican merchants, outside the British trading orbit. But he was not alone in his estimate, and if he erred on the brighter side, observers with a different bias erred on the darker side. Things were worse in New York than in Boston. In May an English observer, actually a spy sent down from Halifax, reported eighty bankruptcies, hundreds of debtors in jail, and thousands out of work. Philadelphia approved the embargo and, in fact, turned it to good account, as did some of the cities in New England, by the diversion of mercantile capital to manufactures and the exploitation of markets in the interior. Jefferson rejoiced in Philadelphia: the city exemplified that "spring" to manufactures which in the end became his solace, almost his vindication. Household manufactures sprang up everywhere in 1808; textile mills and other factories increased at a rapid rate, above all in Pennsylvania.

The economic incidence of the embargo in the vast agricultural spaces of the country, while less visible, was at least as severe and, in the South, more damaging in the long run. Farmers had no control over their prices; they could, however, withhold crops from market for a time, indeed almost indefinitely in the case of non-perishables, if sufficiently affluent. But few were affluent. An astute Vermonter described the chain of pressures in that state, the same as in most rural areas: "The staple commodities . . . are reduced to low prices, consequently money is scarce. They [the farmers] cannot remit.

The merchant delivers his account to an attorney. He sues A, B, C, etc. A, B, C, etc., curse the embargo, because they cannot sell their produce and pay their debts. And sue D, E, F, etc., indebted to them, who in turn curse the embargo and sue G, H, I, etc., who in turn curse the embargo and proceed to persecute those indebted to them in a course of eternal litiguity." Lawyers as a class, it need hardly be said, blessed the embargo. In Virginia, where debt was a chronic disease, creditors showed more leniency than elsewhere. Courts closed in some counties. The legislature, in February, revived an old relief law permitting the extension of debts for twelve months under certain conditions. Executions in federal courts continued, of course, and reports from some quarters indicate that British and urban merchants out-of-state pushed the country debtors hard. In the southern states generally, where the embargo found its best support, it also caused the most enduring economic damage. The South was the nation's leading exporter. Its destiny remained agricultural, while the North's lay in the direction of manufacturing, which the embargo promoted. Southern planters, unlike northern merchants, had enjoyed only modest profits from the neutral trade; and unlike their farming counterparts above the Potomac, they manufactured almost nothing for themselves, had a permanent labor force to keep up, and discovered no collateral sources of income, legitimate or otherwise, from the embargo. Ultra-Federalists invented the myth of a Virginia experiment to destroy eastern commerce and navigation; in fact, no other section suffered as much as the South, which seemed to be martyring itself to save the eastern carrying trade. The President himself, with many planters more opulent than he, would never recover from the blow.

While not insensitive to the distresses of the citizens, the President's cold and lofty response to petitioners for relief failed to meet the reality of their sufferings. They blasted the embargo—"O grab me" in reverse—and cursed the President. Better their petitions be addressed to London and Paris, to the enemies of mankind who had brought this grievous stringency on the nation, he replied. Every complaint, every obstruction, every unrest gave aid and comfort to the enemies and prolonged the real cause of distress. The government, at any rate, could do nothing to relieve personal hardships incident to a measure for the nation's good. Playing for higher stakes,

Jefferson hardened himself to censures often grounded, he felt, in petty profit-seeking motives. His philosophy taught him that the embargo was an easy scapegoat for virtually all the ills men suffered. Among the numerous scraps of song and verse inspired by the embargo was one that expressed his view exactly:

> There's knaves and fools and dupes and tools
>   Debas'd enough to argue
> That every ill the people feel
>   Is owing to *The Embargo*
>
>   . . .
>
> Do party men incline to pen
>   A false and foolish farr'go,
> No other theme so fruitful seem
>   As "*Jefferson's d—d Embargo*"
>
>   . . .
>
> Should Hessian Fly our wheat destroy,
>   Or granaries crowd with weevil,
> *The Embargo's* curst in language worst
>   As source of all the evil.

The second of these verses points to what Jefferson considered a still more powerful motive of complaint and opposition. His political enemies exploited the embargo for all it was worth, and it was worth a good deal, especially in New England, where Federalism had still to be reckoned with. The bulk, perhaps nine out of ten, of the ever increasing addresses and resolutions against the embargo came from that quarter of the Union. That distress should be translated into political opposition was natural; but that the assault on the law should be directed by extreme Federalists suggested a power play aimed at political revolution or something worse. Opposition on the score of hardship caused the President little pain. The problem became serious when a dangerous faction hitched a ride on these disturbances and converted them into a political engine against the Republican administration.

The embargo was a screaming partisan issue from the first—only the volume changed during its fourteen-month history. Arguments that would become hackneyed in press and assembly were heard in acrimonious debate on the supplementary legislation in Congress.

Barent Gardenier, a New York Federalist, shocked the House by the violence of his speech on the second supplementary bill in February. The proposed interdiction of land commerce bore no relationship to the alleged purposes of the original act. That "sly, cunning measure" must now be seen for what it was: an act not to protect the nation's resources but to destroy its trade. And for whose benefit? "Do not go on forging chains to fasten us to the car of the Imperial Conqueror," he declared. Cries of "order" did not deter him. "Yes, sir, I do fear that there is an unseen hand which is guiding us to the most dreadful destinies—unseen, because it cannot endure the light. Darkness and mystery overshadow this House and the whole nation. We know nothing—we are permitted to know nothing. We sit here as mere automata. . . ." Replying to Gardenier, the majority leader, George W. Campbell of Tennessee, patiently examined the causes of the embargo. One of its objects, he said, though not the principal one at the beginning, was coercion of the belligerents by a denial of American commerce, and he went on to denounce the charges of acting under French influence as "infamous, groundless falsehoods." Gardenier promptly challenged him. The two gentlemen met on the dueling ground, and the challenger barely escaped with his life. Leading Federalists also questioned the motives of military measures. The administration asked for, and got, authorization for the President to raise 6000 regulars. The request wrenched the President's principles, but he was getting used to that. This, with other measures, was all part of a two-stage policy, first to back up the persuasions of the embargo abroad, and second to prepare the nation for war should it fail. Wrong, said the Federalists: the bill secretly aimed at an army to enforce the embargo at home with bullets and bayonets. It was marvelous how their imaginings of the starry-eyed visionary faded into delusions of the dark Machiavel.

As the spring elections came on in New York and Massachusetts, the Federalists mounted the dragons of discontent in a bold bid to return to power, immediately to the state houses and just beyond to the national capital. In March the President's inveterate foe, Senator Pickering, published a blast in the form of a letter to Governor Sullivan. Had not the embargo been mandated by Napoleon? (Why else, Pickering mused privately, would the President destroy his popularity?) Why had the President secretly withheld intelligence from Paris? Had Britain done the United States any "essential injury"? Was not the embargo enacted in hostility to northern commerce? Pickering defended the British ministry against the administration, predicted national ruin from the embargo, and warned the northern states to look to their defenses. Twenty thousand copies of the pamphlet were said to have circulated in Massachusetts alone. Jefferson wrote to Lincoln with some alarm. The petty scribblings of the newspaper herd were beneath contempt, but lies were freighted with influence when they came from the pen of an honorable senator. Lincoln calmly reassured the President. The letter was regrettable but it would have little effect. "It is the comparative few that make all the noise, the desperate in politics, the desperate in property. . . . The great body of the people, all the Republicans and many Federalists, believe in the necessity of the [embargo]." Yet the Federalists, stirred by Pickering's blast, regained control of the legislature, narrowly, though Sullivan won re-election as governor. In New York, where Pickering's letter also fired up the Federalists, the Republicans scored a hard victory. Nearly all the newspapers were Federalist or Clintonian, and the latter would not defend the embargo. "At present the arguments appear to be all on the other side," a worried Republican wrote to Madison. Like many others, he wished the administration would make a public case for the embargo. So far as diplomatic documents could speak the administration had done that. Near the end of March the President sent a veritable flood of papers to Congress covering the Monroe-Pinkney negotiations, the *Chesapeake* imbroglio, and the Rose mission, just terminated in stalemate, as well as Armstrong's correspondence. Jefferson believed this mass of papers, which were published, contained the best and ablest answers to the brawlers against the embargo. Perhaps they did. Lincoln thought the publication helped to discredit Pickering and save the Republicans from disaster in Massachusetts. But diplomatic correspondence was not a substitute for executive appeal to the public understanding.

Assessing the damage from the attack, Jefferson feared, above all, its ill effects abroad. The madcap Federalists, he said in June, were playing a dangerous game without perhaps being aware of it. "They are endeavoring to convince England that we suffer more by the embargo than they do, and if they will hold out awhile, we must abandon it." Of course we must, to be followed by war if the embargo failed in its mission. "But the fact is, that if we have war with England, it will be solely produced by their maneuvers." Increasingly, Jefferson transferred the blame of failure from himself and his policy to the party that opposed both. If most Federalists knew not what they were doing, Timothy Pickering surely did. He was trying to revive the disunionist plot of 1804, drawing the eastern states into a separate confederacy under British protection. Adams, his Massachusetts colleague in the Senate, warned the President in March of British collusion in these designs. (Since the *Chesapeake* affair Adams had gravitated toward the administration, causing the Massachusetts Federalists to deprive him of his seat in 1808.) Sullivan backed this warning with hysterical predictions of a British expedition to Halifax to receive the returning eastern states. Rose carried Pickering's inflamatory pamphlet to London in the spring, where it was at once reprinted, widely read, and applauded by the ministry as evidence of the administration's collusion with France and groaning public opposition to the embargo.

By this time the experiment appeared for what it was, peaceable coercion, and the administration pretended nothing else. Everything, Jefferson said, must be subordinated to the test of this great weapon until it became more burdensome than war. Time was required for it to work on the belligerents; unfortunately, as Jefferson began to realize, every hour gained abroad was an hour lost at home. In this race he steadily tightened the screws of the enforcing machine and, against the efforts to subvert the embargo, endeavored to make it a convincing measure in foreign courts. He outlined the diplomatic strategy to Madison in March. Armstrong and Pinkney should demand revocation of the obnoxious decrees. If both belligerents complied, the United States would remain neutral. If not, they should be told, without any bullying gestures, that when the time came to drop the embargo, if either one withdrew its decrees we would war on the other, and if neither relented we would choose the enemy. The policy seemed to hinge success of the experiment with one power to war on the other—a sorry half-victory for peaceable coercion. Actually, of course, Jefferson reasoned that success with one

898

must produce success with the other, since neither would risk American belligerency. Prompted by the administration, Congress passed resolutions in April authorizing the President to suspend the embargo against any or all belligerents. For the present then, and until Congress resumed in the fall, the duration of the embargo hung on the decrees. The ministers were at once instructed on the offer to suspend, holding out the idea of American hostilities against the power that persisted in its edicts.

In Britain, meanwhile, the embargo was just beginning to be felt. Leading Whigs and spokesmen of manufacturing and mercantile interests in the American trade—Lord Grenville, Alexander Baring, Lord Erskine, Henry Brougham, the editors of the *Edinburgh Review*, and others—launched a campaign against the orders in council. The orders formed a system, adopted under the fiction of military reprisal, to establish Britain as the grand emporium of trade with the Continent. In 1793 Britain had tried to starve the enemy into submission; now she intended to feed it by forcing the produce of the empire upon the market and making the Americans either carry it and pay the price in British ports or retire from the oceans. The government frankly conceded the monopolitic purpose. Canning's instructions to Erskine stated it, and Spencer Perceval, Chancellor of the Exchequer, summed it up when the November orders were signed: "Our orders . . . say to the enemy, 'If you will not have *our* trade, as far as we can help it you shall have *none*." The policy was ruinous, said the adversaries. Britain could not expect to command the American market, worth 12,000,000 pounds a year to her manufacturers alone, and rob the Americans of ability to pay by forcing them from the neutral trade. No respectable nation, no neutral, could submit to the monopolistic license system. American neutrality was advantageous to Britain. The produce of the West Indies found vent through it and the planters were fed by it, though in their rage against the competition of the enemy islands they had blindly turned on the Americans. Stores for the navy, cotton for the spindles, food for the people came from the United States; the trade gave employment to factory workers, artisans, and seamen; and the growing country was Britain's best customer. Even if the embargo were removed, the orders would still be ruinous, Brougham declared in Commons. For the orders, not the embargo, which were cause and effect respectively, produced the stoppage of the American trade.

Jefferson was delighted by these strictures. They were his own, and they proved him right, at least in the light of reason. He was being condemned for destroying American commerce, Canning the British, one by embargo, the other by monopoly, one sacrificing gain for peace, the other prosecuting war for profit. It was only a question of who would yield first. Unfortunately for Jefferson the forces ranged behind Canning were much more powerful than his opposition, which centered in a manufacturing interest still weak and isolated politically. The embargo threw seamen out of work, merchants out of business, farmers out of markets instantly in the United States; its impact on the British economy took time, though when it occurred it would be felt in men's stomachs as well as in their pocketbooks. Manchester manufacturers were laying off workers in March—the distress began. But in the spring and on through the summer, morale was high in Britain, the press spoke of the embargo with contempt, and the Tory ministry had nothing to fear from King or Parliament. When Congress adjourned without lifting the embargo, no change of policy or opinion occurred.

Jefferson attributed this obstinance to two factors. First, the misrepresentation of the law's effectiveness and support, together with the belief it would produce a political revolution in the United States, threw dust in the eyes of the nation. Second, the unforeseen Spanish revolt against Napoleonic domination revived British fortunes in the war and opened a vast new market, the peninsula and the Spanish colonies, to her commerce. This turn of affairs, Jefferson remarked in August, put the British "on their stilts again." The new trade more or less compensated for the loss of the old. Jefferson felt the jolt at home too. Merchants, eager to enter the race for the riches of the crumbling Spanish empire, pressed for the removal of the embargo as to that sector. He thought the request preposterous, given the objectives of the embargo and the utter confusion of Spanish affairs, knowing full well, however, the advantage conceded to the British rival. "Considering the narrow and selfish policy of the present cabinet," Madison observed, "it is possible that it may be tempted to continue its orders lest a removal of our embargo should interfere with her in the new commercial prospect. But I suspect she is still more swayed by the hopes of producing a revolution in the public counsels here, which might be followed by a coalition with her in the war."

The embargo was never intended to have the same effect in France as in Britain. An impartial measure in law, its potential for economic damage was much greater on the island empire than on the continental one. Moreover the sister measure, non-importation, applied to Britain alone. The administration's diplomacy with France turned on this differential effect of peaceable coercion. "The embargo which appears to hit France and Britain equally," Jefferson told Turreau, "is for a fact more prejudicial to the latter than the other by reason of a greater number of colonies which England possess and the infirmity in local resources." These were only two items in the comparative balance. What the Federalists interpreted as a partiality of motive and cause was, in fact, a partiality in effect produced by the very different circumstances of the belligerents. By impressing Napoleon with the strength of the American commitment to neutral rights against British pretensions, Jefferson expected two favors in return: first, the revocation of his decrees as to American trade, and second, his aid in securing the Floridas from Spain. The decrees were largely futile against the United States for the same reason that the embargo was largely futile against France: neither effectively reached the object. But the former were the pretext for the British orders; hence by their revocation Napoleon would place the United States in position to demand British repeal at the penalty of war.

Instead of snatching at this bait, Napoleon toyed with Jefferson and played games with the embargo. The Milan Decree, in retaliation against the November orders, declared every vessel going to or coming from a British port, trading under her regulations, as in effect British and lawful prize. Many American vessels fell captives of this extension of the laws of the Continental System to the sea. Armstrong learned they would be sequestered, not confiscated, pending Washington's declaration of war on Britain. This tilt at blackmail was followed in April by the Bayonne Decree. American flags entering Continental ports were seized on the pretext that, in view of the embargo, they must be British in disguise. The American loss ran to $10,000,000. Napoleon said he was simply helping Jefferson enforce the embargo! Mocking Jefferson's system, believing American commerce hopelessly entangled with the British, and American pacificism incorrigible, the Emperor would not abate any part of his own system. "This is no doubt madness," Armstrong wrote, "and what is worse it is . . . incurable." Once again he advised the United States to take its interests into its own hands, beginning with the seizure of the Floridas. No one could be sure from one moment to the next who was the protector of the Floridas in 1808. Jefferson's first concern, as always, was to prevent the Floridas from falling to either major power, and near the end of the year he let it be known to officials in Cuba and Mexico that the United States was "extremely unwilling" that either of these colonies should pass into the hands of Britain or France. This was the germ of the "no transfer" principle of the Monroe Doctrine fifteen years later.

The spectacle of both belligerents cynically trampling on American rights, neither consenting to be "played off" against the other in Jefferson's neutral game, led him to embark on diplomatic relations with Russia. Alexander's reputation for liberalism impressed the President. His hostility to British maritime pretensions, his commitment to neutral rights and freedom of the seas, and the superficial resemblances between his empire and the American, convinced Jefferson that Russia was "the most cordially friendly to us of any power on earth." He was pleased in 1804 when the Emperor, who reciprocated these feelings, invited a correspondence. An exchange ensued. In 1806 Alexander presented Jefferson with a bust of himself, and he, in return, endeavored to satisfy the Emperor's curiosity about the government of the United States. Pacific nations, he said, looked to Alexander's influence to secure their rights when peace finally came to Europe. In addition to neutral rights, Jefferson suggested that the treaty of peace make provision for collective economic sanctions against aggressor nations. In 1808, when there were persistent rumors of an Austrian mediated peace, he grew more anxious for Alexander's patronage of principles abandoned by every other sovereign, including the French Emperor. So he decided to send William Short on a secret mission as minister plenipotentiary to St. Petersburg. The chief object, he told Short, was "to avail ourselves of the Emperor's marked dispositions of friendly regard for us, whenever a treaty of peace shall be on the tapis, and to engage him to patronize our interests there, so as the benefit of the maritime rights which shall then be settled, may be extended to us, and nothing plotted to sacrifice us by France or England, neither of which wish us success." Short sailed in September. Not until the following February, in his last official communication to Congress, did Jefferson present his name to the Senate. Secrecy had been called for, in large part, because of apprehensions that neither Short nor the mission would be approved. The apprehensions proved correct. The Senate rejected the nomination of Short and then, on Madison's authority, that of J. Q. Adams, though Adams was later approved; and in 1810 the Emperor sent a minister to the United States. Diplomatic relations between the two countries thus began as a sidewind of embargo diplomacy. Jefferson's purpose was perfectly clear but his confidence in the Emperor of Russia proved delusory.

During the early summer the President was guardedly optimistic about his "last appeal to the reason and reputation of nations." The mass of Americans regardless of section, interest, or party supported the embargo, and but for the criminal rage of Tory Federalists, "subjects for a mad-house," all would be well. The irksome business of enforcing the law claimed nearly all the President's energies. The embargo was the government—government was the embargo. Defense preparations suffered except as they related to current operations. Always on the lookout for new and unconventional weapons of coastal defense, the President took an interest in Robert Fulton's torpedo. The French and British had passed up this invention, and Smith was skeptical, but Jefferson ordered the Navy Department to co-operate with Fulton in a demonstration finally performed at Kalorama, Barlow's Washington residence, the succeeding February. The threat of Indian warfare in the Illinois country, very alarming a year ago, had receded. Jefferson concluded that the agitation of the Shawnee chief Tecumseh and his brother the Prophet turned not on hostile alliance with the British, as earlier feared, but on the rejection of advancing civilization and reversion to "the ancient habits, customs and superstitions of their fathers." It was only a transient delusion, Jefferson said, and he continued to press his policy of land cessions followed by "intercourse, civilization, and incorporation." The Indians above the Ohio ceded their lands by the millions of acres but got precious little "civilization" in return. The negative half of Jefferson's policy succeeded brilliantly; the positive half failed from administrative and, more fundamentally, moral inadequacy. Demoralization and the reviving primitivism of Tecumseh and the Prophet were the upshot in the Northwest. Jefferson was right: their system could not prevail. But neither could his. The program red men spurned white men would not support. West of the Mississippi, control, not civilization, was the policy. The President was delighted by John Jacob Astor's formation of the American Fur Company to trap and trade on the far Missouri. Jefferson promised "every reasonable patronage" of the government. American merchants, taking possession of this trade, would exclude foreigners who poisoned the minds of the Indians against us, Jefferson said, and their factories would have the same effect as so many armies.

On the 4th of July the President set the style for the nation by appearing at his noon reception in a suit of homespun. His guests on that occasion could view the great collection of bones recently brought from Big Bone Lick on the Ohio and displayed in the "mammoth room." Several days later Caspar Wistar came down to study the collection and take back to the American Philosophical Society the parts necessary to complete the specimen he was mounting. Jefferson shipped the remainder to the National Institute in Paris, then set out for home. Monticello, during August and September, offered no refuge from the toils of the embargo. Petitioners cried out for suspension and relief, so many that Jefferson had a standard printed reply prepared; and every mail brought venomous productions directed at him personally, some ribald:

> Thomas Jefferson
> You are the damdest
>   fool that God put
>   life into
>   God damn you.

and some threatening:

> I have agreed to pay four of my friends $400 to shoot you if you don't take off the embargo by the 10th of October. . . .

Libelous verse filled the columns of the Federalist press. Among the most elaborate of these productions was "The Embargo" by a youthful prodigy of thirteen, William Cullen Bryant.

> Go, wretch, resign the president's chair,
> Disclose secret measures foul or fair,
> Go, search with curious eye, for horned frogs,
> 'Mongst the wild wastes of Louisiana bogs;
> Or where Ohio rolls his turbid stream,
> Dig for huge bones, thy glory and thy theme.
> Go sean, philosophist, thy . . . charms,
> And sink supinely in her sable arms;
> But quit to abler hands the helm of state,
> Nor image ruin on the country's fate.

Jefferson continued to trace the vehemently personal attack to the desperation of an opposition bereft of principles. "Lamentations and invective were all that remained to them. . . . I became of course the butt of everything which reason, ridicule, malice and falsehood could supply. They have concentrated all their hatred on me, till they have really persuaded themselves that I am the sole source of all their imaginary evils."

The libels and lampoons, while painful, had no weight with him politically; the waywardness of respectable Republicans, on the other hand, gave cause for concern. One of the first danger signals came from the judiciary. On the circuit bench in South Carolina, Justice William Johnson, a political associate who had been Jefferson's first appointment to the Supreme Court in 1804, issued a writ of mandamus to the collector at Charleston obliging him to clear a vessel detained under regulations of the executive for the enforcement of the Fourth Embargo Act. That the President and the Secretary of Treasury could prescribe uniform rules for the collectors in the execution of an act of Congress seemed reasonable, but Johnson ruled that the whole discretion to detain a suspicious vessel lay with the collector. The decision amazed Jefferson, especially in view of its source, and on the opinion of the Attorney General sustaining the executive authority, he directed the collectors to conduct themselves as before. Federalists screamed "executive usurpation" and "subservience of the judiciary." On Jefferson's theory, of course, the President was not bound to obey every judicial mandate, and certainly not one where a court's own authority was doubtful (Rodney denied the circuit court's right to issue writs of mandamus) and where a single opinion, if allowed to prevail, would bring down a whole system of legislation. Collectors continued to be harassed with suits, mostly private, in state courts. Surprisingly, in the only test of constitutionality in a federal court, the Massachusetts district bench emphatically upheld the embargo as a proper exercise of the congressional power to regulate commerce. Ironically, the judge, John Davis, was a firm Federalist. The Federalist doctrine of loose construction thus came to the aid of a measure Jefferson would have found difficulty defending on the constitutional doctrine he took into office.

Rising opposition to the embargo frightened the party cadre in New York and New England. Their first commitment was to office, not to policy, and they would sacrifice the President before they would sacrifice their standing at the polls. Sullivan warned of the turn things were taking. "These men consider the embargo as operating very forcibly to the subversion of the Republican interest," he said. And should the measure continue much longer without decisive effect abroad, it would surely sink all the Republicans east of the Delaware. Gallatin was of the same opinion. New England would be Federalized—the Essex Junto mounted for disunion—probably New York and New Jersey, possibly even Pennsylvania. Casting the odds in August, he feared the presidential contest was lost.

The Secretary was tired and sore. Despite all his efforts the frauds of the embargo persisted. "The consciousness of having done what was right in itself is doubtless sufficient," he wrote gloomily, "but for the inefficacy of the measure on the Lakes and to the northward there is no consolation, and that circumstance alone is the strongest argument that can be brought against the measure itself." Yet he did not despair. Barring redress abroad, the embargo must be continued with means of enforcement equal to the ends of the measure itself. Two things were essential, he told his chief: first, not a single vessel should be permitted to move without the permission of the executive; and second, collectors should be empowered to seize property anywhere, not just along the frontiers, without liability to personal suit and with the assistance of military force. "I am sensible that such arbitrary powers are equally dangerous and odious," he said. But they had been made necessary by Federalist incitement to evasion and the natural selfishness incited by a system so far above the common understanding as to render ordinary patriotism of little account.

Jefferson himself, so deeply committed to the policy he could not entertain the thought of abandoning it, entered fully into Gallatin's resolution to put the embargo to the test of force. He must have sometimes recalled his experience in the Virginia governorship, when he had been called to account for jeopardizing the safety of the commonwealth by feeble and temporizing measures. In this crisis he would not run the same risks. "The embargo law is certainly the most embarrassing one we have ever had to execute," he replied cheerlessly to Gallatin. "I did not expect a crop of so sudden and rank growth of fraud and opposition by force could have grown up in the United States. I am satisfied with you that if the orders and decrees are not repealed, and a continuance of the embargo is preferred to war (which sentiment is universal here), Congress should legalize all *means* which may be necessary to obtain its *end*." No one could dissent from the general proposition that the means, if legitimate, should be equal to the end. As Jefferson said on another occasion, it is the responsibility of the executive to do whatever he can to save the public the benefit of the law. "Its intention is the important thing: the means of attaining it quite subordinate." Yet a measure like the embargo, which would strain the capacities of an authoritarian government, could not long co-exist with the ends of a free one. The main question was not whether it was being enforced. Obviously it was, otherwise there would not have been such a hue and cry against it; and doubtlessly enforcement powers could be strengthened. But was the end of coercion abroad any longer supportable in the face of increasing deprivation, loss of liberties, alienation of opinion, division of the Union, and Republican collapse at home? How much was it worth to the American people to discover another arbiter than war among nations? How far could the experiment in peaceable coercion be carried against the dynamics of American freedom? How long could the nation endure an experiment submitted to the sufferance of foreign powers? These questions transcended the relationship of means to ends and weighed different ends themselves in the balance.

Jefferson was not oblivious to these considerations. He took it as axiomatic that at some point the embargo would become more costly than war. No other alternative was available. He had committed the nation to a system from which there could be no honorable escape but war. Yet, on the premises of the system itself, war was the great behemoth of evil; and to concede now, after so much sacrifice for peace, that the American people could no more avoid war than the common run of humanity was to concede his best hopes not only for his own country but for the rule of reason and enlightenment among nations. Other more immediately practical questions had to be asked. War with whom? With what honor could the United States align itself with either of the tyrant nations of Europe? With what risks of danger from the other? And at what costs to unity and sanity at home? Weighing the alternatives, Jefferson unhesitatingly stuck with the embargo. The experiment was not yet desperate. All reports spoke of squirming and suffering in Britain. Bonaparte had his hands full in Spain. Peace might suddenly return to Europe. A little more patience, more strength of means, more loyalty to government, more tolerance of trifling sacrifices in the interest of great ends, he reasoned, would lead to success.

Nothing happened to change Jefferson's opinion between his return to Washington in October and the meeting of Congress on November 7. First the *St. Michael* and then the *Hope* brought dispatches from Britain. Pinkney urged the government to persevere in its course. Repeal of the embargo would be fatal. Britain would never tolerate the rivalry of our neutral trade, and war would only open "a new career in vassalage and meanness." "The embargo, and the loss of our trade, are deeply felt here, and will be felt with more severity every day," the minister advised. "The wheat harvest is likely to be alarmingly short, and the state of the continent will augment the evil. The discontents among their manufacturers are only quieted for the moment from temporary causes. Cotton is rising, and will soon be scarce. Unfavorable events on the continent will subdue the temper, unfriendly to wisdom and justice, which now prevails." But this temper, as expressed in Canning's communications of September 23 to Pinkney, showed no disposition to reform. Responding to the proposition to suspend the embargo, Canning evaded the issue in an idle parade of insult and recrimination. Since the November orders had not been known in Washington when the President moved the embargo, their repeal could not be linked to the suspension of that measure. It was "manifestly unjust" to Britain and came to the aid of the Continental System at a critical hour. Alluding to conversations between the two, Canning treated Pinkney's offer to suspend as "unauthorized," as something advanced privately but not on the instructions of government, and therefore requiring nothing official from him. With this ruse he dismissed embargo repeal, persisted in the policy of commercial warfare, and left Jefferson to get out of the scrape as best he could. The tone as well as the substance of Canning's letters distressed the President. They were "written in the high ropes," he told Erskine, and when known "would be stinging to every American breast." He included one of them in the foreign correspondence sent to Congress at the time of the annual message; the other, on the offer to suspend, was held back pending Pinkney's vindication.

The message reported the unhappy outcome of the overture to Britain and the silence of France on the similar overture to her. Considering that each government had pledged to withdraw retaliatory decrees on the action of the other, it was "reasonably expected that the occasion would have been seized by both for evincing the sincerity of their profession, and for restoring to the commerce of the United States its legitimate freedom." But the appeal to justice had fared no better under peaceable coercion than before. What was to be done? In cabinet discussions prior to the meeting of Congress, none of the secretaries had a new policy to suggest, except Smith who would call home the ministers and prepare for war against both powers, and he stood alone in this opinion. All agreed the embargo should not be continued much longer; but when it should be taken off, under what formula, and with what replacement—minds boggled at these questions. Federalists trooped into Congress, backed by new electoral victories in the eastern states, demanding immediate repeal and careless of the consequences. Some of Jefferson's Republican friends sought to prepare his mind for acceptance of the inevitable. Nicholas, for example, tried to switch the train of Jefferson's thought from the rightness of the measure to the reality of failure. The experiment had been fairly tried. Its defeat because of unforeseen events abroad and misconduct in one section of the Union was no reproach to the President. He should get clear of the tottering system as fast as possible in order to control the alternative, which otherwise would be forced on the government by a desperate opposition. Jefferson's popularity was identified with the national welfare, Nicholas said; hence the burden of leadership rested squarely on his shoulders. The implication, apparently, was that Madison's shoulders were not big enough. Jefferson did not like the implication or respond to the plea. On the contrary, he virtually surrendered his leadership when the electoral result became known in November. Madison won handily over the Federalist candidate C. C. Pinckney—122 to 47 in the final tally of electoral votes. The result marked a decline in Republican strength, but it was far from the disaster many had predicted, and viewed as a referendum on the embargo genuinely encouraging to the President.

The President's message spoke of failure but offered no suggestion for recovery. It belonged to Congress to "weigh and compare the painful alternatives out of which a choice is to be made." In his own mind, though he did not disclose it to Congress, the alternatives were submission, war, and embargo for another six months if necessary. The first was out of the question, the second painful in the extreme and the last thing wanted, unless against France, by the vociferous enemies of the embargo. After surveying the state of the national defenses, he called Congress to fix its attention "unremittingly" on "the safety of our country." The message was grim. But Jefferson introduced several cheerful notes. Retirement of the debt continued. During seven and one-half years over $33,000,000 of funded debt had been extinguished, liberating the treasury of $2,000,000 annual interest. Jefferson was understandably proud of this achievement, though it had not come about by way of economy in operating expenses, which had risen, and owed less to Gallatin's fiscal management than to the bonanza of European war. Defense now laid first claim on the surplus, yet Jefferson again asked Congress to inaugurate "a system of improvement." He congratulated the country on the conversion of industry and capital from foreign commerce and navigation to domestic manufactures, and expressed confidence that these establishments formed behind the protective wall of the embargo would become permanent. The passage was bolder as originally written. But Gallatin had objected to the suggestion of positive benefit to the nation from the annihilation of foreign commerce. Even as amended, Jefferson's encomium on manufactures fed the jealousies and fears of commercial interests already convinced the embargo aimed at their destruction; and the same anxieties were now felt by spokesmen of the agricultural interest. From Virginia, where Federalists and Quids had never accepted the embargo, John Taylor, one of the latter, read Jefferson a lecture on the rise of a "tyrannical manufacturing interest" that threatened to plunder the farmers as Hamilton's paper and stock interest had done in the past. Taylor was prophetic. In time Jefferson would understand the merits, if not the validity, of his fears.

But Jefferson's conspectus of the state of the Union in 1808 foreshadowed a significant revision of the principles of his political economy. Instead of the old reliance on agriculture with commerce as its handmaid, looking to an expansive foreign trade, he now spoke of "a due balance between agriculture, manufactures and commerce," focusing on the home market. The opposition of the commercial interest was, indeed, wonderful. The carrying trade had kept the nation in "hot water" from the beginning until the embargo, the very measure complained of, was undertaken to protect it. "Their doctrine goes to the sacrificing agriculture and manufactures to commerce," Jefferson wrote privately, "to the calling all our people from the interior country into a city of Amsterdam." The embargo had rescued the United States from this delusion, negatively by disclosing its costs, positively by disclosing the undeveloped potential of the national economy. Neither navigation nor agriculture had anything to fear from the rise of manufactures. All would benefit by the shift from the primacy of external to the primacy of internal trade. "My idea is that we should encourage home manufactures to the extent of our own consumptions of everything of which we raise the raw materials. . . . Our agriculture will still afford surplus produce enough to employ a due proportion of navigation."

Throwing the embargo into the hornets' nest on Capitol Hill was an act of supreme folly. Gallatin and Madison, whose own indecision contributed to the act, soon realized the error and begged the President to point out a "precise and distinct course" to Congress. You must, Gallatin said, "decide the question absolutely." But Jefferson declined. "On this occasion," he had already stated, "I think it is fair to leave to those who are to act on them, the decisions they prefer, being . . . myself but a spectator." Madison and Gallatin, the latter slated for Secretary of State, were the principal executors. And they did, on the President's retreat from responsibility, endeavor to lay out a path for Congress; but lacking Jefferson's prestige, uncertain what the path should be, and timid to pursue it when known, the executors lost control of the options to a leaderless herd of the demoralized, the faint-hearted, and the disgusted. Jefferson's policy was what it had always been: embargo or war, the latter to be determined, and the enemy chosen, when the former could no longer be borne, allowing perhaps another six months to the trial. The election, the testimony of support from three-quarters of the Union, strengthened enforcement of the embargo, the manifest fairness of the government's dealings with France and Britain as disclosed in diplomatic correspondence read by the entire nation, Bonaparte's reascendancy in Spain which, if it did not put him on better terms, would compel Britain to be more accommodating—these events sustained his fantastic expectations of public endurance which would allow him to go out of office without a humiliating reversal of policy.

"A great confusion and perplexity reign in Congress," Gallatin observed. Despite the avalanche of petitions against the embargo, the House refused to debate a motion for its repeal, and the Senate defeated such a motion by the same margin, 25 to 6, as was recorded on the passage of the measure a year before. While senators pummeled their colleagues with tiresome arguments, a committee under Giles's chairmanship drafted the fifth and last of the embargo laws, the Enforcing Act. Tailored to Gallatin's specific request, in accordance with the determination to legalize "all means to the end," Giles's bill drastically raised the bonds on coastal traders, gave collectors a free hand to seize suspicious property anywhere, and authorized the President to employ the army, navy, and militia to enforce the embargo laws. Republicans discovered legal precedents for these provisions. Yet some of them clearly violated guarantees of

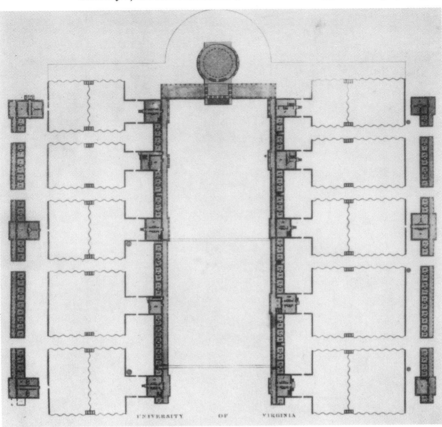

Plan of the University of Virginia. Engraving by Peter Maverick from a drawing by Jefferson in 1822.

The University of Virginia. Engraving by B. Tanner, 1827.

Jefferson at eighty-two. Plaster life mask by John H. I. Browere, 1825.

could the dead feel any interest in Monu
-ments or other remembrances of them, when, as
Anacreon says: Ολιγη δε κεισομεσθα
               Κονις, οςεων λυθεντων
the following would be to my Manes the most
gratifying.
On the grave   a plain die or cube of 3.f without any
mouldings, surmounted by an Obelisk
of 6.f. height, each of a single stone:
on the faces of the Obelisk the following
inscription, & not a word more
         Here was buried
            Thomas Jefferson
Author of the Declaration of American Independance
      of the Statute of Virginia for religious freedom
  & Father of the University of Virginia.

because by these, as testimonials that I have lived, I wish most to
be remembered. ~~it is to~~ to be of the coarse stone of which
my columns are made, that no one might be tempted
hereafter to destroy it for the value of the materials.
my bust by Ciracchi, with the pedestal and truncated
column on which it stands, might be given to the University
if they would place it in the Dome room of the Rotunda.
on the Die of the Obelisk might be engraved
         Born apr. 2. 1743. O.S.
         Died ——   ,

Jefferson's design and inscription for his tombstone.

Monticello, west front, after Jefferson's death. Engraving after a
painting by George Cooke.

personal liberty (the searches and seizures clause of the Fourth Amendment, for instance) and, over-all, so vast was the concentration of power in the President and in minor functionaries, the measure mocked every principle Jefferson held except the one principle, that of the embargo itself, which he believed the crisis of affairs had made a national imperative. The bill passed the Senate on the usual party division; the House stiffened the measure and approved it, 71 to 32. If Congress represented the will of the people, no more decisive test of public support for the embargo was ever recorded.

It was a hollow victory, however. Public support nationally had never been in question; the politically manipulated opposition in the Northeast, especially in Massachusetts, was the critical problem. Now, in January, the Enforcing Act hurried Massachusetts to the brink of resistance and, possibly, disunion. Pickering and associates grew bold. Warned ten months earlier by Adams of this brewing conspiracy, repeatedly alarmed by Sullivan, Jefferson said it was now believed the Bay State legislature just coming into session would call a convention and propose the separation of the New England states. The *New England Palladium,* in Boston, spiced the discontents with the publication of the Canning to Pinkney letter Jefferson had withheld from Congress. The insinuation of government duplicity and the sarcastic tone of the British minister delighted the ultraists, while the publication itself suggested the complicity of the Essex Junto in the policy of a foreign power against their own government. No Federalist congressman undertook to defend the publication and one of them, the Marylander Francis Scott Key, roundly denounced this "direct and insidious attempt of a foreign government to take advantage of and influence the parties of this country." But the spirit of revolt in Massachusetts rose higher. Collectors resigned before the wrath of an angry public. Newspapers and handbills portrayed the President as a tyrant—worse than George III in 1776—and called for open resistance. "Nerve your arms with vengeance against the despot who would wrest the inestimable germ of independence from you, and you shall be conquerors. Give ear no longer to the siren voice of democracy and Jeffersonian liberty. It is a cursed delusion, adopted by traitors, and recommended by sycophants." All along the coast town meetings passed defiant resolutions in an awesome display of grassroots democracy that impressed Jefferson even as he reeled under its blows. Early in February the Bay State legislature, while not calling a convention, adopted a report directing Congress to repeal the embargo forthwith, resume trade with Britain, and "unfurl the republican banner against the imperial standard" of Bonaparte. It further declared the Enforcing Act "unconstitutional, and not legally binding." The Connecticut legislature followed this action by declaring the state's non-compliance with the "unconstitutional and despotic acts" of the federal government.

In Congress, meanwhile, the administration forces tried to ride out the storm. On January 20 the House passed a resolution calling for a special session of the new Congress on the fourth Monday of May. In the course of debate a caustic young Massachusetts representative, Josiah Quincy, arraigned the President for imposture and deceit and declared the administration so patently spineless it could not be kicked into war. Yet Quincy opposed war; *laissez faire*, including submission to Britain, was his policy, as it was Randolph's. The Republican majority held firm and the resolution passed 80 to 26. The implicit assumption, as Jefferson explained to his son-in-law in Virginia, was that Congress would lift the embargo in June, if it had not done its work by then, and letters of marque and reprisal would at once issue against either or both belligerents as the preliminary to hostilities. This was satisfactory to him, and he hoped it would quiet discontents to the eastward. Nicholas made the next move: a resolution declaring that beyond a certain date, to be supplied, the embargo would be repealed, navigation resumed, and also defended by marque and reprisal against nations persisting in their decrees. Nicholas moved to fill the blank with June 1.

But now the New England Republicans bolted. Joined by Clintonians, Randolphians, and assorted Republicans frightened by war, disunion, and loss of office, they defeated the administration repeal date, 73 to 40, then approved with three additional votes the substitution of March 4. This revolution would not have occurred but for the fumbling and tardiness of the administration. The plan embodied in the Nicholas resolution would surely have passed earlier in the session; brought forward after nearly three months of tearing dissension in Congress and explosion in Massachusetts, it was too late. The troubles in the East, Jefferson said, communicated "a kind of panic" to several representatives from that quarter and produced "this sudden and unaccountable revolution of opinion." In the retrospect of eighteen months he was more specific: "I ascribe all this to one pseudo-Republican, Story. He came on . . . and stayed only a few days; long enough, however, to get complete hold of Bacon, who giving in to his representations became panic struck, and communicated his panic to his colleagues, and they to a majority of the sound members of Congress. They believed in the alternative of repeal or civil war, and produced the fatal measure of repeal." Whether the shame or the glory of embargo repeal belonged primarily to Joseph Story or to his Massachusetts colleague Ezekiel Bacon —Story gave the credit to Bacon—is of no importance, but they were the exciting force. Until January no sounder Republicans sat in the House. Young Story, who came on just before Christmas in replacement of Crowninshield for the Salem district, at first stood out against repeal, defended the Enforcing Act, and deplored the seditious tactics of the Essex Junto, which he held responsible for British obstinacy. He voted for the June session but then became convinced that the embargo would have to be sacrificed to allay the dangerous spirit of rebellion and disunionism in New England. Nicholas, Campbell, and other administration leaders pressed him to stick with them. "In the course of these consultations," Story later recalled, "I learned the whole policy of Mr. Jefferson; and was surprised as well as grieved to find, that in the face of the clearest proofs of the failure of his plan, he continued to hope against facts. . . . The very eagerness with which the repeal was supported by a majority of the Republican party ought to have taught Mr. Jefferson that it was already considered by them as a miserable and mischievous failure."

The only honorable alternative to repeal, the administration held, was war. But the·anti-war party outnumbered the anti-embargo party. And instant war was out of the question. Desperate to salvage a policy of some kind, the administration fell back on the plan of non-intercourse first broached in November. As finally passed near the end of February, the Non-Intercourse Act reopened trade with all countries except Britain and France, and authorized the President to resume trade with either of them upon the repeal of the offensive edicts. A provision directing marque and reprisal against the refractory nation was stricken by the House—a final crushing defeat for the administration. The new policy exposed the country to all the risks of war without any of the coercive benefits of the old. Its saving grace, its only excuse, was profit. No one doubted that the belligerents would get everything wanted from the United States via indirect or covert channels and that British goods would be smuggled wholesale into the country. The United States would indeed become "a city of Amsterdam, a mere headquarters for carrying on the commerce of all nations," and a city of smugglers besides. "Thus were we driven," Jefferson sadly concluded, "from the high and wise ground we had taken, and which, had it been held, would have either restored us our free trade or have established manufactures among us."

To the end of his days Jefferson believed that the embargo, if endured a little longer, would have forced justice from Britain and thus put a stop to the long train of degradation that finally terminated, ingloriously, in the War of 1812. The case was a hard one, he conceded. At any other time, with any other nations, the fairness and liberality of the American effort would have won respect, but the hurricane then blasting the world—the twin furies of the "tyrant of the ocean" and "the scourge of the land"—prostrated all principles of reason and right. "All those calculations which, at any other period, would have been deemed honorable, of the existence of a moral sense in man, individually or associated, of the connection which the laws of nature have established between his duties and his interests, of a regard for honest fame and the esteem of our fellow men, have been a matter of reproach to us, as evidences of imbecility. As if it could be folly for an honest man to suppose that others could be honest also, when it is in their interest to be so. And when is this state of things to end?" For Jefferson, the hopes of the Enlightenment, of a new nation, even a world, conceived in its spirit, were wrapped up in the experiment of peaceable coercion. Hence its defeat, his defeat, was more than personal or political or diplomatic; it was a moral defeat as well, and the whole revolutionary edifice of peace and benevolence, reason and law, and freedom of intercourse among nations was involved in the destruction. The New Englanders were only the agents of this disaster. The experiment was undertaken because of the mania of Europe, above all because of Britain's inveterate hostility to the nation wrenched from her loins in revolution; and Britain crushed the experiment, not because her survival demanded it but for commercial monopoly and profit, and not from her intrinsic power but from the persistent colonial subserviency of the new nation. All his life, it seemed, he had been combating the "mother country," and now he and the embargo were going out together—poignant testimony to the nation's untransacted destiny. "The proof she exhibited on that occasion," Jefferson confessed some months later, "that she can exercise such an influence in this country as to control the will of its government and three-fourths of its people, and oblige the three-fourths to submit to one-fourth, is to me the most mortifying circumstance that has occurred since the establishment of our government."

Justifying the embargo to himself, Jefferson closed his eyes to the faults of the policy. Perseverance for six months might very well have brought Britain to her knees. The American minister, Pinkney, fervently shared this conviction. Riots in Manchester, disorders in the countryside, the sufferings of workers, artisans, and West Indian slaves, rising food prices, shortages of raw materials, shrinkage of mercantile income, the damaging loss of the Amercian market—a nation at war could bear great hardships for a time and government could risk the consequences; but the limits of endurance were breached in the early months of 1809, and the ministry did, in fact, relax its orders in April partly because of the embargo's impact, though not until after its repeal became known. This consideration lost its force, however, when weighed in the balance with the mounting discords, casualties, and sufferings of the embargo at home. The nation plunged from unparalleled prosperity into an economic decline from which it would not fully recover for a quarter of a century. And despite Jefferson's plea in the name of manufactures, there were no solidly redeeming economic rewards of the policy. The political damage reckoned in Republican losses and Federalist revival, in torn morale and shrinkage of principle as well as of votes, in subversive plots and disunionism, and the shock to Jefferson's hopes of harmony and reconciliation—these injuries were also incalculable. It was a tribute to the President's power and the trust he inspired that the people endured the embargo for so long and would, in fact, have endured it longer but for the revolt in one quarter of the Union.

But to have contained the rising discontents in 1809 would have required more force and energy than the American government could command and more obedience than a free and enterprising people could give. They had gone a long way with Jefferson's project to prove a principle they never fully understood, in part because he never fully explained it. Patriotism beyond the ordinary degree was required, but the motives of loyalty and sacrifice available to a nation at war were not so readily enlisted or maintained for a hard experiment in the ways of peace. When it appeared to exact more from them than from the intended victims many lost heart while others turned on the government in savage rage. It was the "failure of nerve" among the Republicans, more than the opposition of the Federalists, that defeated the embargo. Jefferson, for all the freight of idealism, had always steered a close-reefed political craft. The voyage of the embargo was under full sail, and the helmsman's single-minded commitment to the principle, with the rational hope it embodied, obscured his view of the navigational hazards. They were false, mere phantasms, in his vision of the truth; but they were, in fact, very real, and as such demanded recognition from a government he had himself made responsive to the popular will and from a federal union that, on his own principle, exacted compromise as the price of existence. Not only politically but diplomatically as well he had allowed himself to become the captive of a policy. When it failed, when the European powers refused to play his neutral game, when foreign events turned up nothing favorable to American aims, when commercial coercion was treated as a "paper tiger," Jefferson had no retreat but to war—the last of all evils—a war he might have had but did not want in 1807 and which neither he nor his executors nor the Congress had the courage to undertake in 1809. The result was drift. His popularity, though shaken, remained high during his last months in office. He might have controlled the sequel, but considering himself a "lame-duck," choosing not to meddle, policy was surrendered to the turbulence in Congress; and not until Andrew Jackson would a President regain control of the reins of government.

A deluge of addresses, all congratulatory, many championing the doomed embargo, poured in upon the President as the hour of retirement neared. They came from Republican meetings, from state legislatures, municipal bodies, colleges, military units, churches and religious associations, and associations of all kinds. The words of the prophet, "Every man has sat under his own vine and under his fig tree, and none to make him afraid," ran like a theme through the encomium. And whatever the errors or failures of his presidency, the public seemed to say, they arose from nothing vicious but from the virtuous heart of a statesman who repelled the Machiavellian teachings of "how not to be good." The "affectionate farewell" of the Virginia General Assembly, penned by William Wirt, was especially eloquent:

> We have to thank you for the model of an administration conducted on the purest principles of republicanism; for pomp and state laid aside; patronage discarded; internal taxes abolished; a host of superfluous offices disbanded; the monarchic maxim "that a national debt is a national blessing" renounced, and more than thirty-three millions of our debt discharged; the native right to nearly one hundred millions of acres of our national domain extinguished; and without the guilts or calamities of conquest, a vast and fertile region added to our Country, far more extensive than the original possessions, bringing along with it the Mississippi and the port of Orleans, the trade of the West to the Pacific Ocean, and in the intrinsic value of the land itself, a source of permanent and almost inexhaustible revenue. These are points in your administration, which the historian will not fail to seize, to expound and teach posterity to dwell upon with delight. Nor will he forget our peace with the civilized world, preserved through a season of uncommon difficulty and trial, the good will cultivated with the unfortunate aborigines of our Country, and the civilization humanely extended among them; the lesson taught the inhabitants of the coast of Barbary, that we have the means of chastising their piratical encroachments and awing them into justice; and that theme on which, above all others, the historic genius will hang with rapture, the liberty of speech and of press preserved inviolate, without which genius and science are given to man in vain.

Jefferson answered these numerous addresses with flourishes to freedom, union, and peace—and a pang of regret that the dragons still breathed. To the citizens of Washington he offered a somewhat anxious reaffirmation of the revolutionary faith declared in 1776 and embellished in 1789:

> Trusted with the destinies of this solitary republic of the world, the only monument of human rights, and the sole depository of the sacred fire of freedom and self-government from hence it is to be lighted up in other regions of the earth, if other regions of the earth shall ever become susceptible to its benign influence, all mankind ought then, with us, to rejoice in its prosperous, and sympathize in its adverse fortunes, as involving everything dear to man. And to what sacrifices of interest or convenience ought not these considerations to animate us, and to what compromises of opinion and inclination, to maintain harmony and union among ourselves, and to preserve from all danger this hallowed ark of human hope and happiness.

Madison asked Jefferson to ride with him in his carriage to the inauguration, but he declined, saying all the honors of the day belonged to him. The retiring President rode up Pennsylvania Avenue on horseback, unattended, hitched his steed to the paling, and went into the Capitol with the rest of the procession. "This day I return to the people and my proper seat is among them." He dined with but a solitary guest, his young grandson Jeff, and that night attended the Inaugural Ball. "Am I too early?" he asked a friend when he found himself among the first arrivals. "You must tell me how to behave, for it is more than forty years since I have been to a ball." With what deliverance he had looked forward to this day is suggested by a letter he wrote to Dupont. "Never did a prisoner, released from his chains, feel such relief as I shall on shaking off the shackles of power," he said. "Nature intended me for the tranquil pursuits of science, by rendering them my supreme delight. But the enormities of the time in which I have lived, have forced me to take a part in resisting them, and to commit myself to the boisterous ocean of political passions. I thank God for the opportunity of retiring from them without censure, and carrying with me the most consoling proofs of public approbation."

He took a week to wind up his personal affairs in Washington and then, following a caravan of wagons, set out for Monticello. The roads were especially treacherous at this season; he rode the last three days in the saddle, part of the time through a blinding snow-storm, and came safely into port at the last on the 15th. His friends and neighbors, the citizens of Albemarle, presented him a cordial address. No testimony, Jefferson said in reply, could be more grateful than that of "the triers of the vicinage." "Of you, then, my neighbors, I may ask, in the face of the world, 'whose ox have I taken, or whom have I defrauded? Whom have I oppressed, or of whose hand have I received a bribe to blind mine eyes therewith?' On your verdict I rest with conscious security."

CHAPTER ELEVEN

Sage of Monticello

Oh, the blessings of privacy and leisure! The wish of the powerful and eminent, but the privilege only of inferiors, who are the only people that live to themselves; nay, the very thought of it is a consolation, even in the tumults and hazards that attend greatness. . . . But it is one thing to retire for pleasure, and another thing for virtue, which must be active even in that retreat, and give proof of what it has learned: for a good and wise man does in privacy consult the well-being of posterity. Zeno and Chrysippus did greater things in their studies than if they had led armies, borne offices, or given laws, which in truth they did, not to one city alone, but to all mankind: their quiet contributed more to the common benefit than the sweat and labor of other people.

Seneca, Moral Essays.

ALL MY WISHES END where I hope my days will end, at Monticello." Many more days than Jefferson calculated, seventeen years and four months of days, lay before him, during which the dream of felicity became a delusion, yet with his confidence in a universe framed on benevolence and his affirmative response to life, he remained a cheerful worker in the vineyard until the end.

The mansion was finished now, all but the final touches, just in time for the decay to commence. Jefferson had turned his thoughts to the gardens, nothing elaborate on the style of English landscape such as he had once envisioned and so much admired in William Hamilton's "Woodlands," in Philadelphia, which would have been awkward in the thick woods and hanging hollows and ridges of Monticello, but flower and vegetable gardens on an ample plan. Trees had always been his passion, he wrote to Madame de Tessé, whom he continued to keep in American seed and whose courage in planting trees he admired; as for himself, he thought it was time to begin planting flowers. "The labors of the year, in that line, are repaid within the year, and death, which will be at my door, shall find me unembarrassed by long-lived undertakings." He said he had scarcely ever planted a flower, and though he had laid out whole orchards of fruits and gardens of vegetables, he had never been free to indulge his calling in this direction. "No occupation is so delightful to me as the culture of the earth, and no culture comparable to that of the garden," he said in the third year of retirement. "Such a variety of subjects, some are always coming to perfection, the failures of one being repaired by the successes of another, and instead of one harvest a continued one through the year." How much more rewarding than the political calling! The flower gardens on the west lawn, planned in 1807 but not completed for five years, featured a winding walk, bordered on either side, with oval beds set in the hollows. "I remember well," one of his granddaughters recalled, "when he first returned to Monticello, how immediately he began to prepare new beds for his flowers." A great variety was planted, and he felt renewed by the annual cycle. A new vegetable garden was laid out, too, in three long tiers on the sunny slope of the mountain; and for the second and last time Jefferson renewed the orchard that had gone to decay while he was attending to public business.

Jefferson's estate was in sad repair when he left the presidency. His farms had suffered grievously, he felt, from the absence of close personal supervision, and he expected to remedy this by becoming a farmer again. Yet by his own admission he was an indifferent farmer. The causes of deterioration lay deeper: in the cursed labor system, in soil exhaustion and erosion, and the depression of the market. Hazards of pests and weather the farmer always had with him, but they were especially unkind to Jefferson during several successive seasons. And under the restraints of embargo, non-intercourse, and war, the market was seldom favorable. On paper he suffered no loss of assets. He continued to own approximately 10,000 acres of land and 200 slaves. The total value of his estate has been estimated at $200,000. But Virginia lands declined more or less steadily in value and produced a paltry return. At the time of his retirement Jefferson estimated an annual income from his farms of $4000, to which might be added perhaps $1500 to $2000 from other sources, such as the flour mill, the naillery (this too had to be restored, with poor results), a cooper's shop, and slave hire on occasion. He intended to tighten his belt at Monticello and live as a plain farmer; but he would be denied this fate. Living expenses at home increased without improvement of capital or income. Worst of all he was still plagued with debts. The blight ate into his happiness and finally consumed a great part of his estate.

Winding up his affairs during the winter in Washington, Jefferson suddenly found himself overwhelmed with a multitude of forgotten accounts, $10,000 to $12,000 above his resources. It dawned on him for the first time how far he had lived beyond his income. Recalling the shock in later years, he said the deficit arose from turning the President's House into "a general tavern" for the Washington community. Whatever the cause, he had to borrow to pay these debts. Eight thousand dollars came from a private lender in Virginia, the remainder from the Bank of the United States on a note endorsed by James Madison. Uneasy about the liability thus assumed by the President, Jefferson soon transferred this debt to Thaddeus Kosciusko, whose American investments he had managed for many years. (He was a much better manager of other men's money than of his own.) These were only the debts run up in Washington. He had not altogether rid himself of the old debts dating back to the Revolution. Altogether, he owed something like $25,000 at the time of his retirement; and no sooner would he begin to see the end of this bondage than new liabilities would befall him. As before, his Bedford plantation, Poplar Forest, much the more productive of the two, was mortgaged to his creditors. He tried to sell several small detached parcels of land, but this was slow work and had no appreciable effect on his estate until the last years of life. To round-out his holdings in Albemarle and Bedford, he also bought some additional acreage. He considered his property and Randolph's "common stock," and since his son-in-law was also heavily in debt, Edgehill, too, operated under mortgage.

The Randolphs and their children, reaching the number of

eleven in 1818, lived with the patriarch at Monticello. With Francis Eppes, Maria's offspring, a part-time resident, the grandchildren came to an even dozen. To say that they worshiped their grandfather is an understatement. "Cheerfulness, love, benevolence, wisdom, seemed to animate his whole form," one of them recalled. "I cannot describe the feelings of veneration, admiration, and love that existed in my heart towards him. I looked upon him as a being too great and good for my comprehension; and yet I felt no fear to approach him, and be taught by him some of the childish sports I delighted in. When he walked in the garden, and would call the children to go with him, we raced after and before him. . . . He would gather fruit for us, seek out the ripest figs, or bring down the cherries from on high above our heads with a long stick, at the end of which there was a hook and a little net bag. . . . One of our earliest amusements was in running races on the terrace or around the lawn. He placed us according to our ages, giving the youngest and smallest the start of all the others by some yards, and so on; and then he raised his arm high with his white handkerchief and we started off to finish the race by returning to the starting-place and receiving our reward of dried fruit—three figs or prunes or dates to the victor, two to the second, and one to the lagger who came in last." Their mother managed the busy household at Monticello, tutored the children, and received the same adoration as her father. Everyone observed the resemblance of father and daughter. One of the neighboring Gilmers, who formed part of the Albemarle circle centered at Monticello, thought Martha Randolph the most accomplished woman he ever knew: "her person tall, largely, loosely made, and awkward, but her actions and manners are graceful, easy, and engaging; her face not what would be esteemed beautiful, but her features are flexible and playful and agreeable. An expression of intelligence always animates her countenance; a turn for the ludicrous, a sweet and variable voice, the contraction of muscles about the eyes when she speaks, vast and various information, frankness and eloquence far above what I have ever met with in any person of her sex. . . ." Between these two paragons, Martha and her father, Randolph cut a poor figure. For all his talents, such as raised him to the governorship of the commonwealth in 1819, he was volatile, eccentric, and little loved by his children. Even Jefferson slowly cooled in his affection for him. The Monticello family had its trials and tribulations like any other. What distinguished it finally was the virtuous character of the patriarch, honored and loved in his domestic circle "above all earthly beings."

Monticello was not only a home; it was a monument. People came from all over: "People of wealth, fashion, men in office, professional men, military and civil, lawyers, doctors, Protestant clergymen, Catholic priests, members of Congress, foreign ministers, missionaries, Indian agents, tourists, travellers, artists, strangers, friends." Some came as idle curiosity seekers, some as seekers of Delphi, others as pilgrims to Mecca. They came to see the renowned Sage of Monticello, statesman, scientist, philanthropist, whose life was identified with the prodigy of the New World, and whose home was among the most interesting of his creations. The monument was even a kind of museum. Visitors noticed "the strange furniture on its walls." In the entrance hall hung heads of elk, deer, buffalo, and mammoth, Indian curiosities from the Lewis and Clark journey, and a variety of paintings, which overflowed into the parlor—portraits of New World discoverers, of Franklin, Adams, Paine, and other Americans, some native landscapes, several of Trumbull's historical canvases, and many Biblical scenes from European galleries—together with busts of various luminaries, including Ceracchi's of Jefferson and Hamilton, who, it was said, stood opposed on marble pedestals in the great hall.

Among the numerous visitors were many Jefferson enjoyed; as for the rest, he had not the heart to turn them away. They came, most of them, to do him honor; hospitality was the custom of the country, and there was no nearby inn to which they could go. So Monticello became a tavern, as the President's House had been. During the summers, when travel commenced from the lowcountry, they came in gangs, Edmund Bacon, the farm manager recalled, "the whole family, with carriage and riding horses and servants; sometimes three or four such gangs at a time." Often the stable, which would take twenty-six horses in addition to the family's stock, was full. Martha put up as many as fifty guests a night on the mountain. Of course, they had to be fed. "I have killed a fine beef, and it would all be eaten in a day or two," Bacon said. More than anything else, he felt that the expense of so much company sank Jefferson's fortune. However that may be, he never complained of the company or the expense, though it was a far cry from the simple, quiet retirement he had imagined. Always on display at Monticello, he escaped two or three times a year to Poplar Forest, ninety miles and two days to the south. Before he left the presidency, as building drew to a close at Monticello, he began to build a house at this plantation, and it became more necessary to him when he retired. This second home and refuge, a lovely brick octagon, occupied him for a dozen years.

In 1810, after a year's retirement, Jefferson described his daily routine to Kosciusko. "My mornings are devoted to correspondence. From breakfast to dinner, I am in my shops, my garden, or on horseback among my farms; from dinner to dark, I give to society and recreation with my neighbors and friends; and from candle light to early bed-time, I read." His health was excellent for a man of sixty-seven years. He used spectacles only to read at night, and another decade passed before he lost a tooth. He said he read but a single newspaper, Thomas Ritchie's *Richmond Enquirer*, though he continued to subscribe to Duane's *Aurora* and the *National Intelligencer.* "But I wish at length to indulge myself in more favorite reading, in Tacitus and Horace and the writers of that philosophy which is the old man's consolation and preparation for what is to come." He occasionally read new books and grew fond of the *Edinburgh Review*. But the ancient writers were his favorites. "I saw him more frequently with a volume of the classics in his hand than with any other book," a granddaughter recalled. He once told an old political associate that he knew more of what passed two or three thousand years ago, "of the heroes of Troy, of the wars of Lacedaemon and Athens, of Pompey and Caesar, and of Augustus too," than of what passed from day to day. Still he was not dead to the world around him. "I talk of ploughs and harrows, of seeding and harvesting with my neighbors," he said, "and of politics too, if they choose, with as little reserve as the rest of my fellow citizens, and feel, at length, the blessings of being free to say and do what I please, without being responsible to any mortal." Among his most pleasing occupations was the direction of the studies of youths who came to him for books and learning and inspiration, often settling nearby. Some, like William Cabell Rives, had distinguished careers before them. "I endeavor," Jefferson said, "to keep their attention fixed on the main object of all science, the freedom and happiness of man."

Less pleasing, in time a drudgery against which he revolted, was a mammoth correspondence. In a single year he received over 1200 letters. "They are letters of inquiry, for the most part, always of good will, sometimes from friends whom I esteem, but much oftener from persons whose names are unknown to me, but written kindly and civilly, and to which therefore, civility requires answers." Many went unanswered of necessity, but he wrote literally thousands of letters, on every conceivable subject, some of them masterpieces of the epistolary art, and all with his own hand until the last years of his life. The early morning hours from sun-up until breakfast were set aside for this task; often, however, Jefferson sat at his writing table, "under the whip and spur, from morning to night." "Is this life?" he once asked John Adams, his most famous correspondent, who was not afflicted in the same way. "At best it is but the life of a mill-horse, who sees no end to his circle but death. To such a life, that of a cabbage is paradise." The stiffness of his right wrist, the legacy of misadventure in Paris now compounded by the miseries of age, led him to declare a "state of insurgency" in 1817. But he never found any relief from this burden of his life.

The Sage of Monticello was many times blessed. Good health, good conscience, benign temperament, indefatigable industry, loving family, pleasant country society, honors of a life well spent—all these and more were his. But for his debts and the perilous state of Virginia agriculture, he said in 1810, his private happiness would be unalloyed. For a decade he remained cheerful about the prospects, only then to discover that his hopes were blasted. It was not a tranquil retirement, a life of study and ease and affection untroubled by the cares of the world, such as had always been his dream for Monticello. Once again he realized how much his private happiness belonged to his public happiness. Every renunciation of interest in affairs of state was followed by ejaculations of deep concern. During forty years in the public service he had accumulated quite an agenda of unfinished business. He could not attend to all of it but certain items, above all education, made an irresistible claim upon him. In his private station, aged and remote from the seats of power, he was still a public man, and in the eyes of many the chief personage in the United States. No one, certainly, embodied so well the history and the hopes of the new nation; and although this dream, too, dimmed for him in the last years of life, he remained its most authentic voice until his death on the fiftieth anniversary of its birth.

Kaleidoscope in Twilight

Many people found it difficult to believe that Jefferson had really surrendered the helm of state. The idea that he secretly directed the administration of his successor from Monticello was wholly mistaken, but Madison had stood for so long in Jefferson's shadow it seemed unlikely he could stand in the sunshine of his own. Jefferson naturally had a stake in the new administration, nor only for reasons of friendship and patriotism but because Madison was, in a very positive sense, the heir of measures he had started. The ultimate fate of his own presidency was involved with the fate of his successor. Conscious of this, conscious of Madison's unfortunate reputation as "a mere appendage" of himself, Jefferson leaned over backwards not to interfere. Each man knew the other's mind almost as well as his own, and they had implicit confidence in each other, so advice was rarely asked or volunteered. As in the past, Madison and his wife usually visited at Monticello in September. What passed in these conversations it is impossible to say, but their correspondence in these years was neither voluminous nor especially informative on matters of state.

Jefferson's influence with the President was most often requested in the business of patronage. Considering himself *hors de combat*, he at once had a circular printed to answer all the pleading office-seekers. Only in the cases of two or three Virginia friends of many years did he actively intercede. In 1810 the death of Justice William Cushing at last opened the way to a Republican majority on the Supreme Court. Jefferson could not be indifferent to this event. For ten years the Court had "braved the spirit and the will of the nation," and at this very time he found himself the defendant in a huge damage suit likely to be heard at Chief Justice Marshall's bench. The vacancy fairly belonged to Massachusetts, Cushing's state. Jefferson recommended Levi Lincoln, a Republican tried and true. Madison offered the seat to Lincoln, who declined, and then, again on his friend's recommendation, to Gideon Granger, whom the Senate rejected. Only after all other possibilities failed did Madison name Joseph Story, the man he may have wanted in the first place but whom Jefferson had ruled out for his insurgency against the embargo.

The former President rendered an important political service by helping to restore the friendship of Madison and Monroe. Monroe had found no new public employment since his return from England. Alienated from Madison, associated with the Randolph junto, there seemed to be no place for him in the administration. He soon returned to Albemarle, and Jefferson made it his business to draw him away from his quondam friends and to revive the old cordiality between the second and third of the Virginia triumvirs. When Meriwether Lewis took his own life in October 1809, Madison offered the Louisiana governorship to Monroe. Jefferson had pressed the same office on him in the past and now did so again, again without success. The next year the General Assembly brought Monroe back to the governorship; but no sooner did he take up the reins than a cabinet shake-up in Washington led him to resign to accept the post of Secretary of State under Madison. From that moment, barring misadventure, Monroe's eventual succession to the presidency was assured, to Jefferson's enormous satisfaction.

The cabinet shake-up, which might better be described as an explosion, had its origins in the rivalry between Albert Gallatin and Robert Smith. These gentlemen had suppressed their differences and worked more or less in unison while Jefferson was at the helm; but the harmony he had managed during eight years Madison could not manage during one. Gallatin had wanted and been promised the State Department. Madison, at the last minute, fearing the opposition of Gallatin's enemies and Smith's friends in the Senate, not only Samuel Smith but William B. Giles and others as well, named Smith to this first post in the cabinet and kept Gallatin in the Treasury. Visiting at Monticello in the fall, Gallatin poured his heart out to his former chief and threatened to resign. Jefferson urged him to stay on, emphasizing the importance of finally sinking the debt and moving ahead with works of improvement and peace. Gallatin stayed on but dissension increased. William Duane, who blamed Gallatin for the ascendancy of the more moderate faction of Pennsylvania Republicans, launched a torrid campaign of invective in the *Aurora*. The spreading feud split the administration and threatened to split the party in 1810. Several Republicans begged Jefferson's intervention to restore harmony. He declined but exhorted Duane, with the other dissidents, to curb their zeal in the interest of unity. The Republicans were not just a party—the name was degrading— "the Republicans are the *nation*," he thundered. "The last hope of human liberty in the world rests on us. We ought, for so dear a stake, to sacrifice every attachment and every enmity." Poor Duane, hopelessly in debt, harassed by creditors, slapped with one libel suit after another, all in the cause of Republicanism, seemed doomed to spend his life in courts of law. Just before leaving office, Jefferson had commissioned him a lieutenant colonel in the provisional army (the editor was a student of the art of war), and despite his vexation at him for "schismatizing" the administration, he now undertook to raise $8000 among Virginia Republicans to keep the *Aurora* in operation. It was a hard cause, and it became desperate the succeeding April when the peppery editor turned on the President himself. Forced at length to choose between Gallatin and Smith, Madison chose Gallatin without hesitation. Smith was dismissed and Monroe brought in. Jefferson, with nine-tenths of the Republican party, would have chosen the same way. He put no credence in reports of Gallatin's enmity to him on the score of Anglophobism—they emanated from David Erskine, the former British minister—and his merits placed him in a class by himself. To Madison he explained his efforts on Duane's behalf, for his "incalculable services to Republicanism," lest the President suppose he endorsed the editor's attack on the administration. He made one last effort to reform Duane and save the *Aurora* but feared the editor had become so much the victim of his passions that he would go the way of Randolph. And so he went, yet Jefferson never abandoned him.

For three years the country drifted toward war. Within a few weeks of his retirement, Jefferson watched the hope of peace dawn brightly and then sink as suddenly as it rose. On the assurances of Erskine that the orders in council would be revoked in June, Madison issued a proclamation restoring trade with Britain. Jefferson hailed this "triumph of our forbearing and yet persevering system." But George Canning at once disavowed the Erskine Agreement and recalled the errant minister. The embarrassed President restored non-intercourse. It was a "dirty trick," Jefferson commiserated with his friend. "Should Bonaparte have the wisdom to correct his injustice towards us, I consider war with England inevitable." Bonaparte ran true to form; even so, after other awkward passages in the pursuit of peace, war with Britain became inevitable in 1812.

Jefferson expressed mingled feelings of disappointment and relief. War, on the one hand, would cut out the lingering cancer of British influence: "the second weaning from British principles, British attachments, British manners and manufactures will be salutary, and will form an epoch of the spirit of nationalism and of consequent prosperity, which would never have resulted from a continued subordination to the interests and influence of England." The American strategy, obviously, was to attack Canada and drive Britain from the continent. "The acquisition of Canada this year, as far as the neighborhood of Quebec, will be a mere matter of marching," Jefferson boasted. Halifax would fall in the next campaign. The Floridas, too, would become an object. The world would then see such an "empire of liberty" as had never been surveyed since the creation. This conception of the war as an epoch of liberty and nationality had firm roots in Jefferson's thought. It was a war against Britain, of course, but in the larger sense it was against Europe, the Old World, and in this sense it promised the consummation of that hemispheric "American system" toward which New World ideology had aimed from the beginning. "What in short is the whole system of Europe towards America but an atrocious and insulting tyranny," Jefferson wrote to one of his unknown correspondents. "One hemisphere of the earth, separated from the other by wide seas on both sides, having a different system of interests flowing from different climates, different soils, different productions, different modes of existence, and its own local relations and duties, is made subservient to all the petty interests of the other, to *their* laws, *their* regulations, their passions and wars, and interdicted from social intercourse, from the interchange of mutual duties and comforts with their neighbors, enjoined on all men by the laws of nature." A war commenced under such favorable auspices as he believed this one to be, holding the promise of so much gain in liberty and dignity and independence, he had almost come to think a blessing to the nation.

On the other hand, what was war itself but the curse of the Old World blighting the hopes of the New? Jefferson contemplated this chapter as a mournful necessity. "Farewell all hope of extinguishing the public debt! Farewell all visions of applying the surplus revenue to the improvements of peace, rather than the ravages of war. Our enemy has indeed the consolation of Satan on removing our first parents from Paradise; from a peaceful and agricultural nation he makes us a military and manufacturing one." The country was meant to be, and might have become, "a garden for the delight and multiplication of mankind," he said. "But the lions and tigers of Europe must be gorged in blood, and some of ours must go, it seems, to their maws, their ravenous and insatiable maws." The United States would win the contest, of course, and get back on the track of destiny, but it would never shine quite so brightly for Jefferson again.

The conduct of the war was itself disillusioning. The crushing military defeats of 1812, beginning with General William Hull's "treacherous" surrender of Detroit in August, shattered Jefferson's easy optimism. It was farewell to Canada too. "So wretched a succession of generals never before destroyed the fairest expectations of a nation," he wrote in disgust. Some Republicans cherished the hope that he might be called back into service, perhaps as President or, more likely, as Secretary of State in Madison's cabinet, relieving Monroe to energize the feeble War Department. Jefferson refused to consider it and counseled the despondent to rally to the administration. The military failures, he felt, proved the case for the reinvigorated militia system he had first recommended to Congress in 1805. Monroe, when he became Secretary of War in 1814, took up the plan, but Congress again registered its opposition. On no problem did Jefferson express himself as strongly as that of war finances. The Bank of the United States died with the expiration and non-renewal of its charter in 1811, which was gratifying; but Congress, instead of adopting his system of Treasury notes redeemed by taxes, abandoned its control over the currency to a multiplying horde of state banks, which flooded the country with worthless paper, drove out specie, drove up prices, and upset property values everywhere.

"Instead of funding issues of paper on the hypothecation of specific redeeming taxes (the only method of anticipating in time of war, the resources of times of peace, tested by the experience of nations)," he wrote, "we are trusting to tricks of jugglers of the cards, to the illusions of banking schemes for the resources of the war, and for the cure of colic to inflations of more wind." His views were well known to the administration, yet when it finally came to grips with financial disaster after two years of war, the remedy chosen was a second national bank, the Hamiltonian solution, rather than his own. He felt the effect of inflation in his own purse, for although it should have raised his income with his expenses, and helped him pay his debts, it did not even by half, largely because the British blockade of the Chesapeake barred access to foreign markets. He pleaded with Madison to send a naval force to break the blockade, but frigates could not be spared and gunboats, though Jefferson seemed to think them servicable in this situation, could not do the job. As a result, at any rate, he and his neighbors were feeding their wheat to the horses in 1814 and tobacco was not worth the pipe that smoked it. Whiskey was one recourse, "but all mankind must become drunkards to consume it," Jefferson quipped. "To me this state of things brings a sacrifice of all tranquillity and comfort through the residue of life. . . . [By] the total annihilation in value of the produce that was to give me subsistence and independence, I shall be like Tantalus, up to the shoulders in water, yet dying of thirst." Thus the war was a great personal as well as national misfortune.

Jefferson took what pleasure he could in the Peace of Ghent at the end of 1814. Andrew Jackson's victory at New Orleans, even if it came after the signing of the peace, had not been wasted, he said. It proved once again that the West was sound and "that our militia are heroes when they have heroes to lead them." The peace was, he thought, only an armistice. The treaty returned the belligerents to the status quo ante bellum, omitting provisions on impressment and neutral rights that had caused the war in the first place. So the country must prepare for the resumption of hostilities at the first crack of the cannon in Europe. The Hartford Convention, called at the invitation of the Massachusetts legislature in December, bespoke the strength of British attachments and disunionist sentiments in that quarter of the Union. "Oh Massachusetts! How have I lamented the degradation of your apostacy!" Fortunately, the peace made a laughing-stock of the New England Federalists and the Hartford Convention a synonym of political degradation. "The cement of the Union is in the heart-blood of every American," Jefferson wrote. "I do not believe there is on earth a government established on so un-movable a basis. Let them, in any state, even in Massachusetts itself, raise the standard of separation, and its citizens will rise in mass, and do justice themselves on their own incendiaries." Still, in other letters, Jefferson did not dismiss this threat to peace and union. British jealousy and hostility, now unchecked by Bonaparte, had yet to run its course. "We were safe from the British fleets because they had Bonaparte at their back," he warned nine months after the war ended, "but the British fleets and the conquerors of Bonaparte being now combined, and the Hartford nation drawn off to them, we have uncommon reason to look to our own affairs." The only limits on the overwhelming power of Britain were bankruptcy and the "ascendancy which nature destines for us by immutable laws."

Distrusting Britain as before, even as he ardently wished peace and friendship with her, Jefferson could not take unalloyed pleasure in the downfall of Napoleon. If the allies succeeded in carving up Europe to suit themselves, he said, "we can expect no other favor than that of being the last devoured." He had penned many scorch-ing indictments of "the beast," the "moral monster" who had "in-flicted more misery on mankind than any other who . . . ever lived," and some of them had found their way into the press against his will and to the chagrin of Republicans, like Duane, who in their hatred of Britain persisted in seeing Napoleon as the champion of liberty. On balance, despite the unlucky loss of France in the scales of European power, Jefferson thought the downfall of Napoleon a blessing to humanity. The return of the Bourbons offered the only solution for France. This melancholy event, writing *finis* to the epoch of European liberty commenced with such glorious hopes in 1789, led Jefferson to reflect with Lafayette, Dupont, and other old comrades on the causes of the catastrophe. "Possibly you may re-member," he wrote to the Marquis, "at the date of the *jeu de paume* (June 20, 1789), how earnestly I urged yourself, and the patriots of my acquaintance, to enter into a compact with the King, securing freedom of religion, freedom of the press, trial by jury, habeas corpus, and a national legislature, all of which it was known he would yield, to go home, and let them work on the amelioration of the condition of the people. . . . This was as much as I then thought them able to bear, soberly and usefully for themselves. You thought otherwise, and that the dose might be larger. And I found you were right, for subsequent events proved they were equal to the constitution of 1791. Unfortunately, some of the most honest and enlightened of our patriotic friends . . . thought more still could be obtained and borne. They did not weigh the hazards of a transition from one form of government to another, the value of what they had already rescued from those hazards, and might hold in security if they pleased, nor the imprudence of giving up the certainty of such a degree of liberty, under a limited monarch, for the uncertainty of a little more under the form of a republic . . . , and from this fatal error of the republicans . . . flowed all the subsequent sufferings of the French nation." For it to be a matter of congratulation that France, and Europe, had reverted to the ante-revoltuionary condition was mournful in the extreme. "I fear from the experience of the last 25 years that morals do not, of necessity, advance hand in hand with the sciences," Jefferson confessed. Still he could not rest in darkness and doubt. Conceding to John Adams that he had been the better prophet on the French Revolution, Jefferson nevertheless felt that in the longer race of history Adams and his faithless tribe would be left at the starting gate. "But altho' your prophesy has proved true so far," he wrote in 1816, "I hope it does not preclude a better final result. The same light from our West seems to have spread and illuminated the very engines employed to extinguish it. It has given them [the Europeans] a glimmering of their rights and their power. The idea of representative government has taken root and growth among them . . . ." And so he continued to steer "with Hope in the head, leaving Fear astern."

The light of the American Revolution had spread to the southern precincts of the New World too. Jefferson rejoiced in the colonial revolts and the new independent states of Latin America. Although he trembled for their survival against the maraudings of Old World imperialism and feared their governments would end in priestly ignorance and military despotism, Jefferson placed this development in the ongoing epoch of American liberty. "But in whatever governments they end," he wrote to Humboldt in 1813, "they will be *American* governments, no longer to be involved in the never ceasing broils of Europe. The European nations constitute a separate division of the globe; their localities make them part of a distinct system, they have a set of interests of their own in which it is our interest never to engage ourselves. America has a hemisphere to itself." This conception of a hemispheric "American system," rooted in the Jeffersonian "empire of liberty," would not be realized in a year or a decade but its day would surely come. For a time Jefferson hoped that the European powers, excluding Britain because of her naval supremacy, might mutually guarantee the peace and independence of the Latin American states until they could stand on their own legs. But the Holy Alliance was little inclined in this direction; and in 1823 Jefferson counseled and supported the declaration of President Monroe that sought to close the hemisphere to Old World powers and make the United States the guardian of the "American system."

All during the war Jefferson made improvements in his Rivanna mill, in agricultural economy, and, above all, in household manufactures. The flour mill had cost him a great deal and continued to involve him in expense and litigation that consumed most of the meager profits. As finished in 1806 the mill incorporated certain improvements, including elevators, conveyor buckets, and hopperboys, on which the ingenious Oliver Evans claimed patents. Evans's agent later presented Jefferson with a bill for $89.60 for the use of these improvements. He paid willingly, as a tribute to a man whose talents were so useful to mankind, but at the same time denied he was under legal obligation to pay. In 1813, when Evans sued for his patent claim in Baltimore, Isaac McPherson, of that city, wrote to ask Jefferson's opinion of the case. His reply was a remarkable essay not just on patent law but on the rights of mankind to ideas. The Rivanna manufacturing mill, he said, had been erected after the expiration of Evans's first patent and before his second. But this was a technicality. By consulting a number of books on the mechanical arts, he showed that the principles of Evans's patent were very old and had been applied to many uses the world around. A man cannot, he went on to argue, patent a new application of a known principle

937

or an old machine. "If nature has made any one thing less susceptible than all others of exclusive property, it is the action of the thinking power called an idea, which an individual may exclusively possess as long as he keeps it to himself; but the moment it is divulged, it forces itself into the possession of every one, and the receiver cannot dispossess himself of it. Its peculiar character, too, is that no one can possess the less, because every other possesses the whole of it. He who receives an idea from me, receives instruction himself without lessening mine; as he who lights his taper at mine, receives light without darkening me. That ideas should freely spread from one to another over the globe, for the moral and mutual instruction of man, and improvement of his condition, seems to have been peculiarly and benevolently designed by nature, when she made them, like fire, expandable over all space, and like the air in which we breathe, move, and have our physical being, incapable of confinement or exclusive appropriation." This was fundamental—a law of nature. Yet Jefferson had written the patent law under which Evans claimed monopoly. Explaining the history of this misadventure, he said that under the original law Evans's patent would have been refused on the principle stated, but the inability of the patent commissioners to examine each request for title had led to the registration system, which installed the English principle of monopoly and left the only challenge to litigants in the courts. Evans won his suit in Baltimore. McPherson then published a pamphlet attacking the claim and offering Jefferson's letter in evidence. The pamphlet went to every member of Congress in the form of a memorial for revision of the patent law. Evans replied publicly, and privately to Jefferson. To adapt and combine known mechanisms for a new purpose, he claimed, vested in him an exclusive right to the use. Jefferson, who had always admired and encouraged Evans, repeated the argument of his letter to McPherson. If the patent law conferred monopoly on the application of ideas that had become the property of mankind, it took much more from the nation than it gave in return.

The rage for household manufactures, begun under the embargo, continued thoughout the war. The spinners and weavers were more daring adversaries of Britain than all the generals, Jefferson remarked. In 1812 he hired a married couple to manage his works at

Monticello. Two years later he and Randolph together had four jennies in operation, a total of 112 spindles, and the carders and looms to go with them. Chiefly, he aimed to clothe his plantation family with 2000 yards of coarse linens, cottons, and woolens yearly, looking to finer things once this was accomplished. Apparently he never got much beyond the first object. He experimented with new and larger spinning machines, but patent fees again became a problem, and their complexity was such that no one could keep them in repair; so he favored the ancient jenny. To make woolens he must have sheep. Jefferson had been raising sheep, mainly for mutton, for twenty years. Now he went into woolgrowing and shared the fantastic hopes of his countrymen for the silken wool of the Spanish merinos. The country became "sheep mad"—above all merino mad. The first merinos had been smuggled out of Spain by David Humphreys, Robert Livingston, the Duponts, and others about 1800. Jefferson supposed some of his flock, the offspring of European imports in the 1790's, were genuine merinos, but learned in 1809 that their wool fell far below the grade. Not until the next year, when prices of merinos soared out of sight, did he obtain a ram and ewe, of the variety called Acquines, as a gift from William Jarvis in Lisbon. "What shall we do with them?" he asked Madison, similarly blessed. "I have been so disgusted with the scandalous extortions lately practiced in the sale of these animals, and with the description of patriotism and praise to the sellers, as if the thousands of dollars apiece they have not been ashamed to receive were not reward enough, that I am disposed to consider as right, whatever is the reverse of what they have done." He proposed that they make gifts of the offspring to Virginia farmers less fortunate than themselves; in seven years the whole state would be covered with this valuable breed. Some farmers bred their stock at Monticello, and apparently Jefferson gave away some of his merino lambs, for two years later he had only a ram and two ewes. But the ravages of dogs and disease took others. And by 1812 the merino craze had so far subsided in Virginia, he said, that farmers would not even take them as gifts. The merinos produced less wool than hardier breeds and of a finer quality than was wanted for Virginia household manufactures. Few farmers understood the husbandry of merinos. All over the United States, when the breed failed to live up to expectations, whole flocks were slaughtered for mutton. Within a few years the merino enthusiasm turned into a fiasco.

Jefferson's experience in his own household strengthened his commitment to manufacturing enterprise as a branch of national economy. An English traveler, John Melish, who had interviewed him in Washington, and whose *Travels* appeared in 1812, was perhaps the first to call the public's attention to Jefferson's revision of the well-known opinion of domestic manufactures advanced in the *Notes on Virginia*. Melish's two volumes, in turn, with their wealth of detail on the progress of American manufactures, astonished Jefferson. In a number of private letters he explained that while he had earlier believed the workshops should remain in Europe and the United States should concentrate on what it could most advantageously produce "as a member of the great family of mankind," exchanging its agriculutral surpluses for European manufactures, he had been forced to conclude the world was not ready for this system—it was two worlds rather than one—and, therefore, "we must endeavor to make everything we want within ourselves, and have as little intercourse as possible with Europe in its present demoralized state." "We must now place the manufacturer by the side of the agriculturist," he declared in the most widely publicized of these letters, addressed to the Massachusetts Republican Benjamin Austin, in 1816. The independence and welfare of the nation required it. And to this end protectionism on a moderate scale won Jefferson's endorsement. He had come by degrees to the conception of a balanced economy of agriculture, commerce, and manufactures, fulfilling the Revolutionary prophesy of the new nation as "a world within itself." Yet he had not embraced the spirit and substance of the industrial revolution. As he did not wish his country to become "a city of Amsterdam," so he did not wish it to become "a city of Manchester." The usual insignia of industrialism—cities of spindles and smoke and steam, great stock companies, masses of propertyless operatives huddled in the poet's "dark satanic mills"—had no place in his thought. The clatter of spindles and the smoke of shops at Monticello was one thing; massed in a different environment, unredeemed by the virtues of nature, quite another. "I concur with you," he wrote to his old friend Peale, "in doubting whether the great establishments, by associated companies, are advantageous in this country. It is the household manufacture which is really precious." It was moral, healthy, and paternal within the beneficent circle of nature. What he embraced, then, was the household-handicraft-mill complex of an advanced agricultural society. He realized, of course, that manufacturing on a larger and more sophisticated scale, by "associated companies," would accompany this growth, at least in the populous eastern centers; but he hoped, quite literally, to place the manufacturer *by the side* of the husbandman and in this way to preserve the values of an agricultural society within an emerging manufacturing one.

Manufacturing was his hobby, agriculture his business, during these years. He continued to experiment with crops and rotations, fertilizers, plows, and threshing machines. For a time he was an enthusiast for benne (sesame), supposedly planted with great success in South Carolina and Georgia, and expected its oil would replace olive oil, butter, and lard in the American diet. But after a trial of three successive seasons in Albemarle, the net product extracted by the cast-iron press he had built was one gallon of oil. The good earth of Albemarle had deteriorated under his feet. To restore it he experimented with plaster, as a fertilizer, on the "Loudoun system" popularized by John A. Binns. In addition to deeper plowing, Jefferson championed the horizontal, or contour, plowing introduced in the Albemarle region by his son-in-law. The innovation materially reduced erosion and leaching. "The improvement of our soil from this course . . . ," Jefferson reported, "strikes everyone with wonder." And in point of beauty nothing could equal "the waving lines and rows winding along the face of the hills and vales." In 1817 he joined with other prominent planters of the region in founding the Albemarle Agricultural Society, a lively center of improving science for many years. Yet the condition of Virginia agriculture went from bad to worse. The sequel to peace was drought. Seeing that his own situation was becoming desperate, Jefferson placed his grandson Jeff in charge of the Albemarle farms in 1815 and several years later gave him the management of Poplar Forest as well. In effect, Jefferson ceased to be a practicing farmer.

Pressures of debt mixed with motives of patriotism in his decision to sell his great library to the nation in 1815. The consummate act of British barbarity, the burning of the Capitol near the close of the war, made ashes of the little congressional library. Three weeks after learning of this event, Jefferson wrote to Samuel Harrison Smith, asking him to act as his agent in the tender of his library to Congress. "You know my collection, its condition and extent," he said. "I have been fifty years making it, and have spared no pains, opportunity or expense, to make it what it is." Into the making had gone books purchased from Virginia estates, from Parisian booksellers, from friends and agents all over Europe, from American publishers and dealers, scoured from attics and the dustbins of courthouses, and many acquired *gratis* or by way of legacy, as from George Wythe. Jefferson supposed the library now numbered 9000 to 10,000 volumes (an overestimate), and while it embraced all branches of knowledge, it was peculiarly a library for American statesmen. "It is long since I have been sensible it ought not to continue private property, and had provided that, at my death, Congress should have the refusal of it, at their own price. But the loss they have incurred makes the present the proper moment for this accommodation without regard to the small remnant of time and the barren use of my enjoyment." Perhaps he might be permitted to retain during his life a few books chiefly classical and mathematical, which were the favorite amusements of his declining years. He enclosed the catalogue commenced in 1783 and kept up ever since. Included in its three main divisions, History, Philosophy, and Fine Arts, and the numerous sub-divisions, were 6500 volumes, not only books but rare colonial newspaper files and precious manuscripts in Virginia history, some of incalculable value, such as the records of the Virginia Company of London. They were arranged in his study in plain pine cases, stacked in tiers nine feet high, and so sturdy and compact that the cases needed only to be boarded and nailed up in front for shipment.

When Congress met in October the joint library committee at once reported a resolution authorizing a contract for purchase of the library. Some opposition arose in the House, chiefly from Massachusetts Federalists. The library was much too large, they said, and it contained many philosophical and infidel productions of no use to congressmen and insulting to the nation. The resolution passed with an amendment requiring the sanction of Congress before the purchase was completed. A Washington bookseller, Joseph Milligan, who knew the collection and was acceptable to both parties, returned an appraisal of $24,000. This was arbitrary to say the least. Milligan simply took the catalogue and allowing $10 for a folio, $6 for a quarto, $3 for an octavo, and $1 for a duodecimo added up the total. Had the library been appraised volume by volume, whether on original cost or replacement value, the figure would have been much higher. William Thornton, for one, thought Congress paid less than half the true value. But Jefferson seemed satisfied, and in December, over renewed opposition, Congress appropriated $23,950 for the acquisition. In March Jefferson described himself as "to the elbows in the dust of my book-shelves." Many books on loan had to be called in, each volume labeled and placed in accordance with the catalogue, and the cases nailed up. Eleven wagons carried the library to Washington in May. There it reposed in temporary quarters for four years before a commodious room in the north wing of the Capitol, now restored, was ready to receive it. Jefferson's books thus became the nucleus of one of the great libraries of the world. Unfortunately, the pyromania that took his first library also eventually consumed his second—two-thirds of the volumes were lost in the Library of Congress fire of 1851.

Jefferson applied three-quarters of the money received from Congress to the payment of pressing debts and at once laid out several hundred dollars of the remainder in the purchase of books. (He had, finally, reserved nothing from the sale.) Thus began his third library, a highly personal collection, especially notable for new editions of classical authors, running eventually to about a thousand volumes. While still in the dust of his old books, he was visited by a brilliant young Bostonian, George Ticknor, and his companion Francis C. Gray, who bore flattering letters of introduction from John Adams. Gray's journal of the visit is a poignant reminder that Monticello, in the waning years of Jefferson's life, was not the resplendent mansion it is today. Unkempt grounds, cluttered house, furnishings falling into decay: the picture, for Gray, was one of genteel shabbiness. Jefferson took to Ticknor at once, called him "the best bibliograph" he had ever encountered, and commissioned him to purchase a whole catalogue of books in Europe, whither he was bound to study modern languages and literature. He finally settled at the University of Gottingen together with another Massachusetts son, Edward Everett, later joined by a third, George Bancroft. This "Gottingen trio," drawn to new fountainheads of learning while Virginia's sons basked in twilight at home, later returned to their native land and opened exciting vistas of German romantic philosophy and literature to the mind. Ticknor saw that Jefferson's catalogue was attended to, though most of the books came from other hands in Paris and London. Common sense told Jefferson that he ought to leave off buying books. Consulting the morality tables some years earlier, in his sixty-ninth year, he discovered that he had but seven years to live. Of all the books he then owned there were not many he cared to read and he would probably decamp before he could read fifty by choice. Solicited to subscribe to a compendius European atlas, he said, "I have, at different periods, bought several 'present states of Europe, geographical and political,' and while I have been reading them, Bonaparte has shuffled all together and dealt out new hands." Riding had become more important than reading: "This is more likely to baffle the tables of morality than reading a $30 book." Still he could not live without books—certain books—and never ceased to acquire them.

In the varied intellectual life of retirement, Jefferson was midwife and nurse to several books, helped to translate two, and, while he wrote none himself, published a lengthy pamphlet in 1812 that was a dazzling piece of erudition. This purported to be a history of the facts and the law arising on them in the angry controversy between Edward Livingston and the government of the United States over the ownership of the Batture St. Marie adjacent to New Orleans. The batture was a long shoal or beach formed by the silt of the Mississippi. Covered with water during half the year, it was used as a free anchorage by the thousands of boats and rafts that descended the river; and during the other months, when above water-level, it served as a quay and source of sand and dirt for the city inhabitants. From time beyond memory the batture had been considered public property. Livingston, having defaulted to the Treasury and accepted a judgment in the amount of $100,000, had gone to New Orleans in 1803 to recoup his fortune. He at once became active against the Claiborne regime, of course; and realizing the great potential value of the batture, by some estimates in the neighborhood of half a million dollars, he acquired a financial stake in the property by taking up the legal case of the landholder fronting the beach. In 1807 the supreme court of the territory ruled, in behalf of Livingston and his client, that the batture, as alluvium, rightfully belonged to the owner of the land bordering the river. The public was outraged. Riot and bloodshed threatened when Livingston, now the principal claimant, commenced improvements that would, some feared, alter the channel of the river, embarrass navigation, and possibly even drown New Orleans during the annual spring inundation. Governor Claiborne, supposing title to the batture passed to the United States with the acquisition of Louisiana, appealed to Washington for aid. In November 1807, after full cabinet discussion and approval, Jefferson ordered Livingston's eviction, by force if necessary, as an intruder on the public lands. The decision of the territorial court was considered a nullity. The United States had not been a party to it and, besides, answered to no court on account of the national domain. The eviction notice was served, in part, under provision of the Squatters' Act of 1807. Jefferson viewed the action as a restoration of the batture to its former condition pending any adjudication of the title by Congress or land commissioners. Driven off in January, Livingston then went to Washington to argue his case. He was unsuccessful. Jefferson had laid the matter before Congress but it acquiesced in the executive's defense of the public title. Livingston did not acquiesce, however; and in May 1810, with amazing effrontery, he filed suit for trespass against Jefferson in the circuit court at Richmond and asked personal damages of $100,000, the same amount, as it happens, for which he was still in hock to the Treasury.

The suit broke like a summer's storm over Monticello. On the face of it, the idea that a former President could be hauled into court and possibly sent into bankruptcy for official actions taken on his judgment of the public interest seemed absurd. Jefferson trusted the government would come to his rescue if that became necessary; for the present, however, he had to defend himself, and indeed preferred the government to keep hands off lest the Federalists make a partisan scandal of the case. He would have felt little anxiety for the outcome but for the court, which was Marshall's circuit, and depending on the result there the case might go to the Supreme Court. Livingston, who had been a thorn in Jefferson's side for seven years, had obviously calculated the Chief Justice's "twistifications" of the law and enmity to the defendant in lodging the suit at Richmond. Jefferson retained three prestigious Virginia lawyers, George Hay, William Wirt, and Littleton W. Tazewell, and began to prepare a statement of the case for their guidance. It was hard work. Quite a volume of literature had already accumulated. The batture had a long and involved history. The law of the case ramified into French, Spanish, and Roman sources and called up the whole history of sovereign and riparian rights to navigable waters from Herodotus forward. Thirty years had passed since Jefferson had been at the bar, but he had not lost his touch with the law. Aided by his friends in Washington, especially Gallatin, his coadjutors in New Orleans, and the Richmond counsel, he developed his statement over eighteen months. How to plea presented a dilemma. He had three main options: the merits of the case, embracing defense of the public title; the discretion of the executive acting, even if in error, in the people's interest; the want of jurisdiction in the court at Richmond for a trespass committed in New Orleans. He preferred the first course, which would place the case before the public and, it was to be hoped, confirm the government's title to the batture. Still, in the torpor of years, he shrank from the immense labor and prolonged anxiety this must entail. Counsel finally presented all three pleas, plus three others, to the court in December 1811. The first, dismissal for want of jurisdiction, prevailed—reluctantly on the part of one of the two judges, Marshall.

Now Jefferson felt it was his duty to lay the facts before the public. He arranged to have 250 copies of his statement printed under the title, *The Proceedings of the Government of the United States in Maintaining the Public Right to the Beach of the Mississippi.* . . . The details are intricate. Basically, he argued that the batture, even if alluvium, belonged to the sovereign in French law governing navigable waters, and therefore passed to the United States in 1803; however, the batture was, in fact, part of the bed of the river and as such could never be alienated. A single individual, Livingston, had no right "to drown the city of New Orleans, or to injure, or change, of his own authority, the course or current of a river which is to give outlet to the productions of two-thirds of the whole area of the United States." Jefferson could scarcely restrain his indignation. And suppose his executive action had been in error, he asked, did he therefore become liable for his whole fortune? Certainly he could not be accused of malice or corruption when his conduct accorded with the custom of the city, the will of the people, the opinion of the governor, the attorney general, and the legislature of the territory, as well as of his own cabinet and, apparently, of Congress. "If a functionary of the highest trust, acting under every sanction which the Constitution has provided for his aid and guide, and with the approbation, expressed or implied, of its highest councils, still acts on his own peril, the honors of his country would be but snares to ruin him." Wirt described Jefferson's production very well when he called it "a piece of Greecian architecture" uniting airiness and solidity, beauty and power. Livingston published his answer; and by sheer persistence he eventually obtained title to the batture, enabling him, at last, to close his account with the government in 1830. It is pleasing to record that he enjoyed a friendly correspondence with the Sage of Monticello before his death.

Frequent requests came to Jefferson to revise the *Notes on Virginia*. He had collected materials for this purpose and recognized, of course, that certain opinions expressed in this pivotal work, while still spoken as gospel in some quarters, had undergone change or required elucidation; but he never found time to revise the *Notes*. Requests came for permission to publish his familiar letters to deceased friends, such as George Wythe, Thomas Paine, and Benjamin Rush. He declined. "To fasten a man to all his unreflected expressions, and to publish him to the world in that as his serious and settled form is a surprise on his own judgment and character." If the world would show a little patience, it would have time enough to judge his acts and character from the ample record of his life. He declined autobiography as well, except for the benefit of his family, and while he assembled personal notes and memoranda on the political history of the 1790's, he left this time-bomb to explode after his death. He was not indifferent to posthumous fame, otherwise he would not have so systematically preserved his papers, but he was remarkably patient about it.

His labors as a translator were in connection with two manuscripts of the French political economist, Destutt de Tracy. One of

947

the group of *Idéologues*, which included several of Jefferson's friends in France, Tracy had written a critical commentary on Montesquieu which he feared to publish at home. He asked Jefferson to attend to its translation and publication, anonymously, in the United States, whence its influence would reverberate back to France. Jefferson admired the work, thought it soundly republican and liberal, a useful corrective of Montesquieu's heresies, and, on the whole, "the most valuable political work of the present age." He induced Duane to undertake the translation and publication, though he contributed to the former, and the work appeared in 1811 under the title *A Commentary and Review of Montesquieu's Spirit of Laws*, with Jefferson's "author's preface" in the disguise of an unnamed Frenchman. So true, in fact, were its doctrines to those of the Sage of Monticello that the book was adopted as a text at William and Mary and some Frenchmen ascribed the authorship to him. Even Dupont was fooled and began to translate the book back into French. Jefferson persuaded him to desist. After Napoleon's exile, Tracy appeared publicly as the author of the original French version. So successful was this venture that he asked the same favor of Jefferson for his treatise on political economy. Duane botched the translation. Jefferson had to revise the whole—a daily drudgery of many weeks in the winter of 1815-16—and Milligan finally published it, with Tracy's name, in Washington.

As the years passed and death took its toll of the Founding Fathers, Jefferson and Adams became the great patriarchs of the nation's heritage. For the Virginian, at least, remembrance did not come easily. He derived little enjoyment from looking back over the ground he had traveled, the field strewn with the bodies of dead friends, himself standing "like a solitary tree . . . , its trunk indeed erect but its branches fallen off and its neighboring plants eradicated from around it." With the decay of memory, and its damnable tricks, he sometimes felt like a stranger to his own life. Public events—a remorseless crowding of events—had passed with such rapidity and confusion, he said, that they seemed like scenes in a magic lantern, vanishing quickly, leaving only a blur in the mind. He was little inclined to stare into the shadows of his own reflection and generally preferred to broach the future rather than recall the past. Still the history of his country was of immense importance to posterity. He could not and would not write it; but he opened himself freely to those who would, and there were many calls upon him for assistance.

His principal venture thus far in this enterprise was with Joel Barlow. It came to nought, as Barlow in 1811 returned seven boxes of Jefferson's papers and set off on a futile mission to bring Napoleon to his senses, dying instead with his retreating army in the snows of Poland in 1812. Another project, William Waller Hening's collection of the laws of Virginia, which Jefferson may be fairly said to have inspired, came to fruition after he left the presidency. He had gone to much trouble and expense to collect texts of the missing or forgotten laws of the province from the legislative beginnings in 1619. In 1796, when he loaned some of "these precious monuments of our history" to Wythe for an edition of the laws relative to lands, Jefferson wrote a letter, subsequently published by the General Assembly, imploring an edition of all the laws ever passed in Virginia. Hening, then a young Albemarle lawyer, undertook this work a decade later. Jefferson placed his indispensable collection at Hening's disposal and gave him every encouragement. The monumental *Statutes at Large*, the first work of its kind in the United States, began to appear in 1809 and concluded with the 13th volume in 1823. Jefferson had earlier loaned historical materials to John Daly Burk, whose *History of Virginia*, in three volumes to the Revolution, was dedicated to him "by a sort of national right." Louis Hue Girardin and Skelton Jones continued the work in a fourth volume, published in 1816, over which Jefferson's muse presided pencil in hand. Especially notable was the book's defense of his wartime governorship; indeed in these chapters it could be read as his personal vindication. His lawyer-friend Wirt, who had married an Albemarle lady and resided in the neighborhood in earlier years, repeatedly pumped him for recollections of Revolutionary times and, more especially, of Patrick Henry, whose biography he had undertaken to write. "Mr. Henry," said Wirt confidently in 1810, "seems to me a good text for a discourse on rhetoric, patriotism and morals." Jefferson could not unreservedly accept the premise; still, Wirt had literary as well as legal talents, as demonstrated by many Addisonian essays, so Jefferson encouraged him. Recalling Henry in all candor, lauding him as the greatest orator who ever lived, yet portraying him neither as saint nor as hero but as a lazy and ignorant backwoodsman, Jefferson sent the admiring author into a tailspin. "I despair of the subject," he declared. Torn between his splendid conception and unheroic, even impious, image Jefferson set before him, Wirt was sorry he had ever taken it up. He kept returning to the biography, however, and in 1816 pleaded with Jefferson to read the nearly complete manuscript. He agreed and offered some rather withering criticisms in the form of polite suggestions: "that Mr. Henry read Livy thro' once a year is a known impossibility," many passages were "too flowery for the sober taste of history," and some should be stricken altogether. Still he pronounced the work excellent. The judgment seemed more courteous than candid. Wirt shot back, should he publish it? Yes, by all means, said Jefferson, suppressing his fears. Published it was—a landmark in American hagiography.

While Jefferson steadfastly refused to dredge up his own past for the benefit of would-be biographers, he wrote a number of felicitous sketches of famous contemporaries, some of which became famous themselves. In the aftermath of the second war with England the nation decided to celebrate itself. A virtual industry grew up around the publication of elegant "repositories" of the lives and portraits of Revolutionary heroes and signers of the Declaration of Independence. The fame of that document soared, and the fame of its author, who was often consulted on its history, soared with it. Several of his biographical sketches, of Wythe and Franklin and Peyton Randolph, were written at the solicitation of compilers and publishers of Revolutionary lives. Others, such as the brilliant characterization of General Washington, occurred in the normal course of correspondence. In all this patriotic ferment little controversies arose. Was the Revolution set in motion by Massachusetts or Virginia? Marshall credited the former province with the origination of committees of correspondence. Wirt's *Henry* cited Jefferson's authority for the prior claim of Virginia and, also, of Henry over the Bay State hero, James Otis, in the Revolutionary vanguard. Jefferson did not become a polemicist in these matters, however. Undoubtedly his most important contribution to the annals of biography was the fifteen-page sketch of the life of Meriwether Lewis published in the two-volume *History* of the Lewis and Clark Expedition in 1814.

Jefferson had waited impatiently for this work for several years. Lewis had arranged for the publication of a definitive record before his death, and on that event General Clark assumed the responsibility. But neither knew anything of writing or publishing. What finally materialized, unfortunately, was not the journals themselves but a hurried narrative derived from the journals by two young authors in Philadelphia. A great deal remained to be done before this momentous chapter of history and science could be closed. The most precious parts—geographical, botanical, zoological, linguistic, and so on—had yet to go before the world. But despite Jefferson's continuing interest, the skill that presided over the performance of the expedition was not available for its liquidation.

Nature meant him to be a scientist, Jefferson had told himself many times, and he fancied he might take up this calling at last in studious retirement at Monticello. But it was too late: "Forty-two years of entire absorption by political duties scarcely permitting me as much attention to the more beloved studies of the natural sciences as would keep me where I once was, disqualify me from instructing those daily versed in their exercise and practice." Whole new worlds of natural science and philosophy and literature were coming into existence beyond his ken. Ticknor gave him glimpses of the astounding new intellectual world of Germany; but knowing neither the language nor the climate of romanticism he was barred from entrance. The principal diversions of his old age, as of his youth, were the ancient classics and mathematics. "My business," he wrote in his seventy-sixth year, "is to beguile the weariness of declining life, as I endeavor to do by the delights of classical reading and of mathematical truths and by the consolations of a sound philosophy, equally indifferent to hope and fear." In the realms of science, he advanced nothing new. One important contribution he had hoped to make, on the Indian languages, had been washed away in the waters of the James River as the trunk containing his collection of vocabularies fell to pirates on its passage from Washington in 1809. He remained president of the American Philosophical Society, very much in his climate, for six more years, finally insisting that he withdraw from this "sinecure" at the end of 1814. His learned letters ranged over a wide, and generally familiar, terrain: the "poison" of Hume and Blackstone, the moral sense, Epicurean philosophy, the history of the Greek ablative, Lord Napier's theorem for the solution of right-angled spherical triangles, the superiority of Linnaean classification to the systems of Cuvier and Blumenbach, the comparison of the American and Siberian mammoth, the new Spanish constitution, the history of hopperboys, weights and measures on a universal standard, and the value of neology in the enrichment and growth of language. Of the latter it might be observed that he had often been criticized, from the *Notes on Virginia* forward, for using words not to be found in standard dictionaries. As late as 1820 the citadel of New England letters, *The North American Review*, called him to account for *location, centrality, sparse*, and *grade*. To these purists who made grammar rather than strength or usage their guide, he replied that necessity obliged the Americans to invent new words for new things, to write and speak anew as they must think anew, "and should the language of England continue stationary, we shall probably enlarge our employment of it, until its new character may separate it in name as well as in power, from the mother tongue."

Jefferson was the magnet of the country intellectual circle in Albemarle. Over the years some of its brightest stars, like William Short and Robert Mills, had fled to Philadelphia, others to Richmond or elsewhere, and Jefferson's hope of attracting enlightened Europeans, like the French political economist Jean-Baptiste Say and the Portuguese savant Correa de Serra, never materialized, though his university became a magnet of another sort. But the prominent families, Randolphs, Carrs, Coleses, Cabells, Gilmers, and others, contained a wealth of talent, to which newcomers like Louis Girardin, William C. Rives, Nicholas P. Trist, and so on made impressive additions. Monticello was a country philosophical hall. In the late afternoons, when Jefferson gave himself up to society, friends and neighbors gathered around and were enthralled by his conversation, "light and attic," one observed, "having sometimes the agreeable levity of the French, at others the graver instruction of a philosopher, but always the simplicity and pleasantry which are among the characteristics of greatness." A stranger who had spent only a few days in this Socratic company said he could have spent an age without ennui: "so much freshness of character; nothing worn out or exhausted; such a magnanimous carelessness in the promulgation of his opinions; such various knowledge, so easy and cheerful a hospitality." Within the Albemarle circle, young Francis Walker Gilmer, earlier a pupil, was now his greatest pride. "In the vast dearth of scientific education in our state he presents almost the solitary object," Jefferson said of Gilmer. It was a melancholy confession of Virginia backwardness. Even Gilmer, with his fine talents for science of literature, became a slave to the law, like nearly every member of the Albemarle circle. The Abbé Correa, a regular summer guest from Philadelphia during eight years, shone in the opinion of everyone. He came on in 1813 with flattering introductions from Caspar Wistar, Dupont and others. Jefferson at once pronounced him "the greatest collection and best digest of science in books, men, and things" he had ever met with, "and with these the most amiable and engaging character." Correa was an *encyclopédist* of the old school, though especially well versed in geology and botany. During the fall of 1815 he and Gilmer accompanied Jefferson on a tour of the Peaks of Otter, the highest in Virginia's Blue Ridge, which he measured, and of the Natural Bridge, that "most sublime of nature's works," his own property, which he had not viewed for several decades. Jefferson had hoped that Correa might become a permanent member of the country circle, but he returned to Portugal in 1820.

The finest literary legacy of these autumn years was his correspondence with John Adams. The first essay toward renewal of the old friendship occurred in 1804 when Mrs. Adams wrote a letter of condolence to Jefferson on the death of his younger daughter. Jefferson had then invited a reunion, but political wounds had not healed and the exchange terminated on a sour note. In 1810 Benjamin Rush, a great friend of both men, took up the task of reconciliation. In response Jefferson sent his correspondence with Mrs. Adams to explain the difficulty. Some months later Edward Coles, Madison's private secretary at the time, called on Adams at Quincy. He talked freely of Jefferson and their political differences, and complained of his treatment by him; but after Coles assured him of Jefferson's continued affection, Adams burst out, "I always loved Jefferson, and still love him." When Coles's report reached Monticello, Jefferson at once wrote to Rush. "This is enough for me," he declared. Rush passed the word to Quincy, and Adams seized the olive branch. On January 1, 1812, he opened the correspondence with greetings on the new year and the promise of "two pieces of homespun" produced in his quarter of the Union. Jefferson, caught off-guard by Adams's humor, responded with a lecture on domestic manufactures, only the next day to discover that the "homespun" consisted of two volumes of *Lectures on Rhetoric and Oratory* by John Quincy Adams.

In a sense the contrast between humor and gravity in these opening letters characterized the entire correspondence of over fourteen years. Adams tended to be rollicking, Jefferson serious; Adams garrulous, Jefferson spare of diction; Adams bold, even reckless, in expression of opinion, Jefferson studied and reserved; Adams egocentric, Jefferson detached and, on the whole, much more interested in things observed and reflected upon than in himself. Adams's letters, which are the more sprightly, ran off in half-a-dozen directions at once. Jefferson's, more felicitous, tended to be rounded essays on some topic of learning—Indian ethnology, Greek pronunciation, the uses and abuses of grief, Christianity and the common law. Adams liked to speculate on history and politics and theology; Jefferson, while he ventured in these realms, was more drawn to scientific ones. Adams inclined to look back and reflect over the ground they had traversed, even to settle an old score or two; Jefferson seldom looked back and never engaged in recriminations. Adams wrote much more, about four times as much. The correspondence was a godsend to him. Jefferson, burdened with correspondents, could not keep up with him. The Quincy sage read more too. "Forty-three volumes read in one year, and twelve of them quartos!" Jefferson exclaimed. "Dear Sir, how I envy you! Half a dozen 8 vos. in that space of time are as much as I am allowed." Both men were keenly aware of their place in history, and as their Revolutionary comrades passed away one by one (Rush went in 1813), the bond between them strengthened.

"You and I ought not to die, before we have explained ourselves to each other," Adams declared. This seemed much more important to him than it did to Jefferson, who resisted all the way; and in the end, at least in the branch of Adams's chief concern, political philosophy, it cannot be said that they succeeded. About most things they agreed, or at any rate did not choose to differ, from the metaphysical nonsense of Plato to the despotism of Napoleon. But between them there remained fundamental differences of opinion. One that was aired, quite pleasantly, concerned aristocracy. Adams broached the subject. Aristocracy had always been his *bête noire*, but considering it inevitable and in some ways valuable in any society, he had supposed even republican constitutions must arrange for it. Jefferson, in reply, distinguished between *natural* and *artificial* aristocracy, the former founded on virtue and talents, the latter on wealth and birth. "The natural aristocracy I consider as the most precious gift of nature, for the instruction, the trusts, and government of society. . . . May we not even say," he opined, "that that form of government is the best, which provides most effectually for a pure selection of these natural aristoi into the offices of government? The artificial aristocracy is a mischievous ingredient in government, and provision should be made to prevent its ascendancy." How? Adams would lock "the pseudo-aristoi" into a separate chamber of the legislature. But that would institutionalize the evil. It was an unjust intrusion on the popular will; nor was it necessary to protect wealth from numbers. "I think the best remedy," Jefferson said, "is that provided in all our constitutions, to leave to the citizens the free election and separation of the aristoi from the pseudo-aristoi, of the wheat from the chaff. In general they will elect the really good and wise." And he went on to speak of the one thing, the general diffusion of knowledge, still wanted in his own state to secure the happy result. Adams, answering with his usual candor, rejected Jefferson's basic distinction. The natural and the pseudo-aristoi were one and the same, he said, and every aristocracy tends to become hereditary. While he could match Jefferson's expletives against Calvinism, there was still a gloomy predestinarianism in Adams's view of society, which suggested his Puritan lineage, and which the sunny Virginian repelled. Again and again Adams gloatingly recalled his friend to the exploded hopes—Jefferson's, not his—of the French Revolution. "Let me ask you, very seriously my friend, Where are now in 1813, *the perfection and perfectibility* of human nature? Where is now, the progress of the human mind? Where is the amelioration of society?" *Touché!* Nevertheless, despite the shock to his best hopes, Jefferson serenely pointed to progress in the face of catastrophe and voiced his faith in the ultimate triumph.

The reconciliation was but a year and a half old when Adams called Jefferson to account for portraying him as a kind of vandal against science and progress in a letter written to Joseph Priestley in 1801. The letter had turned up in the *Memoirs of the Late Reverend Theophilus Lindsay*, published in London. Jefferson offered a tactful explanation and expressed indignation at the publication of his private letters. He was less anxious about this particular letter, offensive to Adams, than another to Priestley in April 1803 on the subject of religion. In this epistle, now published, he had sketched the plan of a comparative view of the moral doctrines of the ancients, the Jews, and Jesus. He had hoped Priestley might undertake this work. The great philosopher-theologian died a few months later, though not before he had written *The Doctrines of Heathen Philosophy Compared with Revelation* in response to Jefferson's request. Adams now, in 1813, encouraged his friend to take up the work on his own account. Jefferson explained that he had, just after his letter to Priestley, written a brief syllabus, or outline, of the proposed inquiry. Only Priestley and Rush, to whom he had sent copies, were let in on the secret. Actually, the privileged circle had been somewhat larger, and Jefferson now admitted Adams to it.

This important chapter in the history of Jefferson's religious opinions had its beginnings in a promise made to Rush, a devout Christian, in the course of evening conversations in 1798–99 which, as Jefferson remembered, "served as an anodyne to the afflictions of the crisis through which our country was then laboring." Rush believed Christianity laid the groundwork of republicanism. Jefferson could not follow him to the acceptance of revelation or sectarian dogma of any sort but promised to give him a view of the subject, the result of a life of inquiry and reflection, very different from the "anti-Christian system" ascribed to him by clerical and political enemies. Rush reminded him of the promise during the election of 1800. Jefferson had not forgotten it. His views, he said, while they should be acceptable to rational Christians, would probably not reconcile the *genus irratabile vatum* who had seized upon the recent delusion to aid their pretensions of establishing a particular form of Christianity in the United States. "The returning good sense of our country threatens abortion to their hopes, and they believe that any portion of power confided to me will be executed in opposition to their schemes, and they believe truly, for I have sworn upon the altar of God eternal hostility against every form of tyranny over the mind of man." As the tone of this passage suggests, Jefferson's religious libertarianism became more deeply involved in anti-clericalism under the attack of pulpit politicians in 1800.

Not until April 1803 did he fulfill, in some part, his commitment to Rush. At the moment of leaving Monticello he received Priestley's little book, *Socrates and Jesus Compared.* This touched his own view, and he ruminated the subject on the road back to Washington. There he at once set down his Syllabus of an Estimate of the Merit of the Doctrines of Jesus, Compared with Those of Others. In this outline of less than a thousand words he reached the conclusion that the system of morals broached by Jesus, "if filled up in the true style and spirit of the rich fragments he left us, would be the most perfect and sublime that has ever been taught by man." The ancient heathen moralists, their teachings uncluttered by the corruptions and superstitions of Christianity, had won his allegiance when young, but he now thought them deficient on two serious counts. So far as they aimed at "tranquillity of mind" they were "really great." This was always an important consideration with Jefferson, and he continued to seek instruction from Seneca, Cicero, Epicurus, and other ancient moralists to the day of his death. But they had not developed man's duties to his fellows "within the circle of benevolence" or pushed their scrutinies into the recesses of the human heart. Neither had the Jews, whose ideas of the deity were degrading and whose ethics were "repulsive and anti-social." This was left to Jesus. Many disadvantages attended his teachings: he wrote nothing himself; the rich patrons of learning opposed him, and so the commitment of his teachings to writing fell to unlettered men who, moreover, wrote from memory after the transactions of his life had passed; a victim of the "combination of the altar and the throne" at an early age, he was not spared the time or the maturity to perfect his system; only fragments survived, which descended to posterity "mutilated, misstated, and often unintelligible," and still more disfigured by "the corruptions of schismatizing followers." Even so, the universal philanthropy Jesus inculcated, gathering all mankind into one family, together with his juster notions of God, his appeal to the tribunal of the heart, and his teaching of a future state of rewards and punishments as an incentive to moral conduct—in this his system was sublime.

Such is "my religious creed," Jefferson said. Whether or not it made him a Christian in the theological sense, he did not care. The moral branch of religion alone concerned him; the dogmatic branch of the priests and metaphysicians corrupted the pure and simple principles of Jesus. "I am a Christian," he declared, "in the only sense he wished any one to be; sincerely attached to his doctrines, in preference to all others; ascribing to himself every *human* excellence; and believing he never claimed any other." The question of Christ's humanity or divinity, being theological, was purposely omitted from the Syllabus. He sent copies to Rush, Priestley, several members of the cabinet, John Page, and his two daughters. All were under strict instructions not to expose it to anyone. It was a matter between God and himself; nor did he wish to countenance by any act of his the presumption of those who would erect a public tribunal over the rights of conscience. He had placed the document in these few friendly hands, he said, that they might judge the libels published against him and, presumably, secure the sanctity of his grave after death. He did not proselytize; he had no public object in view. Still he believed that his opinions, if fully developed, might form the basis of a broad common faith, a *consenus gentium*, uniting all men of reason and liberality around a hard core of morality, discovered in the moral sense, and a benevolent god discovered by inquiry into nature. Christianity might thus be saved from both the priests and the infidels. He was fond of saying, with Bolingbroke, "there would never have been an infidel, if there had never been a priest." Jesus was the greatest reformer of morals and scourger of priestcraft who ever lived, Jefferson declared, and on these points natural religionists like himself had underestimated his character. For this reason he encouraged Priestley to take up the work of inquiry and reconciliation along the lines sketched in the Syllabus and, indeed, already carried some way by the great Unitarian. Jefferson had been deeply influenced by Priestley's *Corruptions of Christianity* (1782) and other works which, with Conyers Middleton's writings, he said, formed the groundwork of his religious faith. Priestley was a Socinian, who denied the Trinity, virgin birth, original sin, vicarious atonement, the divine inspiration of Scripture, and so on. Yet he subscribed to revelation and the miracles, preached such curious doctrines as the resurrection of the body, though not of the

958

soul, and prophesied a second coming—a millennium of the Enlightenment. If much of Priestley's theology was unacceptable to the secular-minded Jefferson, he fully entered into the spirit of his return to primitive Christianity. And Priestley, who championed Jefferson's political cause, recognized in him a religious friend as well, and even had the temerity to dedicate his last major book, the huge *General History of the Christian Church* (1802–03), to Jefferson.

There was still a second part of the work Jefferson had in mind. On the premises of the Syllabus the teachings of Jesus had been disfigured and corrupted; so it was necessary to strip away the impurities and lay bare the plain and unsophisticated moral texts. Sometime after Priestley's death, during several desultory evenings in Washington, Jefferson took a New Testament, cut from the books of the Evangelists those verses that had the authentic stamp of Jesus' mind and imagination, "as easily distinguished as diamonds in a dunghill," and arranged the text in an octavo of forty-six pages which he called the "Philosophy of Jesus." He mentioned this to no one until several years after his retirement. The publication in 1813 of his letters to Priestley alerted him to the danger of his Syllabus bursting upon the public. When Rush died in that year, Jefferson implored his son to return this document. The Syllabus remained a secret. In 1816 Francis Adrian Van der Kemp, a versatile scholar and Unitarian preacher who had come to the United States in 1788, a refugee of the abortive Dutch revolution, asked Jefferson for a copy of the Syllabus he had seen while visiting Adams at Quincy. Jefferson complied, adding the usual injunction. Van der Kemp liked it so much he begged Jefferson to permit its publication, quite anonymously, in an English theological journal. Surprisingly, he consented; and it appeared in the *Monthly Repository of Theological and General Literature* in 1816 with ascription to "an eminent American statesman." This was more ascription than Jefferson had bargained for. Fortunately, so obscure was the journal in the United States, it was never picked up.

Yet at this very time the word circulated that Jefferson had changed his religious opinions and planned to publish a book on the subject. He received letters welcoming his conversion to Christ. Part of the the mysterious infection stemmed from the republication of the letters to Priestley in a Boston volume, *American Unitarianism.*

The principal source, however, was a letter to Charles Thomson, his old comrade, who had let it go into the press. In the letter Jefferson spoke of his Philosophy of Jesus. "It is a document in proof that *I am a real Christian*, that is to say, a disciple of the doctrines of Jesus, very different from the Platonists, who call *me* infidel. . . ." He went on to say that if he had the time he would improve this first essay by the addition of Greek, Latin, and French texts ranged in columns side by side with the English, perhaps subjoining a translation of Gassendi's Syntagma of the doctrines of Epicurus, which he still thought the most virtuous and rational system of the ancients. To those who inquired, mainly on the basis of this letter, of his conversion to Christianity, Jefferson denied it, at least in so far as any change of opinion was implied, and as for writing a book he "should as soon think of writing for the reformation of Bedlam." All he had in mind, solely for his personal satisfaction, was the project mentioned to Thomson: a bible of primitive Christianity. For this he needed New Testaments in the four languages, all of roughly the same typography. (The Hebrew text should have been included but Jefferson did not know the language.) He began to assemble these in 1816. Either because the bibles or the time failed him, the work was not completed until 1819. He called this scissors-and-paste book of 164 pages, two columns to the page, "The Life and Morals of Jesus of Nazareth," and had it bound in red morocco. Apparently no one, not even in his immediate family, knew of its existence until after his death. The Syllabus with this work constitute what is sometimes called The Jefferson Bible.

Jefferson said he was a sect to himself so far as he knew. He continued, as in younger days, to aid churches of different denominations in his neighborhood and often attended their services; but he belonged to no church. He followed with interest the Unitarian controversy in New England and once predicted "there is not a young man living in the United States who will not die a Unitarian." In Unitarianism he saw the possibilities of a unifying religion of humanity, and this new accent counterpointed the earlier individualism of Jefferson's religious creed. But he was not a Unitarian. Rather than seeking "the country of spirits," he preferred to rest his head on "that pillow of ignorance which the benevolent Creator has made so soft for us, knowing how much we should be forced to use it." Deep or moving religious experience seems never to have touched him. He had discovered in his youth that reason was the only oracle given to man by God. And as he wrote confidently in 1814: "I have followed it faithfully in all important cases, to such a degree at least as leaves me without uneasiness, and if on minor occasions I have erred from its dictates, I have trust in him who made us what we are, and knows it was not his plan to make us always unerring. He has formed us moral agents, not that, in the perfection of his state, he can feel pain or pleasure from anything we may do: he is far above our power: but that we may promote the happiness of those with whom he has placed us in society, by acting honestly towards all, benevolently to those who fall within our way, respecting sacredly their rights bodily and mental, and cherishing especially their freedom of conscience, as we value our own. I must ever believe that religion substantially good which produces an honest life, and we have been authorized . . . to judge the tree by its fruits. Our particular principles of religion are a subject of accountability to our god alone. I inquire after no man's and trouble none with mine: nor is it given to us in this life to know whether yours or mine, our friend's or our foe's, is exactly right." Given this summation, what had he changed? Not much. He still rejected revelation, the divinity of Christ, the miracles, the atonement, and so on, without which Christianity was nothing in the eyes of believers. He did not even accept Jesus on his own terms, for Jesus was a spiritualist by the grace of God and he a materialist by the grace of science. But he had brought the morals of Jesus, above all the love of man, within the perimeters of the older faith of the Enlightenment. The simple precepts of Jesus infused a universal ethic founded on the natural rights of man. In this sense Jesus *was* the savior, not of priests and metaphysicians only, but of all men; and Jefferson was the *real* Christian he professed to be.

Founding the University

On his agenda of unfinished business the septuagenarian Jefferson gave first place to education. "I have two great measures at heart, without which no republic can maintain itself in strength," he wrote soon after his retirement. "1. That of general education, to enable every man to judge for himself what will secure or endanger his freedom. 2. To divide every county into hundreds, of such size that all the children of each will be within reach of a central school in it." On these "two hooks," he often said, the future of republican government depended. The wards, or hundreds, while associated with primary education, would be miniature republics, drawing every citizen immediately into the administration of local affairs and voicing the will of the people through all the expanding circles— county, state, and federal—of Jefferson's concentric commonwealth. The wards would be the Virginia equivalent of New England townships, which had proven their strength and vitality in the embargo repeal. Both proposals, wards and general education, traced back to Jefferson's Bill for the More General Diffusion of Knowledge in 1778. The crucial defeat of his young years, he hoped it might ripen into the triumph of his old age.

Virginia had never been very hospitable to his reforms, and was perhaps less so now than at the crest of the Revolutionary wave. The prophet was honored but unarmed in his native country. The constitution of 1776 still stood as an obstacle to democratic government. A new movement for its reform arose west of the Blue Ridge. Jefferson furnished it with an ideology and a platform, marking the farthest advance of his democratic thought, but he declined to become a gladiator in this embattled cause. Reform, such as it was, came only after his death and could not have come sooner because of conservative fears of his influence. Slavery emancipation, on the gradual plan he had formed during the Revolution and publicized, like the constitutional reforms, in the *Notes on Virginia,* was another crucial item on the agenda. But Jefferson despaired of its success; and he would not waste the waning energies of the years that remained to him in a cause certain to deprive him of all power for good in other and more promising directions. So he made education, arduous yet not impossible of fulfillment, his "holy cause." "I have only this singular anxiety in the world," he wrote in 1817. "It is a bantling of 40 years birth and nursing, and if I can once see it on its legs, I will sing with sincerity and pleasure my nunc dimittis." In the end he could sing indeed, though not for the plan of general education. Again it went down to defeat. In the process, however, he brought to fruition his dream of a university. This had been part of the original plan—the apex of a comprehensive system of public education arising like a pyramid from the primary schools. To erect the apex without the base was doubtless an act of folly; yet this is what the Virginians attempted, and Jefferson, knowing it was folly, took what pleasure he could in the result.

The University of Virginia, chartered in 1819, was as much his personal creation as Monticello, the Declaration of Independence, or the Lewis and Clark expedition. And perhaps nothing contained so well the dominant forces of his life and mind, of democracy and enlightenment and nationality, as his vision of a great university. The vision passed through several phases before it came to realization. Initially, in 1779, Jefferson sought to transform William and Mary into a secular institution of university caliber. He failed in this and gradually lost all hope of reforming his alma mater. In 1794 he felt keen interest in the proposal of a Swiss exile from revolution, François d'Ivernois, to remove the whole College of Geneva to the United States. When the General Assembly passed up the opportunity, Jefferson recommended it to President Washington in the belief that this seminary, one of the finest in Europe in his opinion, might become the foundation of a national university. But Washington thought the hazards of transplanting a foreign college, and a foreign-speaking faculty, too great. Jefferson himself had earlier warned against one experiment in this line, the establishment of a French academy of arts and sciences in Richmond under the direction of Quesnay de Beaurepaire, which had already failed.

In 1800 he first seriously turned his thoughts to the creation of a wholly new institution in his native state. From his friends Priestley and Dupont he requested the plan of a university "so broad and liberal and modern as to be worth patronizing with public support, and be a temptation to the youth of other states to come and drink of the cup of knowledge and fraternize with us." Priestley offered a series of useful suggestions, while Dupont furnished an elaborate plan of national education. Neither altogether suited Jefferson's purposes. At this stage he aimed at a state university, modestly begun but large in conception, and national in spirit and service and outline. In January 1805 he wrote a four-page prospectus for such a university in reply to the request of Littleton Waller Tazewell, who seemed to believe the General Assembly had been brought to the point of action. Already Georgia, North Carolina, South Carolina, and Tennessee had established state universities, and though they existed mostly on paper, Virginia could not be indifferent to this movement. The letter to Tazewell was the genesis of Jefferson's plan for the University of Virginia. Emphasizing the modernity of his conception, he called not only for a redefinition of higher education but for a university geared to the constantly advancing knowledge of the times. "Science is progressive," he wrote. "What was useful two centuries ago is now become useless; e.g., one half of the professorships of William and Mary. What is now deemed useful will in some of its parts become useless in another century. . . . Everyone knows that Oxford, Cambridge, the Sorbonne, etc. are now a century or two behind the sciences of the age." Perhaps as an inducement to the legislature, Jefferson offered the legacy of his library to the meditated university. But it was not to be. When Virginia remained mute after the passage of two years, Jefferson set aside his hopes in this direction, and in December 1806 recommended a national university to Congress. The project concerted with Joel Barlow and others was still another engagement in the forty-year campaign.

Jefferson had been in retirement for five years before he became associated with the enterprise that led to the establishment of the University of Virginia. Several of his neighbors, including Peter Carr as president of the board, were endeavoring in 1814 to set up a private secondary school, Albemarle Academy, in Charlottesville. Petty academies of this kind, Jefferson told Adams, dotted the state. "They commit their pupils to the theatre of the world with just taste enough of learning to be alienated from industrious pursuits, and not enough to do service in the ranks of science." Placed on the board of the fledgling academy, he at once set out to escalate it into a college and then into a university. In September he drafted a bill to accomplish the first step, the conversion of Albemarle Academy into Central College. The bill failed in the ensuing session of the legislature but passed in February 1816. By the act of incorporation Central College was a private non-sectarian seminary with no other resources than it could raise from the sale of the two glebes in Albemarle (the parish lands of the old Established Church), from voluntary subscriptions, and from lottery. However, the charter provided for a liberal enlargement of the educational plan to reach the objects of a state university and divested the college of its local character by placing the appointment of the Board of Visitors in the governor and making him an ex officio member. The Governor, Wilson Cary Nicholas, named Jefferson's friends, including Madison and Monroe, to the board. In the space of two years a lifeless academy had been transformed into the design of a state university.

But Jefferson aimed at more than a university. That remained, as in 1778, the capstone of a general plan of public education. He revived this plan in his letter to Carr transmitting the college bill in 1814. Three grades of instruction, elementary, general, and professional, corresponded more or less to the three classes of society, the laboring, the gentry, and the learned. The primary schools, again as in 1778, contemplated the division of counties into wards and three years of rudimentary education at the public expense to ensure that everyone was equipped for the business of life and the duties of citizenship. In 1796 the General Assembly had given the county courts the option of laying out aldermanic districts, like Jefferson's wards, and assessing the populace for public schools. But the local magistrates had not exercised this option, which aroused Jefferson against these "oligarchs," and Virginia slid into deeper ignorance than she had known at her birth. The "General Schools" of Jefferson's second grade combined the features of a secondary or grammar school and a college. They would be terminal for youth whose position or calling required modest polish, while they would be preparatory for those destined to the pursuits of science and the learned professions. Essentially classical schools, they would also embrace philosophy, mathematics, and natural science. These "colleges," as Jefferson began to call them, would be established by the commonwealth in districts within a day's ride of every citizen. Although aided by the state, they would not be free except for the few "public foundationers," the natural aristoi of the poor, as proposed in the original plan. In the third grade, the professional, "each science is to be taught in the highest degree it has yet attained." His conception was still vague, but he envisioned a university with specialized instruction in the useful sciences and learned professions of the time. The most novel feature of this plan was the provision for a school of technical philosophy serving artisans and workmen—machinists, brewers, ship-wrights, glassmakers—through evening courses and maintained, like the ward schools, at public expense. While one might wish Jefferson had persevered with this idea of an evening trades school, he probably realized its impracticality in Virginia and, accordingly, dropped it from later plans. The letter to Carr throughout was quite abstract, a philosophical view, and addressed to no specific institution.

Over a year later the scheme Jefferson had sketched for his nephew, who had died in the interim, came prominently into the deliberations at Richmond. It was published, and Charles Fenton Mercer drafted a general education bill based on the plan. The bill passed the House but came to grief in the Senate. Both houses concurred in February 1816 in a resolution requesting the Directors of the Literary Fund to report a comprehensive plan of education from the primary schools through the university. The Literary Fund had been set up in 1810 to receive state income from miscellaneous sources and to aid, principally, the education of the poor. Jefferson eyed this resource for the state university postulated by the February resolution. If the Literary Fund went to the support of primary schools nothing would be left for the university or the district colleges. The decision of the legislature on the destiny of the Literary Fund would largely determine the future of public education in Virginia. While he proceeded to build Central College as the shell of the state university, Jefferson worked to shape the whole system of education. The Governor, Nicholas, gave him a sympathetic ear, of course, as did certain members of the assembly; but his principal liaison with that body, and his leading coadjutor in the establishment of the university, was Joseph C. Cabell.

A friend and neighbor, deeply interested in the cause of public education, one of the trustees of Central College, and the representative of the Albemarle district in the Senate, Cabell headed the cadre of "Monticello men" at Richmond. He conferred at length with Jefferson in the summer of 1817. At his request Jefferson drafted bills for the three grades of education. The Bill for Establishing Elementary Schools was on the usual plan. Requiring the support of these schools by tax levies on the residents of each ward, proportioned to property, Jefferson's system reserved the Literary Fund for the colleges and the university. Cabell presented this bill, with the companion Bill for the Establishment of District Colleges and University, to the chairman of the Committee on Schools and Colleges, after striking certain interesting provisions. Jefferson had wished to exclude clergymen as visitors (trustees) of the elementary schools, to bar religious instruction inconsistent with the tenets of any sect or denomination, and, borrowing from the example of the new Spanish constitution, to impose a test of literacy for citizenship on the rising generation. On the advice of Nicholas, Thomas Ritchie, and others, Cabell omitted these invitations to political cavil. Objections to the plan arose on the score of practicality; the mass of people, it was said, would not submit to taxation for education, and the rich would not contribute to the education of the poor. Jefferson answered in a letter to Cabell published in Ritchie's *Enquirer*. Among other things, he pointed out that the cost of the lower schools amounted to only three and three-quarter cents per capita for the entire state and that the rich had an important stake in raising up honest and useful citizens from the mass of poor. Indeed, in the equalitarian society of the United States, their children or grandchildren might well be poor. But Jefferson's bill did not emerge from the committee. Offered as a substitute in the House, it received few votes. What passed was an act providing for appropriations of the Literary Fund to the education of the poor only in "charity schools," so far as they might be conducted in the counties. This was a grave disappointment, and it proved decisive for elementary education in Virginia until after the Civil War. Nor was any provision made for district colleges. Yet the defeat breathed life into the university. When the school bill came to the Senate, Cabell engrafted upon it a $15,000 annuity from the Literary Fund for the support of a state university. A commission was to be appointed by the Governor to fix the site of the institution and develop its educational plan.

Jefferson rejoiced in this half-victory. He felt confident that the commission would choose the site of Central College for the university. During the past year the board under Jefferson's direction as Rector had bought 200 acres of high ground just west of Charlottesville, commenced the building, and even begun to assemble a faculty. Precious little money had been raised. Determined to call attention to this struggling infant, Jefferson assumed the disguise of an itinerant correspondent to write a flattering prospectus of the university-to-be for publication in the *Richmond Enquirer*. The cornerstone of the first building was laid with appropriate ceremony in the presence of Jefferson, Madison, and Monroe on October 6, 1817.

By then the architectural plan had been settled. The conception of an "academical village" had taken form in Jefferson's mind at least a dozen years before. He had broached it in his letter to Tazewell. Consulted in 1810 on a new college in Tennessee, he advised against the common practice of erecting a large central building, unfriendly to health, study, morals, and manners. "It is infinitely better," he said, "to erect a small and separate building for each separate professorship, with only a hall below for his class, and two chambers above for himself; joining the lodges by barracks for a certain portion of students, opening into a covered way to give a dry communication between all the schools. The whole of these arranged around an open square of grass and trees, would make it, what it should be in fact, an academical village, instead of a large and common den of noise, of filth and of fetid air." What evolved from this conception in 1817 was a rectangle open at one of the longer sides, alternating modest two-story pavilions with a series of flat-roofed barracks, or dormitories, of one story, the whole united in front by a covered colonnade. Jefferson wished the pavilions to be "chaste models of the orders of architecture taken from the finest remains of antiquity," not alone for their inherent beauty but in order to instruct and elevate the taste of the students. He asked William Thornton and Benjamin Latrobe to sketch their ideas. Both responded generously. They influenced the design of some of the pavilions, no two alike, though in the final analysis the architectural work, like everything else, was Jefferson's. Latrobe suggested the idea of a dominant central building, which Jefferson matured into the Rotunda, a scale model of the Roman Pantheon adapted to the service of a library.

The plan underwent some change when Jefferson became better acquainted with the terrain. The site offered a narrow ridge declining from north to south and allowing but 200 feet of level ground between the buildings on either side. So Jefferson rearranged the three-sided rectangle into two long porticoed rows, descending in three levels with the slope of the ground, and open at both ends, though to be filled at the north by the Rotunda. Latrobe objected to the east-west exposure thereby given to the conjoined residences of professors and students. The west winds would freeze them in winter and the sun bake them in summer. Jefferson conceded the objection but the terrain was a law of nature. Other parts of the plan were settled as the building went forward. The gardens of the professors would be placed at the rear of their pavilions and separated by serpentine walls. The "hotels" for feeding the students, conducted by French families speaking their native tongue, would be thrown on rear streets, and joined by additional dormitories in arcaded ranges paralleling the rows on the lawn. How far Jefferson would be able to go with his plan remained to be seen. In 1817, in the *Enquirer* article, he hoped for four professors, hence four pavilions and the dormitories to go with them, by 1820. But he was then writing under the restraint of a college plan. The university bill drafted for Cabell called for ten professors, each a separate school, each with its own pavilion.

Jefferson lavished his love of classical architecture on the pavilions. "We are sadly at a loss here for a Palladio," he wrote to Madison in November 1817. All of his three editions had gone to Washington and nobody in the neighborhood had one. Obviously Madison or someone came to his rescue, for the façades of the pavilions were derived from Palladio and, in some instances, from the antique models themselves, such as the Theater of Marcellus and the Bath of Diocletian. Some of the first occupants of the buildings complained of Jefferson's "logarithmic" adherence to Palladian rule for the sake of external appearance to the sacrifice of interior livability. The criticism may have been just. He believed a degree of splendor would contribute to the success of the institution, most immediately in the attraction of a superior faculty. And certainly his great achievement was not in the individual buildings themselves, whether viewed from the outside or the inside—only the Rotunda qualified in this respect as a monument of architectural genius—but in the unified articulation of the whole, not alone for its dramatic beauty but for its exquisite adaptation to the educational purposes to be served. Ticknor, when he first gazed on this serried mass of red brick and white columns in 1824, called it "more beautiful than anything architectural in New England, and more appropriate to a university than is to be found, perhaps, in the world." And Lewis

Mumford, a century later, placed Jefferson's creation in a rank by itself in the nation's architecture for the succeeding fifty years. Imitative in classical details, the over-all design was one of unparalleled originality. No prototype has ever been discovered for it. Reference has sometimes been made to the Reverend Samuel Knox's *Essay on the Best System of Liberal Education,* winner of an Amercian Philosophical Society prize in 1799. Jefferson had surely read this essay and learned from it; indeed, Knox was the first man offered an appointment to the faculty of Central College. In his discussion of the physical design of a university, Knox proposed the grouping of buildings around a square in a manner similar to Jefferson's "academical village"; but he imposed smaller squares, like graduated blocks, one inside the other until all freedom and openness was lost. Classical sources have sometimes been cited. And undoubtedly the layout of Roman country villas entered into Jefferson's conception, as it did into Monticello, which itself bears visual resemblances to the University; but this is the most that can be said. During these years Jefferson designed a number of buildings in the Albemarle region—courthouses, jails, country houses, even a church—but before the University they pale into insignificance. This was a masterpiece, and a heroic one at that, for the raising of columns, capitals, and entablatures in the Virginia upcountry was not easy work, and Jefferson made himself personally responsible for every last detail.

In the spring of 1818 he was appointed to the commission charged with choosing the site and developing the plan of the state university. The principal competition to Charlottesville came from Williamsburg, in the tidewater, and Lexington and Staunton in the Valley. William and Mary, at the former place, feared the rivalry of a state university. The old college had declined steadily. Jefferson never gave a thought to its rehabilitation, nor did he consider it a serious threat to his ambitions for Central College. The claims of the Valley were more troublesome from the standpoint both of geography and population. The Valley was the fastest growing section of Virginia. Jefferson supported its claims, and the claims of the Transmontane beyond, for political equality through the reform of the Virginia constitution. Staunton aspired to become the new capital of the commonwealth, and feared the location of the university in Charlottesville would impair its chances. Lexington, farther to the south, boasted a going seminary, Washington College (later Washington and Lee), for elevation to higher status. Sectarian religionists gathered around both William and Mary and Washington College, the former Episcopal, the latter Presbyterian; and neither could look with equanimity on a secular institution fathered by the Sage of Monticello. The commission, being formed on senatorial districts, gave the balance of influence to the country east of the Blue Ridge. During the summer Jefferson confidently developed his strategy and wrote a report that might serve as a draft for the commission's educational plan.

The commission met at Rockfish Gap, high in the Blue Ridge nearly thirty miles west of Monticello, on August 1–4. Jefferson made the strenuous journey on horseback. From the moment the commission gathered around tables in the room of a local tavern and chose him to preside, everything went his way. He had prepared a large map showing Charlottesville's location exactly at the geographical and population center of the state. If this argument was not conclusive in itself, there were the added persuasions of his fame and reputation, his leadership in the cause of education, and the prospects of a new institution neither wearied by age nor fettered by parochial or sectarian ties. The commission chose Charlottesville and Central College with little difficulty. And as chairman of a committee to draw up the proposed plan of education, Jefferson offered the report he had already written.

The Rockfish Gap Report, one of the great documents from his pen, was not addressed to "an assembly of philosophers," he said, but to the Virginia General Assembly, which must act on the recommendations of the commission. Written with a view to influencing the legislative decision, it was, in this sense, a political production, and should not be taken as a complete or definitive guide to Jefferson's mind on the subject of higher education. In his educational labors, as in others, he never articulated his whole thought. His ideas were in constant motion and seldom abstracted from immediately practical objectives. Still the Report of 1818 has exceptional theoretical interest. He began with definitions of the aims and character of primary and secondary education. It was impossible to plan a university in an educational vacuum or to expect it to succeed in its mission without strong foundations in the lower schools. So he entered an impassioned plea for public education in general. "Education . . . engrafts a new man on the native stock, and improves what in his nature was vicious and perverse into qualities of virtue and social worth. And it cannot be but that each generation succeeding to the knowledge acquired by all those who preceded it, adding to it their own acquisitions and discoveries, and handing the mass down for successive and constant accumulation, must advance the knowledge and well-being of mankind, not *infinitely*, as some have said, but *indefinitely*, and to a term which no one can fix or foresee." Voicing once again this hope of the Enlightenment, Jefferson showed little patience with owl-like creatures only fitted for the habitations of the night. The values of education, moral, political, and economical, were above all estimate, not alone for the individual but for the state and the nation. Education was the only road to "the prosperity, the power, and happiness of a nation."

Jefferson collected the useful sciences to be taught in the university into ten branches: Ancient Languages (Latin, Greek, Hebrew), Modern Languages (including Anglo-Saxon), Pure Mathematics (adding military and naval architecture), Physico-Mathematics (mechanics, optics, pneumatics and so on, plus astronomy and geography), Natural Philosophy (physics, chemistry, mineralogy), Natural History, Anatomy and Medicine, Government (including civil history), Law, and Ideology (the science of thought, embracing moral philosophy, belles lettres, and fine arts). The actual grouping of the subjects in the schools would be finally determined by the ten professors in the light of their qualifications. The conception, overall, broke completely with the traditional classical curriculum in higher education. In England certainly, to a lesser extent in the United States, the colleges and universities had been at the service of wealth and religion, dispensing a mixture of humanistic refinement and Christian piety. Some American educators were beginning to recognize the need to reform the curriculum in directions both secular and modern, giving scope to new sciences like chemistry and political economy, to modern languages, and to professional and applied subjects. Innovations along this line had been attempted at some places, but without much success. The University of Pennsylvania, as Jefferson knew, had made a promising start in modern studies a quarter-century ago. Recent reports from Wistar and others had been discouraging, however, and by 1818 Jefferson thought better of Harvard than of Pennsylvania. Abroad only the Scottish universities, Edinburgh most notably, had reached out to the larger community and introduced the practical element into the higher learning. The educational plan, like the architectural plan, of the University of Virginia had no model; still the University of Edinburgh, with which Jefferson and many Virginians had affinities, scientific or theological, exerted a pervasive influence.

Jefferson hoped to dispense altogether with conventional study of the ancient languages, not because he, with so many modernists, thought them dead and useless, but because these languages were "the foundations common to all the sciences," and so should form the core of instruction in the collegiate or secondary schools. He worried lest the University be dragged down to the level of a classical school full of "the noisy turbulence of a multitude of small boys." He again entered a plea for the district colleges, which would take boys to the fifteenth year of age or beyond. "These institutions . . . ," he wrote, "might then be the passage of entrance for youths into the University, where their classical learning might be critically completed, by a study of the authors of highest degree; and it is at this stage only that they should be received at the University." While he would have liked to embrace such applied studies as agriculture, commerce, diplomacy, and manufacturing in his scheme, he was unwilling to do so at the expense of the basic sciences and, practically, knew the legislature would never support more than ten schools. (He finally had to settle for eight.) Medicine, occupying the shady ground between science and charlatanism, would be taught only in its theoretical aspects and as a part of general culture. It could not be taught clinically, or professionally, without a hospital, which did not exist in Charlottesville. Young men preparing to become physicians and surgeons would have to complete their education elsewhere.

The Report called attention to the unprecedented omission of religious instruction and a chair of divinity. The constitutional principles of religious freedom and equality presented an insuperable bar, Jefferson said. He sometimes spoke of theology as "the charlatanism of the mind," as medicine was "the charlatanism of the body," and so far as this view prevailed he could not consider it a branch of

973

useful knowledge to be taught in any university, public or private. He did not express this view in the Report. On the contrary, anticipating pious objections to a godless university, he emphasized that religion in its moral, literary, and historical aspects had a place in the curriculum. These would be taught as a branch of ethics, through the languages, and so on. Since the study of languages involved for Jefferson the whole history of civilization, the student of Hebrew, Greek, and Latin, for instance, would learn a great deal of primitive Christianity. In a larger sense all education was moral. It exercised man's moral sense, overcame any of its "innate obliquities," and developed one's duties to others and to God. By purely secular studies, cultivating those moral obligations in which all sects agree, Jefferson prophesied, "a basis will be formed common to all sects." A common faith uniting the multitude of Americans in a secular religion of peace and reason and humanity would surely advance hand in hand with the progress of enlightenment.

Jefferson addressed himself briefly to certain "accessories" of formal education—manual exercise, manual arts, and "the arts which embellish life, dancing, music, and drawing"—which, while not incorporated in the schools, would be available to the students; and also to the parietal functions of a resident university. Here he expressed an unusually liberal attitude. Most American colleges and universities were nurseries for growing boys. Discipline was a serious problem everywhere; and such was the reputed indulgence of southern parents toward their children that the president of Yale had once declared there could never be a university below the Potomac. Nevertheless, Jefferson repudiated the common appeal to motives of fear in the government of youth. "Hardening them by disgrace, to corporal punishments, and servile humiliations cannot be the best process for producing erect character." He recommended instead "the affectionate deportment" of the home environment. And noting the experience of some universities abroad in allowing the students to police and govern themselves, he thought the example worthy of emulation in America for the initiation of youth into the duties of civil life. The government of a university, unlike that of a school, ought to be a portico to manhood. If founded in reason and comity, he said, "it will be more likely to nourish in the minds of our youth the combined spirit of order and self-respect, so con-

genial with our political institutions, and so important to be woven
into the American character."

One of Jefferson's most liberal ideas was not contained in the
Rockfish Gap Report, presumably because it had not yet occurred
to him. This was the principle of free election. Jefferson came to it
in 1820. He had sent his grandson Francis Eppes to Columbia College, in South Carolina, where Thomas Cooper was teaching while
waiting to take up his appointment in Charlottesville. Young Eppes
soon found himself in a regimented curriculum, forced into courses
he did not want or need, and to proceed, not as he was capable, but
in the lockstep of the four-class system. In this respect Columbia
College (later the University of South Carolina) was like every
other. The regimen was wasteful and arbitrary, Jefferson wrote
sympathetically to young Eppes. It will be "the fundamental law of
our university to leave everyone free to attend whatever branches of
instruction he wants, and to decline what he does not want." And so
it became. Furthermore, the marshaled classes (freshman, sopho-
more, and so on) would be abolished. Students became simply students, all on an equal footing, and free to proceed according to ability. Very likely Jefferson would have arrived at this position without the shock of his grandson's experience. It was a logical outcome
of the revolt against the standard curriculum, of the introduction of
specialized courses of study, and the spirit of individualism. George
Ticknor, just beginning his tenure as Professor of Modern Languages at Harvard, soon hit on the same idea in his efforts to reform
that institution. The reform did not take hold, not at Harvard or anywhere outside the University of Virginia, for half a century. The
"elective system," like most of the liberal reforms proposed in the
Report of 1818, was admired in theory but had little practical influence in the educational world of the time.

The published Report made a strong impression in Richmond.
Sectarian and local interests in the General Assembly opposed the
commission's site recommendation, but many legislators, east and
west, Episcopal and Presbyterian, set aside their prejudices and
voted, in January 1819, to charter the University of Virginia in
Charlottesville. The pride and the interest of the commonwealth demanded a university; it was too late in the day to quarrel about location or other details. A new Board of Visitors was constituted in

the shell of the old, Jefferson still the Rector, and the University arose on the foundations of Central College. Nothing but the name had changed. The University existed on paper only. With but one pavilion completed and a meager $15,000 a year committed by the state, its future was still at hazard. Jefferson at once pressed Nicholas and Cabell for additional funds. Most of the counties had not claimed the money in the Literary Fund for the support of local charity schools. Jefferson proposed the diversion of these derelict funds, amounting to $45,000, to the University. The assembly would not now hear of it or vote another cent for the University, Cabell informed him. One victory at a time was all the "Monticello men" could expect. Some legislators feared the University would drain the Literary Fund. Very few shared Jefferson's splendid conception of the institution. Motives of mean economy were reinforced by economic disaster. Unfortunately, the University came into existence in the year of the Panic of 1819, the nation's first great depression. Retrenchment was the order of the day, and for the next several years Jefferson's pleas for help fell on reluctant ears in Richmond.

He was determined not to open the institution until it could be opened in style, buildings completed, faculty assembled, and all the insignia of a university in evidence. He had a horror of its becoming a petty college filled with mediocre professors and student cast-offs of Harvard or Princeton or Pennsylvania. Tentatively, the opening was scheduled for 1822. Meanwhile, Jefferson and the board arranged for a classical school to be set up in Charlottesville to prepare youth for the University. On the grounds Arthur S. Brokenborough, named Proctor, assumed oversight of the building; but Jefferson and John Hartwell Cocke, the board's committee of superintendence, were constantly active. The buildings had first priority and Jefferson gave them steady attention. To carve the Ionic and Corinthian capitals of several façades, he imported two Italian artisans, only then to discover that the native stone, even some hauled from a quarry 70 miles distant, was not susceptible to this delicate art. So he arranged for the capitals to be executed in Carrara and shipped to Charlottesville. Later the capitals and marble blocks of the Rotunda came in this way.

He also began to recruit a faculty. Indeed one professor, Thomas Cooper, had already been appointed and invitations had gone out to others before the University was chartered. In October 1818, on his return to Monticello from Warm Springs, which he had visited after the meeting at Rockfish Gap, seeking relief of rheumatism and becoming desperately ill instead, Jefferson invited Ticknor and Nathaniel Bowditch to join the faculty of the embryo university. Bowditch, also of Massachusetts, he considered the nation's premier mathematician. And had he obtained their services, together with Cooper's, he would have had the nucleus of a faculty without peer in the United States. But Ticknor and Bowditch declined. Discouraged, Jefferson felt he had no choice but to go abroad for a faculty. From the beginning, as far back as 1800, he had insisted that the professors be of the first order of science, "supereminent professors," American if possible, European if necessary. They should be scholars as well as teachers, consistent with his idea of a university dedicated both to the discovery and the dissemination of knowledge. Edinburgh best exemplified this idea. Aided by Dugald Stewart, the luminary of Scottish "common sense" philosophy, whose friendship Jefferson had made in Paris, he hoped to recruit several of the professors from Edinburgh and her sister institutions. Oxford, the citadel of classical studies, Cambridge, of mathematics—these too, and possibly the new German universities, should be explored. Brushing aside difficulties, Jefferson exuded optimism. "With scientists and men of letters," he said, "the globe itself is one great commonwealth, in which no geographical divisions are acknowledged; but all compose one fraternity of fellow citizens." The school of law and government alone must go to an American. Although several talented Americans applied for one chair or another, none measured up to Jefferson's standards. By 1819 he was not only resigned to a mainly European faculty but exultant over the celebrity it would confer on the University at the outset.

The one American already named, Cooper, "the greatest man in America in the powers of mind and acquired information," in Jefferson's opinion, was lost to the institution in 1820. The storm that blew up around this man of all science, Priestley's companion and disciple, victim of the Sedition Law, Republican ideologue and Unitarian publicist, threatened irreparable harm to the University. At the last meeting of the old board in February 1819, which Jefferson, sick and weary, braved a snowstorm to attend at Madison's place, he proposed to bring Cooper on at once to teach the upper classes in the classical school. Several of the Visitors, including Cabell, expressed surprise that the College, or University, was still obligated to Cooper, who had taken a position in South Carolina. They also raised the question of his moral character. Jefferson assured them of the obligation—the post at Columbia was temporary—and of Cooper's good character, as evidenced during his visit at Monticello the previous fall. The first meeting of the new board in March confirmed Cooper in his appointment, on leave, as it were, in South Carolina. He would teach chemistry, mineralogy, and natural philosophy, perhaps law for a time. Jefferson considered him "the cornerstone of the edifice."

Now the evangelical clergy, spearheaded by the Presbyterians, attacked Cooper's appointment. John Holt Rice, the pope of Virginia Presbyterianism, climaxed the campaign in January 1820 with a long article in his *Evangelical Magazine*. Cooper's theological writings, Rice argued, showed little philosophy and much prejudice, and his Socinianism would alienate a substantial portion of the people of Virginia from the state university. Rice feared an invasion of Unitarianism. He did not call for a Calvinistic university but for one where religion had a respectable place in the curriculum, in the faculty, in divine worship. In his eyes a university without religion was a monstrosity. He was equally concerned for the success of the institution, however. As Cabell informed Jefferson, Rice and the Presbyterians had rallied to the charter bill in the assembly. And the University, Rice felt, could not succeed in hostility to the prevailing opinion of the community. A university conducted without preference as to religious sect was one thing, a university without religion, or indeed motivated by rationalistic zeal against orthodoxy, quite another. Well, Jefferson had been on this hook before—forty years before. The priests driven out of their monopoly, sought reentrance under cover of equality; and when he attempted to exclude them, in affairs of education as in affairs of state, they accused him of proselytizing infidelity.

Jefferson reacted to the furor on several levels. Privately he was outraged at this assault on the integrity of the University, and he flailed the Presbyterians in characteristic fashion. All the priests, he wrote to Correa, "dread the advance of science as witches do the approach of daylight; and scowl on the fatal harbinger announcing the subversion of the duperies in which they live." The Presbyterians were the loudest, he declaimed to Short: "The most intolerant of all sects, the most tyrannical, and ambitious; ready at the word of the lawgiver, if such a word could be obtained, to put the torch to the pile, and to rekindle in this virgin hemisphere the flames in which their oracle Calvin consumed the poor Servetus." This reflex action, wired into Jefferson's brain and nerves and tissue over fifty years, was neither quite fair to the Presbyterians nor responsive to the real issue he faced. How could a democratic state university, supported by the people of the state and in their service, maintain its integrity without alienation of its constituency? Jefferson never really saw the issue. It was inconceivable to him that freedom of mind—academic freedom in this case—could be opposed to the will of a free people in "this virgin hemisphere." Democracy could not defeat enlightenment. In fact, of course, the history of the higher learning in America proved that it could, not generally but sometimes. However that may be, Jefferson realized, practically, something had to be done to appease the sectarians. Cooper himself offered no problem. He was being well paid in Columbia, better than he would be in Charlottesville; and he doubted Jefferson's prodigy would ever spring to life. The clergy would not permit it. At Columbia, as earlier at Carlisle, in Pennsylvania, he was assailed by bigotry. He had not the courage to face the *odium theologicum* still another time and offered to resign. Jefferson at first refused to accept his resignation; but he relented gracefully, reluctantly, at the April meeting of the board, convinced by Cabell and others that the cornerstone had become the millstone of the University. Cooper's contract of three years' standing was annulled by mutual consent in October.

The crusade continued despite Cooper's sacrifice. Fighting for money in the assembly, Cabell repeatedly warned the Rector of the widespread opinion in evangelical circles, Presbyterian especially, "that the Socinians are to be installed at the University for the purpose of overthrowing the religious opinions of the country." (Had the clergy known of the overtures to Ticknor and Bowditch, both Unitarians, though of the mild New England variety, the alarm would surely have been greater.) "The clergy have succeeded in spreading the belief of their intended exclusion," Cabell said, "and in my opinion it is the source of much of our trouble." At the meeting of the Visitors in October 1822, someone, probably Jefferson himself, brought forward a resolution to conciliate the sectarians. The various denominations would be invited to establish theological schools "on the confines" of the University and entirely independent of it. The Visitors adopted the proposal and it formed part of their annual report to the legislature. The purpose was not, as has sometimes been said, to enable the University students to obtain formal religious instruction, though they might avail themselves of the religious services of these schools outside regular University hours; the purpose, rather, was to extend the secular instruction of the University to the theological students. Without in any way compromising the University, the arrangement might open the minds of a new generation of clergy. "And by bringing the sects together," Jefferson explained to Cooper, "and mixing them with the mass of other students, we shall soften their asperities, liberalize and neutralize their prejudices, and make the general religion a religion of peace, reason and morality." The schools "on the confines" resolution was an astute move to placate the sectarians. Cabell credited it with great influence in Richmond. "It is the Franklin that has drawn the lightning from the cloud of opposition." Jefferson confidently expected some of the churches to take up the invitation. They did not, and the evangelicals eyed the University with suspicion and jealousy for years to come.

From beginning to end a grudging legislature offered the main obstacle to Jefferson's plans for the University. "All the states but our own are sensible that knowledge is power," he wrote. Kentucky, the daughter of Virginia, already boasted a going university. Must Virginia send her sons to Kentucky, or to Harvard or Princeton or Columbia, for their education? Jefferson estimated Virginia's annual debt to the other states on account of education at $300,000. Constantly, he appealed to the pride and reputation of the state, not only in behalf of the University but of education generally. Massachusetts, one-tenth the size of Virginia and the fourth smallest state, had more influence than any other. "Whence this ascendancy?" he asked. "From her attention to education, unquestionably. There can be no stronger proof knowledge is power, and . . . ignorance is weakness." Virginia, by contrast, seemed destined to become "the Barbary of the Union." The degeneration over half a century was indeed appalling. "The mass of education in Virginia before the Revolution placed her with the foremost of her sister colonies. What is her education now? Where is it?" he demanded. "The little we have we import, like beggars, from other states; or import their beggars to bestow on us their miserable crumbs."

These appeals to pride and interest were joined in 1820 by appeals to political sentiment. Jefferson had envisioned the University as a national institution; increasingly, under the reaction produced by the Panic of 1819 and the Missouri Compromise south of the Potomac, he came to think of it as a state or sectional bulwark of Old Republicanism against the advance of "consolidation" and kindred political heresies in the North. The line of division between free and slave states marked out by the Missouri Compromise pointed up the gravity of "trusting to those who are against us in position and principle to fashion to their own form the mind and affections of our youth." Send them to Harvard, Jefferson warned, and they will be returned "fanatics and tories." Yet there were probably, in 1821, some 500 of Virginia's future leaders enrolled in northern seminaries, learning the lessons of "anti-Missourism" and imbibing heretical opinions. "This canker is eating at the vitals of our existence," he lectured, "and if not arrested at once will be beyond remedy." The appeal accurately expressed Jefferson's deep distress over the course of national affairs, yet it must also be seen as part of his strategy of argument with a legislature that shared his political anxieties and might discover more enthusiasm for an institution devoted to Virginia's, and the South's, sovereign interests that for one devoted to liberality and enlightenment in the abstract. At any rate, whether conviction or strategy, Jefferson tended to give a political cast to his conception of the University; and while he did not abandon the ideal of a fountainhead of learning for the entire nation, it slowly receded from view.

Jefferson and his friends waged a relentless five year campaign to obtain the money to build the University. The General Assembly had committed the state to $15,000 a year. The legislature would not divert the surplus of the Literary Fund, as Jefferson wanted, but it would permit the Visitors to borrow the capital for the buildings.

Three loans of $60,000 each were authorized over a four-year pe-
riod. The trick then became, first to liberate the loans of interest,
which must otherwise be paid from the annuity, or possibly the
meager private subscriptions, and finally to sponge the principal.
The state had a claim on the government of the United States for
expenses incurred in the prosecution of the War of 1812. Jefferson
angled for legislative extermination of the whole of the University's
debt by means of this hypothetical claim. While he failed in this, he
succeeded in liberating the annuity of interest and, in 1824, obtained
an outright grant of $50,000 for the purchase of books and scientific
apparatus, contingent on Washington's payment of the Virginia
claim. Pressure from Jefferson, Cabell, and others, with the personal
intervention of President Monroe, led to prompt settlement of the
claim. As for the $180,000 debt, Jefferson never gave it another
thought; it was already remitted in the eyes of everyone, including
the enemies of the institution.

During these years Jefferson's hopes for the University sometimes faltered. "I perceive that I am not to live to see it opened," he
wrote gloomily to Cabell in 1821. Cabell was struggling to obtain
approval of the second loan; and convinced that the legislature
would never again vote one cent for the institution, he announced
his intention to retire. Jefferson begged him to reconsider. He did,
and continued his leadership of the cause at Richmond. Senators and
delegates complained that the University was on too grand a scale,
that too much money went into finery, that it was costing twice as
much as originally estimated, and so on. Jefferson answered these
critics and also those, including some of the Visitors, who wanted to
open the University before the library was completed and all the essentials of academic excellence secured. "It would be an impatience
defeating its own object, by putting on a subordinate character in
the outset, which never would be shaken off," he said. Jealous local
interests continued to snipe at the University. Staunton and Richmond feared that behind its elegant façade the state capital would be
seated in Charlottesville. William and Mary had not altogether given
up the fight. In 1823, after the assembly voted the third loan to
build the Rotunda, Cabell thought the resistance of the College had
been broken, in fact that all the enemy battalions had struck their
colors. But the friends of William and Mary made one last challenge

the next year, proposing to transfer the College, lock, stock, and barrell, to Richmond, where it would have all the advantages of location at the seat of government. Jefferson countered this move by threatening legislation to consolidate the endowment of the College with the University. The former would lose its identity and the latter would become the beneficiary of $6000 a year, easily making up the deficit of two professors in Jefferson's plan, for the annuity alone, he realized, would support only eight professors of distinction. Although he did not expect the old college to submit to this death decree, he did expect the threat to quiet the removal petition in the legislature. Apparently it did, for the petition was withdrawn.

While fighting for the University, Jefferson kept the whole system of education steadily in view. It was mortifying to be charged, as he was, with sacrificing primary to higher education. He denied this and blamed the curious reversal of priorities on the legislature. If the state chose to place the cart before the horse, he could only make the best of it. "If we cannot do everything at once, let us do one thing at a time," he philosophized. The system of charity schools, after several years experience, was a complete bust. The money might better have been spent on the University, he felt, pending the institution of common schools on the ward plan, which required no preliminary outlay by the legislature. When the third loan was on the carpet, in 1823, he wrote to Cabell: "Were it necessary to give up either the Primaries or the University, I would rather abandon the last, because it is safer to have a whole people respectably enlightened than a few in a high state of science and the many in ignorance. This last is the most dangerous state in which a nation can be. The nations and governments of Europe are so many proofs of it." Young Rives had gone to Richmond with his mentor's encouragement to push a new plan of primary schools. Cabell now told Jefferson this was a mistake. The odious reputation of the charity schools had produced a reaction in favor of the University and nothing should be done to divert the current. Persuaded by Cabell's reasoning, Jefferson asked Rives to let the primaries sink, meanwhile "availing ourselves of the present state of discredit under which that plan is, and profiting of the current it produces toward the University." The regional colleges must also wait. Expediency dictated his course, but in championing the University he did not sacrifice any-thing attainable at the lower levels of the educational pyramid.

In May 1824 the Visitors announced the opening of the Univer-sity nine months hence. Ten pavilions, 109 dormitories (for 218 students), and 6 hotels had been completed. The Rotunda was up, though the columns stood gaping for their capitals en route from Italy and the vast cavernous interior awaited books and ornamenta-tion. In the summer Jefferson drew up a catalogue of the library—6860 volumes—and arranged for the purchase of the books. A fac-ulty remained the principal problem. None of the professors, reluc-tantly only eight at the start, had been appointed. (Law and Gov-ernment, separate schools in the Rockfish Gap Report, were com-bined, and the chair in Physico-Mathematics dropped.) Cabell, who was familiar with the British and Continental universities from a grand tour twenty years ago, had been scheduled to undertake the recruiting mission abroad. He was not well, however, and declined. Jefferson entrusted this delicate responsibility to Francis Walker Gilmer, throwing the law professorship into the bargain. Gilmer hesitated on the professorship but agreed to the mission. The 34-year-old attorney, almost a son to Jefferson, set forth in the spring with flattering letters of introduction to Richard Rush, the Ameri-can Minister in London, to Dugald Stewart and others. He was to go to Oxford for a classicist, to Cambridge for a mathematician, to Edinburgh for an anatomist; either Edinburgh or Cambridge might provide professors of natural history or natural philosophy, while a scholar in modern languages should be obtained from the Continent. This last was the first secured. George Blaetterman, a German ear-lier recommended by Ticknor, talked to Gilmer in London and agreed to terms. On the other posts Gilmer met with great diffi-culty. No one knew anything of this embryo university in the wilds of Virginia; and while Gilmer spoke eloquently of the buildings, the Rector, and the prospects, he had mountains of ignorance and preju-dice and conceit to overcome. Moreover, the income of British uni-versity professors turned out to be much greater than Jefferson had been led to believe. (Virginia offered $1500 in salary, plus student tuitions of perhaps $500 a year and a house and garden.) Expansion at places like Cambridge had suddenly brightened the opportunities for younger scholars; and the Britishers did not look with favor on the long term, practically the year around, or the assortment of subjects they would be expected to cover in Virginia.

Hearing all this from Gilmer in October, Jefferson said he had never received a greater blow to his hopes. "I think therefore," he wrote to Madison in the depths of dismay, "he had better bring the best professors he can get, although of secondary standing." The whole idea of going abroad was to obtain professors of the first rank, which struck some patriots as un-American to begin with; and if Jefferson had to settle for foreigners of "secondary standing," he might better have recruited his faculty at home. But within a week another letter from Gilmer revived his spirits. Before he left England in the fall Gilmer had engaged five of the six professors sought abroad: Blaetterman (modern languages), Thomas Key (a Cambridge M.A., for mathematics), George Long (a fellow of Trinity College, Cambridge, for classics), Charles Bonneycastle (son of a noted mathematician, for natural philosophy), and Robley Dunglison (a London physician, for anatomy and medicine). Gilmer arranged for the sixth, in natural history, in New York. Thomas Addis Emmet, nephew of the Irish refugee-patriot, took this post. On the whole, they were men of broad general culture and able scholars. But they were not the "supereminent professors" Jefferson had hoped for, nor is it certain that the chairs could not have been filled by Americans of equal or higher rank.

The chairs of law and, subsequently, of moral philosophy had been reserved for Americans. The latter, including *belles lettres*, went to George Tucker on Madison's suggestion. Fifty years of age in 1825—much the eldest of the eight professors—Tucker belonged to a prominent Virginia clan, had served three terms in Congress, published two volumes of essays, at least one of them known to Jefferson, and recently completed a long novel, *The Valley of the Shenandoah*. All considered, he was one of the most literate Virginians of his day. Jefferson summoned him to Monticello and finally argued him into the professorship just as the University opened. The law chair remained empty for another year. Jefferson insisted the occupant be politically sound—none of "the honied Mansfieldism of Blackstone" or the "toryism" of Marshall and his ilk was admissible—and this requirement, together with the loss of income any prominent lawyer must suffer in the post, made the prospects desperate. Gilmer finally accepted but died before he could occupy the chair; and it was offered to six other Virginia Republicans before a Fredericksburg lawyer, John Tayloe Lomax, consented in April 1826.

Jefferson's anxiety for the political purity of the law school led him to propose the prescription of certain texts in government. There was nothing unusual about this; as he said, it was the common practice for the trustees of colleges and universities to determine the *norma docendi* in the various schools. The founders of the University of Virginia, by leaving this matter to the professors, registered another advance for educational liberalism. But in the case of the law school, so far as it was a school of government, Jefferson thought the Visitors had a duty to lay down the first principles to be taught. He sent the proposal to Madison and Cabell in Feburary 1825, when the occupant of the law chair remained very uncertain. "He may be a Richmond lawyer, or one of that school of quondam Federalism, now consolidation," Jefferson observed. "It is our duty to guard against such principles being disseminated among our youth, and the diffusion of that poison, by a previous prescription of the texts to be followed in their discourses." He suggested Locke on civil government, Sidney's *Discourses,* and with particular reference to the United States, the Declaration of Independence, *The Federalist,* and Madison's Virginia Report of 1799 on the Alien and Sedition Laws. Madison and Cabell concurred in the proposal. The former suggested the addition of Washington's Farewell Address, to which Jefferson readily agreed. At its next meeting, in March, the Board adopted the Rector's resolution. Its intent was somewhat ambiguous, as if the author knew he transgressed the legitimate boundaries of academic freedom. It began with a mere expression of *opinion* that the *best guides* to the true principles of government were to be found in the given texts; but it ended with the statement that they *shall be used as the texts and documents of the school.* Clearly, if the resolution meant to prescribe certain texts, it did not mean to proscribe others. The purpose was to ensure that the students received the correct principles of government, "in the common opinion" of their elders, before they trusted the researches and convictions of their own minds. Whatever the intent, the resolution assailed the liberatarian spirit of the University. "This institution,"

Jefferson had written, "will be based on the illimitable freedom of the human mind. For here we are not afraid to follow truth wherever it may lead, nor to tolerate any error so long as reason is left free to combat it." But the personal and political distresses of the final years of the founder's life eroded this conception. The resolution on political texts expressed his deepening anxieties for the survival of the Union and Republicanism. In a sense it was not partisan, for the canon was acceptable to men of all parties—"all federalists, all republicans"—yet it would not have been ventured at all but for the partisan fears of consolidation in the surrounding political environment of Jefferson's last unquiet years.

The faculty arrived, the library filled up, and the students dribbled in, only fifty or so at the start but over a hundred a year later. Jefferson was pleased with the professors, all but Tucker utter strangers to him. The young Europeans faced a season of acclimatization both educational and environmental. Trifling problems arose but, in the main, they adjusted satisfactorily; and at Monticello all the professors learned of the founder's prejudices in the different schools of instruction—his rage against Hume and Blackstone, his skepticism of medicine, his enthusiasm for Anglo-Saxon. The students were less pleasing. They had been very poorly prepared by Jefferson's lights. At once the University had to relax its admission standards and recede from the lofty conception of a post-collegiate institution. There were no "classes," but had there been most the entrants would have qualified as freshmen or sophomores rather than as the juniors and seniors contemplated by Jefferson's plan. And there were no degrees, only diplomas offered by the several schools, but had there been the only realistic degree would have been the B.A., though in 1831 when the faculty bowed to the univeral practice of awarding degrees, it chose to award the M.A. Moreover, the students were inclined to rowdy and riotous behavior quite beyond Jefferson's expectations. The idea had got into circulation of a lax "democratic" code of government in the University. Hearing this from Philadelphia in August, Jefferson blandly answered that two-thirds of the students, the older ones, required no government and their example controlled the younger third. "The University may be said to be as quiet as a Convent." Within a month rampage and riot rolled over the tranquil lawn. Three students were expelled and eleven severely reprimanded. Jefferson, 82 years of age, rode down from Monticello to help restore order; and the Visitors, meeting just after the disturbance, stiffened the regulations governing students. The refusal of the students to bear witness against their fellows undermined Jefferson's plan for the denizens to police themselves.

Other hopes and plans would also fail, but a dream had become a reality and the founder would not live to trace its tortuous history. Jefferson's labors for the University absorbed him almost to the hour of his death. At the end of April 1826, he laid out the plan of a botanical garden. On his last visit to the grounds, as he watched the raising of the great marble capitals atop the columns of the Rotunda, he must have reflected on the agony and the ecstasy of this triumph. "I have long been sensible," he had written three months before, "that while I was endeavoring to render my country the greatest of all services, that of regenerating the public education, and placing the rising generation on the level of our sister states . . . , I was discharging the odious function of a physician pouring medicine down the throat of a patient insensible of needing it." Yet with courage, faith, and skill rarely equalled, he had succeeded—at least with the University. It was *his* monument. If Emerson's aphorism, "An institution is the lengthened shadow of one man," has any truth, it belongs to Jefferson and the University of Virginia. It contained himself. Jefferson knew this. So when he came to write his epitaph, reflecting on his varied services, he chose for inscription on his tombstone, " 'Author of the Declaration of Independence, of the Statute of Virginia for Religious Freedom, and Father of the University of Virginia,' because by these, as testimonials that I have lived, I wish most to be remembered."

Unquiet Sage

Jefferson's last years were etched with sadness and even a little bitterness. A siege of illness came upon him in the fall of 1818, and he was never really free of bodily misery again. The waters of insolvency rose steadily until he despaired of his estate. Deterioration was all around him, not only at Monticello but in his beloved Virginia, shriveling into drab decay only half a century after the sun rose and without ever reaping the promises of the green springtime. Perhaps the University would charm back the sun; but the affliction ran too deep, as Jefferson knew in his heart, and so far as the University was committed to peculiar Virginia principles and tired Virginia defenses it became an ally of the mournful sickness it was intended to cure. The years 1819–20 were years of crisis for the entire nation. Economic depression and sectional discord were succeeded by rancorous political discontent. The crisis involved several vital areas of national policy but settled most grievously on the issue of slavery restriction, eventuating in the Missouri Compromise. This "firebell in the night," as Jefferson called it, shook his hopes for the Union and, in association with other tendencies in the national government, drove him back to old political fears, back to the "principles of '98," overlaid now with a sectional consciousness he had not known before. For a decade in retirement he had quietly drifted with the currents of nationalism. His political feelings revived in 1819, not with the zest of new wine, but with the musty acridity of a wine soured by age. The anguish of his personal affairs entered into the reaction. To an extent he transferred the burden of his own problems to the public, particularly to the national government, whose disastrous course had brought on himself, on his family, and on his state great vexations of life and spirit.

The Panic of 1819 struck when Jefferson's fortunes were at low ebb yet still showed promise of improvement. In 1815, after years of Napoleonic wars, the starved European markets soaked up American agricultural surpluses and prices soared. Unfortunately, Jefferson, like many Virginia farmers, derived little benefit from this boom. Two years of drought were followed by invasion of fly, which left him, in 1817, only enough wheat to seed the next year's crop. His Bedford tobacco was so miserably bad during successive seasons that he discharged the two overseers there. Prospects improved in 1818. Plaster and clover were restoring his farms in Albemarle. Fields that formerly produced five or six bushels to the acre, he said, were yielding two or three times as much under his grandson's management. But for his debts he might have trusted in God, husbandry, and the weather. Not until Jeff took a hand in the plantation business did Jefferson realize how far his estate was mortgaged to his creditors. His total indebtedness at this time is not easily calculated, but it was probably not less than when he returned to Monticello. Borrowing from Richmond banks to pay interest on his old debts and to make up deficiencies in accounts with his Richmond factor, he steadily increased his obligations without substantially improving his income.

The chain of pressures released by the panic began with these banks, specifically in Jefferson's case with the Richmond branch of the Second Bank of the United States. The BUS, after feeding the post-war inflation by allowing the state banks recklessly to expand their note issues, suddenly put on the brakes in the summer of 1818. Just as he was setting out for Rockfish Gap, Jefferson learned that the Richmond branch had curtailed his credit 12-1/2 per cent. So on his $3000 loan he had to come up with $375 at once. This, he said, "is really like a clap of thunder to me, for god knows I have no means in the world of raising money on so sudden a call, my whole and sole dependence being only in the annual income of my farm." It was only the beginning. Contraction by the BUS forced contraction by the state banks, among them the Bank of Virginia, to which Jefferson was indebted; and one curtailment was followed by a second, then a third, until the early months of the next year he had to borrow an additional $4000, most of it from still another Richmond bank, in order to meet the demands and keep up his credit. His bank debt alone rose to over $10,000. Meanwhile, as money vanished, agricultural prices dropped precipitously. "Never were such times seen as we have now here," Jefferson wrote despondently. "Not a dollar is passing from one to another. Everyone had been so pressing and so pressed that finding it useless they from necessity give it up and bear and forbear with one another." The price deflation and the money stringency, he estimated with pardonable extravagance, had tripled his debts. He tried to sell land but there were few buyers, though he did manage to dispose of one tract. Bankruptcy knocked at his door, as at so many others, in 1819, just when improved management and husbandry and markets had once again brightened his hopes of a better tomorrow.

Jefferson blamed the panic on the banks, above all the national bank at the head of a vicious system. Banks, by their easy paper issues, seduced ambitious farmers from the labors of the plow into careers of gambling and speculation, then to save their own skins bankrupted the farmers. Jefferson had sworn many Jeremiads against the system; now, for the first time, he was himself a victim of it. "We have been truly sowing the wind, and are now reaping the whirlwind." The distresses, he said, were no greater than he had always expected and freely predicted from the moment of the creation of the Bank of the United States in 1791. "Hamilton . . . let in this torrent of swindling institutions which have spread ruin and wretchedness over the face of our country." But he could take small comfort in this political vindication, if vindication it was, amidst personal catastrophe in 1819.

What he called the *coup de grâce* to his fortunes was administered by one of his dearest friends, Governor Nicholas, who sank under the weight of the panic and took part of Jefferson's estate with him. On May 1, 1818, he had endorsed two BUS loans, each of $10,000, for Nicholas. This was more than a routine service in view of Jefferson's circumstances and the precarious state of the Virginia economy. But Nicholas, a director of one of the Richmond banks, had endorsed for him and been helpful in other ways. As Governor he had been a good friend of the University. Through the marriage of a daughter to Jeff he had become almost a member of the family. The two promissory notes were for twelve months only, and Nicholas was thought to be worth upwards to $300,000. But the panic "revolutionized" his fortune. Nicholas defaulted, the bank protested the notes, and the liability fell on the first endorser. Jefferson was at Poplar Forest, wracked by rheumatism, in August 1819 when he learned of this new affliction. "A call on me to the amount of my endorsements for you," he wrote Nicholas, "would indeed close my course by a catastrophe I had never contemplated." The bankrupt's property would be committed to trustees with the hope, of course, it might prove sufficient to protect his endorsers and cover his debts. Jefferson took encouragement from a recent ruling of the state Court of Appeals freeing usurious debts from liability—this would wipe-off nine-tenths of Nicholas's, he casually remarked. Meanwhile, to cover the $20,000 obligation at the bank, Jefferson executed a bond which, in effect, mortgaged part of Poplar Forest. The interest itself now drained off $1200 yearly from his income and ate into his capital. He pressed some of Nicholas's debtors, but without success, and tried to sell more land, with the same result. He never got free of the debt. Amazingly, in all this he showed not a trace of enmity toward Nicholas, tried to persuade Monroe to give him a federal office, and remained an affectionate friend until the penniless man went to his death three years later.

Prices turned upward in 1821 but Jefferson dropped farther and farther behind every year. Unable to sell land he sold slaves, realizing $3500 in one transaction to furnish a labor force for his grandson Francis Eppes. Jefferson consoled himself that the Negroes at least remained in the family. His bank loans increased, although on one occasion, in 1822, all three Richmond banks turned him down for additional credit. A statement of the next year listed debts in excess of $40,000, as well as the $20,000 obligation on Nicholas's account. Randolph's position was similar. He fell into despondency, withdrew from his family, and finally became quite alienated from Jefferson. In order to protect his property from liability for the Colonel's debts, and thus to secure it for Martha and the children, Jefferson named his dutiful grandson, Jeff, executor of his estate—another blow to Randolph's pride. In the end, all else failing, Jefferson was reduced to the humiliation of begging permission of the legislature to dispose of most of his property by way of lottery in the expectation of saving the splendid remnant, Monticello, for Martha.

These anxieties drove Jefferson back on his political heels. While he did not inspire, he gave aid and comfort to the Virginia revival of state rights politics led by a phalanx of Old Republicans, which included his former nemesis John Randolph of Roanoke, the planter-philosopher John Taylor, Judge Spencer Roane of the state's supreme bench, Thomas Ritchie, editor of the *Richmond Enquirer*, William B. Giles, and other lesser lights. With these men he made a *bête noire* of "consolidation" and from this protean enemy sought to save Virginia, indeed the entire South, by drawing the national government back into the narrow channels of the "principles of '98." Awakened from his political slumbers by the Panic of 1819, the Sage of Monticello was haunted for the rest of his life by ghosts of departed Federalism. Banking, as already noted, was the root of the evil; but it was associated in his mind with a whole system of measures, sometimes called "the American System," for the development of national wealth and power. The protective tariff for the support of manufactures and internal improvements for the creation of a home market were integral parts of the system. These measures, while they may have been Hamiltonian in origin, had been assimilated into Jeffersonian nationalism. The American System, generally, was the legitimate offspring of Jefferson's mature politics. Yet in 1819 he disowned these latter-day children: the national bank, which Madison and Gallatin had approved if he had not, because of the rage of speculation; the tariff because it taxed agriculture, chiefly southern and western, for the support of manufactures, chiefly northern; and internal improvements because, without the safeguard of a constitutional amendment, they hastened the federal government down the disastrous road of consolidation. Even more alarming was the aggressive underpining of consolidation by the federal judiciary, highlighted by several broad nationalistic opinions of Chief Justice Marshall in and around 1819. The Federalism of the bench seemed incurable, unless by drastic surgery; and Jefferson feared that the old political hydra, Federalism, nothing changed but its name, had sneaked back into power under the camouflaged "good feelings" of the Monroe era and renewed its grip on the entire federal establishment. Most alarming of all was the Missouri Compromise of 1820. This new species of Federalist trickery, as he saw it, "fanaticized" the North against the South, and it drove him toward sectionalism in spite of himself.

In all this Jefferson's political feelings consorted with the ascendant Old Republican ideology in Virginia. He did not take an active role but neither did he disguise his approval of this movement. To Judge Roane, who led the state judiciary's fight against encroachments of the federal courts, Jefferson said he subscribed to "every tittle" of his essays in the *Enquirer*. "They contain the true principles of the revolution of 1800, for that was as real a revolution in the principles of our government as that of '76 was in its form." The principles denied the supremacy of the Supreme Court to decide constitutional questions for the other branches of the government, for the states, and for the people. "The judiciary of the United States," he wrote in 1820, "is the subtle corps of sappers and miners constantly working under ground to undermine the foundations of our confederated fabric. They are construing our Constitution from a coordination of a general [national] and special [state] government to a general and supreme one alone. This will lay all things at their feet . . . ." Jefferson read John Taylor's turgid polemics, beginning in 1820 with *Construction Construed and Constitutions Vindicated*, a slashing attack on the Supreme Court, especially its opinion in *McCulloch v. Maryland* upholding the constitutionality of the Second Bank on the Hamiltonian logic of implied powers. To Ritchie, Roane, and the Caroline planter himself, Jefferson did not hesitate to pronounce this work orthodox. Taylor's writings against the Court, the tariff, internal improvements, and every other avenue of consolidation ought to be "standing instruction" to Congress, he said. For six months he stoutly resisted the pressures of Old Republicans to bring him forth publicly, "like a Priam in armor," in support of Taylor's doctrines. He finally yielded, however. The endorsement, drawn from Jefferson's previous letters, declared that on all important public questions Taylor espoused "the true political faith, to which every Republican should stedfastly hold."

But many Republicans of the nationalist persuasion, friends of the American System and the coalescence of parties in the "era of good feelings," expressed surprise and regret at this evidence of Jefferson's patronage of a new state rights party. "I am pelted for it in print," he observed unhappily. Further efforts to draw him into the leadership of this cause were unavailing. Yet when Ritchie, pressed to defend the partisan conscription of Jefferson's name and reputation, disclosed his authorship of the Kentucky Resolutions of 1798, the Sage of Monticello confessed "the naked truth." The truth should be known at last, he said in 1821, for after the passage of twenty-three years the country faced another crisis such as that of '98, only now the federal judiciary spearheaded the assault on the Constitution. This spiritual return to the partisan climate of the 1790's, this revival of the Republican feelings and symbols and slogans of '98, had a profound influence on the course of American politics in the ensuing decade; and in the South especially, the cause of state rights, strict construction, and limited government paraded under the Jeffersonian banner of "nullification" nailed to the Kentucky Resolutions.

The judiciary was the great unresolved problem of Jeffersonian Republicanism, as the Hamiltonian outburst of 1819 made abundantly clear. Jefferson's prescription for reform contained two main elements. First, in order to secure the responsibility of the federal courts to the Constitution and the people, judges should be appointed to six-year terms renewable by the President with the consent of both houses of Congress. Judicial independence, running to judicial absolutism, could not coexist with democracy. "Independence can be trusted nowhere but in the people in mass," Jefferson declared. Nor could the Union survive if the Supreme Court arrogated to itself the authority to decide fundamental issues arising in the federal system. The Court seemed not to realize that the Constitution "is a compact of many independent powers, every single one of which claims an equal right to understand it, and to require its observance. However strong the cord of compact may be," he warned, "there is a point of tension at which it will break." But, it was usually said in reply, there must be an ultimate arbiter somewhere. To be sure, Jefferson answered: the people of two-thirds of the states. They had adopted the Constitution and were competent to amend it. "Let them decide to which they meant to give an authority claimed by two of their organs. And it has been the peculiar wisdom and felicity of our Constitution to have provided this peaceable appeal, where that of other nations is at once to force." Jefferson also called for the courts, above all the Supreme Court, to adopt the practice of seriatim opinions, each judge pronouncing for himself rather than through the mouth of a single one. He pressed the point with Justice William Johnson, who acknowledged its merits but was not entirely convinced. Marshall dominated his fellows and huddled up unanimous opinions in secret conclave, Jefferson believed. By forcing each judge on his mettle, he hoped to neutralize the engine of consolidation under the Chief Justice's command. Neither reform made headway. The Court, while never impervious to political influence, remained impervious to reform; and Jefferson went to his death badly worsted in the recurrent battle of a quarter-century with John Marshall.

It was slavery, raising a mighty storm in national affairs for the first time, that gave a peculiar pungency to Jefferson's fears of judicial nationalism, bank mania, and the consolidating American System. The Missouri Question, brought on by the application of the territory for admission to statehood, embraced the larger issue of congressional authority to prohibit slavery in the Louisiana Purchase lands and, ultimately, to control the destiny of the institution itself. "In the gloomiest moments of the Revolutionary War," Jefferson wrote at the height of the debate in February 1820, "I never had any apprehensions equal to what I feel from this source." A compromise resolved the immediate crisis. Missouri was admitted as a slave state, Maine (a simultaneous applicant) as a free state, thereby maintaining the sectional balance in Congress, and slavery was henceforth prohibited above the latitudinal line 36° 30′. Jefferson vehemently disapproved of the Missouri Compromise. The fact that former Federalists like Rufus King, now United States Senator from New York, headed the anti-slavery forces in Congress bore out his fears of resurgent Toryism within the Republican amalgam. "The Missouri question is a mere party trick," he declared. "The leaders of Federalism, defeated in their schemes of obtaining power by rallying partisans to the principles of monarchism . . . have changed their track, and thrown out another burr to the whale. They are taking advantage of the virtuous feelings of the people [against slavery] to effect a division of parties by a geographical line. They expect that this will insure them, on local principles, the majority they could never obtain on the principles of Federalism." Having labored to build a national party to cement the Union together, Jefferson perceived not merely a revival of the old party conflict but of a conflict fanaticized by sectionalism. "The old schism of Federal and Republican," he explained to Short, "threatened nothing because it existed in every state, and united them together by the fraternism of party. But the coincidence of a marked principle, moral and political, with a geographcial line, once conceived, I feared would never more be oblitered from the mind; that it would be recurring on every occasion and renewing irritations until it would kindle such mutual and mortal hatred as to render separation preferable to eternal discord. I have been among the most sanguine in believing that our Union should be of long duration," he continued gravely. "I now doubt it much, and see the event [of disunion] at no great distance, and the direct consequence of this question." It was, he prophesied, "the knell of the Union."

While he did not deny the moral aspect of the question, Jefferson believed the northern restrictionists were politically motivated or, in some instances, honestly deluded by their righteousness against slavery. "They are wasting Jeremiads on the miseries of slaves as if we were advocates for it." For himself, at least, the cession of slave property was "a bagatelle" unworthy of a second thought *if* a scheme of emancipation and expatriation could be effected. "But as it is," he sighed, "we have the wolf by the ears, and we can neither hold him, nor safely let go. Justice is in one scale, self-preservation in the other." The dangers of slave revolt and racial warfare, embedded in every southerner's mind, surfaced in Jefferson's in 1820. "Are our slaves to be presented with freedom and a dagger?" he asked Adams. For if Congress could regulate the condition of the inhabitants of new states it could presumably declare all the slaves free in the existing states. "In which case," he told Gallatin, "all the whites south of the Potomac and Ohio must evacuate their states; and most fortunate those who can do it first." Virtue would become vice if pushed to the lengths of destruction and disunion. Who then would be the sinners, the slaveholders or the abolitionists? Moreover, the restriction of slavery would not, in fact, free a single human being. Restriction had only the semblance of morality; morality itself, Jefferson said, indulging a delusion of his own, lay on the side of the diffusion of slaves into the territories, "because by spreading them over a larger surface their happiness would be increased, and the burden of their future liberation lightened by bringing a greater number of shoulders under it." In truth, between a question of power and a question of existence, North and South, morality was hard to find anywhere. In 1784 Jefferson had proposed the exclusion of slavery from the territories. Indeed he was the father of the principle he now opposed in circumstances so entirely different he could not recognize the claim of the principle upon him.

Amidst the deluge of woe, the Missouri Compromise threw Jefferson into the deepest political malaise of his entire life. "I regret," he wrote seven weeks after the measure became law, "that I am now to die in the belief, that the . . . sacrifice of themselves by the generation of 1776, to acquire self-government and happiness to their country, is to be thrown away by the unwise and unworthy passions of their sons, and that my only consolation is to be that I live not to weep over it. If they would but dispassionately weigh the blessings they will throw away, against an abstract principle more likely to be effected by union than by scission, they would pause before they would perpetrate this act of suicide on themselves, and of treason against the hopes of the world." The melancholy testament of an old man in a dark season, it was not, fortunately, his final one.

If this chapter had any power for good it should spur the country to adopt a plan of gradual emancipation and colonization such as he had advocated in the Revolutionary era. Black slavery, this first and last curse visited on the country by European despotism, still mocked the nation's pretensions and blighted the promises of the American Revolution. All of Jefferson's values and goals dictated the extermination of slavery. This was as self-evident as the principles of 1776 themselves. But the Revolutionary generation could not be brought up to the mark. The Virginians of that day, Jefferson reflected, daily nursed and educated in the habits of slavery, had no more doubted the legitimacy of this species of property than of horses and cattle. "The quiet and monotonous course of colonial life had been disturbed by no alarm, and little reflection on the value of liberty." And drawn into the tasks of nation-building, choosing not to waste his influence in the advocacy of an untimely cause, he had patiently awaited the "revolution of opinion" sure to come. "I had always hoped that the younger generation," he wrote in 1814, "receiving their early impressions after the flame of liberty had been kindled in every breast, and had become, as it were, the vital spirit of every American, that the generous temperament of youth, analogous to the motion of their blood and above the suggestions of avarice, would have sympathized with oppression wherever found, and proved the love of liberty beyond their own share of it." He had been disappointed in this hope; and contrary to all reasonable expectations, domestic slavery had taken deeper root despite the bar to the African trade, and interest, instead of going over to the side of morality, had found new sustenance of exploitation in the burgeoning cotton lands of the South. While President, in response to resolutions of the Virginia legislature seeking an asylum for free Negroes and criminal slaves, he had endeavored to make arrangements with a British company colonizing Negroes in Sierra Leone. A similar overture had been made to the government of Portugal. These efforts failed; but the principle of colonization, which Jefferson and nearly

998

all liberal southerners considered the *sine qua non* of emancipation, had been set in motion. Virginians were prominent in the American Colonization Society founded in 1817. Under its auspices Liberia was soon established as an independent republic for the colonization of freed blacks from the United States. Although Jefferson encouraged, and in a larger sense inspired, this movement, he neither took an active role in the Society nor supposed that a tiny colony on the distant coast of Africa (he favored Santo Domingo as an asylum) offered a realistic solution to the mammoth problem of slavery in the United States.

In 1814 Jefferson's young friend and neighbor, Edward Coles, beseeched him to become a Hercules against slavery. "This difficult task [of emancipation] could be . . . more successfully performed by the revered father of our political and social blessings than by any succeeding statesman," Coles argued, "and would seem to come with peculiar propriety and force from those whose valor, wisdom and virtue have done so much in meliorating the condition of mankind. And it is a duty, as I conceive, that devolves particularly on you, from your known philosophical and enlarged view of subjects, and from the principles you have professed and practiced through a long and useful life." Coles had already embarked on an experiment to free and educate his own slaves, an experiment that necessitated his removal to free soil and took him, finally, to Illinois in 1819. Jefferson welcomed his "solitary voice" but thought his proposed course mistaken. He tried to persuade Coles to remain in Virginia, becoming, even as a slaveholder, the public missionary of emancipation and persevering until it was accomplished. As for himself, it was out of the question. "No, I have outlived the generation with which mutual labors and perils begat mutual confidence and influence. This enterprise is for the young—for those who can follow it up, and bear it through to its consummation." Instead he took up another and more agreeable cause, education.

Whether he might have effectively wielded the club against slavery, as Coles thought, is very doubtful. And it was not now, nor had it ever been, a labor consonant with his personal or political style. He could preach emancipation, plan it, encourage it, all from high principles and humanitarian feelings; but he could not lead so unpopular or so desperate a cause. That required moral enthusiasm and political audacity he neither possessed nor trusted. At bottom he did not care enough to sacrifice himself, or even put himself to great inconvenience, for the freedom of slaves, certainly not in the declining years of life. His dear friend Kosciusko, dying in Swizerland in 1817, had named Jefferson executor of his estate and provided for the disposition of his property in the United States, about $17,000 in securities, to the purchase, manumission, and education of young blacks. Jefferson declined this testamentary trust. He tried to get his younger neighbor John Hartwell Cocke, whose sentiments were in perfect accord, to take it on, but he too declined, citing the obstacle of Virginia laws. The object of the will was lost. Had Jefferson felt stronger about the object he would have ventured the experiment, despite statutory obstacles and the shortness of years, for the experiment was one he often commended to others and, indeed, one he may have himself suggested to Kosciusko, whose will was executed in Philadelphia prior to his departure under the shadow of the Alien Law in May 1798.

Jefferson adhered to the plan of gradual emancipation sketched in the *Notes on Virginia* in 1785. All the slaves born after a certain day would be emancipated, left in the care of their families until able to work, placed under state guardianship, and then deported at a proper age to Santo Domingo or elsewhere. "This would give time for a gradual extinction of that species of labor, and substitution of another, and lessen the severity of the shock, which an operation so fundamental cannot fail to produce." The expenses of the plan might be met by revenue from the public lands, a large part of which had been ceded by the southern states. Until 1820 Jefferson had thought the entire burden must fall on the slaveholding states. With the Missouri Compromise he concluded that the survival of the Union itself depended on the solution of this problem; accordingly, that the responsibility belonged jointly to the federal and state governmets. Such was the fillip of hope in that egregious measure. The magnitude of the object overcame Jefferson's constitutional scruples. The plan was difficult but feasible. "And who could estimate its blessed effects?" he asked. "I leave this to those who will live to see their accomplishment, and to enjoy a beatitude forbidden to my age. But I leave it with the admonition, to rise and be doing." For in another generation the problem would escape control and the country would go the way of Santo Domingo multiplied to the hundredth power. He did not despair utterly. What was right and good must prevail in the end, he philosophized. But would right prevail before disaster? Or would righteousness itself, exalted to hysteria in one section, hysterically resisted in the other, produce disaster? There was a solemn note of resignation in Jefferson's last letter on the subject only two weeks before his death. "A good cause is often injured more by ill-timed efforts of its friends than by the arguments of its enemies," he wrote partly as warning, partly as justification. "Persuasion, perseverance, and patience are the best advocates on questions depending on the will of others. The revolution in public opinion which this cause requires, is not to be expected in a day, or perhaps in an age; but time, which outlives all things, will outlive this evil also. My sentiments have been forty years before the public. Had I repeated them forty times, they would only have become the more stale and threadbare. Although I shall not live to see them consummated," he concluded, "they will not die with me; but living or dying, they will ever be in my most fervent prayer."

Jefferson's anti-slavery opinions, while generally known, only scratched the surface of the public mind during these last unquiet years. His political reaction, on the other hand, moving with the current of Virginia opinion, exposed him to the buffetings of parties and gave him an unwanted prominence in the presidential election of 1824. He had been disappointed in Monroe. Consolidation had reared its ugly head during his administration. Monroe had nursed the illusion of an amalgamation of parties, "that the lion and the lamb are lying down together," and while this might seem the culmination of Jefferson's own strategy of conciliation—"all federalists, all republicans"—it had, in fact, permitted the lions to return in the disguise of the lambs. Monroe approved of the Missouri Compromise, gave up Texas to Spain, acquiesced in rising protectionism, and even yielded on internal improvements without benefit of constitutional amendment. Of course, with some of the President's measures Jefferson concurred, above all the Monroe Doctrine, on which he was fully consulted. The famous pronouncement, declaring the Western Hemisphere off-limits to European powers, expressed the true spirit of Jeffersonian foreign policy, summed up in one of the former President's letters to Monroe while the doctrine was being formulated in Washington: "Our first and fundamental maxim should be, never to entangle ourselves in the broils of Europe. Our second—never to suffer Europe to intermeddle with cis-Altantic affairs. America, North and South, have a set of interests distinct from those of Europe, and perculiarly her own. She should therefore have a system of her own, separate and apart from that of Europe. While the last is laboring to become the domicile of despotism, our endeavor should surely be, to make our hemisphere that of freedom." So long as Jefferson's differences with Monroe were political, they did not intrude on an old friendship. In 1824, however, he asked the favor of a federal office, the Richmond postmastership, for his long-suffering commercial agent, Bradford Peyton, and was turned down. "I asked it as for myself . . . ," he explained bitterly to Peyton. "It was the first opportunity, too, I had ever given him of obliging me. I have miscalculated, and shall better understand my place hereafter." The friendship survived but never recovered its old footing of intimacy.

With the passing of the Virginia Dynasty, the incipient revival of parties, and rising political passions, the succession to the presidency aroused unusual interst. As early as December 1821 attempts were made to enlist Jefferson's name and reputation on the side of one candidate or another. "Numerous have been the attempts to entangle me in the imbroglio," he said a year and some months later. Scrupulously withholding public endorsement of any one of the four or five leading candidates, he nevertheless made it abundantly clear in private letters that William H. Crawford, of Georgia, a Republican of "the old school" was his favorite. And some of these letters were dressed-up for partisan purposes and published in the press, causing the usual perturbations at Monticello. Death eliminated Crawford. No candidate receiving a majority of the electoral vote, the choice fell to the House of Representatives, where John Quincy Adams emerged victorious over Andrew Jackson. Adams represented the consolidationist wing of the amalgamated party, the National Republicans; and while Jefferson had reservations about Jackson, he at once became the rallying point for the Democratic Republicans committed to Jeffersonian restoration on the principles of 1800.

Adams's first message to Congress, in December 1825, produced consternation and dismay at Monticello. Boldly nationalistic, laying out a vast program of internal improvements, embracing not only roads and canals but moral and intellectual objects as well, the message again transported Jefferson back to the Federalist decade. Virginia Republicans turned to him for counsel. He drafted for the legislature a solemn protest against federal usurpations, but then suppressed it on the appearance of firm resolutions from South Carolina and resistance in Congress to the Adams regime. "We had better at present rest awaile on our oars and see which way the tide will set," he prudently advised. Patience and longer endurance was also his directive to Giles, now Governor, who tried, unsuccessfully, to enlist him in the campaign to discredit the motives of Adams's "political conversion" of 1808 and to reveal him as a pseudo-Republican. But in a second and confidential letter to Giles, Jefferson lashed out at the new breed of Republicans, "who having nothing in them of the principles of '76 now look back to a single and splendid government of an aristocracy, founded on banking institutions and monied incorporations under the guise and cloak of their favored branches of manufactures, commerce, and navigation, riding and ruling over the plundered ploughman and beggared yeomanry." With this Taylor-like utterance, he also fixed the limits to patience and endurance. The states must be ever vigilant, he said, and when the sole alternatives become "dissolution of our Union . . . 'or submission to a government without limitation of powers," there should be no hesitation in the choice of liberty. Giles sat on this bombshell while the Sage of Monticello lived; releasing it soon after his death, it created havoc in the National Republican camp and inspired the motley assemblage of democrats and state rightists, northerners, southerners, weterners, aristocratic planters and petty bourgeois, nostalgic Old Republicans and freewheeling entrepreneurs following Andrew Jackson back, figuratively, to the "revolution of 1800."

So, nursing his wounds at Monticello, Jefferson helped to transact the political future. Ironically, the rebel against the past, the prophet of progress and enlightenment, the champion of the living generation ended his days haunted by demons he had vanquished a quarter-century before and left a legacy of fetish and dogma, jealousy and fear, to American politics. This was not the whole of it, of course—only the sadder part. The political shadows that darkened

Jefferson's last years had a reality of their own—they were not imaginary—yet they loomed larger than they were and grew darker still from the gloom around him. The decay of his own fortune was simply an incident to the decay of Virginia. From the richest and most populous state at the beginning of the new nation, Virginia had become one of the poorest, giving up her unfortunates to people the West, and falling farther and farther behind in the race for improvement and power. Too many of her talented sons in the sciences and the arts went north to Philadelphia or elsewhere; those who stayed behind faced blighted careers with a dilettantish sideboard of learning and wit or condemned to the galleys of law and politics. Virginia was not barren culturally or intellectually, as the little circle in Albemarle attested, but she was living on old capital and an ineradicable amateurism lay over everything. Nothing is more likely to evoke the sense of degeneracy than the sense of a "golden age"; and in Virginia the fame of the Revolutionary generation hung like a pall over the sons. In culture as in politics Virginia cherished this grandiose image of herself. Its various parts, truncated and distorted now, held the mind enthralled. In the North things were starting into life—a new age—not only industrially but intellectually. Jefferson's granddaughter Ellen, who married Joseph Coolidge of a prominent Boston family in 1825, felt she was entering a whole new world on her journey northward. The prosperous look of the people, the lands, and the villages, the great improvements of art and industry—why, she exclaimed, "they are at least a century in advance of us." The future lay with Ellen, not with Jeff in Albemarle or the other grandchildren. Jefferson sensed this. Had he not given the last dozen years of his life to rescuing Virginia from that awful destiny,"the Barbary of the Union," by building the University? But he had better reason to know than William Short that it had been "got up against the grain" and that redemption was beyond his powers. (Short predicted the University would collapse within two or three years of the founder's death.) Perhaps there was no redemption, from slavery or ignorance or debt; but the crisis of 1819–20 sent him charging back to 1800 for a political cure of the Virginia malaise. It was indeed the sadder part of a chapter otherwise glorious and full of faith.

Men who visited the Sage of Monticello near the end of his life said he appeared a man twenty years younger than he was. The ravages of age were more evident to him than to the casual observer, but his mind remained lively, his senses sharp, his countenance warm, his manners as bright and urbane as ever. He attributed his good health, generally, to temperate habits of living. He ate moderately, an essentially vegetable diet, and drank light wines only. He kept regular hours, exercised daily on horseback, and bathed his feet every morning in cold water, as he had done for sixty years, to which he ascribed his remarkable freedom from colds. With little trust in physic and less in physicians—three of them together were enough to bring buzzards to the neighborhood, he jested—he was fortunate in rarely needing either.

Nevertheless, the toll of physical affliction mounted from his seventy-fifth year. After the conference at Rockfish Gap, it may be recalled, he rode to Warm Springs to seek relief from the aches and pains of rheumatism. But the waters, finding no disease to heal, made one instead. He returned home prostrated by a severe intestinal disturbance, which grew worse under treatment, and actually brought him to death's door for a time. The illness lasted many months and he never got entirely free of it. In 1822 he broke his left arm in a fall; the crippled state of his right hand and wrist, badly swollen from the old dislocation, made writing increasingly painful. On occasion he employed one of the grandchildren as a secretary. Except at brief intervals, until the final illness came on in 1825, he was able to continue his accustomed rounds. He could often be seen trudging to and from the University. Horseback riding had long ago replaced walking as the "sovereign invigorator" of mind and body; indeed, said Jefferson, "so delightful and so necessary is this daily revival to me, that I would wish to lose that and life together."

Monticello continued to receive its stream of visitors. The rising University offered an additional attraction to some. Early in November 1824, General Lafayette, then on a triumphal tour of the United States—an unparalleled patriotic extravaganza—wound up the mountain in a wave of Revolutionary banners, stepped from his carriage at the east lawn, and met Jefferson halfway to the door, where the old comrades fell tearfully into each other's arms. They traversed a vast field of history during the General's visit of several days. Jefferson, ill and feeble, attended a great banquet for the "nation's guest" in the Rotunda, still under scaffolding, at the University. Three Presidents of the United States sat at the head-table. It was Jefferson's last public appearance. He made a little address, through the voice of another, extolling Lafayette's services in war and peace and closing with a prayer for the eternal duration of the nation's freedom.

Perhaps the best description of Jefferson at this time comes from Daniel Webster, then a rising political star, though in another firmament than Jefferson's. Tall and thin, head set forward on the shoulders, neck wiry and limber, hair long and graying—Thomas Sully captured the main features in his full-length portrait of 1821 which, adding the life-mask by J.H.I. Browere in 1825, offers the best likeness of the aged Sage. "His eyes are small," said Webster, "very light, and now neither brilliant nor striking. His chin is rather long, but not pointed. His nose small, regular in its outline, and the nostrils a little elevated. His mouth is well-formed and still filled with teeth; it is strongly compressed, bearing an expression of contentment and benevolence. His complexion, formerly light and freckled, now bears the marks of age and cutaneous affection. His limbs are uncommonly long; his hands and feet very large, and his wrists [both swollen from fractures] of an extraordinary size. His walk is . . . easy and swinging. He stoops a little . . . . When sitting, he appears short, partly from a rather lounging habit of sitting and partly from the disproportionate length of his limbs." Webster thought his dress neglected but not slovenly. Even in the house—it was December 1824—he wore a long gray overcoat (surtout) and two waistcoats underneath. "His pantaloons are very long and loose, and of the same color as his coat." He wore glasses only to read at night and his hearing was good. His conversation, easy and natural, touched everything with lightness and grace. On the whole, Webster thought, he showed "an extraordinary degree of health, vivacity, and spirit."

The last illness, urinary in nature, descended the following May. For long intervals Jefferson lay on a couch of pain. But he was often up and about, if not in the saddle then in the carriage. "The little of the powers of life which remains to me I consecrate to our university," he wrote in October. But for the specter of bankruptcy he could go peacefully in the confidence of Seneca that "he who had dedicated his mind to virtue, and to the good of human society, whereof he is a member, had consummated all that is either profitable or necessary for him to know or to do toward the establishment of his peace." But on his death the creditors would flock like buzzards over the mountain, and his family, even his beloved daughter, would be driven penniless and propertyless from the land of their birth. From this gloomy prospect he sought relief in January 1826 by appealing to the legislature for permission to dispose of most of his property by lottery. This last mortifying solution had become "almost a question of life and death." Lotteries were not uncommon in Virginia for eleemosynary purposes, but the privilege had very rarely, in recent decades, been extended to individuals and in no instances analogous to Jefferson's. For the first time in his life he begged a personal favor from the state he had served. Mainly he urged the prostration in the value of lands, which if sold on the market must be sacrificed at one-third or one-fourth of their true worth. Raffled in a lottery on a fair valuation, his property should realize enough money to pay his debts and leave to him and Martha Monticello with an adjoining farm. The General Assembly, after some hesitation, bowed to his request in February. As the lottery was set in motion, the American public learned of Jefferson's plight. Gratitude, it had often been said, is a virtue unknown to republics. As if to refute the slur, Jefferson's friends and admirers in New York, Philadelphia, Baltimore, and elsewhere organized subscription funds in his behalf. The lottery was suspended. Jefferson died in the belief, quite delusory as it turned out, that this outpouring of public sympathy and affection would save his estate.

He slowly sank from the middle of February. The urinary disease, compounded by a renewed attack of diarrhea, drained the life from his body. In March, knowing he must die, he drew his last will. It provided for the emancipation, subject to legislative confirmation, of five of his ablest and most faithful slaves. Neither the state of his property nor the state of the laws, he felt, permitted him to do more. The fatal crisis arrived in June. (The last entry in his account book was on June 20: "Isaacs for cheese 4.84.") Dr. Dunglison, the University Professor of Medicine who was at his bedside, remarked on the clarity and vigor of his mind to the end. "Until the 2nd and 3rd of July," the Doctor recalled, "he spoke freely of his approaching death; made all his arrangements with his grandson, Mr. Randolph, in regard to his private affairs; and expressed his anxiety for the prosperity of the University and his confidence in the exertion in its behalf of Mr. Madison and the other Visitors . . . . In the course of the day and night of the 2nd of July, he was affected with stupor, with intervals of wakefulness and consciousness; but on the 3rd, the stupor became permanent. About seven o'clock of the evening of that day, he awoke, and seeing my staying at his bedside exclaimed, 'Oh Doctor, are you still there?' in a voice, however, that was husky and indistinct. He then asked, 'Is it the Fourth?' to which I replied, 'It soon will be.' These were the last words I heard him utter."

The patriarch died at Monticello, surrounded by his family, at approximately one o'clock in the afternoon on the fiftieth anniversary of the Declaration of Independence. (On his reading table were two French political pamphlets, Aristotle's *Politics*, and a volume of Seneca.) John Adams also died on that memorable day at Quincy. His last words, "Thomas Jefferson still survives," prophesied a long history still to come, for Jefferson could not escape the future. More than any of his great contemporaries he had given form to the ideas, the values, even the dilemmas of the new nation, and thus involved himself with its destiny. He had inspired its democracy, which was egalitarian and progressive and inherently centralizing, yet within a coherent frame of law committed to the protection of individual and provincial rights and to the guardianship of enlightened intelligence. He had inspired the nationality of the Americans, not only the elements of independence and empire but those of character and ethos as well, yet under an overarching vision of the revolutionary nation's responsibilities to the freedom and peace and happiness of mankind. He had inspired the new nation with the hopes of the Enlightenment, embracing the paired directives toward nature and progress, science and humanism, power and civility, self-discovery and universality.

It was a mighty legacy. Posterity could comprehend it only in fragments. Lying on his deathbed, Jefferson's mind wandered backwards to the American Revolution, when the dream of the new nation was born. He had been invited to attend the anniversary ceremonies in Washington. Ten days before he died he penned his last letter, declining the invitation but affirming the faith of his life in a noble last testament to the nation on its jubilee. "May it be to the world, what I believe it will be (to some parts sooner, to others later, but finally to all), the signal of arousing men to burst the chains under which monkish ignorance and superstition had persuaded them to bind themselves, and to assume the blessings and security of self-government. That form which we have substituted, restores the free right to the unbounded exercise of reason and freedom of opinion. All eyes are opened, or opening, to the rights of man. The general spread of the light of science has already laid open to every view the palpable truth, that the mass of mankind has not been born with saddles on their backs, nor a favored few booted and spurred, ready to ride them legitimately, by the grace of God. These are grounds of hope for others. For ourselves, let the annual return of this day, forever refresh our recollections of these rights, and an undiminished devotion to them." And so he went to his death in the knowledge that the end of a man is nothing weighed in the scales with the history he has made.

Select

Bibliography

THE BIBLIOGRAPHY lists the sources of principal interest for this study. The bibliographical essay in *The Jefferson Image in the American Mind* offers a view of the literature from the time of Jefferson's death. Many items cited there are not repeated here. Also omitted are the books that Jefferson read—the books that shaped and informed his mind—to which the best guide is Sowerby's *Catalogue* of Jefferson's library, cited below.

PRIMARY SOURCES

a) *Jefferson Papers*

Three major manuscript collections:

Library of Congress. (Principally letters to and from Jefferson, it is of first importance for his public career.) Microfilm Edition.

Massachusetts Historical Society. (Sometimes called the Coolidge Collection, it is of special interest for Jefferson's private affairs.) Microfilm Edition.

University of Virginia. (A varied collection most useful for family and local concerns. A calendar is available: *The Jefferson Papers of the University of Virginia*, Constance E. Thurlow and Francis L. Berkeley, Jr., comp.)

The Account Books (1767–1826). Typescript photocopy, University of Virginia.

Published Editions:

The Writings of Thomas Jefferson. 10 v. Paul L. Ford, ed. (New York, 1892–99)

The Writings of Thomas Jefferson. 20 v. A. A. Lipscomb and A. E. Bergh, eds. (Washington, 1903)

The Papers of Thomas Jefferson. 17 v. to date. Julian P. Boyd and others, eds. (Princeton, 1950–65)

Other Published Works:

The Commonplace Book of Thomas Jefferson. Gilbert Chinard, ed. (Baltimore, 1926)

The Literary Bible of Thomas Jefferson. Gilbert Chinard, ed. (Baltimore, 1928)

Thomas Jefferson's Garden Book, 1766–1824. Edwin M. Betts, ed. (Philadelphia, 1944)

Thomas Jefferson's Farm Book. Edwin M. Betts, ed. (New York, 1953)

Notes on the State of Virginia. William Peden, ed. (Chapel Hill, 1955)

"A Memoir on the Discovery of Certain Bones of a Quadruped of the Clawed Kind in the Western Parts of Virginia," American Philosophical Society *Transactions*, v. 4 (1799)

The Complete Anas of Thomas Jefferson. F. B. Sawvel, ed. (New York, 1903)

Catalogue of the Library of Thomas Jefferson. 5 v. E. Millicent Sowerby, ed. (Washington, 1952)

The Complete Jefferson. Saul K. Padover, ed. (New York, 1943)

b) *State Papers and Related Documents*

American Archives. 9 v. Peter Force, ed. (Washington, 1837–53)

American State Papers. 38 v. Walter Lowrie and Matthew S. Clarke, eds. (Washington, 1836–61)

Calendar of Virginia State Papers and Other Manuscripts. 11 v. W. P. Palmer and others, eds. (Richmond, 1875–93)

Collection of Interesting and Important Reports and Papers on Navigation and Trade. (London, 1807)

A Compilation of the Messages and Papers of the Presidents. 10 v. J. D. Richardson, ed. (Washington, 1907)

Correspondence of the French Ministers to the United States, 1791–97. F. J. Turner, ed. American Historical Association *Annual Report,* 1903. (Washington, 1904)

Debates and Proceedings in the Congress of the United States, v. 1–19 (Washington, 1834–53)

Instructions to the British Ministers to the United States, 1791–1812. Bernard Mayo, ed. American Historical Association *Annual Report,* 1936. (Washington, 1941)

Journal of the House of Delegates of Virginia, 1776–1790. (Richmond, 1827–28)

Journals of the Council of State of Virginia, 1776–1781. 2 v. H. R. McIlwaine, ed. (Richmond, 1931–32)

Journals of the Continental Congress. 34 v. Worthington C. Ford, ed. (Washington, 1904–36)

Louisiana Under the Rule of Spain, France, and the United States, 1785–1807. 2 v. James A. Robertson, ed. (Cleveland, 1911)

Papers Relating to America. (London, 1810)

Reports of the Trials of Aaron Burr. 2 v. D. Robertson, ed. (Philadelphia, 1808)

The Statutes at Large . . . Virginia. 13 v. W. W. Hening, ed. (Richmond, 1809–23)

The Territorial Papers of the United States, 24 v. Clarence E. Carter, ed. (Washington, 1934–52)

c) *Contemporary Letters, Journals and Writings*

(Letters are incorporated in some of the biographical works listed under Secondary Sources—Other Books.)

Adams, Abigail: *Letters of Mrs. Adams.* 4th ed. Charles F. Adams, ed. (Boston, 1848)
New Letters of Abigail Adams, 1788–1801. Stewart Mitchell, ed. (Boston, 1947)

Adams, John: *Works.* 10 v. Charles F. Adams, ed. (Boston, 1850–56)
Diary and Autobiography. 4 v. L. H. Butterfield, ed. (Cambridge, 1961)
Papers of John Adams. (Letters 1797–1801) Microfilm Edition.
The Adams-Jefferson Letters. 2 v. Lester Cappon, ed. (Chapel Hill, 1959)

The Spur of Fame: Dialogues of John Adams and Benjamin Rush, 1805–1813. John A. Schutz and Douglass Adair, eds. (San Marino, Calif., 1966)

Adams, John Quincy: *Memoirs.* 12 v. Charles Adams, ed. (Philadelphia, 1874–77)

Writings. 7 v. Worthington C. Ford, ed. (New York, 1913–17)

Adams, Samuel: *Writings.* 4 v. H. A. Cushing, ed. (New York, 1904–08)

Ames, Fisher: *Works.* 2 v. Seth Ames, ed. (Boston, 1854)

Bayard, James A.: *Papers.* Elizabeth Donnan, ed. American Historical Association *Annual Report,* 1913 (Washington, 1915)

Bland, Theodorick, Jr.: *Papers.* 2 v. Charles Campbell, ed. (Petersburg, Va., 1840–43)

Bond, Phineas: *Letters.* J. F. Jameson, ed. American Historical Association *Annual Report,* 1896–97 (Washington, 1897–98)

Bowdoin, James: *The Bowdoin and Temple Papers,* Part II. Massachusetts Historical Society *Collections,* 7th ser., v. 6 (Boston, 1907)

Burwell, William A.: "Private Memoir . . . ." MS, Library of Congress

Cabell, Joseph C.: *Early History of the University of Virginia as Contained in the Letters of Thomas Jefferson and Joseph C. Cabell.* Nathaniel F. Cabell, ed. (Richmond, 1856)

Carter, Landon: *Diary . . . , 1752–1758.* 2 v. Jack P. Greene, ed. (Charlottesville, 1965)

Clark, George Rogers: *Papers, 1771–1781.* James A. James, ed. Illinois Historical Society *Collections.* (Springfield, 1912)

Cutler, Manasseh: *Life, Journals and Correspondence.* 2 v. (Cincinnati, 1888)

Daggett, David: "Selections from the Letters Received . . . , 1786–1802." Franklin B. Dexter, ed. American Antiquarian Society *Proceedings,* new ser., v. 4 (1855–87)

Duane, William: "Letters." Worthington C. Ford, ed. Massachusetts Historical Society *Proceedings,* 3rd ser., v. 20 (1906–07)

Dunbar, William: *Life, Letters and Papers.* Mrs. Dunbar Rowland, ed. (Jackson, Miss., 1930)

Dunlap, William: *Diary.* 3 v. (New York, 1930)

Dupont de Nemours, Pierre Samuel: *Correspondence . . . Jefferson.* Dumas Malone, ed. (Boston, 1930)

Erskine, David M.: "Letters from America, 1798–1799." Patricia H. Menk, ed. *William and Mary Quarterly,* 3rd ser., v. 6 (1949)

Fenwick, Joseph: "Letters . . . , 1787–1795." Richard K. MacMaster, ed. *Maryland Historical Magazine*, v. 60 (1965)

Few, Frances: "Diary . . . , 1808–1809." Noble E. Cunningham, Jr., ed. *Journal of Southern History*, v. 29 (1963)

Fithian, Phillip V.: *Journal and Letters . . . , 1773–1774*. H. D. Farish, ed. (Williamsburg, 1943)

Foster, Sir Augustus: *Jeffersonian America*. Richard Beale Davis, ed. (San Marino, Calif., 1954)

Gallatin, Albert: *Writings*. 3 v. Henry Adams, ed. (Philadelphia, 1879)

Grenville, William W.: *The Manuscripts of J. B. Fortesque. . . .* v. 9. Royal Historical Manuscripts Commission (London, 1915)

Griswold, Roger: Papers (1797–1801). Library of Congress. Microfilm Edition.

Hamilton, Alexander: *Works*. 7 v. John C. Hamilton, ed. (New York, 1850–51)
Works. 12 v. Henry Cabot Lodge, ed. (New York, 1904)
Papers. v. 1–14. Harold Syrett and others, eds. (New York, 1961–69)

Higginson, Stephen: "Letters . . . , 1783–1804." J. F. Jameson, ed. American Historical Association *Annual Report*, 1896. (Washington, 1897)

Honyman, Robert: "Diary and Journal . . . , 1776–1782." MS, Library of Congress

Howe, John: "Secret Reports .·. . , 1808." David W. Parker, ed. *American Historical Review*, v. 17 (1911–12)

Iredell, James: *Life and Correspondence*. 2 v. G. J. McRee, ed. (New York, 1857–58)

Jay, John: *Correspondence and Public Papers*. 4 v. Henry P. Johnston, ed. (New York, 1890–93)

Jones, Joseph: *Letters . . . , 1777–1787*. Worthington C. Ford, ed. (New York, 1889)

King, Rufus: *Life and Correspondence*. 6 v. Charles R. King, ed. (New York, 1894–1900)

Latrobe, Benjamin H.: *Journal* (New York, 1905)

Lee, Richard Henry: *Letters*. 2 v. James C. Ballagh, ed. (New York, 1911–14)

Letters of Members of the Continental Congress. 8 v. Edmund C. Burnett, ed. (Washington, 1921–36)

Lewis, Meriwether, and William Clark: *Letters of the Lewis and Clark Expedition*. Donald Jackson, ed. (Urbana, Ill., 1962)

Original Journals of the Lewis and Clark Expedition, 1804–06. 8 v. Reuben G. Thwaites, ed. (New York, 1904–05)

Liston, Henrietta: "Letters . . . , 1796–1801." Bradford Perkins, ed. *William and Mary Quarterly,* 3rd ser., v. 11 (1954)

Maclay, William: *Journal.* E. S. Maclay, ed. (New York, 1890)

Madison, James: *Letters and Other Writings.* 4 v. (Washington, 1894)

Writings. 9 v. Gaillard Hunt, ed. (New York, 1900–10)

Papers. v. 1–5. William T. Hutcheson and Willam M. E. Rachel, eds. (Chicago, 1962–69)

Presidential Papers. Library of Congress. Microfilm Edition.

Marshall, Christopher: *Passages from the Diary.* William Duane, ed. (Philadelphia, 1849)

Miscellaneous State Department Papers, 1801–09. Microfilm Edition.

Mitchill, Samuel L.: "Letters from Washington, 1801–1813." *Harper's Magazine,* v. 58 (1879)

Monroe, James: *Writings.* 7 v. S. M. Hamilton, ed. (New York, 1898–1903)

Presidential Papers. Library of Congress. Microfilm Edition.

Morris, Gouverneur: *A Diary of the French Revolution.* 2 v. Beatrix C. Davenport, ed. (Boston, 1939)

Murray, William Vans: "Letters . . . to John Quincy Adams, 1797–1803." Worthington C. Ford, ed. American Historical Association *Annual Report,* 1912 (Washington, 1914)

Nicholas, Wilson Cary: Papers. Library of Congress. Microfilm Edition.

Otto, Louis W.: "A French Diplomat's View of the First Congress, 1790." Margaret M. O'Dwyer, ed. *William and Mary Quarterly,* 3rd ser., v. 21 (1964)

Paine, Thomas: *Writings.* 2 v. Philip Foner, ed. (New York, 1945)

Pendleton, Edmund: *Letters and Papers.* 2 v. David J. Mays, ed. (Charlottesville, 1967)

Pickering, Timothy: *Calendar of Pickering Papers.* Massachusetts Historical Society *Collections,* v. 58 (Boston, 1896)

Plumer, William: *Memorandum of Proceedings in the Senate, 1803–07.* E. S. Brown, ed. (New York, 1923)

Riedesel, Friederich von: *Memoirs, Letters and Journals.* 2 v. W. L. Stone, tr. (Albany, 1868)

Riedesel, Madame: *Letters and Journals.* W. L. Stone, tr. (Albany, 1867)

Rush, Benjamin: *Letters.* 2 v. Lyman H. Butterfield, ed. (Princeton, 1951)
Old Family Letters (Philadelphia, 1892)

Simcoe, John Graves: *Military Journal.* (New York, 1844)

Smith, Abigail Adams: *Journal and Correspondence of Miss Adams.* Ed. by her daughter. (New York, 1841)

Smith, John Cotton: *Correspondence and Miscellanies.* (New York, 1847)

Smith, Robert: "Some Papers . . . ." Bernard C. Steiner, ed. *Maryland Historical Magazine,* v. 15 (1925)

Smith, Samuel: Papers. Library of Congress. Microfilm Edition.

"South Carolina Federalist Correspondence, 1789-1797." Ulrich B. Phillips, ed. *American Historical Review,* v. 14 (1909)

Steele, John: *Papers.* 2 v. H. M. Wagstaff, ed. (Raleigh, N.C., 1924)

Taggart, Samuel: "Letters . . . , 1803-1814." George H. Haynes, ed. American Antiquarian Society *Proceedings,* new ser., v. 33 (1923)

Taylor, John: "Letters, 1793-1823." *John P. Branch Historical Papers of Randolph-Macon College,* v. 2 (1908)

Thornton, Edward: "A Young Englishman Reports on the New Nation . . . , 1791-1793." S. W. Jackman, ed. *William and Mary Quarterly,* 3rd ser., v. 18 (1961)

Von Humboldt, Alexander: "Correspondence with Jefferson, Madison and Gallatin." Helmut de Terra, ed. American Philosophical Society *Proceedings,* v. 103 (1959)

Washington, George: *Correspondence of the American Revolution, Being Letters of Eminent Men to George Washington,* 4 v. Jared Sparks, ed. (Boston, 1853)
Diaries, 1748-1799. 4 v. J. C. Fitzpatrick, ed. (Boston, 1925)
Washington's Farewell Address. Victor H. Paltsits, ed. (New York, 1935)
Writings. 39 v. J. C. Fitzpatrick, ed. (Washington, 1931-41)

Webster, Noah: *Letters.* Harry R. Warfel, ed. (New York, 1953)

Wilson, James: *Works.* 2 v. James D. Andrews, ed. (Chicago, 1896)

d) *Contemporary Newspapers, Magazines, Pamphlets, and Political Miscellany*

Newspapers:

Aurora (Philadelphia), 1797-1809
Gazette of the United States (New York, Philadelphia), 1790-93, 1798-1800

General Advertiser (Philadelphia), 1790–93
National Gazette (Philadelphia), 1791–93
National Intelligencer (Washington), 1800–09
Niles' Weekly Register (Baltimore), 1811–26
Virginia Gazette(s) (Williamsburg), 1769–76

Magazines:

American Museum (Philadelphia), 1787–92
North American Review (Boston), 1815–26

Pamphlets and Miscellany:

Austin, Benjamin, *Constitutional Republicanism* (Boston, 1803)

Baring, Alexander, *An Inquiry Into the Causes and Consequences of the Order in Council* . . . . (London, 1808)

Barlow, Joel, *Advice to the Privileged Orders* (New York, 1794)

[Beckley, John], *An Address to the People of the United States with an Epitome and Vindication of the Public Life and Character of Thomas Jefferson* (Philadelphia, 1800)

Brougham, Henry, *The Speech . . . Before the House of Commons . . . April 1, 1808* (London, 1808)

Callender, James T., *The Political Progress of Britain*. 2 v., 3rd ed. (Philadelphia, 1795)
The Prospect Before Us. 3 v. (Richmond, 1800–01)

Cobbett, William, *Porcupine's Works*. 12 v. (London, 1801)

Cooper, Thomas, *Political Essays* (Northumberland, Pa., 1799)

Coxe, Tench, *Reflections on the State of the Union* (Philadelphia, 1792)
A View of the United States of America (Philadelphia, 1794)

Daveiss, Joseph Hamilton, *A View of the President's Conduct Concerning the Conspiracy of 1806* (Frankfort, Ky., 1807)

Fenno, John, Jr., *New Political Aspects* (Philadelphia, 1799)

[Fessenden, William G.], *Democracy Unveiled*. 2 v., 3rd ed. (New York, 1806)

Hay, George, *An Essay on the Liberty of the Press* . . . . (Richmond, 1803)

Knox, Samuel, *A Vindication of the Religion of Mr. Jefferson* (Baltimore. 1801)

An Essay on the Best System of Liberal Education (Baltimore, 1799)

Magruder, Allan B., *Political, Commercial, and Moral Reflections on the Late Cession of Louisiana to the United States* (Lexington, Ky., 1803)

Mason, John M., *The Voice of Warning to Christians* . . . . (New York, 1800)

Moore, Frank, comp., *Diary of the American Revolution, from Newspapers and Original Documents*. 2 v. (New York, 1859–60)

Pickering, Timothy, *A Letter to the Honorable William Sullivan* . . . . (Hartford, 1808)

Pownall, Thomas, *A Memorial . . . to the Sovereigns of Europe*. . . . 2nd ed. (London, 1780)

Price, Richard, *Observations on the Nature of Civil Liberty* (London, 1776)
Observations on the Importance of the American Revolution (London, 1784)

Roscoe, William, *Consideration on the Causes, Objects, and Consequences of the Present War* (London, 1808)

Schlegel, J. F. W., *Neutral Rights* . . . . (Philadelphia, 1801)

Sheffield, Lord [John Baker Holroyd], *Observations on the Commerce of the United States* (London, 1783)

[Smith, William Loughton], *The Politicks and Views of a Certain Party Displayed* (n.p., 1792)
The Pretensions of Thomas Jefferson to the Presidency Examined . . . . (Philadelphia, 1796)

[Stephen, James], *War in Disguise; or The Frauds of the Neutral Flags* (London, 1805)

Taylor, John, *Arator*. 2nd ed. (Georgetown, 1814)
An Examination of the Late Proceedings of Congress Respecting the Official Conduct of the Secretary of the Treasury (Philadelphia, 1793)
An Inquiry Into the Principles and Policy of the Government of the United States (New Haven, 1950)
Construction Construed and Constitutions Vindicated (Richmond, 1820)

Tucker, St. George, ed., Notes and Appendices, *Blackstone's Commentaries*. 5 v. (Philadelphia, 1803)
A Dissertation on Slavery (Philadelphia, 1796)

Reflections on the Cession of Louisiana to the United States (Washington, 1803)

e) *Travels*

Anburey, Thomas, *Travels Through the Interior Parts of America.* 2 v. (London, 1789)

Bayard, Ferdinand-Marie, *Travels of a Frenchman in Maryland and Virginia . . . , in 1791.* Ben C. McCary, ed. (Williamsburg, 1950)

Bernard, John, *Retrospections of America, 1797–1811* (New York, 1887)

Boudinot, Elias, *Journey to Boston in 1809.* M. H. Thomas, ed. (Princeton, 1955)

Bradbury, John, *Travels in the Interior of America* (Liverpool, 1817)

Brissot de Warville, J. P., *New Travels in the United States of America.* 2nd ed. (London, 1794)

Burnaby, Andrew, *Travels through North America.* [1759–60] Rufus R. Wilson, ed. (New York, 1904)

Caldwell, John Edwards, *A Tour Through Part of Virginia in . . . 1808.* (New York, 1809)

Chastellux, Marquis de, *Travels in North America, 1780, 1781.* Howard C. Rice, tr. and ed. (Chapel Hill, 1963)

Crevecoeur, M. G. St. Jean de, *Letters from An American Farmer* (London, 1782)

Davis, John, *Travels in the United States* (New York, 1803)

Du Roi, August Wilhelm, *Journal.* Charlotte S. J. Epping, tr. (New York, 1911)

Hunter, Robert, Jr., *Quebec to Carolina in 1785–1786.* Louis B. Wright and Marion Tinling, eds. (San Marino, 1943)

Kendall, Edward A., *Travels Through the Northern Parts of the United States, in 1807–1808.* 3 v. (New York, 1809)

La Rochefoucauld Liancourt, Francois A. F., Duc de, *Travels Through the United States of North America.* 2 v. (London, 1799)

Melish, John, *Travels in the United States of America, in the Years 1806 and 1807.* 2 v. (Philadelphia, 1812)

Moreau de Saint-Méry, *American Journey, 1793–1798.* Kenneth Roberts and Anna M. Roberts, tr. and ed. (Garden City, 1947)

Schoepf, Johann David, *Travels in the Confederation*. 2 v. Alfred J. Morrison, tr. and ed. (Philadelphia, 1911)

Smyth, John F. D., *A Tour of the United States of America, 1784*. 2 v. (Dublin, 1784)

Strickland, William, *Observations on the Agriculture of the United States of America* (London, 1801)

Sutcliffe, Robert, *Travels in Some Parts of North America in the Years 1804, 1805, and 1806*. (Philadelphia, 1812)

Weld, Isaac, Jr., *Travels Through the States of North America . . . During the Years 1795, 1796, and 1797* (London, 1799)

Young, Arthur, *Travels in France During the Years 1787, 1788, 1789*. M. Betham-Edwards, ed. (London, 1913)

SECONDARY SOURCES

a) *Books on Jefferson*

Berman, Eleanor D., *Thomas Jefferson Among the Arts* (New York, 1947)

Boorstin, Daniel, *The Lost World of Thomas Jefferson* (New York, 1948)

Bullock, Helen D., *My Head and My Heart* (New York, 1945)

Caldwell, Lynton K., *The Administrative Theories of Hamilton and Jefferson* (Chicago, 1944)

Chinard, Gilbert, *Thomas Jefferson, The Apostle of Americanism*. Rev. ed. (New York, 1939)

Dumbauld, Edward, *Thomas Jefferson, American Tourist* (Norman, Okla., 1946)

Frary, I. T., *Thomas Jefferson, Architect and Builder* (Richmond, 1931)

Healey, Robert M., *Jefferson on Religion in Public Education* (New Haven, 1962)

Honeywell, Roy J., *The Educational Work of Thomas Jefferson*, (Cambridge, 1931)

Kimball, Fiske, *The Life Portraits of Jefferson and Their Replicas* (Philadelphia, 1944)
  Thomas Jefferson, Architect (Boston, 1916)

Kimball, Marie, *Jefferson: The Road to Glory* (New York, 1943)

Jefferson: War and Peace (New York, 1947)

Jefferson: The Scene of Europe (New York, 1950)

Koch, Adrienne, *Jefferson and Madison: The Great Collaboration* (New York, 1951)

The Philosophy of Thomas Jefferson (New York, 1943)

Lehman, Karl, *Thomas Jefferson, American Humanist* (Chicago, 1947)

Levy, Leonard, *Jefferson and Civil Liberties* (Cambridge, 1963)

Malone, Dumas, *Jefferson the Virginian* (Boston, 1948)

Jefferson and the Rights of Man (Boston, 1951)

Jefferson and the Ordeal of Liberty (Boston, 1962)

Martin, Edwin T., *Thomas Jefferson, Scientist* (New York, 1952)

Nichols, Frederick D., *Thomas Jefferson's Architectural Drawings* (Boston, 1960)

Nock, Albert J., *Jefferson* (New York, 1926)

Parton, James, *Life of Thomas Jefferson* (Boston, 1874)

Peterson, Merrill D., *The Jefferson Image in the American Mind* (New York, 1960)

Randall, Henry S., *Life of Thomas Jefferson.* 3 v. (Philadelphia, 1857)

Randolph, Sarah N., *The Domestic Life of Thomas Jefferson.* American Classics Edition (New York, 1958)

Tucker, George, *Life of Thomas Jefferson*, 2 v. (Philadelphia, 1837)

Wiltse, Charles M., *The Jeffersonian Tradition in American Democracy* (Chapel Hill, 1935)

b) *Other Books*

Abel, Anna H., *The History of Events Resulting in Indian Consolidation West of the Mississippi.* American Historical Association *Annual Report*, 1906 (Washington, 1908)

Abernethy, Thomas P., *The Burr Conspiracy* (New York, 1954)

The South in the New Nation, 1789–1819 (Baton Rouge, 1961)

Western Lands and the American Revolution (New York, 1937)

Acomb, Frances, *Anglophobia in France, 1763–1789* (Durham, N.C., 1950)

Adams, Henry, *History of the United States During the Administrations of Jefferson and Madison.* 9 v. (New York, 1891–93)

The Life of Albert Gallatin (Philadelphia, 1879)

ed., *Documents Relating to New England Federalism, 1800–1815* (Boston, 1877)

Adams, Herbert B., *The College of William and Mary* (Washington, 1887)

Thomas Jefferson and the University of Virginia (Washington, 1888)

Adams, Randolph G., *Political Ideas of the American Revolution* (Durham, N.C., 1922)

Agar, Herbert, *The Price of Union* (Boston, 1950)

Alden, John R., *John Stuart and the Southern Colonial Frontier* (Ann Arbor, 1944)

The South in the Revolution, 1763–1789 (Baton Rouge, 1957)

Allen, Harry C., *Great Britain and the United States: A History of Anglo-American Relations* (London, 1954)

Alvord, Clarence W., *The Mississippi Valley in British Politics.* 2 v. (Cleveland, 1917)

Anderson, Dice R., *William Branch Giles* (Menasha, Wisc., 1914)

Arendt, Hannah, *On Revolution* (New York, 1963)

Arieli, Yehoshua, *Individualism and Tradition in American Ideology* (Cambridge, 1964)

Aronson, Sidney H., *Status and Kinship in the Higher Civil Service* (Cambridge, 1964)

Bacon-Foster, Corra, *The Potomac Route to the West* (Washington, 1912)

Bailyn, Bernard, "General Introduction," *Pamphlets of the American Revolution.* v. 1 (Cambridge, 1965)

Baldwin, Simeon E., *Life and Letters of Simeon Baldwin* (New Haven, 1918)

Balinky, Alexander, *Albert Gallatin: Fiscal Theories and Policies* (New Brunswick, 1958)

Barnes, Harry Elmer, *The Evolution of Penology in Pennsylvania* (Indianapolis, 1927)

Barnhart, John D., *Henry Hamilton and George Rogers Clark . . . .* (Crawfordsville, Ind., 1951)

Beard, Charles A., *Economic Origins of Jeffersonian Democracy* (New York, 1915)

and Mary R. Beard, *The American Spirit* (New York, 1942)

Becker, Carl, *The Declaration of Independence* (New York, 1922)

Bemis, Samuel F., *Jay's Treaty* (New York, 1923)

John Quincy Adams and the Foundations of American Foreign Policy (New York, 1949)

ed., *The American Secretaries of State and Their Diplomacy.* v. 1 and 2 (New York, 1927)

Bernhard, Winfred E. A., *Fisher Ames, Federalist Statesman, 1758–1808.* (Chapel Hill, 1965)

Beveridge, Albert J., *Life of John Marshall.* 4 v. (Boston, 1916–19)

Blake, John B., *Benjamin Waterhouse and the Introduction of Vaccination . . . .* (Philadelphia, 1957)

Boorstin, Daniel, *The Americans: The Colonial Experience* (New York, 1958)

Borden, Morton, *The Federalism of James A. Bayard* (New York, 1955)

Boudinot, Jane J., ed., *The Life of Elias Boudinot.* 2 v. (Boston, 1896)

Boulton, James T., *The Language of Politics in the Age of Wilkes and Burke* (Toronto, 1963)

Boyd, Julian P., *The Declaration of Independence: The Evolution of the Text. . . .* (Washington, 1943)

Number 7, Alexander Hamilton's Secret Attempts to Control American Foreign Policy (Princeton, 1964)

Brant, Irving, *James Madison: The Virginia Revolutionist* (Indianapolis, 1941)

James Madison: Father of the Constitution (Indianapolis, 1950)

James Madison: Secretary of State (Indianapolis, 1953)

James Madison: The President (Indianapolis, 1959)

James Madison: Commander-in-Chief (Indianapolis, 1961)

Bridenbaugh, Carl, *Myths and Realities: Societies of the Colonial South* (Baton Rouge, 1952)

Seat of Empire: The Political Role of Eighteenth Century Williamsburg (Charlottesville, 1963)

Briggs, Herbert W., *The Doctrine of Continuous Voyage* (Baltimore, 1926)

Brown, Everett S., *Constitutional History of the Louisiana Purchase, 1803–1812* (Berkeley, 1920)

Brown, Glenn, *History of the United States Capitol.* v. 1 (Washington, 1900)

Brown, Robert E., and B. Katherine Brown, *Virginia, 1705–1786: Democracy or Aristocracy?* (East Lansing, Mich., 1964)

Brown, Roger H., *The Republic in Peril: 1812* (New York, 1964)

Bruce, Philip Alexander, *History of the University of Virginia.* v. 1 and 2 (New York, 1920)

Bruce, William C., *John Randolph of Roanoke* (New York, 1939)

Bruchey, Stuart, *The Roots of American Economic Growth* (New York, 1965)

Bryan, Wilhemus B., *A History of the National Capital.* v. 1 (New York, 1914)

Brydon, George M., *Virginia's Mother Church.* 2 v. (Philadelphia, 1952)

Bryson, Gladys, *Man and Society: The Scottish Inquiry of the Eighteenth Century* (Princeton, 1945)

Bulfinch, Ellen S., ed., *The Life and Letters of Charles Bulfinch* (Boston, 1896)

Burk, John Daly, and others, *History of Virginia.* 4 v. (Richmond, 1804–16)

Burnett, Edmund C., *The Continental Congress* (New York, 1941)

Burt, A. L., *The United States, Great Britain, and British North America* . . . . (New Haven, 1940)

Butts, R. Freeman, *The American Tradition in Religion and Education* (Boston, 1950)
The College Charts Its Course (New York, 1939)

Callender, Guy S., ed., *Selections from the Economic History of the United States* (Boston, 1909)

Carroll, John A., and Mary W. Ashworth, *George Washington.* v. 7 (New York, 1957). Cf. Freeman, Douglas S.

Cassirer, Ernst, *The Philosophy of the Enlightenment.* Fritz C. A. Koelln and James P. Pettegrove, trs. (Boston, 1951)

Chambers, William N., *Political Parties in a New Nation* (New York, 1963)

Channing, Edward, *A History of the United States.* 6 v. (New York, 1905–25)

Charles, Joseph, *The Origins of the American Party System* (Williamsburg, Va., 1951)

Chitwood, Oliver P., *Justice in Colonial Virginia* (Baltimore, 1905)

Clark, Allen C., ed., *Life and Letters of Dolly Madison* (Washington, 1914)

Clauder, Anna C., *American Commerce as Affected by the Wars of the French Revolution* . . . . (Philadelphia, 1932)

Colbourn, H. Trevor, *The Lamp of Experience* (Chapel Hill, 1965)

Commager, Henry S., and Elmo Giardonetti, eds., *Was America a Mistake? An Eighteenth Century Controversy* (Columbia, S.C., 1967)

Conant, James B., *Thomas Jefferson and the Development of American Public Education* (Berkeley, 1962)

Conway, Moncure D., *Omitted Chapters of History Disclosed in the Life and Public Papers of Edmund Randolph* (New York, 1888)

The Life of Thomas Paine. 2 v. (New York, 1892)

Cooper, James Fenimore, *The History of the Navy of the United States.* 2 v. (Philadelphia, 1839)

Corwin, Edward S., *The Doctrine of Judicial Review* (Princeton, 1914)

John Marshall and the Constitution (New Haven, 1919)

The President: Office and Powers (New York, 1940)

Cox, Isaac J., *The West Florida Controversy, 1789–1813* (Baltimore, 1918)

Craven, Avery, *Soil Exhaustion as a Factor in the Agricultural History of Virginia and Maryland, 1606–1860* (Urbana, Ill., 1926)

Cresson, William P., *James Monroe* (Chapel Hill, 1946)

Crosskey, William W., *Politics and the Constitution in the History of the United States.* 2 v. (Chicago, 1953)

Cunningham, Noble E., Jr., *The Jeffersonian Republicans: The Formation of Party Organization, 1789–1801* (Chapel Hill, 1957)

The Jeffersonian Republicans in Power (Chapel Hill, 1963)

Curtler, W. H. R., *A Short History of English Agriculture* (Oxford, 1909)

Dangerfield, George, *Chancellor Robert R. Livingston of New York* (New York, 1960)

The Era of Good Feelings (New York, 1952)

Darling, Arthur B., *Our Rising Empire, 1763–1803* (New Haven, 1940)

Dauer, Manning J., *The Adams Federalists* (Baltimore, 1953)

Davis, David Brion, *The Problem of Slavery in Western Culture* (Ithaca, N.Y., 1966)

Davis, Joseph S., *Essays in the Earlier History of American Corporations.* 2 v. (Cambridge, 1917)

Davis, Matthew L., *Memoirs of Aaron Burr.* 2 v. (New York, 1936–37)

Davis, Richard Beale, *Francis Walker Gilmer: Life and Learning in Jefferson's Virginia* (Richmond, 1939)

Intellectual Life in Jefferson's Virginia (Chapel Hill, 1964)

De Conde, Alexander, *Entangling Alliance: Politics and Diplomacy Under George Washington* (Durham, N.C., 1958)

The Quasi-War: The Politics and Diplomacy of the Undeclared War with France, 1797–1801 (New York, 1966)

Dewey, Davis R., *Financial History of the United States*. 12th ed. (New York, 1936)

Dewey, John, *Freedom and Culture* (New York, 1939)

Dickerson, Oliver M., *The Navigation Acts and the American Revolution* (Philadelphia, 1951)

Dictionary of American Biography. 22 v. Allen Johnson, Dumas Malone, Harris E. Starr, eds. (New York, 1928–58)

Dorfman, Joseph, *The Economic Mind in American Civilization*. v. 1 and 2. (New York, 1946)

Douglass, Elisha P., *Rebels and Democrats* (Chapel Hill, 1955)

Echeverria, Durand, *Mirage in the West: A History of the French Image of American Society to 1815* (Princeton, 1957)

Eckenrode, Hamilton J., *The Revolution in Virginia* (Boston, 1916)
Separation of Church and State in Virginia (Richmond, 1910)

Ellery, Eloise, *Brissot de Warville* (Boston, 1915)

Ernst, Robert, *Rufus King, American Federalist* (Chapel Hill, 1968)

Ferguson, E. James, *The Power of the Purse* (Chapel Hill, 1961)

Fischer, David H., *The Revolution of American Conservatism* (New York, 1965)

Foster, Roger, *Commentaries on the Constitution of the United States*. v. 1 (Boston, 1895)

Freeman, Douglas S., *George Washington: A Biography*. v. 5 and 6. (New York, 1952–54) Cf. Carroll and Ashworth.

Gaines, William H., *Thomas Mann Randolph* (Baton Rouge, 1966)

Garlick, Richard C., Jr., *Philip Mazzei, Friend of Jefferson* (Baltimore, 1933)

Gay, Peter, *The Enlightenment: An Interpretation. The Rise of Modern Paganism* (New York, 1966)

Gibbs, George, *Memoirs of the Administrations of Washington and Adams*. 2 v. (New York, 1846)

Gilbert, Felix, *To the Farewell Address* (New York, 1961)

Godechot, Jacques, *France and the Atlantic Revolution of the Eighteenth Century, 1770–1799*. Herbert Rowen, tr. (New York, 1965)

Goldsborough, Charles W., *The United States Naval Chronicle*. v. 1 (Washington, 1824)

Goodman, Paul, *The Democratic-Republicans of Massachusetts* (Cambridge, 1964)

Gottschalk, Louis, *Lafayette, 1783–1789* (Chicago, 1950)

Gough, J. W., *John Locke's Political Philosophy* (Oxford, 1950)

Graham, Gerald S., *Sea Power and British North America, 1783–1802* (Cambridge, 1941)

Gras, N. S. B., *A History of Agriculture in Europe and America* (New York, 1925)

Gray, Francis C., *Thomas Jefferson in 1814. Being an Account of a Visit to Monticello* (Boston, 1924)

Gray, Lewis C., *History of Agriculture in the Southern United States to 1860.* 2 v. (Washington, 1933)

Graydon, Alexander, *Memoirs of His Own Time.* J. S. Littell, ed. (Philadelphia, 1846)

Green, Constance M., *Washington, Village and Capital, 1800–1878* (Princeton, 1962)

Greene, Jack P., *The Quest for Power . . . , 1689–1776* (Chapel Hill, 1963)

Grigsby, Hugh Blair, *The Virginia Convention of 1776* (Richmond, 1855)

Griswold, Rufus W., *The Republican Court; or American Society in the Days of Washnigton* (London, 1854)

Gummere, Richard M., *The American Colonial Mind and the Classical Tradition* (Cambridge, 1963)

Guttridge, G. H., *English Whiggism and the American Revolution* (Berkeley, 1942)

Haines, Charles G., *The Role of the Supreme Court in American Government and Politics, 1789–1835* (Berkeley, 1944)

Hammond, Bray, *Banks and Politics in America from the Revolution to the Civil War* (Princeton, 1957)

Handler, Edward G., *America and Europe in the Political Thought of John Adams* (Cambridge, 1964)

Haraszti, Zoltan, *John Adams and the Prophets of Progress* (Cambridge, 1952)

Harlow, Vincent T., *The Founding of the Second British Empire, 1763–1793* (London, 1952)

Harrell, Isaac S., *Loyalism in Virginia* (Durham, N.C., 1926)

Harris, Neil, *The Artist in American Society: The Formative Years, 1790–1860* (New York, 1966)

Hart, Freeman H., *The Valley of Virginia in the American Revolution* (Chapel Hill, 1942)

Hartz, Louis, *The Founding of New Societies* (New York, 1964)

Hastings, G. E., *Life and Works of Francis Hopkinson* (Chicago, 1926)

Hatcher, William B., *Edward Livingston* (Baton Rouge, 1940)

Hawke, David, *A Transaction of Free Men: The Birth and Career of the Declaration of Independence* (New York, 1964)

Hazelton, John H., *The Declaration of Independence: Its History* (New York, 1960)

Hazen, Charles D., *Contemporary American Opinion of the French Revolution* (Baltimore, 1897)

Hechscher, Eli, *The Continental System: An Economic Interpretation* (Oxford, 1922)

Heimann, Edward, *History of Economic Doctrines* (New York, 1945)

Henderson, Archibald, *Dr. Thomas Walker of the Loyal Company of Virginia* (Worcester, 1951)

Herr, Richard, and Harold T. Parker, eds., *Ideas in History: Essays Presented to Louis Gottschalk* . . . . (Durham, N.C., 1965)

Higginbotham, Sanford W., *The Keystone in the Democratic Arch: Pennsylvania Politics, 1800–1816* (Harrisburg, 1952)

Higgins, Earl Leroy, ed., *The French Revolution as Told by Contemporaries* (Cambridge, 1938)

Hildreth, Richard, *The History of the United States*. 6 v. (New York, 1849–56)

Hindle, Brooke, *The Pursuit of Science in Revolutionary America* (Chapel Hill, 1956)

Holmes, Jack D. L., *Gayoso. The Life of a Spanish Governor in the Mississippi Valley, 1789–1799* (Baton Rouge, 1965)

Hook, Sidney, *The Paradoxes of Freedom* (Berkeley, 1962)

Horsman, Reginald, *The Causes of the War of 1812* (Philadelphia, 1962)

Expansion and American Indian Policy, 1783–1812 (East Lansing, Mich., 1967)

Howe, John R., Jr., *The Changing Political Thought of John Adams* (Princeton, 1966)

Humphrey, Edward F., *Nationalism and Religion in America, 1774–1789* (Boston, 1924)

Humphreys, Francis L., *Life and Times of David Humphreys*. 2 v. (New York, 1917)

Hunt, Gaillard, *The Department of State of the United States* (New Haven, 1894)

Hutcheson, Harold, *Tench Coxe* (Baltimore, 1938)

Hynemann, Charles S., *The First American Neutrality* (Urbana, Ill., 1934)

Irwin, Ray W., *Diplomatic Relations of the United States with the Barbary Powers, 1776–1816* (Chapel Hill, 1931)

Jackson, Henry F., *Scholar in the Wilderness, Francis Adrian Van der Kemp* (Syracuse, 1963)

Jacob, John I., *A Biographical Sketch of the Life of the Late Michael Cresap* (Cincinnati, 1866)

Jacobs, James R., *The Beginnings of the United States Army, 1783–1812* (Princeton, 1947)

Tarnished Warrior, Major General James Wilkinson (New York, 1938)

James, Charles F., *Documentary History of the Struggle for Religious Liberty in Virginia* (Danville, Va., 1900)

[Jefferson, Isaac], *Memoirs of a Monticello Slave*. Rayford W. Logan, ed. (Charlottesville, 1951)

Jennings, Walter W., *The American Embargo, 1807–1809* (Iowa City, 1921)

Jensen, Merrill, *The Founding of a Nation* (New York, 1968)

The New Nation . . . (New York, 1950)

Jones, Howard Mumford, *O Strange New World* (New York, 1965)

Jordon, Winthrop D., *White over Black: American Attitudes toward the Negro, 1550–1812* (Chapel Hill, 1968)

Kaplan, Lawrence S., *Jefferson and France: An Essay . . . .* (New Haven, 1967)

Kapp, Friedrich, *The Life of Frederick William von Steuben*. 2nd ed. (New York, 1859)

Kehoe, Vincent, *Virginia 1774* (Málaga, Spain, 1958)

Keller, Charles R., *The Second Great Awakening in Connecticut* (New Haven, 1942)

Kennedy, John P., *Memoirs of the Life of William Wirt*. 2 v. (New York, 1872)

Koch, Adrienne, *Power, Morals, and the Founding Fathers* (Ithaca, N.Y., 1961)

Koebner, Richard, *Empire* (Cambridge, England, 1961)

Kurtz, Stephen G., *The Presidency of John Adams* (Philadelphia, 1957)

Landers, H. L., *The Virginia Campaign and the Blockade and Siege of Yorktown . . . .* (Washington, 1931)

Leary, Lewis G., *That Rascal Freneau* (New Brunswick, 1941)

Leder, Lawrence H., *Liberty and Authority: Early American Political Ideology, 1689–1763* (Chicago, 1968)

Lee, Henry, *Memoirs of the War in the Southern Department of the United States* (Philadelphia, 1812)

Lefebvre, George, *The Coming of the French Revolution.* R. R. Palmer, tr. (New York, 1960)

Levy, Leonard W., *The Legacy of Suppression: Freedom of Speech and Press in Early American History* (Cambridge, 1960)

Lewis, O. F., *The Development of American Prisons and Prison Customs, 1775–1845* (New York, 1922)

Lingley, Charles R., *The Transition in Virginia from Colony to Commonwealth* (New York, 1910)

Lipset, Seymour Martin, *The First New Nation* (New York, 1963)

Little, Lewis P., *Imprisoned Preachers and Religious Liberty in Virginia* (Lynchburg, Va., 1938)

Lodge, Henry Cabot, *The Life and Letters of George Cabot* (Boston, 1877)

Logan, Deborah, *Memoir of Dr. George Logan of Stenton* (Philadelphia, 1899)

Logan, John A., Jr., *No Transfer: An American Security Principle* (New Haven, 1961)

Logan, Rayford W., *The Diplomatic Relations of the United States with Haiti, 1776–1891* (Chapel Hill, 1941)

Lokke, Carl L., *France and the Colonial Question . . . , 1763–1801* (New York, 1932)

Lough, John, *An Introduction to Eighteenth Century France* (New York, 1960)

Lyon, E. Wilson, *Louisiana in French Diplomacy, 1759–1804* (Norman, Okla., 1934)

Macmillan, Margaret B., *The War Governors in the American Revolution* (New York, 1943)

Magrath, C. Peter, *Yazoo: Law and Politics in the New Republic . . . .* (Providence, 1966)

Mahan, Alfred Thayer, *Sea Power in Its Relation to the War of 1812.* 2 v. (Boston, 1905)

Mahon, John K., *The American Militia: Decade of Decision, 1789–1799* (Gainesville, Fla., 1960)

Main, Jackson T., *The Antifederalists: Critics of the Constitution* (Chapel Hill, 1961)

Malone, Dumas, *The Public Life of Thomas Cooper* (New York, 1926)

Martin, Francis-Xavier, *The History of Louisiana* (New Orleans, 1882)

Marx, Leo, *The Machine in the Garden: Technology and the Pastoral Ideal in America* (New York, 1964)

Mayo, Bernard, *Myths and Men: Patrick Henry, George Washington, Thomas Jefferson* (Athens, 1959)

Mays, David John, *Edmund Pendleton, A Biography*. 2 v. (Cambridge, 1952)

Maxwell, Lloyd W., *Discriminatory Duties and the American Merchant Marine* (New York, 1926)

Maxwell, William, *Memoir of the Reverend John H. Rice* (Philadelphia, 1835)

Mazzei, Philip, *Memoirs. . . .* Howard R. Marraro, tr. (New York, 1942)

McBain, Howard L., *De Witt Clinton and the Origin of the Spoils System in New York* (New York, 1907)

McCaleb, Walter F., *The Aaron Burr Conspiracy*. Rev. ed. (New York, 1936)

McColley, Robert, *Slavery in Jeffersonian Virginia* (Urbana, Ill., 1964)

McDonald, Forrest, *We the People: The Economic Origins of the Constitution* (Chicago, 1958)

McIlwain, Charles H., *The American Revolution: A Constitutional Interpretation* (New York, 1924)

McLean, Robert C., *George Tucker, Moral Philosopher and Man of Letters* (Chapel Hill, 1961)

McLaughlin, Andrew C., *A Constitutional History of the United States* (New York, 1935)

The Foundations of American Constitutionalism (New York, 1932)

McMaster, John B., *A History of the People of the United States*. v. 1 and 2 (New York, 1883)

Meade, Robert, *Patrick Henry: Patriot in the Making* (Philadelphia, 1957)

Meade, William, *Old Churches, Ministers and Families of Virginia* 2 v. (Philadelphia, 1861)

Miller, John C., *Alexander Hamilton: Portrait in Paradox* (New York, 1959)

Triumph of Freedom, 1775-1783 (Boston, 1948)

Miller, Samuel, *A Brief Retrospect of the Eighteenth Century*. 2 v. (New York, 1803)

Minnigerode, Meade, *Jefferson, Friend of France, 1793* (New York, 1928)

Mitchell, Broadus, *Alexander Hamilton.* 2 v. (New York, 1957–62)

Mitchell, Julia Post, *St. Jean de Crevecoeur* (New York, 1916)

Mordecai, Samuel, *Richmond in By-Gone Days* (Richmond, 1946)

Morgan, Edmund S., *Virginians at Home* (Charlottesville, 1963) and Helen M. Morgan, *The Stamp Act Crisis* (Chapel Hill, 1953)

Morison, Samuel E., *The Life and Letters of Harrison Gray Otis.* 2 v. (Boston, 1913)

Morris, Richard B., ed., *The Era of the American Revolution* (New York, 1939)

Morton, Louis, *Robert Carter of Momini Hall* (Williamsburg, Va., 1941)

Mudge, E. T., *The Social Philosophy of John Taylor of Caroline* (New York, 1939)

Mumford, Lewis, *The South in Architecture* (New York, 1941)

Munroe, John A., *Federalist Delaware, 1775–1815* (New Brunswick, 1954)

Nagel, Paul C., *One Nation Indivisible: The Union in American Thought, 1776–1861* (New York, 1964)

Nelson, William H., *The American Tory* (New York, 1962)

Nettels, Curtis P., *The Emergence of a National Economy, 1775–1815* (New York, 1962)

North, Douglass C., *The Economic Growth of the United States, 1790–1860* (Englewood Cliffs, N.J., 1961)

Nye, Russel B., *The Cultural Life of the New Nation, 1776–1830* (New York, 1960)

Palmer, Robert R., *The Age of the Democratic Revolution.* 2 v. (Princeton, 1959–64)

Pattison, William D., *Beginnings of the American Rectangular Land Survey System, 1784–1806* (Chicago, 1957)

Paullin, Charles O., *The Navy and the American Revolution* (Cleveland, 1906)

Pearce, Roy Harvey, *The Savages of America: A Study of the Indian and the Idea of Civilization* (Baltimore, 1953)

Perkins, Bradford, *The First Rapprochement: England and the United States, 1795–1805* (Philadelphia, 1955)

Prologue to War: England and the United States, 1805–1812 (Berkeley, 1961)

Perry, Ralph Barton, *Puritanism and Democracy* (New York, 1944)

Philbrick, Francis S., "Introduction," *The Laws of Illinois Territory, 1809–1818*, Illinois State Historical Library *Collections*, v. 25 (Springfield, 1950)
The Rise of the West, 1754–1830 (New York, 1965)

Pickering, Octavius, and C. W. Upham, *The Life of Timothy Pickering*. 4 v. (Boston, 1867–73)

Pierson, Hamilton, W., *Jefferson at Monticello* (New York, 1962)

Pitkin, Timothy, *A Statistical View of the Commerce of the United States of America* (New Haven, 1835)

Pocock, J. G. A., *The Ancient Constitution and the Feudal Law* (Cambridge, England, 1957)

Pole, J. R., *Political Representation in England and the Origin of the American Revolution* (New York, 1966)

Porter, Albert O., *County Government in Virginia* (New York, 1947)

Pound, Merritt C., *Benjamin Hawkins, Indian Agent* (Athens, Ga., 1951)

Powell, J. H. *Bring Out Your Dead: The Great Plague of Yellow Fever in Philadelphia in 1793* (Philadelphia, 1949)

Prince, Carl E., *New Jersey's Jeffersonian Republicans* (Chapel Hill, 1967)

Prucha, Francis P., *American Indian Policy in the Formative Years* (Cambridge, 1962)

Purcell, Richard J., *Connecticut in Transition, 1775–1818* (Washington, 1918)

Quaife, Milo M., ed., *The Capture of Old Vincennes* (Indianapolis, 1927)

Quincy, Edmund, *Life of Josiah Quincy of Massachusetts* (Boston, 1867)

Ragatz, Lowell J., *The Fall of the Planter Class in the British Caribbean, 1763–1833* (New York, 1928)

Reps, John W., *The Making of Urban America: A History of City Planning in the United States* (Princeton, 1965)

Risjord, Norman K., *The Old Republicans: Southern Conservatives in the Age of Jefferson* (New York, 1965)

Ritcheson, Charles R., *British Politics and the American Revolution* (Norman, Okla., 1954)

Robbins, Caroline, *The Eighteenth-Century Commonwealthman* (Cambridge, 1959)

Rogers, George C., *Evolution of a Federalist: William Loughton Smith of South Carolina* (Columbia, 1962)

Rose, Lisle A., *Prologue to Democracy: The Federalists in the South, 1789–1800* (Lexington, Ky., 1968)

Rossiter, Clinton, *Alexander Hamilton and the Constitution* (New York, 1964)

Seedtime of the Republic (New York, 1953)

Rowland, Kate Mason, *Life of Charles Carroll of Carrollton, 1737–1832* . . . . 2 v. (New York, 1898)

Life of George Mason, 1725–1792. 2 v. (New York, 1892)

Rudolph, Frederich, *The American College and University* (New York, 1962)

Rush, Benjamin, *Autobiography.* George W. Corner, ed. (Princeton, 1948)

Rutman, Darrett B., ed., *The Old Dominion: Essays for Thomas Perkins Abernethy* (Charlottesville, 1964)

Saricks, Ambrose, *Pierre Samuel Du Pont de Nemours* (Lawrence, Kans., 1965)

Schachner, Nathan, *Aaron Burr* (New York, 1937)

Schaff, Philip, *Church and State in the United States* (New York, 1888)

Scharf, J. T., and Thompson Westcott, *History of Philadelphia, 1609–1884.* 3 v. (Philadelphia, 1884)

Scott, Arthur P., *Criminal Law in Colonial Virginia* (Chicago, 1930)

Sears, Louis, *George Washington and the French Revolution* (Detroit, 1960)

Jefferson and the Embargo (Durham, N.C., 1927)

Sellers, Charles Coleman, *Charles Willson Peale.* 2 v. (Philadelphia, 1947)

Semmes, John E., *John H. B. Latrobe and His Times, 1803–1891* (Baltimore, 1917)

Semple, R. B., *History of the Rise and Progress of the Baptists in Virginia* (Richmond, 1810)

Setser, Vernon G., *The Commercial Reciprocity Policy of the United States, 1774–1829* (Philadelphia, 1937)

Shulim, Joseph I., *The Old Dominion and Napoleon Bonaparte* (New York, 1952)

Singleton, Esther, *Story of the White House.* v. 1 (New York, 1907)

Smallwood, William M., *Natural History and the American Mind* (New York, 1941)

Smelser, Marshall, *The Congress Founds the Navy, 1787–1789* (South Bend, Ind., 1959)

Smith, Henry Nash, *Virgin Land: The American West as Symbol and Myth* (Cambridge, 1950)

Smith, James Morton, *Freedom's Fetters: The Alien and Sedition Laws and American Civil Liberties* (New York, 1956)

[Smith, Margaret Bayard], *The First Forty Years of Washington Society*. Gaillard Hunt, ed. (New York, 1906)

Smith, Page, *John Adams*. 2 v. (New York, 1962)

Spalding, E. Wilder, *His Excellency George Clinton* (New York, 1938)

Sparks, Jared, *The Life of Gouverneur Morris*. 2 v. (Boston, 1832)

Sprout, Harold, and Margaret Sprout, *The Rise of American Naval Power, 1776–1918* (Princeton, 1939)

Spurlin, Paul M., *Montesquieu in America, 1760–1801* (Baton Rouge, 1940)

Staples, William R., *Rhode Island in the Continental Congress* (Providence, 1870)

Steiner, B. C., *The Life and Correspondence of James McHenry* (Cleveland, 1907)

Stephen, Sir Leslie, *History of English Thought in the Eighteenth Century*. 2 v. Harbinger Ed. (New York, 1962)

Stewart, Robert A., *History of Virginia's Navy of the Revolution* (Richmond, 1933)

Stillé, Charles J., *The Life and Times of John Dickinson* (Philadelphia, 1891)

Stokes, Anson P., *Church and State in the United States*. v. 1 and 2. (New York, 1950)

Story, William W., ed., *Life and Letters of Joseph Story*. 2 v. Boston, 1851)

Stourzh, Gerald, *Benjamin Franklin and American Foreign Policy* (Chicago, 1954)

Sullivan, William, *Familiar Letters on Public Characters and Public Events* (Boston, 1834)

Sydnor, Charles, *The Development of Southern Sectionalism, 1819–1843* (Baton Rouge, 1953)

Gentlemen Freeholders: Political Parties in Washington's Virginia (Chapel Hill, 1952)

Tarleton, Banastre, *History of the Campaign of 1780 and 1781* (London, 1787)

Thayer, Theodore, *Nathanael Greene: Strategist of the American Revolution* (New York, 1960)

Thom, William T., *The Struggle for Religious Freedom in Virginia: The Baptists* (Baltimore, 1900)

Thomas, Charles M., *American Neutrality in 1793* . . . . (New York, 1931)

Thompson, J. M., *The French Revolution* (Oxford, 1945)

Tinkcom, Harry M., *Republicans and Federalists in Pennsylvania, 1790–1801* (Harrisburg, 1950)

Tocqueville, Alexis de, *The Old Regime and the French Revolution.* Stuart Gilbert, tr. (Garden City, 1955)

Tolles, Frederich B., *George Logan of Philadelphia* (New York, 1953)

Trumbull, John, *Autobiography.* Theodore Sizer, ed., (New Haven, 1953)

Turner, Lynn W., *William Plumer of New Hampshire* (Chapel Hill, 1962)

Van Doren, Carl, *Benjamin Franklin* (New York, 1938)

Van Tyne, Charles, *Loyalists in the American Revolution* (New York, 1929)

Varg, Paul A., *Foreign Policies of the Founding Fathers* (East Lansing, Mich., 1963)

Vile, M. J. C., *Constitutionalism and the Separation of Powers* (Oxford, 1967)

Von Eckhardt, Ursula M., *The Pursuit of Happiness in the Democratic Creed* (New York, 1959)

Walters, Raymond, Jr., *Albert Gallatin: Jeffersonian Financier and Diplomat* (New York, 1957)

Alexander James Dallas (Philadelphia, 1943)

Warren, Charles, *A History of the American Bar* (Boston, 1911)

The Supreme Court in United States History. 2 v., Rev. ed. (Boston, 1937)

Jacobin and Junto (Cambridge, 1931)

Odd Byways in American History (Cambridge, 1942)

Watkins, Frederick, *The Political Tradition of the West* (Cambridge, 1948)

Watson, John S., *The Reign of George III, 1760–1815* (New York, 1960)

Weinberg, Albert K., *Manifest Destiny. A Study of Nationalist Expansion in American History* (Baltimore, 1935)

Welch, Richard E., Jr., *Theodore Sedgwick, Federalist* (Middletown, Conn., 1965)

Whitaker, Arthur P., *The Spanish-American Frontier, 1783–1795* (Boston, 1927)

The Mississippi Question, 1795–1803 (New York, 1934)

White, Leonard D., *The Federalists: A Study in Administrative History* (New York, 1948)

The Jeffersonians . . . . (New York, 1951)

Whitney, Lois, *Primitivism and the Idea of Progress in the English Popular Literature of the Eighteenth Century* (Baltimore, 1934)

Willey, Basil, *The Eighteenth Century Background* (London, 1949)

Wilkinson, James, *Memoirs of My Own Times*. 3 v. (Philadelphia, 1816)

Willcox, William B., *Portrait of a General. Sir Henry Clinton in the War of Independence* (New York, 1964)

Wirt, William, *The Letters of the British Spy*. 10th ed. (New York, 1832)

Sketches of the Life and Character of Patrick Henry (Philadelphia, 1817)

Wolf, A., *A History of Science, Technology, and Philosophy in the 18th Century*. Torchbook Edition. 2 v. (New York, 1961)

Woodress, James, *A Yankee's Odyssey: The Life of Joel Barlow* (Philadelphia, 1958)

Woods, Edgar, *Albemarle County in Virginia* (Charlottesville, 1901)

Woodward, C. Vann, ed., *The Comparative Approach to American History* (New York, 1968)

Woolery, William K., *The Relation of Thomas Jefferson to American Foreign Policy* (Baltimore, 1927)

Wright, Benjamin F., *American Interpretations of Natural Law* (Cambridge, 1931)

Wright, Louis B., *The Atlantic Frontier* (New York, 1947)

The Cultural Life of the American Colonies (New York, 1957)

Young, Alfred, *The Jeffersonian Republicans of New York. The Origins, 1763–1797* (Chapel Hill, 1967)

Young, James Sterling, *The Washington Community, 1800–1828* (New York, 1966)

Zahniser, Marvin L., *Charles Cotesworth Pinckney* (Chapel Hill, 1967)

Zimmerman, James F., *Impressment of American Seamen* (New York, 1925)

c) *Articles and Essays*

Two anthologies may be consulted: *The Jefferson Reader*, Francis Coleman Rosenberger, ed. (New York, 1953) and *Thomas Jefferson: A Profile*, Merrill D. Peterson, ed. (New York, 1967). The latter contains articles or essays by Dixon Wecter, Carl Becker, John Dos Passos, Robert R. Palmer, Merrill D. Peterson, William D. Grampp, Dumas Malone, Julian P. Boyd, Louis B. Wright, Horace M. Kallen, and George Harmon Knoles, none of which is cited below.

Adams, Mary P., "Jefferson's Reaction to the Treaty of San Ildefonso," *Journal of Southern History*, v. 21 (1955)

Adams, Randolph G., "Thomas Jefferson, Librarian," in *Three Americanists* (Philadelphia, 1939)

Ammon, Harry, "The Formation of the Republican Party in Virginia," *Journal of Southern History*, v. 19 (1953)

"The Genêt Mission and the Development of American Political Parties," *Journal of American History*, v. 52 (1966)

"James Monroe and the Election of 1808 in Virginia," *William and Mary Quarterly*, 3rd ser., v. 20 (1963)

"The Jeffersonian Republicans in Virginia: An Interpretation," *Virginia Magazine of History and Biography*, v. 71 (1963)

Anderson, Dice R., "Jefferson and the Virginia Constitution," *American Historical Review*, v. 21 (1916)

Appleby, Joyce, "The Jefferson-Adams Rupture and the First French Translation of John Adams' *Defence*," *American Historical Review*, v. 73 (1968)

Arena, C. Richard, "Landholding and Political Power in Spanish Louisiana," *Louisiana Historical Quarterly*, v. 38 (1955)

Bailyn, Bernard, "Boyd's Jefferson: Notes for a Sketch," *New England Quarterly*, v. 33 (1960)

"Butterfield's Adams: Notes for a Sketch," *William and Mary Quarterly*, 3rd ser., v. 19 (1962)

"Political Experience and Enlightenment Ideas in Eighteeth Century America," *American Historical Review*, v. 67 (1962)

Bestor, Arthur, "Thomas Jefferson and the Freedom of Books," in Bestor and others, *Three Presidents and Their Books* (Urbana, Ill., 1955)

Bigelow, John, "Jefferson's Financial Diary," *Harper's Magazine*, v. 70 (1885)

Bowman, Albert H., "Jefferson, Hamilton, and American Foreign Policy," *Political Science Quarterly*, v. 81 (1956)

Boyd, Julian P., "The Megalonyx, the Megatherium, and Thomas Jefferson's Lapse of Memory," *American Philosophical Society Proceedings*, v. 102 (1958)

"Two Diplomats Between Revolutions: John Jay and Thomas Jefferson," *Virginia Magazine of History and Biography*, v. 66 (1958)

Brant, Irving, "Edmund Randolph, 'Not Guilty'," *William and Mary Quarterly*, 3rd ser., v. 7 (1950)

Brown, Ira V., "The Religion of Joseph Priestley," *Pennsylvania History*, v. 24 (1957)

Buron, Edmund, "Statistics on Franco-American Trade, 1778–1806," *Journal of Economic and Business History*, v. 4 (1931–32)

Busey, Samuel C., "The Centennial of the First Inauguration of a President at the Permanent Seat of the Government," Columbia Historical Society *Records*, v. 5 (1902)

Butterfield, Lyman H., "Elder John Leland, Jeffersonian Itinerant," American Antiquarian Society *Proceedings*, v. 62 (1952)

Chinard, Gilbert, "Eighteenth Century Theories on America as a Human Habitat," American Philosophical Society *Proceedings*, v. 91 (1947)

"Jefferson Among the Philosophers," *Ethics*, v. 53 (1943)

"Jefferson's Influence Abroad," *Mississippi Valley Historical Review*, v. 30 (1943)

Coatsworth, John H., "American Trade with European Colonies in the Caribbean and South America, 1790–1812," *William and Mary Quarterly*, 3rd ser., v. 24 (1967)

Coles, Harry L., Jr., "The Confiscation of Foreign Land Titles in Louisiana," *Louisiana Historical Quarterly*, v. 38(1955)

Cometti, Elizabeth, "John Rutledge, Jr., Federalist," *Journal of Southern History*, v. 13 (1947)

Corwin, Edward S., "The 'Higher Law' Background of American Constitutional Law," *Harvard Law Review*," v. 42 (1928–29)

Cox, Isaac J., "Hispanic-American Phases of the Burr Conspiracy," *Hispanic-American Historical Review*, v. 12 (1932)

"The Pan-American Policy of Jefferson and Wilkinson," *Mississippi Valley Historical Review*, v. 1 (1914–15)

Dauer, Manning J., "The Two John Nicholases: Their Relationship to Washington and Jefferson," *American Historical Review*, v. 45 (1940)

De Conde, Alexander, "Washington's Farewell Address, the French Alliance, and the Election of 1796," *Mississippi Valley Historical Review*, v. 38 (1957)

Detwiler, Philip F., "The Changing Reputation of the Declaration of Independence: The First Fifty Years," *William and Mary Quarterly*, 3rd ser., v. 19 (1962)

Downes, Randolph, "Thomas Jefferson and the Removal of Governor St. Clair in 1802," *Ohio Archeological and Historical Quarterly*, v. 36 (1927)

Duff, Stella F., "The Case Against the King: The *Virginia Gazettes* Indict George III," *William and Mary Quarterly*, 3rd ser., v. 6 (1949)

Dungan, James R., "Sir William Dunbar of Natchez, Planter, Explorer, and Scientist, 1792–1810," *Journal of Mississippi History*, v. 23 (1961)

Evans, Edith R., "Thomas Jefferson in Annapolis," *Maryland Historical Magazine*," v. 41 (1946)

Evans, Emory G., "Planter Indebtedness and the Coming of the Revolution in Virginia," *William and Mary Quarterly*, v. 19 (1962)

Ewers, John C., "Chiefs from the Missouri and Mississippi," *Smithsonian Journal of History*, v. 1 (1966)

Fabian, Bernhard, "Jefferson's *Notes on Virginia:* The Genesis of Query XVII . . . ," *William and Mary Quarterly*, 3rd ser., v. 12 (1955)

Farnham, Thomas J., "The Federal-State Issue and the Louisiana Purchase," *Louisiana History*, v. 6 (1965)

Faulkner, Robert K., "John Marshall and the Burr Trial," *Journal of American History*, v. 53 (1966)

Fischer, David H., "The Myth of the Essex Junto," *William and Mary Quarterly*, 3rd ser., v. 21 (1964)

Fisher, John E., "Slavery and the Slave Trade in the Louisiana Purchase, 1803–1812," *Essays in History*, v. 13 (1968)

Fowler, Samuel, "The Political Opinions of Jefferson," *North American Review*, v. 101 (1865)

Franklin, Mitchell, "The Place of Thomas Jefferson in the Expulsion of Spanish Medieval Law from Louisiana," *Tulane Law Review*, v. 16(1942)

Friis, Herman, R., "Baron Alexander von Humboldt's Visit to Washington . . . ," Columbia Historical Society *Records* (1960–62)

Gaines, Edwin M., "Governor Cabell and the Republican Schism in Virginia, 1805–08," *Essays in History*, v. 2 (1955)

Ganter, Herbert L., "William Small, Jefferson's Beloved Teacher," *William and Mary Quarterly*, 3rd ser., v. 4 (1947)

Graham, Gerald S., "The Migration of the Nantucket Whale Fishery . . . ," *New England Quarterly*, v. 8 (1935)

Greene, Jack P., "The Currency Act of 1764 in Imperial-Colonial Relations, 1764–1776," *William and Mary Quarterly*, 3rd ser., v. 18 (1961)

Greene, John C., "Some Early Speculations on the Origin of Human Races," *American Anthropologist*, v. 56 (1954)

Hatfield, Joseph T., "William C. C. Claiborne, Congress and Republicanism, 1797–1804," *Tennessee Historical Quarterly*, v. 24 (1964)

Haynes, Robert V., "The Revolution of 1800 in Mississippi," *Journal of Mississippi History*," v. 19 (1957)

"Historical Philadelphia," American Philosophical Society *Transactions*, new ser., v. 43 (1953)

Howell, Wilbur Samuel, "The Declaration of Independence and Eighteenth Century Logic," *William and Mary Quarterly*, 3rd ser., v. 18 (1961)

Hunt, Gaillard, "Office Seeking During Jefferson's Administration," *American Historical Review*, v. 3 (1898)

Hyslop, Beatrice F., "The American Press and the French Revolution of 1789," American Philosophical Society *Proceedings*, v. 104 (1960)

"American Press Reports of the French Revolution, 1789–1794," *New York Historical Society Quarterly*, v. 42 (1958)

Jellison, Charles A., "That Scoundrel Callender," *Virginia Magazine of History and Biography*, v. 67 (1959)

Jensen, Merrill, "Democracy and the American Revolution," *Huntington Library Quarterly*, v. 20 (1957)

"The Idea of a National Government During the American Revolution," *Political Science Quarterly*, v. 58 (1943)

Keim, C. Ray, "Primogeniture and Entail in Colonial Virginia," *William and Mary Quarterly*, 3rd ser., v. 25 (1968)

Kenyon, Cecilia M., "Republicanism and Radicalism in the American Revolution: An Old-Fashioned Interpretation," *William and Mary Quarterly*, 3rd ser., v. 19 (1962)

Koch, Adrienne, and Harry Ammon, "The Virginia and Kentucky Resolutions: An Episode in Jefferson's and Madison's Defense of Civil Liberties," *William and Mary Quarterly*, 3rd ser., v. 5 (1948)

Krislov, Samuel, "Jefferson and Judicial Review: Refereeing Cahn, Commager and Mendelson," *Journal of Public Law*, v. 9 (1960)

Laub, C. H., "Revolutionary Virginia and the Crown Lands, 1775–1783," *William and Mary Quarterly*, 2nd ser., v. 11 (1931)

Lerche, Charles O., Jr., "Jefferson and the Election of 1800: A Case Study of the Political Smear," *William and Mary Quarterly*, 3rd ser., v. 5 (1948)

Leubke, Fred C., "The Origins of Thomas Jefferson's Anti-Clericalism," *Church History*, v. 33 (1963)

Lewis, Anthony M., "Jefferson and Virginia's Pioneers, 1774–1781," *Mississippi Valley Historical Review*, v. 34 (1948)

"Jefferson's *Summary View* as a Chart of Political Union," *William and Mary Quarterly*, 3rd ser., v. 5 (1948)

Loehr, Rodney C., "The Influence of English Agriculture on American Agriculture," *Agricultural History*, v. 11 (1937)

Lokke, Carl L., "Jefferson and the Leclerc Expedition," *American Historical Review*, v. 33 (1928)

Lovejoy, Arthur O., "The Parallel of Deism and Classicism," *Modern Philology*, v. 19 (1932)

Low, W. A., "Merchant and Planter Relations in Post-Revolutionary Virginia, 1783–1789," *Virginia Magazine of History and Biography*, v. 61 (1953)

Lyon, E. Wilson, "The Directory and the United States," *American Historical Review*, v. 43 (1938)

Macloed, Julia H., "Jefferson and the Navy: A Defense," *Huntington Library Quarterly*, v. 8 (1945)

Main, Jackson T., "The Distribution of Property in Post-Revolutionary Virginia," *Mississippi Valley Historical Review*, v. 41 (1954)

"Government By the People: The American Revolution and the Democratization of the Legislature," *William and Mary Quarterly*, 3rd ser., v. 23 (1966)

Marraro, Howard R., "The Four Versions of Jefferson's Letter to Mazzei," *William and Mary Quarterly*, 2nd ser., v. 22 (1942)

Mayo, Bernard, "A Peppercorn for Mr. Jefferson," *Virginia Quarterly Review*, v. 19 (1943)

McDonald, Forrest, "The Anti-Federalists, 1781–1789," *Wisconsin Magazine of History*, v. 46 (1963)

Merriam, J. M., "Jefferson's Use of the Executive Patronage," *American Historical Association Papers* (1888)

Miller, Ralph N., "American Nationalism as a Theory of Nature," *William and Mary Quarterly*, 3rd ser., v. 12 (1955)

Mott, Royden J., "Sources of Jefferson's Ecclesiastical Views," *Church History*, v. 3 (1934)

Nash, Gary B., "American Clergy and the French Revolution," *William and Mary Quarterly*, 3rd ser., v. 22 (1965)

Nussbaum, F. L., "American Tobacco and French Politics," *Political Science Quarterly*, v. 40 (1926)

"The French Colonial Arrêt of August 30, 1784," *South Atlantic Quarterly*, v 27 (1928)

"The Revolutionary Vergennes and Lafayette versus the Farmers General," *Journal of Modern History*, v. 3 (1931)

Palmer, Robert R., ed., "A Neglected Work: Otto Vossler on Jefferson and the Revolutionary Era," *William and Mary Quarterly*, 3rd ser., v. 12 (1955)

Pancake, John S., "Aaron Burr: Would Be Usurper," *William and Mary Quarterly*, 3rd ser., v. 8 (1951)

Peden, William, "Some Notes Concerning Thomas Jefferson's Libraries," *William and Mary Quarterly*, 3rd ser., v. 1 (1944)
ed., "A Book Peddler Invades Monticello," *William and Mary Quarterly*, 3rd ser., v. 6 (1949)

Pocock, J. G. R., "Machiavelli, Harrington, and English Political Ideologies in the Eighteenth Century," *William and Mary Quarterly*, 3rd ser., v. 22 (1965)

Praeger, Frank D., "Trends and Developments in American Patent Law from Jefferson to Clifford, Part Two," *American Journal of Legal History*, v. 6 (1962)

Pritchard, Walter, "Selecting a Governor for the Territory of Orleans," *Louisiana Historical Quarterly*, v. 31 (1948)

Pulley, Judith P., "An Agent of Nature's Republic Abroad: Thomas Jefferson in Pre-Revolutionary France," *Essays in History*, v. 11 (1966)

Randolph, Edmund, "Essay on the Revolutionary History of Virginia,"*Virginia Magazine of History and Biography*, v. 43–45 (1935–37)

Reid, David S., "An Analysis of British Parliamentary Opinion on American Affairs at the Close of the War of Independence," *Journal of Modern History*, v. 18 (1946)

Reynolds, Donald E., "Ammunition Supply in Revolutionary Virginia," *Virginia Magazine of History and Biography*, v. 73 (1965)

Rhinesmith, W. Donald, "Joseph Dennie, Critic of Jeffersonian Democracy," *Essays in History*, v. 7 (1962)

Rice, Howard C., Jr., "Jefferson's Gift of Fossils to the Museum of Natural History in Paris," American Philosophical Society *Proceedings*, v. 95 (1951)

Risjord, Norman K., "The Virginia Federalists," *Journal of Southern History*, v. 33 (1967)

Ritcheson, Charles R., "The London Press and the First Decade of American Independence, 1783–1793," *Journal of British Studies*, v. 2 (1963)

Robbins, Caroline, "Honest Heretic: Joseph Priestley in America," *American Philosophical Society Proceedings*, v. 106 (1962)

Scanlon, James E., "A Sudden Conceit: Jefferson and the Louisiana Government Bill of 1804," *Louisiana History*, v. 9 (1968)

Schneider, Herbert W., "The Enlightenment in Thomas Jefferson," *Ethics*, v. 53 (1943)

Sée, Henri, "Commerce Between France and the United States," *American Historical Review*, v. 31 (1926)

Seeber, Edward D., "Critical Views on Logan's Speech," *Journal of American Folklore*, v. 60 (1947)

Sifton, Paul G., ed., "Otto's Memoir to Vergennes, 1785," *William and Mary Quarterly*, 3rd ser., v. 22 (1965)

Simpson, George Gaylord, "The Beginnings of Vertebrate Paleontology in the United States," *American Philosophical Society Proceedings*, v. 86 (1942)

Smelser, Marshall, "The Jacobin Phrenzy: The Menace of Monarchy, Plutocracy, and Anglophilia, 1789–1798," *Review of Politics*, v. 21 (1959)

Smith, T. V., "Thomas Jefferson and the Perfectibility of Mankind," *Ethics*, v. 53 (1943)

Sowerby, E. Millicent, "Thomas Jefferson and His Library," *Bibliographical Society of America Publications*, v. 50 (1956)

Steel, Anthoney, "Impressment in the Monroe-Pinkney Negotiations, 1806–1807," *American Historical Review*, v. 57 (1952)

Stover, John F., "French-American Trade During the Confederation, 1781–1789," *North Carolina Historical Review*, v. 35 (1958)

Tanner, Douglas W., "Thomas Jefferson, Impressment, and the Rejection of the Monroe-Pinkney Treaty," *Essays in History*, v. 13 (1968)

Tate, Thad W., "The Coming of the Revolution in Virginia: Britain's Challenge to Virginia's Ruling Class, 1763–1776," *William and Mary Quarterly*, 3rd ser., v. 19 (1962)

Terra, Helmut de, "Motives and Consequences of Alexander von Humboldt's Visit to the United States," *American Philosophical Society Proceedings*, v. 104 (1960)

Thomas, Robert, "The Virginia Convention of 1788," *Journal of Southern History*, v. 19 (1953)

Trent, William P., "The Case of Josiah Philips," *American Historical Review*, v. 1 (1895–96)

Turner, Kathryn, "Federalist Policy and the Judiciary Act of 1801," *William and Mary Quarterly*, 3rd ser., v. 22 (1965)

"The Midnight Judges," *University of Pennsylvania Law Review*, v. 109 (1960–61)

Verner, Coolie, "The Maps and Plates Appearing with the Several Editions of Mr. Jefferson's 'Notes on the State of Virginia'," *Virginia Magazine of History and Biography*, v. 59 (1951)

Viner, Jacob, "Power versus Plenty as Objectives of Foreign Policy in the Seventeenth and Eighteenth Centuries," *World Politics*, 1 (1948)

Wall, A. J., "The Story of the Convention Army," New York Historical Society *Quarterly Bulletin*, v. 11 (1927–28)

Waterman, Julius S., "Thomas Jefferson and Blackstone's *Commentaries*," *Illinois Law Review*, v. 27 (1933)

Wheat, Carl I., "Mapping the American West, 1540–1857," American Antiquarian Society *Proceedings*, v. 64 (1954)

Wolford, Thorp L., "Democratic-Republican Reaction in Massachusetts to the Embargo of 1807," *New England Quarterly*, v. 15 (1942)

Wood, Gordon S., "Rhetoric and Reality in the American Revolution," *William and Mary Quarterly*, 3rd ser., v. 23 (1966)

Woodfin, Maude H., "Contemporary Opinion in Virginia of Thomas Jefferson," in *Essays in Honor of William E. Dodd*, Avery Craven, ed. (Chicago, 1935)

Zook, George F., "Proposals for a New Commercial Treaty Between France and the United States, 1778–1793," *South Atlantic Quarterly*, v. 8 (1909)

d) *Unpublished Theses and Dissertations*

Adams, Mary P., "Jefferson's Military Policy with Special Reference to the Frontier, 1805–1809," Ph.D. Dist., Univ. of Va., 1958

Brewer, Paul, "Jefferson's Administration of the Patronage: New York, 1801–1804," M.A. Thesis, Univ. of Va., 1968

Coyner, M. Boyd, "John Hartwell Cocke of Bremo: Agriculture and Slavery in the Ante-Bellum South," Ph.D. Dist., Univ. of Va., 1961

Cross, Jack L., "Thomas Pinckney's London Mission," Ph.D. Dist., Univ. of Chicago, 1957

Dabney, William M., "Jefferson's Albemarle: History of Albemarle County, Virginia, 1727–1819," Ph.D. Dist., Univ. of Va., 1951

Elsmere, Mary Jane Shaffer, "The Impeachment Trial of Justice Samuel Chase," Ph.D. Dist., Indiana Univ., 1962

Gaines, Edwin M., "Outrageous Encounter: The Chesapeake-Leopard Affair of 1807," Ph.D. Dist., Univ. of Va., 1960

Harrison, Joseph Hopson, Jr., "The Internal Improvements Issue in the Politics of the Union, 1783–1825," Ph.D. Dist., Univ. of Va., 1954

Harrison, Lowell H., "John Breckinridge, Western Statesman," Ph.D. Dist., New York Univ., 1951

Knudson, Jerry W., "The Jefferson Years: Response by the Press, 1801–1809," Ph.D. Dist., Univ. of Va., 1962

Lacy, Alex B., "Jefferson and Congress: Congressional Methods and Politics, 1801–1809," Ph.D. Dist., Univ. of Va., 1963

McGrath, Rosemarie, "The Issue of the Foreign Slave Trade in the Louisiana Territory," M.A. Thesis, Univ. of Va., 1967

Mumper, Jamse M., "The Jefferson Image in the Federalist Mind, 1801–1809," Ph.D. Dist., Univ. of Va., 1966

Pancake, John S., "The General from Baltimore: The Public Life of General Samuel Smith, 1752–1812," Ph.D. Dist., Univ. of Va., 1947

Pulley, Judith P., "Thomas Jefferson at the Court of Versailles: An American *Philosophe* and the Coming of the French Revolution," Ph.D. Dist., Univ. of Va., 1966

Rasmusson, Ethel Elise, "Capital on the Delaware: The Philadelphia Upper Class in Transition, 1789–1801," Ph.D. Dist., Brown Univ., 1962

Shackelford, George Green, "William Short, Jefferson's Adopted Son, 1758–1849," Ph.D. Dist., Univ. of Va., 1955

Sheehan, Bernard W., "Civilization and the American Indian in the Thought of the Jeffersonian Era," Ph.D. Dist., Univ. of Va., 1965

Smith, Robert H., "Albert Gallatin's Fiscal Policy," Ph.D. Dist., Syracuse Univ., 1954

Stampp, Norman, "Political Parties in Connecticut," Ph.D. Dist., Yale Univ., 1952

Stewart, Donald H., "Jeffersonian Journalism: Newspaper Propaganda and the Development of the Democratic-Republican Party, 1791–1801," Ph.D. Dist., Columbia Univ., 1951

Wheeler, William Bruce, "Urban Politics in Nature's Republic: The Development of Political Parties in the Seaport Cities in the Federalist Era," Ph.D. Dist., Univ. of Va., 1967

Index

Bartram, John, 5
Bartram, William, 420
Bastrop grant, 850
Batture St. Marie, and TJ, 944-47
Bayard, James A., 676, 677, 678, 728;
in Burr-TJ contest, 646, 649-51, 845
Bayonne Decree, 901
Beaurepaire, Quesnay de, 963
Beccaria, Marchese di, 47, 124, 126, 128
Beckley, John, 437, 468, 554, 555, 575, 640
Beckwith, Major General George, 416, 417, 428, 439
Bérard, Simon, 319, 328
Berkeley, Admiral George C., 875, 876, 877, 879
Berlin Decree, 826, 860, 861, 862, 882, 901
Bermuda, 188, 216, 617
Berni agreement, 320, 321, 356
Beverley, Robert, quoted, 166
Bible, The, TJ and, 959-60
Bidwell, Barnabas, 817-18, 820, 821
Big Bone Lick, 736, 904
Bill of Rights, U.S., TJ and, 106, 360-61. *See also* Constitution, First Amendment, Kentucky Resolutions
Bingham, Mrs. William, 420
Binns, John A., 941
Bishop, Abraham, 672
Bishop, Samuel, 672
Blackstone, William: TJ's view of, 16, 17, 951, 985, 987; on allegiance, 73, 154; on escheat, 123
Blaetterman, George, 984, 985
Blanchard, Jean Pierre, 479
Bland, Richard, 44; imperial theory of, 72, 77; TJ on, 72
Bland, Theodorick, 414
Blennerhassett, Harman, 847, 870, 871
Blennerhassett's Island, 847, 850, 854, 871, 872
blockade, 546, 831, 863
Board of Agriculture (English), 527, 589, 735
Bolingbroke, Lord, 50, 51, 53, 63, 64, 958
Bollman, Eric, 854, 868, 870, 871
Bonaparte, Jerome, 732
Bonaparte, Mme (Elizabeth Patterson), 732-33
Bonaparte, Joseph, 757-758
Bonaparte, Napoleon, 565, 732, 833-34, 954; TJ's opinion of, 628, 677, 878, 935; and Convention of 1800, 631, 665; First Consul, 677; and

Louisiana, 747-62; and Florida negotiations, 768, 808, 814, 825-26; Emperor, 801; and Berlin Decree, 882; and TJ's embargo diplomacy, 901-2; and War of 1812, 932
Bonneycastle, Charles, 985
Boone, Daniel, 119
Boré, Etienne, 784, 785
Boston Port Act, 71, 75
Boston Tea Party, 70
"botanizing excursion," 439-40
botany, 250; American-European exchanges, 335-36, 337-38, 735
Botetourt, Norborne Berkeley, Baron de, 33, 35, 36
Boulton, Matthew, 343, 402
Bowditch, Nathaniel, 977, 979
Bowdoin, James, 823, 825, 826
Boyd, Julian P., quoted, 112, 415
Bracton, Henry, 18, 60
Bradley, Stephen, 729
Brand-Hollis, Thomas, 342
Brant, Irving, cited, 586
Braxton, Carter, 101, 104, 120
Breckinridge, John: and Kentucky Resolutions, 612, 613, 614, 624; Senate leader, 691, 696-97; and Louisiana, 770, 776, 780-82; Attorney General, 805, 846
Breckinridge Act, TJ and, 780-83
Brehan, Marquise de, 369
Brent, Robert, 740
Brienne, Comte de, 372
Briggs, Isaac, 735, 779, 852, 857
Brodhead, General William, 218
"broken voyage," doctrine of, 807
Brokenborough, Arthur S., 976
Brougham, Henry, 899
Browere, J. H. I., 1006
Brown, James, 583
Brown, John, 846
Brown, Mather, 345
Brunswick, Duke of, 479
Bryant, William Cullen, quoted, 905
Buffon, Comte de, 47, 262, 287, 577; and degeneracy theory, 253, 254, 255, 256, 258, 578, 581; TJ meets in France, 338-39
Burgh, James, 59, 63
Burk, John Daly, 949
Burke, Edmund: on the sublime, 23-24; on American character, 67; on imperial relationship, 72-73; and French Revolution, 384, 437, 439
Burr, Aaron: elected to Senate, 439; TJ's relations with, 553, 557, 570, 671, 791-92, 845; vice presidential

Muhlenberg, General J. P. G., 209, 231

Mumford, Lewis, cited, 969-70

Murray, William Vans, 619, 620, 621, 631

music, TJ and, 15, 27, 164, 333, 343, 723

Muter, George, 210

National Capital: New York, 405-7; Philadelphia, 419-20, 420-21, 492-93, 505-6, 507-8; Washington, 644, 653-54, 721, 723-24, 731, 739; permanent site determined, 412-14; TJ in planning of, 418, 447-49, 739-44

National Capitol, 449, 653, 741, 742-43

national domain: creation of, 278, 280; land system, 285

National Gazette, 445-46, 461, 464, 470-71, 473-74, 490, 508

National Institute, of France, 734-35, 736-37, 859, 904

National Intelligencer, 691, 698, 699, 711, 927

National Road, 857

national university, 858-60, 964

nationality, American, 1008; before Revolution, 65-68; in *Notes on Virginia*, 247-48, 254-59, 265; and TJ's European experience, 314, 331-32, 338, 380, 387-89; and foreign policy, 566-68, 627-29; and TJ's presidency, 734, 794, 854, 858; War of 1812, 932-33

"natural aristocracy," 152, 679, 955

Natural Bridge, Virginia, 246, 251, 953

natural history, in *Notes on Virginia*, 249-65. *See also* ethnology, paleontology, etc.

Natural History Museum (Peale's), 419, 737, 859

natural law, 25, 29, 31, 47, 49, 64, 66, 255, 404

natural rights: in general, 57, 64; in Declaration of Independence, 93-96; in landholding, 113-15, 118-19; in criminal justice, 129; in religion, 134; and expatriation, 154; and slavery, 260; in trade, 304, 329-30, 388; on navigable waters, 457; of speech and press, 606; and state rights, 615

naturalization, TJ on: bill in Virginia, 153; as President, 686, 692, 827

Naturalization Act, 603; repeal of, 686, 692

Nature, American: and nationality,

251, 253-57, 265, 337-38, 338-39; and civilization, 255, 257, 369, 1008

Navy, U.S.: TJ's proposed creation of, 312-14; in Quasi War, 599, 600, 617; founded, 664; peacetime establishment in 1801, 664; and fiscal policy, 688, 692; establishment in 1806, 833; character of the naval system, 835-37; TJ's "lock-dock," 836; gunboats, 836-39; after *Chesapeake* encounter, 877; embargo and, 887, 912

Navy, Virginia, in Revolutionary War, 168-69, 222, 231

Navy Department, 599, 661-62

Navy Yard, Washington, 740, 741

Necker, Jacques, 335, 375, 377, 379

Necker, Mme, 335

Negroes, TJ's thoughts on, 259-64

Nelson, Admiral Horatio, 618

Nelson, Thomas, 108

Nelson, General Thomas, 199, 206, 207, 212; succeeds TJ as Governor, 236, 239

Nelson, William, 43

neology, 952

neutrality, U.S., 292, 329, 357, 389; in TJ's policy, 416; in 1793, 481-513; and Jay Treaty, 546, 566; in War of Third Coalition, 805-8, 826, 831, 860, 862, 863, 882, 899-901

New Haven Remonstrance, 672; answer to, 673-75

New Jersey, 680

New Orleans: TJ on its importance, 752-53; closure of, 755-56, 757; U.S. authority in, 776-77, 783, 786; and Burr Conspiracy, 849, 850, 852, 853, 854; and Batture St. Marie, 944-46

New World: images of, 66-68, 255-56, 331, 369; degeneracy theory of, 252-53; TJ's attack on, 254-59, 265, 338-39, 578; in TJ's conception, 745-46, 932

New York: and Revolution, 34-35; party contests in, 439, 469; in election of 1800, 625, 631-32; in TJ's patronage decisions, 669-71, 680; Burr-Lewis contest, 791-93; and embargo, 896, 897

New York *Evening Post*, 792, 881

newspapers: English, 300, 408; European, 408; U.S., 408, 444-46; partisan warfare in Philadelphia, 464, 466, 469, 470-71, 473-74; in election of 1800, 626; TJ's views of, 713-14, 715-16, 927

Newton, Sir Isaac, 47, 54, 386, 403

Nicholas, George, 237; and censure of TJ, 237-39, 241-42
Nicholas, John, 650
Nicholas, "Clerk John," 573, 710
Nicholas, Robert Carter, 70, 109, 120, 140
Nicholas, Wilson Cary: TJ's political associate, 575, 612, 615, 623, 624; and TJ's administration, 662, 691, 775, 825, 909-10, 915; and University of Virginia, 965, 967; bankruptcy of, and TJ, 991-92
Nicholson, Joseph, 796, 815, 817, 829, 840, 854, 864
Nock, Albert J.: quoted, 29; cited, 531
Nolan, Philip, 588-89
Non-Importation Act, of 1806, 828-30, 882, 885, 901
Non-Intercourse Act, of 1809, 915-16
Nootka Sound affair, 415-18
North, Lord Frederick, 36, 69, 76; his "conciliatory proposition," 78; TJ's replies to, 78-79, 82
North American Review, 952
Northern Confederacy, in 1804, 793-94, 898
Northwest Ordinance, 278, 284, 778, 780, 787, 788
Notes on Coinage (TJ), 276-78
Notes on Virginia (TJ), 153, 237, 245, 267, 302, 587; writing of, 247-48; publication of, 248-49, 334, 381; as work of natural history, 249-65, 586; influence and reputation of, 264-65, 295, 334, 581, 584, 639, 738, 940, 947, 952, 962; appendix to, 584; quoted, 137, 289-90
nullification, doctrine of, 614, 624, 994

Observations on the Whale-Fishery (TJ), 325-26
Ohio, 692, 857. See also Indians, Northwest
Ordinance of 1784, 278, 281-84
Orleans Territory, 783; TJ's policy for defense of, 834-35, 855
Osborne's, 231
Ossian, 245, 302
Otis, James, 72, 950
Otto, Louis Guillaume: protests Tonnage Act, 423; on TJ, 424; quoted, 409, 556
Oxford University, 964, 977, 984

Page, John, 17, 166, 958; quoted, 19, 98, 144, 202

Page, Mann, 583
Paine, Thomas, 63, 241, 440, 560, 665, 709, 947; *Common Sense*, 85-86, quoted 67-68, 68, 85, 95, 96, 289; and TJ, 337, 360, 444; and French Revolution, 384, 437, 438, 439; return to U.S., 681-82, 711-13; champion of gunboats, 838
painting, TJ and, 351-52
paleontology, 255, 576-79, 736-37
Palladio, Andrea, and TJ's architecture, 24-26, 341, 354, 539, 969
Panic of 1819: and University of Virginia, 976, 981; and TJ's personal fortune, 989-92; and political reaction, 992-94
Parson's Cause, 8, 22
Parton, James, quoted, 31
patents, TJ and, 450, 589-90, 937-38
Patterson, Robert, 589
Peace of Amiens, 754
Peace of Ghent, 934
peaceable coercion, 829-30, 863-64, 865, 883-86, 898, 916-18. See also commercial policy
Peale, Charles Willson, 738, 742; museum, 419-20, 737; and the mammoth, 736; and polygraph, 737
Peale, Raphael, 736
Peale, Rembrandt, 718, 766
Pendleton, Edmund, 126, 288; as lawyer, 13, 20; in colonial politics, 41, 71, 81, 83, 101; and Virginian reforms, 102, 104, 108, 109, 110, 111, 114, 115, 140; in election of 1800, 626; and after, 682-83, 695
Penet, Windel & Company, 172, 188
penitentiary system, 130
Pennsylvania: in Revolution, 81, 91; in election of 1796, 554, 555-56, 557; of 1800, 625, 634, 641, 642; in TJ's administration, 667, 714-15, 793, 857
Perceval, Spencer, 899
Pestalozzi, Johann, 148
Peter the Great, 836
Petersburg, Virginia, 230, 231, 234
Peterson, Jeffrey and Kent, dedication page
Petit, Adrien, 355, 400, 421
Petite Démocrate, 498-501
Petrarch, 354
Petty, Sir William, quoted, 152
Peyton, Bradford, 1002
Philadelphia, USS, 199
Philips, Josiah, 131, 156
Phillips, Major General William, 163, 164, 165, 180-81; campaign in Virginia, 226, 230-31